CONTEMPORARY WORLD HISTORY

SIXTH
EDITION

CONTEMPORARY WORLD HISTORY

WILLIAM J. DUIKER

The Pennsylvania State University

CENGAGE
Learning

Australia • Brazil • Mexico • Singapore • United Kingdom • United States

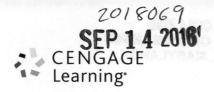
CENGAGE
Learning

Contemporary World History, Sixth Edition
William J. Duiker

Product Director: Suzanne Jeans

Product Manager: Brooke Barbier

Senior Content Developer: Margaret McAndrew Beasley

Content Coordinator: Cara D. Swan

Product Assistant: Katie Coaster

Media Developer: Kate MacLean

Marketing Manager: Valerie Hartman

Market Development Manager: Kyle Zimmerman

Senior Content Project Manager: Jane Lee

Associate Art Director: Hannah Wellman

Manufacturing Planner: Sandee Milewski

Senior Rights Acquisition Specialist: Jennifer Meyer Dare

Production Service: Cenveo Publisher Services

Cover Designer: Shawn Girsberger

Cover Image: © Vittoriano Rastelli/Corbis

Compositor: Cenveo Publisher Services

For product information and technology assistance, contact us at **Cengage Learning Customer & Sales Support, 1-800-354-9706**

For permission to use material from this text or product, submit all requests online at **www.cengage.com/permissions**. Further permissions questions can be e-mailed to **permissionrequest@cengage.com**.

Library of Congress Control Number: 2013950398

ISBN 13: 978-1-285-44790-2
ISBN 10: 1-285-44790-5

Cengage Learning
200 First Stamford Place, 4th Floor
Stamford, CT 06902
USA

Cengage Learning is a leading provider of customized learning solutions with office locations around the globe, including Singapore, the United Kingdom, Australia, Mexico, Brazil and Japan. Locate your local office at **international.cengage.com/region**.

Cengage Learning products are represented in Canada by Nelson Education, Ltd.

For your course and learning solutions, visit **www.cengage.com**. Purchase any of our products at your local college store or at our preferred online store **www.cengagebrain.com**.
Instructors: Please visit **login.cengage.com** and log in to access instructor-specific resources.

Printed in Canada
1 2 3 4 5 6 7 17 16 15 14 13

ABOUT THE AUTHOR

WILLIAM J. DUIKER is liberal arts professor emeritus of East Asian studies at The Pennsylvania State University. A former U.S. diplomat with service in Taiwan, South Vietnam, and Washington, D.C., he received his doctorate in Far Eastern history from Georgetown University in 1968, where his dissertation dealt with the Chinese educator and reformer Cai Yuanpei. At Penn State, he has written extensively on the history of Vietnam and modern China, including the highly acclaimed *The Communist Road to Power in Vietnam* (revised edition, Westview Press, 1996), which was selected for a Choice Outstanding Academic Book Award in 1982–1983 and 1996–1997. Other recent books are *China and Vietnam: The Roots of Conflict* (Berkeley, 1987); *Sacred War: Nationalism and Revolution in a Divided Vietnam* (McGraw-Hill, 1995); and *Ho Chi Minh* (Hyperion, 2000), which was nominated for a Pulitzer Prize in 2001. He is the author, with colleague Jackson Spielvogel, of *World History* (seventh edition, Wadsworth, 2013). While his research specialization is in the field of nationalism and Asian revolutions, his intellectual interests are considerably more diverse. He has traveled widely and has taught courses on the history of communism and non-Western civilizations at Penn State, where he was awarded a Faculty Scholar Medal for Outstanding Achievement in the spring of 1996.

TO JULES F. DIEBENOW (1929–2013),
INVETERATE FELLOW TRAVELER, MENTOR, AND FRIEND.
W.J.D.

BRIEF CONTENTS

DETAILED CONTENTS

DOCUMENTS

MAPS

FEATURES

FILM & HISTORY

OPPOSING VIEWPOINTS

PREFACE

THE TWENTIETH CENTURY was an era of paradox. When it began, Western civilization was an emerging powerhouse that bestrode the world like a colossus. Internally, however, the continent of Europe was a patchwork of squabbling states that within a period of less than three decades engaged in two bitter internecine wars that threatened to obliterate two centuries of human progress. As the century came to an end, the Western world had become prosperous and increasingly united, yet there were clear signs that global economic and political hegemony was beginning to shift to the East. In the minds of many observers, the era of Western dominance had come to a close.

In other ways as well, the twentieth century was marked by countervailing trends. While parts of the world experienced rapid industrial growth and increasing economic prosperity, other regions were still mired in abject poverty. The century's final decades were characterized by a growing awareness of not only global interdependence, but also burgeoning ethnic and national consciousness; the period witnessed both the rising power of science and fervent religiosity and growing doubts about the impact of technology on the human experience. As the closing chapters of this book indicate, these trends have continued and even intensified in the decade that has ensued since the advent of the new millennium.

Contemporary World History (formerly titled *Twentieth-Century World History*) attempts to chronicle the key events in this revolutionary century and its aftermath while seeking to throw light on some of the underlying issues that shaped the times. Did the beginning of a new millennium indeed mark the end of the long period of Western dominance? If so, will recent decades of European and American superiority be followed by a "Pacific century," with economic and political power shifting to the nations of eastern Asia? Will the end of the Cold War eventually lead to a "new world order" marked by global cooperation, or are we now entering an unstable era of ethnic and national conflict? Why has a time of unparalleled prosperity and technological advance been accompanied by deep pockets of poverty and widespread doubts about the role of government and the capabilities of human reason? Although this book does not promise final answers to such questions, it seeks to provide a framework for analysis and a better understanding of some of the salient issues of modern times.

Any author who seeks to encompass in a single volume the history of our turbulent times faces some important choices. First, should the book be arranged in strict chronological order, or should separate chapters focus on individual cultures and societies in order to place greater emphasis on the course of events taking place in different regions of the world? In this book, I have sought to achieve a balance between a global and a regional approach. I accept the commonplace observation that the world we live in is increasingly interdependent in terms of economics as well as culture and communications. Yet the inescapable reality is that this process of globalization is at best a work in progress, as ethnic, religious, and regional differences continue to proliferate and to shape the course of our times. To many observers around the world, the oft-predicted inevitable victory of the democratic capitalist way of life is by no means a preordained vision of the future of the human experience. In fact, influential figures in many countries, from China to Russia and the Middle East, emphatically deny that the forces of globalization will inevitably lead to the worldwide adoption of the Western model.

This issue has practical observations as well. College students today are often not well informed about the distinctive character of civilizations such as China, India, and sub-Saharan Africa. Without sufficient exposure to the historical evolution of such societies, students will assume all too readily that the peoples in these countries have had historical experiences similar to their own and react to various stimuli in a fashion similar to those living in western Europe or the United States. If it is a mistake to ignore the forces that link us together, it is equally erroneous to underestimate the factors that divide us.

Balancing the global and regional perspectives means that some chapters focus on issues that have a global impact, such as the Industrial Revolution, the era of imperialism, and the two world wars. Others center on individual regions of the world, while singling out contrasts and comparisons that link them to the broader world community. The book is divided into five parts. The first four parts are each followed by a short section labeled "Reflections," which attempts to link events in a broad comparative and global framework. The chapter in the fifth and final part examines some of the common problems of our time—including environmental pollution, the population explosion, and spiritual malaise—and takes a cautious look into the future to explore how such issues will evolve in the twenty-first century.

Another issue that has recently attracted widespread discussion and debate among historians is how to balance the treatment of Western civilization with other parts of the world. The modern world has traditionally been viewed essentially as the history of Europe and the United States, with other regions treated as mere appendages of the industrial countries. It is certainly true that much of the twentieth century was dominated by events that were initiated in Europe and North America, and in recognition of this fact, the opening chapters in this book focus on the Industrial Revolution and the age of imperialism, both issues related to the rise of the West in the modern world. In recent decades, however, other parts of the world have assumed greater importance, thus restoring a global balance that had existed prior to the scientific and technological revolution that transformed the West in the eighteenth and nineteenth centuries. Later chapters examine this phenomenon in more detail, according to regions such as Africa, Asia, and Latin America the importance that they merit today.

In sum, this sixth edition of *Contemporary World History* seeks to present a balanced treatment of the most important political, economic, social, and cultural events of the modern era within an integrated and chronologically ordered synthesis. In my judgment, a strong narrative, linking key issues in a broad interpretive framework, is still the most effective way to present the story of the past to young minds.

To supplement the text, I have included a number of boxed documents that illustrate key issues within each chapter. A new feature, Opposing Viewpoints, presents a comparison of two or more primary sources to facilitate student analysis of historical documents, including examples such as "Islam in the Modern World: Two Views" (Chapter 5), "Two Visions for India" (Chapter 13), and "Africa: Dark Continent or Radiant Land?" (Chapter 14). Film & History features present a brief analysis of the plot as well as the historical significance, value, and accuracy of nine films, including such movies as *Khartoum* (1966), *Gandhi* (1982), *The Last Emperor* (1987), *The Lives of Others* (2006), and *Persepolis* (2007). Extensive maps and illustrations, each positioned at the appropriate place in the chapter, serve to deepen the reader's understanding of the text. "Spot maps" provide details not visible in the larger maps. Suggested Readings, now available on the companion website, review the most recent literature on each period while referring also to some of the older "classic" works in the field.

The following supplements are available to accompany this text.

Instructor Resources

Online PowerLecture with Cognero® [ISBN: 9781285458212] This PowerLecture is an all-in-one online multimedia resource for class preparation, presentation, and testing. It is accessible through Cengage.com/login with your faculty account. There you will find available for download: book-specific Microsoft® PowerPoint® presentations; a Test Bank in both Microsoft® Word® and Cognero® formats; an Instructor's Manual; Microsoft® PowerPoint® Image Slides; and a JPEG Image Library.

The Test Bank, offered in Microsoft® Word® and Cognero® formats, contains multiple-choice and essay questions for each chapter. Cognero® is a flexible online system that allows you to author, edit, and manage test bank content for *Contemporary World History, 6e*. Create multiple test versions instantly and deliver through your LMS from your classroom, or wherever you may be, with no special installs or downloads required.

The Instructor's Manual contains the following for each chapter: an outline, discussion questions, learning objectives, lecture launching suggestions, suggested student projects, essay topics, and Web resources.

The Microsoft® PowerPoint® presentations are ready-to-use, visual outlines of each chapter. These presentations are easily customized for your lectures and offered along with chapter-specific Microsoft® PowerPoint® Image Slides and JPEG Image Libraries. Access your Online PowerLecture at www.cengage.com/login.

Companion Site [ISBN: 9781285458229] This website for instructors features all of the free student assets, plus an Instructor's Resource Manual (instructional objectives, chapter outlines, discussion questions, suggested lecture topics, suggested paper topics, and related Internet resources) and PowerPoint® presentations (lecture outlines, images, and maps).

CourseReader CourseReader is an online collection of primary and secondary sources that lets you create a customized electronic reader in minutes. With an easy-to-use interface and assessment tool, you can choose exactly what your students will be assigned—simply search or browse Cengage Learning's extensive document database to preview and select your customized collection of readings. In addition to print sources of all types (letters, diary entries, speeches, newspaper accounts, etc.), the collection includes a growing number of images and video and audio clips.

Each primary source document includes a descriptive headnote that puts the reading into context and is further supported by both critical thinking and multiple-choice questions designed to reinforce key points. For more information visit www.cengage.com/coursereader.

Cengagebrain.com Save your students time and money. Direct them to www.cengagebrain.com for a choice in formats and savings and a better chance to succeed in your class. *Cengagebrain.com*, Cengage Learning's online store, is a single destination for more than 10,000 new textbooks, eTextbooks, eChapters, study tools, and audio supplements. Students have the freedom to purchase à la carte exactly what they need when they need it. Students can save 50 percent on the electronic textbook and can pay as little as $1.99 for an individual eChapter.

Student Resources

Book Companion Site [ISBN: 9781285458229] This website provides a variety of resources to help you review for class. These study tools include a glossary, crossword puzzles, short quizzes, essay questions, critical thinking questions, and primary sources.

Doing History: Research and Writing in the Digital Age, 2e [ISBN: 9781133587880] Prepared by Michael J. Galgano, J. Chris Arndt, and Raymond M. Hyser of James Madison University. Whether you're starting down the path as a history major, or simply looking for a straightforward and systematic guide to writing a successful paper, you'll find this text to be an indispensable handbook to historical research. This text's "soup to nuts" approach to researching and writing about history addresses every step of the process, from locating your sources and gathering information, to writing clearly and making proper use of various citation styles to avoid plagiarism. You'll also learn how to make the most of every tool available to you—especially the technology that helps you conduct the process efficiently and effectively. The second edition includes a special appendix linked to CourseReader (see above), where you can examine and interpret primary sources online.

The History Handbook, 2e [ISBN: 9780495906766] Prepared by Carol Berkin of Baruch College, City University of New York, and Betty Anderson of Boston University. This book teaches students both basic and history-specific study skills such as how to take notes, get the most out of lectures and readings, read primary sources, research historical topics, and correctly cite sources. Substantially less expensive than comparable skill-building texts, *The History Handbook* also offers tips for Internet research and evaluating online sources.

Additionally, students can purchase and download the *eAudio* version of *The History Handbook* or any of its eighteen individual units at www.cengagebrain.com to listen to on the go.

Writing for College History, 1e [ISBN: 9780618306039] Prepared by Robert M. Frakes, Clarion University. This brief handbook for survey courses in American history, Western civilization/European history, and world civilization guides students through the various types of writing assignments they encounter in a history class. Providing examples of student writing and candid assessments of student work, this text focuses on the rules and conventions of writing for the college history course.

The Modern Researcher, 6e [ISBN: 9780495318705] Prepared by Jacques Barzun and Henry F. Graff of Columbia University. This classic introduction to the techniques of research and the art of expression is used widely in history courses, but is also appropriate for writing and research methods courses in other departments. Barzun and Graff thoroughly cover every aspect of research, from the selection of a topic through the gathering, analysis, writing, revision, and publication of findings. They present the process not as a set of rules but through actual cases that put the subtleties of research in a useful context. Part One covers the principles and methods of research; Part Two covers writing, speaking, and getting one's work published.

Rand McNally Historical Atlas of the World, 2e [ISBN: 9780618841912] This valuable resource features more than seventy maps that portray the rich panoply of the world's history from preliterate times to the present. They show how cultures and civilization were linked and how they interacted. The maps make it clear that history is not static. Rather, it is about change and movement across time. The maps show change by presenting the dynamics of expansion, cooperation, and conflict. This atlas includes maps showing the world from the beginning of civilization; the political development of all major areas of the world; extensive coverage of Africa, Latin America, and the Middle East; the current Islamic world; and the world population change in 1900 and 2000.

Custom Options

Nobody knows your students like you, so why not give them a text that is tailor-fit to their needs? Cengage Learning offers custom solutions for your course—whether it's making a small modification to *Contemporary World History, 6e* to match your syllabus or combining multiple sources to create something truly unique. You can pick and choose chapters, include your own material, and add additional map exercises along with the *Rand McNally Atlas* to create a text that fits the way you teach. Ensure that your students get the most out of their textbook dollar by giving them exactly what they need. Contact your

Cengage Learning representative to explore custom solutions for your course.

Acknowledgments

I would like to express my appreciation to the reviewers who have read individual chapters and provided useful suggestions for improvement on this edition: Marjorie Berman, Red Rocks Community College; Elizabeth Clark, West Texas A&M University; Margaret B. Denning, Slippery Rock University; Hayley Froysland, Indiana University, South Bend; Irwin Halfond, McKendree University; Eduardo Magalhaes, Simpson College; and Jeffrey Martinson, Meredith College.

Jackson Spielvogel, coauthor of our textbook *World History*, was kind enough to permit me to use some of his sections in that book for the purposes of writing this one. Several of my other colleagues at Penn State—including Kumkum Chatterjee, E-tu Zen Sun, On-cho Ng, and Arthur F. Goldschmidt—have provided me with valuable assistance in understanding parts of the world that are beyond my own area of concentration. Ian Bell, Carol Coffin, Ruth Petzold, and my daughter Claire L. Duiker have provided useful illustrations, while Dale and Jan Peterson have been stimulating travel companions and a steady source of useful books and news items. I have also benefited from Nan Johnson's broad understanding of the growth of the women's movement in the United States. To Clark Baxter, whose unfailing good humor, patience, and sage advice have so often eased the trauma of textbook publishing, I offer my heartfelt thanks. I am also grateful to Brooke Barbier, product manager, Margaret McAndrew Beasley, senior development editor, and Jane Lee, senior content project manager, for their assistance in bringing this project to fruition, and to John Orr of Orr Book Services, Chris Schoedel of Cenveo Publisher Services, and Pat Lewis, copyeditor, for production services.

Finally, I am eternally grateful to my wife, Yvonne V. Duiker, Ph.D. Her research and her written contributions on art, architecture, literature, and music have added sparkle to this book. Her presence at my side has added immeasurable sparkle to my life.

William J. Duiker
The Pennsylvania State University

PART I

New World in the Making

The Crystal Palace in London

The Rise of Industrial Society in the West

SHEFFIELD SMOKE.
From a Drawing by A. MORROW.

Sheffield became one of England's greatest manufacturing cities during the nineteenth century.

Hulton Archive/Getty Images

THE TWENTIETH CENTURY was a turbulent era, marked by two violent global conflicts, a bitter ideological struggle between two dominant world powers, explosive developments in the realm of science, and dramatic social change. When the century began, the vast majority of the world's peoples lived on farms, and the horse was still the most common means of transportation. By its end, human beings had trod on the moon and lived in a world increasingly defined by urban sprawl and modern technology.

What had happened to bring about these momentous changes? Although a world as complex as ours cannot be assigned a single cause, a good candidate for consideration is the Industrial Revolution, which began on the British Isles at the end of the eighteenth century and spread steadily throughout the world during the next two hundred years. The Industrial Revolution was unquestionably one of the most important factors in laying the foundation of the modern world. It not only transformed the economic means of production and distribution, but also altered the political systems, the social institutions and values, and the intellectual and cultural life of all the societies that it touched. The impact has been both massive and controversial. While proponents have stressed the enormous material and technological benefits that industrialization has brought, critics have pointed out the high costs involved, from growing economic inequality and environmental pollution to the dehumanization of everyday life. Already in the nineteenth century, the German philosopher Karl Marx charged that factory labor had reduced workers to a mere

"appendage of the machine," and the English novelist Charles Dickens wrote about an urban environment of factories, smoke, and ashes that seemed an apparition from Dante's Hell. ❧

CRITICAL THINKING

Q What factors appear to explain why Great Britain was the first nation to enter the industrial age?

The Industrial Revolution in Great Britain

Why the Industrial Revolution occurred first in Great Britain rather than in another part of the world has been a subject for debate among historians for many decades. Some observers point to cultural factors, such as the Protestant "work ethic" that predisposed British citizens to risk taking and the belief that material rewards in this world were a sign of heavenly salvation to come.

Others point out more tangible factors that contributed to the rapid transformation of eighteenth-century British society from a predominantly agricultural to an industrial and commercial economy. First, improvements in agriculture during the eighteenth century had led to a significant increase in food production. British agriculture could now feed more people at lower prices with less labor; even ordinary British families no longer had to use most of their income to buy food, giving them the potential to purchase manufactured goods. At the same time, a rapidly growing population in the second half of the eighteenth century provided a pool of surplus labor for the new factories of the emerging British industrial sector.

Another factor that played a role in promoting the Industrial Revolution in Great Britain was the rapid increase in national wealth. Two centuries of expanding trade had provided Britain with a ready supply of capital for investment in the new industrial machines and the factories that were required to house them. As the historian Kenneth Pomeranz has recently pointed out, it was the country's access to cheap materials from other parts of the world—notably from Asia and the Americas—that provided the assets that fueled Britain's entrance into the industrial age (see Chapter 2).[1]

In addition to profits from trade, Britain possessed an effective central bank and well-developed, flexible credit facilities. Many early factory owners were merchants and entrepreneurs who had profited from the eighteenth-century cottage industry. The country also possessed what might today be described as a "modernization elite"—individuals who were interested in making profits if the opportunity presented itself. In that objective, they were generally supported by the government.

Moreover, Britain was richly supplied with important mineral resources, such as coal and iron ore, needed in the manufacturing process. Britain was also a small country and the relatively short distances made transportation facilities readily accessible. In addition to nature's provision of abundant rivers, from the mid-seventeenth century onward, both private and public investment poured into the construction of new roads, bridges, and canals. By 1780, roads, rivers, and canals linked the major industrial centers of the north, the Midlands, London, and the Atlantic coast.

During the last decades of the eighteenth century, technological innovations, including the flying shuttle, the spinning jenny, and the power loom, led to a significant increase in textile production. The cotton textile industry—fueled by the import of cheap cotton fibers from Britain's growing empire in South Asia—achieved even greater heights of productivity with the invention of the steam engine, which proved invaluable to Britain's Industrial Revolution. The steam engine was a tireless source of power and depended for fuel on a substance—namely, coal—that seemed then to be available in unlimited quantities. The success of the steam engine increased the demand for coal and led to an expansion in coal production. In turn, new processes using coal furthered the development of an iron industry, the production of machinery, and the invention of the railroad.

The Spread of the Industrial Revolution

By the turn of the nineteenth century, industrialization had begun to spread to the continent of Europe, where it took a different path than had been followed in Great Britain (see Map 1.1). Governments on the Continent were accustomed to playing a major role in economic affairs and continued to do so as the Industrial Revolution got under way, subsidizing inventors, providing incentives to factory owners, and improving the transportation network. By 1850, a network of iron rails (described by the French novelist Émile Zola as a "monstrous great steel skeleton") had spread across much of western and central Europe, while water routes were improved by the deepening and widening of rivers and canals.

Across the Atlantic Ocean, the United States experienced the first stages of its industrial revolution in the first half of the nineteenth century. In 1800, America was still a predominantly agrarian society, as six out of every seven workers were farmers. Sixty years later, only half of all workers were farmers, while the total population had grown from 5 to 30 million people, larger than Great Britain itself.

The initial application of machinery to production was accomplished by borrowing from Great Britain. Soon, however, Americans began to equal or surpass British technical achievements. The Harpers Ferry arsenal, for example, built muskets with interchangeable parts. Because all the individual parts of a musket were identical (for example, all triggers were the same), the final product could be put together quickly and easily; this innovation enabled Americans to avoid the more costly system in which skilled craftsmen fitted together individual parts made separately. The so-called American system reduced costs and revolutionized production by saving labor, an important consideration in a society that had few skilled artisans.

Unlike Britain, the United States was a large country, and the lack of a good system of internal transportation initially seemed to limit American economic development by making the transport of goods prohibitively expensive. This difficulty was gradually remedied, however. Thousands of miles of roads and canals were built linking east and west. The steamboat facilitated transportation on rivers and the Great Lakes and in Atlantic coastal waters. Most important of all in the development of an American transportation system was the railroad. Beginning with 100 miles in 1830, more than 27,000 miles of railroad track were laid in the next thirty years. This transportation revolution turned the United States into a single massive market for the manufactured goods of the Northeast, the early center of American industrialization, and by 1860, the United States was well on its way to being an industrial nation.

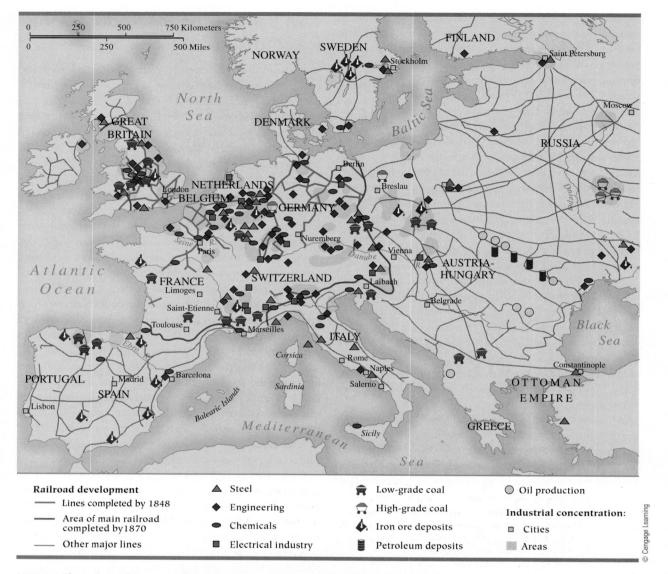

MAP 1.1 The Industrial Regions of Europe at the End of the Nineteenth Century. By the end of the nineteenth century, the Industrial Revolution—in steelmaking, electricity, petroleum, and chemicals—had spurred substantial economic growth and prosperity in western and central Europe; it had also sparked economic and political competition between Great Britain and Germany.

Q *Which parts of Europe became industrialized most quckly in the nineteenth century? Why do you think this was?*

New Products and New Patterns

During the fifty years before the outbreak of World War I in 1914, the Western world witnessed a dynamic age of material prosperity. Thanks to new industries, new sources of energy, and new technological achievements, a second stage of the Industrial Revolution transformed the human environment and led people to believe that their material progress would improve world conditions and solve all human problems.

The first major change in industrial development after 1870 was the substitution of steel for iron. Steel, an alloy stronger and more malleable than iron, soon became an essential component of the Industrial Revolution. New methods for rolling and shaping steel made it useful in the construction of lighter, smaller, and faster until the 1870s. By 1910, hydroelectric power stations and coal-fired steam-generating plants enabled entire districts to be tied into a single power distribution system that provided a common source of power for homes, shops, and industrial enterprises.

Electricity spawned a whole series of new products. The invention of the incandescent filament lamp opened homes and cities to illumination by electric lights. Although most electricity was initially used for lighting, it was eventually put to use in transportation. By the 1880s, streetcars and subways had appeared in major European cities. Electricity also transformed the factory. Conveyor belts, cranes, machines, and machine tools could all be powered by electricity and located anywhere. Meanwhile, a revolution in communications ensued when Alexander Graham Bell invented the telephone in 1876 and Guglielmo Marconi sent the first radio waves across the Atlantic in 1901.

THE INTERNAL COMBUSTION ENGINE The development of the internal combustion engine had a similar effect. The processing of liquid fuels—petroleum and its distilled derivatives—made possible the widespread use of the internal combustion engine as a source of power in transportation. An oil-fired engine was made in 1897, and by 1902, the Hamburg-Amerika Line had switched from coal to oil on its new ocean liners. By the beginning of the twentieth century, some naval fleets had been converted to oil burners as well.

The internal combustion engine gave rise to the automobile and the airplane. In 1900, world production, initially led by the French, stood at 9,000 cars, but by 1906, Americans had taken the lead. It was an American, Henry Ford, who revolutionized the automotive industry with the mass production of the Model T. By 1916, Ford's factories were producing 735,000 cars a year. In the meantime, air transportation had emerged with the Zeppelin airship in 1900. In 1903, at Kitty Hawk, North Carolina, the Wright brothers made the first flight in a fixed-wing plane powered by a gasoline engine. World War I stimulated the aircraft industry, and in 1919 the first regular passenger air service was established.

TRADE AND MANUFACTURING The growth of industrial production depended on the development of markets for the sale of manufactured goods. Competition for foreign markets was keen, and by 1870, European countries were increasingly compelled to focus on promoting domestic demand. Between 1850 and 1900, real wages increased in Britain by two-thirds and in Germany by one-third. A decline in the cost of food combined with lower prices for manufactured goods because of reduced production and transportation costs made it easier for Europeans to buy consumer products. In the cities, new

The Colossus of Paris. When it was completed for the Paris World's Fair in 1889, the Eiffel Tower became, at 1,056 feet, the tallest human-made monument in the world. The colossus, which seemed to be rising from the shadows of the city's feudal past like some new technological giant, symbolized the triumph of the Industrial Revolution and machine-age capitalism, proclaiming the dawn of a new era of endless possibilities and power. Constructed of wrought iron with more than 2.5 million rivet holes, the structure was completed in two years and was paid for entirely by the builder himself, the engineer Gustave Eiffel. From the outset, the monument was wildly popular. Nearly 2 million people lined up at the fair to visit this gravity-defying marvel.

machines and engines as well as for railways, shipbuilding, and armaments. It also paved the way for the building of the first skyscrapers, a development that would eventually transform the skylines of the cities of the West. In 1860, Great Britain, France, Germany, and Belgium produced 125,000 tons of steel; by 1913, the total was 32 million tons.

THE INVENTION OF ELECTRICITY Electricity was a major new form of energy that proved to be of great value since it moved relatively effortlessly through space by means of transmitting wires. The first commercially practical generators of electric current were not developed methods for retail distribution—in particular, the department store—were used to expand sales of a whole new range of consumer goods made possible by the development of the steel and electric industries. The desire to own sewing machines, clocks, bicycles, electric lights, and typewriters generated a new consumer ethic that has since become a crucial part of the modern economy.

Meanwhile, increased competition for foreign markets and the growing importance of domestic demand led to a reaction against the free trade that had characterized the European economy between 1820 and 1870. By the 1870s, Europeans were returning to the use of protective **tariffs** to guarantee domestic markets for the products of their own industries. At the same time, cartels were being formed to decrease competition internally. In a **cartel**, independent enterprises worked together to control prices and fix production quotas, thereby restraining the kind of competition that led to reduced prices. The Rhenish-Westphalian Coal Syndicate, founded in 1893, controlled 98 percent of Germany's coal production by 1904.

The formation of cartels was paralleled by a move toward larger and more efficient manufacturing plants, especially in the iron and steel, machinery, heavy electric equipment, and chemical industries. The result was a desire to streamline or rationalize production as much as possible. The development of precision tools enabled manufacturers to produce interchangeable parts, which in turn led to the creation of the assembly line for production.

By 1900, much of western and central Europe had entered a new era, characterized by rising industrial production and material prosperity. With its capital, industries, and military might, the region dominated the world economy. Eastern and southern Europe, however, was still largely agricultural and relegated by the industrialized countries to providing food and raw materials. The presence of Romanian oil, Greek olive oil, and Serbian pigs and prunes in western Europe served as reminders of an economic division in Europe that continued well into the twentieth century.

The Emergence of a Mass Society

The new world created by the Industrial Revolution led to the emergence of a **mass society** in western Europe and the United States by the end of the nineteenth century. A mass society meant new forms of expression for the lower classes as they benefited from the extension of voting rights, an improved standard of living, and compulsory elementary education. But there was a price to pay. Urbanization and rapid population growth led to overcrowding in the burgeoning cities and increasing public health problems. As the number and size of cities continued to mushroom, by the 1880s governments came to the reluctant conclusion that private enterprise could not solve the housing crisis. In 1890, a British law empowered local town councils to construct cheap housing for the working classes. Similar activity had been set in motion in Germany by 1900. In general, however, such measures failed to do much to meet the real housing needs of the working classes. Nevertheless, the need for planning had been recognized, and in the 1920s, municipal governments moved into housing construction on a large scale. More and more, governments were stepping into areas of social engineering that they would never have touched earlier.

Social Structures

At the top of European society stood a wealthy elite, constituting only 5 percent of the population but controlling between 30 and 40 percent of its wealth. This privileged minority was an amalgamation of the traditional landed aristocracy that had dominated European society for centuries and the emerging upper middle class, sometimes called the bourgeoisie (literally "burghers" or "city people"). In the course of the nineteenth century, aristocrats coalesced with the most successful industrialists, bankers, and merchants to form a new elite.

Increasingly, aristocrats and the affluent bourgeoisie fused as the latter purchased landed estates to join the aristocrats in the pleasures of country living, while the aristocrats bought lavish town houses for part-time urban life. Common bonds were also created when the sons of wealthy bourgeois families were admitted to the elite schools dominated by the children of the aristocracy. This educated elite assumed leadership roles in the government and the armed forces. Marriage also served to unite the two groups. Daughters of tycoons gained titles, and aristocratic heirs gained new sources of cash. When the American heiress Consuelo Vanderbilt married the duke of Marlborough, the new duchess brought £2 million (approximately $10 million) to her husband.

A NEW MIDDLE CLASS Below the upper class was a middle level of the bourgeoisie that included professionals in law, medicine, and the civil service as well as moderately well-to-do industrialists and merchants. The industrial expansion of the nineteenth century also added new vocations to Western society such as business managers, office workers, engineers, architects, accountants, and chemists, who formed professional associations as the symbols of their newfound importance. At the lower end of the middle class were the small shopkeepers, traders, manufacturers, and prosperous peasants. Their chief preoccupation was the provision of goods and services for the classes above them.

The moderately prosperous and successful members of this new mass society shared a certain style of life, one whose values tended to dominate much of nineteenth-century society. They were especially active in preaching their worldview to their children and to the upper and lower classes of their society. This was especially evident in Victorian Britain, often considered a model of middle-class society. It was the European middle classes who accepted and promulgated the importance of progress and science. They believed in hard work, which they viewed as the primary human good, open to everyone and guaranteed to have positive results. They also believed in the good conduct associated with traditional Christian morality.

Such values were often scorned at the time by members of the economic and intellectual elite, and in later years, it became commonplace for observers to mock the Victorian era—the years of the long reign of Queen Victoria (r. 1837–1901) in Great Britain—for its vulgar materialism, cultural philistinism, and conformist values. As the historian Peter Gay has recently shown, however, this harsh portrayal of the "bourgeois" character of the age distorts the reality of an era of complexity and contradiction, with diverse forces interacting to lay the foundations of the modern world.[2]

THE WORKING CLASS The working classes constituted almost 80 percent of the population of Europe. In rural areas, many of these people were landholding peasants, agricultural laborers, and sharecroppers, especially in eastern Europe. Only about 10 percent of the British population worked in agriculture, however; in Germany, the figure was 25 percent.

There was no homogeneous urban working class. At the top were skilled artisans in such traditional handicraft trades as cabinetmaking, printing, and jewelry making. The Industrial Revolution also brought new entrants into the group of highly skilled workers, including machine-tool specialists, shipbuilders, and metalworkers. Many skilled workers attempted to pattern themselves after the middle class by seeking good housing and educating their children.

Semiskilled laborers, including such people as carpenters, bricklayers, and many factory workers, earned wages that were about two-thirds of those of highly skilled workers (see the box on p. 8). At the bottom of the hierarchy stood the largest group of workers, the unskilled laborers. They included day laborers, who worked irregularly for very low wages, and large numbers of domestic servants. One of every seven employed persons in Great Britain in 1900 was a domestic servant.

Urban workers did experience a betterment in the material conditions of their lives after 1870. A rise in real wages, accompanied by a decline in many consumer costs, especially in the 1880s and 1890s, made it possible for workers to buy more than just food and housing. Workers' budgets now included money for more clothes and even leisure at the same time that strikes and labor agitation were winning ten-hour days and Saturday afternoons off. The combination of more income and more free time produced whole new patterns of mass leisure.

Among the least attractive aspects of the era, however, was the widespread practice of child labor. Working conditions for underage workers were often abysmal. According to a report commissioned in 1832 to inquire into the conditions for child factory workers in Great Britain, children as young as six years of age began work before dawn. Those who were drowsy or fell asleep were tapped on the head, doused with cold water, strapped to a chair, or flogged with a stick. Another commission convened in the 1840s described conditions for underage workers in the coal mines as follows: "Chained, belted, harnessed like dogs in a go-cart, black, saturated with wet, and more than half naked—crawling upon their hands and feet, and dragging their heavy loads behind them—they present an appearance indescribably disgusting and unnatural."[3]

Changing Roles for Women

The position of women during the Industrial Revolution was also changing. During much of the nineteenth century, many women adhered to the ideal of femininity popularized by writers and poets. Tennyson's poem *The Princess* expressed it well:

> Man for the field and woman for the hearth:
> Man for the sword and for the needle she:
> Man with the head and woman with the heart:
> Man to command and woman to obey; All else confusion.

The reality was somewhat different. Under the impact of the Industrial Revolution, which created a wide variety of service and white-collar jobs, women began to accept employment as clerks, typists, secretaries, and salesclerks. Compulsory education opened the door to new opportunities in the teaching profession, and the expansion of hospital services enabled more women to find employment as nurses. In some countries in western Europe, women's legal rights increased. Still, most women remained confined to their traditional roles of homemaking and child rearing. The less fortunate were compelled to undertake marginal work as domestic servants or as pieceworkers in sweatshops.

Paradoxically, however, employment in the new textile mills in the United States served as an effective means for young women in New England to escape their homes and

Discipline in the New Factories

Workers in the new factories of the Industrial Revolution had been accustomed to a lifestyle free of overseers. Unlike the cottage industry, where home-based workers spun thread and wove cloth in their own rhythm and time, the factories demanded a new, rigorous discipline geared to the requirements and operating hours of the machines. This selection is taken from a set of rules for a factory in Berlin in 1844. They were typical of company rules everywhere the factory system had been established.

Factory Rules, Foundry and Engineering Works, Royal Overseas Trading Company

In every large works, and in the coordination of any large number of workmen, good order and harmony must be looked upon as the fundamentals of success, and therefore the following rules shall be strictly observed.

1. The normal working day begins at all seasons at 6 A.M. precisely and ends, after the usual break of half an hour for breakfast, an hour for dinner, and half an hour for tea, at 7 P.M., and it shall be strictly observed. . . .

2. Workers arriving 2 minutes late shall lose half an hour's wages; whoever is more than 2 minutes late may not start work until after the next break, or at least shall lose his wages until then. Any disputes about the correct time shall be settled by the clock mounted above the gatekeeper's lodge. . . .

3. No workman, whether employed by time or piece, may leave before the end of the working day, without having first received permission from the overseer and having given his name to the gatekeeper. Omission of these two actions shall lead to a fine of ten silver groschen payable to the sick fund.

4. Repeated irregular arrival at work shall lead to dismissal. This shall also apply to those who are found idling by an official or overseer, and refused to obey their order to resume work. . . .

6. No worker may leave his place of work otherwise than for reasons connected with his work.

7. All conversation with fellow-workers is prohibited; if any worker requires information about his work, he must turn to the overseer, or to the particular fellow-worker designated for the purpose.

8. Smoking in the workshops or in the yard is prohibited during working hours; anyone caught smoking shall be fined five silver groschen for the sick fund for every such offense. . . .

10. Natural functions must be performed at the appropriate places, and whoever is found soiling walls, fences, squares, etc., and similarly, whoever is found washing his face and hands in the workshop and not in the places assigned for the purpose, shall be fined five silver groschen for the sick fund. . . .

12. It goes without saying that all overseers and officials of the firm shall be obeyed without question, and shall be treated with due deference. Disobedience will be punished by dismissal.

13. Immediate dismissal shall also be the fate of anyone found drunk in any of the workshops. . . .

14. Every workman is obliged to report to his superiors any acts of dishonesty or embezzlement on the part of his fellow workmen. If he omits to do so, and it is shown after subsequent discovery of a misdemeanor that he knew about it at the time, he shall be liable to be taken to court as an accessory after the fact and the wage due to him shall be retained as punishment.

 Which, if any, of these regulations do you believe would be acceptable to employers and employees in today's labor market? Why?

SOURCE: From *Documents of European Economic History* by Sidney Pollard and Colin Holmes (New York: St. Martin's Press, 1968). Copyright © 1968 by S. Pollard and C. Holmes.

---

establish an independent existence. As one female factory worker expressed it:

Despite the toil we all agree
Out of the mill or in,
Dependent on others we ne'er will be
As long as we're able to spin.[4]

Many of the improvements in women's position occurred as a result of the rise of the first feminist movements. **Feminism** in Europe had its origins in the social upheaval of the French Revolution, when some women advocated equality for women based on the doctrine of natural rights. In the 1830s, a number of women in the United States and Europe sought improvements for women by focusing on family and marriage law to strengthen the property rights of wives and enhance their ability to secure a divorce (see the box on p. 10). Later in the century, attention shifted to the issue of equal political rights. Many feminists

Cracks in the Glass Ceiling. Women were largely excluded from male-dominated educational institutions in the United States before 1900. Consequently, the demand for higher education for women led to the establishment of women's colleges, as well as specialized institutes and medical schools. The Women's Medical College of Pennsylvania in the city of Philadelphia was the world's first medical school created specifically for women. In this 1911 photograph, we see an operation performed by women surgeons as they instruct their students in the latest medical techniques.

believed that the right to vote was the key to all other reforms to improve the position of women.

The British women's movement was the most vocal and active in Europe, but it was divided over tactics. Moderates believed that women must demonstrate that they would use political power responsibly if they wanted Parliament to grant them the right to vote. Another group, however, favored a more radical approach. In 1903, Emmeline Pankhurst (1858–1928) and her daughters, Christabel and Sylvia, founded the Women's Social and Political Union, which enrolled mostly middle- and upper-class women. The members of Pankhurst's organization realized the value of the media and used unusual publicity stunts to call attention to their insistence on winning women the right to vote and other demands. They pelted government officials with eggs, chained themselves to lampposts, smashed the windows of department stores on

fashionable shopping streets, burned railroad cars, and went on hunger strikes in jail.

Before World War I, demands for women's rights were being heard throughout Europe and the United States, although only in Norway and a few American states as well as in Australia and New Zealand did women actually receive the right to vote before 1914. It would take the dramatic upheaval of World War I before male-dominated governments capitulated on this basic issue.

Reaction and Revolution: The Decline of the Old Order

While the Industrial Revolution shook the economic and social foundations of European society, similar revolutionary developments were reshaping the political map of the Continent. These developments were the product of a variety of factors, including not only the Industrial Revolution itself but also the Renaissance, the Enlightenment, and the French Revolution at the end of the eighteenth century. The influence of these new forces resulted in a redefinition of political conditions in Europe. The conservative order—based on the principle of hereditary monarchy and the existence of great multinational states such as Russia, the Habsburg Empire, and the Ottoman Empire—had emerged intact from the defeat of Napoleon Bonaparte at the Battle of Waterloo in 1815, but by mid-century, it had come under attack along a wide front. Arrayed against the conservative forces was a set of new political ideas that began to come into their own in the first half of the nineteenth century and continue to affect the entire world today.

Liberalism and Nationalism

One of these new political ideas was **liberalism**. Liberalism owed much to the Enlightenment of the eighteenth century and the American and French Revolutions that erupted at the end of that century, all of which proclaimed the autonomy of the individual against the power of the state. Opinions diverged among people classified as liberals—many of them members of the emerging middle class—but all began with a common denominator, a conviction that in both economic and political terms, people should be as free from restraint as possible. Economic liberalism, also known as classical economics, was based on the tenet of *laissez-faire*—the belief that the state should not interfere in the free play of natural economic forces, especially supply and demand. Political liberalism was based on the concept of a constitutional monarchy or constitutional state, with limits on the powers of government and a written charter to protect the basic civil rights of the people.

Escaping the Doll's House

Although a majority of women probably followed the nineteenth-century middle-class ideal of women as keepers of the household and nurturers of husband and children, an increasing number of women fought for the rights of women. This selection is taken from Act III of Henrik Ibsen's *A Doll's House* (1879), in which the character Nora Helmer declares her independence from her husband's control over her life.

Henrik Ibsen, *A Doll's House*

NORA: *(Pause)* Does anything strike you as we sit here?

HELMER: What should strike me?

NORA: We've been married eight years: does it not strike you that this is the first time we two, you and I, man and wife, have talked together seriously?

HELMER: Seriously? What do you mean, seriously?

NORA: For eight whole years, and more—ever since the day we first met—we have never exchanged one serious word about serious things. . . .

HELMER: Why, my dearest Nora, what have you to do with serious things?

NORA: There we have it! You have never understood me. I've had great injustice done to me, Torvald; first by father, then by you.

HELMER: What! Your father and me? We, who have loved you more than all the world?

NORA: *(Shaking her head)* You have never loved me. You just found it amusing to think you were in love with me.

HELMER: Nora! What a thing to say!

NORA: Yes, it's true, Torvald. When I was living at home with father, he told me his opinions and mine were the same. If I had different opinions, I said nothing about them, because he would not have liked it. He used to call me his doll-child and played with me as I played with my dolls. Then I came to live in your house.

HELMER: What a way to speak of our marriage!

NORA: *(Undisturbed)* I mean that I passed from father's hands into yours. You arranged everything to your taste and I got the same tastes as you; or pretended to—I don't know which—both, perhaps: sometimes one, sometimes the other. When I look back on it now, I seem to have been living here like a beggar, on handouts. I lived by performing tricks for you, Torvald. But that was how you wanted it. You and father have done me a great wrong. It is your fault that my life has come to naught.

HELMER: Why, Nora, how unreasonable and ungrateful! Haven't you been happy here?

NORA: No, never. I thought I was, but I never was.

HELMER: Not—not happy! . . .

NORA: I must stand quite alone if I am ever to know myself and my surroundings; so I cannot stay with you.

HELMER: Nora! Nora!

NORA: I am going at once. I daresay [my friend] Christina will take me in for tonight.

HELMER: You are mad! I shall not allow it! I forbid it!

NORA: It's no use your forbidding me anything now. I shall take with me only what belongs to me; from you I will accept nothing, either now or later.

HELMER: This is madness!

NORA: Tomorrow I shall go home—I mean to what was my home. It will be easier for me to find a job there.

HELMER: Oh, in your blind inexperience—

NORA: I must try to gain experience, Torvald.

HELMER: Forsake your home, your husband, your children! And you don't consider what the world will say.

NORA: I can't pay attention to that. I only know that I must do it.

HELMER: This is monstrous! Can you forsake your holiest duties?

NORA: What do you consider my holiest duties?

HELMER: Need I tell you that? Your duties to your husband and children.

NORA: I have other duties equally sacred.

HELMER: Impossible! What do you mean?

NORA: My duties toward myself.

HELMER: Before all else you are a wife and a mother.

NORA: That I no longer believe. Before all else I believe I am a human being, just as much as you are—or at least that I should try to become one. I know that most people agree with you, Torvald, and that they say so in books. But I can no longer be satisfied with what most people say and what is in books. I must think things out for myself and try to get clear about them.

 Why is Nora dissatisfied with her life in the "doll's house"? What is her husband's response?

SOURCE: From Wesley D. Camp, *Roots of Western Civilization*. Copyright © 1988 McGraw-Hill Companies.

Nineteenth-century liberals, however, were not democrats in the modern sense. Although they held that people were entitled to equal civil rights, the right to vote and to hold office would be open only to men who met certain property qualifications.

Nationalism was an even more powerful ideology for change in the nineteenth century. The idea arose out of an awareness of being part of a community that had common institutions, traditions, language, and customs. In some cases, that sense of identity was based on shared ethnic or linguistic characteristics. In others, it was a consequence of a common commitment to a particular religion or culture. Such a community came to be called a "nation," and the primary political loyalty of individuals would be to this "nation" rather than, as was the case in much of Europe at that time, to a dynasty or a city-state or some other political unit. Nationalism did not become a popular force for change until the French Revolution, when the concept arose that governments should coincide with nationalities. Thus, a divided people such as the Germans wanted national unity in a German nation-state with one central government. Subject peoples, such as the Czechs and the Hungarians, wanted national self-determination, or the right to establish their own autonomy rather than be subject to a German minority in a multinational state such as the Habsburg Empire.

Liberalism and nationalism began to have an impact on the European political scene in the 1830s, when a revolt led by reformist forces installed a constitutional monarchy in France, and nationalist uprisings, often given active support by liberal forces, took place in Belgium (which was then attached to the Dutch Republic), in Italy, and in Poland (then part of the Russian Empire). Only the Belgians were successful, as Russian forces crushed the Poles' attempt to liberate themselves from foreign domination, while Austrian troops intervened to uphold reactionary governments in a number of Italian states.

In the spring of 1848, a new series of uprisings against established authority broke out in several countries in central and western Europe. The most effective was in France, where an uprising centered in Paris overthrew the so-called bourgeois monarchy of King Louis Philippe and briefly brought to power a new republic composed of an alliance of workers, intellectuals, and progressive representatives of the urban middle class.

The Unification of Germany and Italy

Within a few months, however, it became clear that optimism about the imminence of a new order in Europe had not been justified. In France, the shaky alliance between workers and the urban bourgeoisie was ruptured when workers' groups and their representatives in the government began to demand extensive social reforms to provide guaranteed benefits to the poor. Moderates, frightened by rising political tensions in Paris, resisted such demands. Facing the specter of class war, the French nation drew back and welcomed the rise to power of Louis Napoleon, a nephew of Napoleon Bonaparte. Within three years, he declared himself Emperor Napoleon III. Elsewhere in Europe—in Germany, in the Habsburg Empire, and in Italy—popular uprisings failed to unseat autocratic monarchs and destroy the existing political order.

But the rising force of nationalism was not to be quenched. Nationalist sentiment, at first restricted primarily to the small educated elite, began to spread among the general population with the rise in literacy rates and the increasing availability of books, journals, and newspapers printed in the vernacular languages. Ordinary Europeans, previously unconcerned about political affairs, now became increasingly aware of the nationalist debate and sometimes became involved in the political process.

Italy, long divided into separate kingdoms, was finally united in the early 1860s. Germany followed a few years later. Unfortunately, the rise of nation-states in central Europe did not herald the onset of liberal principles or greater stability. To the contrary, it inaugurated a period of heightened tensions as an increasingly aggressive Germany began to dominate the politics of Europe. In 1870, Prussian Prime Minister Otto von Bismarck (1815–1898) had provoked a war with France. After the latter's defeat, a new German Empire was declared in the Hall of Mirrors at the Palace of Versailles, just outside Paris.

Many German liberals were initially delighted at the unification of their country after centuries of division. But they were soon to discover that the new German Empire would not usher in a new era of peace and freedom. Under Prussian leadership, the new state quickly proclaimed the superiority of authoritarian and militaristic values and abandoned the principles of liberalism and constitutional government. Nationalism had become a two-edged sword, as advocates of a greater Germany began to exert an impact on domestic politics.

Liberal principles made similarly little headway elsewhere in central and eastern Europe. After the transformation of the Habsburg Empire into the dual monarchy of Austria-Hungary in 1867, the Austrian part received a constitution that theoretically recognized the equality of the nationalities and established a parliamentary system with the principle of **ministerial responsibility**. But the problem of reconciling the interests of the various nationalities remained a difficult one. The German minority that governed Austria felt increasingly threatened by the Czechs,

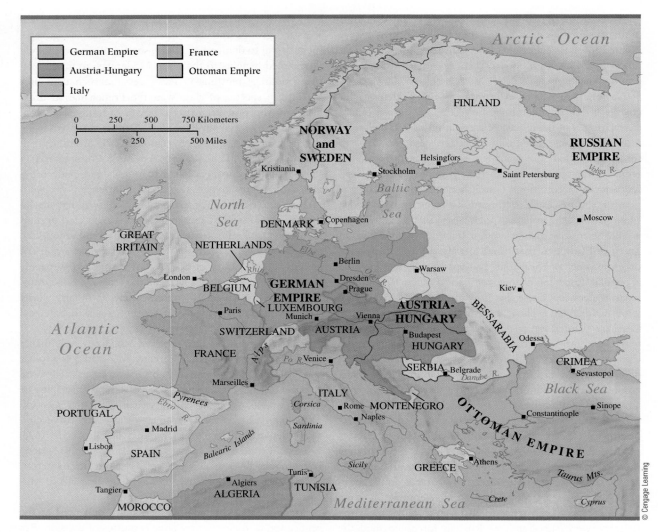

MAP 1.2 Europe in 1871. German unification in 1871 upset the balance of power that had prevailed in Europe for more than half a century and eventually led to a restructuring of European alliances. By 1907, Europe was divided into two opposing camps: the Triple Entente of Great Britain, Russia, and France and the Triple Alliance of Germany, Austria-Hungary, and Italy.

 Which of the countries identified on this map could be described as multinational empires?

Poles, and other Slavic groups within the empire, and when representatives of the latter began to agitate for autonomy, the government ignored the parliament and relied increasingly on imperial emergency decrees to govern. On the eve of World War I, the Austro-Hungarian Empire was far from solving its minorities problem (see Map 1.2).

Roots of Revolution in Russia

To the east, in the vast Russian Empire, neither the Industrial Revolution nor the European Enlightenment had

exerted much impact. At the beginning of the nineteenth century, Russia was overwhelmingly rural, agricultural, and autocratic. The Russian tsar was still regarded as a divine-right monarch with unlimited power, although the physical extent of the empire made the claim impracticable. For centuries, Russian farmers had groaned under the yoke of an oppressive system that tied the peasants to poverty conditions and the legal status of serfs under the authority of their manor lord. An enlightened tsar, Alexander II (r. 1855–1881), had emancipated the serfs in 1861, but under conditions that left most Russian peasants still poor and with little hope for social or economic betterment. In desperation, the Russian peasants periodically lashed out at their oppressors in sporadic rebellions, but all such uprisings were quelled with brutal efficiency by the tsarist regime.

In western Europe, as we have seen, it was the urban bourgeoisie that took the lead in the struggle for change. In preindustrial Russia, the middle class was still small in size and lacking in self-confidence. A few, however, had traveled to the West and were determined to import Western values and institutions into the Russian environment. At mid-century, a few progressive intellectuals went out to the villages to arouse their rural brethren to the need for change. Known as *narodniks* (from the Russian term *narod*, for "people" or "nation"), they sought to energize the peasantry as a force for the transformation of Russian society. Although many saw the answer to Russian problems in the western European model, others insisted on the uniqueness of the Russian experience and sought to bring about a revitalization of the country on the basis of the communal traditions of the native village.

For the most part, such efforts achieved little. The Russian peasant was resistant to change and suspicious of outsiders. In desperation, some radicals turned to terrorism in the hope that assassinations of public officials would spark tsarist repression, thereby demonstrating the brutality of the system and galvanizing popular anger. Chief among such groups was the Narodnaya Volya ("the People's Will"), a terrorist organization that assassinated Tsar Alexander II in 1881.

The assassination of Alexander II convinced his son and successor, Alexander III (r. 1881–1894), that reform had been a mistake, and he quickly returned to the repressive measures of earlier tsars. When Alexander III died, his son and successor, Nicholas II (r. 1894–1917), began his rule armed with his father's conviction that the absolute power of the tsars should be preserved.

But it was too late, for conditions were changing. Although industrialization came late to Russia, it progressed rapidly after 1890, especially with the assistance of foreign investment. By 1900, Russia had become the fourth-largest producer of steel, behind the United States, Germany, and Great Britain. At the same time, Russia was turning out half of the world's production of oil. Conditions for the working class, however, were abysmal, and opposition to the tsarist regime from workers, peasants, and intellectuals finally exploded into revolt in 1905. Facing an exhausting war with Japan in Asia (see Chapter 3), Tsar Nicholas reluctantly granted civil liberties and agreed to create a legislative assembly, the Duma, elected directly by a broad franchise. But real constitutional monarchy proved short-lived. By 1907, the tsar had curtailed the power of the Duma and fell back on the army and the bureaucracy to rule Russia.

The Ottoman Empire and Nationalism in the Balkans

Like the Austro-Hungarian Empire, the Ottoman Empire was threatened by the rising nationalist aspirations of its subject peoples. Beginning in the fourteenth century, the Ottoman Turks had expanded from their base in the Anatolian peninsula into the Balkans and southern Russia, and along the northern coast of Africa. Soon they controlled the entire eastern half of the Mediterranean Sea. But by the nineteenth century, despite state reform programs designed to modernize the empire, increasing social unrest and the intervention of the European powers in Ottoman affairs challenged the legitimacy of the Ottoman state.

Gradually, the emotional appeal of nationhood began to make inroads among the various ethnic and linguistic groups in southeastern Europe. In the course of the nineteenth century, the Balkan provinces of the Ottoman Empire began to gain their freedom, although the intense rivalry in the region between Austria-Hungary and Russia complicated the process. Greece became an independent kingdom in 1830 after a successful revolt. After Russia's defeat of the Ottoman Empire in 1878, Serbia and Romania were recognized as independent states. Bulgaria achieved autonomous status under Russia's protection, and the Balkan territories of Bosnia and Herzegovina were placed under Austria's. Despite such changes, the force of Balkan nationalism was by no means stilled.

Meanwhile, other parts of the empire began to break away from central control. In Egypt, the ambitious governor Muhammad Ali declared the region's autonomy from Ottoman rule and initiated a series of reforms designed to promote economic growth and government efficiency. During the 1830s, he sought to improve agricultural production and reform the educational system, and he imported machinery and technicians from Europe to carry out the first industrial revolution on African soil. In the end, however, the effort failed, partly because Egypt's manufactures could not compete with those of Europe and also because much of the profit from the export of cash crops went into the hands of conservative landlords.

Measures to promote industrialization elsewhere in the empire had even less success. By mid-century, a small industrial sector, built with equipment imported from Europe, took shape, and a modern system of transport and communications began to make its appearance. By the end of the century, however, the results were meager, and members of the empire's small Westernized elite became increasingly restive (see Chapter 5).

Liberalism Triumphant

In western Europe, where an affluent urban middle class represented a growing political force, liberal principles experienced a better fate. The British political and economic elites had been frightened by the specter of social revolution that periodically raged on the Continent, and by 1871 the country had a functioning two-party parliamentary system. Both the governing Liberal and Conservative parties were dominated by a coalition of aristocratic landowners, who were also frequently involved in industrial and financial activities, and upper-middle-class businessmen. But both parties also saw the necessity of adopting political reforms and competed in supporting legislation that expanded the right to vote. Reform acts in 1867 and 1884 greatly expanded the number of adult males who could vote, and by the end of World War I, all males over twenty-one and women over thirty had that right.

The political reforms grudgingly enacted in the last half of the nineteenth century led eventually to the growth of **trade unions** and the emergence in 1900 of the Labour Party, which dedicated itself to workers' interests. As a result, the Liberals felt pressure to seek the workers' support by promoting a program of social welfare. The National Insurance Act of 1911 provided benefits for workers in case of sickness or unemployment, to be paid for by compulsory contributions from workers, employers, and the state. Additional legislation provided a small pension for those over seventy and compensation for those injured in accidents at work.

A similar process was under way in France, where the overthrow of Napoleon III's Second Empire in 1870 led to the creation of a republican form of government. France failed, however, to develop a strong parliamentary system on the British two-party model because the existence of a dozen political parties forced the premier to depend on a coalition of parties to stay in power. The Third Republic was notorious for its changes of government. Between 1875 and 1914, there were no fewer than fifty cabinet changes; during the same period, the British had eleven. Nevertheless, the government's political and social reforms gradually won more and more middle-class and peasant support, and by 1914, the Third Republic commanded the loyalty of most French people.

By 1870, Italy had emerged as a geographically united state, but sectional differences (a poverty-stricken south and an industrializing north) weakened any sense of community. Chronic turmoil between labor and industry undermined the social fabric, as did the prevalence of extensive corruption among government officials and the lack of stability created by ever-changing government coalitions. Abroad, Italy's pretensions to great-power status proved equally hollow when it became the first European power to lose a war to an African state, Ethiopia, a humiliation that later led to the costly (but successful) attempt to compensate by conquering Libya in 1911 and 1912.

The United States and Canada

Between 1860 and World War I, the United States made the shift from an agrarian to a mighty industrial nation. American heavy industry stood unchallenged in 1900. In that year, the Carnegie Steel Company alone produced more steel than Great Britain's entire steel industry. Industrialization also led to urbanization. While established cities, such as New York, Philadelphia, and Boston, grew even larger, other moderate-size cities, such as Pittsburgh, grew by leaps and bounds because of industrialization and the arrival of millions of immigrants from eastern Europe. Whereas 20 percent of Americans lived in cities in 1860, more than 40 percent did in 1900. One factor underlying the change was a vast increase in agricultural productivity, creating a food surplus that enabled millions of Americans to move from the farm to the factory.

By 1900, the United States had become the world's richest nation and greatest industrial power. Less inclined than their European counterparts to accept government intervention as a means of redressing economic or social ills, Americans experienced both the benefits and the disadvantages of unfettered capitalism. In 1890, the richest 9 percent of Americans owned an incredible 71 percent of all the wealth. Labor unrest over unsafe working conditions, strict work discipline, and periodic cycles of devastating unemployment led workers to organize. By the turn of the twentieth century, one national organization, the American Federation of Labor, emerged as labor's dominant voice. Its lack of real power, however, is reflected in its membership figures: in 1900, it constituted but 8.4 percent of the American industrial labor force. And part of the U.S. labor force remained almost entirely disenfranchised. Although the victory of the North in the Civil War led to the abolition of slavery, political, economic, and social opportunities for the African American population remained limited, and racist attitudes were widespread.

During the so-called Progressive Era after 1900, the reform of many features of American life became a primary issue. At the state level, reforming governors sought to achieve clean government by introducing elements of direct democracy, such as direct primaries for selecting nominees for public office. State governments also enacted economic and social legislation, including laws that governed hours, wages, and working conditions, especially for women and children. The realization that state laws were ineffective in dealing with nationwide problems, however, led to a progressive movement at the national level.

National progressivism was evident in the administrations of Theodore Roosevelt and Woodrow Wilson. Under Roosevelt (1901–1909), the Meat Inspection Act and Pure Food and Drug Act provided for a limited degree of federal regulation of corrupt industrial practices. Wilson (1913–1921) was responsible for the creation of a graduated federal income tax and the Federal Reserve System, which gave the federal government a role in important economic decisions formerly made by bankers. Like many European nations, the United States was moving into policies that extended the functions of the state.

Canada, economically somewhat more homogeneous than its southern neighbor, faced fewer problems in addressing issues related to social and economic equality. The larger issue for Canada was that of national unity. At the beginning of 1870, the Dominion of Canada had only four provinces: Quebec, Ontario, Nova Scotia, and New Brunswick. With the addition of two more provinces in 1871—Manitoba and British Columbia—the Dominion now extended from the Atlantic Ocean to the Pacific. But real unity was difficult to achieve because of the distrust between the English-speaking and the French-speaking peoples of Canada, most of whom lived in the province of Quebec. Fortunately for Canada, Sir Wilfrid Laurier, who became the first French Canadian prime minister in 1896, was able to reconcile Canada's two major groups and resolve the issue of separate schools for French Canadians. Laurier's administration also witnessed increased industrialization and successfully encouraged immigrants from central and eastern Europe to help populate Canada's vast territories.

Tradition and Change in Latin America

In the three centuries following the arrival of Christopher Columbus in the Western Hemisphere in 1492, South and Central America fell increasingly into the European orbit. Portugal dominated Brazil, and Spain created a vast empire that included most of the remainder of South America as well as Central America. Hence, the entire area is generally described as Latin America. Almost from the beginning, it was a multicultural society composed of European settlers, indigenous American Indians, immigrants from Asia, and black slaves brought from Africa to work on the sugar plantations and in other menial occupations. Intermarriage among the four groups resulted in the creation of a diverse population with a less rigid view of race than was the case in North America. Latin American culture also came to reflect a rich mixture of Iberian, Asian, African, and Native American themes.

THE EMERGENCE OF INDEPENDENT STATES Until the beginning of the nineteenth century, the various Latin American societies were ruled by colonial officials appointed by monarchical governments in Europe. An additional instrument of control was the Catholic Church, which undertook a major effort to Christianize the indigenous peoples and transform them into docile and loyal subjects of the Portuguese and Spanish Empires. By 1800, however, local elites, mostly descendants of Europeans who had become permanent inhabitants of the Western Hemisphere, became increasingly affected by the spirit of nationalism that had emerged after the Napoleonic era in Europe. During the first quarter of the nineteenth century, under great leaders like Simón Bolívar of Venezuela and José de San Martín of Argentina, they launched a series of revolts that led to the eviction of the monarchical regimes and the formation of independent states from Argentina and Chile in the south to Mexico in North America. Brazil received its independence from Portugal in 1825.

Many of the new states were based on the administrative divisions that had been established by the Spanish in the early colonial era. Although all shared the legacy of Iberian culture brought to the Americas by the **conquistadors**, the particular mix of European, African, and indigenous peoples resulted in distinctive characteristics for each country.

One of the goals of the independence movement had been to free the economies of Latin America from European control and to exploit the riches of the continent for local benefit. In fact, however, political independence did not lead to a new era of prosperity for the people of Latin America. Most of the powerful elites in the region earned their wealth from the land and had few incentives to follow the European model of promoting an industrial revolution. As a result, the previous trade pattern persisted, with Latin America exporting raw materials and foodstuffs (wheat and sugar) as well as tobacco and hides in exchange for manufactured goods from Europe and the United States.

PROBLEMS OF ECONOMIC DEPENDENCE With economic growth came a boom in foreign investment. Between 1870 and 1913, British investments—mostly in railroads, mining, and public utilities—grew from £85 million to £757 million, which constituted two-thirds of all foreign investment in Latin America. By the end of the century, however, the U.S. economic presence began to increase dramatically. As Latin Americans struggled to create more balanced economies after 1900, they concentrated

The Opera House at Manaus. The discovery of rubber in the mid-nineteenth century was one of the most significant events in the history of Brazil. Natural rubber, much of it produced by slave labor, became the source of great wealth for Brazilian plantation owners until the rubber boom declined after 1900. The most visible symbol of "king rubber" is the Opera House at Manaus, the largest city on the Amazon. Built in 1896 in an opulent style that included the profligate use of Italian marble, it has recently been renovated and stands as a beacon of promise for one of Latin America's fastest-growing regions, as well as a reminder of a shameful period in the history of Latin America.

on building a manufacturing base, notably in textiles, food processing, and construction materials.

Nevertheless, the growth of the Latin American economy came largely from the export of raw materials, and the gradual transformation of the national economies in Latin America simply added to the region's growing dependence on the capitalist nations of the West. Modernization was basically a surface feature of Latin American society; past patterns still largely prevailed. Rural elites dominated their estates and their rural workers. Although slavery was abolished by 1888, former slaves and their descendants were still at the bottom of society. The Native Americans remained poverty-stricken, debt servitude was still a way of life, and the region remained economically dependent on foreigners. Despite its economic growth, Latin America was still sorely underdeveloped.

One potential bright spot for the future economic prosperity of Latin America was the discovery of natural rubber in Brazil. Derived from the sap of a tree native to the Amazon River basin, rubber rapidly achieved popularity throughout the world as products made of it—from erasers, footwear, and raincoats to automobile tires—flooded the markets of Europe and the United States. The boom was short-lived, however. After seeds of the rubber tree were secretly shipped to Great Britain in the 1870s, rubber plantations began to be established by European growers in colonial Southeast Asia, and the Brazilian industry—plagued by poor management practices—quickly declined in the first quarter of the twentieth century (see Chapter 2).

The surface prosperity that resulted from the emergence of an export economy had a number of repercussions. One result was the modernization of the elites, who grew determined to pursue their vision of progress. Large landowners increasingly sought ways to rationalize their production methods to make greater profits. As a result, cattle ranchers in Argentina and coffee barons in Brazil became more aggressive entrepreneurs.

Another result of the new prosperity was the growth of a small but increasingly visible middle class—lawyers, merchants, shopkeepers, businessmen, schoolteachers, professors, bureaucrats, and military officers. Living mainly in the cities, these people sought education and decent incomes and increasingly regarded the United States as the model to emulate, especially in regard to industrialization and education.

As Latin American export economies boomed, the working class expanded, and this in turn led to the growth of labor unions, which often advocated the use of the general strike as an instrument for change. By and large, however, the governing elites succeeded in stifling the political influence of the working class by restricting the right to vote. The need for industrial labor also led Latin American countries to encourage European immigrants. Between 1880 and 1914, 3 million Europeans, primarily Italians and Spaniards, settled in Argentina. More than 100,000 Europeans, mostly Italian, Portuguese, and Spanish, arrived in Brazil each year between 1891 and 1900.

SOCIAL AND POLITICAL CHANGES As in Europe and the United States, industrialization led to urbanization. Buenos Aires (known as the "Paris of South America" for its European atmosphere) had 750,000 inhabitants by 1900 and 2 million by 1914—one-fourth of Argentina's population. By that time, urban dwellers made up 53 percent of Argentina's population overall. Brazil and Chile also witnessed a dramatic increase in the number of urban dwellers.

Latin America also experienced a political transformation after 1870. Large landowners began to take a more direct interest in national politics, sometimes expressed by a direct involvement in governing. In Argentina and Chile, for example, landholding elites controlled the governments, and although they produced constitutions similar to those of the United States and European countries, they were careful to ensure their power by regulating voting rights.

In some countries, large landowners made use of dictators to maintain their interests. Porfirio Díaz, who ruled Mexico from 1876 to 1911, established a conservative government with the support of the army, foreign capitalists, large landowners, and the Catholic Church, all of whom benefited from their alliance. But there were forces for change in Mexico that sought to precipitate a true social revolution. Díaz was ousted from power in 1911, opening an extended era of revolutionary unrest.

Sometimes political instability led to foreign intervention. In 1898, the United States sent military forces in support of an independence movement in Cuba, bringing an end to four hundred years of Spanish rule on the island. U.S. occupation forces then remained for several years, despite growing opposition from the local population. The United States also intervened militarily in Nicaragua, Honduras, and the Dominican Republic to restore law and order and protect U.S. economic interests in the region, sparking cries of "Yankee imperialism."

The Rise of the Socialist Movement

One of the less desirable consequences of the Industrial Revolution was the yawning disparity in the distribution of wealth. While industrialization brought increasing affluence to an emerging middle class, it brought grinding hardship to millions of others in the form of low-paying jobs in mines or factories characterized by long working hours under squalid conditions. The underlying cause was clear: because of the rapid population growth taking place in most industrializing societies in Europe, factory owners remained largely free to hire labor on their own terms, based on market forces.

Beginning in the last decades of the eighteenth century, radical groups, inspired by the egalitarian ideals of the French Revolution, began to seek the means to rectify the problem. Some found the answer in intellectual schemes that envisaged a classless society based on the elimination of private property. Others prepared for an armed revolt

to overthrow the ruling order and create a new society controlled by the working masses. Still others began to form trade unions to fight for improved working conditions and higher wages. Only one group sought to combine all of these factors into a comprehensive program to destroy the governing forces and create a new egalitarian society based on the concept of "scientific socialism." The founder of that movement was Karl Marx, a German who had abandoned an academic career in philosophy to take up radical political activities in Paris.

The Rise of Marxism

Marxism made its first appearance in 1847 with the publication of a short treatise, *The Communist Manifesto*, written by Karl Marx (1818–1883) and his close collaborator, Friedrich Engels (1820–1895). In the *Manifesto*, the two authors predicted the outbreak of a massive uprising that would overthrow the existing ruling class and bring to power a new revolutionary regime based on their ideas (see the box on p. 18).

Marx, the son of a Jewish lawyer in the city of Trier in western Germany, was trained in philosophy and became an admirer of the German philosopher Georg W. F. Hegel, who viewed historical change as the result of conflict between contending forces. The clash between such forces would eventually lead to synthesis in a new and higher reality.

Marx appropriated Hegel's ideas and applied them to the economic and social conditions of mid-nineteenth-century Europe, where he envisioned an intense struggle between the owners of the means of production and distribution and the oppressed majority who labored on their behalf. During the feudal era, landless serfs rose up to overthrow their manor lords, giving birth to capitalism. In turn, Marx predicted, the **proletariat** (the urban working class) would eventually revolt against subhuman conditions to bring down the capitalist order and establish a new classless society to be called communism. According to Marx, the achievement of communist societies throughout the world would represent the final stage of history.

When revolutions broke out all over Europe in the eventful year of 1848, Marx and Engels eagerly but mistakenly predicted that the uprisings would spread throughout Europe and lead to a new revolutionary regime led by workers, dispossessed bourgeois, and communists. When that did not occur, Marx belatedly concluded that urban merchants and peasants were too conservative to support the workers and would oppose revolution once their own immediate economic demands were satisfied. As for the worker movement itself, it was clearly still too weak to seize power and could not expect

The Classless Society

In *The Communist Manifesto*, Karl Marx and Friedrich Engels predicted the creation of a classless society as the end product of the struggle between the bourgeoisie and the proletariat. In this selection, they discuss the steps by which that classless society would be reached.

Karl Marx and Friedrich Engels,
The Communist Manifesto

We have seen . . . that the first step in the revolution by the working class is to raise the proletariat to the position of ruling class. . . . The proletariat will use its political supremacy to wrest, by degrees, all capital from the bourgeoisie, to centralize all instruments of production in the hands of the State, i.e., of the proletariat organized as the ruling class; and to increase the total of productive forces as rapidly as possible.

Of course, in the beginning, this cannot be effected except by means of despotic inroads on the rights of property, and on the conditions of bourgeois production; by means of measures, therefore, which appear economically insufficient and untenable, but which, in the course of the movement, outstrip themselves, necessitate further inroads upon the old social order, and are unavoidable as a means of entirely revolutionizing the mode of production.

These measures will of course be different in different countries.

Nevertheless, in the most advanced countries, the following will be pretty generally applicable:

1. Abolition of property in land and application of all rents of land to public purposes.
2. A heavy progressive or graduated income tax.
3. Abolition of all right of inheritance. . . .
5. Centralization of credit in the hands of the State, by means of a national bank with State capital and an exclusive monopoly.

6. Centralization of the means of communication and transport in the hands of the State.
7. Extension of factories and instruments of production owned by the State. . . .
8. Equal liability of all to labor. Establishment of industrial armies, especially for agriculture.
9. Combination of agriculture with manufacturing industries; gradual abolition of the distinction between town and country, by a more equable distribution of the population over the country.
10. Free education for all children in public schools. Abolition of children's factory labor in its present form. . . .

When, in the course of development, class distinctions have disappeared, and all production has been concentrated in the whole nation, the public power will lose its political character. Political power, properly so called, is merely the organized power of one class for oppressing another. If the proletariat during its contest with the bourgeoisie is compelled, by the force of circumstances, to organize itself as a class, if, by means of a revolution, it makes itself the ruling class, and, as such, sweeps away by force the old conditions of production, then it will, along with these conditions, have swept away the conditions for the existence of class antagonisms and of classes generally, and will thereby have abolished its own supremacy as a class.

In place of the old bourgeois society, with its classes and class antagonisms, we shall have an association, in which the free development of each is the condition for the free development of all.

 How did Marx and Engels define the proletariat? The bourgeoisie? Why did Marxists come to believe that this distinction was paramount for understanding history? For shaping the future?

SOURCE: From Karl Marx and Friedrich Engels, *The Communist Manifesto.*

to achieve its own objectives until the workers had become politically more sophisticated and better organized. In effect, Marx concluded that revolution would not take place in western Europe until capitalism had "ripened," leading to a concentration of capital in the hands of a wealthy minority and an "epidemic of overproduction" because of inadequate purchasing power by the impoverished lower classes. Then a large and increasingly alienated proletariat could drive the capitalists from power and bring about a classless utopia.

For the remainder of his life, Marx acted out the logic of these conclusions. From his base in London, he undertook a massive study of the dynamics of the capitalist system, a project that resulted in the publication of the first volume of his most ambitious work, *Das Kapital (Capital)*, in 1869. In the meantime, he attempted to prepare for the future revolution by organizing the scattered radical parties throughout Europe into a cohesive revolutionary movement, called the International Workingmen's Association (usually known today as the First International), that would be ready to rouse the workers to action when the opportunity came.

Unity was short-lived. Although all members of the First International shared a common distaste for the capitalist system, some preferred to reform it from within (many of the labor groups from Great Britain), whereas others were convinced that only violent insurrection would suffice to destroy the existing ruling class (Karl Marx and the **anarchists** around Russian revolutionary Mikhail Bakunin). Even the radicals could not agree. Marx believed that revolution could not succeed without a core of committed communists to organize and lead the masses; Bakunin contended that the general insurrection should be a spontaneous uprising from below. In 1871, the First International disintegrated.

Capitalism in Transition

While Marx was grappling with the problems of preparing for the coming revolution, European society was undergoing significant changes. The advanced capitalist states such as Great Britain, France, and the Low Countries (Belgium, Luxembourg, and the Netherlands) were gradually evolving into mature, politically stable societies in which Marx's dire predictions were not being borne out. His forecast of periodic economic crises was correct enough, but his warnings of concentration of capital and the impoverishment of labor were somewhat wide of the mark, as capitalist societies began to eliminate or at least reduce some of the more flagrant inequities apparent in the early stages of capitalist development. These reforms occurred because workers and their representatives had begun to use the democratic political process to their own advantage, organizing labor unions and political parties to improve working conditions and enhance the role of workers in the political system. Some of these political parties were led by Marxists, who were learning that in the absence of a social revolution to bring the masses to power, the capitalist democratic system could be reformed from within to improve the working and living conditions of its constituents. In 1889, after Marx's death, several such parties (often labeled "social democratic" parties) formed the Second International, dominated by reformist elements committed to achieving **socialism** within the bounds of the Western parliamentary system.

Marx had also underestimated the degree to which nationalism would appeal to workers in most European countries. Marx had viewed nation and culture as false idols diverting the interests of the oppressed from their true concern, the struggle against the ruling class. In his view, the proletariat would throw off its chains and unite in the sacred cause of "internationalist" world revolution. In reality, workers joined peasants and urban merchants in defending the cause of the nation against its foreign enemies. A generation later, French workers would die in the trenches defending France from workers across the German border.

A historian of the late nineteenth century might have been forgiven for predicting that Marxism, as a revolutionary ideology, was dead. To the east, however, in the vast plains and steppes of central Russia, it was about to be reborn (see Chapter 4).

Toward the Modern Consciousness: Intellectual and Cultural Developments

The physical changes that were taking place in societies exposed to the Industrial Revolution were accompanied by an equally significant transformation in the arena of culture. Before 1914, most Westerners continued to believe in the values and ideals that had been generated by the impact of the Scientific Revolution and the Enlightenment. The ability of human beings to improve themselves and achieve a better society seemed to be well demonstrated by a rising standard of living, urban improvements, and mass education. Between 1870 and 1914, however, a dramatic transformation in the realm of ideas and culture challenged many of these assumptions. A new view of the physical universe, alternative views of human nature, and radically innovative forms of literary and artistic expression shattered old beliefs and opened the way to a modern consciousness. Although the real impact of many of these ideas was not felt until after World War I, they served to provoke a sense of confusion and anxiety before 1914 that would become even more pronounced after the war.

Developments in the Sciences: The Emergence of a New Physics

A prime example of this development took place in the realm of physics. Throughout much of the nineteenth century, Westerners adhered to the mechanical conception of the universe postulated by the classical physics of Isaac Newton (1642–1727). In this perspective, the universe was a giant machine in which time, space, and matter were objective realities that existed independently of the parties observing them. Matter was thought to be composed of indivisible, solid material bodies called atoms.

But these views began to be questioned at the end of the nineteenth century. Some scientists had discovered that certain elements such as radium and polonium spontaneously gave off rays or radiation that apparently came from within the atom itself. Atoms were therefore not hard material bodies but small worlds containing such subatomic particles as electrons and protons that behaved in a seemingly random and inexplicable fashion. Inquiry into the disintegrative process within atoms became a central theme of the new physics.

Building on this work, in 1900, a Berlin physicist, Max Planck (1858–1947), rejected the belief that a heated body radiates energy in a steady stream but maintained instead that it did so discontinuously, in irregular packets of energy that he called "quanta." The quantum theory raised fundamental questions about the subatomic realm of the atom. By 1900, the old view of atoms as the basic building blocks of the material world was being seriously questioned, and Newtonian physics was in trouble.

Albert Einstein (1879–1955), a German-born patent officer working in Switzerland, pushed these new theories of thermodynamics into new terrain. In 1905, Einstein published a paper setting forth his theory of relativity. According to relativity theory, space and time are not absolute but relative to the observer, and both are interwoven into what Einstein called a four-dimensional space-time continuum. Neither space nor time has an existence independent of human experience. Moreover, matter and energy reflect the relativity of time and space. Einstein concluded that matter was nothing but another form of energy. His epochal formula $E = mc^2$—each particle of matter is equivalent to its mass times the square of the velocity of light—was the key theory explaining the vast energies contained within the atom. It led to the atomic age.

Charles Darwin and the Theory of Evolution

Equally dramatic changes took place in the biological sciences, where the British scientist Charles Darwin (1809–1882) stunned the world in 1859 with the publication of his book *The Origin of Species*. Drawing from evidence obtained during a scientific expedition to the Galapagos Islands, Darwin concluded that plants and animals were not the product of divine creation but evolved over time from earlier and simpler forms of life through a process of **natural selection**. In the universal struggle for existence, only the fittest species survived. Later, Darwin provoked even more controversy by applying his theory of **organic evolution** to human beings. Speculating that modern humans had evolved over millions of years from primates and were thus not the unique creation of God but "a co-descendant with other mammals of a common progenitor," Darwin's theory represented a direct affront to the biblical interpretation of the creation of man as described in the book of Genesis (see the box on p. 21).

Critics mocked his ideas as demeaning to human dignity and made scathing references to his own forebears.

Sigmund Freud and the Emergence of Psychoanalysis

Although poets and mystics had revealed a world of unconscious and irrational behavior, many scientifically oriented intellectuals under the impact of Enlightenment thought continued to believe that human beings responded to conscious motives in a rational fashion. But at the end of the nineteenth century, the Viennese doctor Sigmund Freud (1856–1939) put forth a series of theories that undermined optimism about the rational nature of the human mind. Freud's thought, like the new physics, added to the uncertainties of the age. His major ideas were published in 1900 in *The Interpretation of Dreams*, which laid the basic foundation for what came to be known as psychoanalysis.

According to Freud, human behavior is strongly determined by the unconscious—former experiences and inner drives of which people are largely oblivious. To explore the contents of the unconscious, Freud relied not only on hypnosis but also on dreams, which were dressed in an elaborate code that needed to be deciphered if the contents were to be properly understood.

Why do some experiences whose influence persists in controlling an individual's life remain unconscious? According to Freud, repression is a process by which unsettling experiences are blotted from conscious awareness but still continue to influence behavior because they have become part of the unconscious. To explain how repression works, Freud elaborated an intricate theory of the inner life of human beings.

Although Freud's theory has had numerous critics, his insistence that a human being's inner life is a battleground of contending forces undermined the prevailing belief in the power of reason and opened a new era of psychoanalysis, in which a psychotherapist assists a patient in probing deep into memory to retrace the chain of repression back to its childhood origins and bring about a resolution of the inner psychic conflict. Belief in the primacy of rational thought over the emotions would never be the same.

Literature and the Arts: The Culture of Modernity

The revolutions in physics and psychology were paralleled by similar changes in literature and the arts. Throughout much of the late nineteenth century, literature was dominated by Naturalism. Naturalists accepted the material

The Theory of Evolution

Darwin published his theory of organic evolution in 1859, followed twelve years later by *The Descent of Man*, in which he argued that human beings, like other animals, evolved from lower forms of life. The theory provoked a firestorm of criticism, especially from the clergy. One critic described Darwin's theory as a "brutal philosophy—to wit, there is no God, and the ape is our Adam."

Charles Darwin, *The Descent of Man*

The main conclusion here arrived at, and now held by many naturalists, who are well competent to form a sound judgment, is that man is descended from some less highly organized form. The grounds upon which this conclusion rests will never be shaken, for the close similarity between man and the lower animals in embryonic development, as well as in innumerable points of structure and constitution, both of high and of the most trifling importance,—the rudiments which he retains, and the abnormal reversions to which he is occasionally liable,—are facts which cannot be disputed. They have long been known, but until recently they told us nothing with respect to the origin of man. Now when viewed by the light of our knowledge of the whole organic world, their meaning is unmistakable. The great principle of evolution stands up clear and firm, when these groups of facts are considered in connection with others, such as the mutual affinities of the members of the same group, their geographical distribution in past and present times, and their geological succession. It is incredible that all these facts should speak falsely. He who is not content to look, like a savage, at the phenomena of nature as disconnected, cannot any longer believe that man is the work of a separate act of creation.

He will be forced to admit that the close resemblance of the embryo of man to that, for instance, of a dog—the construction of his skull, limbs and whole frame on the same plan with that of other mammals, independently of the uses to which the parts may be put—the occasional reappearance of various structures, for instance of several muscles, which man does not normally possess . . . —and a crowd of analogous facts—all point in the plainest manner to the conclusion that man is the co-descendant with other mammals of a common progenitor. . . .

Man may be excused for feeling some pride at having risen, though not through his own exertions, to the very summit of the organic scale; and the fact of his having thus risen, instead of having been aboriginally placed there, may give him hope for a still higher destiny in the distant future. But we are not here concerned with hopes or fears, only with the truth as far as our reason permits us to discover it; and I have given the evidence to the best of my ability. We must, however, acknowledge, as it seems to me, that man with all his noble qualities, with sympathy which feels for the most debased, with benevolence which extends not only to other men but to the humblest living creature, with his god-like intellect which has penetrated into the movements and constitution of the solar system—with all these exalted power—Man still bears in his bodily frame the indelible stamp of his lowly origin.

 What evidence does Darwin cite to defend his theory of evolution? What is the essence of the theory?

SOURCE: From Charles Darwin, *The Descent of Man* (New York: Appleton, 1876), pp. 606–607, 619.

---

world as real and believed that literature should be realistic. By addressing social problems, writers could contribute to an objective understanding of the world.

The novels of the French writer Émile Zola (1840–1902) provide a good example of Naturalism. Against a backdrop of the urban slums and coalfields of northern France, Zola showed how alcoholism and different environments affected people's lives. The materialistic science of his age had an important influence on Zola. He had read Darwin's *Origin of Species* and had been impressed by its emphasis on the struggle for survival and the importance of environment and heredity.

By the beginning of the twentieth century, however, the belief that the task of literature was to represent "reality" had lost much of its meaning. By that time, the new psychology and the new physics had made it evident that many people were not sure what constituted reality anyway. The same was true in the realm of art, where in the late nineteenth century, painters were beginning to respond to ongoing investigations into the nature of optics and human perception by experimenting with radical new techniques to represent the multiplicity of reality. The changes that such cultural innovators produced have since been called **Modernism**.

The first to embark on the challenge were the Impressionists. Originating in France in the 1870s, they rejected indoor painting and preferred to go out to the countryside to paint nature directly. As Camille Pissarro (1830–1903), one of the movement's founders, expressed it: "Don't proceed according to rules and principles, but paint what you observe and feel. Paint generously and unhesitatingly, for it is best not to lose the first impression." The most influential of the Impressionists was Claude Monet (1840–1926), who painted several series of canvases on the same object—such as haystacks, Rouen Cathedral, and water lilies in the garden of his house on the Seine River—in the hope of breaking down the essential lines, planes, colors, and shadows of what the eye observed. His paintings that deal with the interplay of light and reflection on a water surface are considered to be among the wonders of modern painting.

The growth of photography gave artists another reason to reject visual realism. Invented in the 1830s, photography became popular and widespread after George Eastman created the first Kodak camera for the mass market in 1888. What was the point of an artist's doing what the camera did better? Unlike the camera, which could only

mirror reality, artists could *create* reality. As in literature, so also in modern art, individual consciousness became the source of meaning. Between the beginning of the new century and the outbreak of World War I in 1914, this search for individual expression produced several new schools of painting that would have a significant impact on the world of art for decades to come.

In Expressionism, the artist employed an exaggerated use of colors and distorted shapes to achieve emotional expression. Painters such as the Dutchman Vincent van Gogh (1853–1890) and the Norwegian Edvard Munch (1863–1944) were interested not in capturing the optical play of light on a landscape but in projecting their inner selves onto the hostile universe around them. Who cannot be affected by the intensity of van Gogh's dazzling sunflowers or by the ominous swirling stars above a church steeple in his *Starry Night* (1890)?

Another important artist obsessed with finding a new way to portray reality was the French painter Paul

PRISMA ARCHIVO/Alamy

Paul Cézanne, *Bathing Women.* Paul Cézanne (1839–1906) was one of the outstanding figures in modern art, propelling it to seek new ways of expressing reality. Abandoning the one-point perspective of Renaissance painting, he tried to extract the internal dimension underlying the panorama of his canvases. In *Bathing Women,* he is not interested in re-creating the surface details of individual women, but rather the inner pulse of energy emanating from a group of women in harmony with their surroundings. The blue of the lake and the sky is reflected on their skin as they relax, chat, and embrace one another in the midst of a natural scene.

Cézanne (1839–1906). Scorning the photographic duplication of a landscape, he sought to isolate the pulsating structure beneath the surface. During the last years of his life, he produced several paintings of Mont Sainte-Victoire, located near Aix-en-Provence in the south of France. Although each canvas differed in perspective, composition, and color, they all reflect the same technique of reducing the landscape to virtual geometric slabs of color to represent the interconnection of trees, earth, tiled roofs, mountain, and sky.

Following Cézanne was the Spaniard Pablo Picasso (1881–1973), one of the giants of twentieth-century painting. Settling in Paris in 1904, he and the French artist Georges Braque (1882–1963) collaborated in founding Cubism, the first truly radical approach in representing visual reality. To the Cubist, any perception of an object was a composite of simultaneous and different perspectives.

Modernism in the arts also revolutionized architecture and architectural practices. A new principle known as functionalism motivated this revolution by maintaining that buildings, like the products of machines, should be "functional" or useful, fulfilling the purpose for which they were constructed. Art and engineering were to be unified, and all unnecessary ornamentation was to be stripped away.

The United States took the lead in this effort. Unprecedented urban growth and the absence of restrictive architectural traditions allowed for new building methods, especially in the relatively new city of Chicago. The Chicago school of the 1890s, led by Louis H. Sullivan (1856–1924), used reinforced concrete, steel frames, electric elevators, and sheet glass to build skyscrapers virtually free of external ornamentation. One of Sullivan's most successful pupils was Frank Lloyd Wright (1867–1959), who became known for innovative designs in domestic architecture. Wright's private houses, built chiefly for wealthy patrons, featured geometric structures with long lines, overhanging roofs, and severe planes of brick and stone. The interiors were open spaces and included cathedral ceilings and built-in furniture and lighting features. Wright pioneered the modern American house.

At the beginning of the twentieth century, developments in music paralleled those in painting. Expressionism in music was a Russian creation, the product of composer Igor Stravinsky (1882–1971) and the Ballet Russe, the dance company of Sergei Diaghilev (1872–1929). Together they revolutionized the world of music with Stravinsky's ballet *The Rite of Spring*. When it was performed in Paris in 1913, the savage and primitive sounds and beats of the music and dance caused a near riot among an audience outraged at its audacity.

By the end of the nineteenth century, then, traditional forms of literary, artistic, and musical expression were in a state of rapid retreat. Freed from conventional tastes and responding to the intellectual and social revolution that was getting under way throughout the Western world, painters, writers, composers, and architects launched a variety of radical new ideas that would revolutionize Western culture in coming decades.

CONCLUSION

DURING THE COURSE OF THE NINETEENTH century, Western society underwent a number of dramatic changes. Countries that were predominantly agricultural in 1750 had by 1900 been transformed into essentially industrial and urban societies. The amount of material goods available to consumers had increased manyfold, and machines were rapidly replacing labor-intensive methods of production and distribution. The social changes were equally striking. Human beings were becoming more mobile and enjoyed more creature comforts than at any time since the Roman Empire. A mass society, based on the principles of universal education, limited government, and an expanding franchise, was in the process of creation.

The Industrial Revolution had thus vastly expanded the horizons and the potential of the human race. It had also broken down many walls of aristocratic privilege and opened the door to a new era based on merit. Yet the costs had been high. The distribution of wealth was as unequal as ever, and working and living conditions for millions of Europeans had deteriorated. The psychological impact of such rapid changes had also produced feelings of anger, frustration, and alienation on the part of many who lived through them. With the old certainties of religion and science now increasingly under challenge, many faced the future with doubt or foreboding.

Meanwhile, along the borders of Europe—in Russia, in the Balkans, and in the vast Ottoman Empire—the Industrial Revolution had not yet made an impact or was just getting under way. Old autocracies found themselves under increasing pressure from ethnic minorities and other discontented subjects but continued to resist pressure for reform. As the world prepared to enter a new century, the stage was set for dramatic change.

TIMELINE

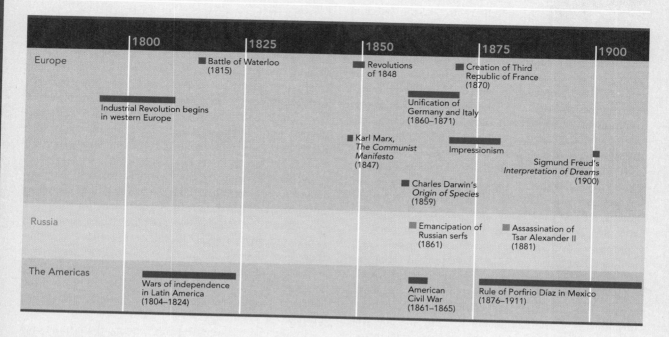

	1800	1825	1850	1875	1900

Europe

- Battle of Waterloo (1815)
- Industrial Revolution begins in western Europe
- Revolutions of 1848
- Creation of Third Republic of France (1870)
- Unification of Germany and Italy (1860–1871)
- Karl Marx, *The Communist Manifesto* (1847)
- Impressionism
- Sigmund Freud's *Interpretation of Dreams* (1900)
- Charles Darwin's *Origin of Species* (1859)

Russia

- Emancipation of Russian serfs (1861)
- Assassination of Tsar Alexander II (1881)

The Americas

- Wars of independence in Latin America (1804–1824)
- American Civil War (1861–1865)
- Rule of Porfirio Díaz in Mexico (1876–1911)

CHAPTER NOTES

1. See Kenneth Pomeranz, *The Great Divergence: China, Europe, and the Making of the Modern World Economy* (Princeton, 2000).
2. See Peter Gay, *Pleasure Wars: The Bourgeois Experience: Victoria to Freud* (New York, 1998).
3. Quoted in Barbara Freese, *Coal: A Human History* (New York, 2003), p. 78.
4. From Stephen Yafa, *Cotton: The Biography of a Revolutionary Fiber* (New York, 2005), p. 94, citing William Moran, *The Belles of New England* (New York, 2002), p. 23.

2

The High Tide of Imperialism: Africa and Asia in an Era of Western Dominance

Revere the conquering heroes: British rule in Africa

© Time Life Pictures/Getty Images

IN 1877, THE YOUNG BRITISH EMPIRE builder Cecil Rhodes drew up his last will and testament. He bequeathed his fortune, achieved as a diamond magnate in South Africa, to two of his close friends and acquaintances. He also instructed them to use the inheritance to form a secret society with the aim of bringing about "the extension of British rule throughout the world, the perfecting of a system of emigration from the United Kingdom . . . especially the occupation of the whole continent of Africa, the Holy Land, the valley of the Euphrates, the Islands of Cyprus and Candia [Crete], the whole of South America . . . the ultimate recovery of the United States as an integral part of the British Empire . . . [and] finally the foundation of so great a power to hereafter render wars impossible and promote the best interests of humanity."[1] A fervent supporter of the British imperial vision, Rhodes actively promoted the extension of British rule until his untimely death in 1902.

Nowhere were Rhodes's ambitious ideas more evident than in Africa, as he and many of his contemporaries sought to bring much of that enormous continent under the paternal sway of British colonial rule. During the last quarter of the nineteenth century, British troops and civilian administrators fanned out across the region in a bid to create the most extensive empire the world had ever known. ❧

CRITICAL THINKING

Q What were the consequences of the new imperialism of the nineteenth century for the colonies of the European powers? How should the motives and stated objectives of the imperialist countries be evaluated?

The Spread of Colonial Rule

Preposterous as Cecil Rhodes's ideas seem to us today, they serve as a graphic reminder of the hubris that characterized the worldview of Rhodes and many of his European contemporaries during the Age of Imperialism, as well as the complex union of moral concern and vaulting ambition that motivated their actions on the world stage. During the nineteenth and early twentieth centuries, Western colonialism spread throughout much of the non-Western world. Spurred by the demands of the Industrial Revolution, a few powerful states—notably Great Britain, France, Germany, Russia, and the United States—competed avariciously for consumer markets and raw materials for their expanding economies. By the end of the nineteenth century, virtually all of the traditional societies in Asia and Africa were under direct or indirect colonial rule.

The Myth of European Superiority

To many Western observers at the time, the ease of the European conquest provided a clear affirmation of the innate superiority of Western civilization to its counterparts elsewhere in the world. Influenced by the popular theory of **social Darwinism**, which applied Charles Darwin's theory of natural selection to the evolution of human societies (see Chapter 1 and "The Philosophy of Colonialism" later in this chapter), historians in Europe and the United States began to view world history as essentially the story of the inexorable rise of the West, from the glories of ancient Greece to the emergence of modern Europe after the Enlightenment and the Industrial Revolution. The extension of Western influence to Africa and Asia, a process that began with the arrival of European fleets in the Indian Ocean in the early sixteenth century, was thus viewed as a reflection of Western cultural superiority and represented a necessary step in bringing civilization to the peoples of that area.

The truth, however, was quite different, for Western global hegemony was a relatively recent phenomenon. Prior to the age of Christopher Columbus, Europe was only an isolated appendage of a much larger world system of states stretching across the Eurasian landmass from the Atlantic Ocean to the Pacific. The center of gravity in this trade network was not in Europe or even in the Mediterranean Sea but much farther to the east, in the Persian Gulf and in Central Asia. The most sophisticated and technologically advanced region in the world was not Europe but China, whose proud history could be traced back several thousand years to the rise of the first Chinese state in the Yellow River valley.

As for the transcontinental trade network that linked Europe with the nations of the Middle East, South Asia, and the Pacific basin, it had not been created by Portuguese and Spanish navigators but had already developed under the Arab empire, which had its capital in Baghdad. Later the Mongols took control of the land trade routes during their conquest of much of the Eurasian supercontinent in the thirteenth and fourteenth centuries. During the long centuries of Arabic and Mongolian hegemony, the caravan routes and sea lanes stretching across Eurasia and the Indian Ocean between China, Africa, and Europe carried not only commercial goods but also ideas and inventions such as the compass, paper, Arabic numerals, and gunpowder. Inventions such as these, many of them originating in China or India, would later play a major role in the emergence of Europe as a major player on the world's stage. Only in the sixteenth century, with the onset of the Age of Exploration, did Europe become important in the process. For the next three centuries, the ships of several European nations crossed the seas in quest of the spices, silks, precious metals, and porcelains of the Orient.

For the first time since the decline of the Roman Empire, Europe now became a major player in the global trade network. In a few cases, Europeans engaged in military conquest as a means of seeking their objective. They were aided by technological advances in shipbuilding and weaponry that gave them a distinct advantage over their rivals. Spain, Portugal, and later other nations of western Europe divided up the Americas into separate colonial territories. During the eighteenth century, the islands of the Indonesian archipelago were gradually brought under Dutch colonial rule, and the British inexorably extended their political hegemony over the South Asian subcontinent. For the most part, however, European nations were satisfied to trade with their Asian and African counterparts from coastal enclaves that they had established along the trade routes that threaded across the seas from the ports along the Atlantic and the Mediterranean Sea to their far-off destinations.

The Advent of Western Imperialism

In the nineteenth century, a new phase of Western expansion into Asia and Africa began. Whereas European aims in the East before 1800 could be summed up in the Portuguese explorer Vasco da Gama's famous phrase "Christians and spices," in the early nineteenth century, a new relationship took shape: European nations began to view Asian and African societies as a source of industrial raw materials and a market for Western manufactured goods. No longer were Western gold and silver exchanged for cloves, pepper, tea, silk, and porcelain. Now the prodigious output of European factories was sent to Africa and Asia in return for oil, tin, rubber, and the other resources needed to fuel the Western industrial machine.

THE IMPACT OF THE INDUSTRIAL REVOLUTION The reason for this change, of course, was the Industrial Revolution. Now industrializing countries in the West needed vital raw materials that were not available at home as well as a reliable market for the goods produced in their factories. The latter factor became increasingly crucial as capitalist societies began to discover that their home markets could not always absorb domestic output. When consumer demand lagged, economic depression threatened.

As Western economic expansion into Asia and Africa gathered strength during the last quarter of the nineteenth century, it became fashionable to call the process **imperialism**.

Although the term *imperialism* has many meanings and can trace its linguistic heritage back to the glories of ancient Rome, in this instance it referred to the efforts of capitalist states in the West to seize markets, cheap raw materials, and lucrative areas for capital investment beyond traditional Western countries. In this interpretation, the primary motives behind the Western expansion were economic. The best-known promoter of this view was the British political economist John A. Hobson, who in 1902 published a major analysis, *Imperialism: A Study*. In this influential book, Hobson maintained that modern imperialism was a direct consequence of the modern industrial economy. In his view, the industrialized states of the West often produced more goods than could be absorbed by the domestic market and thus had to export their manufactures to make a profit.

The issue was not simply an economic one, however, since economic concerns were inevitably tinged with political ones and with questions of national grandeur and moral purpose as well. In nineteenth-century Europe, economic wealth, national status, and political power went hand in hand with the possession of a colonial empire, at least in the minds of observers at the time. To global strategists of the day, colonies brought tangible benefits in the world of power politics as well as economic profits, and many nations became involved in the pursuit of colonies as much to gain advantage over their rivals as to acquire territory for its own sake.

The relationship between colonialism and national survival was expressed directly in a speech by the French politician Jules Ferry in 1885. A policy of "containment or abstinence," he warned, would set France on "the broad road to decadence" and initiate its decline into a "third- or fourth-rate power." British imperialists agreed. To Cecil Rhodes, the extraction of material wealth from the colonies was only a secondary matter. "My ruling purpose," he remarked, "is the extension of the British Empire."[2] That British Empire, on which (as the saying went) "the sun never set," was the envy of its rivals and was viewed as the primary source of British global dominance during the latter half of the nineteenth century.

TACTICS OF CONQUEST With the change in European motives for colonization came a corresponding shift in tactics. Earlier, when their economic interests were more limited, European states had generally been satisfied to deal with existing independent states rather than attempt to establish direct control over vast territories. There had been exceptions where state power at the local level was on the point of collapse (as in India), where European economic interests were especially intense (as in Latin America and the East Indies), or where there was no centralized authority (as

in North America and the Philippines). But for the most part, the Western presence in Asia and Africa had been limited to controlling the regional trade network and establishing a few footholds where the foreigners could carry on trade and missionary activity.

After 1800, the demands of industrialization in Europe created a new set of dynamics. Maintaining access to industrial raw materials, such as oil and rubber, and setting up reliable markets for European manufactured products required more extensive control over colonial territories. As competition for colonies increased, the colonial powers sought to solidify their hold over their territories to protect them from attack by their rivals. During the last two decades of the nineteenth century, the quest for colonies became a scramble as all the major European states, now joined by the United States and Japan, engaged in a global land grab. In many cases, economic interests were secondary to security concerns or national prestige. In Africa, for example, the British engaged in a struggle with their rivals to protect their interests in the Suez Canal and the Red Sea. In Southeast Asia, the United States seized the Philippines from Spain at least partly to keep them out of the hands of the Japanese, and the French took over Indochina for fear that it would otherwise be occupied by Germany, Japan, or the United States.

By 1900, virtually all the societies of Africa and Asia were either under full colonial rule or, as in the case of China and the Ottoman Empire, on the point of virtual collapse. Only a handful of states, such as Japan in East Asia, Thailand in Southeast Asia, Afghanistan and Iran in the Middle East, and mountainous Ethiopia in East Africa, managed to escape internal disintegration or political subjection to colonial rule. As the twentieth century began, European hegemony over the ancient civilizations of Asia and Africa seemed complete.

The Colonial System

Once they had control of most of the world, what did the colonial powers do with it? As we have seen, their primary objective was to exploit the natural resources of the subject areas and to open up markets for manufactured goods and capital investment from the mother country. In some cases, that goal could be realized in cooperation with local political elites, whose loyalty could be earned (or purchased) by economic rewards or by confirming them in their positions of authority and status in a new colonial setting. Sometimes, however, this policy of **indirect rule** was not feasible because local leaders refused to cooperate with their colonial masters or even actively resisted the foreign conquest. In such cases, the

The Company Resident and His Puppet. The British of the East India Company gradually replaced the sovereigns of the once independent Indian states with puppet rulers who carried out the company's policies. Here we see the company's resident dominating a procession in Tanjore in 1825, while the Indian ruler, Sarabhoji, follows like an obedient shadow. As a boy, Sarabhoji had been educated by European tutors and had filled his life and home with English books and furnishings.

right." Western powers viewed industrial resources as vital to national survival and security and felt that no moral justification was needed for any action to protect access to them. By the end of the nineteenth century, that attitude received pseudoscientific validity from the concept of social Darwinism, which maintained that only societies that moved aggressively to adapt to changing circumstances would survive and prosper in a world governed by the Darwinist law of "survival of the fittest."

THE WHITE MAN'S BURDEN
Some people, however, were uncomfortable with such a brutal view of the law of nature and sought a moral justification that appeared to benefit the victim. Here again, social Darwinism pointed the way: since human societies, like living organisms, must adapt to survive, the advanced nations of the West were obliged to assist the backward peoples of Asia and Africa so that they, too, could adjust to the challenges of the modern world. Few expressed this view as graphically as the English poet Rudyard Kipling, who called on the Anglo-Saxon peoples (in particular, the United States) to take up the "white man's burden" in Asia (see the box on p. 29).

Buttressed by such comforting theories, humane souls in Western countries could ignore the brutal aspects of the colonial process and persuade themselves that in the long run, the results would be beneficial to both sides. Some saw the issue primarily in religious terms. During the nineteenth century, Christian missionaries by the thousands went to Asia and Africa to bring the gospel to the "heathen masses." To others, the objective was the more secular one of bringing the benefits of Western democracy and capitalism to the tradition-ridden societies of the Orient. Either way, sensitive Western minds could console themselves with the belief that their governments were bringing civilization to the primitive peoples of the world. If commercial profit and national prestige happened to be by-products of that effort, so much the better. Few were as effective at making the case as the silver-tongued French colonial official Albert Sarraut. Conceding

local elites were removed from power and replaced with a new set of officials recruited from the mother country.

The distinction between **direct rule** and indirect rule was not always clearly drawn, and many colonial powers vacillated between the two approaches, sometimes in the same colonial territory. The decision often had fateful consequences for the peoples involved. Where colonial powers encountered resistance and were forced to overthrow local political elites, they often adopted policies designed to eradicate the source of resistance and destroy the traditional culture. Such policies often had corrosive effects on the indigenous societies and provoked resentment that not only marked the colonial relationship but even affected relations after the restoration of national independence (see Part V).

The situation in Latin America was a special case. There the Western powers sought to protect their economic interests and preserve access to crucial raw materials and markets by propping up pseudo-independent regimes. The United States, in particular, sent troops to protect its interests in Central America and the Caribbean on several occasions.

The Philosophy of Colonialism

To justify their conquests, the colonial powers appealed, in part, to the time-honored maxim of "might makes

White Man's Burden, Black Man's Sorrow

One of the justifications for modern imperialism was the notion that the supposedly "more advanced" white peoples had the moral responsibility to raise presumably ignorant indigenous peoples to a higher level of civilization. Few captured this notion better than the British poet Rudyard Kipling (1865–1936) in his famous poem *The White Man's Burden*. His appeal, directed to the United States, became one of the most famous sets of verses in the English-speaking world.

That sense of moral responsibility, however, was often misplaced or, even worse, laced with hypocrisy. All too often, the consequences of imperial rule were detrimental to those living under colonial authority. Few observers described the destructive effects of Western imperialism on the African people as well as British journalist Edmund Morel. His book *The Black Man's Burden*, as well as a number of articles written during the first decade of the twentieth century, pointed out some of the more horrific aspects of colonialism in the Belgian Congo. Morel's reports on the brutal treatment of Congolese workers involved in gathering rubber, ivory, and palm oil for export helped to spur the formation of an investigative commission, whose report in 1904 ultimately led to reforms.

Rudyard Kipling, *The White Man's Burden*

> Take up the White Man's burden—
> Send forth the best ye breed—
> Go bind your sons to exile
> To serve your captives' need;
> To wait in heavy harness,
> On fluttered folk and wild—
> Your new-caught sullen peoples,
> Half-devil and half-child.
>
> Take up the White Man's burden—
> In patience to abide,
> To veil the threat of terror
> And check the show of pride;
> By open speech and simple,
> An hundred times made plain
> To seek another's profit,
> And work another's gain.
>
> Take up the White Man's burden—
> The savage wars of peace—
> Fill full the mouth of Famine

> And bid the sickness cease;
> And when your goal is nearest
> The end for others sought,
> Watch Sloth and heathen Folly
> Bring all your hopes to nought.

Edmund Morel, *The Black Man's Burden*

It is [the Africans] who carry the "Black man's burden." They have not withered away before the white man's occupation. Indeed . . . Africa has ultimately absorbed within itself every Caucasian and, for that matter, every Semitic invader, too. In hewing out for himself a fixed abode in Africa, the white man has massacred the African in heaps. The African has survived, and it is well for the white settlers that he has. . . .

What the partial occupation of his soil by the white man has failed to do; what the mapping out of European political "spheres of influence" has failed to do; what the Maxim and the rifle, the slave gang, labour in the bowels of the earth and the lash, have failed to do; what imported measles, smallpox and syphilis have failed to do; whatever the overseas slave trade failed to do; the power of modern capitalistic exploitation, assisted by modern engines of destruction, may yet succeed in accomplishing.

For from the evils of the latter, scientifically applied and enforced, there is no escape for the African. Its destructive effects are not spasmodic; they are permanent. In its permanence resides its fatal consequences. It kills not the body merely, but the soul. It breaks the spirit. It attacks the African at every turn, from every point of vantage. It wrecks his polity, uproots him from the land, invades his family life, destroys his natural pursuits and occupations, claims his whole time, enslaves him in his own home.

 According to Kipling, why should Western nations take up the "white man's burden"? What was the "black man's burden," in the eyes of Edmund Morel?

SOURCES: Rudyard Kipling, *The White Man's Burden*. From Rudyard Kipling, "The White Man's Burden," *McClure's Magazine* 12 (Feb. 1899). Edmund Morel, *The Black Man's Burden*. From Edmund Morel, *The Black Man's Burden* (New York: Metro Books, 1972).

that colonialism was originally an "act of force" taken for material profit, he declared that the end result would be a "better life on this planet" for conqueror and conquered alike.

But what about the possibility that historically and culturally, the societies of Asia and Africa were fundamentally different from those of the West and could not, or would not, be persuaded to transform themselves along Western lines? After all, even Kipling had remarked that "East is East and West is West, and never the twain shall meet." Was the human condition universal, in which case the Asian and African peoples could be transformed, in the quaint American phrase for the subject Filipinos, into "little brown Americans"? Or were human beings so shaped by their history and geographic environment that their civilizations would inevitably remain distinctive from those of the West? If so, a policy of cultural transformation could not be expected to succeed.

ASSIMILATION AND ASSOCIATION In fact, colonial theory never decided this issue one way or the other. The French, who were most inclined to philosophize about the problem, adopted the terms **assimilation** (which implied an effort to transform colonial societies in the Western image) and **association** (collaborating with local elites while leaving local traditions alone) to describe the two alternatives and then proceeded to vacillate between them. French policy in Indochina, for example, began as one of association but switched to assimilation under pressure from liberal elements who felt that colonial powers owed a debt to their subject peoples. But assimilation aroused resentment among the local population, many of whom opposed the destruction of their culture and traditions.

Most colonial powers were not as inclined to debate the theory of colonialism as the French were. The United States, in formulating a colonial policy for the Philippines, adopted a strategy of assimilation in theory but was not quick to put it into practice. The British refused to entertain the possibility of assimilation and generally treated their subject peoples as culturally and racially distinct (as Queen Victoria declared in 1858, her government disclaimed "the right and desire to impose Our conditions on Our subjects"). Although some observers have ascribed this attitude to a sense of racial superiority, not all agree. In his recent book *Ornamentalism: How the British Saw Their Empire*, historian David Cannadine argues that the British simply attempted to replicate their own hierarchical system, based on the institutions of monarchy and aristocracy, and apply it to the peoples of the empire.

India Under the British Raj

The first of the major Asian civilizations to fall victim to European predatory activities was India. An organized society (commonly known today as the Harappan civilization) had emerged in the Indus River valley in the fourth and third millennia B.C.E. After the influx of Aryan peoples across the Hindu Kush into the Indian subcontinent around 1500 B.C.E., a new civilization based on sedentary agriculture and a regional trade network gradually emerged, with its central focus in the Ganges River basin in north central India. A religious faith brought to the subcontinent by the Aryan people, known today as **Hinduism**, evolved into the dominant religion of the Indian people.

Beginning in the eleventh century, much of northern India fell under the rule of Turkic-speaking people who penetrated into the subcontinent from the northwest and introduced the Islamic religion and civilization. Indian society, however, was not entirely receptive to the new faith. Where **Islam** was fiercely monotheistic, the Indian cosmos was peopled with a multiplicity of deities, each representing different aspects of an all-knowing world spirit known as Brahma. While Islam was egalitarian, Indian society since early times had been divided into several classes (known as *varna*, or "color"), each historically identified with a particular economic or social function—priests, warriors, merchants, and farmers. Although such functions had blurred over time, the system also possessed a religious component that determined not only one's status in society but also one's hope for heavenly salvation. At the bottom of the social and religious scale were the "untouchables," individuals who were assigned to carry out the myriad "unclean" tasks in Indian society.

The Indian people did not belong to one of the classes as individuals, but as part of a larger kinship group, a system of extended families known in English as **castes**. Each caste was identified with a particular *varna*, creating a highly stratified society in which social movement along the scale was extremely unusual; individuals thus lived their entire lives within the boundaries of caste distinctions.

At the end of the fifteenth century, a powerful new force penetrated the Indian subcontinent from the mountains to the north. The Mughals, as they were known, were a Turkic-speaking people whose founding ruler Babur (1483–1530) traced his ancestral heritage back to the great Mongol chieftain Genghis Khan. Although foreigners and Muslims like many of their immediate predecessors, the Mughals nevertheless brought India to a level of political power and cultural achievement that inspired admiration and envy throughout the entire region.

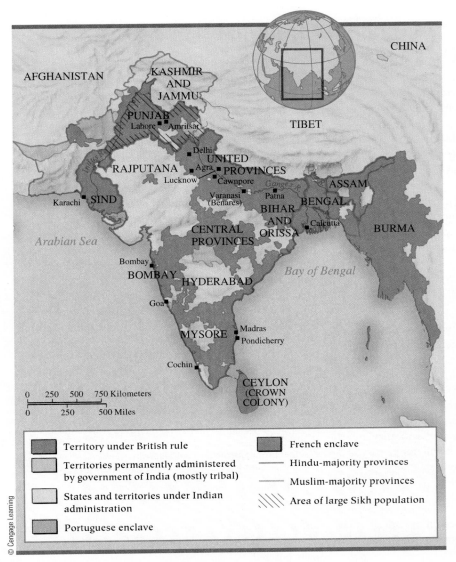

regional trade routes and to meddle in the internal politics of the subcontinent. Soon nothing remained of the empire but a shell. Into the vacuum left by its final decay stepped the British, who used a combination of firepower and guile to consolidate their power over the subcontinent. Some territories were taken over directly by the privately run East India Company, which at that time was given authority to administer Asian territories under British occupation, while others were ruled indirectly through their local **maharajas** (see Map 2.1). British rule extended northward as far as present-day Afghanistan, where British fears of Russian expansionism led to a lengthy imperialist rivalry that was popularly labeled "the Great Game."

The Nature of British Rule

British rule in India brought stability to a region that had been wracked by civil strife, as the British adopted reforms that led to a relatively honest and efficient government that in some respects operated to the benefit of the average Indian. For example, heightened attention was given to education. Through the efforts of the British administrator and historian Lord Macaulay, a new school system was established to train the children of Indian elites, and the British civil service examination was introduced (see the box on p. 32).

MAP 2.1 India Under British Rule, 1805–1931. This map shows the different forms of rule that the British applied in India under their control. The Sikhs, located primarily in the Punjab, were adherents of a religion that began in the sixteenth century as an attempt to reconcile the Hindu and Muslim traditions and ultimately developed into an alternative to both.

Q *Where were the major cities of the subcontinent located, and under whose rule did they fall?*

The Mughal Empire reached the peak of its greatness under the famed Emperor Akbar (r. 1556–1605). Eventually, however, the dynasty began to weaken as Hindu forces in southern India sought to challenge the authority of the Mughal court in Delhi. This process of fragmentation was probably hastened by the growing presence of European traders, who began to establish enclaves along the fringes of the subcontinent. By the end of the eighteenth century, the British and the French had begun to seize control of the

British rule also brought an end to some of the more inhumane aspects of Indian tradition. The practice of *sati* (cremation of a widow on her husband's funeral pyre) was outlawed, and widows were legally permitted to remarry. The British also attempted to put an end to the brigandage (known as *thuggee*, which gave rise to the English word *thug*) that had plagued travelers in India since time immemorial. Railroads, the telegraph, and the postal service were introduced to India shortly after they appeared in

Indian in Blood, English in Taste and Intellect

Thomas Babington Macaulay (1800–1859) was named a member of the Supreme Council of India in the early 1830s. In that capacity, he was responsible for drawing up a new educational policy for British subjects in the area. In his *Minute on Education*, he considered the claims of English and various local languages to become the vehicle for educational training and decided in favor of the former. It is better, he argued, to teach Indian elites about Western civilization so as "to form a class who may be interpreters between us and the millions whom we govern; a class of persons, Indian in blood and color, but English in taste, in opinions, in morals, and in intellect." Later Macaulay became a prominent historian.

Thomas Babington Macaulay, *Minute on Education*

We have a fund to be employed as government shall direct for the intellectual improvement of the people of this country. The simple question is, what is the most useful way of employing it?

All parties seem to be agreed on one point, that the dialects commonly spoken among the natives of this part of India contain neither literary or scientific information, and are moreover so poor and rude that, until they are enriched from some other quarter, it will not be easy to translate any valuable work into them. . . .

What, then, shall the language [of education] be? One half of the Committee maintain that it should be the English. The other half strongly recommend the Arabic and Sanskrit. The whole question seems to me to be, what language is the best worth knowing?

I have no knowledge of either Sanskrit or Arabic—I have done what I could to form a correct estimate of their value. I have read translations of the most celebrated Arabic and Sanskrit works. I have conversed both here and at home with men distinguished by their proficiency in the Eastern tongues. I am quite ready to take the Oriental learning at the valuation of the Orientalists themselves. I have never found one among them who could deny that a single shelf of a good European library was worth the whole native literature of India and Arabia. . . .

It is, I believe, no exaggeration to say that all the historical information which has been collected from all the books written in the Sanskrit language is less valuable than what may be found in the most paltry abridgments used at preparatory schools in England.

 How does Macaulay justify the teaching of the English language in India? How might a critic respond?

SOURCE: From *Speeches by Lord Macaulay, With His Minute on Indian Education* by Thomas B. MacAuley. AMS Press, 1935.

Great Britain. A new penal code based on the British model was adopted, and health and sanitation conditions were improved.

AGRICULTURAL REFORMS But in some ways the Indian people paid dearly for the peace and stability brought by the British raj (from the Indian *raja*, or prince). Perhaps the most flagrant cost was economic. In rural areas, the British adopted the existing *zamindar* system, according to which local landlords were authorized to collect taxes from peasants and turn the taxes over to the government. The British mistakenly anticipated that by continuing the system, they would not only facilitate the collection of agricultural taxes but also create a landed gentry that could, as in Britain itself, become the conservative foundation of imperial rule. But the local gentry took advantage of their authority to increase taxes and force the less fortunate peasants to become tenants or lose their land entirely. When rural unrest threatened, the government passed legislation protecting farmers against eviction and unreasonable rent increases, but this measure had little effect outside the southern provinces, where it was originally enacted.

MANUFACTURING British colonialism was also remiss in bringing modern science and technology to India. Industrial development was still in its infancy during the Mughal era, although foreign trade thrived, as Indian goods, notably textiles, tropical food products, spices, and precious stones, were exported in return for gold and silver. Under the British, limited forms of industrialization took place, notably in the manufacturing of textiles and rope. The first textile mill opened in 1856; seventy years later, there were eighty mills in the city of Bombay (now Mumbai) alone. Nevertheless, the lack of local capital and the advantages given to British imports prevented the emergence of other vital new commercial and manufacturing operations, and the introduction of British textiles put thousands of Bengali women out of work and severely damaged the village textile industry.

A CIVILIZING MISSION? Foreign rule also had an effect on the psyche of the Indian people. Although many British colonial officials sincerely tried to improve the lot of the people under their charge, the government made few efforts to introduce democratic institutions and values to the Indian people. Moreover, British arrogance and contempt for local traditions cut deeply into the pride of many Indians, especially those of high caste who were accustomed to a position of superior status in India.

By the end of the nineteenth century, increasingly disillusioned with the failure of the British to live up to their "civilizing mission," educated Indians began to clamor for a greater role in the governance of their country, and in 1885 a new organization designed to represent the interests of the indigenous population—the Indian National Congress—was born (see Chapter 5).

The Colonial Takeover of Southeast Asia

Southeast Asia had been one of the first destinations for European fleets en route to the East. Lured by the riches of the Spice Islands (at the eastern end of present-day Indonesia), European adventurers sailed to the area in the early sixteenth century in the hope of seizing control of the spice trade from Arab and Indian merchants. A century later, the trade was fast becoming a monopoly of the Dutch, whose sturdy ships and ample supply of capital gave them a significant advantage over their rivals.

Well before the arrival of the first Europeans, however, Southeast Asia had been an active participant in the global trade network, purchasing textiles from India and luxury goods from China in return for spices, precious metals, and various tropical woods and herbs. Although no single empire had ever controlled all of Southeast Asia, several powerful states had emerged in the region since the early centuries of the first millennium C.E. Some, like Sailendra and Srivijaya in the Indonesian archipelago, were primarily trading states. Others, like Vietnam, Angkor (in present-day Cambodia), and the Burmese empire of Pagan on the subcontinent, were predominantly agricultural. Most had patterned their political systems and their religious beliefs after those of the Indian subcontinent. Vietnam was strongly influenced by China. Then, by the thirteenth century, Islam began to make inroads into the southern part of the region, promoted by Muslim merchants from India and the Middle East who were active in the spice trade.

In 1800, only two societies in Southeast Asia were under effective colonial rule: the Spanish Philippines and the Dutch East Indies. The British had been driven out of the Spice Islands trade by the Dutch in the seventeenth century and possessed only a small enclave on the southern coast of the island of Sumatra and some territory on the Malay peninsula. The French had actively engaged in trade with states on the Asian mainland, but their activity in the area was eventually reduced to a small missionary effort run by the Society for Foreign Missions. The only legacy of Portuguese expansion in the region was the possession of half of the small island of Timor. The remainder of the region continued to be governed by indigenous rulers.

The Imposition of Colonial Rule

During the second half of the nineteenth century, however, European interest in Southeast Asia grew rapidly, and by 1900, virtually the entire area was under colonial rule (see Map 2.2). The process began after the Napoleonic wars, when the British, by agreement with the Dutch, abandoned their claims to territorial possessions in the East Indies in return for a free hand in the Malay peninsula. In 1819, the colonial administrator Stamford Raffles founded a new British colony on a small island at the tip of the peninsula. Called Singapore ("City of the Lion"), it had previously been used by Malay pirates as a base for raiding ships passing through the Strait of Malacca. When the invention of steam power enabled merchant ships to save time and distance by passing through the strait rather than sailing with the westerlies across the southern Indian Ocean, Singapore became a major stopping point for traffic to and from China and other commercial centers in the region. A few decades later, the British took over the kingdom of Burma and placed it under the colonial administration in India.

The British advance into Burma was watched nervously in Paris, where French geopoliticians were ever anxious about British operations in Asia and Africa. The French still maintained a clandestine missionary organization in Vietnam despite harsh persecution by the local authorities, who viewed Christianity as a threat to imperial rule and internal stability. But Vietnamese efforts to prohibit Christian missionary activities were hindered by the internal rivalries that had earlier divided the country into two separate and mutually hostile governments in the north and south.

In 1857, the French government decided to compel the Vietnamese to accept French protection to prevent the British from obtaining a monopoly of trade in South China. A naval attack launched a year later was not a total success, but the French eventually forced the Vietnamese court to cede territories in the southern part of the country. A generation later, French rule was extended over the

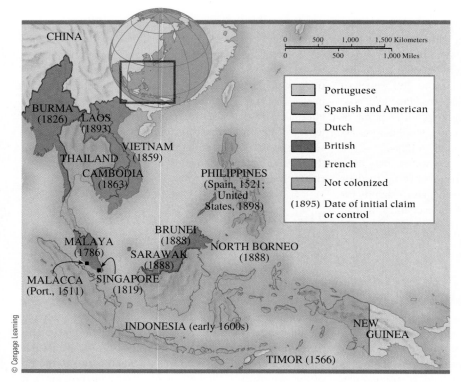

MAP 2.2 **Colonial Southeast Asia.** European colonial rule spread into Southeast Asia between the sixteenth century and the end of the nineteenth.

Q *What was the significance of Malacca?*

remainder of Vietnam. By the end of the century, French seizure of neighboring Cambodia and Laos had led to the creation of the French-ruled Indochinese Union.

With the French conquest of Indochina, Thailand—then known as Siam—was the only remaining independent state on the Southeast Asian mainland. During the last quarter of the century, British and French rivalry threatened to place the Thai, too, under colonial rule. But under the astute leadership of two remarkable rulers, King Mongkut (familiar to millions in the West as the monarch—played by actor Yul Brynner—in the 1956 film *The King and I*) and his son King Chulalongkorn, the Thai sought to introduce Western learning and maintain relations with the major European powers without undermining internal stability or inviting an imperialist attack. In 1896, the British and French agreed to preserve Thailand as an independent buffer zone between their possessions in Southeast Asia.

The final piece of the colonial edifice in Southeast Asia was put in place in 1898, when U.S. naval forces under Commodore George Dewey defeated the Spanish fleet in Manila Bay on the island of Luzon in the Spanish Philippines. Since gaining independence in the late eighteenth century, the United States had always considered itself to be an anticolonialist nation, but by the end of the nineteenth century, many Americans believed that the United States was ready to expand abroad. The Pacific islands were the scene of great-power competition and witnessed the entry of the United States on the imperialist stage. Eastern Samoa became the first important American colony; the Hawaiian Islands were the next to fall. Soon after an American naval station had been established at Pearl Harbor in 1887, American settlers gained control of the sugar industry on the islands. When the local Hawaiians tried to reassert their authority, the U.S. Marines were brought in to "protect" American lives. Hawaii was annexed by the United States in 1898 during the era of American nationalistic fervor generated by the Spanish-American War, which broke out after an explosion damaged a U.S. battleship anchored at Havana on the Spanish-held island of Cuba.

The defeat of Spain encouraged the Americans to extend their empire by acquiring Puerto Rico, Guam, and the Philippine Islands. Although President William McKinley justified the seizure of the Philippines on moral grounds, the real reason was to prevent them from falling into the hands of the Japanese. In fact, the Americans (like the Spanish before them) found the islands a convenient jumping-off point for the China trade (see Chapter 3). Although guerrilla forces led by Emilio Aguinaldo fought bitterly against U.S. troops to maintain independence, the resistance collapsed in 1901. President McKinley had his stepping-stone to the rich markets of China.

Colonial Regimes in Southeast Asia

In Southeast Asia, economic profit was the immediate and primary aim of the colonial enterprise. For that purpose, colonial powers tried wherever possible to work with local elites to facilitate the exploitation of natural resources. Indirect rule reduced the cost of training European administrators and had a less corrosive impact on the local culture.

COLONIAL ADMINISTRATION In the Dutch East Indies, for example, officials of the Dutch East India Company

(VOC, from the initials of its Dutch name) entrusted local administration to the indigenous landed aristocracy, known as the *priyayi*. The *priyayi* maintained law and order and collected taxes in return for a payment from the VOC. The British followed a similar practice in Malaya. While establishing direct rule over areas of crucial importance, such as the commercial centers of Singapore and Malacca and the island of Penang, the British signed agreements with local Muslim rulers to maintain princely power in the interior of the peninsula.

In some instances, however, local resistance to the colonial conquest made such a policy impossible. In Burma, faced with staunch opposition from the monarchy and other traditionalist forces, the British abolished the monarchy and administered the country directly through their colonial government in India. In Indochina, the French used both direct and indirect means. They imposed direct rule on the southern provinces in the Mekong delta, which had been ceded to France as a colony after the first war in 1858–1860. The northern parts of the country, seized in the 1880s, were governed as a protectorate, with the emperor retaining titular authority from his palace in Hué. The French adopted a similar policy in Cambodia and Laos, where local rulers were left in charge with French advisers to counsel them. Even the Dutch were eventually forced into a more direct approach. When the

development of plantation agriculture and the extraction of oil in Sumatra made effective exploitation of local resources more complicated, they dispensed with indirect rule and tightened their administrative control over the archipelago. Whatever method was used, colonial regimes in Southeast Asia, as elsewhere, were slow to create democratic institutions. The first legislative councils and assemblies were composed almost exclusively of European residents in the colonies. The first representatives from the indigenous population were wealthy and conservative in their political views. When Southeast Asians began to complain, colonial officials gradually and reluctantly began to broaden the franchise, but even such liberal thinkers as Albert Sarraut advised patience in awaiting the full benefits of colonial policy. "I will treat you like my younger brothers," he promised, "but do not forget that I am the older brother. I will slowly give you the dignity of humanity."[3]

ECONOMIC DEVELOPMENT Colonial powers were equally reluctant to shoulder the "white man's burden" in the area of economic development. As we have seen, their primary goals were to secure a source of cheap raw materials and to maintain markets for manufactured goods. So colonial policy concentrated on the export of raw materials—teakwood from Burma; rubber and tin from

The Production of Rubber. Natural rubber was one of the most important cash crops in the European colonies in Asia. Rubber trees, native to the Amazon River basin in Brazil, were eventually transplanted to Southeast Asia, where they became a major source of profit. Workers on the plantations received few benefits, however. Once the sap of the tree, called latex, was extracted, as shown on the left, it was hardened and pressed into sheets (right photo) and then sent to Europe for refining.

Malaya; spices, tea, coffee, and palm oil from the East Indies; and sugar and copra from the Philippines.

In some Southeast Asian colonial societies, a measure of industrial development did take place to meet the needs of the European population and local elites. Major manufacturing cities, including Rangoon in lower Burma, Batavia on the island of Java, and Saigon in French Indochina, grew rapidly. Although the local middle class benefited in various ways from the Western presence, most industrial and commercial establishments were owned and managed by Europeans or, in some cases, by Indian or Chinese merchants who had long been active in the area. In Saigon, for example, even the manufacture of *nuoc mam*, the traditional Vietnamese fish sauce, was under Chinese ownership. Most urban residents were coolies (laborers), factory workers, or rickshaw drivers or eked out a living in family shops as they had during the traditional era.

RURAL POLICIES Despite the growth of an urban economy, the vast majority of people in the colonial societies continued to farm the land. Many continued to live by subsistence agriculture, but the colonial policy of emphasizing cash crops for export also led to the creation of a form of plantation agriculture in which peasants were recruited to work as wage laborers on rubber and tea plantations owned by Europeans. To maintain a competitive edge, the plantation owners kept the wages of their workers at the poverty level. Many plantation workers were "shanghaied" (the English term originated from the practice of recruiting laborers, often from the docks and streets of Shanghai, by the use of force, alcohol, drugs, or other unscrupulous means) to work on plantations, where conditions were often so inhumane that thousands died. High taxes, enacted by colonial governments to pay for administrative costs or improvements in the local infrastructure, were a heavy burden for poor peasants.

The situation was made even more difficult by the steady growth of the population. Peasants in Asia had always had large families on the assumption that a high proportion of their children would die in infancy. But improved sanitation and medical treatment resulted in lower rates of infant mortality and a staggering increase in population. The population of the island of Java, for example, increased from about a million in the precolonial era to about 40 million at the end of the nineteenth century. Under these conditions, the rural areas could no longer support the growing populations, and many young people fled to the cities to seek jobs in factories or shops. The migratory pattern gave rise to squatter settlements in the suburbs of the major cities.

IMPERIALISM IN THE BALANCE As in India, colonial rule did bring some benefits to Southeast Asia. It led to

the beginnings of a modern economic infrastructure, and the development of an export market helped create an entrepreneurial class in rural areas. On the outer islands of the Dutch East Indies (such as Borneo and Sumatra), for example, small growers of rubber, palm oil, coffee, tea, and spices began to share in the profits of the colonial enterprise.

A balanced assessment of the colonial legacy in Southeast Asia must take into account that the early stages of industrialization are difficult in any society. Even in western Europe, industrialization led to the creation of an impoverished and powerless proletariat, urban slums, and displaced peasants driven from the land. In much of Europe, however, the bulk of the population eventually enjoyed better material conditions as the profits from manufacturing and plantation agriculture were reinvested in the national economy and gave rise to increased consumer demand. In contrast, in Southeast Asia, most of the profits were repatriated to the colonial mother country, while displaced peasants fleeing to cities such as Rangoon, Batavia, and Saigon found little opportunity for employment. Many were left with seasonal employment, with one foot on the farm and one in the factory. The old world was being destroyed, and the new had yet to be born.

Empire Building in Africa

The last of the equatorial regions of the world to be placed under European colonial rule was the continent of Africa. European navigators had first established contacts with Africans south of the Sahara during the late fifteenth century, when Portuguese fleets sailed down the Atlantic coast on their way to the Indian Ocean. During the next three centuries, Europeans established port facilities along the coasts of East and West Africa to facilitate their trade with areas farther to the east and to engage in limited commercial relations with African societies. Although European exploration of the area was originally motivated by the search for gold and a route to the Spice Islands of the mysterious Orient, eventually the trade in slaves took precedence, and over the next three centuries several million unfortunate Africans were loaded onto slave ships destined to serve on the sugar and cotton plantations of the Americas. For a variety of reasons, however, Europeans made little effort to penetrate the vast continent and were generally content to deal with African intermediaries along the coast to maintain their trading relationship. The Western psyche developed a deeply ingrained image of "darkest Africa"—a continent without a history, its people living out their days bereft of cultural contact with the outside world.

Africa Before the Europeans

There was a glimmer of truth in the Western image of sub-Saharan Africa as a region outside the mainstream of civilization on the Eurasian landmass. Although Africa was the original seedbed of humankind and the site of much of its early evolutionary experience, the desiccation of the Sahara during the fourth and third millennia B.C.E. had erected a major obstacle to communications between the peoples south of the desert and societies elsewhere in the world. The barrier was never total, however. From ancient times, caravans crossed the Sahara from the Niger River basin to the shores of the Mediterranean carrying gold and tropical products in exchange for salt, textile goods, and other manufactured articles from the north. By the seventh century C.E., several prosperous trading societies, whose renown extended to medieval Europe and the Middle East, had begun to arise in the savanna belt (a region of grasslands on the southern edge of the desert) of West Africa.

One crucial consequence of this new trade network was the introduction of Islam to the peoples of the region. Arab armies sweeping westward along the coast of the Mediterranean Sea had already brought the message of the Prophet Muhammad as far as Morocco and the Iberian peninsula. Soon, Islamic religion and culture began to cross the Sahara in the baggage of Muslim merchants. Along with the Qur'an, Islam's holy book, the new faith introduced its African converts to a new code of law and ethics—the *Shari'a*—and to the Prophet's uncompromising message of the equality of all in the eyes of God. The city of Timbuktu, on the banks of the Niger River, soon became a major center of Islamic scholarship and schools providing education in the Arabic language.

In the eastern half of the continent, the Sahara posed no obstacle to communication beyond the seas. The long eastern coast had played a role in the trade network of the Indian Ocean since the time of the pharaohs along the Nile. Ships from India, the Persian Gulf, and as far away as China made regular visits to the East African ports of Kilwa, Malindi, and Sofala, bringing textiles, metal goods, and luxury articles in return for gold, ivory, and various tropical products from Africa. With the settlement of Arab traders along the eastern coast, the entire region developed a new synthetic culture, known as **Swahili**, that combined elements of Arabic and indigenous cultures. Although the Portuguese briefly seized or destroyed most of the trading ports along the eastern coast, by the eighteenth century the Europeans had been driven out, and local authority was restored.

In the vast interior of the continent, from the Congo River basin southward to the Cape of Good Hope, contacts with the outside world were rare, and the majority of the population lived in autonomous villages organized by clans or a local chieftain; they supported themselves by farming, pastoral pursuits, or hunting and gathering. In a few cases, some of these individual communities had begun to consolidate into small states, which took part in a growing interregional trade network based on the exchange of metal goods and foodstuffs. It was here, above all, that the Western image of "the dark continent" carried the most plausibility.

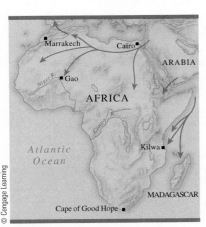

The Spread of Islam in Africa

The Growing European Presence in West Africa

By the beginning of the nineteenth century, the slave trade was in decline. One reason was the growing sense of outrage in Europe over the purchase, sale, and exploitation of human beings. Traffic in slaves by Dutch merchants effectively came to an end in 1795 and by Danes in 1803. The slave trade was declared illegal in Great Britain in 1807 and in the United States in 1808. The British began to apply pressure on other nations to follow suit, and most did so after the end of the Napoleonic wars in 1815, leaving only Portugal and Spain as practitioners of the trade south of the equator. Meanwhile, the demand for slaves began to decline in the Western Hemisphere, although an illegal trade in slaves across the Atlantic persisted for some time (see the box on p. 38). By the 1880s, slavery had been abolished in all major countries of the world.

The decline of the slave trade in the Atlantic during the nineteenth century, however, did not lead to an overall reduction in the European presence in West Africa. On the contrary, European interest in what was sometimes called "legitimate trade" in natural resources increased. Exports of peanuts, timber, hides, and palm oil increased substantially during the first decades of the century, and imports of textile goods and other manufactured products also rose.

Tragedy at Caffard Cove

The slave trade was declared illegal in France in 1818, but the clandestine shipment of Africans to the Americas continued for many years afterward. At the same time, slavery was widely tolerated in the French colonies, especially in the Caribbean, where sugar plantations on the islands of Guadeloupe and Martinique depended on cheap labor for their profits. It was not until 1849 that slavery was abolished throughout the French Empire.

Among the tragic events that characterized the shipment of slaves to the Americas (often called the "Middle Passage"), few are as poignant as the incident described in the passage below, which took place in 1830 on the island of Martinique. The text, which includes passages from the original official report of the incident, is taken from a memorial erected at the site many years later. Laurent Valère, a local sculptor, erected fifteen statues to commemorate the victims. The name of the ship and the name and nationality of the ship's captain, as well as the ultimate fate of the surviving victims, remain a mystery to this day.

The Caffard Memorial

Around noon on the 8th of April 1830, a sailing ship [was observed] carrying out odd maneuvers off the coast of [the town of] Diamant [on the southern coast of Martinique]; at about five P.M. [the vessel] cast anchor off the dangerous coast of nearby Caffard Cove. François Dizac, a resident of the neighborhood and manager of the Plage du Diamant, a plantation owned by the Count de Latournelle, realized that the ship's situation was perilous, but a heavy swell prevented him from launching a boat to warn the captain that the vessel was in imminent danger of running aground. He therefore sent signals that the captain either could not, or chose not, to acknowledge.

At 11 P.M. that evening, anguished cries and cracking sounds suddenly began to shatter the silence of the night. Dizac and a party of slaves from the nearby plantation rushed promptly to the scene, only to encounter a horrifying sight: the ship had been dashed on the rocks and its passengers thrown into the fury of the raging seas. The rescuers on shore then observed a large number of panic-stricken males clinging desperately to the ship's foremast, which suddenly broke in two, tossing them into the foam or onto the rocks. Broken masts lying on the rocks, fragments of torn sails floating alongside ropes caught in the reef where the ship itself lay on the rocks all provided visual evidence of the frightful incident that had just occurred.

Forty-six bodies, four of whom were white males, were lying amidst the rocks. . . . "I ordered the bodies of the black victims to be buried at a short distance from the shore, then directed that those of the white males be carried to the cemetery of Diamant parish, where they received a Christian burial. I was then taken to the cabin of a certain Borromé, a free man of color, where those black castaways who had been rescued from the shipwreck had been given temporary shelter. Among the victims, six were found to be in such poor condition that they could not be taken to the Latournelle plantation. The other 80 survivors were handed over to the naval authorities at Fort Royal. In all, 86 African captives, of whom 60 were women or girls, were rescued out of a ship's "cargo" estimated at nearly 300 persons.

"I ordered the interrogation of the surviving black castaways by interpreters, and it became clear from their testimony that the ship had been at sea for four months, and that most of the white sailors on board had died during the crossing [of the Atlantic], and that an additional 70 blacks had died from illness and had been thrown overboard during the voyage. Another 260 individuals remained on the ship when it was sunk off the coast of Diamant. . . . Only a few males had thus survived, since all of them were shackled together in the ship's hold with irons on their feet at the time of the wreck."

At that point, a legal issue was raised: what should be done with the surviving castaways who, although they could not be classified as slaves under existing law (since they were victims of illegal trade), yet could not be considered in this colony as men and therefore couldn't be freed. In May 1830, the Privy Council of Martinique ordered that the captured Negroes were to be shipped to Cayenne [the capital of French Guiana] in order to avoid having in the [French] West Indies a special class of people who could not be classified either as slaves or as free individuals. . . .

Thus, in July 1830, a second deportation followed the first, adding to the ordeal of the [African] slaves who had survived the shipwreck at Caffard Cove.

 How were the surviving victims of the shipwreck at Caffard Cove dealt with by the government authorities in Martinique? Under what provisions of the law was the decision reached?

SOURCE: Association de Sauvegarde du Patrimoine du Diamant. Text by Merlande, MOANDA SATURNIN, historian. Translation from the original French by the author.

Stimulated by growing commercial interests in the area, European governments began to push for a more permanent presence along the coast. During the first decades of the nineteenth century, the British established settlements along the Gold Coast (present-day Ghana) and in Sierra Leone, where they attempted to set up agricultural plantations for freed slaves who had returned from the Western Hemisphere or had been liberated by British ships while en route to the Americas. A similar haven for ex-slaves was developed with the assistance of the United States in Liberia. The French occupied the area around the Senegal River near Cape Verde, where they attempted to develop peanut plantations.

The growing European presence in West Africa led to tensions with African governments in the area. British efforts to increase trade with Ashanti, in the area of the present-day state of Ghana, led to conflict in the 1820s. British influence in the area intensified in later decades. Most African states, especially those with a fairly high degree of political integration, were able to maintain their independence from this creeping European encroachment, called "informal empire" by some historians, but eventually, in 1874, the British stepped in and annexed the Ashanti kingdom as Britain's first African colony of the Gold Coast. At about the same time, the British extended an informal protectorate over warring tribal groups in the Niger delta.

Imperialist Shadow over the Nile

A similar process was under way in the Nile valley. Ever since the voyages of the Portuguese explorers at the close of the fifteenth century, European trade with the East had been carried on almost exclusively by the route around the Cape of Good Hope at the southern tip of Africa. But from the outset, there was interest in shortening the route by digging a canal east of Cairo, where only a low, swampy isthmus separated the Mediterranean from the Red Sea. The Ottoman Turks, who controlled the area, had considered constructing a canal in the sixteenth century, but nothing was accomplished until 1854, when the French entrepreneur Ferdinand de Lesseps signed a contract to begin construction of the canal, which was completed in 1869. The project brought little immediate benefit to Egypt, however, which was attempting to adopt reforms on the European model under the vigorous rule of the Ottoman official Muhammad Ali. The costs of construction imposed a major debt on the Egyptian government and forced a growing level of dependence on foreign financial support. When an army revolt against the increasing foreign influence broke out in 1881, the British stepped in to protect their investment (they had bought Egypt's canal

company shares in 1875) and set up an informal protectorate that would last until World War I.

Rising discontent in the Sudan added to Egypt's internal problems. In 1881, the Muslim cleric Muhammad Ahmad, known as the Mahdi (in Arabic, the "rightly guided one"), led a religious revolt that brought much of

The Suez Canal

the upper Nile under his control. The famous British general Charles Gordon led a military force to Khartoum to restore Egyptian authority, but his besieged army was captured in 1885 by the Mahdi's troops, thirty-six hours before a British rescue mission reached Khartoum. Gordon himself died in the battle (see the Film & History feature on p. 40).

The weakening of Turkish rule in the Nile valley had a parallel farther along the Mediterranean coast to the west, where autonomous regions had begun to emerge under local viceroys in Tripoli, Tunis, and Algiers. In 1830, the French, on the pretext of reducing the threat of piracy to European shipping in the Mediterranean, seized the area surrounding Algiers and annexed it to the kingdom of France. By the mid-1850s, more than 150,000 Europeans had settled in the fertile region adjacent to the coast, though Berber resistance continued in the desert to the south. In 1881, the French imposed a protectorate on neighboring Tunisia. Only Tripoli and Cyrenaica (Ottoman provinces that make up modern-day Libya) remained under Turkish rule until the Italians took them in 1911–1912.

The Scramble for Africa

At the beginning of the 1880s, most of Africa was still independent. European rule was limited to the fringes of the continent, and a few areas, such as Egypt, lower Nigeria, Senegal, and Mozambique, were under various forms of loose protectorate. But the trends were ominous, as the pace of European penetration was accelerating and the constraints that had limited European rapaciousness were fast disappearing.

The scramble began in the mid-1880s, when several European states engaged in what today would be called a

Khartoum (1966)

The tragic mission of General Charles "Chinese" Gordon to Khartoum in 1884 was one of the most dramatic news stories of the last quarter of the nineteenth century. Gordon was already renowned in his native Great Britain for his successful efforts to bring an end to the practice of slavery in North Africa. He had also attracted attention for helping the Manchu Empire suppress the Taiping Rebellion in China in the 1860s (see Chapter 3), hence his nickname. The Khartoum affair not only marked the culmination of his storied career but also symbolized in broader terms the epic struggle in Britain between advocates and opponents of imperial expansion. The battle for Khartoum thus became an object lesson in modern British history. Proponents of British imperial expansion argued that the country must assert its power in the Nile River valley to protect the Suez Canal as its main trade route to the East. Critics argued that imperial overreach would inevitably entangle the country in unwinnable wars in far-off places.

The movie *Khartoum* (1966) dramatically captures the ferocity of the battle for the Nile as well as its significance for the future of the British Empire. General Gordon, stoically played by the American actor Charlton Heston, is a devout Christian who has devoted his life to carrying out the moral imperative of imperialism in the continent of Africa. When peace in the Sudan (then a British protectorate in the upper Nile River valley) is threatened by the forces of radical Islam led by the Muslim mystic Muhammad Ahmad—known as the Mahdi—Gordon leads a mission to Khartoum under orders to prevent catastrophe there. But Prime Minister William Ewart Gladstone, admirably portrayed by the British actor Sir

General Charles Gordon (Charlton Heston) astride his camel in Khartoum, Sudan.

Cinerama/United Artists/The Kobal Collection/Art Resource NY

Ralph Richardson, fears that Gordon's messianic desire to save the Sudan will entrap his government in an unwinnable war; he thus orders Gordon to lead an evacuation of the city. The most fascinating character in the film is the Mahdi himself (played brilliantly by Sir Laurence Olivier), who firmly believes that he has a sacred mandate to carry the Prophet's words to the global Muslim community.

The conclusion of the film, set in the breathtaking beauty of the Nile River valley, takes place as the clash of wills reaches a climax in the battle for control of Khartoum. Although the film's portrayal of a face-to-face meeting between Gordon and the Mahdi is not based on fact, the narrative serves as an object lesson on the dangers of imperial overreach and as an eerie foretaste of the clash between militant Islam and Christendom in our own day. ■

feeding frenzy. All sought to seize a piece of African territory before the carcass had been picked clean. By 1900, virtually the entire continent had been placed under one form or another of European rule (see Map 2.3). The British had consolidated their authority over the Nile valley and seized additional territories in East Africa. The French retaliated by advancing eastward from Senegal into the central Sahara, where they eventually came eyeball to eyeball with the British in the Nile valley They also occupied the island of Madagascar and other coastal territories in West and Central Africa. In between, the Germans claimed the hinterland opposite Zanzibar, as well as coastal strips in West and Southwest Africa north of the Cape, and King Leopold II of Belgium claimed the Congo.

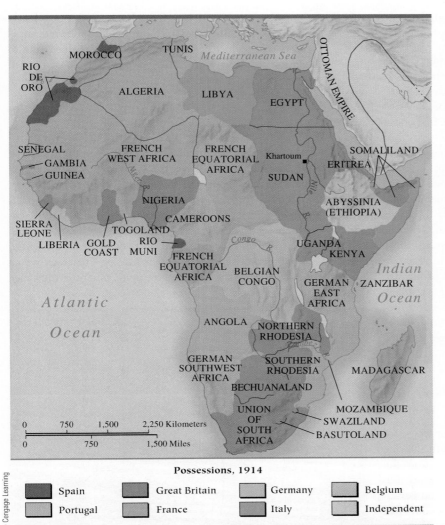

MAP 2.3 **Africa in 1914.** By the beginning of 1900, virtually all of Africa was under some form of European rule. The territorial divisions established by colonial powers on the continent of Africa on the eve of World War I are shown here.

Q *Which European countries possessed the most colonies in Africa? Why did Ethiopia remain independent?*

THE MOTIVES What had happened to spark the sudden imperialist hysteria that brought an end to African independence? Economic interests in the narrow sense were not at stake as they had been in South and Southeast Asia: the level of trade between Europe and Africa was simply not sufficient to justify the risks and the expense of conquest. Clearly, one factor was the growing rivalry among the imperialist powers. European leaders might be provoked into an imperialist takeover not by economic considerations but by the fear that another state might do so, leaving them at a disadvantage.

Another consideration might be called the "missionary factor," as European religious interests lobbied with their governments for a colonial takeover to facilitate their efforts to convert the African population to Christianity. In fact, considerable moral complacency was inherent in the process. The concept of the "white man's burden" persuaded many that it was in the interests of the African people to be introduced more rapidly to the benefits of Western civilization. Even the highly respected Scottish missionary David Livingstone had become convinced that missionary work and economic development had to go hand in hand, pleading to his fellow Europeans to introduce the "three Cs" (Christianity, commerce, and civilization) to the continent. How much easier such a task would be if African peoples were under benevolent European rule! There were more prosaic reasons as well. Advances in Western technology and European superiority in firearms made it easier than ever for a small European force to defeat superior numbers. Furthermore, life expectancy for Europeans living in Africa had improved. With the discovery that quinine (extracted from the bark of the cinchona tree) could provide partial immunity from the ravages of malaria, the mortality rate for Europeans living in Africa dropped dramatically in the 1840s. By the end of the century, European residents in tropical Africa faced only slightly higher risks of death by disease than individuals living in Europe.

Under these circumstances, King Leopold of Belgium used missionary activities as an excuse to claim vast territories in the Congo River basin—Belgium, he said, as "a small country, with a small people," needed a colony to enhance its image.[4] The royal land grab set off a desperate race among European nations to stake claims throughout sub-Saharan Africa. Leopold ended up with the territories south of the Congo River, while France occupied areas to the north. Rapacious European adventurers established

Empire Building in Africa ❧ **41**

plantations in the new Belgian Congo to grow rubber, palm oil, and other valuable export products.

THE BERLIN CONFERENCE As rivalry among the competing powers heated up, a conference was convened at Berlin in 1884 to avert war and reduce tensions among European nations competing for the spoils of Africa. It proved reasonably successful at achieving the first objective but less so at the second. During the next few years, African territories were annexed without provoking a major confrontation between Western powers, but in the late 1890s, Britain and France reached the brink of conflict at Fashoda, a small town on the Nile River in the Sudan. The French had been advancing eastward across the Sahara with the transparent objective of controlling the regions around the upper Nile. In 1898, British and Egyptian troops seized the Sudan and then marched southward to head off the French. After a tense face-off between units of the two European countries at Fashoda, the French government backed down, and British authority over the area was secured. Except for Djibouti, a tiny portion of the Somali coast, the French were restricted to equatorial Africa.

Bantus, Boers, and British in South Africa

Nowhere in Africa did the European presence grow more rapidly than in the south. During the eighteenth century, Dutch settlers from the Cape Colony began to migrate eastward into territory inhabited by local Khoisan- and Bantu-speaking peoples, the latter of whom had recently entered the area from the north. Internecine warfare among the Bantus had largely depopulated the region, facilitating occupation of the land by the Boers, the Afrikaans-speaking farmers descended from the original Dutch settlers in the seventeenth century. But in the early nineteenth century, a Bantu people called the Zulus, under the talented ruler Shaka, counterattacked, setting off a series of wars between the Europeans and the Zulus. Eventually, Shaka was overthrown, and the Boers continued their advance northeastward during the so-called Great Trek of the mid-1830s (see Map 2.4). By 1865, the total European population of the area had risen to nearly 200,000 people.

The Boers' eastward migration was provoked in part by the British seizure of the Cape from the Dutch during the Napoleonic wars. The British government was generally more sympathetic to the rights of the local African population than were the Afrikaners, many of whom saw white superiority as ordained by God and fled from British rule to control their own destiny. Eventually, the Boers formed their own independent republics, the Orange Free State and the South African Republic (usually known as Transvaal). Much of the African population in these areas was confined to reserves.

THE BOER WAR The discovery of gold and diamonds in the Transvaal complicated the situation. Clashes between the Afrikaner population and foreign (mainly British) miners and developers led to an attempt by Cecil Rhodes, prime minister of the Cape Colony and a prominent entrepreneur in the area, to subvert the Transvaal and bring it under British rule. In 1899, the so-called Boer War broke out between Britain and the Transvaal, which was backed by the Orange Free State. Guerrilla resistance

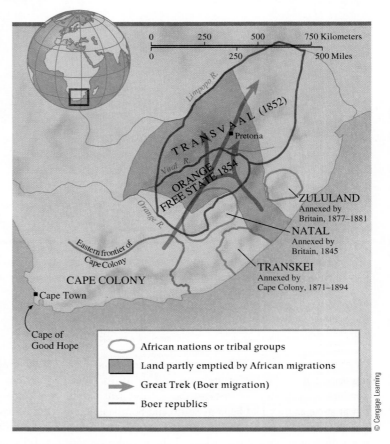

MAP 2.4 The Struggle for Southern Africa. Shown here is the expansion of European settlers from the Cape Colony into adjacent areas of southern Africa in the nineteenth century. The arrows indicate the routes taken by the Afrikaans-speaking Boers.

Q *Who were the Boers, and why did they migrate eastward?*

by the Boers was fierce, but the vastly superior forces of the British were able to prevail by 1902. To compensate the defeated Afrikaner population for the loss of independence, the British government agreed that only whites would vote in the now essentially self-governing colony. The Boers were placated, but the brutalities committed during the war (the British introduced an institution later to be known as the concentration camp) created bitterness on both sides that continued to fester for decades.

Colonialism in Africa

In general, Western economic interests were more limited in Africa than elsewhere. As a result, most colonial governments settled down to govern their new territories with the least effort and expense possible. In many cases, they pursued a form of indirect rule reminiscent of the British approach to the princely states in the Indian peninsula.

BRITISH RULE IN NIGERIA Nigeria offers a typical example of British-style indirect rule. British officials operated at the central level, but local authority was assigned to Nigerian chiefs, with British district officers serving as intermediaries with the central administration. The local authorities were expected to maintain law and order and to collect taxes from the indigenous population. A dual legal system was instituted that applied African laws to Africans and European laws to foreigners.

One advantage of such an administrative system was that it did not severely disrupt local customs and institutions. At the same time, it was misleading because all major decisions were made by the British administrators while the African authorities served primarily as the means of enforcing the decisions. Moreover, indirect rule served to perpetuate the autocratic system that often existed prior to colonial takeover since there was a natural tendency to view the local aristocracy as the African equivalent of the traditional British ruling class. Such a policy provided few opportunities for ambitious and talented young Africans from outside the traditional elite and thus sowed the seeds for class tensions after the restoration of independence in the twentieth century.

THE BRITISH IN EAST AFRICA The situation was somewhat different in Kenya, which had a relatively large European population attracted by the temperate climate in the central highlands. The local government had encouraged Europeans to migrate to the area as a means of promoting economic development and encouraging financial self-sufficiency. To attract them, fertile farmlands in the central highlands were reserved for European settlement while, as in South Africa, specified reserve lands were set aside for Africans. The presence of a privileged European minority had an impact on Kenya's political development. The European settlers actively sought self-government and dominion status similar to that granted to such former British possessions as Canada and Australia. The British government, however, was not willing to run the risk of provoking racial tensions with the African majority and agreed only to establish separate government organs for the European and African populations.

SOUTH AFRICA The situation in South Africa, of course, was unique, not only because of the high percentage of European settlers but also because of the division between English-speaking and Afrikaner elements within the European population. In 1910, the British agreed to the creation of the independent Union of South Africa, which combined the old Cape Colony and Natal with the two Boer republics. The new union adopted a representative government, but only for the European population. The African reserves of Basutoland (now Lesotho), Bechuanaland (now Botswana), and Swaziland were subordinated directly to the crown. The union was now free to manage its own domestic affairs and possessed considerable autonomy in foreign relations. Remaining areas south of the Zambezi River, eventually divided into the territories of Northern and Southern Rhodesia, were also placed under British rule. British immigration into Southern Rhodesia was extensive, and in 1922, after a popular referendum, it became a crown colony.

DIRECT RULE Most other European nations governed their African possessions through a form of direct rule. The prototype was the French system, which reflected the centralized administrative system introduced in France by Napoleon. As in the British colonies, at the top of the pyramid was a French official, usually known as a governor-general, who was appointed from Paris and governed with the aid of a bureaucracy in the capital city. At the provincial level, French commissioners were assigned to deal with local administrators, but the latter were required to be conversant in French and could be transferred to a new position to meet the needs of the central government.

After World War I, European colonial policy in Africa entered a new and more formal phase. Colonial governments paid more attention to improving social services, including education, medicine, sanitation, and communications. More Africans were now serving in colonial administrations, though relatively few were in positions of responsibility. On the other hand, race consciousness probably increased during this period. Segregated clubs, schools, and churches were established as more European officials brought their wives with them and began to raise families in the colonies.

More directly affected by the colonial presence than the small African elite were ordinary Africans, who were routinely exposed to unbelievably harsh conditions as they were put to use as manual laborers to promote the cause of imperialism.

The most flagrant example was in the Belgian Congo. Conditions on the plantations there were so abysmal that an international outcry eventually led to the formation of a commission under British consul Roger Casement to investigate. The commission's report, issued in 1904, helped to bring about reforms (see the box on p. 29).

WOMEN IN COLONIAL AFRICA Colonial rule had a mixed impact on the rights and status of women in Africa. Sexual relationships changed profoundly during the colonial era, sometimes in ways that could justly be described as beneficial. Colonial governments attempted to put an end to forced marriage, bodily mutilation such as clitoridectomy, and **polygyny**. Missionaries introduced women to Western education and encouraged them to organize to defend their interests.

But the colonial system had some unfavorable consequences as well. African women had traditionally benefited from the prestige of **matrilineal** systems and were empowered by their traditional role as the primary agricultural producers in their community. Under colonialism, European settlers not only took the best land for themselves but also, in introducing new agricultural techniques, tended to deal exclusively with males, encouraging the latter to develop lucrative cash crops, while women were restricted to traditional farming methods. Whereas African men applied chemical fertilizer to the fields, women continued to use manure. While men began to use bicycles, and eventually trucks, to transport goods, women still carried their goods on their heads, a practice that continues today. In British colonies, Victorian attitudes of female subordination led to restrictions on women's freedom, and positions in government that they had formerly held were now closed to them.

Legacy of Shame. By the mid-nineteenth century, most European nations had prohibited the trade in African slaves, but slavery continued to exist in Africa well into the next century. In the Belgian Congo, the mistreatment of conscript laborers led to a popular outcry and the formation of a commission to look into the situation and recommend reforms. Shown here are two manacled members of a chain gang in the Belgian Congo. The photograph was taken in 1904.

subjected to countless indignities reminiscent of Western practices in Asia. While the institution of slavery was discouraged in much of the continent, African workers were

CONCLUSION

BY THE EARLY TWENTIETH CENTURY, virtually all of Africa and a good part of South and Southeast Asia were under some form of colonial rule. With the advent of the Age of Imperialism, a global economy was finally established, and the domination of Western civilization over those of Africa and Asia appeared to be complete.

Defenders of colonialism argue that the system was a necessary if sometimes painful stage in the evolution of human societies. Although its immediate consequences were admittedly sometimes unfortunate, Western imperialism was ultimately beneficial to colonial powers and subjects alike because it created the conditions for global economic development and the universal application of democratic institutions. Critics, however, charge that the Western colonial powers were driven by an insatiable lust for profits. They dismiss the Western civilizing mission as a fig leaf to cover naked greed and reject the notion that imperialism played a salutary role in hastening the adjustment of traditional societies to the demands of industrial civilization. Rather, it locked them in to what many social scientists today describe as a "dependency relationship" with their colonial masters. "Why is Africa (or for that matter Latin America and much of Asia) so poor?" asked one Western critique of imperialism. "The answer is very brief: we have made it poor."[5]

Between these two irreconcilable views, where does the truth lie? It is difficult to provide a simple answer to this question, as the colonial record varied from country to country. In some cases, the colonial experience was probably beneficial in introducing Western technology, values, and democratic institutions into traditional societies. As its defenders are quick to point out, colonialism often laid the foundation for preindustrial societies to play an active and rewarding role in the global economic marketplace.

Still, the critics have a point. Although colonialism did introduce the peoples of Asia and Africa to new technology and the expanding economic marketplace, it was unnecessarily brutal in its application and all too often failed to realize the exalted claims and objectives of its promoters. Existing economic networks—often potentially valuable as a foundation for later economic development—were ruthlessly swept aside in the interests of providing markets for Western manufactured goods. Potential sources of local industrialization were nipped in the bud to avoid competition for factories in Amsterdam, London, Pittsburgh, or Manchester. Training in Western democratic ideals and practices was ignored out of fear that the recipients might use them as weapons against the ruling authorities.

The fundamental weakness of colonialism, then, was that it was ultimately based on the self-interests of the citizens of the colonial powers. When those interests collided with the needs of the colonial peoples, the former always triumphed. However sincerely the David Livingstones, Albert Sarrauts, and William McKinleys of the world were convinced of the rightness of their civilizing mission, the ultimate result was to deprive the colonial peoples of the right to make their own choices about their destiny.

In general, the peoples of Latin America were able to avoid some of the worst consequences of the era of Western imperialism by virtue of having won their independence from colonial control during the nineteenth century. As we saw in Chapter 1, however, some imperialist nations continued to exert influence over regional economies through their dominant position in local export markets. When those interests were threatened, as occurred frequently in Central America and the Caribbean, imperialist governments—and especially the United States—were not shy about employing military force to protect them. Eventually, this form of "**informal empire**" would come to be known as **neocolonialism**, provoking sharp criticism from commentators in Africa, Asia, and Latin America.

In one area of Asia, the spreading tide of imperialism did not result in the establishment of formal Western colonial control. In East Asia, the traditional societies of China and Japan were buffeted by the winds of Western expansionism during the nineteenth century but successfully resisted foreign conquest. In the next chapter, we will see how they managed this and how they fared in their encounter with the West.

TIMELINE

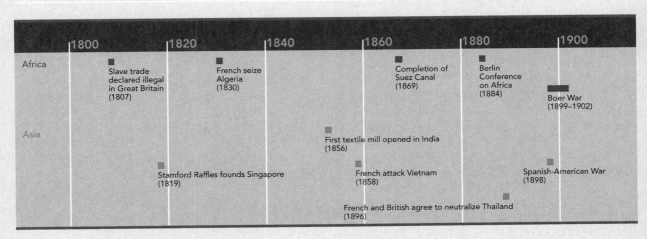

	1800	1820	1840	1860	1880	1900
Africa	Slave trade declared illegal in Great Britain (1807)	French seize Algeria (1830)		Completion of Suez Canal (1869)	Berlin Conference on Africa (1884)	Boer War (1899–1902)
Asia		Stamford Raffles founds Singapore (1819)	First textile mill opened in India (1856) / French attack Vietnam (1858)	French and British agree to neutralize Thailand (1896)		Spanish-American War (1898)

CHAPTER NOTES

1. J. G. Lockhart and C. M. Woodehouse, *Rhodes: The Colossus of Southern Africa* (New York, 1953), pp. 69–70.
2. The quotations are from Henri Brunschwig, *French Colonialism, 1871–1914* (London, 1961), p. 80.
3. Quoted in Louis Roubaud, *Vietnam: La Tragédie Indochinoise* (Paris, 1926), p. 80.
4. Quoted in T. Pakenham, *The Scramble for Africa* (New York, 1991), p. 13.
5. Quoted in Tony Smith, *The Pattern of Imperialism: The United States, Great Britain and the Late-Industrializing World Since 1815* (Cambridge, 1981), p. 81.

3

Shadows over the Pacific: East Asia Under Challenge

The Macartney mission to China, 1793

Eileen Tweedy/The Art Archive/Art Resource NY

IN AUGUST 1793, a British diplomatic mission led by Lord Macartney arrived at the North Chinese port of Dagu and embarked on the road to Beijing. His caravan, which included six hundred cases filled with presents for the emperor, bore flags and banners provided by the Chinese that proclaimed in Chinese characters "Ambassador bearing tribute from the country of England." Upon his arrival in the capital, Macartney refused his hosts' demand that he perform the **kowtow**, a traditional symbol of submission to the emperor. Eventually, the dispute over protocol was resolved with a compromise: Macartney agreed to bend on one knee, a courtesy that he displayed to his own sovereign.

In other respects, however, the mission was a failure, for China rejected the British request for an increase in trade between the two countries, and Macartney left Beijing in October with nothing to show for his efforts. Not until half a century later would the ruling Qing dynasty—at the point of a gun—agree to the British demand for an expansion of commercial ties.

Historians have often viewed the failure of the Macartney mission as a reflection of the disdain of Chinese rulers toward their counterparts in other countries and their serene confidence in the superiority of Chinese civilization in a world inhabited by barbarians. If that was the case, the Chinese emperor Qianlong's confidence was misplaced, for in the decades immediately following the abortive Macartney mission to Beijing, China faced a growing challenge not only from the escalating power and ambitions of the West but

also from its own growing internal weaknesses. Backed by European guns, European merchants and missionaries pressed insistently for the right to carry out their activities in China and the neighboring islands of Japan. Despite their initial reluctance, the Chinese and Japanese governments were eventually forced to open their doors to the foreigners, whose presence and threat to the local way of life escalated rapidly during the final years of the nineteenth century.

CRITICAL THINKING

Q How did China and Japan each respond to Western pressures in the nineteenth century, and what implications did their different responses have for each nation's history?

China at Its Apex

In 1800, the Qing or Manchu dynasty (1644–1911) appeared to be at the height of its power. The Manchus, a seminomadic people whose original homeland was north of the Great Wall, had invaded North China in the mid-seventeenth century and conquered the tottering Ming dynasty in 1644. Under the rule of two great emperors, Kangxi (1661–1722) and Qianlong (1736–1795), China had then experienced a long period of peace and prosperity. Its borders were secure, and its culture and intellectual

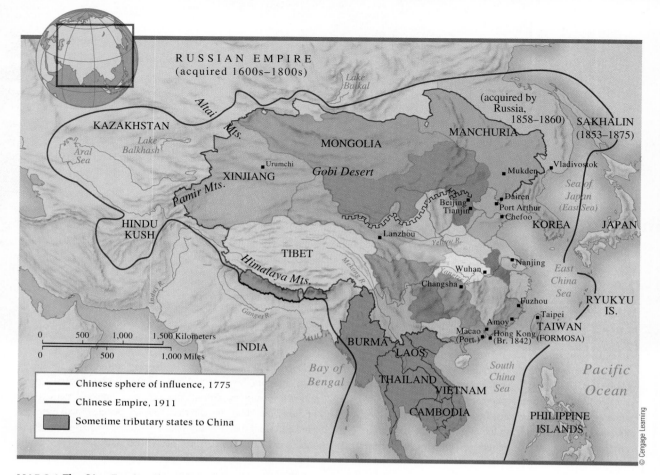

MAP 3.1 The Qing Empire. Shown here is the Qing Empire at the height of its power in the late eighteenth century, together with its shrunken boundaries at the moment of its dissolution in 1911.

Q *Where are China's tributary states on the map? How had their status changed by 1911?*

achievements were the envy of the world. Its rulers, hidden behind the walls of the Forbidden City in Beijing, had every reason to describe their patrimony as the Central Kingdom, China's historical name for itself. But a little over a century later, humiliated and harassed by the black ships and big guns of the Western powers, the Qing dynasty, the last in a series that had endured for more than two thousand years, collapsed in the dust (see Map 3.1).

Changeless China?

Historians once assumed that the primary reason for the rapid decline and fall of the Manchu dynasty was the intense pressure applied to a proud but somewhat complacent traditional society by the modern West. There is indeed some truth in that allegation. On the surface, China had long appeared to be an unchanging society

patterned after the Confucian vision of a Golden Age in the remote past. This, in fact, was the image presented by China's rulers, who referred constantly to tradition as a model for imperial institutions and cultural values. That tradition was based firmly on **Confucianism**, a set of ideas that were identified with the ancient philosopher Confucius (551–479 B.C.E.), who emphasized such qualities as obedience, hard work, rule by merit, and the subordination of the individual to the interests of the community. Such principles, which had emerged out of the conditions of a continental society based on agriculture as the primary source of national wealth, had formed the basis for Chinese political and social institutions and values since the rise of the Han dynasty in the late third century B.C.E.

When European ships first appeared off the coast of China in the sixteenth and seventeenth centuries, they brought with them dangerous new ideas and values that were strikingly at variance with those of imperial China. China's rulers soon came to recognize the nature of the threat represented by European Christian missionaries and merchants and attempted to expel the former while restricting the latter to a limited presence in the southern coastal city of Canton. For the next two centuries, China was, at least in intent, an essentially closed society.

It was the hope of influential figures at the imperial court in Beijing that by expelling the barbarians, they could protect Chinese civilization from the virus of foreign ideas. Their effort to freeze time was futile, however, for in reality, Chinese society was already beginning to change under their feet—and changing rather rapidly. Although few observers may have been aware of it at the time, by the beginning of the Manchu era in the seventeenth century, many traditional precepts were becoming increasingly irrelevant in a society that was becoming ever more complex.

CHANGES IN RURAL AREAS Nowhere was change more evident than in the economic sector. During the early modern period, China was still a predominantly agricultural society, as it had been throughout recorded history. Nearly 85 percent of the people were farmers. In the south, the main crop was rice; in the north, it was wheat or dry crops. But even though China had few urban centers, the population was beginning to increase rapidly. Thanks to a long era of peace and stability, the introduction of new crops from the Americas, and the cultivation of new, fast-ripening strains of rice, the Chinese population doubled between the time of the early Qing and the end of the eighteenth century. And it continued to grow during the nineteenth century, reaching the unprecedented level of 400 million by 1900.

Of course, this population increase meant much greater pressure on the land, smaller farms, and an ever-thinner margin of safety in the event of climatic disaster. The imperial court had attempted to deal with the problem by various means—most notably by preventing the concentration of land in the hands of wealthy landowners—but by the end of the eighteenth century, almost all the land that could be irrigated was already under cultivation, and the problems of rural hunger and landlessness became increasingly serious. Not surprisingly, economic hardship quickly translated into rural unrest.

SEEDS OF INDUSTRIALIZATION Another change that took place during the Qing dynasty was the steady growth of manufacturing and commerce. Trade and manufacturing had existed in China since early times, but they had been limited by a number of factors, including social prejudice, official restrictions, and state monopolies on

mining and on the production of such commodities as alcohol and salt. Now, taking advantage of the long era of peace and prosperity under the Qing, merchants and manufacturers began to expand their operations beyond their immediate provinces. Trade in silk, metal and wood products, porcelain, cotton goods, and cash crops such as tea and tobacco developed rapidly, and commercial networks began to operate on a regional and sometimes even a national basis.

With the growth of trade came an expansion of commercial contacts and guild organizations nationwide. Merchants began organizing guilds in cities and market towns throughout the country to provide legal protection, an opportunity to do business, and food and lodging for merchants from particular provinces. Foreign trade also expanded, as Chinese merchants, mainly from the coastal provinces of the south, established extensive contacts with countries in Southeast Asia. In many instances, the contacts in Southeast Asia were themselves ethnic Chinese who had settled in the area during the seventeenth and eighteenth centuries.

Some historians have suggested that this rise in industrial and commercial activity would, under other circumstances, have led to an indigenous industrial revolution and the emergence of a capitalist society such as that taking shape in Europe. The significance of these changes should not be exaggerated, however, for there were some key differences between China and western Europe that would have impeded the emergence of capitalism in China. In the first place, although industrial production in China was on the rise, it was still based almost entirely on traditional methods of production. China had no uniform system of weights and measures, and the banking system was still primitive by European standards. The use of paper money, invented centuries earlier, was still relatively limited. There were few paved roads, and the Grand Canal, long the most efficient means of carrying goods between the north and the south, was silting up. As a result, merchants had to rely more and more on the coastal route, where they faced increasing competition from foreign shipping.

There were other, more deep-seated differences as well. The bourgeois class in China was not as independent as its European counterpart. Reflecting an ancient preference for agriculture over manufacturing and trade, the state levied heavy taxes on manufacturing and commerce while seeking to keep agricultural taxes low. Such attitudes were still shared by key groups in the population. Although much money could be made in commerce, most merchants who accumulated wealth used it to buy their way into the ranks of the landed gentry. The most that can really be said, then, is that during the Qing dynasty, China was beginning to undergo major economic and social changes that might have led, in due time, to the emergence of an industrialized society.

Traditional China in Decline

When Western pressure on the Manchu Empire began to increase during the early nineteenth century, it served to exacerbate the existing strains in Chinese society. By 1800, the trade relationship that restricted Western merchants to a small commercial outlet at Canton was no longer acceptable to the British, who were increasingly concerned about the trade imbalance resulting from the growing appetite for Chinese tea in Britain. Their solution was opium. A product more addictive than tea, opium was grown in northeastern India under British East India Company sponsorship and then shipped directly to the Chinese market. Soon demand for the product in South China became insatiable, despite an official prohibition on its use. Bullion now flowed out of the Chinese imperial treasury into the pockets of British merchants and officials.

Opium and Rebellion

When the Qing attempted to prohibit the opium trade, the British declared war. The Opium War, as it was called, lasted three years (1839–1842) and graphically demonstrated the superiority of British firepower and military tactics. China sued for peace and, in the Treaty of Nanjing, agreed to open five coastal ports to British trade, limit tariffs on imported British goods, grant extraterritorial rights to British citizens in China, and pay a substantial indemnity to cover the British costs of the war. Beijing also agreed to cede the island of Hong Kong (dismissed by a senior British official as a "barren rock") to Great Britain. Nothing was said in the treaty about the opium trade.

Although the Opium War is now considered the beginning of modern Chinese history, it is unlikely that many Chinese at the time would have seen it that way. This was not the first time that a ruling dynasty had been forced to make concessions to foreigners, and the opening of five coastal ports to the British hardly constituted a serious threat to the security of the empire. Although a few concerned Chinese argued that the court should learn more about European civilization to find the secret of the

Eileen Tweedy/The Art Archive/Art Resource NY

The Opium War. The Opium War, waged between China and Great Britain between 1839 and 1842, was China's first conflict with a European power. Lacking modern military technology, the Chinese suffered a humiliating defeat. In this painting, heavily armed British steamships destroy unwieldy Chinese junks along the Chinese coast. China's humiliation at sea was a legacy of its rulers' lack of interest in maritime matters since the middle of the fifteenth century, when Chinese junks were among the most advanced sailing ships in the world.

British success, others contended that China had nothing to learn from the barbarians and that borrowing foreign ways would undercut the purity of Confucian civilization.

The Taiping Rebellion

The Manchus attempted to deal with the problem in the traditional way of playing the foreigners off against each other. Concessions granted to the British were offered to other Western nations, including the United States, and soon thriving foreign concession areas were operating in treaty ports along the southern Chinese coast from Canton in the south to Shanghai, a bustling new port on a tributary of the Yangtze, in the center.

In the meantime, the Qing court's failure to deal with pressing internal economic problems led to a major peasant revolt that shook the foundations of the empire. On the surface, the so-called Taiping Rebellion owed something to the Western incursion; the leader of the uprising, Hong Xiuquan, a failed candidate for the civil service examination, was a Christian convert who viewed himself as a younger brother of Jesus Christ and hoped to establish what he referred to as a "Heavenly Kingdom of Supreme Peace" in China. With their ranks swelled by impoverished peasants and other discontented elements throughout the southern provinces, the rebels swept northward, seizing the Yangtze River port of Nanjing in March 1853. The revolt continued for ten more years but gradually lost momentum, and in 1864, the Qing, though weakened, retook Nanjing and destroyed the remnants of the rebel force. The rebellion had cost the lives of millions of Chinese.

One reason for the dynasty's failure to deal effectively with internal unrest was its continuing difficulties with the Western imperialists. In 1856, the British and the French, smarting from trade restrictions and limitations on their missionary activities, launched a series of attacks and seized the capital of Beijing in 1860. In the ensuing Treaty of Tianjin, the Qing agreed to humiliating new concessions: legalization of the opium trade, the opening of additional ports to foreign trade, and cession of the peninsula of Kowloon (opposite the island of Hong Kong) to the British.

Efforts at Reform

By the late 1870s, the old dynasty was on the verge of collapse. In fending off the Taiping Rebellion, the Manchus had been compelled to rely for support on armed forces under regional command. After quelling the revolt, many of these regional commanders refused to disband their units and, with the support of the local gentry, continued to collect local taxes for their own use. The dreaded pattern of imperial breakdown, so familiar in Chinese history, was beginning to appear once again.

In their weakened state, the Qing rulers finally began to listen to the appeals of reform-minded officials for a new policy called **self-strengthening**, in which Western technology would be adopted while Confucian principles and institutions were maintained intact. This policy, popularly known by its slogan "East for essence, West for practical use," remained the guiding standard for Chinese foreign and domestic policy for decades. Some people even called for reforms in education and in China's hallowed political institutions. Pointing to the power and prosperity of Great Britain, the journalist Wang Tao (1828–1897) remarked, "The real strength of England . . . lies in the fact that there is a sympathetic understanding between the governing and the governed, a close relationship between the ruler and the people. . . . My observation is that the daily domestic political life of England actually embodies the traditional ideals of our ancient Golden Age"[1] (see the box on p. 52). Such democratic ideas were too radical for most moderate reformers, however. One of the leading court officials of the day, Zhang Zhidong, countered:

> The doctrine of people's rights will bring us not a single benefit but a hundred evils. Are we going to establish a parliament? . . . Even supposing the confused and clamorous people are assembled in one house, for every one of them who is clear-sighted, there will be a hundred others whose vision is beclouded; they will converse at random and talk as if in a dream—what use will it be?[2]

For the time being, Zhang Zhidong's arguments won the day. During the last quarter of the century, the Manchus attempted to modernize their military establishment and build up an industrial base without disturbing the essential elements of traditional Chinese civilization. Railroads, weapons arsenals, and shipyards were built, but the value system remained essentially unchanged.

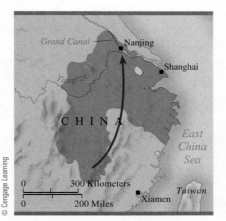

Area Under Taiping Rebellion Control

© Cengage Learning

An Appeal for Change in China

After the humiliating defeat at the hands of the British in the Opium War, a few Chinese intellectuals began to argue that China must change its ways if it was to survive. One of these reformist thinkers was the journalist and author Wang Tao. After a trip to Europe in the late 1860s, Wang returned to China convinced of the technological superiority of the West and the need for his country to adopt reforms that would enable it to compete effectively in a changing world. He had only limited success in persuading his contemporaries of the need for dramatic change. Many Chinese were undoubtedly reluctant to believe his claim that China was not the Middle Kingdom or "all under Heaven" but only one nation among many in a rapidly changing world.

Wang Tao on Reform

I know that within a hundred years China will adopt all Western methods and excel in them. For though both are vessels, a sailboat differs in speed from a steamship; though both are vehicles, a horse-drawn carriage cannot cover the same distance as a locomotive train. Among weapons, the power of the bow and arrow, sword and spear, cannot be compared with that of firearms; and of firearms, the old types do not have the same effect as the new. Although it be the same piece of work, there is a difference in the ease with which it can be done by machine and by human labor. When new methods do not exist, people will not think of changes; but when there are new instruments, to copy them is certainly possible. Even if the Westerners should give no guidance, the Chinese must surely exert themselves to the utmost of their ingenuity and resources on these things.

Alas! People all understand the past, but they are ignorant of the future. Only scholars whose thoughts run deep and far can grasp the trends. As the mind of Heaven changes above, so do human affairs below. Heaven opens the minds of the Westerners and bestows upon them intelligence and wisdom. Their techniques and skills develop without bound. They sail eastward and gather in China. This constitutes an unprecedented situation in history, and a tremendous change in the world. The foreign nations come from afar with their superior techniques, contemptuous of us in our deficiencies. They show off their prowess and indulge in insults and oppression; they also fight among themselves. Under these circumstances, how can we not think of making changes? . . .

If China does not make any change at this time, how can she be on a par with the great nations of Europe, and compare with them in power and strength? Nevertheless, the path of reform is beset with difficulties. What the Western countries have today are regarded as of no worth by those who arrogantly refuse to pay attention. Their argument is that we should use our own laws to govern the empire, for that is the Way of our sages. They do not know that the Way of the sages is valued only because it can make proper accommodations according to the times. If Confucius lived today, we may be certain that he would not cling to antiquity and oppose making changes. . . .

 What arguments did Wang Tao use in his efforts to persuade readers to accept his point of view? Would Confucius have found Wang Tao's arguments persuasive? Why or why not?

SOURCE: Excerpt from *Sources of Chinese Tradition* by William Theodore de Bary. Copyright © 1960 by Columbia University Press, New York.

The Climax of Imperialism in China

In the end, the results spoke for themselves. During the last two decades of the nineteenth century, the European penetration of China, both political and military, intensified. Rapacious imperialists began to bite off territory at the outer edges of the Qing Empire. The Gobi Desert north of the Great Wall, Chinese Central Asia (known in Chinese as Xinjiang), and Tibet, all inhabited by non-Chinese peoples and never fully assimilated into the Chinese Empire, were now gradually removed totally from Beijing's control. In the north and northwest, the main beneficiary was Russia, which took advantage of the dynasty's weakness to force the cession of territories north of the Amur River in Siberia. In Tibet, competition between Russia and Great Britain prevented either power from seizing the territory outright but at the same time enabled Tibetan authorities to revive local autonomy never recognized by the Chinese. On the southern borders of the empire, British and French advances in mainland Southeast Asia removed Burma and Vietnam from their traditional vassal relationship with the Manchu court.

Even more ominous developments were taking place in the Chinese heartland, where European economic penetration led to the creation of so-called **spheres of influence** dominated by diverse foreign powers. Although the imperial court retained theoretical sovereignty throughout the country, in practice its political, economic, and administrative influence beyond the region of the capital was increasingly circumscribed.

The breakup of the Manchu dynasty accelerated during the last five years of the nineteenth century. In 1894, the Qing went to war with Japan over Japanese incursions into the Korean peninsula, which threatened China's long-held suzerainty over the area (see "Joining the Imperialist Club" later in this chapter). To the surprise of many observers, the Chinese were roundly defeated, confirming to some critics the devastating failure of the policy of self-strengthening by halfway measures.

More humiliation came in 1897, when Germany, a new entrant in the race for spoils in East Asia, used the pretext of the murder of two German missionaries by Chinese rioters to demand the cession of territories in the Shandong peninsula. The imperial court's approval of this demand set off a scramble for territory by other interested powers. Russia now demanded the Liaodong peninsula with its ice-free harbor at Port Arthur, and Great Britain obtained a hundred-year lease on the New Territories, adjacent to Hong Kong, as well as a coaling station in northern China.

The latest scramble for territory had taken place at a time of internal crisis in China. In the spring of 1898, an outspoken advocate of reform, the progressive Confucian scholar Kang Youwei, won the support of the young emperor Guangxu for a comprehensive reform program patterned after recent changes initiated in Japan. Without change, Kang argued, China would perish. During the next several weeks, the emperor issued edicts calling for major political, administrative, and educational reforms. Not surprisingly, Kang's ideas for reform were opposed by many conservatives, who saw little advantage to copying the West. Most important, the new program was opposed by the emperor's aunt, the Empress Dowager Cixi, the real source of power at court. Cixi had begun her political career as a concubine to an earlier emperor. After his death, she became a dominant force at court and in 1878 placed her infant nephew, the future emperor Guangxu, on the throne. For two decades, she ruled in his name as regent. Cixi interpreted Guangxu's action as a British-supported effort to reduce her influence at court. With the aid of conservatives in the army, she arrested and executed several of the reformers and had the emperor

The Art Archive/Art Resource NY

The Empress Dowager Cixi. Portraits of ruling figures have traditionally been designed to inspire admiration or devotion and thus tend to emphasize the majestic or charismatic quality of the subject. After the disastrous Boxer Rebellion of 1900, however, the Empress Dowager Cixi sought to improve her image in the Western world and turned to the modern medium of photography as a means of doing so. In this photograph, taken in 1903, she appeared in an elaborate costume in a traditional Chinese setting, but her casual stance was apparently intended to soften her image among foreign observers.

incarcerated in the palace. Kang Youwei managed to flee abroad. With Cixi's palace coup, the so-called One Hundred Days of reform came to an end.

OPENING THE DOOR TO CHINA During the next two years, foreign pressure on the dynasty intensified (see Map 3.2 on p. 54). With encouragement from the British, who hoped to avert a total collapse of the Manchu Empire, U.S. Secretary of State John Hay presented the other imperialist powers with a proposal to ensure equal economic access to the China market for all nations. Hay also suggested that all powers join together to guarantee the territorial and administrative integrity of the Chinese

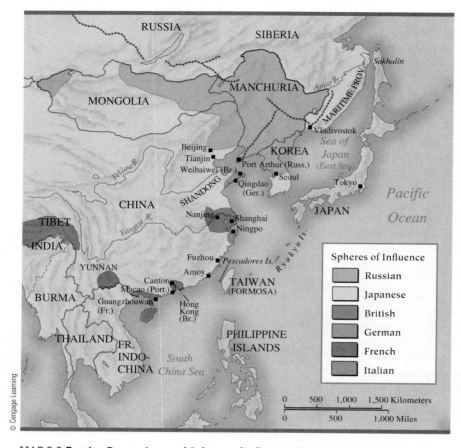

MAP 3.2 Foreign Possessions and Spheres of Influence About 1900. At the end of the nineteenth century, China was being carved up like a melon by foreign imperialist powers.

Q *Which of the areas marked on the map were removed from Chinese control during the nineteenth century?*

THE BOXER REBELLION In the long run, then, the Open Door was a positive step that brought a measure of sanity to the imperialist meddling in East Asia. Unfortunately, it came too late to stop the domestic explosion known as the Boxer Rebellion. The Boxers (literally, "righteous and harmonious fists"), so called because of the physical exercises they performed, were members of a secret society operating primarily in rural areas in North China. Provoked by a damaging drought and high levels of unemployment caused in part by foreign economic activity (the introduction of railroads and steamships, for example, undercut the livelihood of boat workers who traditionally carried merchandise on the rivers and canals), the Boxers attacked foreign residents and besieged the foreign legation quarter in Beijing until the foreigners were rescued by an international expeditionary force in the late summer of 1900. As punishment, the foreign troops destroyed a number of temples in the capital suburbs, and the Chinese government was compelled to pay a heavy indemnity to the foreign governments involved in suppressing the uprising.

The Collapse of the Old Order

During the next few years, the old dynasty tried desperately to reform itself. The empress dowager, who had long resisted change, now embraced a number of reforms in education, administration, and the legal system. The venerable **civil service examination** system, based on knowledge of the Confucian classics, was replaced by a new educational system patterned after the Western model. In 1905, a commission was formed to study constitutional changes, and over the next few years, legislative assemblies were established at the provincial level. Elections for a national assembly were held in 1910.

Such moves helped shore up the dynasty temporarily, but history shows that the most dangerous period for an

Empire. When none of the other governments flatly opposed the idea, Hay issued a second note declaring that all major nations with economic interests in China had agreed to an "Open Door" policy in China.

Though probably motivated more by a U.S. desire for open markets than by a benevolent wish to protect China, the **Open Door Notes** did have the practical effect of reducing the imperialist hysteria over access to the China market. That hysteria—the product of decades of mythologizing among Western commercial interests about the "400 million" Chinese customers—had accelerated at the end of the century as fears of China's imminent collapse increased. The "gentlemen's agreement" about the Open Door (it was not a treaty but merely a pious and nonbinding expression of intent) served to diminish fears in Britain, France, Germany, and Russia that other powers would take advantage of China's weakness to dominate the China market.

authoritarian system is when it begins to reform itself, because change breeds instability and performance rarely matches rising expectations. Such was the case in China. The emerging new provincial elite, composed of merchants, professionals, and reform-minded gentry, soon became impatient with the slow pace of political change and were disillusioned to find that the new assemblies were intended to be primarily advisory rather than legislative. The government also alienated influential elements by financing railway development projects through lucrative contracts to foreign firms rather than by turning to local investors. The reforms also had little meaning for peasants, artisans, miners, and transportation workers, whose living conditions were being eroded by rising taxes and official venality. Rising rural unrest, as yet poorly organized and often centered on secret societies such as the Boxers, was an ominous sign of deep-seated resentment to which the dynasty would not, or could not, respond.

THE RISE OF SUN YAT-SEN

To China's reformist elite, such signs of social unrest were a threat to be avoided; to its tiny revolutionary movement, they were a harbinger of promise. The first physical manifestations of future revolution appeared during the last decade of the nineteenth century with the formation of the Revive China Society by the young radical Sun Yat-sen (1866–1925). Born to a peasant family in a village south of Canton, Sun was educated in Hawaii and returned to China to practice medicine. Soon he turned his full attention to the ills of Chinese society, leading bands of radicals in small-scale insurrections to attract attention.

At first, Sun's efforts yielded few positive results other than creating a symbol of resistance and the new century's first revolutionary martyrs. But at a convention in Tokyo in 1905, Sun managed to unite radical groups from across China in the so-called Revolutionary Alliance (Tongmenghui). The new organization's program was based on Sun's **Three People's Principles**: nationalism (meaning primarily the destruction of Manchu rule over China), democracy, and "people's livelihood," which was a program to improve social and economic conditions (see the box on p. 56). Although the new organization was small and relatively inexperienced, it benefited from rising popular discontent with the failure of Manchu reforms to improve conditions in China.

THE 1911 REVOLUTION

In October 1911, followers of Sun Yat-sen launched an uprising in the industrial center of Wuhan, in central China. With Sun traveling in the United States, the insurrection lacked leadership, but the decrepit government's inability to react quickly encouraged political forces at the provincial level to take measures into their own hands. The dynasty was now in a state of virtual collapse: the dowager empress had died in 1908, one day after her nephew Guangxu; the throne was now occupied by the infant Puyi, the son of Guangxu's younger brother. Sun's party, however, had neither the military strength nor the political base necessary to seize the initiative and was forced to turn to a representative of the old order, General Yuan Shikai (1859–1916). A prominent figure in military circles since the beginning of the century, Yuan had been placed in charge of the imperial forces sent to suppress the rebellion, but now he abandoned the Manchus and acted on his own behalf. In negotiations with representatives of Sun Yat-sen's party (Sun himself had arrived in China in January 1912), he agreed to serve as president of a new Chinese republic. The old dynasty and the age-old system it had attempted to preserve were no more.

Propagandists for Sun Yat-sen's party have often portrayed the events of 1911 as a glorious revolution that brought two thousand years of imperial tradition to an end. But a true revolution does not just destroy an old order; it also brings new political and social forces into power and creates new institutions and values that provide a new framework for a changing society. In this sense, the 1911 revolution did not live up to its name. Sun and his followers were unable to consolidate their gains. The Revolutionary Alliance found the bulk of its support in an emerging urban middle class and set forth a program based generally on Western liberal democratic principles. That class and that program had provided the foundation for the capitalist democratic revolutions in western Europe and North America in the late eighteenth and nineteenth centuries, but the bourgeois class in China was too small to form the basis for a new post-Confucian political order. The vast majority of the Chinese people still lived on the land. Sun had hoped to win their support with a land reform program that relied on fiscal incentives to persuade landlords to sell excess lands to their tenants, but few peasants had participated in the 1911 revolution. In effect, then, the events of 1911 were less a revolution than a collapse of the old order. Undermined by imperialism and its own internal weaknesses, the old dynasty had come to an abrupt end before new political and social forces were ready to fill the vacuum.

What China had experienced was part of a historical process that was bringing down traditional empires across the globe, both in regions threatened by Western imperialism and in Europe itself, where tsarist Russia, the Austro-Hungarian Empire, and the Ottoman Empire all came to an end within a few years of the collapse of the Qing (see Chapters 4 and 5). The circumstances of their demise were not all the same, but all four regimes bore

Program for a New China

In 1905, Sun Yat-sen united a number of anti-Manchu groups into a single patriotic organization called the Revolutionary Alliance (Tongmenghui). The new organization was eventually renamed the Guomindang, or Nationalist Party. This excerpt is from the organization's manifesto, published in 1905 in Tokyo. Note that Sun believed that the Chinese people were not ready for democracy and required a period of tutelage to prepare them for constitutional political government. This was a formula that would be adopted by many other political leaders in Asia and Africa after World War II.

Sun Yat-sen, Manifesto for the Tongmenghui

By order of the Military Government, . . . the Commander-in-Chief of the Chinese National Army proclaims the purposes and platform of the Military Government to the people of the nation:

Therefore we proclaim to the world in utmost sincerity the outline of the present revolution and the fundamental plan for the future administration of the nation.

1. *Drive out the Tartars:* The Manchus of today were originally the eastern barbarians beyond the Great Wall. They frequently caused border troubles during the Ming dynasty; then when China was in a disturbed state they came inside Shanhaikuan [the eastern terminus of the Great Wall], conquered China, and enslaved our Chinese people. . . . The extreme cruelties and tyrannies of the Manchu government have now reached their limit. With the righteous army poised against them, we will overthrow that government, and restore our sovereign rights.

2. *Restore China:* China is the China of the Chinese. The government of China should be in the hands of the Chinese. After driving out the Tartars we must restore our national state. . . .

3. *Establish the Republic:* Now our revolution is based on equality, in order to establish a republican government. All our people are equal and all enjoy political rights. . . .

4. *Equalize land ownership:* The good fortune of civilization is to be shared equally by all the people of the nation. We should improve our social and economic organization, and assess the value of all the land in the country. Its present price shall be received by the owner, but all increases in value resulting from reform and social improvements after the revolution shall belong to the state, to be shared by all the people, in order to create a socialist state, where each family within the empire can be well supported, each person satisfied, and no one fail to secure employment. . . .

The above four points will be carried out in three steps in due order. The first period is government by military law. When the righteous army has arisen, various places will join the cause. . . . Evils like the oppression of the government, the greed and graft of officials, . . . the cruelty of tortures and penalties, the tyranny of tax collections, shall all be exterminated together with the Manchu rule. Evils in social customs, such as the keeping of slaves, the cruelty of foot binding, the spread of the poison of opium, should also all be prohibited. . . .

The second period is that of government by a provisional constitution. When military law is lifted in each *hsien* [district], the Military Government shall return the right of the self-government to the local people. . . .

The third period will be government under the constitution. Six years after the provisional constitution has been enforced, a constitution shall be made. The military and administrative powers of the Military Government shall be annulled; the people shall elect the president, and elect the members of parliament to organize the parliament.

 What are Sun Yat-sen's key proposals for the modernization of Chinese society? Why can he be described as a revolutionary rather than a reformer?

SOURCE: From *Sources of Chinese Tradition* by Wm. Theodore de Bary. Copyright © 1964 Columbia University Press. Reprinted with permission of the publisher.

responsibility for their common fate because they had failed to meet the challenges posed by the times. All had responded to the forces of industrialization and popular participation in the political process with hesitation and reluctance, and their attempts at reform were too little and too late. All paid the supreme price for their folly.

Chinese Society in Transition

The growing Western presence in China during the late nineteenth and early twentieth centuries had provided the imperial government with an opportunity to benefit from the situation. The results, however, were meager.

Although foreign concession areas in the coastal cities provided a conduit for the importation of Western technology and modern manufacturing methods, the Chinese borrowed less than they might have. Foreign manufacturing enterprises could not legally operate in China until the last decade of the nineteenth century, and their methods had little influence beyond the concession areas. Chinese efforts to imitate Western methods, notably in shipbuilding and weapons manufacture, were dominated by the government and often suffered from mismanagement.

Equally serious problems persisted in the countryside. The rapid increase in population had led to smaller plots and growing numbers of tenant farmers. Whether per capita consumption of food was on the decline is not clear from the available evidence, but apparently rice as a staple of the diet was increasingly being replaced by less nutritious foods, many of which depleted the soil, already under pressure from the dramatic increase in population. Some farmers benefited from switching to commercial agriculture to supply the markets of the growing coastal cities. The shift entailed a sizable investment, however, and many farmers went so deeply into debt that they eventually lost their land. At the same time, the traditional patron-client relationship was frayed as landlords moved to the cities to take advantage of the glittering urban lifestyle introduced by the West.

The Impact of Western Imperialism

The advent of the imperialist era in the second half of the nineteenth century thus came in a society already facing serious problems. Whether the Western intrusion was beneficial or harmful is debated to this day. The Western presence undoubtedly accelerated the development of the Chinese economy in some ways: the introduction of modern means of production, transport, and communications; the expansion of an export market; and the steady integration of the Chinese market into the nineteenth-century global economy. To many Westerners at the time, it was self-evident that such changes would ultimately benefit the Chinese people. Critics retorted that Western imperialism actually hindered the process of structural change in preindustrial societies because the imperialist powers thwarted the rise of local industrial and commercial sectors in order to maintain colonies and semicolonies as a market for Western manufactured goods and a source of cheap labor and materials. If the West had not intervened, some argued, China would have found its own road to becoming an advanced industrial society.

Whatever the truth of these conjectures, the hesitant efforts of the Qing to cope with these challenges suggest that the most important obstacle to reform was at the top:

Qing officials often seemed overwhelmed by the combination of external pressure and internal strife. At a time when other traditional societies, such as Russia, the Ottoman Empire, and Japan, were making vigorous attempts to modernize their economies, the Manchu court, along with much of the elite class, still exhibited an alarming degree of complacency.

Daily Life in Qing China

At the beginning of the nineteenth century, daily life for most Chinese was not substantially different from what it had been in earlier centuries. Most were farmers, living in millions of villages in rice fields and on hillsides throughout the countryside. Their lives were governed by the harvest cycle, village custom, and family ritual. Their roles in society were firmly fixed by the time-honored principles of Confucian social ethics. Male children, at least the more fortunate ones, were educated in the Confucian classics, while females remained in the home or in the fields. All children were expected to obey their parents, and wives to submit to their husbands.

A visitor to China a hundred years later would have seen a very different society, although still recognizably Chinese. Change was most striking in the coastal cities, where the educated and affluent had been visibly affected by the growing Western cultural presence. Confucian social institutions and behavioral norms were declining rapidly in influence, while those of Europe and North America were on the ascendant. Change was much less noticeable in the countryside, but even there, the customary bonds had been dangerously frayed by the rapidly changing times.

Some of the change can be traced to the educational system. During the nineteenth century, the importance of a Confucian education steadily declined because up to half of the degree holders had purchased their degrees. After 1906, when the government abolished the civil service examinations, a Confucian education ceased to be the key to a successful career, and Western-style education became more desirable. The old dynasty attempted to modernize by establishing an educational system on the Western model with universal education at the elementary level. Such plans had some effect in the cities, where public schools, missionary schools, and other private institutions educated a new generation of Chinese with little knowledge of or respect for the past.

Changing Roles for Women

The status of women was also in transition. During the mid-Qing era, women were still expected to remain in the

Women with Bound Feet. To provide the best possible marriage for their daughters, upper-class families began to perform foot binding during the Song dynasty. Eventually, the practice spread to all social classes in China. Although small feet were supposed to denote a woman of leisure, most Chinese women with bound feet were in the labor force, working mainly in textiles and handicrafts to supplement the family income.

home. Their status as useless sex objects was painfully symbolized by the practice of foot binding, a custom that had probably originated among court entertainers in the eighth century and later spread to the common people. By the mid-nineteenth century, more than half of all adult women probably had bound feet.

During the second half of the nineteenth century, signs of change began to appear. Women began to seek employment in factories—notably in the cotton mills and in the silk industry, established in Shanghai in the 1890s. Some women were active in dissident activities, such as the Taiping Rebellion and the Boxer movement, and a few fought beside men in the 1911 revolution. Qiu Jin, a well-known female revolutionary, wrote a manifesto calling for women's liberation and then organized a revolt against the Manchu government, only to be captured and executed at the age of thirty-two in 1907.

By the end of the century, educational opportunities for women appeared for the first time. Christian missionaries began to open girls' schools, mainly in the foreign concession areas. Although only a relatively small number of women were educated in these schools, they had a significant impact on Chinese society as progressive intellectuals began to argue that ignorant women produced ignorant children. In 1905, the court announced its intention to open public schools for girls, but few such schools ever materialized. The government also began to take steps to discourage the practice of foot binding, initially with only minimal success.

Traditional Japan and the End of Isolation

While Chinese rulers were coping with the dual problems of external threat and internal instability, similar developments were taking place in Japan. An agricultural society like its powerful neighbor, Japan had borrowed extensively from Chinese civilization for more than a millennium; its political institutions, religious beliefs, and cultural achievements all bore the clear imprint of the Chinese model. Nevertheless, throughout the centuries, the Japanese were able to retain not only their political independence but also their cultural uniqueness and had created a distinct civilization.

One reason for the historical differences between China and Japan is that China is a large continental country and Japan a small island nation. Proud of their own considerable cultural achievements and their dominant position throughout the region, the Chinese have traditionally been reluctant to dilute the purity of their culture with foreign innovations. Often subject to invasion by nomadic peoples from the north, the Chinese viewed culture rather than race as a symbol of their sense of identity. By contrast, the island character of Japan probably had the effect of strengthening the Japanese sense of ethnic and cultural distinctiveness. Although the Japanese self-image of ethnic homogeneity may not be entirely justified, it enabled them to import ideas from abroad without the risk of destroying the uniqueness of their own culture.

As a result, although the Japanese borrowed liberally from China over the centuries, they turned Chinese ideas and institutions to their own uses. In contrast to China, where a centralized political system was viewed as crucial to protect the vast country from foreign conquest or internal fractionalization, a decentralized political system reminiscent of the feudal system in medieval Europe held sway in Japan under the hegemony of a powerful military leader, or **shogun**, who ruled with varying degrees of effectiveness in the name of the hereditary emperor. This system lasted until the early seventeenth century, when a strong shogunate called the Tokugawa rose to power after a protracted civil war. The Tokugawa managed to revitalize the traditional system in a somewhat more centralized form that enabled it to survive for another 250 years.

A "Closed Country"

One of the many factors contributing to the rise of the Tokugawa was the impending collapse of the old system. Another was contact with the West, which had begun with the arrival of Portuguese ships in Japanese ports in the mid-sixteenth century. Japan initially opened its doors eagerly to European trade and missionary activity, but later Japanese elites became concerned about the corrosive effects of Western ideas and practices and attempted to evict the foreigners. For the next two centuries, the Tokugawa adopted a policy of "closed country" (to use the contemporary Japanese phrase) to keep out foreign ideas and protect Japanese values and institutions. In spite of such efforts, however, Japanese society was changing from within, and by the early nineteenth century, it was quite different from what it had been two centuries earlier. Traditional institutions and the aristocratic feudal system were under increasing strain, not only from the emergence of a new merchant class but also from the centralizing tendencies of the powerful shogunate.

Some historians have noted strong parallels between Tokugawa Japan and early modern Europe, which developed centralized empires and a strong merchant class at the same time. Certainly, there were signs that the **shogunate system** was becoming less effective. Factionalism and corruption plagued the central bureaucracy. Feudal lords in the countryside (known as **daimyo**, or "great names") reacted to increasing economic pressures by intensifying their exactions from the peasants who farmed their manorial holdings and by engaging in manufacturing and commercial pursuits, such as the sale of textiles, forestry products, and *sake* (Japanese rice wine). As peasants were whipsawed by rising manorial exactions and a series of poor harvests caused by bad weather, rural unrest swept the countryside.

Japan, then, was ripe for change. Some historians maintain that the country was poised to experience an industrial revolution under the stimulus of internal conditions. As in China, the resumption of contacts with the West in the middle of the nineteenth century rendered the question somewhat academic. To the Western powers, the continued isolation of Japanese society was an affront and a challenge. Driven by growing rivalry among themselves and convinced by their own propaganda and the ideology of world capitalism that the expansion of trade on a global basis would benefit all nations, Western nations began to approach Japan in the hope of opening up the country to foreign economic interests.

The Opening of Japan

The first to succeed was the United States. American ships following the northern route across the Pacific needed a fueling station before completing their long journey to China and other ports in the area. The efforts to pry the Japanese out of their cloistered existence in the 1830s and 1840s failed, but the Americans persisted. In the summer of 1853, an American fleet of four warships under Commodore Matthew C. Perry arrived in Edo Bay (now Tokyo Bay) with a letter from President Millard Fillmore addressed to the shogun. A few months later, Japan agreed to the Treaty of Kanagawa, providing for the opening of two ports and the establishment of a U.S. consulate on Japanese soil. In 1858, U.S. Consul Townsend Harris signed a more elaborate commercial treaty calling for the opening of several ports to U.S. trade and residence, an exchange of ministers, and extraterritorial privileges for U.S. residents in Japan. The Japanese soon signed similar treaties with several European nations.

The decision to open relations with the Western barbarians was highly unpopular in some quarters, particularly in regions distant from the shogunate headquarters in Edo. Resistance was especially strong in two of the key daimyo territories in the south, Satsuma and Choshu, both of which had strong military traditions. In 1863, the "Sat-Cho" alliance forced the hapless shogun to promise to bring relations with the West to an end, but the rebellious groups soon disclosed their own weakness. When Choshu troops fired on Western ships in the Strait of Shimonoseki, the Westerners fired back and destroyed the Choshu fortifications. The incident convinced the rebellious **samurai** ("retainers," the traditional warrior class) of the need to strengthen their own military and intensified their unwillingness to give in to the West. Having strengthened their influence at the imperial court in Kyoto, they demanded the resignation of the shogun and the restoration of the power of the emperor.

In January 1868, rebel armies attacked the shogun's palace in Kyoto and proclaimed the restored authority of the emperor. After a few weeks, resistance collapsed, and the venerable shogunate system was brought to an end.

Rich Country, Strong Army

Although the victory of the Sat-Cho faction over the shogunate appeared on the surface to be a triumph of tradition over change, the new leaders soon realized that Japan must modernize to survive and embarked on a policy of comprehensive reform that would lay the foundations of a modern industrial nation within a generation. The symbol of the new era was the young emperor himself, who had taken the reign name Meiji ("enlightened rule") on ascending the throne after the death of his father in 1867. Although the post-Tokugawa period was termed a "restoration," the Meiji ruler was controlled by the new leadership, just as the shogun had controlled his predecessors. In tacit recognition of the real source of political power, the new capital was located at Edo, which was renamed Tokyo ("Eastern Capital"), and the imperial court was moved to the shogun's palace in the center of the city.

The Transformation of Japanese Politics

Once in power, the new leaders launched a comprehensive reform of Japanese political, social, economic, and cultural institutions and values. They moved first to abolish the remnants of the old order and strengthen their executive power. To undercut the power of the daimyo, hereditary feudal privileges were abolished in 1871, and the great lords lost title to their lands. As compensation, they were named governors of the territories formerly under their control. The samurai received a lump-sum payment to replace their traditional stipends but were forbidden to wear the sword, the symbol of their hereditary status.

The abolition of the legal underpinnings of the Tokugawa system permitted the Meiji modernizers to embark on the creation of a modern political system based on the Western model. In the Charter Oath of 1868, the new leaders promised to create a new deliberative assembly within the framework of continued imperial rule. Although senior positions in the new government were given to the daimyo, the key posts were dominated by modernizing samurai, known as the *genro*, from the Sat-Cho clique.

During the next two decades, the Meiji government undertook a systematic study of Western political systems. A constitutional commission under Prince Ito Hirobumi traveled to several Western countries, including Great Britain, Germany, Russia, and the United States, to study their political institutions. As the process evolved, a number of factions appeared, each representing different ideas. The most prominent were the Liberals, who favored political reform on the Western liberal democratic model, and the Progressives, who called for a division of power between the legislative and executive branches, with a slight nod to the latter. There was also an imperial party that advocated the retention of supreme authority in the hands of the emperor.

THE MEIJI CONSTITUTION During the 1870s and 1880s, these factions competed for preeminence. In the end, the Progressives emerged victorious. The Meiji constitution, adopted in 1890, vested authority in the executive branch, although the imperialist faction was pacified by the statement that the constitution was the gift of the emperor. Members of the cabinet were to be handpicked by the Meiji oligarchs. The upper house of parliament was to be appointed and have equal legislative powers with the lower house, called the Diet, whose members would be elected. The core ideology of the state, called the **kokutai** (national polity), embodied (although in very imprecise form) the concept of the uniqueness of the Japanese system based on the supreme authority of the emperor.

The result was a system that was democratic in form but despotic in practice, modern in external appearance but still recognizably traditional in that power remained in the hands of a ruling oligarchy. The system permitted the traditional ruling class to retain its influence and economic power while acquiescing in the emergence of a new set of institutions and values.

Meiji Economics

With the end of the daimyo domains, the government needed to establish a new system of land ownership that would transform the mass of the rural population from indentured serfs into citizens. To do so, it enacted a land reform program that redefined the domain lands as the private property of the tillers while compensating the previous owner with government bonds. One reason for the new policy was that the government needed operating revenues. At the time, public funds came mainly from customs duties, which were limited by agreement with the foreign powers to 5 percent of the value of the product. To remedy the problem, the Meiji leaders added a new agriculture tax, which was set at an annual rate of 3 percent of the estimated value of the land. The new tax proved to be a lucrative and dependable source of income for the government, but it was quite onerous for the farmers, who had previously paid a fixed percentage of their harvest to the landowner. As a result, in bad years, many peasants were unable to pay their taxes and were forced to sell their lands to wealthy neighbors. Eventually, the government reduced the tax to 2.5 percent of the land value. Still, by the end of the century, about 40 percent of all farmers were tenants.

LAUNCHING THE INDUSTRIAL REVOLUTION With its budget needs secured, the government turned to the promotion of industry. A small but growing industrial economy had already existed under the Tokugawa. In its early stages, manufacturing in Japan had been the exclusive responsibility of an artisan caste, who often worked for the local daimyo. Eventually, these artisans began to expand their activities, hiring workers and borrowing capital from merchants. By the end of the seventeenth century, manufacturing centers had developed in Japan's growing cities, such as Edo, Kyoto, and Osaka. According to one historian, by 1700, Japan already had four cities with a population over 100,000 and was one of the most urbanized societies in the world.

Japan's industrial sector received a massive stimulus from the **Meiji Restoration**. The government provided financial subsidies to needy industries, imported foreign advisers, improved transport and communications, and established a universal system of education emphasizing applied science. In contrast to China, Japan was able to achieve results with minimum reliance on foreign capital. Although the first railroad—built in 1872—was underwritten by a loan from Great Britain, future projects were all financed locally. Foreign currency holdings came largely from tea and silk, which were exported in significant quantities during the latter half of the nineteenth century.

During the late Meiji era, Japan's industrial sector began to grow. Besides tea and silk, other key industries were weaponry, shipbuilding, and *sake*. From the start, the distinctive feature of the Meiji model was the intimate relationship between government and private business in terms of operations and regulations. Once an individual enterprise or industry was on its feet (or sometimes, when it had ceased to make a profit), it was turned over entirely to private ownership, although the government often continued to play some role even after its direct involvement in management was terminated.

Also noteworthy is the effect that the Meiji reforms had on rural areas. As we have seen, the new land tax provided the government with funds to subsidize the industrial sector, but it imposed severe hardship on the rural population, many of whom abandoned their farms and fled to the cities in search of jobs. This influx of people in turn benefited Japanese industry by providing an abundant source of cheap labor. As in early modern Europe, the industrial revolution in Japan was built on the strong backs of the long-suffering peasantry.

Building a Modern Social Structure

The Meiji Restoration also transformed several other feudal institutions. A key focus of their attention was the army. The Sat-Cho reformers had been struck by the weakness of the Japanese armed forces in clashes with the Western powers and embarked on a major program to create a modern military force that could compete in a Darwinist world in which only the fittest would survive. The old feudal army based on the traditional warrior class was abolished, and an imperial army based on universal conscription was formed in 1871. The army also played an important role in Japanese society, becoming a means of upward mobility for many rural males.

EDUCATION Education also underwent major changes. The Meiji leaders recognized the need for universal education, including instruction in modern technology. After a few years of experimenting, they adopted the American model of a three-tiered system culminating in a series of universities and specialized institutes. In the meantime, they sent bright students to study abroad and brought foreign specialists to Japan to teach in the new schools. Much of the content of the new system was inspired by Western models. Yet its ethical foundations, as embodied in the Imperial Rescript on Education promulgated in 1890, had a distinctly Confucian orientation, emphasizing such values as filial piety and loyalty to the emperor.

THE ROLE OF WOMEN The Meiji reforms also had an impact on the role of women in Japan. In the traditional era, women were constrained by the "**three obediences**" imposed on them: child to father, wife to husband, and widow to son. Husbands could easily obtain a divorce, but wives could not (supposedly, a husband could divorce his spouse if she drank too much tea or talked too much). Marriages were arranged, and the average age of marriage for females was sixteen years. Females did not share inheritance rights with males, and few received any education outside the family.

By the end of the nineteenth century, women were beginning to play a crucial role in their nation's effort to modernize. Urged by their parents to augment the family income as well as by the government to fulfill their patriotic duty, young girls were sent en masse to work in the textile mills. From 1894 to 1912, women made up 60 percent of the Japanese labor force. Thanks to them, by 1914, Japan was the world's leading exporter of silk and dominated cotton manufacturing. If it had not been for the export revenues earned from textile exports, Japan might not have been able to develop its heavy industry and military prowess without an infusion of foreign capital.

Japanese women received few rewards, however, for their contribution to the nation. In 1900, new regulations prohibited women from joining political organizations or attending public meetings. Beginning in 1905, a group of independent-minded women petitioned the Japanese parliament to rescind this restriction, but it was not repealed until 1922.

Joining the Imperialist Club

Japan's rapid advance was viewed with proprietary pride and admiration by sympathetic observers around the world. Unfortunately, the Japanese did not just imitate the domestic policies of their Western mentors; they also emulated the latter's aggressive approach to foreign affairs. That they adopted this course is perhaps not surprising. In their own minds, the Japanese were particularly vulnerable in the world economic arena. Their territory was small, lacking in resources, and densely populated, and they had no natural outlet for expansion. To observant Japanese, the lessons of history were clear. Western nations had amassed wealth and power not only because of their democratic systems and high level of education but also because of their colonies, which provided them with sources of raw materials, cheap labor, and markets for their manufactured products.

Traditionally, Japan had not been an expansionist country. The Japanese had generally been satisfied to remain on their home islands and had even deliberately isolated themselves from their neighbors during the Tokugawa era. Perhaps the most notable exception was a short-lived attempt at the end of the sixteenth century to extend Japanese control over the Korean peninsula.

The Japanese began their program of territorial expansion (see Map 3.3) close to home. In 1874, they claimed compensation from China for fifty-four sailors from the Ryukyu Islands who had been killed by the local population on the island of Taiwan and sent a Japanese fleet to Taiwan to punish the perpetrators. When the Qing dynasty evaded responsibility for the incident while agreeing to pay an indemnity to Japan to cover the cost of the expedition, it weakened its claim to ownership of the island of Taiwan. Japan was then able to claim suzerainty over the Ryukyu Islands, long tributary to the Chinese Empire. Two years later, Japanese naval pressure forced the opening of Korean ports to Japanese commerce.

During the 1880s, as the Meiji leaders began to modernize their military forces along Western lines, Sino-Japanese rivalry over Korea intensified. In 1894, China and Japan intervened on opposite sides of an internal rebellion in Korea. When hostilities broke out between the two powers, Japanese ships destroyed the Chinese fleet and seized the Manchurian city of Port Arthur (see the box on p. 63). In the Treaty of Shimonoseki, the Manchus were forced to recognize the independence of

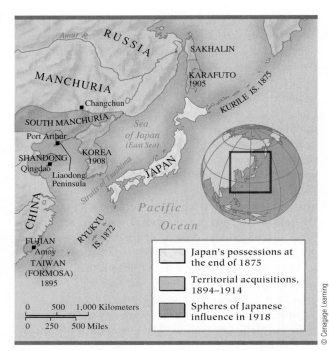

MAP 3.3 Japanese Overseas Expansion During the Meiji Era. Beginning in the late nineteenth century, Japan ventured beyond its home islands and became an imperialist power. The extent of Japanese colonial expansion through World War I is shown here.

Q *Which parts of the Chinese Empire came under Japanese influence?*

Korea and to cede Taiwan and the Liaodong peninsula, with its strategic naval base at Port Arthur, to Japan.

Shortly thereafter, under pressure from the European powers, the Japanese returned the Liaodong peninsula to China, but in the early twentieth century, they returned to the offensive. Rivalry with Russia over influence in Korea led to increasingly strained relations between the two countries. In 1904, Japan launched a surprise attack on the Russian naval base at Port Arthur, which Russia had taken from China in 1898. The Japanese armed forces were weaker, but Russia faced difficult logistical problems along its new Trans-Siberian Railway and severe political instability at home. In 1905, after Japanese warships sank almost the entire Russian fleet off the coast of Korea, the Russians agreed to a humiliating peace, ceding the strategically located Liaodong peninsula back to Japan, along with southern Sakhalin and the Kurile Islands. Russia also agreed to abandon its political and economic influence in Korea and southern Manchuria, which now came increasingly under Japanese control. The Japanese victory stunned the world, including the colonial peoples of Southeast Asia, who now began to realize that Europeans were not necessarily invincible.

Two Views of the World

During the nineteenth century, China's hierarchical way of looking at the outside world came under severe challenge, not only from European countries avid for new territories in Asia but also from the rising power of Japan, which accepted the Western view that a colonial empire was the key to national greatness. Japan's first objective was Korea, long a dependency of China, and in 1894, the competition between China and Japan in the peninsula led to war. The following declarations of war by the rulers of the two countries are revealing. Note the Chinese use of the derogatory term *Wojen* ("dwarf people") in referring to the Japanese.

Declaration of War Against China

Korea is an independent state. She was first introduced into the family of nations by the advice and guidance of Japan. It has, however, been China's habit to designate Korea as her dependency, and both openly and secretly to interfere with her domestic affairs. At the time of the recent insurrection in Korea, China dispatched troops thither, alleging that her purpose was to afford a succor to her dependent state. We, in virtue of the treaty concluded with Korea in 1882, and looking to possible emergencies, caused a military force to be sent to that country.

Wishing to procure for Korea freedom from the calamity of perpetual disturbance, and thereby to maintain the peace of the East in general, Japan invited China's cooperation for the accomplishment of the object. But China, advancing various pretexts, declined Japan's proposal. . . . Such conduct on the part of China is not only a direct injury to the rights and interests of this Empire, but also a menace to the permanent peace and tranquillity of the Orient. . . . In this situation, . . . we find it impossible to avoid a formal declaration of war against China.

Declaration of War Against Japan

Korea has been our tributary for the past two hundred odd years. She has given us tribute all this time, which is a

matter known to the world. For the past dozen years or so Korea has been troubled by repeated insurrections and we, in sympathy with our small tributary, have as repeatedly sent succor to her aid. . . . This year another rebellion was begun in Korea, and the King repeatedly asked again for aid from us to put down the rebellion. We then ordered Li Hung-chang to send troops to Korea; and they having barely reached Yashan the rebels immediately scattered. But the *Wojen*, without any cause whatever, suddenly sent their troops to Korea, and entered Seoul, the capital of Korea, reinforcing them constantly until they have exceeded ten thousand men. In the meantime the Japanese forced the Korean king to change his system of government, showing a disposition every way of bullying the Koreans. . . .

As Japan has violated the treaties and not observed international laws, and is now running rampant with her false and treacherous actions commencing hostilities herself, and laying herself open to condemnation by the various powers at large, we therefore desire to make it known to the world that we have always followed the paths of philanthropy and perfect justice throughout the whole complications, while the *Wojen*, on the other hand, have broken all the laws of nations and treaties which it passes our patience to bear with. Hence we commanded Li Hung-chang to give strict orders to our various armies to hasten with all speed to root the *Wojen* out of their lairs.

 Compare the worldviews of China and Japan at the end of the nineteenth century, as expressed in these declarations. Which point of view do you find more persuasive?

Source: From H.F. McNair, *Modern Chinese History* pp. 530–534, quoted in Franz Schurmann and Orville Schell, eds., *The China Reader: Imperial China* (New York: Vintage, 1967), pp. 251–259.

During the next few years, the Japanese consolidated their position in northeastern Asia, annexing Korea in 1908 as an integral part of Japan. When the Koreans protested the seizure, Japanese reprisals resulted in thousands of deaths. The United States was the first nation to recognize the annexation in return for Tokyo's declaration of respect for U.S. authority in the Philippines. In 1908, the

two countries reached an agreement in which the United States recognized Japanese interests in the region in return for Japanese acceptance of the principles of the Open Door. But mutual suspicion between the two countries was growing, sparked in part by U.S. efforts to restrict immigration from all Asian countries. President Theodore Roosevelt, who mediated the Russo-Japanese War, had aroused the anger of many Japanese by turning down a Japanese demand for reparations from Russia. In turn, some Americans began to fear the "yellow peril," manifested by Japanese expansion in East Asia.

Japanese Culture in Transition

The wave of Western technology and ideas that entered Japan in the second half of the nineteenth century greatly altered the shape of traditional Japanese culture. Literature in particular was affected as European models eclipsed the repetitive and frivolous tales of the Tokugawa era. Dazzled by this "new" literature, Japanese authors began translating and imitating the imported models. Experimenting with Western verse, Japanese poets were at first influenced primarily by the British but eventually adopted such styles as Symbolism, Dadaism, and Surrealism, although some traditional poetry was still composed.

As the Japanese invited technicians, engineers, architects, and artists from Europe and the United States to teach their "modern" skills to a generation of eager students, the Meiji era became a time of massive consumption of Western artistic techniques and styles. Japanese architects and artists created huge buildings of steel and reinforced concrete adorned with Greek columns and cupolas, oil paintings reflecting the European concern with depth perception and shading, and bronze sculptures of secular subjects. European influence even affected the familiar Japanese technique of woodblock printing, as in the print of the Ginza, which uses a traditional technique to depict Tokyo's most modern thoroughfare complete with streetcar and electric lights (see the illustration below).

Cultural exchange also went the other way as Japanese arts and crafts, porcelains, textiles, fans, folding screens, and woodblock prints became the vogue in Europe and North America. Japanese art influenced Western painters such as Vincent van Gogh, Edgar Degas, and James Whistler, who experimented with flatter compositional perspectives and unusual poses. Japanese gardens, with their exquisite attention to the positioning of rocks and falling water, became especially popular.

After the initial period of mass absorption of Western art, a national reaction occurred at the end of the nineteenth century as many artists returned to pre-Meiji techniques. In 1889, the Tokyo School of Fine Arts (today the Tokyo National University of Fine Arts and Music) was founded to promote traditional Japanese art. Over the next several decades, Japanese art underwent a dynamic resurgence, reflecting the nation's emergence as a prosperous and powerful state. While some artists attempted to synthesize Japanese and foreign techniques, others returned to past artistic traditions for inspiration.

The Ginza in Downtown Tokyo. This 1877 woodblock print shows the Ginza, a major commercial thoroughfare in downtown Tokyo, with modern brick buildings and a horse-drawn streetcar. The centerpiece and focus of public attention is a new electric streetlight. In combining traditional form with modern content, this print symbolizes the unique ability of the Japanese to borrow ideas from abroad while preserving much of the essence of their traditional culture.

CONCLUSION

THE MEIJI RESTORATION was one of the great success stories of modern times. Not only did the Meiji leaders put Japan firmly on the path to economic and political development, but they also managed to remove the unequal treaty provisions that had been imposed at mid-century. Japanese achievements are especially impressive when compared with the difficulties experienced by China, which was not only unable to effect significant changes in its traditional society but had not even reached a consensus on the need for doing so. Japan's achievements more closely resemble those of Europe, but whereas the West needed a century and a half to achieve a significant level of industrial development, the Japanese achieved it in forty years.

The differences between the Japanese and Chinese responses to the West have sparked considerable debate among students of comparative history. Some have argued that Japan's success was partly due to good fortune; lacking abundant natural resources, it was exposed to less pressure from the West than many of its neighbors. That argument, however, is not very persuasive, since it does not explain why nations under considerably less pressure, such as Laos and Nepal, did not advance even more quickly.

One possible explanation has already been suggested: Japan's unique geographic position in Asia. China, a continental nation with a heterogeneous ethnic composition, was distinguished from its neighbors by its Confucian culture. By contrast, Japan was an island nation, ethnically and linguistically homogeneous, that had never been conquered. Unlike the Chinese, the Japanese had little to fear from cultural change in terms of its effect on their national identity. If Confucian culture, with all its accoutrements, was what defined the Chinese gentleman, his Japanese counterpart, in the familiar image, could discard his sword and kimono and don a modern military uniform or a Western business suit and still feel comfortable in both worlds.

Whatever the case, the Meiji Restoration was possible because aristocratic and capitalist elements managed to work together in a common effort to achieve national wealth and power. The nature of the Japanese value system, with its emphasis on practicality and military achievement, may also have contributed. Finally, the Meiji benefited from the fact that the pace of urbanization and commercial and industrial development had already begun to quicken under the Tokugawa. Japan, it has been said, was ripe for change, and nothing could have been more suitable as an antidote for the collapsing old system than the Western emphasis on wealth and power. It was a classic example of challenge and response.

TIMELINE

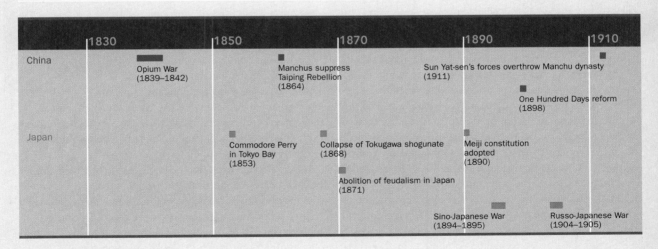

CHAPTER NOTES

1. Quoted in Ssu-yu Teng and John K. Fairbank, eds., *China's Response to the West: A Documentary Survey, 1839–1923* (New York, 1970), p. 140.

2. Ibid., p. 167.

THE LATE NINETEENTH CENTURY witnessed two major developments: the Industrial Revolution and European domination of the world. The first was clearly the more important, for it created the conditions for the latter. It was, of course, the major industrial powers—Great Britain, France, and later Germany and the United States—that took the lead in building large colonial empires that spanned the globe.

EXPLAINING THE WINNERS AND LOSERS Why some societies were able to master the challenge of industrialization and others were not has been a matter of considerable scholarly debate. Some observers have found the answer in the cultural characteristics of individual societies, such as the Protestant work ethic in parts of Europe or the tradition of social discipline and class hierarchy in Japan. According to historian David Landes, cultural differences are the key reason the Industrial Revolution took place first in Europe rather than elsewhere in the world.

While admitting that other factors, such as climate and the presence of natural resources, played a role in the process, what is most important, he maintains in his provocative book *The Wealth and Poverty of Nations*, are "work, thrift, honesty, patience, and tenacity," all characteristics that are present to a greater or lesser degree in European civilization. Other societies were entangled in a "web of tradition" composed of political authoritarianism, religious prejudice, and a suspicion of material wealth. Thus, they failed to overcome obstacles to rapid economic development. Only Japan, with its own tradition of hard work and self-sacrifice, succeeded in emulating the European experience.

Other observers argue that more practical considerations may have played a crucial role in determining the winners and losers in the race to achieve economic wealth and power. Historian Kenneth Pomeranz, in *The Great Divergence: China, Europe, and the Making of the Modern World Economy*, maintains that access to crucial raw materials like coal and water power, along with the capital and experience accumulated during the early stages of European expansion in the early modern era, may have provided the initial impetus for the Industrial Revolution in Great Britain. The importance of the early modern era was also emphasized by the sociologist Andre Gunder Frank, who argued that the Industrial Revolution was less important as the driving force of the modern age than the age of exploration and expansion in the sixteenth and seventeenth centuries—a period marked by Western military conquest and degradation of many non-Western peoples.

It is clear that neither side possesses a monopoly of truth in this debate. Although culture clearly matters, other factors, such as climate, geography, the quality of political leadership, and what has been called "social capital" (such as the strength of the civil society), are also important. On the other hand, the argument that imperialism is the main culprit cannot explain why some previously colonial societies have succeeded in mounting the ladder of economic success so much more successfully than others. What is increasingly evident is that there is no single answer, or solution, to the question.

THE LEGACY OF THE INDUSTRIAL REVOLUTION Whatever the ultimate causes, the advent of the industrial age had a number of lasting consequences for the world at large. On the one hand, the material wealth of those nations that successfully passed through the process increased significantly. In many cases, the creation of advanced industrial societies strengthened democratic institutions and led to a higher standard  of living for the majority of the population. The spread of technology and trade outside of Europe created the basis for a new international economic order based on the global exchange of goods.

On the other hand, as we have seen, not all the consequences of the Industrial Revolution were beneficial. In the industrializing societies themselves, rapid economic change often led to resentment over the vast disparities in the distribution of wealth and a sense of rootlessness and alienation among much of the population. Some societies were able to manage these problems with a degree of success, but others experienced a breakdown of social values and the rise of widespread political instability. Industrialization in Europe also had destabilizing consequences for the global scene as rising economic competition among the industrial powers contributed to heightened tensions in the world.

Even along the periphery of Europe where the Industrial Revolution had not yet had much of an impact, old empires found it increasingly difficult to respond to new problems. The Ottoman Empire appeared helpless to curb unrest in the Balkans. In Imperial Russia, internal tensions became too much for the traditional landholding elites to handle, leading to significant political and social unrest in the first decade of the twentieth century. In Austria-Hungary, deep-seated ethnic and class antagonisms remained under the surface but reached a point where they might eventually threaten the survival of that multinational state.

IMPERIALISM: INDUSTRIALIZATION'S "EVIL TWIN"?

In the meantime, the Industrial Revolution was creating the technological means by which the West would achieve domination of much of the rest of the world. Europeans had begun to explore the world in the fifteenth century, but even as late as 1870, they had not yet completely penetrated North America, South America, and Australia. In Asia and Africa, with a few notable exceptions, the Western presence was limited to trading posts. Between 1870 and 1914, Western civilization expanded into the rest of the Americas and Australia, while most of Africa and Asia were divided into European colonies or spheres of influence. Two major factors explain this remarkable expansion: the need by Europe's industrializing economies for raw materials and new markets for their products outside the continent and the strengthening of the imperialist powers made possible by the West's technological advances.

Beginning in the 1880s, European states began an intense scramble for overseas territory. This "new imperialism," as some have called it, led Europeans to carve up

Asia and Africa. Imperialism was not really a new phenomenon. Since the Crusades of the Middle Ages and the overseas expansion of the sixteenth and seventeenth centuries, when Europeans established colonies in North and South America and trading posts around Africa and the Indian Ocean, Europeans had shown a marked proclivity for the domination of less technologically oriented, non-European peoples. Nevertheless, the imperialism of the late nineteenth century was different from that of earlier periods. First, it was more rapid and resulted in greater and deeper penetrations into non-European societies. Second, it was directed primarily toward Africa and Asia, two regions that had been largely ignored until then.

The new imperialism had a dramatic effect on Africa and Asia as Western powers competed for control of these two continents. Like the debate over the Industrial Revolution, the debate among historians over the consequences of the imperialist era has been marked by sharp disagreements, as opposing sides have drawn starkly contrasting portraits of its ultimate effects on the colonized societies. This divergence of views has occurred in part because colonialism had different consequences in various parts of the world. Also, some observers have focused on the immediate impact, whereas others have emphasized the long-term effects of colonial rule. Critics have argued that under imperialism, millions of people in Asia, Africa, and Latin America were uprooted from their traditional environments and exposed to a new life marked by poverty and degradation. Defenders point out that whatever its faults, the era of colonial rule introduced traditional societies around the world to the technology, institutions, and values that characterize the advanced nations of the modern world. This too is an argument that will never end.

THE EAST ASIAN DIFFERENCE It is important to keep in mind that a few countries managed to evade total domination by the imperialist powers. The new nations in Latin America managed to retain their independence at the end of the nineteenth century, although many of them remained highly vulnerable to political manipulation and penetration by U.S. or European economic interests. In East Asia, China and Japan were able to maintain at least the semblance of national independence during the height of the Western onslaught. For China, once the most advanced country in the world, survival was very much in doubt for many decades as the waves of Western political, military, and economic influence lapped at the edges of the Chinese Empire and the imperialist powers appeared on the verge of dividing up the Chinese heartland into separate spheres of influence. Only Japan responded with vigor and effectiveness, launching a comprehensive reform program that by the end of the century had transformed the island nation into an industrial power in its own right.

What explains the ability of the two major societies in East Asia to avoid total domination by the Western powers? In the case of China, the answer may lie in the sheer size of that continental empire and the fact that rivalry among the covetous industrial nations prevented any single power from placing the nation within its own orbit. Japan, however, stands out as the one true exception. By its own efforts, it not only fended off the Western challenge, but by the end of the century threatened to become an emerging member of the imperialists club. As the new century dawned, the industrialized nations' stranglehold on the world appeared virtually complete. 🕮

PART II

Cultures in Collision

The Japanese attack on Pearl Harbor, December 7, 1941

Library of Congress Prints & Photographs Division[LC-USE6-D-007405]

War and Revolution: World War I and Its Aftermath

The excitement of war

NEGOTIATIONS AMONG THE great powers had been going on for weeks. Anguished messages had been exchanged between Berlin, Vienna, and Saint Petersburg as the crowned heads of three empires—William II of Germany, Francis Joseph of Austria, and Nicholas II of Russia—alternated between threats and appeals as they sought to avoid the outbreak of all-out war in Europe. Their efforts were in vain: on August 1, 1914, Germany declared war on Russia. Three days later, France and Great Britain had entered the fray. In London, British Foreign Secretary Edward Grey remarked sorrowfully to an acquaintance: "The lamps are going out all over Europe; we shall not see them lit again in our lifetime."[1] As it turned out, his comment was all too prescient. A century of peace and progress was about to come to an end in four years of bloody conflict on the battlefields of Europe. The continent would take more than a generation to recover from the slaughter. ❧

CRITICAL THINKING

Q For years, historians have debated the underlying reasons for the outbreak of World War I. Based on the information available to you, what do you think caused the war?

The Coming of War

The new century had dawned on a much brighter note. To some contemporaries, the magnificent promise offered by recent scientific advances and the flowering of the Industrial Revolution appeared about to be fulfilled. Few expressed this mood of optimism better than the renowned British historian Arnold Toynbee. In a retrospective look at the opening of a tumultuous century written many years later, Toynbee remarked:

> [We had expected] that life throughout the world would become more rational, more humane, and more democratic and that, slowly, but surely, political democracy would produce greater social justice. We had also expected that the progress of science and technology would make mankind richer, and that this increasing wealth would gradually spread from a minority to a majority. We had expected that all this would happen peacefully. In fact we thought that mankind's course was set for an earthly paradise.[2]

Such bright hopes for the future of humankind were sadly misplaced. In the summer of 1914, simmering rivalries between the major imperialist powers erupted into full-scale war. By the time it ended, Europe had suffered extensive physical destruction and the deaths of millions. Several venerable empires across the continent were in a state of collapse, and the rising power of nationalism appeared unstoppable. The Great War, as it came to be called, was an eerie prelude to a tumultuous century marked by widespread violence and dramatic change.

Rising Tensions in Europe

Between 1871 and 1914, Europeans experienced a long period of peace as the great powers sought to maintain a fragile balance of power in an effort to avert the reemergence of the destructive forces unleashed during the Napoleonic era. But rivalries among the major world powers continued, and even intensified, leading to a series of crises that might have erupted into a general war. Some of these crises, as we have seen in Chapters 2 and 3, took place outside Europe, as the imperialist nations scuffled for advantage in the race for new colonial territories. But the main focus of European statesmen remained on Europe itself, where the emergence of Germany as the most powerful state on the Continent threatened to upset the fragile balance of power that had been established at the Congress of Vienna in 1815. Fearful of a possible anti-German alliance between France and Russia, German Chancellor Otto von Bismarck signed a defensive treaty with Austria in 1879. Three years later, the alliance was enlarged to include Italy, which was angry with the French over conflicting colonial ambitions in North Africa. The so-called Triple Alliance of 1882 committed the three powers to support the existing political and social order while maintaining a defensive alliance against France.

While Bismarck was chancellor, German policy had been essentially cautious, as he sought to prevent rival powers from conspiring against Berlin. But in 1890 Emperor William II dismissed the "iron chancellor" from office and embarked on a more aggressive foreign policy dedicated to providing Germany with its rightful "place in the sun." As Bismarck had feared, France and Russia responded by concluding a military alliance in 1894. By 1907, a loose confederation of Great Britain, France, and Russia—known as the Triple Entente—stood opposed to the Triple Alliance of Germany, Austria-Hungary, and Italy. Europe was divided into two opposing camps that became more and more inflexible and unwilling to compromise. The stage was set for war.

Crisis in the Balkans, 1908–1913

The dispute that led to world war began in the Balkans, where the decline of Ottoman power had turned the region into a tinderbox of ethnic and religious tensions. In 1908, Austria decided to annex its two protectorates of Bosnia and Herzegovina to prevent them from being seized by neighboring Serbia, whose leaders had visions of creating a large kingdom that would include most of the southern Slavic-speaking peoples. When Russia backed its protégé Serbia, Germany announced its support of Austria. The standoff ended when Russia backed down, but tensions within the Balkans had intensified, leading in 1912 and 1913 to a brief and inconclusive struggle for territory among the newly independent states in the region (see Map 4.1). In the meantime, Great Britain and France drew closer to Saint Petersburg.

MAP 4.1 Europe in 1914. By 1914, two alliances dominated Europe: the Triple Entente of Britain, France, and Russia and the Triple Alliance of Germany, Austria-Hungary, and Italy. Russia sought to bolster fellow Slavs in Serbia, whereas Austria-Hungary was intent on increasing its power in the Balkans and thwarting Serbia's ambitions. Thus, the Balkans became the flash point for World War I.

Q *Which nonaligned nations were positioned between the two alliances?*

The Outbreak of War

By now Austrian officials in Vienna had become convinced that Serbia was a mortal threat to their empire and must be crushed. When Archduke Francis Ferdinand (the heir to the Austrian throne) and his wife, Sophia, were assassinated on June 28, 1914, in the Bosnian city of Sarajevo by a Serbian terrorist organization, the Austrian government issued an ultimatum to Serbia. The demands were so extreme that Serbia felt it had little choice but to reject them in order to preserve its sovereignty. Austria then declared war on Serbia on July 28. Still smarting from its humiliation in the Bosnian crisis of 1908, Russia was determined to support Serbia's cause. On July 28, Tsar Nicholas II ordered a partial mobilization of the Russian army against Austria (see the box on p. 73). The Russian general staff informed the tsar that their mobilization plans were based on a war against both Germany and Austria simultaneously. They could not execute a partial mobilization without creating chaos in the army. Consequently, the Russian government ordered a full mobilization on July 29, knowing that the Germans would consider this an act of war against them. Germany responded by demanding that the Russians halt their mobilization within twelve hours. When the Russians ignored the ultimatum, Germany declared war on Russia on August 1.

The World at War

Before 1914, many political leaders had become convinced that war entailed so many political and economic risks that it was not worth fighting. Others believed that "rational" diplomats could control any situation and prevent the outbreak of war. At the beginning of August 1914, both of these illusions were shattered, but the new illusions that replaced them soon proved to be equally foolish.

Illusions and Stalemate, 1914–1915

Europeans went to war in 1914 with remarkable enthusiasm. Government propaganda had been successful in stirring up national antagonisms before the war. Now, in August 1914, the urgent pleas of governments for defense against aggressors fell on receptive ears in every belligerent nation. Most people seemed genuinely convinced that their nation's cause was just. A new set of illusions also fed the enthusiasm for war. In August 1914, almost everyone believed that because of the risk of damage to the regional economy, the war would be over in a few weeks. People were reminded that the major battles in European wars since 1815 had in fact ended in

a matter of weeks. Both the soldiers who exuberantly boarded the trains for the war front in August 1914 and the jubilant citizens who bombarded them with flowers as they departed believed that the warriors would be home by Christmas.

German hopes for a quick end to the war rested on a military gamble. The so-called Schlieffen Plan (named after its creator, Alfred von Schlieffen, the German Chief of Staff from 1891 to 1905) had called for the German army to proceed through Belgium into northern France with a vast encircling movement that would sweep around Paris and surround most of the French army. But the high command had not heeded Schlieffen's advice to place sufficient numbers of troops on the western salient near the English Channel to guarantee success, and the German advance was halted only 20 miles from Paris at the First Battle of the Marne (September 6–10). The war quickly turned into a stalemate as neither the Germans nor the French could dislodge the other from the trenches they had begun to dig for shelter. Two lines of trenches soon extended from the English Channel to the frontiers of Switzerland (see Map 4.2). The Western Front had become bogged down in **trench warfare** that kept both sides immobilized in virtually the same positions for four years.

THE WAR IN THE EAST German strategists had counted on achieving a rapid victory on the Western Front before launching their offensive against Russia. But the unexpected success of the French changed the equation. At the beginning of the war, the Russian army moved into eastern Germany but was decisively defeated at the Battles of Tannenberg on August 30 and the Masurian Lakes on September 15. The Russians were no longer a threat to German territory. The Austrians, Germany's allies, fared less well initially. After they were defeated by the Russians in Galicia and thrown out of Serbia as well, the Germans came to their aid. A German-Austrian army defeated and routed the poorly equipped Russian army in Galicia and pushed the Russians back 300 miles into their own territory. Russian casualties stood at 2.5 million killed, captured, or wounded; the Russians had almost been knocked out of the war. Buoyed by their success, the Germans and Austrians, joined by the Bulgarians in September 1915, attacked and eliminated Serbia from the war.

The Great Slaughter, 1916–1917

The successes in the east enabled the Germans to move back to the offensive in the west. The early trenches dug in 1914 had by now become elaborate systems of defense. Both lines of trenches were protected by barbed-wire

"You Have to Bear the Responsibility for War or Peace"

After Austria declared war on Serbia on July 28, 1914, Russian support of Serbia and German support of Austria threatened to escalate the conflict in the Balkans into a wider war. As we can see in these last-minute telegrams between the Russians and Germans (known as the "Willy-Nicky letters"), the rigidity of the military war plans on both sides made it difficult to avoid a confrontation once the process got under way.

Communications Between Berlin and Saint Petersburg on the Eve of World War I

Emperor William II to Tsar Nicholas II, July 28, 10:45 P.M.

I have heard with the greatest anxiety of the impression which is caused by the action of Austria-Hungary against Servia [Serbia]. The inscrupulous agitation which has been going on for years in Servia has led to the revolting crime of which Archduke Franz Ferdinand has become a victim. . . . Doubtless You will agree with me that both of us, You as well as I, and all other sovereigns, have a common interest to insist that all those who are responsible for this horrible murder shall suffer their deserved punishment. . . .

Your most sincere and devoted friend and cousin
(*Signed*) WILHELM

Tsar Nicholas II to Emperor William II, July 29, 1 P.M.

I am glad that you are back in Germany. In this serious moment I ask You earnestly to help me. An ignominious war has been declared against a weak country and in Russia the indignation which I fully share is tremendous. I fear that very soon I shall be unable to resist the pressure exercised upon me and that I shall be forced to take measures which will lead to war. To prevent a calamity as a European war would be, I urge You in the name of our old friendship to do all in Your power to restrain Your ally from going too far.
(*Signed*) NICOLAS

Emperor William II to Tsar Nicholas II, July 29, 6:30 P.M.

I have received Your telegram and I share Your desire for the conservation of peace. However: I cannot—as I told You in my first telegram—consider the action of Austria-Hungary as an "ignominious war." Austria-Hungary knows from experience that the promises of Servia as long as they are merely on paper are entirely unreliable. . . . I believe that a direct understanding is possible and desirable between Your

Government and Vienna, an understanding which—as I have already telegraphed You—my Government endeavors to aid with all possible effort. Naturally military measures by Russia, which might be construed as a menace by Austria-Hungary, would accelerate a calamity which both of us desire to avoid and would undermine my position as mediator which—upon Your appeal to my friendship and aid—I willingly accepted.
(*Signed*) WILHELM

Emperor William II to Tsar Nicholas II, July 30, 1 A.M.

My Ambassador has instructions to direct the attention of Your Government to the dangers and serious consequences of a mobilization. I have told You the same in my last telegram. Austria-Hungary has mobilized only against Servia, and only a part of her army. If Russia, as seems to be the case, according to Your advice and that of Your Government, mobilizes against Austria-Hungary, the part of the mediator with which You have entrusted me in such friendly manner and which I have accepted upon Your express desire, is threatened if not made impossible. The entire weight of decision now rests upon Your shoulders; You have to bear the responsibility for war or peace.
(*Signed*) WILHELM

German Chancellor to German Ambassador at Saint Petersburg, July 31, URGENT

In spite of negotiations still pending and although we have up to this hour made no preparations for mobilization, Russia has mobilized her entire army and navy, hence also against us. On account of these Russian measures, we have been forced, for the safety of the country, to proclaim the threatening state of war, which does not yet imply mobilization. Mobilization, however, is bound to follow if Russia does not stop every measure of war against us and against Austria-Hungary within 12 hours, and notifies us definitely to this effect. Please to communicate this at once to M. Sazonoff and wire hour of communication.

 Based on these telegrams, what was the chief issue that led to the outbreak of war? Was Emperor William II correct when he told Tsar Nicholas II that the latter would "have to bear the responsibility for war or peace"?

SOURCE: *The Western World: From 1700*, Vol. II, by W. E. Adams, R. B. Barlow, G. R. Kleinfeld, and R. D. Smith (Dodd, Mead, and Co., 1968), pp. 421–442.

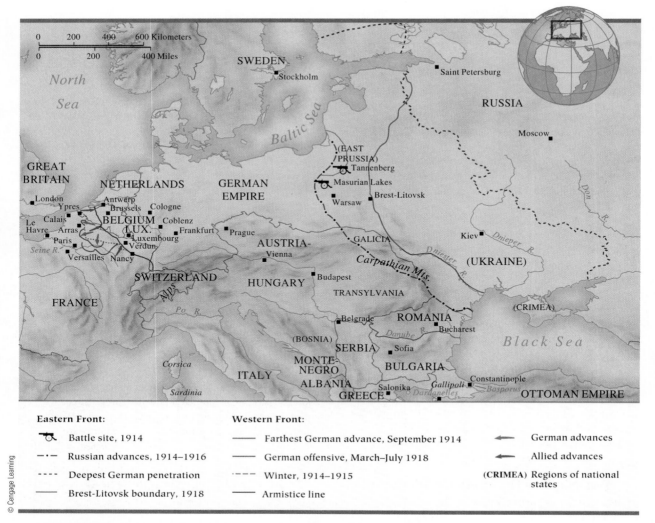

Eastern Front:

🔫 Battle site, 1914

–·– Russian advances, 1914–1916

- - - - Deepest German penetration

—— Brest-Litovsk boundary, 1918

Western Front:

—— Farthest German advance, September 1914

—— German offensive, March–July 1918

- - - - Winter, 1914–1915

—— Armistice line

◄— German advances

◄— Allied advances

(CRIMEA) Regions of national states

MAP 4.2 World War I, 1914–1918. This map shows how greatly the Western and Eastern Fronts of World War I differed. After initial German gains in the west, the war became bogged down in trench warfare, with little change in the battle lines throughout the war. The Eastern Front was marked by considerable mobility, with battle lines shifting by hundreds of miles.

Q *How do you explain the difference in the two fronts?*

entanglements 3 to 5 feet high and 30 yards wide, concrete machine-gun nests, and mortar batteries, supported farther back by heavy artillery. Troops lived in holes in the ground, separated from the enemy by a no-man's land.

The unexpected development of trench warfare baffled military leaders who had been trained to fight wars of movement and maneuver. Taking advantage of the recent American invention of the Caterpillar tractor, the British introduced tanks on the Western Front in 1915, but their effectiveness in breaking through enemy defenses was not demonstrated. The only plan generals could devise was to attempt a breakthrough by throwing masses of men

against enemy lines that had first been battered by artillery barrages. Periodically, the high command on either side would order an offensive that would begin with an artillery barrage to flatten the enemy's barbed wire and leave the enemy in a state of shock. After "softening up" the enemy in this fashion, a mass of soldiers would climb out of their trenches with fixed bayonets and hope to work their way toward the opposing trenches. The attacks rarely worked, as the machine gun put hordes of men advancing unprotected across open fields at a severe disadvantage. In 1916 and 1917, millions of young men were sacrificed in the search for the elusive breakthrough. In

The Horrors of War. The slaughter of millions of men in the trenches of World War I created unimaginable horrors for the participants. For the sake of survival, many soldiers learned to harden themselves against the stench of decomposing bodies and the sight of bodies horribly dismembered by artillery barrages.

ten months at Verdun in 1916, 700,000 men lost their lives over a few miles of terrain.

Warfare in the trenches of the Western Front produced unimaginable horrors. Battlefields were hellish landscapes of barbed wire, shell holes, mud, and injured and dying men (see the box on p. 76). The introduction of poison gas in 1915 produced new forms of injuries, but the first aerial battles were a rare sideshow and gave no hint of the horrors to come with air warfare in the future.

Soldiers in the trenches also lived with the persistent presence of death. Since combat went on for months, soldiers had to carry on in the midst of countless dead bodies and the remains of men dismembered by artillery barrages. Many soldiers remembered the stench of decomposing bodies and the swarms of rats that grew fat in the trenches. At one point, battlefield conditions became so bad that units of the French army erupted in open mutiny. The high command responded by carrying out widespread executions of suspected ringleaders.

The Widening of the War

As the war settled into a long, grueling struggle that consumed almost the entire continent, its tentacles began to stretch into other parts of the world as well. Faced with high casualties on the battlefield, the major imperialist countries began to recruit troops from their colonies to serve on the front lines. Punjabis and Gurkhas from India, Zouaves from North Africa, Cossacks from Central Asia, and infantry units from Australia and New Zealand fought side by side with their European counterparts. Thousands of others, mainly from Africa and French Indochina, served in factories to replace workers who had been drafted into military service.

The Middle East, in particular, became an important front in the war. The German war planners had hoped that the Ottoman Empire, as an influential force in the Middle East, could be persuaded to conduct a holy war that would eliminate British and French influence throughout the region, especially in the oil-rich Arabian peninsula. The Turks, always suspicious of the Russians, did agree to enter the war on the German side, causing the British to launch a disastrous attack at Gallipolli, south of Constantinople, in 1915. But Berlin had miscalculated. In 1917, the dashing but eccentric British adventurer T. E. Lawrence (1888–1935), popularly known as Lawrence of Arabia, incited Arab princes to revolt against their Ottoman overlords (see the Film & History feature on p. 78). In 1918, British forces from Egypt destroyed the rest of the Ottoman Empire in the Middle East. For these campaigns, the British mobilized forces from India, Australia, and New Zealand. The Allies (Britain, France, Russia, and their allies) also took advantage of Germany's preoccupations in Europe and lack of naval strength to seize German colonies in Africa. Japan seized a number of German-held islands in the Pacific, and Australia took over German New Guinea (for further discussion of these events, see Chapter 5).

THE YANKS ARE COMING Most important to the Allied cause was the entry of the United States into the war. At first, the United States tried to remain neutral, but that became more difficult as the war dragged on. The naval conflict between Germany and Great Britain was the immediate reason for U.S. concern. Britain took advantage of its superior naval power to impose a naval blockade on Germany. The latter retaliated with a counterblockade enforced by unrestricted submarine warfare. Strong U.S. protests over the German sinking of passenger liners—especially the British ship *Lusitania* on May 7, 1915, when more than one hundred Americans lost their lives—forced the German government to suspend unrestricted submarine warfare to avoid further antagonizing the Americans.

In January 1917, however, German naval officers convinced Emperor William II that the renewed use of

The World at War 🦋 **75**

The Excitement and the Reality of War

The incredible outpouring of patriotic enthusiasm that greeted the declaration of war at the beginning of August 1914 in many European countries demonstrated the power that nationalistic feeling had attained at the beginning of the twentieth century. Many Europeans seemingly believed that the war had given them a higher purpose, a renewed dedication to the greatness of their nation. That sense of enthusiasm was captured by the Austrian writer Stefan Zweig in his book *The World of Yesterday*.

The reality of war was entirely different. Soldiers who had left for the front in August 1914 in the belief that they would be home by Christmas found themselves shivering and dying in the vast networks of trenches along the battlefront. Few expressed the horror of trench warfare as well as the German writer Erich Maria Remarque in his famous novel *All Quiet on the Western Front*, first published in a German newspaper in 1928.

Stefan Zweig, *The World of Yesterday*

The next morning I was in Austria. In every station placards had been put up announcing general mobilization. The trains were filled with fresh recruits, banners were flying, music sounded, and in Vienna I found the entire city in a tumult. . . . There were parades in the street, flags, ribbons, and music burst forth everywhere, young recruits were marching triumphantly, their faces lighting up at the cheering. . . .

And to be truthful, I must acknowledge that there was a majestic, rapturous, and even seductive something in this first outbreak of the people from which one could escape only with difficulty. And in spite of all my hatred and aversion for war, I should not like to have missed the memory of those days. As never before, thousands and hundreds of thousands felt what they should have felt in peace time, that they belonged together.

What did the great mass know of war in 1914, after nearly half a century of peace? They did not know war, they had hardly given it a thought. It had become legendary, and distance had made it seem romantic and heroic. They still saw it in the perspective of their school readers and of paintings in museums; brilliant cavalry attacks in glittering uniforms, the fatal shot always straight through the heart, the entire campaign a resounding march of victory—"We'll be home at Christmas," the recruits shouted laughingly to their mothers in August of 1914. . . .

A rapid excursion into the romantic, a wild, manly adventure—that is how the war of 1914 was painted in the imagination of the simple man, and the younger people were honestly afraid that they might miss this most wonderful and exciting experience of their lives; that is why they hurried and thronged to the colors, and that is why they shouted and sang in the trains that carried them to the slaughter; wildly and feverishly the red wave of blood coursed through the veins of the entire nation.

Erich Maria Remarque, *All Quiet on the Western Front*

We wake up in the middle of the night. The earth booms. Heavy fire is falling on us. We crouch into corners. . . . Every man is aware of the heavy shells tearing down the parapet, rooting up the embankment and demolishing the upper layers of concrete. . . . Already by morning a few of the recruits are green and vomiting. . . .

No one would believe that in this howling waste there could still be men, but steel helmets now appear on all sides out of the trench, and fifty yards from us a machine-gun is already in position and barking.

[Finally the attack begins.]

The wire-entanglements are torn to pieces. Yet they offer some obstacle. We see the storm-troops coming. . . . We recognize the distorted faces, the smooth helmets: they are French. They have already suffered heavily when they reach the remnants of the barbed wire entanglements.

I see one of them, his face upturned, fall into a wire cradle. His body collapses, his hands remain suspended as though he were praying. Then his body drops clear away and only his hands with the stumps of his arms, shot off, now hang in the wire.

 According to Stefan Zweig, why did so many Europeans welcome the outbreak of war in 1914? Why had they so badly underestimated the cost?

SOURCES: From *The World of Yesterday* by Stefan Zweig, translated by Helmut Ripperger. Translation copyright 1943 by the Viking Press, Inc. *All Quiet on the Western Front* by Erich Maria Remarque. *Im Westen nichts Neues*, copyright 1928 by Ullstein A. G.; copyright renewed © 1956 by Erich Maria Remarque. *All Quiet on the Western Front*, copyright 1929, 1930 by Little, Brown and Company. Copyright renewed © 1957, 1958 by Erich Maria Remarque. All Rights Reserved.

unrestricted submarine warfare could starve the British into submission within five months. To create a distraction in case the administration of U.S. president Woodrow Wilson should decide to enter the war on the Allied side, German Foreign Minister Alfred von Zimmerman secretly encouraged the Mexican government to launch a military attack to recover territories lost to the United States in the American Southwest.

The resumption of unrestricted submarine warfare, combined with outrage over the Zimmerman telegram (which had been decoded by the British and provided to U.S. diplomats in London), finally brought the United States into the war on April 6, 1917. Although American troops did not arrive in Europe in large numbers until 1918, the U.S. entry into the war gave the Allies a badly needed psychological boost. The year 1917 was not a good year for them. Allied offensives on the Western Front were disastrously defeated. Then, in November 1917, the Bolshevik Revolution in Russia (see "Revolution in Russia" later in this chapter) led to Russia's withdrawal from the war, leaving Germany free to concentrate entirely on the Western Front.

The Home Front: The Impact of Total War

Because most of the participants had expected the war to be short, they had given little thought to economic problems and long-term wartime needs. Governments had to respond quickly, however, when the war machines failed to achieve their knockout blows and made ever-greater demands for men and matériel. The extension of government power was a logical outgrowth of these needs. Most European countries had already devised some system of mass conscription or military draft. It was now carried to unprecedented heights as countries mobilized tens of millions of young men for that elusive breakthrough to victory.

Throughout Europe, wartime governments also expanded their powers over their economies. Free market capitalistic systems were temporarily shelved as governments experimented with price, wage, and rent controls; the rationing of food supplies and matériel; the regulation of imports and exports; and the nationalization of transportation systems and industries. Some governments even moved toward compulsory employment. In effect, to mobilize the entire resources of the nation for the war effort, European countries had moved toward planned economies directed by government agencies.

WOMEN IN WORLD WAR I The war also created new roles for women. Because so many men went off to fight at the front, women were called on to take over jobs and responsibilities that had not been available to them before. Overall, the number of women employed in Britain who held new jobs or replaced men rose by 1,345,000. Their occupations included chimney sweeps, truck drivers, farm laborers, and factory workers in heavy industry. By 1918, some 38 percent of the workers in the Krupp armaments factories in Germany were women.

While male workers expressed concern that the employment of females at lower wages would depress their own wages, women began to demand equal pay legislation. A law passed by the French government in July 1915 established a minimum wage for women home-workers in textiles, an industry that had grown dramatically thanks to the demand for military uniforms. Later in 1917, the government decreed that men and women should receive equal rates for piecework. Despite the noticeable increase in women's wages that resulted from government regulations, women's industrial wages still were not equal to men's wages by the end of the war.

MORALE PROBLEMS As the Great War dragged on and both casualties and privations worsened, internal dissatisfaction replaced the patriotic enthusiasm that had marked the early stages of the conflict. By 1916, there were numerous signs that civilian morale was beginning to crack under the pressure of total war. War governments, however, fought back against the growing opposition to the war, as even parliamentary regimes resorted to an expansion of police powers to stifle internal dissent. At the very beginning of the war, the British Parliament passed the Defence of the Realm Act (DORA), which allowed the public authorities to arrest dissenters as traitors. The act was later extended to authorize public officials to censor newspapers by deleting objectionable material and even to suspend newspaper publication. In France, government authorities had initially been lenient about public opposition to the war, but by 1917, they began to fear that open opposition to the war might weaken the French will to fight. When Georges Clemenceau (1841–1929) became premier near the end of 1917, the lenient French policies came to an end, and basic civil liberties were suppressed for the duration of the war. When a former premier publicly advocated a negotiated peace, Clemenceau's government had him sentenced to prison for two years for treason.

The Last Year of the War

For Germany, the withdrawal of the Russians from the war in March 1918 offered renewed hope for a favorable

Lawrence of Arabia (1962)

The conflict in the Middle East produced one of the great romantic heroes of World War I. T. E. Lawrence, a British army officer popularly known as Lawrence of Arabia, organized Arab tribesmen and led them in battle against the Ottoman Turks, who had become allies of the Central Powers (Germany and its allies). Although the military significance of Lawrence's exploits was limited, their long-term implications for the region were enormous. During the peace negotiations that followed the German surrender in November 1918, most Ottoman possessions in the Middle East were replaced by British and French mandates, while the Arabian peninsula embarked on the road to independence under the tribal chieftain Ibn Saud. The political implications of that settlement are still important today.

Columbia/The Kobal Collection/Art Resource NY

T. E. Lawrence (Peter O'Toole in white) at the head of the Arab tribes.

The movie *Lawrence of Arabia* (1962), directed by the great British filmmaker David Lean, won seven Oscars and made an instant star of actor Peter O'Toole, who played the eccentric Lawrence with mesmerizing perfection. The photography and the acting are both superb, and Lean's deft portrayal of the behavior and motives of all participants makes the lengthy film (more than three hours) essential viewing for those interested in comprehending the complex roots of the current situation in the Middle East.

British objectives, as voiced by the British general Viscount Edmund Allenby (played by the veteran actor Jack Hawkins), were unabashedly military in nature—use Arab unrest in the region as a means of taking the Ottomans out of the war. Arab leaders such as Prince Faisal—languidly played by the consummate actor Alec Guinness—openly sought their independence from Turkish rule, but initially appeared hopelessly divided. It was Major Lawrence who provided the spark and the determination to knit together a coalition of Arab forces capable of winning crucial victories in the final year of the war. Faisal himself would eventually be chosen by the British to become the king of the artificial state of Iraq.

Lawrence himself remains an enigma—in the movie as in real life. Combining a fervent idealism about the Arab cause with an overweening sense of self-promotion, he played to the end an ambiguous role in the geopolitics of the Middle East. Disenchanted with the postwar peace settlement, he eventually removed himself from the public eye and died in a motorcycle accident in 1935. ∎

end to the conflict. Erich von Ludendorff (1865–1937), who guided German military operations, persuaded civilian leaders to make one final gamble—a grand offensive in the west to break the military stalemate. The German attack was launched in March and lasted into July, but an Allied counterattack, supported by the arrival of 140,000 fresh American troops, defeated the Germans at the Second Battle of the Marne on July 18. Ludendorff's gamble had failed. With the arrival of 2 million more American troops on the Continent, Allied forces began to advance steadily toward Germany.

On September 29, 1918, General Ludendorff informed German leaders that the war was lost and demanded that the government sue for peace. When German officials discovered that the Allies were unwilling to make peace with the wartime leadership, reforms were instituted to create a liberal government. But these constitutional reforms came too late for the exhausted and restive German people. On November 3, naval units in Kiel mutinied, and within days, councils of workers and soldiers were forming throughout northern Germany and taking over civilian and military administrations. William II, bowing to public pressure, abdicated on November 9, and the Socialists under Friedrich Ebert (1871–1925) announced the establishment of a republic. Two days later, on November 11, 1918, the new German government agreed to an armistice. The war was over.

The final tally of casualties from the war was appalling. Nearly 10 million soldiers were dead, including 5 million on the Allied side and 3.5 million from the Central Powers. Civilian deaths were nearly as high. France, which had borne much of the burden of the war, suffered nearly 2 million deaths, including one out of every four males between eighteen and thirty years of age.

Seeking Eternal Peace

In January 1919, the delegations of twenty-seven victorious Allied nations gathered at the palace of Versailles near Paris to conclude a final settlement of the Great War. Some delegates hoped that this conference would avoid the mistakes made at Vienna in 1815 by aristocrats who rearranged the map of Europe to meet the selfish desires of the great powers. As Harold Nicolson, one of the British delegates, remarked: "We were journeying to Paris not merely to liquidate the war, but to found a New Order in Europe. We were preparing not Peace only, but Eternal Peace. There was about us the halo of some divine mission. . . . For we were bent on doing great, permanent and noble things."[3]

The Vision of Woodrow Wilson

National expectations, however, made Nicolson's quest for "eternal peace" a difficult one. Over the years, the reasons for fighting World War I had been transformed from selfish national interests to idealistic principles. No one expressed the latter better than Woodrow Wilson (1856–1924). The American president outlined to the U.S. Congress "Fourteen Points" that he believed justified the enormous military struggle then being waged. Later, Wilson spelled out additional steps for a truly just and lasting peace. Wilson's proposals included "open covenants of peace, openly arrived at" instead of secret diplomacy; the reduction of national armaments to a "point consistent with domestic safety"; and the self-determination of peoples so that "all well-defined national aspirations shall be accorded the utmost satisfaction." Wilson characterized World War I as a people's war waged against "absolutism and militarism," two scourges of liberty that could be eliminated only by creating democratic governments and a "general association of nations" that would guarantee "political independence and territorial integrity to great and small states alike." As the spokesman for a new world order based on democracy and international cooperation, Wilson was enthusiastically cheered by many Europeans when he arrived in Europe for the peace conference.

Wilson soon found, however, that other states at the conference were guided by considerably more pragmatic motives. The secret treaties and agreements that had been made before and during the war could not be totally ignored, even if they conflicted with Wilson's principle of self-determination. National interests also complicated the deliberations of the conference. David Lloyd George (1863–1945), prime minister of Great Britain, had won a decisive electoral victory in December 1918 on a platform of making the Germans pay for this dreadful war.

France's approach to peace was determined primarily by considerations of national security. To Georges Clemenceau, the feisty French premier who had led his country to victory, the French people had borne the brunt of German aggression and deserved security against any possible future attack. Clemenceau wanted a demilitarized Germany, vast reparations to pay for the costs of the war, and a separate Rhineland as a buffer state between France and Germany—demands that Wilson viewed as vindictive and contrary to the principle of national self-determination. The Europeans, he once complained to a colleague, just want to "divide the swag."[4]

Although twenty-seven nations were represented at the Paris Peace Conference, the most important decisions were made by Wilson, Clemenceau, and Lloyd George. Italy was considered one of the so-called Big Four powers but played a much less important role than the other three countries. Germany was not invited to attend, and Russia could not because it was embroiled in civil war.

FORMING THE LEAGUE OF NATIONS In view of the many conflicting demands at Versailles, it was inevitable that the Big Three would quarrel. Wilson was determined to create a League of Nations to prevent future wars. Clemenceau and Lloyd George were equally determined to punish Germany. In the end, only compromise made it possible to achieve a peace settlement. On January 25, 1919, the conference adopted the principle of the League of Nations (the details of its structure were left for later sessions); Wilson willingly agreed to make compromises on territorial arrangements to guarantee the League's establishment, believing that a functioning League could later rectify bad arrangements. Clemenceau also compromised to obtain some guarantees for French security. He renounced France's desire for a separate Rhineland and instead accepted a defensive alliance with Great Britain and the United States, both of which pledged to help France if it was attacked by Germany.

The Peace Settlement

The final peace settlement at Paris consisted of five separate treaties with the defeated nations—Germany, Austria, Hungary, Bulgaria, and Turkey. The Treaty of Versailles with Germany, signed on June 28, 1919, was by far the most important one. The Germans considered it a harsh peace and were particularly unhappy with Article 231, the so-called **war guilt clause**, which declared Germany (and Austria) responsible for starting the war and ordered Germany to pay **reparations** for all the damage to which the Allied governments and their people had been subjected as a result of the war "imposed upon them by the aggression of Germany and her allies."

The military and territorial provisions of the treaty also rankled the Germans. Germany was required to lower its army to 100,000 men, reduce its navy, and eliminate its air force. German territorial losses included the return of Alsace and Lorraine to France and sections of Prussia to the new Polish state. German territory west and as far as 30 miles east of the Rhine was established as a demilitarized zone and stripped of all armaments or fortifications to serve as a barrier to any future German military moves westward against France. Outraged by the "dictated peace," the new German government complained but accepted the treaty.

The separate peace treaties made with the other Central Powers extensively redrew the map of eastern Europe (see Map 4.3). Many of these changes merely ratified what the war had already accomplished. Both Germany and Russia lost considerable territory in eastern Europe; the Austro-Hungarian Empire disappeared altogether. New nation-states emerged from the remnants of these three empires: Finland, Latvia, Estonia, Lithuania, Poland, Czechoslovakia, Austria, and Hungary. Territorial rearrangements were also made in the Balkans. Romania acquired additional lands from Russia, Hungary, and Bulgaria. Serbia formed the nucleus of a new South Slav state, called Yugoslavia, which combined Serbs, Croats, and Slovenes. The Ottoman Empire was also broken up, remaking the map of the Middle East (see Chapter 5).

Although the Paris Peace Conference was supposedly guided by the principle of self-determination, the mixtures of peoples in eastern Europe made it impossible to draw boundaries along neat ethnic lines. Compromises had to be made, sometimes to satisfy the national interest of the victors. France, for example, had lost Russia as its major ally on Germany's eastern border and wanted to strengthen Poland, Czechoslovakia, Yugoslavia, and Romania as much as possible so that those states could serve as barriers against Germany and Communist Russia. As a result of such compromises, virtually every eastern European state was left with national minorities that could lead to future conflicts: Germans in Poland; Hungarians, Poles, and Germans in Czechoslovakia; and the combination of Serbs, Croats, Slovenes, Macedonians, and Albanians in Yugoslavia all became sources of later conflict. Moreover, the new map of eastern Europe was based on the temporary collapse of power in both Germany and Russia. As neither country accepted the new eastern frontiers, it seemed only a matter of time before both would seek to make changes. In retrospect, the fear expressed by U.S. Secretary of State Robert Lansing that the principle of self-determination aroused hopes that "can never be realized" seems all too justified.

Revolution in Russia

One of the more important consequences of the Great War was the impact that it had on Imperial Russia. In the summer of 1914, Tsar Nicholas II had almost appeared to welcome the prospect of a European war. Such a conflict, he hoped, would unite his subjects at a time when his empire was passing through a period of rapid social change and political unrest. The imperial government had survived the popular demonstrations that erupted during the Russo-Japanese War of 1904–1905, although the tsar had been forced to grant a series of reforms in a desperate effort to forestall the collapse of the traditional system (see Chapter 1).

As it turned out, the onset of war served not to revive the Russian monarchy, but rather—as is so often the case with decrepit empires undergoing dramatic change—to undermine its already fragile foundations. World War I halted the trajectory of Russia's economic growth and set the stage for the final collapse of the old order. After stirring victories in the early stages of the war, news from

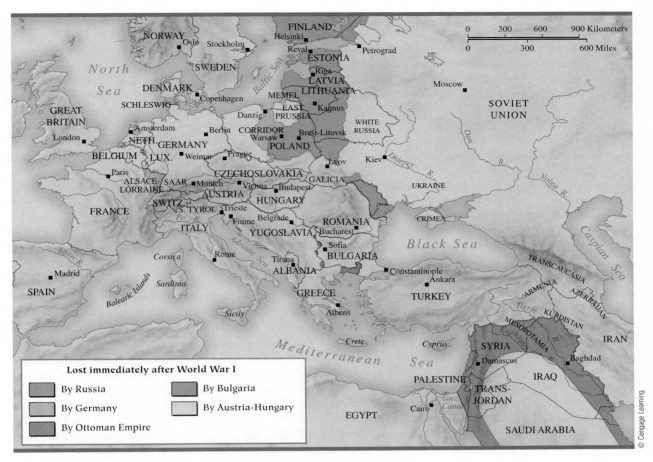

MAP 4.3 Territorial Changes in Europe and the Middle East After World War I. The victorious Allies met in Paris to determine the shape and nature of postwar Europe. At the urging of U.S. President Woodrow Wilson, many nationalist aspirations of former imperial subjects were realized with the creation of several new countries from the prewar territory of Austria-Hungary, Germany, Russia, and the Ottoman Empire.

 What new countries emerged in Europe and the Middle East?

the battlefield turned increasingly grim as poorly armed Russian soldiers were slaughtered by the modern armies of the German emperor. Between 1914 and 1916, 2 million Russian soldiers were killed, and another 4 to 6 million were wounded or captured. The conscription of peasants from the countryside caused food prices to rise and led to periodic bread shortages in the major cities. Workers grew increasingly restive at the wartime schedule of long hours with low pay and joined army deserters in angry marches through the capital of Saint Petersburg (now for patriotic reasons renamed Petrograd).

It was a classic scenario for revolution—discontent in the big cities fueled by mutinous troops streaming home from the battlefield and a rising level of lawlessness in rural areas as angry peasants seized land and burned the manor houses of the wealthy. Even the urban middle class, always a bellwether on the political scene, grew impatient with the economic crisis and the bad news from the front and began to question the competence of the tsar and his advisers. In March 1917 (late February according to the old style Julian calendar still in use in Russia), government troops fired at demonstrators in the streets of the capital and killed several. An angry mob marched to the Duma, where restive delegates demanded the resignation of the tsar's cabinet.

The March Revolution

Nicholas II, whose character combined the fatal qualities of stupidity and stubbornness, had never wanted to share the supreme power he had inherited. After a brief period of hesitation, he abdicated, leaving a vacuum that was quickly seized by leading elements in the Duma, who formed a provisional government to steer Russia through the crisis. On the left, reformist and radical political parties—including the Social Revolutionaries (the legal successors of the outlawed terrorist organization **Narodnaya Volya**) and the Russian Social Democratic Labor Party (RSDLP), the only orthodox Marxist party active in Russia—cooperated in creating a shadow government called the Saint Petersburg Soviet. It supported the provisional government in pursuing the war but attempted to compel it to grant economic and social reforms that would benefit the masses.

The March 1917 uprising had brought about the collapse of the monarchy but showed little promise of solving the deeper problems that had led Russia to the brink of civil war. As the crisis continued, radical members of the RSDLP began to hope that a social revolution was at hand.

Marxism had first appeared in Russia in the 1880s. Early Marxists, aware of the primitive conditions in their country, asked Karl Marx himself for advice. The Russian proletariat was oppressed—indeed, brutalized—but small in numbers and unsophisticated. Could agrarian Russia make the transition to socialism without an intervening stage of capitalism? Marx, who always showed more tactical flexibility than the rigid determinism of his system suggested, replied that Russia might be able to avoid the capitalist stage by building on the communal traditions of the Russian village, known as the *mir*.

But as Russian Marxism evolved, its leaders turned more toward Marxist orthodoxy. Founding member George Plekhanov saw signs in the early stages of its industrial revolution that Russia would follow the classic pattern. In 1898, the RSDLP held its first congress.

LENIN AND THE BOLSHEVIKS During the last decade of the nineteenth century, a new force entered the Russian Marxist movement in the figure of Vladimir Ulyanov, later to be known as Lenin (1870–1924). Initially radicalized by the execution of his older brother for terrorism in 1886, he became a revolutionary and a member of Plekhanov's RSDLP. Like Plekhanov, Lenin believed in the revolution, but he was a man in a hurry. Whereas Plekhanov sought to prepare patiently for revolution by education and mass work, Lenin wanted to build up the party rapidly as a vanguard instrument to galvanize the masses and spur the workers to revolt. In a pamphlet titled *What Is to Be Done?* he proposed the transformation of the RSDLP into a compact and highly disciplined group of professional revolutionaries that would not merely ride the crest of the revolutionary wave but would unleash the storm clouds of revolt.

At the Second National Congress of the RSDLP, held in 1903 in Brussels and London, Lenin's ideas were supported by a majority of the delegates (thus, the term **Bolsheviks**, or "majorityites," for his followers). His victory was short-lived, however, and for the next decade, Lenin was a brooding figure living in exile on the fringe of the Russian revolutionary movement, which was now dominated by the **Mensheviks** ("minorityites"), who opposed Lenin's single-minded pursuit of violent revolution. Scoffing at his more cautious rivals, Lenin declared that revolution was "a tough business" and could not be waged "wearing white gloves and with clean hands."[5]

From his residence in exile in Switzerland, Lenin heard the news of the collapse of the tsarist monarchy and decided to return to Russia. The German government secretly provided him and his followers with a sealed railroad car to travel through Germany, undoubtedly in the hope that his presence would promote instability in Russia. On his arrival in Petrograd in April 1917, Lenin laid out a program for the RSDLP: all power to the **soviets** (locally elected government councils), an end to the war, and the distribution of land to poor peasants. But Lenin's April Theses (see the box on p. 83) were too radical even for his fellow Bolsheviks, who continued to cooperate with the provisional government while attempting to push it to the left. His onetime mentor Plekhanov remarked that Lenin's plans for a general uprising were "delirious."

The Bolshevik Revolution

During the summer, the crisis worsened, and in July, riots by workers and soldiers in the capital led the provisional government to outlaw the Bolsheviks and call for Lenin's arrest. The "July Days," raising the threat of disorder and class war, aroused the fears of conservatives and split the fragile political consensus within the provisional government. In September, General Lavr Kornilov, commander in chief of Russian imperial forces, launched a coup d'état to seize power from Alexander Kerensky, now the dominant figure in the provisional government. The revolt was put down with the help of so-called Red Guard units, formed by the Bolsheviks within army regiments in the capital area (these troops would later be regarded as the first units of the Red Army), but Lenin now sensed the weakness of the provisional government and persuaded his colleagues to prepare for revolt. On the night of November 7 (October 25

All Power to the Soviets!

On his return to Petrograd in April 1917, the revolutionary Marxist Vladimir Lenin issued a series of proposals designed to overthrow the provisional government and bring his Bolshevik Party to power in Russia. At the time his April Theses were delivered, his ideas appeared to be too radical, even for his closest followers. But the Bolsheviks' simple slogan of "Peace, Land, and Bread" soon began to gain traction on the streets of the capital. By the end of the year, Lenin's compelling vision had been realized, and the world would never be the same again.

Lenin's April Theses, 1917

1. The specific feature of the present situation in Russia is that the country is *passing* from the first stage of the revolution—which, owing to the insufficient class-consciousness and organization of the proletariat, placed power in the hands of the bourgeoisie—to its *second* stage, which must place power in the hands of the proletariat and the poorest sections of the peasants. . . .

     This peculiar situation demands of us an ability to adapt ourselves to the *special* conditions of Party work among unprecedentedly large masses of proletarians who have just awakened to political life. . . .

2. No support for the Provisional Government: the utter falsity of all the promises should be made clear, particularly of those relating to the renunciation of annexations. Exposure in place of the impermissible, illusion-breeding "demand" that *this* government of capitalists should *cease* to be an imperialist government.

The masses must be made to see that the Soviets of Workers' Deputies are the *only possible* form of revolutionary government, and that therefore our task is, as long as *this* government yields to the influence of the bourgeoisie, to present a patient, systematic and persistent explanation of the errors of their tactics, an explanation especially adapted to the practical needs of the masses.

As long as we are in the minority we carry on the work of criticizing and exposing errors and at the same time we preach the necessity of transferring the entire state power to the Soviets of Workers' Deputies, so that the people may overcome their mistakes by experience.

Nationalization of *all* lands in the country, the land to be disposed of by the local Soviets of Agricultural Laborers' and Peasants' Deputies. The organization of separate Soviets of Deputies of Poor Peasants. The setting up of a model farm on each of the large estates (ranging in size from 100 to 300 dessiatines [about 270 to 810 acres], according to local and other conditions, and to the decisions of the local bodies) under the control of the Soviets of Agricultural Laborers' Deputies and for the public account.

 What were the key provisions of Lenin's April Theses? To what degree were they carried out?

SOURCE: V. I. Lenin, *Collected Works*, 4th ed. (Moscow: Progress, 1964), Vol. XXIV, pp. 21–24.

old style), forces under the command of Lenin's lieutenant, Leon Trotsky (1879–1940), seized key installations in the capital area, while other units loyal to the Bolsheviks, including mutinous sailors from the battleship *Aurora* stationed nearby on the Neva River, stormed the Winter Palace, where supporters of the provisional government were quickly overwhelmed. Alexander Kerensky was forced to flee from Russia in disguise.

The following morning, at a national congress of delegates from soviet organizations throughout the country, the Bolsheviks declared a new socialist order. Moderate elements from the Menshevik faction and the Social Revolutionary Party protested the illegality of the Bolshevik action and left the conference hall in anger. They were derided by Trotsky, who proclaimed that they were relegated "to the dustbin of history."

With the Bolshevik Revolution of November 1917, Lenin was now in command. His power was tenuous and extended only from the capital to a few of the larger cities, such as Moscow and Kiev, that had waged their own insurrections. There were, in fact, few Bolsheviks in rural areas, where most peasants supported the moderate leftist Social Revolutionaries. On the fringes of the Russian Empire, restive minorities prepared to take advantage of the anarchy to seize their own independence, while supporters of the monarchy began raising armies to destroy the "Red menace" in Petrograd. Lenin was in power, but for how long?

Lenin Addresses a Crowd. Vladimir Lenin was the driving force behind the success of the Bolsheviks in seizing power in Russia and creating the Union of Soviet Socialist Republics. Here Lenin is seen addressing a rally in Moscow in 1917.

THE BOLSHEVIK REVOLUTION IN RETROSPECT The Bolshevik Revolution of 1917 has been the subject of vigorous debate by scholars and students of world affairs. Could it have been avoided if the provisional government had provided more effective leadership, or was it inevitable? Did Lenin stifle Russia's halting progress toward a Western-style capitalist democracy, or was the Bolshevik victory preordained by the autocratic conditions and lack of democratic traditions in Imperial Russia? Such questions have no simple answers, but some hypotheses are possible. The weakness of the moderate government created by the March revolution was probably predictable, given the political inexperience of the urban middle class and the deep divisions within the ruling coalition over issues of peace and war. At the same time, it seems highly unlikely that the Bolsheviks would have possessed the self-confidence to act without the presence of their leader, Vladimir Lenin, who almost single-handedly employed his strength of will to urge his colleagues to make their bid for power. The November revolution in Russia is often cited as a cardinal example of the role that a single individual can sometimes have on the course of history. Without Lenin, it would probably have been left to the army to intervene in an effort to maintain law and order, as would happen so often elsewhere during the turbulent twentieth century.

In any event, the Bolshevik Revolution was a momentous development for Russia and for the entire world. Not only did it present Western capitalist societies with a brazen new challenge to their global supremacy, but it also demonstrated that Lenin's concept of revolution, carried through at the will of a determined minority of revolutionary activists "in the interests of the masses," could succeed in a society going through the difficult early stages of the Industrial Revolution. It was a repudiation of orthodox "late Marxism" and a return to Marx's pre-1848 vision of a multiclass revolt leading rapidly from a capitalist to a proletarian takeover (see Chapter 1). It was, in short, a lesson that would not be ignored by radical intellectuals throughout the world, as we shall see in the chapter to follow.

The Civil War

The Bolshevik seizure of power in Petrograd (soon to be renamed Leningrad after Lenin's death in 1924) was only the first, and not necessarily the most difficult, stage in the Russian Revolution. Although the Bolshevik slogan of "Peace, Land, and Bread" had considerable appeal among workers, petty merchants, and soldiers in the vicinity of the capital and other major cities, the party—only 50,000 strong in November—had little representation in the rural areas, where the majority of the peasants supported the moderate leftist Social Revolutionary Party. On the fringes of the Russian Empire, ethnic minority groups took advantage of the confusion in Petrograd to launch movements to restore their own independence or achieve a position of autonomy within the Russian state. In the meantime, supporters of the deposed Romanov dynasty and other political opponents of the Bolsheviks, known as White Russians, attempted to mobilize support to drive the Bolsheviks out of the capital and reverse the verdict of "Red October." And beyond all that, the war with Germany continued.

Lenin was aware of these problems and hoped that a wave of socialist revolutions in the economically advanced countries of central and western Europe would bring the world war to an end and usher in a new age of peace, socialism, and growing economic prosperity. In the meantime, his first priority was to consolidate the rule of the working class and its party vanguard (now to be renamed the Communist Party) in Russia. The first step was to set up a new order in Petrograd to replace the provisional government that had been created after the March Revolution. For lack of a better alternative, outlying areas were simply informed of the change in government—a "revolution by telegraph," as Leon Trotsky termed it. Then Lenin moved to create new organs of proletarian power, setting up the Council of People's Commissars (the word "commissar," Lenin remarked "smells of revolution") to serve as a provisional government. Lenin was unwilling to share power with moderate leftists who had resisted the Bolshevik coup in November, and he created security forces (popularly called the Cheka, or "extraordinary commission"), which imprisoned and brutally executed opponents of the new regime. In January 1918, the Constituent Assembly, which had been elected on the basis of plans established by the previous government, convened in Petrograd. Composed primarily of delegates from the Social Revolutionary Party and other parties opposed to the Bolsheviks, it showed itself critical of the new regime and was immediately abolished.

Lenin was determined to prevent the Romanov family from becoming a rallying cry for opponents of the new Bolshevik regime. In the spring of 1918, the former tsar and his family were placed under guard in Ekaterinburg, a small mining town in the Ural Mountains. On the night of July 16, the entire family was murdered on Lenin's order. The bodies were dropped into a nearby mine shaft. For decades, rumors persisted that one of Nicholas II's daughters, Anastasia, had survived execution.

In foreign affairs, Lenin's first major decision was to seek peace with Germany in order to permit the new government to focus its efforts on the growing threat posed by White Russian forces within the country. In March 1918, a peace settlement with Germany was reached at Brest-Litovsk, although at enormous cost. Soviet Russia lost nearly one-fourth of the territory and one-third of the population of the prewar Russian Empire. In retrospect, however, Lenin's controversial decision to accept a punitive peace may have been a stroke of genius, for it gained time for the regime to build up its internal strength and defeat its many adversaries still operating in the territories that once composed the empire of the tsars.

Indeed, the odds for a Bolshevik success must have seemed dim in the immediate aftermath of the seizure of power. Lenin himself initially predicted that defeat was likely in the absence of successful revolutionary outbreaks elsewhere in Europe. Support for the Bolsheviks in Russia was limited, and the regime antagonized farmers by the harsh measures it used to obtain provisions for its troops. Although Leon Trotsky showed traces of genius in organizing the Red Army, he was forced to station trusted lieutenants as "political commissars" in army units to guarantee the loyalty of his commanders.

In the end, Lenin's gamble that the Russian people were desperate enough to embrace radical change paid off. The White Russian forces were larger than those of the Red Army, and they were supported by armed contingents sent by Great Britain, France, and the United States to assist in the extinction of the "Red menace." Nevertheless, they were also rent by factionalism and hindered by a tendency to fight "red terror" with "white terror" and to return conquered land to the original landowners, thereby driving many peasants to support the Soviet regime. By 1920, the civil war was over, and Soviet power was secure.

The Failure of the Peace

In the years following the end of World War I, many people hoped that the world was about to enter a new era of international peace, economic growth, and political democracy. In all of these areas, the optimistic hopes of the 1920s failed to be realized.

The Search for Security

The peace settlement at the end of World War I had tried to fulfill the nineteenth-century dream of nationalism by creating new boundaries and new states out of the now-defunct empires in central and eastern Europe. From the outset, however, the settlement had left many unhappy. Conflicts over disputed border regions between Germany and Poland, Poland and Lithuania, Poland and Czechoslovakia, Austria and Hungary, and Italy and Yugoslavia poisoned mutual relations in eastern Europe for years. Many Germans viewed the peace of Versailles as a dictated peace and vowed to seek its revision.

To its supporters, the League of Nations was the place to resolve such problems. The League, however, proved ineffectual in maintaining the peace. One of the reasons for its weakness was the lack of adequate provisions for enforcement. Because many nations were reluctant to compromise their own national security, the League could use only economic sanctions to halt aggression. The French attempt to strengthen the League's effectiveness as an instrument of collective security by creating a peacekeeping force was rejected by nations that feared giving up any of their sovereignty to a larger international body.

Another reason that the League failed to achieve its promise was that the United States, where many were disillusioned by the disputes at Versailles, failed to join the new organization. The U.S. Senate also rejected President Wilson's proposal for a defensive alliance with Great Britain and France.

FRANCE GOES IT ALONE The weakness of the League of Nations and the failure of both the United States and Great Britain to honor their promise of a defensive military alliance with France led the latter to insist on a strict enforcement of the Treaty of Versailles. This tough policy toward Germany began with the issue of reparations—the payments that the Germans were supposed to make to compensate for the "damage done to the civilian population of the Allied and Associated Powers and to their property," as the treaty asserted. In April 1921, the Allied Reparations Commission settled on a sum of 132 billion marks ($33 billion) for German reparations, payable in annual installments of 2.5 billion (gold) marks. Allied threats to occupy the Ruhr valley, Germany's chief industrial and mining center, induced the new German republic to accept the reparations settlement and to make its first payment in 1921. By the following year, however, facing rising inflation, domestic turmoil, and lack of revenues because of low tax rates, the German government announced that it was unable to pay more. Outraged by what they considered to be Germany's violation of one aspect of the peace settlement, the French government sent troops to occupy the Ruhr valley. If the Germans would not pay reparations, the French would collect reparations in kind by operating and using the Ruhr mines and factories.

French occupation of the Ruhr seriously undermined the fragile German economy. The German government adopted a policy of passive resistance to French occupation that was largely financed by printing more paper money, thus intensifying the inflationary pressures that had already begun at the end of the war. The German mark became worthless. Economic disaster fueled political upheavals as Communists staged uprisings in October and nationalist elements under the leadership of an as yet little known army veteran by the name of Adolf Hitler attempted to seize power in Munich in 1923. The following year, a new conference of experts was convened to reassess the reparations problem.

SOLVING THE REPARATIONS PROBLEM The formation of liberal-socialist governments in both Great Britain and France opened the door to conciliatory approaches to Germany and the reparations problem. At the same time, a new German government led by Gustav Stresemann (1878–1929) ended the policy of passive resistance and committed Germany to carry out the provisions of the Versailles Treaty while seeking a new settlement of the reparations question.

In August 1924, an international commission produced a new plan for reparations. Named the Dawes Plan after the American banker who chaired the commission, it reduced reparations and stabilized Germany's payments on the basis of its ability to pay. The Dawes Plan also granted an initial $200 million loan for Germany's recovery, which opened the door to heavy American investments in Europe that helped create a new era of European prosperity between 1924 and 1929.

THE SPIRIT OF LOCARNO A new approach to European diplomacy accompanied the new economic stability. A spirit of international cooperation was fostered by the foreign ministers of Germany and France, Gustav Stresemann and Aristide Briand (1862–1932), who concluded the Treaty of Locarno in 1925. This treaty guaranteed Germany's new western borders with France and Belgium. Although Germany's new eastern borders with Poland were conspicuously absent from the agreement, the Locarno pact was viewed by many as the beginning of a new era of European peace. On the day after the pact was concluded, the headline in the *New York Times* read "France and Germany Ban War Forever," and the London *Times* declared "Peace at Last."[6]

Germany's entry into the League of Nations in March 1926 soon reinforced the atmosphere of conciliation engendered at Locarno. Two years later, similar attitudes prevailed in the Kellogg-Briand Pact, drafted by U.S. Secretary of State Frank B. Kellogg and French Foreign Minister Briand. Sixty-three nations signed this accord, in which they pledged "to renounce war as an instrument of national policy." Nothing was said, however, about what would be done if anyone violated the treaty.

The spirit of Locarno was based on little real substance. Germany lacked the military power to alter its western borders even if it wanted to. Pious promises to renounce war without mechanisms to enforce them were virtually worthless. And the issue of disarmament soon proved that paper promises could not bring nations to cut back on their weapons. The League of Nations Covenant had recommended the "reduction of national armaments to the lowest point consistent with national safety." Numerous disarmament conferences, however, failed to achieve anything substantial as states proved unwilling to trust their security to anyone but their own military forces. By the time the World Disarmament Conference finally met in Geneva in 1932, the issue was already dead.

A Return to Normalcy?

According to Woodrow Wilson, World War I had been fought to make the world "safe for democracy." During the decade that followed the signing of the Treaty of Versailles, there seemed to be some justification for his optimism. Several major European states, as well as a number of the new countries established in eastern Europe, had functioning political democracies. A number of nations, including the United States, broadened the right to vote to include women, and the individual liberties of citizens were strengthened in other ways as well. Even Germany appeared to share in the shift toward political pluralism, as a new republic based in the city of Weimar took steps to establish democratic political institutions under the able leadership of moderate statesmen like Friedrich Ebert (1871–1925) and Gustav Stresemann.

But the "return to normalcy," as Woodrow Wilson's successor, President Warren Harding (1865–1923), called it, was based on fragile economic foundations, as recovery from the four years of bitter conflict was slow and halting. France was only partially successful in reconstructing areas in the northern parts of the country that had been devastated by the Great War. Great Britain went through its own period of painful adjustment. The country had lost many of its markets for industrial products, especially to the United States and Japan. The postwar decline of such staple industries as coal, steel, and textiles led to a rise in unemployment, which reached the 2 million mark by 1922. An economic recovery began in the next few years but proved to be superficial, and unemployment remained at the 10 percent level throughout the decade. Coal miners were especially affected by the decline of the antiquated and inefficient British coal mines, which suffered from a global glut of coal.

The United States continued its gradual emergence as an industrial powerhouse—marked by the rapid development of the motor car industry under the leadership of Henry Ford. But the benefits of economic expansion were uneven, and rural areas generally did not share in the surface prosperity that had begun to appear in the larger industrialized cities. In the meantime, labor organizations fought with only limited success to improve the working conditions and wages of their constituents in the face of legal hurdles and stiff resistance by corporate interests.

None of the larger Western democracies, however, faced greater challenges than Germany, where the Weimar Republic, burdened by heavy war reparations, encountered serious economic difficulties from the start. The runaway inflation of 1922 and 1923 mentioned earlier had grave social effects, as widows, orphans, the elderly, army officers, civil servants, and others who lived on fixed incomes all watched their monthly stipends become worthless or their lifetime savings disappear. Ominously, these continuing economic difficulties inexorably pushed the middle class, which still lacked experience in using its political influence to achieve its objectives, toward the young German Communist Party or to rightist parties that were equally hostile to the republic.

The Great Depression

During the first few years after the end of World War I, there had been some tantalizing signs that Europe was on the path of recovery from the consequences of that devastating conflict. But that illusion was burst in 1929, with the onset of the Great Depression.

CAUSES Two factors played a major role in the coming of the Great Depression: a downturn in European economies and an international financial crisis created by the collapse of the American stock market in 1929. Already in the mid-1920s, global prices for agricultural goods were beginning to decline rapidly as a result of the overproduction of basic commodities, such as wheat. In 1925, states in central and eastern Europe began to impose tariffs to close their markets to other countries' goods. Meanwhile, an increase in the use of oil and hydroelectricity led to a slump in the coal industry.

Much of the European prosperity in the mid-1920s was built on U.S. bank loans to Germany, but in 1928 and 1929, American investors began to pull money out of Germany to invest in the booming New York stock market. When that market crashed in October 1929, panicky American investors withdrew even more of their funds from Germany and other European markets. The withdrawal of funds seriously weakened the banks of Germany and other central European states. The Credit-Anstalt, Vienna's most prestigious bank, collapsed on May 31, 1931. By that time, trade was slowing down, industrialists were cutting back production, and unemployment was increasing as the ripple effects of international bank failures had a devastating impact on domestic economies.

REPERCUSSIONS Economic downturns were by no means a new phenomenon in the rise of Western capitalism, but the Great Depression was exceptionally severe and had immediate repercussions. In the United States, great fortunes were lost overnight, and, with consumer demand dropping, industrial production fell dramatically, throwing millions out of work. President Herbert Hoover (1874–1964) signed legislation imposing high tariffs on imported goods. In Great Britain, the Labour Party failed to resolve the crisis and fell from power in 1931. A new government dominated by the Conservatives took office and sought to lift the country out of the depression by using the traditional policies of balanced budgets and protective tariffs.

France did not suffer from the effects of the Great Depression as soon as other countries because it was a protected market and a majority of French industrial plants were small enterprises. Consequently, France did not begin to face the crisis until 1931, but then it quickly led to political repercussions. During a nineteen-month period in 1932–1933, six different cabinets were formed as France faced political chaos.

The European nation that suffered the most damage from the depression was probably Germany. Unemployment increased to more than 4 million by the end of 1930. For many Germans, who had already suffered through difficult times in the early 1920s, the democratic experiment represented by the Weimar Republic had become a nightmare. Some reacted by turning to Marxism because Karl Marx had long predicted that capitalism would destroy itself through overproduction. As in several other European countries, communism took on a new popularity, especially with workers and intellectuals. But in Germany, the real beneficiary of the Great Depression was Adolf Hitler, whose Nazi Party came to power in 1933 (see Chapter 6).

The first reaction of all major Western governments faced with the depression was to adopt the traditional policy of tight money and balanced budgets. But as the Great Depression worsened, the Cambridge University economist John Maynard Keynes (1883–1946) took issue with the traditional view that depressions should be left to work themselves out through the self-regulatory mechanisms of a free economy. Keynes argued that unemployment stemmed not from overproduction but from a decline in consumer demand, which could be increased by public works, financed if necessary through **deficit spending** to stimulate production. Such policies, however, could be accomplished only by government intervention in the economy, a measure that most political leaders were unwilling to undertake.

FRANKLIN ROOSEVELT AND THE NEW DEAL After Germany no Western nation was more affected by the Great Depression than the United States. The full force of the depression had struck the United States by 1932. In that year, industrial production fell to 50 percent of what it had been in 1929. By 1933, there were 15 million unemployed. Under these circumstances, Democrat Franklin Delano Roosevelt (1882–1945) was able to win a landslide victory in the presidential election of 1932. A pragmatist who was willing to adopt unorthodox measures to deal with a crisis situation, FDR (as he was popularly known) pursued a Keynesian policy of active government intervention in the economy that came to be known as the **New Deal**.

Initially, the New Deal attempted to restore prosperity by creating the National Recovery Administration (NRA), which required government, labor, and industrial leaders to work out regulations for each industry. Declared unconstitutional by the Supreme Court in 1935, the NRA was soon superseded by other efforts collectively known as the Second New Deal. Its programs included the Works Progress Administration (WPA), established in

© Archive Holdings Inc./Getty Images

Brother, Can You Spare a Job? The Great Depression devastated the world economy and led to a dramatic rise in unemployment throughout the industrialized world. In the United States, manufacturing centers like Chicago, Cleveland, and Detroit were especially hard hit as consumer demand for appliances and automobiles plummeted throughout the decade of the 1930s. In this poignant photograph taken in 1930, an unemployed worker in Detroit pleads for a job at the height of the depression. Unfortunately, full recovery would not come until many years later.

1935, which employed between 2 and 3 million people building bridges, roads, post offices, airports, and other public works. The Roosevelt administration was also responsible for new social legislation that launched the American welfare state. In 1935, the Social Security Act created a system of old-age pensions and unemployment insurance. At the same time, the National Labor Relations Act of 1935 encouraged the rapid growth of labor unions.

The New Deal undoubtedly provided some social reform measures and may even have averted social revolution in the United States. But it did not immediately solve the unemployment problems created by the Great

Depression. In May 1937, during what was considered a period of recovery, American unemployment still stood at 7 million; a recession the following year, triggered in part by a decline in public spending, increased that number to 11 million. Only World War II and the subsequent growth of armaments industries brought American workers back to full employment.

Building Socialism in Soviet Russia

In Russia, Bolshevik leaders had their own plans for the future. With their victory over the White Russians in 1920, Lenin and his colleagues could turn for the first time to the challenging task of building the first socialist society in a world dominated by their capitalist enemies. In his writings, Karl Marx had said little about the nature of the final communist utopia or how to get there. He had spoken briefly of a transitional phase, variously known as "raw communism" or "socialism," that would precede the final stage of communism. During this phase, the Communist Party would establish a "dictatorship of the proletariat" to rid society of the capitalist oppressors, set up the institutions of the new order, and indoctrinate the population in the communist ethic. In recognition of the fact that traces of "bourgeois thinking" would remain among the population, profit incentives would be used to encourage productivity (in Marxist terminology, payment would be on the basis of "work" rather than solely on "need"), but major industries would be nationalized and private landholdings eliminated. After seizing power in 1917, however, the Bolsheviks were too preoccupied with survival to give much attention to the future nature of Soviet society. **War communism**—involving the government seizure of major industries, utilities, and sources of raw materials and the requisition of grain from private farmers—was, by Lenin's own admission, just a makeshift policy to permit the regime to mobilize resources for the civil war.

THE NEW ECONOMIC POLICY In 1920, it was time to adopt a more coherent approach. The realities were sobering. Soviet Russia was not an advanced capitalist society in the Marxist image, blessed with modern technology and an impoverished and politically aware underclass imbued with the desire to advance to socialism. It was poor and primarily agrarian, and its small but growing industrial sector had been ravaged by years of war. Under the circumstances, Lenin called for caution. He won his party's approval for a moderate program of social and economic development known as the **New Economic Policy**, or NEP. The program was based on a combination of capitalist and socialist techniques designed to increase production through the use of profit incentives while at the same time promoting the concept of socialist ownership and maintaining firm party control over the political system and the overall direction of the economy. The "commanding heights" of the Soviet economy (heavy industry, banking, utilities, and foreign trade) remained in the hands of the state, while private industry and commerce were allowed to operate at the lower levels. The forced requisition of grain, which had caused serious unrest among the peasantry, was replaced by a tax, and land remained firmly in private hands. The theoretical justification for the program was that Soviet Russia now needed to go through its own "capitalist stage" (albeit under the control of the party) before beginning the difficult transition to socialism.

As an economic strategy, the NEP succeeded brilliantly. During the early and mid-1920s, the Soviet economy recovered rapidly from the ravages of war and civil war. A more lax hand over the affairs of state allowed a modest degree of free expression of opinion within the ranks of the party and in Soviet society at large. Under the surface, however, trouble loomed. Lenin had been increasingly disabled by a bullet lodged in his neck from an attempted assassination, and he began to lose his grip over a fractious party. Even before his death in 1924, potential successors had begun to scuffle for precedence in the struggle to assume his position as party leader, the most influential position in the state. The main candidates were Leon Trotsky and a rising young figure from the state of Georgia, Joseph Djugashvili, better known by his revolutionary name, Stalin (1879–1953). Lenin had misgivings about all the candidates hoping to succeed him and suggested that a collective leadership would best represent the interests of the party and the revolution. After his death in 1924, however, factional struggle among the leading figures in the party intensified. Although in some respects it was a pure power struggle, it did have policy ramifications as party factions argued about the NEP and its impact on the future of the Russian Revolution.

At first, the various factions were relatively evenly balanced, but Stalin proved adept at using his position as general secretary of the party to outmaneuver his rivals. By portraying himself as a centrist opposed to the extreme positions of his "leftist" (too radical in pursuit of revolutionary goals) or "rightist" (too prone to adopt moderate positions contrary to Marxist principles) rivals, he gradually concentrated power in his own hands.

In the meantime, the relatively moderate policies of the NEP continued to operate as the party and the state vocally encouraged the Soviet people, in a very un-Marxist manner, to enrich themselves. Capital investment and technological assistance from Western capitalist countries were actively welcomed. An observer at the time might reasonably have concluded that the Marxist vision of a world characterized by class struggle had become a dead letter.

STALIN TAKES OVER Stalin had previously joined with the moderate members of the party to defend the NEP against Trotsky, whose "left opposition" wanted a more rapid advance toward socialism. Trotsky, who had become one of Stalin's chief critics, was expelled from the party in 1927. Then, in 1928, Stalin reversed course: he now claimed that the NEP had achieved its purpose and called for a rapid advance to socialist forms of ownership. Beginning in 1929, a series of new programs changed the face of Soviet society. Private capitalism in manufacturing and trade was virtually abolished, and state control over the economy was extended. The first of a series of five-year plans was launched to promote rapid "socialist industrialization," and in a massive effort to strengthen the state's hold over the agricultural economy, all private farmers were herded onto **collective farms**.

The bitter campaign to collectivize the countryside aroused the antagonism of many peasants and led to a decline in food production and in some areas to mass starvation. It also further divided the Communist Party and led to a massive purge of party members at all levels who opposed Stalin's effort to achieve rapid economic growth and the socialization of Russian society. A series of brutal purge trials eliminated thousands of "Old Bolsheviks" (people who had joined the party before the 1917 Revolution) and resulted in the conviction and death of many of Stalin's chief rivals. Trotsky, driven into exile, was dispatched by Stalin's assassin in 1940. Of the delegates who attended the National Congress of the CPSU (Communist Party of the Soviet Union) in 1934, fully 70 percent had been executed by the time of the National Congress in 1939.

THE LEGACY OF STALINISM By the late 1930s, as the last of the great purge trials came to an end, the Russian Revolution had been in existence for more than two decades. It had achieved some successes. Stalin's policy of forced industrialization had led to rapid growth in the industrial sector, surpassing in many respects what had been achieved in the capitalist years prior to World War I. Between 1918 and 1937, steel production increased from 4 to 18 million tons per year, and hard coal output went from 36 to 128 million tons. New industrial cities sprang up overnight in the Urals and Siberia. The Russian people in general were probably better clothed, better fed, and better educated than they had ever been before. The cost had been enormous, however. Millions had died by bullet or starvation. Thousands, perhaps millions, languished in Stalin's concentration camps. The remainder of the population lived in a society now officially described as socialist, under the watchful eye of a man who had risen almost to the rank of a deity, the great leader of the Soviet Union, Joseph Stalin.

The impact of Stalin on Soviet society in one decade had been enormous. If Lenin had brought the party to power and nursed it through the difficult years of the civil war, it was Stalin, above all, who had mapped out the path to economic modernization and socialist transformation. To many foreign critics of the regime, the Stalinist terror and autocracy were an inevitable consequence of the concept of the vanguard party and the centralized state built by Lenin. Others traced Stalinism back to Marx. It was he, after all, who had formulated the idea of the dictatorship of the proletariat, which now provided ideological justification for the Stalinist autocracy. Still others found the ultimate cause in Russian political culture, which had been characterized by autocracy since the emergence of Russian society from Mongol control in the fifteenth century.

Was Stalinism an inevitable outcome of Marxist-Leninist doctrine and practice? Or as the last Soviet leader Mikhail Gorbachev later claimed, were Stalin's crimes "alien to the nature of socialism" and a departure from the course charted by Lenin before his death? Certainly, Lenin had not envisaged a party dominated by a figure who became even larger than the organization itself and who, in the 1930s, almost destroyed the party. On the other hand, recent evidence shows that Lenin was capable of brutally suppressing perceived enemies of the revolution in a way that is reminiscent in manner, if not in scope, of Stalin's actions. In a 1922 letter to a colleague, he declared that after the NEP had served its purpose, "we shall return to the terror, and to economic terror."[7]

It is also true that the state created by Lenin provided the conditions for a single-minded leader like Stalin to rise to absolute power. The great danger that neither Marx nor Lenin had foreseen had come to pass: the party itself, the vanguard organization leading the way into the utopian future, had become corrupted.

The Search for a New Reality in the Arts

The mass destruction brought by World War I precipitated a general disillusionment with Western civilization on the part of artists and writers throughout Europe.

Avant-garde art, which had sought to discover alternative techniques to portray reality, now gained broader acceptance as Europeans began to abandon classical traditions in an attempt to come to grips with the anxieties of the new age.

New Schools of Artistic Expression

A number of the artistic styles that gained popularity during the 1920s originated during the war in neutral Switzerland, where alienated intellectuals congregated at cafés to decry the insanity of the age and exchange ideas on how to create a new and better world. Among them were the **Dadaists**, who sought to destroy the past with a vengeance, proclaiming their right to complete freedom of expression in art.

A flagrant example of Dada's revolutionary approach to art was the decision by French artist Marcel Duchamp (1887–1968) to enter a porcelain urinal in a 1917 art exhibit in New York City. By signing it and giving it a title, Duchamp proclaimed that he had transformed the urinal into a work of art. Duchamp's Ready-Mades (as such art would henceforth be labeled) declared that whatever the artist proclaimed to be art was art. Duchamp's liberating concept served to open the floodgates of the art world, obliging the entire twentieth century to swim in this free-flowing, exuberant, exploratory, and often frightening torrent.

PROBING THE SUBCONSCIOUS While Dadaism flourished in Germany during the Weimar era, a school of **Surrealism** was established in Paris to liberate the total human experience from the restraints of the rational world. By using the subconscious, Surrealists hoped to resurrect the whole personality and reveal a submerged and illusive reality. Normally unrelated objects and people were juxtaposed in dreamlike and frequently violent paintings that were intended to shock the viewer into approaching reality from a totally fresh perspective. Most famous of the Surrealists was the Spaniard Salvador Dalí (1904–1989), who subverted the sense of reality in his painting by using near-photographic detail in presenting a fantastic and irrational world.

Yet another modernist movement born on the eve of World War I was **Abstract**, or Nonobjective, painting. As one of its founders, Swiss artist Paul Klee (1879–1940), observed, "the more fearful this world becomes, . . . the more art becomes abstract."[8] Two of the movement's principal founders, Wassily Kandinsky (1866–1944) and Piet Mondrian (1872–1944), were followers of Theosophy, a religion that promised the triumph of the spirit in a new millennium. Since they viewed matter as an obstacle to salvation, the art of the new age would totally abandon all reference to the material world. Only abstraction, in the form of colorful forms and geometric shapes floating in space, could express the bliss and spiritual beauty of this terrestrial paradise.

A MUSICAL REVOLUTION Just as artists began to experiment with revolutionary ways to represent reality in painting, musicians searched for new revolutionary sounds. Austrian composer Arnold Schoenberg (1874–1951) rejected the traditional tonal system based on the harmonic triad that had dominated Western music since the Renaissance. To free the Western ear from traditional harmonic progression, Schoenberg substituted a radically new "atonal" system in which each piece established its

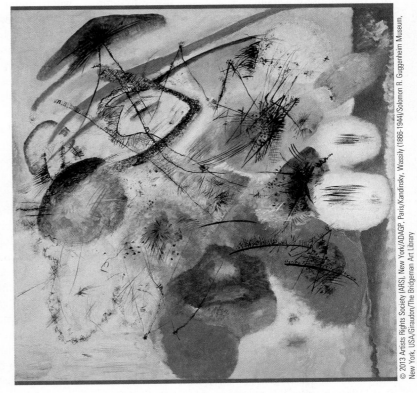

Black Lines No. 189, 1913 (oil on canvas), Wassily Kandinsky. Abstract painting was a renunciation of the material world and a glorification of the spiritual realm. Deeming it no longer necessary to represent objects and people, artists chose to express their emotions solely through color and abstract form. In this painting by Kandinsky, we rejoice in the springlike swirling splashes of color of the artist's abstract world.

own individual set of relationships and structure. In 1923, he devised a twelve-tone system in which he placed the twelve pitches of the chromatic scale found on the piano in a set sequence for a musical composition. The ordering of these twelve tones was to be repeated throughout the piece, for all instrumental parts, constituting its melody and harmony. Even today, such atonal music seems inaccessible and incomprehensible to the uninitiated. Yet Schoenberg, perhaps more than any other modern composer, influenced the development of twentieth-century music.

MODERNISM IN ARCHITECTURE Other fields of artistic creativity, including sculpture, ballet, and architecture, also reflected these new directions. In Germany, a group of imaginative architects called the Bauhaus School created what is widely known as the international school, which soon became the dominant school of modern architecture. Led by the famous German architect Ludwig Mies van der Rohe (1881–1969), the internationalists promoted a new functional and unadorned style (Mies was widely known for observing that "less is more") characterized by high-rise towers of steel and glass that were reproduced endlessly all around the world during the second half of the century.

For many postwar architects, the past was the enemy of the future. In 1925, the famous French architect Le Corbusier (1877–1965) advocated razing much of the old city of Paris, to be replaced by modern towers of glass. In his plan, which called for neat apartment complexes separated by immaculate areas of grass, there was no room for people, pets, or nature. Fortunately, the plan was rejected by municipal authorities.

Culture for the Masses

During the postwar era, writers followed artists and architects in rejecting traditional forms in order to explore the subconscious. In his novel *Ulysses*, published in 1922, Irish author James Joyce (1882–1941) invented the "stream of consciousness" technique to portray the lives of ordinary people through the use of inner monologue. Joyce's technique exerted a powerful influence on literature for the remainder of the century. Some American writers, such as Ernest Hemingway (1899–1961), Theodore Dreiser (1871–1945), and Sinclair Lewis (1885–1951), reflected the rising influence of mass journalism in a new style designed to "tell it like it is." Such writers sought to report the "whole truth" in an effort to attain the authenticity of modern photography.

For much of the Western world, however, the best way to find (or escape) reality was through mass entertainment. The 1930s represented the heyday of the Hollywood studio system, which in the single year of 1937 turned out nearly six hundred feature films. Supplementing the movies were cheap paperbacks and radio, which brought sports, soap operas, and popular music to the mass of the population. The radio was a great social leveler, speaking to all classes with the same voice. Such new technological wonders offered diversion even to the poor while helping to define the twentieth century as the era of the common people.

CONCLUSION

WORLD WAR I SHATTERED the image of a progressive and rational society in early-twentieth-century Europe. The widespread destruction and the deaths of millions of people undermined the Enlightenment belief in human progress. New propaganda techniques had manipulated entire populations into sustaining their involvement in a meaningless slaughter.

Who was responsible for the carnage? To the victorious Allied leaders, it was their defeated former adversaries, on whom they imposed harsh terms at the Paris Peace Conference at the end of the war. In later years, some historians placed the primary blame on Russia for its decision to order full military mobilization in response to events taking place in the Balkans.

Perhaps, however, the real culprit was the system itself. The system of nation-states that began to emerge in

Europe in the second half of the nineteenth century had led not to cooperation, as many liberals had hoped, but to competition. Governments that exercised restraint to avoid war wound up being publicly humiliated; those that went to the brink of war to maintain their national interests were often praised for having preserved national honor. As British historian John Keegan has noted, for European statesmen in the early twentieth century, "the fear of not meeting a challenge was greater than the fear of war." In either case, by 1914, the major European states had come to believe that their allies were important and that their security depended on supporting those allies, even when they took foolish risks.

To make matters worse, the very industrial and technological innovations that had brought the prospect of increased material prosperity for millions had also led to the manufacture of new weapons of mass destruction such as the long-range artillery, tanks, poison gas, and airplanes that would make war a more terrible prospect for those involved, whether military or civilian. If war did come, it would be highly destructive.

The victorious world leaders who gathered at Versailles hoped to forge a peace settlement that would say good-bye to all that. But as it turned out, the turmoil wrought by World War I seemed to open the door to even greater insecurity. Revolutions in Russia and the Middle East dismembered old empires and created new states that gave rise to unexpected problems. Expectations that Europe and the world would return to normalcy were soon dashed by the failure to achieve a lasting peace, economic collapse, and the rise of authoritarian governments that not only restricted individual freedoms but sought even greater control over the lives of their subjects, manipulating and guiding their people to achieve the goals of their totalitarian regimes. In the next chapter, we will examine these events in greater detail.

TIMELINE

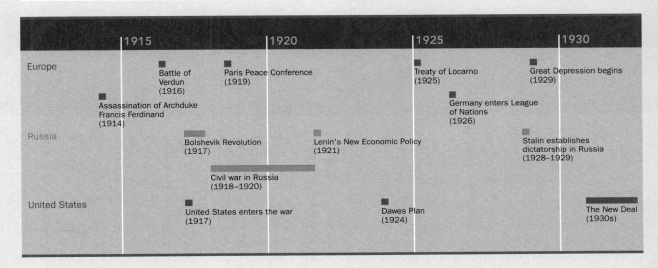

CHAPTER NOTES

1. Cited in Barbara Tuchman, *The Guns of August* (New York, 1962), p. 146.
2. Arnold Toynbee, *Surviving the Future* (New York, 1971), pp. 106–107.
3. Harold Nicolson, *Peacemaking, 1919* (Boston and New York, 1933), pp. 31–32.
4. Margaret MacMillan, *Paris 1919: Six Months That Changed the World* (New York, 2001), p. 103.
5. Dmitri Volkogonov, *Lenin: A New Biography* (New York, 1994), p. 22.
6. Quoted in Robert Paxton, *Europe in the Twentieth Century*, 2nd ed. (San Diego, 1985), p. 237.
7. Volkogonov, *Lenin*, p. 3.
8. Quoted in Nikos Stangos, *Concepts of Modern Art: From Fauvism to Postmodernism*, 3rd ed. (London, 1994), p. 44.

Nationalism, Revolution, and Dictatorship: Asia, the Middle East, and Latin America from 1919 to 1939

Nguyen the Patriot at Tours

The Tours Congress, Ho Chi Minh (1890–1969) from 'L'Humanite', December 1920 (b/w photo), French Photographer, (20th century)/Bibliotheque Nationale, Paris, France/Archives Charmet/The Bridgeman Art Library

ON CHRISTMAS DAY IN 1920, a young Asian man in an ill-fitting rented suit stood up nervously to address the several hundred delegates of the French Socialist Party (FSP) who had gathered in the French city of Tours. The speaker called himself Nguyen Ai Quoc, or Nguyen the Patriot, and was a Vietnamese subject of the French colony of Indochina.

The delegates had assembled to decide whether the FSP would follow the path of violent revolution recommended by the new Bolshevik regime in Soviet Russia. Among those voting in favor of the proposal was Nguyen Ai Quoc, who had decided that only the path of Karl Marx and Lenin could lead to national independence for his compatriots. Later he would become the founder of the Vietnamese Communist Party and become known to the world by the pseudonym Ho Chi Minh.

The meeting in Tours was held at a time when resistance to colonial rule was on the rise, and the decision that Nguyen Ai Quoc faced of whether to opt for violent revolution was one that would be faced by colonial peoples throughout the world. As Europeans devastated their own civilization on the battlefields of Europe, the subject peoples of their vast colonial empires were quick to recognize the opportunity to shake free of foreign domination. In those areas, movements for national independence began to take shape. Some were inspired by the nationalist and liberal movements of the West, while others looked to the new Marxist model provided by the victory of the Communists in Soviet Russia, who soon worked to spread their revolutionary vision to African and Asian societies. In the

Middle East, World War I ended the rule of the Ottoman Empire and led to the creation of new states, many of which were placed under Western domination.

The societies of Latin America were no longer under direct colonial rule and thus, for the most part, did not face the same types of challenges as their counterparts in Asia and Africa. Nevertheless, in some cases the economies of the Latin American countries were virtually controlled by foreign interests. A similar situation prevailed in China and Japan, which had managed with some difficulty to retain a degree of political independence, despite severe pressure from the West. But the political flux and economic disruption that characterized much of the world during the two decades following World War I had affected Latin America, China, and Japan as well, leading many in these regions to heed the siren call of fascist dictatorship or social revolution. For all the peoples of Asia, the Middle East, and Latin America, the end of the Great War had not created a world safe for democracy, as Woodrow Wilson had hoped, but an age of great peril and uncertainty. ◆

CRITICAL THINKING

Q How did the societies discussed in this chapter deal with the political, economic, and social challenges that they faced after World War I, and how did these challenges differ from one region to another?

The Spread of Nationalism in Asia and Africa

Although the West had emerged from World War I relatively intact, its political and social foundations and its self-confidence had been severely undermined by the experience. Within Europe, doubts about the future viability of Western civilization were widespread, especially among the intellectual elite. These doubts were quick to reach the attention of perceptive observers elsewhere and contributed to a rising tide of unrest against Western political domination throughout the colonial and semi-colonial world. That unrest took a variety of forms but was most notably displayed in increasing worker activism, rural protest, and a rising sense of national fervor among anticolonialist intellectuals. In Japan and Latin America, where independent states sought to evade the Western onslaught, the discontent fostered by the war and later by the Great Depression led to a loss of confidence in democratic institutions and the rise of political dictatorships.

As we have seen (see Chapter 1), nationalism refers to a state of mind rising out of an awareness of being part of a community that possesses common institutions, traditions, language, and customs. Unfortunately, even today few nations in the world meet such criteria. Most modern states contain a variety of ethnic, religious, and linguistic communities, each with its own sense of cultural and national identity. How does nationalism differ from tribal, religious, linguistic, or other forms of affiliation? Should every group that resists assimilation into a larger cultural unity be called nationalist?

Such questions complicate the study of nationalism and make agreement on a definition elusive. They create a particular dilemma in discussing Asia and Africa, where most societies are deeply divided by ethnic, linguistic, and religious differences and the very concept of nationalism is a foreign phenomenon imported from the West. Prior to the colonial era, most traditional societies in such regions were unified on the basis of religious beliefs, community loyalties, or devotion to hereditary monarchies. Individuals in some countries identified themselves as members of a particular national group, while others viewed themselves as subjects of a king, members of a caste, or adherents of a particular religion.

The advent of European colonialism brought the consciousness of modern nationhood to many societies outside the West. The creation of colonies with defined borders and a powerful central government weakened local ties and reoriented individuals' sense of political identity. The introduction of Western ideas of citizenship and representative government engendered a new sense of participation in the affairs of government. At the same time, the appearance of a new elite class based not on hereditary privilege or religious sanction but on alleged racial or cultural superiority aroused a shared sense of resentment among the subject peoples who felt a common commitment to the creation of an independent society. By the first quarter of the twentieth century, political movements dedicated to the overthrow of colonial rule had arisen throughout much of the non-Western world.

Nationalist movements in Asia and Africa, then, were a product of colonialism and, in a sense, a reaction to it. But a sense of nationhood does not emerge full-blown in a society. It begins among a few members of the educated elite (most commonly among articulate professionals such as lawyers, teachers, journalists, and doctors) and spreads gradually to the mass of the population. Only then has a true sense of nationhood been created.

Traditional Resistance: A Precursor to Nationalism

If we view the concept of nationalism as a process by which people in a given society gradually become aware of themselves as members of a particular nation, with its own culture and aspirations, then it is reasonable to seek the beginnings of modern nationalism in Asia and Africa in the initial resistance by the indigenous peoples to the colonial conquest itself. Although essentially motivated by the desire to defend traditional institutions, such movements reflected an early awareness of nationhood in that they sought to protect the homeland from the invader. Thus, traditional resistance to colonial conquest may logically be viewed as the first stage in the development of modern nationalism.

Such resistance took various forms. For the most part, it was led by the existing ruling class. In the Ashanti kingdom in West Africa and in Burma and Vietnam in Southeast Asia, the resistance to Western domination was initially directed by the imperial courts. In some cases, however, traditionalist elements continued to oppose foreign conquest even after resistance had collapsed at the center. In Japan, conservative elites opposed the decision of the Tokugawa shogunate in Tokyo to accommodate the Western presence and launched an abortive movement to defeat the foreigners and restore Japan to its previous policy of isolation (see Chapter 3). In India, Tipu Sultan resisted the British in the Deccan plateau region of central India after the collapse of the Mughal dynasty. Similarly, after the decrepit monarchy in Vietnam had bowed to French pressure and agreed to the concession of territory in the south and the establishment of a French protectorate over the remainder of the country, a number of civilian and military officials set up an organization called Can Vuong (literally, "Save the King") and continued their resistance without imperial sanction.

THE SEPOY REBELLION Sometimes traditional resistance had a religious basis, as in the Sudan, where a revolt against the growing British presence in the Nile River valley had strong Islamic overtones, although it was initially provoked by Turkish misrule in Egypt. More significant was the famous Sepoy Rebellion of 1857 in India. The **sepoys** (derived from the Turkish word for "horseman" or "soldier") were Indian troops hired by the East India Company to protect British interests in the region. Unrest within Indian units of the colonial army had been common since early in the century, when it had been sparked by economic issues, religious sensitivities, or nascent anticolonial sentiment. Such attitudes intensified in the mid-1850s when the British instituted a new policy of shipping Indian troops abroad—a practice that exposed Hindus to pollution by foreign cultures. In 1857, tension erupted when the British adopted the new Enfield rifle for use by sepoy infantrymen. The new weapon was a muzzleloader that used paper cartridges covered with animal fat and lard; the cartridge had to be bitten off, but doing so violated strictures against high-caste Hindus' eating animal products and Muslim prohibitions against eating pork. Protests among sepoy units in northern India turned into a full-scale rebellion, supported by uprisings in rural districts in various parts of the country. But the revolt lacked clear goals, and rivalries between Hindus and Muslims and discord among leaders within each community prevented coordination of operations. Although Indian troops often fought bravely and outnumbered the British by 240,000 to 40,000, they were poorly organized, and the British forces (supplemented in many cases by sepoy troops) suppressed the rebellion.

Still, the revolt frightened the British and led to a number of major reforms. The proportion of Indian troops in the army was reduced, and precedence was given to ethnic groups likely to be loyal to the British, such as the **Sikhs** of Punjab and the Gurkhas, an upland people from Nepal in the Himalaya Mountains. To avoid religious conflicts, ethnic groups were spread throughout the service rather than assigned to special units. The British also decided to suppress the final remnants of the hapless Mughal dynasty, which had supported the rebellion, and place the governance of India directly under the British Crown.

As noted earlier, such forms of resistance cannot properly be called nationalist because they were essentially attempts to protect or restore traditional society and its institutions and were not motivated by the desire to create a nation in the modern sense of the word. In any event, such movements rarely met with success. Peasants armed with pikes and spears were no match for Western armies possessing the most terrifying weapons then known to human society, including the Gatling gun, the first rapid-fire weapon and the precursor of the modern machine gun.

Modern Nationalism

The first stage of resistance to the West in Asia and Africa must have confirmed many Westerners' conviction that colonial peoples lacked both the strength and the know-how to create modern states and govern their own destinies.

In fact, however, the process was just beginning. The next phase began to take shape at the beginning of the twentieth century and was the product of the convergence of several factors. The most vocal sources of anticolonialist sentiment were found in a new class of Westernized intellectuals in the urban centers created by colonial rule. In many cases, this new urban middle class, composed of merchants, petty functionaries, clerks, students, and professionals, had been educated in Western-style schools. A few had spent time in the West. In either case, they were the first generation of Asians and Africans to possess more than a rudimentary understanding of the institutions and values of the modern West.

THE PARADOX OF NATIONALISM The results were paradoxical. On the one hand, this new class admired Western culture and sometimes harbored a deep sense of contempt for traditional ways (see the box on p. 97). On the other hand, many strongly resented the gap between ideal and reality, theory and practice, in colonial policy. Although Western political thought exalted democracy, equality, and individual freedom, these values were generally not applied in the colonies. Democratic institutions were primitive or nonexistent, and colonial subjects usually had access to only the most menial positions in the colonial bureaucracy.

Equally important, the economic prosperity of the West was only imperfectly reflected in the colonies. Normally, middle-class Asians did not suffer in the same manner as impoverished peasants or menial workers in coal mines or on sugar or rubber plantations, but they, too, had complaints. They usually qualified only for menial jobs in the government or business. Even when employed, their salaries were normally lower than those of Europeans in similar occupations. The superiority of

The Dilemma of the Intellectual

Sutan Sjahrir (1909–1966) was a prominent leader of the Indonesian nationalist movement who briefly served as prime minister of the Republic of Indonesia in the 1950s. Like many Western-educated Asian intellectuals, he was tortured by the realization that by education and outlook he was closer to his colonial masters—in his case, the Dutch—than to his own people. He wrote the following passage in a letter to his wife in 1935 and later included it in his book *Out of Exile*.

Sutan Sjahrir, *Out of Exile*

Am I perhaps estranged from my people? . . . Why are the things that contain beauty for them and arouse their gentler emotions only senseless and displeasing for me? In reality, the spiritual gap between my people and me is certainly no greater than that between an intellectual in Holland . . . and the undeveloped people of Holland. . . . The difference is rather . . . that the intellectual in Holland does not feel this gap because there is a portion—even a fairly large portion—of his own people on approximately the same intellectual level as himself. . . .

This is what we lack here. Not only is the number of intellectuals in this country smaller in proportion to the total population—in fact, very much smaller—but in addition, the few who are here do not constitute any single entity in spiritual outlook, or in any spiritual life or single culture whatsoever. . . . It is for them so much more difficult than for the intellectuals in Holland. In Holland they build—both consciously and unconsciously—on what is already there. . . . Even if they oppose it, they do so as a method of application or as a starting point.

In our country this is not the case. Here there has been no spiritual or cultural life, and no intellectual progress for centuries. There are the much-praised Eastern art forms but what are these except bare rudiments from a feudal culture that cannot possibly provide a dynamic fulcrum for people of the twentieth century? . . . Our spiritual needs are needs of the twentieth century; our problems and our views are of the twentieth century. Our inclination is no longer toward the mystical, but toward reality, clarity, and objectivity. . . .

We intellectuals here are much closer to Europe or America than we are to the Borobudur or Mahabharata or to the primitive Islamic culture of Java and Sumatra. . . .

So, it seems, the problem stands in principle. It is seldom put forth by us in this light, and instead most of us search unconsciously for a synthesis that will leave us internally tranquil. We want to have both Western science and Eastern philosophy, the Eastern "spirit," in the culture. But what is this Eastern spirit? It is, they say, the sense of the higher, of spirituality, of the eternal and religious, as opposed to the materialism of the West. I have heard this countless times, but it has never convinced me.

 Why did Sutan Sjahrir feel estranged from his own culture? What was his answer to the challenges faced by his country in coming to terms with the modern world?

SOURCE: From *The World of Southeast Asia: Selected Historical Readings*, Harry J. Benda and John A. Larkin, eds. Copyright © 1967 by Harper & Row, Publishers.

---

the Europeans was expressed in a variety of ways, including "whites only" clubs and the use of the familiar form of the language (normally used by adults to children) when addressing members of the local population.

Out of this mixture of hopes and resentments emerged the first stirrings of modern nationalism in Asia and Africa. During the first quarter of the twentieth century, in colonial and semicolonial societies across the entire arc of Asia from the Suez Canal to the shores of the Pacific Ocean, educated indigenous peoples began to organize political parties and movements seeking reforms or the end of foreign rule and the restoration of independence.

At first, many of the leaders of these movements did not focus clearly on the idea of nationhood but tried to

defend the economic interests or religious beliefs of the indigenous population. In Burma, for example, the first expression of modern nationalism came from students at the University of Rangoon, who formed an organization to protest against official persecution of the Buddhist religion and British failure to observe local customs in Buddhist temples, such not removing their footwear. Calling themselves Thakin (a polite term in the Burmese language meaning "lord" or "master," thereby emphasizing their demand for the right to rule themselves), the students began by protesting against British arrogance and lack of respect for local religious traditions. Eventually, however, they began to focus specifically on the issue of national independence.

A similar movement arose in the Dutch East Indies, where the first quasi-political organization dedicated to the creation of a modern Indonesia, the Sarekat Islam (Islamic Association), began as a self-help society among Muslim merchants to fight against domination of the local economy by Chinese interests. Eventually, activist elements began to realize that the source of the problem was not the Chinese merchants but the colonial presence, and in the 1920s, Sarekat Islam was transformed into a new organization—the Nationalist Party of Indonesia (PNI)—that focused on the issue of national independence. Like the Thakins in Burma, this party would eventually lead the country to independence after World War II.

INDEPENDENCE OR MODERNIZATION? THE NATIONALIST QUANDARY Building a new nation, however, requires more than a shared sense of grievances against the foreign invader. By what means was independence to be achieved? Should independence or modernization be the first priority? What kind of political and economic system should be adopted once colonial rule had been overthrown? What national or cultural concept should be adopted as the symbol of the new nation, and which institutions and values should be preserved from the past?

Questions such as these triggered lively and sometimes acrimonious debates among patriotic elements throughout the colonial world. If national independence was the desired end, how could it be achieved? Could the Westerners be persuaded to leave by nonviolent measures, or would force be required? If the Western presence could be beneficial by introducing much-needed reforms in traditional societies, then a gradualist approach made sense. On the other hand, if the colonial regime was viewed as an impediment to social and political change, then the first priority, in the minds of many, was to bring it to an end.

Another problem was how to adopt modern Western ideas and institutions while preserving the essential values that defined the indigenous culture. One of the reasons for using traditional values was to provide ideological symbols that the common people could understand. If the desired end was national independence, then the new political parties needed to enlist the mass of the population in the common struggle. But how could peasants, plantation workers, fishermen, and shepherds be made to understand complicated and unfamiliar concepts like

democracy, industrialization, and nationhood? The problem was often one of communication, for most urban intellectuals had little in common with the teeming population in the countryside. As the Indonesian intellectual Sutan Sjahrir lamented, many Westernized intellectuals had more in common with their colonial rulers than with the local population in the rural villages (see the box on p. 97).

Gandhi and the Indian National Congress

Nowhere in the colonial world were these issues debated more vigorously than in India. Before the Sepoy Rebellion, Indian consciousness had focused primarily on the question of religious identity. But in the latter half of the nineteenth century, a stronger sense of national consciousness began to arise, provoked by the conservative policies and racial arrogance of the British colonial authorities.

The first Indian nationalists were almost invariably upper class and educated. Many of them were from urban areas such as Bombay (now Mumbai), Madras (Chennai), and Calcutta (Kolkata). Some were trained in law and were members of the civil service. At first, many tended to prefer reform to revolution and believed that India needed modernization before it could handle the problems of independence. An exponent of this view was Gopal Gokhale (1866–1915), a moderate nationalist who hoped that he could convince the British to bring about needed reforms in Indian society. Gokhale and other like-minded reformists did have some effect. In the 1880s, the government launched a series of reforms introducing a measure of self-government for the first time. All too often, however, such efforts were sabotaged by local British officials.

British India Between the Wars

(© Cengage Learning)

THE INDIAN NATIONAL CONGRESS The slow pace of reform convinced many Indian nationalists that relying on British benevolence was futile. In 1885, a small group of Indians met in Bombay to form the Indian National Congress (INC). They hoped to speak for all India, but most were high-caste English-trained Hindus. Like their reformist predecessors, members of the INC did not demand immediate independence and accepted the need for reforms to end traditional abuses like child marriage and *sati* (see Chapter 2). At the same time, they called for an Indian share in the governing process and more spending on economic development and less on military campaigns along the frontier.

The British responded with a few concessions, such as accepting the principle of elective Indian participation on government councils, but in general, change was glacially slow. As impatient members of the INC became disillusioned, radical leaders such as Balwantrao Tilak (1856–1920) openly criticized the British while defending traditional customs like child marriage to solicit support from conservative elements within the local population. Tilak's activities split the INC between moderates and radicals, and he and his followers formed the New Party, which called for the use of terrorism and violence to achieve national independence. Tilak was eventually convicted of sedition.

The INC also had difficulty reconciling religious differences within its ranks. The stated goal of the INC was to seek self-determination for all Indians regardless of class or religious affiliation, but many of its leaders were Hindu and inevitably reflected Hindu concerns. By the first decade of the twentieth century, Muslims began to call for the creation of a separate Muslim League to represent the interests of the millions of Muslims in Indian society.

INDIA'S "GREAT SOUL," MOHANDAS GANDHI
In 1915, the return of a young Hindu lawyer from South Africa transformed the movement and galvanized India's struggle for independence and identity. Mohandas Gandhi was born in 1869 in Gujarat, in western India, the son of a government minister. In the late nineteenth century, he studied in London and became a lawyer. In 1893, he went to South Africa to work in a law firm serving Indian émigrés working as laborers there. He soon became aware of the racial prejudice and exploitation experienced by Indians living in the territory and tried to organize them to protest their living conditions.

NONVIOLENT RESISTANCE
On his return to India, Gandhi immediately became active in the independence movement. Using his experience in South Africa, he set up a movement based on nonviolent resistance (the Indian term was **satyagraha**, "hold fast to the truth") to try to force the British to improve the lot of the poor and grant independence to India. Gandhi was particularly concerned about the plight of the millions of "untouchables" (the lowest social class in traditional India), whom he called **harijans**, or "children of God." When the British attempted to suppress dissent, he called on his followers to refuse to obey British regulations. He began to manufacture his own clothes (dressing in a simple *dhoti* made of coarse homespun cotton) and adopted the spinning wheel

as a symbol of Indian resistance to imports of British textiles.

Gandhi, now increasingly known as India's "Great Soul" (*Mahatma*), organized mass protests to achieve his aims, but in 1919, they got out of hand and led to British reprisals. British troops killed hundreds of unarmed protesters in the enclosed square in the city of Amritsar in northwestern India. When the protests spread, Gandhi was horrified at the violence and briefly retreated from active politics. Nevertheless, he was arrested for his role in the protests and spent several years in prison.

Gandhi combined his anticolonial activities with an appeal to the spiritual instincts of all Indians (see the Film & History feature on p. 100). Though born and raised a Hindu, he possessed a universalist approach to the idea of God that transcended individual religion, although it was shaped by the historical themes of Hindu religious belief. At a speech given in London in September 1931, he expressed his view of the nature of God as "an indefinable mysterious power that pervades everything . . . , an unseen power which makes itself felt and yet defies all proof."

In 1921, the British passed the Government of India Act to expand the role of Indians in the governing process and transform the heretofore advisory Legislative Council into a bicameral parliament, two-thirds of whose members would be elected. Similar bodies were created at the provincial level. In a stroke, 5 million Indians were enfranchised. But such reforms were no longer enough for many members of the INC, who wanted to follow the new INC leader, Motilal Nehru, in pushing aggressively for full independence. The British exacerbated the situation by increasing the salt tax and prohibiting the Indian people from manufacturing or harvesting their own salt. In 1930, Gandhi, now released from prison, resumed his policy of **civil disobedience** by openly joining several dozen supporters in a 240-mile walk to the sea, where he picked up a lump of salt and urged Indians to ignore the law. Gandhi and many other members of the INC were arrested.

NEW LEADERS, NEW PROBLEMS
In the 1930s, a new figure entered the movement in the person of Jawaharlal Nehru (1889–1964), son of the INC leader Motilal Nehru. Educated in the law in Great Britain and a *brahmin* (member of the highest social class) by birth, Nehru personified the new Anglo-Indian politician: secular, rational, upper class, and intellectual. In fact, he appeared to be everything that Gandhi was not. With his emergence, the independence movement embarked on dual paths: religious and secular, Indian and Western, traditional and modern. The dichotomous character of the INC leadership may well have strengthened the movement by bringing together the two primary impulses behind the desire for

Gandhi (1982)

To many of his contemporaries, Mohandas Gandhi—the Mahatma, or "great soul"—was the conscience of India. Son of a senior Indian official from the state of Gujarat, he trained as a lawyer at University College in London. Gandhi first dealt with racial discrimination when he sought to provide legal assistance to Indian laborers living under the apartheid regime in South Africa. On his return to India in 1915, he rapidly emerged as a fierce critic of British colonial rule over his country. His message of *satyagraha*—embodying the idea of a steadfast but nonviolent resistance to the injustice and inhumanity inherent in the colonial enterprise—inspired millions of his compatriots in their long struggle for national independence. It also earned the admiration and praise of sympathetic observers around the world. His death by assassination at the hands of a Hindu fanatic in 1948 shocked the world.

Jawaharlal Nehru (Roshan Seth), Mahatma Gandhi (Ben Kingsley), and Muhammad Ali Jinnah (Alyque Padamsee) confer before the partition of India into Hindu and Muslim states.

Time, however, has somewhat dimmed his message. Gandhi's vision of a future India was symbolized by the spinning wheel—he rejected the industrial age and material pursuits in favor of the simple pleasures of the traditional Indian village. Since achieving independence, however, India has followed the path of national wealth and power laid out by Gandhi's friend and colleague Jawaharlal Nehru. Gandhi's appeal for religious tolerance and mutual respect at home rapidly gave way to a bloody conflict between Hindus and Muslims that still persists today. On the global stage, his vision of world peace and brotherly love has been similarly ignored, first during the Cold War and more recently by the "clash of civilizations" between Western countries and the forces of militant Islam.

It was at least partly in an effort to revive and perpetuate the message of the Mahatma that British filmmaker Richard Attenborough directed the film *Gandhi*. Epic in its length and scope, the film seeks to present a faithful rendition of the life of its subject, from his introduction to apartheid in South Africa at the turn of the century to his tragic death after World War II. Actor Ben Kingsley, son of an Indian father and an English mother, plays the title role with intensity and conviction. The film was widely praised and earned eight Academy Awards, including one for Kingsley as Best Actor. ■

---

independence: elite nationalism and the primal force of Indian traditionalism. But it portended trouble for the nation's new leadership in defining India's future path in the contemporary world. In the meantime, Muslim discontent with Hindu dominance over the INC was increasing. In 1940, the Muslim League called for the creation of a separate Muslim state in the northwest, to be known as Pakistan ("Land of the Pure"). As communal strife between Hindus and Muslims increased, many Indians came to realize with sorrow (and some British colonialists with satisfaction) that British rule was all that stood between peace and civil war.

Nationalist Ferment in the Middle East

In the Middle East, as in Europe, World War I hastened the collapse of old empires. The Ottoman Empire, which had dominated the eastern Mediterranean since the seizure of Constantinople in 1453, had been growing steadily weaker since the end of the eighteenth century, troubled by rising governmental corruption, a decline in the effectiveness of the sultans, and the loss of considerable territory in the Balkans and southwestern Russia. In North Africa, Ottoman authority, tenuous at best, had disintegrated in the nineteenth century, enabling the French to seize Algeria and Tunisia and the British to establish a protectorate over the Nile River valley.

THE OTTOMAN EMPIRE IN TRANSITION Reformist elements in Istanbul (as Constantinople was officially renamed in 1930), to be sure, had tried to resist the decline. The first efforts had taken place in the eighteenth century, when Westernizing forces, concerned at the shrinkage of the empire, had tried to modernize the army. One energetic **sultan**, Selim III (r. 1789–1807), tried to establish a "new order" that would streamline both the civilian and military bureaucracies, but conservative elements in the emperor's private guard, alarmed at the potential loss of their power, revolted and brought the experiment to an end. Further efforts during the first half of the nineteenth century were somewhat more successful and resulted in a series of bureaucratic, military, and educational reforms. New roads were built, the power of local landlords was reduced, and an Imperial Rescript issued in 1856 granted equal rights to all subjects of the empire, whatever their religious preference. In the 1870s, a new generation of reformers seized power in Istanbul and pushed through a constitution aimed at forming a legislative assembly that would represent all the peoples in the state. But the sultan they placed on the throne, Abdulhamid (r. 1876–1909), suspended the new charter and attempted to rule by traditional authoritarian means.

THE "YOUNG TURKS" By the end of the nineteenth century, the defunct 1876 constitution had become a symbol of change for reformist elements, now grouped together under the common name **Young Turks**. In 1908, Young Turk elements forced the sultan to restore the constitution, and he was removed from power the following year.

But the Young Turks had appeared at a moment of extreme fragility for the empire. Internal rebellions, combined with Austrian annexations of Ottoman territories in the Balkans, undermined support for the new government and provoked the army to step in. With most minorities from the old empire now removed from Turkish authority, many ethnic Turks began to embrace a new concept of a Turkish state based on all residents of Turkish nationality.

The final blow to the old empire came in World War I, when the Ottoman government allied with Germany in the hope of driving the British from Egypt and restoring Ottoman rule over the Nile valley. In response, the British declared an official protectorate over Egypt and, aided by the efforts of T. E. Lawrence (Lawrence of Arabia), sought to undermine Ottoman rule in the Arabian peninsula by encouraging Arab nationalists there. In 1916, the local governor of Mecca, encouraged by the British, declared Arabia independent from Ottoman rule, while British troops, advancing from Egypt, seized Palestine. In October 1918, having suffered more than 300,000 casualties during the war, the Ottoman Empire negotiated an armistice with the Allied Powers.

During the next two years, Allied diplomats wrestled with how to deal with the remnants of the defeated Ottoman Empire. In 1916, the British and the French had reached a secret agreement to divide up the non-Turkish areas of the empire between themselves. This did not sit well with Woodrow Wilson, who opposed the outright annexation of colonial territories by the victorious Allies. Ultimately, the latter agreed to establish these territories as mandates under the new League of Nations. Mesopotamia and Palestine were assigned to the British, while Syria was given to the French. The Arabian peninsula was dealt with separately, and eventually received its independence as the kingdom of Saudi Arabia in 1932 (see "The Rise of Arab Nationalism" later in the chapter).

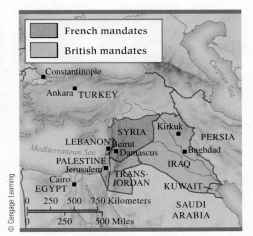

The Middle East in 1923

Other aspects of the Treaty of Sevres, signed in 1920, were even more controversial. Western portions of the Anatolian peninsula were to be occupied by the Greeks in preparation for a future plebiscite to determine the future of the area. Armenia—where the local Christian population had been brutally mistreated by the Turks—was to receive its independence. A proposal for an independent Kurdistan (the Kurds were a non-Arab Muslim people living in mountainous areas throughout the region) was left unresolved.

MUSTAFA KEMAL AND THE MODERNIZATION OF TURKEY The impending collapse of the Ottoman Empire energized key elements in Turkey under the leadership of war hero Colonel Mustafa Kemal (1881–1938), who had commanded Turkish forces in their heroic defense of the Dardanelles against a British invasion during World War I. Now he resigned from the army and convoked a national congress that called for the creation of an elected government and the preservation of the remaining territories of the old empire in a new republic of Turkey. Establishing the new capital at Ankara, Kemal's forces drove the Greeks from the Anatolian peninsula and seized Kurdish lands to the east, thus bringing an end to the dream of an independent Kurdistan. The Allies agreed to sign a new Treaty of Lausanne, incorporating these changes. Armenian leaders, still bitter at their mistreatment at the hands of the Turks, decided to join the Soviet Union. In 1923, the last of the Ottoman sultans fled the country, which was now declared a Turkish republic. The Ottoman Empire had finally come to an end.

During the next few years, President Mustafa Kemal (now popularly known as Atatürk, or "Father Turk") attempted to transform Turkey into a modern secular republic. The trappings of a democratic system were put in place, centered on the elected Grand National Assembly, but the president was relatively intolerant of opposition and harshly suppressed critics of his rule. Turkish nationalism was emphasized, and the Turkish language, now written in the Roman alphabet, was shorn of many of its Arabic elements. Popular education was emphasized, old aristocratic titles like *pasha* and *bey* were abolished, and all Turkish citizens were given family names in the European style.

Atatürk also took steps to modernize the economy, overseeing the establishment of a light industrial sector producing textiles, glass, paper, and cement and instituting a

© William J. Duiker

Hagia Sophia. Nothing more vividly symbolizes the secular character of Kemal Atatürk's Turkish republic than Istanbul's most historic building—the Hagia Sophia. Built as a Christian church at the order of the Byzantine emperor Justinian in the sixth century, Hagia Sophia ("Holy Wisdom" in Greek), became a mosque after the seizure of the city by the Ottoman Turks in 1453. In the 1930s, however, it was transformed into a museum. Today the ecumenical character of the building is readily visible to the eye of the visitor, as Christian mosaics vie with massive gold and black placards in the Arabic script listing the names of Allah, Muhammad, and the early Muslim caliphs.

five-year plan on the Soviet model to provide for state direction over the economy. Atatürk was no admirer of Soviet communism, however, and the Turkish economy can be better described as a form of state capitalism. He also encouraged the modernization of the agricultural sector through the establishment of training institutions and model farms, but such reforms had relatively little effect on the nation's predominantly conservative rural population.

Perhaps the most significant aspect of Atatürk's reform program was his attempt to limit the power of the Islamic religion and transform Turkey into a secular state. The caliphate (according to which the Ottoman sultan was recognized as the temporal leader of the global Islamic community) was formally abolished in 1924, and the *Shari'a* (Islamic law) was replaced by a revised version of the Swiss law code (see the box on p. 104). The fez (the brimless cap worn by Turkish Muslims) was abolished as a form of headdress, and women were discouraged from wearing the traditional Islamic veil. Women received the right to vote in 1934 and were legally guaranteed equal rights with men in all aspects of marriage and inheritance. Education and the professions were now open to both men and women, and some women even began to take part in politics. All citizens were given the right to convert to another religion at will.

The legacy of Mustafa Kemal Atatürk was enormous. Although not all of his reforms were widely accepted in practice, especially by devout Muslims, most of the changes that he introduced were retained after his death in 1938. In virtually every respect, the Turkish republic was the product of his determined efforts to create a modern nation, a Turkish version of the "revolution from above" in Meiji Japan.

MODERNIZATION IN IRAN   In the meantime, a similar process was under way in Persia. Under the Qajar dynasty (1794–1925), the country had not been very successful in resisting Russian advances in the Caucasus or a growing European presence farther south. To secure themselves from foreign influence, the Qajars moved the capital from Tabriz to Tehran, in a mountainous area just south of the Caspian Sea. During the mid-nineteenth century, one modernizing shah attempted to introduce political and economic reforms but faced resistance from tribal and religious forces. The majority of Persians were **Shi'ites**, one of the two main branches of Islam (as opposed to **Sunni** Muslims, who predominated in most of the Muslim world). Both Sunnis and Shi'ites adhered to the fundamental principles of Islam, including the "**Five Pillars of Islam**": belief in Allah and Muhammad

as his prophet; prayer five times a day and public prayer on Friday at midday to worship Allah; observation of the holy month of Ramadan, including fasting from dawn to sunset; making a pilgrimage, if possible, to Mecca at least once in one's lifetime; and giving alms (*zakat*) to the poor and unfortunate. The Shi'ites, however, had broken with the mainstream Sunni form of Islam over leadership issues not long after the death of Muhammad and adopted a more strict interpretation of the Muslim faith.

Eventually, the growing foreign presence led to the rise of an indigenous nationalist movement. Its efforts were largely directed against Russian advances in the northwest and growing European influence in the small modern industrial sector, the profits from which left the country or disappeared into the hands of the dynasty's ruling elite. Supported actively by Shi'ite religious leaders, opposition to the regime rose steadily among both peasants and merchants in the cities, and in 1906, popular pressures forced the reigning shah to grant a constitution on the Western model.

As in the Ottoman Empire and Qing China, however, the modernizers had moved before their power base was secure. With the support of the Russians and the British, the shah was able to retain control, and the two foreign powers began to divide the country into separate spheres of influence. One reason for the growing foreign presence in Persia was the discovery of oil reserves in the southern part of the country in 1908. Within a few years, oil exports increased rapidly, with the bulk of the profits going into the pockets of British investors.

In 1921, a Persian army officer by the name of Reza Khan (1878–1944) led a mutiny that seized power in Tehran. The new ruler had originally intended to establish a republic, but resistance from traditional forces impeded his efforts, and in 1925, the new Pahlavi dynasty, with Reza Khan as shah, replaced the now defunct Qajar dynasty. During the next few years, Reza Khan attempted to follow the example of Mustafa Kemal Atatürk in Turkey, introducing a number of reforms to strengthen the central government, modernize the civilian and military bureaucracy, and establish a modern economic infrastructure.

Unlike Atatürk, Reza Khan did not attempt to destroy the power of Islamic beliefs, but he did encourage the establishment of a Western-style educational system and forbade women to wear the veil in public. To strengthen the sense of nationalism and reduce the power of Islam, he restored the country's ancient name, Iran, in 1935 and attempted to popularize the symbols and beliefs of pre-Islamic times. Like his Qajar predecessors, however, Reza

OPPOSING ✕ VIEWPOINTS

Islam in the Modern World: Two Views

As part of his plan to transform Turkey into a modern society, Mustafa Kemal Atatürk sought to free his country from what he considered to be outdated practices imposed by traditional beliefs. The first selection is from a speech in which he proposed bringing an end to the caliphate, which had been in the hands of Ottoman sultans since the formation of the empire. But not all Muslims wished to move in the direction of a more secular society. Mohammed Iqbal, a well-known Muslim poet in colonial India, was a prominent advocate of the creation of a separate state for Muslims in South Asia. The second selection is from an address he presented to the All-India Muslim League in December 1930, explaining the rationale for his proposal.

Atatürk, Speech to the Assembly (October 1924)

The sovereign entitled Caliph was to maintain justice among the three hundred million Muslims on the terrestrial globe, to safeguard the rights of these peoples, to prevent any event that could encroach upon order and security, and confront every attack which the Muslims would be called upon to encounter from the side of other nations. It was to be part of his attributes to preserve by all means the welfare and spiritual development of Islam. . . .

If the Caliph and Caliphate, as they maintained, were to be invested with a dignity embracing the whole of Islam, ought they not to have realized in all justice that a crushing burden would be imposed on Turkey, on her existence; her entire resources and all her forces would be placed at the disposal of the Caliph? . . .

For centuries our nation was guided under the influence of these erroneous ideas. But what has been the result of it? Everywhere they have lost millions of men. "Do you know," I asked, "how many sons of Anatolia have perished in the scorching deserts of the Yemen? Do you know the losses we have suffered in holding Syria and Egypt and in maintaining our position in Africa? And do you see what has come out of it? Do you know?

"Those who favor the idea of placing the means at the disposal of the Caliph to brave the whole world and the power to administer the affairs of the whole of Islam must not appeal to the population of Anatolia alone but to the great Muslim agglomerations which are eight or ten times as rich in men.

"New Turkey, the people of New Turkey, have no reason to think of anything else but their own existence and their own welfare. She has nothing more to give away to others."

Mohammed Iqbal, Speech to the All-India Muslim League (1930)

It cannot be denied that Islam, regarded as an ethical ideal plus a certain kind of polity . . . has been the chief formative factor in the life history of the Muslims of India. It has furnished those basic emotions and loyalties which gradually unify scattered individuals and groups and finally transform them into a well-defined people. Indeed it is no exaggeration to say that India is perhaps the only country in the world where Islam, as a people-building force, has worked at its best. In India, as elsewhere, the structure of Islam as a society is almost entirely due to the working of Islam as a culture inspired by a specific ethical ideal. . . .

Communalism in its higher aspect, then, is indispensable to the formation of a harmonious whole in a country like India. The units of Indian society are not territorial as in European countries. India is a continent of human groups belonging to different religions. Their behavior is not at all determined by a common race consciousness. Even the Hindus do not form a homogeneous group. The principle of European democracy cannot be applied to India without recognizing the fact of communal groups. The Muslim demand for the creation of a Muslim India within India is, therefore, perfectly justified. . . .

I therefore demand the formation of a consolidated Muslim State in the best interests of India and Islam. For India it means security and peace resulting from an internal balance of power; for Islam an opportunity to rid itself of the stamp that Arabian imperialism was forced to give it, to mobilize its law, its education, its culture, and to bring them into closer contact with its own original spirit and with the spirit of modern times.

 Why did Mustafa Kemal believe that the caliphate no longer met the needs of the Turkish people? Why did Mohammed Iqbal believe that a separate state for Muslims in India would be required? How did he attempt to persuade non-Muslims that this would be to their benefit as well?

SOURCES: From Atatürk's Speech to the Assembly, pp. 432–433. A speech delivered by Ghazi Mustafa Kemal, President of the Turkish Republic, October 1924; Mohammed Iqbal, Speech to the All-India Muslim League, 1930.

Khan was hindered by strong foreign influence. When the Soviet Union and Great Britain decided to send troops into the country during World War II, he resigned in protest and died three years later.

NATION BUILDING IN IRAQ One consequence of the collapse of the Ottoman Empire was the emergence of a new political entity along the Tigris and Euphrates Rivers, once the heartland of ancient empires. Lacking defensible borders and sharply divided along ethnic and religious lines—a Shi'ite majority in rural areas was balanced by a vocal Sunni minority in the cities and a largely Kurdish population in the northern mountains— the region had been under Ottoman rule since the seventeenth century. With the advent of World War I, the lowland area from Baghdad southward to the Persian Gulf was occupied by British forces, who hoped to protect oil-producing regions in neighboring Iran from a German takeover.

In 1920, the country was placed under British control as the mandate of Iraq under the League of Nations. Civil unrest and growing anti-Western sentiment rapidly dispelled any possible plans for the emergence of an independent government, and in 1921, after the suppression of resistance forces, the country became a monarchy under the titular authority of King Faisal, a resistance leader during World War I and a descendant of the Prophet Muhammad. Faisal relied for support primarily on the politically more sophisticated urban Sunni population, although they represented less than a quarter of the population. The discovery of oil near Kirkuk in 1927 increased the value of the area to the British, who granted formal independence to the country in 1932, although British advisers retained a strong influence over the fragile government.

THE RISE OF ARAB NATIONALISM As we have seen, the Arab uprising during World War I helped bring about the demise of the Ottoman Empire. Actually, unrest against Ottoman rule had existed in the Arabian peninsula since the eighteenth century, when the Wahhabi revolt attempted to expel the outside influences and cleanse Islam of corrupt practices that had developed in past centuries. The revolt was eventually suppressed, but the influence of the Wahhabi movement persisted, revitalized in part by resistance to the centralizing and modernizing efforts of reformist elements in the nineteenth century.

World War I offered an opportunity for the Arabs to throw off the shackles of Ottoman rule—but what would replace them? The Arabs were not a nation but an idea, a loose collection of peoples who often did not see eye to eye on what constituted their community. Disagreement over what it means to be an Arab has plagued generations of political leaders who have sought unsuccessfully to knit together the disparate peoples of the region into a single Arab nation.

When the Arab leaders in Mecca declared their independence from Ottoman rule in 1916, they had hoped for British support, but they were sorely disappointed when the British and French assumed control of much of the area as mandates of the League of Nations. To add salt to the wound, the French created a new state of Lebanon along the coastal regions of their mandate of Syria so that the Christian peoples there could be under a Christian administration.

In the early 1920s, a leader of the Wahhabi movement, Ibn Saud (1880–1953), united Arab tribes in the northern part of the Arabian peninsula and drove out the remnants of Ottoman rule. Ibn Saud was a descendant of the family that had led the Wahhabi revolt in the eighteenth century. Devout and gifted, he won broad support among Arab tribal peoples and established the kingdom of Saudi Arabia throughout much of the peninsula in 1932.

At first, his new kingdom, consisting essentially of the vast wastes of central Arabia, was desperately poor. Its financial resources were limited to the income from Muslim pilgrims visiting the holy sites in Mecca and Medina. But during the 1930s, American companies began to explore for oil, and in 1938, Standard Oil made a successful strike at Dahran, on the Persian Gulf. Soon an Arabian-American oil conglomerate, popularly called Aramco, was established, and the isolated kingdom was suddenly inundated by Western oilmen and untold wealth.

THE ISSUE OF PALESTINE The land of Palestine—once the home of the Jews but now inhabited primarily by Muslim Arabs and a few thousand Christians—became a separate mandate and immediately became a thorny problem for the British. In 1897, the Austrian-born journalist Theodor Herzl (1860–1904) had convened an international conference in Basel, Switzerland, which led to the creation of the World Zionist Organization (WZO). Its aim was to create a homeland for the Jewish people— long dispersed widely throughout Europe, North Africa, and the Middle East—in Palestine, which was then under Ottoman rule.

Over the next decade, Jewish immigration into Palestine increased with WZO support. By the outbreak of World War I, about 85,000 Jews lived in Palestine, representing about 15 percent of the total population. In 1917, responding to appeals from the British chemist Chaim Weizmann, British Foreign Secretary Lord Arthur Balfour issued a declaration saying Palestine was to be a national home for the Jews. The Balfour Declaration, which was later confirmed by the League of Nations, was ambiguous on the legal status of the territory and promised that the decision would not undermine the rights of the non-Jewish peoples currently living in the area. But Arab nationalists were incensed. How could a national home for the Jewish people be established in a territory where the majority of the population was Muslim?

After World War I, more Jewish settlers began to arrive in Palestine in response to the promises made in the Balfour Declaration. As tensions between the new arrivals and existing Muslim residents began to escalate, the British tried to restrict Jewish immigration into the territory while Arab voices rejected the concept of a separate state. In a bid to relieve Arab sensitivities, Great Britain created the separate emirate of Trans-Jordan out of the eastern portion of Palestine. After World War II, it would become the independent kingdom of Jordan. The stage was set for the conflicts that would take place in the region after World War II.

THE BRITISH IN EGYPT Great Britain had maintained a loose protectorate over Egypt since the middle of the nineteenth century, although the area remained nominally under Ottoman rule. London formalized its protectorate in 1914 to protect the Suez Canal and the Nile River valley from possible seizure by the Central Powers. After the war, however, nationalist elements became restive and formed the Wafd Party, a secular organization dedicated to the creation of an independent Egypt based on the principles of representative government. The Wafd received the support of many middle-class Egyptians who, like Kemal Atatürk in Turkey, hoped to meld Islamic practices with the secular tradition of the modern West. This modernist form of Islam did not have broad appeal outside the cosmopolitan centers, however, and in 1928 the Muslim cleric Hasan al-Bana organized the Muslim Brotherhood, which demanded strict adherence to the traditional teachings of the Prophet, as set forth in the Qur'an. The Brotherhood rejected Western ways and sought to create a new Egypt based firmly on the precepts of the *Shari'a*. By the 1930s, the organization had as many as a million members.

Nationalism and Revolution

Before the Russian Revolution, to most observers in Asia, "Westernization" meant the capitalist democratic civilization of western Europe and the United States, not the doctrine of social revolution developed by Karl Marx.

Until 1917, Marxism was regarded as a utopian idea rather than a concrete system of government. Moreover, Marxism appeared to have little relevance to conditions in Asia. Marxist doctrine, after all, declared that a communist society could arise only from the ashes of an advanced capitalism that had already passed through the stage of industrial revolution. From the perspective of Marxist historical analysis, most societies in Asia were still at the feudal stage of development; they lacked the economic conditions and political awareness to achieve a socialist revolution that would bring the working class to power. Finally, the Marxist view of nationalism and religion had little appeal to many patriotic intellectuals in the non-Western world. Marx believed that nationhood and religion were essentially false ideas that diverted the attention of the oppressed masses from the critical issues of class struggle and, in his phrase, the exploitation of one person by another. Instead, Marx stressed the importance of an "internationalist" outlook based on class consciousness and the eventual creation of a classless society with no artificial divisions based on culture, nation, or religion.

LENIN AND THE EAST The situation began to change after the Russian Revolution in 1917. The rise to power of Lenin's Bolsheviks demonstrated that a revolutionary party espousing Marxist principles could overturn a corrupt, outdated system and launch a new experiment dedicated to ending human inequality and achieving a paradise on earth. In 1920, Lenin proposed a new revolutionary strategy designed to relate Marxist doctrine and practice to non-Western societies. His reasons were not entirely altruistic. Soviet Russia, surrounded by capitalist powers, desperately needed allies in its struggle to survive in a hostile world. To Lenin, the anticolonial movements emerging in North Africa, Asia, and the Middle East after World War I were natural allies of the beleaguered new regime in Moscow. Lenin was convinced that only the ability of the imperialist powers to find markets, raw materials, and sources of capital investment in the non-Western world kept capitalism alive. If the tentacles of capitalist influence in Asia and Africa could be severed, imperialism itself would ultimately weaken and collapse.

Establishing such an alliance was not easy, however. Most nationalist leaders in colonial countries belonged to the urban middle class, and many abhorred the idea of a comprehensive revolution to create a totally egalitarian society. In addition, others still adhered to traditional religious beliefs and were opposed to the atheistic principles of classical Marxism.

Since it was unrealistic to expect bourgeois support for social revolution, Lenin sought a compromise by which Communist parties could be organized among the working classes in the preindustrial societies of Asia and Africa. These parties would then forge informal alliances with existing middle-class nationalist parties to struggle against the remnants of the traditional ruling class and Western imperialism. Such an alliance, of course, could not be permanent because many bourgeois nationalists in Asia and Africa would reject an egalitarian, classless society. Once the imperialists had been overthrown, therefore, the Communist parties would turn against their erstwhile nationalist partners to seize power on their own and carry out the socialist revolution. Lenin thus proposed a two-stage revolution: an initial "national democratic" stage followed by a "proletarian socialist" stage.

Lenin's strategy became a major element in Soviet foreign policy in the 1920s. Soviet agents fanned out across the world to carry Marxism beyond the boundaries of industrial Europe. The primary instrument of this effort was the **Communist International**, or **Comintern** for short. Formed in 1919 at Lenin's prodding, the Comintern was a worldwide organization of Communist parties dedicated to the advancement of world revolution. At its headquarters in Moscow, agents from around the world were trained in the precepts of world communism and then sent back to their own countries to form Marxist parties and promote the cause of social revolution. By the end of the 1920s, almost every colonial or semicolonial society in Asia had a party based on Marxist principles. The Soviets had less success in the Middle East, where Marxist ideology appealed mainly to minorities such as Jews and Armenians in the cities, or in sub-Saharan Africa, where Soviet strategists in any case felt that conditions were not sufficiently advanced for the creation of Communist organizations.

THE APPEAL OF COMMUNISM According to Marxist doctrine, the rank and file of Communist parties should be urban workers alienated from capitalist society by inhumane working conditions. In practice, many of the leading elements even in European Communist parties tended to be intellectuals or members of the lower middle class (in Marxist parlance, the "petty bourgeoisie"). That phenomenon was even more apparent in the non-Western world. Some were probably drawn into the movement for patriotic reasons and saw Marxist doctrine as a new and more effective means of modernizing their societies and removing the power of exploitative colonialism. Others were attracted by the utopian dream of a classless society. For those who had lost their faith in traditional religion, communism often served as a new secular ideology, dealing not with the hereafter but with the here and now. All who joined found a stirring message of release from oppression and a practical strategy for the liberation of their society from colonial rule. The young Ho Chi Minh, later to become the founder of the Vietnamese Communist Party, was quick to see the importance of Lenin's revolutionary strategy for his own country:

> There were political terms difficult to understand in this thesis. But by dint of reading it again and again, finally I could grasp the main part of it. What emotion, enthusiasm, clear-sightedness, and confidence it instilled in me! I was overjoyed to tears. Though sitting alone in my room, I shouted aloud as if addressing large crowds: "Dear martyrs, compatriots! This is what we need, this is the path to our liberation!"[1]

Of course, the new doctrine's appeal was not the same in all non-Western societies. In Confucian societies such as China and Vietnam, where traditional belief systems had been badly discredited by their failure to counter the Western challenge, communism had an immediate impact and rapidly became a major factor in the anticolonial movement. In Buddhist and Muslim societies, where traditional religion remained strong and actually became a cohesive factor within the resistance movement, communism had less success and was forced to adapt to local conditions to survive.

Sometimes, as in Malaya (where the sense of nationhood was weak) or Thailand (which, alone in Southeast Asia, had not fallen under colonial rule), support for the local Communist Party came from minority groups such as the overseas Chinese community. To maximize their appeal and minimize potential conflict with traditional ideas, Communist parties frequently attempted to adjust Marxist doctrine to indigenous values and institutions. In the Middle East, for example, the Ba'ath Party in Syria adopted a hybrid socialism combining Marxism with Arab nationalism. In Africa, radical intellectuals talked vaguely of a uniquely "African road to socialism."

The degree to which these parties were successful in establishing alliances with existing nationalist parties also varied from place to place. In some instances, the local Communists were briefly able to establish a cooperative relationship with bourgeois parties in the struggle against Western imperialism. In the Dutch East Indies, the Indonesian Communist Party (known as the PKI) allied with the middle-class nationalist group Sarekat Islam but later broke loose in an effort to organize its own mass movement among the poor peasants. Similar problems were encountered in French Indochina, where Vietnamese Communists organized by the Moscow-trained revolutionary Ho Chi Minh sought to cooperate with bourgeois nationalist parties against the colonial regime. In 1928, all such efforts were abandoned when the Comintern, reacting to Chiang Kai-shek's betrayal of the alliance with the Chinese Communist Party (see the next section), declared that Communist parties should restrict their recruiting efforts to the most revolutionary elements in society—notably, the urban intellectuals and the working class. Harassed by colonial authorities and saddled with strategic directions from Moscow that often had little relevance to local conditions, Communist parties in most colonial societies had little success in the 1930s and failed to build a secure base of support among the mass of the population.

Revolution in China

Overall, revolutionary Marxism had its greatest impact in China, where a group of young radicals, including several faculty and staff members from the prestigious Beijing University, founded the Chinese Communist Party (CCP) in 1921. The rise of the CCP was a consequence of the failed revolution of 1911. When political forces are too weak or divided to consolidate their power during a period of instability, the military usually steps in to fill the vacuum. In China, Sun Yat-sen and his colleagues had accepted General Yuan Shikai as president of the new Chinese republic in 1911 because they lacked the military force to compete with his control over the army. Moreover, many feared, perhaps rightly, that if the revolt lapsed into chaos, the Western powers would intervene and the last shreds of Chinese sovereignty would be lost. But some had misgivings about Yuan's intentions. As one remarked in a letter to a friend, "We don't know whether he will be a George Washington or a Napoleon."

As it turned out, he was neither. Showing little comprehension of the new ideas sweeping into China from the West, Yuan ruled in a traditional manner, reviving Confucian rituals and institutions and eventually trying to found a new imperial dynasty. Yuan's dictatorial inclinations led to clashes with Sun's party, now renamed the Guomindang, or Nationalist Party. When Yuan dissolved the new parliament, the Nationalists launched a rebellion. When it failed, Sun Yat-sen fled to Japan.

Yuan was strong enough to brush off the challenge from the revolutionary forces but not to turn back the clock of history. He died in 1916 (apparently of natural causes) and was succeeded by one of his military subordinates. For the next several years, China slipped into anarchy as the power of the central government disintegrated and military warlords seized power in the provinces.

Mr. Science and Mr. Democracy: The New Culture Movement

Although the failure of the 1911 revolution was a clear sign that China was not yet ready for dramatic change, discontent with existing conditions continued to rise in various sectors of Chinese society. The most vocal protests came from radical elements who opposed Yuan Shikai's conservative agenda but were now convinced that political change could not take place until the Chinese people were more familiar with trends in the outside world. Braving the displeasure of Yuan Shikai and his successors, progressive intellectuals at Beijing University launched the **New Culture Movement**, aimed at abolishing the remnants of the old system and introducing Western values and institutions into China. Using the classrooms of China's most prestigious university as well as the pages of newly established progressive magazines and newspapers, they presented the Chinese people with a heady mix of new ideas, from the philosophy of Friedrich Nietzsche and Bertrand Russell to the educational views of the American John Dewey and the feminist plays of Henrik Ibsen. As such ideas flooded into China, they stirred up a new generation of educated Chinese youth, who chanted "Down with Confucius and sons" and talked of a new era dominated by "Mr. Sai" (Mr. Science) and "Mr. De" (Mr. Democracy). No one was a greater defender of free thought and speech than the chancellor of Beijing University, Cai Yuanpei:

> So far as theoretical ideas are concerned, I follow the principles of "freedom of thought" and an attitude of broad tolerance in accordance with the practice of universities the world over. . . . Regardless of what school of thought a person may adhere to, so long as that person's ideas are justified and conform to reason and have not been passed by through the process of natural selection, although there may be controversy, such ideas have a right to be presented.[2]

The problem was that appeals for American-style democracy and women's liberation had little relevance to Chinese peasants, most of whom were still illiterate and concerned above all with survival. Consequently, the New Culture Movement did not win widespread support outside the urban areas. It certainly earned the distrust of conservative military officers, one of whom threatened to lob artillery shells into Beijing University to destroy the poisonous new ideas and their advocates.

Discontent among intellectuals, however, was soon joined by the rising chorus of public protest against Japan's efforts to expand its influence on the mainland. During the first decade of the twentieth century, Japan had taken advantage of the Qing's decline to extend its domination over Manchuria and Korea (see Chapter 3). In 1915, the Japanese government insisted that Yuan Shikai accept a series of twenty-one demands that would have given Japan a virtual protectorate over the Chinese government and economy. Yuan was able to fend off the most far-reaching Japanese demands by arousing popular outrage in China, but at the Paris Peace Conference four years later, Japan received Germany's sphere of influence in Shandong Province as a reward for its support of the Allied cause in World War I. On hearing that the Chinese government had accepted the decision, on May 4, 1919, patriotic students, supported by other sectors of the urban population, demonstrated in Beijing and other major cities of the country. Although this "May Fourth Movement," as it came to be called, did not lead to the restoration of Shandong to China, it did alert a substantial part of the politically literate population to the threat to national survival and the incompetence of the warlord government. A sense of Chinese national identity, long suppressed under Manchu rule, was on the rise in the young republic.

By 1920, central authority had almost ceased to exist in China. Two competing political forces now began to emerge from the chaos. One was Sun Yat-sen's Nationalist Party. Driven from the political arena seven years earlier by Yuan Shikai, the party now reestablished itself on the mainland by making an alliance with the warlord ruler of Guangdong Province in South China. From Canton, Sun sought international assistance to carry out his national revolution. The other was the Chinese Communist Party. Following Lenin's strategy, the CCP sought to link up with the more experienced Nationalists. Sun Yat-sen needed the expertise and the diplomatic support that the Soviet Union could provide because his anti-imperialist rhetoric had alienated many Western powers. In 1923, the two parties formed an alliance to oppose the warlords and drive the imperialist powers out of China.

For three years, with the assistance of a Comintern mission in Canton, the two parties submerged their mutual suspicions and mobilized and trained a revolutionary army to march north and seize control of China. The so-called Northern Expedition began in the summer of 1926

(see Map 5.1). By the following spring, revolutionary forces were in control of all Chinese territory south of the Yangtze River, including the major river ports of Wuhan and Shanghai. But tensions between the two parties now surfaced. Sun Yat-sen had died of cancer in 1925 and was succeeded as head of the Nationalist Party by his military subordinate, Chiang Kai-shek (1887–1975). Chiang feigned support for the alliance with the Communists but actually planned to destroy them. In April 1927, he struck against the Communists and their supporters in Shanghai, killing thousands. The CCP responded by encouraging revolts in central China and Canton, but the uprisings were defeated and their leaders were killed or forced into hiding.

Sun Yat-Sen (1866–1925) and Chiang Kai-Shek (1887–1975) (b/w photo), Chinese Photographer/Private Collection/ Archives Charmet/The Bridgeman Art Library

Masters and Disciples. When the founders of nationalist movements passed leadership over to their successors, the result was often a change in the strategy and tactics of the organizations. In India, when Jawaharlal Nehru replaced Mahatma Gandhi as leader of the Indian National Congress, the movement adopted a more secular posture. In China, Chiang Kai-shek took Sun Yat-sen's Nationalist Party in a more conservative direction after Sun's death in 1925. Here Chiang (standing) is shown with Sun Yat-sen.

Revolution in China ❧ **109**

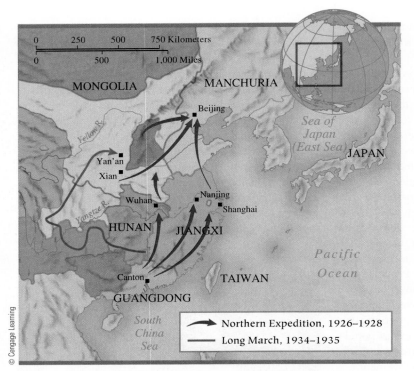

MAP 5.1 **The Northern Expedition and the Long March.** This map shows the routes taken by the combined Nationalist-Communist forces during the Northern Expedition of 1926–1928. The blue arrow indicates the route taken by Communist units during the Long March led by Mao Zedong.

Q *Where did Mao establish his new headquarters after the Long March? Why?*

The Nanjing Republic

In 1928, Chiang Kai-shek founded a new Republic of China at Nanjing, and over the next three years, he managed to reunify China by a combination of military operations and inducements (known as "silver bullets") to various northern warlords to join his movement. One of his key targets was the warlord Zhang Zuolin, who controlled Manchuria under the tutelage of Japan. When Zhang allegedly agreed to throw in his lot with the Nationalists, the Japanese had him assassinated by placing a bomb under his train as he was returning to Manchuria in 1928. The Japanese hoped that Zhang Zuolin's son and successor, Zhang Xueliang, would be more cooperative, but they had miscalculated. Promised a major role in Chiang Kai-shek's government, Zhang began instead to integrate Manchuria politically and economically into the Nanjing republic.

Chiang Kai-shek saw the Japanese as a serious threat to Chinese national aspirations but considered them less dangerous than the Communists. (He once remarked to an American reporter that "the Japanese are a disease of the skin, but the Communists are a disease of the heart.") After the Shanghai massacre of April 1927, most of the Communist leaders went into hiding in the city, where they attempted to revive the movement in its traditional base among the urban working class. Shanghai was a rich recruiting ground for the party. A city of millionaires, paupers, prostitutes, gamblers, and adventurers, it had led one pious Christian missionary to comment, "If God lets Shanghai endure, He owes an apology to Sodom and Gomorrah."[3] Some party members, however, led by the young Communist organizer Mao Zedong (1893–1976), fled to the hilly areas south of the Yangtze River.

Unlike most other CCP leaders, Mao was convinced that the Chinese revolution must be based on the impoverished peasants in the countryside, not on workers in the big cities. The son of a prosperous farmer, Mao had helped organize a peasant movement in South China during the early 1920s and then served as an agitator in rural villages in his home province of Hunan during the Northern Expedition in the fall of 1926. At that time, he wrote a famous report to the party leadership suggesting that the CCP support peasant demands for a land revolution. But his superiors refused, fearing that such radical policies would destroy the alliance with the Nationalists (see the box on p. 111).

After the spring of 1927, the CCP-Nationalist alliance ceased to exist. Chiang Kai-shek attempted to root the Communists out of their urban base in Shanghai. He succeeded in 1931, when most party leaders were forced to flee Shanghai for Mao's rural redoubt in the rugged hills of Jiangxi Province. Three years later, using their superior military strength, Chiang's troops surrounded the Communist base, inducing Mao's young People's Liberation Army (PLA) to abandon its guerrilla lair and embark on the famous Long March, an arduous journey of thousands of miles on foot through mountains, marshes, and deserts to the small provincial town of Yan'an 200 miles north of the modern-day city of Xian in the dusty hills of North China. Of the 90,000 who embarked on the journey in October 1934, only 10,000 arrived in Yan'an a year later. Contemporary observers must have thought that the Communist threat to the Nanjing regime had been averted forever.

Meanwhile, Chiang Kai-shek was trying to build a new nation. When the Nanjing republic was established in

A Call for Revolt

In the fall of 1926, Nationalist and Communist forces moved north from Canton on their Northern Expedition in an effort to defeat the warlords. The young Communist Mao Zedong accompanied revolutionary troops into his home province of Hunan, where he submitted a report to the CCP Central Committee calling for a massive peasant revolt against the ruling order. The report shows his confidence that peasants could play an active role in the Chinese revolution despite the skepticism of many of his colleagues.

Mao Zedong, "The Peasant Movement in Hunan"

During my recent visit to Hunan I made a firsthand investigation of conditions. . . . In a very short time, . . . several hundred million peasants will rise like a mighty storm, . . . a force so swift and violent that no power, however great, will be able to hold it back. They will smash all the trammels that bind them and rush forward along the road to liberation. They will sweep all the imperialists, warlords, corrupt officials, local tyrants, and evil gentry into their graves. Every revolutionary party and every revolutionary comrade will be put to the test, to be accepted or rejected as they decide. There are three alternatives. To march at their head and lead them? To trail behind them, gesticulating and criticizing? Or to stand in their way and oppose them? Every Chinese is free to choose, but events will force you to make the choice quickly.

The main targets of attack by the peasants are the local tyrants, the evil gentry and the lawless landlords, but in passing they also hit out against patriarchal ideas and institutions, against the corrupt officials in the cities and against bad practices and customs in the rural areas. . . . As a result, the privileges which the feudal landlords enjoyed for thousands of years are being shattered to pieces. . . . With the collapse of the power of the landlords, the peasant associations have now become the sole organs of authority, and the popular slogan "All power to the peasant associations" has become a reality.

The peasants' revolt disturbed the gentry's sweet dreams. When the news from the countryside reached the cities, it caused immediate uproar among the gentry. . . . From the middle social strata upwards to the Kuomintang [Nationalist] right-wingers, there was not a single person who did not sum up the whole business in the phrase, "It's terrible!" . . . Even quite progressive people said, "Though terrible, it is inevitable in a revolution." In short, nobody could altogether deny the word "terrible." But . . . the fact is that the great peasant masses have risen to fulfill their historic mission. . . . What the peasants are doing is absolutely right; what they are doing is fine! "It's fine!" is the theory of the peasants and of all other revolutionaries. Every revolutionary comrade should know that the national revolution requires a great change in the countryside. The Revolution of 1911 did not bring about this change, hence its failure. This change is now taking place, and it is an important factor for the completion of the revolution. Every revolutionary comrade must support it, or he will be taking the stand of counterrevolution.

 Why did Mao Zedong believe that rural peasants could help bring about a social revolution in China? How does his vision compare with the reality of the Bolshevik Revolution in Russia?

SOURCE: From *Selected Works of Mao Tse-Tung* (London: Lawrence and Wishart, Ltd., 1954), vol. 1, pp. 21–23.

1928, Chiang publicly declared his commitment to Sun Yat-sen's Three People's Principles. In a program announced in 1918, Sun had written about the all-important second stage of "political tutelage":

> As a schoolboy must have good teachers and helpful friends, so the Chinese people, being for the first time under republican rule, must have a farsighted revolutionary government for their training. This calls for the period of political tutelage, which is a necessary transitional stage from monarchy to republicanism. Without this, disorder will be unavoidable.[4]

In keeping with Sun's program, Chiang announced a period of political indoctrination to prepare the Chinese people for a final stage of constitutional government. In the meantime, the Nationalists would use their dictatorial power to carry out a land reform program and modernize the urban industrial sector.

But it would take more than paper plans to create a new China. Years of neglect and civil war had severely frayed the political, economic, and social fabric of the nation. There were faint signs of an impending industrial revolution in the major urban centers, but most of the people in the

Mao Zedong on the Long March. In 1934, the Communist leader Mao Zedong led his bedraggled forces on the famous Long March from southern China to a new location at Yan'an, in the hills just south of the Gobi Desert. The epic journey has ever since been celebrated as a symbol of the party's willingness to sacrifice for the revolutionary cause. In this photograph, Mao sits astride a white horse as he accompanies his followers on the march. Reportedly, he was the only participant allowed to ride a horse en route to Yan'an.

the failure of the traditional system to solve China's growing problems. Critics also noted that Chiang's government did not practice what it preached. Much of the national wealth was in the hands of the so-called four families, composed of senior officials and close subordinates of the ruling elite. Lacking the political sensitivity of Sun Yat-sen and fearing Communist influence, Chiang repressed all opposition and censored free expression, thereby alienating many intellectuals and political moderates.

PROMOTING ECONOMIC DEVELOPMENT With only a tenuous hold over the vast countryside (the Nanjing republic had total control over just a handful of provinces in the Yangtze valley), Chiang Kai-shek's government had little more success in promoting economic development. Although mechanization was gradually beginning to replace manual labor in a number of traditional industries (notably in the manufacture of textile goods), about 75 percent of all industrial production was still craft produced in the mid-1930s. In addition, traditional Chinese exports, such as silk and tea, were hard-hit by the Great Depression. With military expenses consuming about half the national budget, distressingly little was devoted to economic development. During the decade of precarious peace following the Northern Expedition, industrial growth averaged only about 1 percent annually.

countryside, drained by warlord exactions and civil strife, were still grindingly poor and overwhelmingly illiterate. A Westernized middle class had begun to emerge in the cities and formed much of the natural constituency of the Nanjing government. But this new Westernized elite, preoccupied with bourgeois values of individual advancement and material accumulation, had few links with the peasants in the countryside or the rickshaw drivers "running in this world of suffering," in the poignant words of a Chinese poet. In an expressive phrase, some critics dismissed Chiang Kai-shek and his chief followers as "banana Chinese"—yellow on the outside, white on the inside.

BLENDING EAST AND WEST Chiang was aware of the difficulty of introducing exotic foreign ideas into a society still culturally conservative. While building a modern industrial sector and rejecting what he considered the excessive individualism and material greed of Western capitalism, Chiang sought to propagate traditional Confucian values of hard work, obedience, and moral integrity through the officially promoted New Life Movement, sponsored by his Wellesley-educated wife, Mei-ling Soong.

Unfortunately for Chiang, Confucian ideas—at least in their institutional form—had been widely discredited by

Whether overall per capita consumption declined during the early decades of the century is unclear, but there is no doubt that Chinese farmers were often victimized by high taxes imposed by local warlords and the endemic political and social conflict that marked the period. One of Sun Yat-sen's most prominent proposals had been the redistribution of land to poor peasants in the countryside. A land reform program was enacted in 1930, but it had little effect. Since the urban middle class and the landed gentry were Chiang Kai-shek's natural political constituency, he shunned programs that would lead to a radical redistribution of wealth.

Social Change in Republican China

The transformation of the old order that had commenced at the end of the Qing era continued into the period of the early Chinese republic. By 1915, the assault on the old system and values by educated youth was intense. The main focus of the attack was the Confucian concept of the family—in particular, filial piety and the subordination of women. Young people called for the right to choose their own mates and their own careers. Women began to demand rights and opportunities equal to those enjoyed by men.

More broadly, progressives called for an end to the concept of duty to the community and praised the Western individualist ethos. The prime spokesman for such views was the popular writer Lu Xun, whose short stories criticized the Confucian concept of family as a "man-eating" system that degraded humanity. In a famous short story titled "Diary of a Madman," the protagonist remarks:

> I remember when I was four or five years old, sitting in the cool of the hall, my brother told me that if a man's parents were ill, he should cut off a piece of his flesh and boil it for them if he wanted to be considered a good son. I have only just realized that I have been living all these years in a place where for four thousand years they have been eating human flesh.[5]

Such criticisms did have some beneficial results. During the early republic, the tyranny of the old family system began to decline, at least in urban areas, under the impact of economic changes and the urgings of the New Culture intellectuals. Women, long consigned to an inferior place in the Confucian world order, began to escape their cloistered existence and seek education and employment alongside their male contemporaries. Free choice in marriage and a more relaxed attitude toward sex became commonplace among affluent families in the cities, where the teenage children of Westernized elites aped the clothing, social habits, and musical tastes of their contemporaries in Europe and the United States.

But as a rule, the new consciousness of individualism and women's rights that marked the early republican era in the major cities did not penetrate the villages, where traditional attitudes and customs held sway. Arranged marriages continued to be the rule rather than the exception, and concubinage remained common. According to a survey taken in the 1930s, well over two-thirds of the marriages, even among urban couples, had been arranged by their parents; in one rural area, only 3 of 170 villagers interviewed had heard of the idea of "modern marriage." Even the tradition of binding the feet of female children continued despite efforts by the Nationalist government to eradicate the practice.[6]

DOWN WITH CONFUCIUS AND SONS Nowhere was the struggle between traditional and modern more visible than in the field of culture. Beginning with the New Culture era during the early years of the first Chinese republic, radical reformists criticized traditional culture as the symbol and instrument of feudal oppression that must be entirely eradicated to create a new China that could stand on its feet with dignity in the modern world.

For many reformers, that new culture must be based on that of the modern West. During the 1920s and 1930s, Western literature and art became popular in China, especially among the urban middle class. Traditional culture continued to prevail among more conservative elements of the population, and some intellectuals argued for the creation of a new art that would synthesize the best of Chinese and foreign culture. But the most creative artists were interested in imitating foreign trends, whereas traditionalists were more concerned with preservation.

Literature in particular was influenced by foreign ideas as Western genres like the novel and the short story attracted a growing audience. Although most Chinese novels written after World War I dealt with Chinese subjects, they reflected the Western tendency toward social realism and often dealt with the new Westernized middle class (Mao Dun's *Midnight*, for example, described the changing mores of Shanghai's urban elites) or the disintegration of the traditional Confucian family. Most of China's modern authors displayed a clear contempt for the past.

Japan Between the Wars

By the beginning of the twentieth century, Japan had made steady progress toward the creation of an advanced society on the Western model. Economic and social reforms launched during the Meiji era led to increasing prosperity and the development of a modern industrial and commercial sector. Although the political system still retained many authoritarian characteristics, optimists had reason to hope that Japan was on the road to becoming a full-fledged democracy.

Experiment in Democracy

During the first quarter of the twentieth century, the Japanese political system appeared to evolve significantly toward the Western democratic model. Political parties expanded their popular following and became increasingly competitive, while individual pressure groups such as labor unions began to appear in Japanese society, along with an independent press and a bill of rights. The influence of the old ruling oligarchy, the *genro*, had not yet been significantly challenged, however, nor had that of its ideological foundation, which focused on national wealth and power.

The fragile flower of democratic institutions was able to survive throughout the 1920s. During that period, the military budget was reduced, and a suffrage bill enacted in 1925 granted the vote to all adult Japanese males. Women remained disenfranchised, but women's associations became increasingly visible during the 1920s, and women were active in the labor movement and in campaigns for various social reforms.

But the era was also marked by growing social turmoil, and two opposing forces within the system were gearing up to challenge the prevailing wisdom. On the left, a Marxist labor movement, which reflected the tensions within the working class and the increasing radicalism among the rural poor, began to take shape in the early 1920s in response to growing economic difficulties. Government suppression of labor disturbances led to further radicalization. On the right, ultranationalist groups called for a rejection of Western models of development and a more militant approach to realizing national objectives. In 1919, radical nationalist Kita Ikki called for a military takeover and the establishment of a new system bearing a strong resemblance to what would later be called fascism in Europe (see Chapter 6).

This cultural conflict between old and new, indigenous and foreign, was reflected in literature. The restoration of Japanese self-confidence after the victories over China and Russia launched an age of cultural creativity in the early twentieth century. Fascination with Western literature gave birth to a striking new genre called the "I novel." Defying traditional Japanese reticence, some authors reveled in self-exposure with confessions of their innermost thoughts. Others found release in the "proletarian literature" movement of the early 1920s. Inspired by Soviet literary examples, these authors wanted literature to serve socialist goals and improve the lives of the working class. Finally, some Japanese writers blended Western psychology with Japanese sensibility in exquisite novels reeking of nostalgia for the old Japan. One well-known example is Junichiro Tanizaki's *Some Prefer Nettles* (1929), which delicately juxtaposes the positive aspects of traditional and modern Japan. By the early 1930s, however, military censorship increasingly inhibited literary expression.

A *Zaibatsu* Economy

Japan also continued to make impressive progress in economic development. Spurred by rising domestic demand as well as a continued high rate of government investment in the economy, the production of raw materials tripled between 1900 and 1930, and industrial production increased more than twelvefold. Much of the increase went into the export market, and Western manufacturers began to complain about the rising competition for markets from the Japanese.

As often happens, rapid industrialization was accompanied by some hardship and rising social tensions. A characteristic of the Meiji model was the concentration of various manufacturing processes within a single enterprise, the **zaibatsu**, or financial clique. Some of these firms were existing merchant companies that had the capital and the foresight to move into new areas of opportunity. Others were formed by enterprising samurai, who used their status and experience in management to good account in a new environment. Whatever their origins, these firms gradually developed, often with official encouragement, into large conglomerates that controlled a major segment of the Japanese industrial sector. According to one source, by 1937, the four largest *zaibatsu* (Mitsui, Mitsubishi, Sumitomo, and Yasuda) controlled 21 percent of the banking industry, 26 percent of mining, 35 percent of shipbuilding, 38 percent of commercial shipping, and more than 60 percent of paper manufacturing and insurance.

This concentration of power and wealth in the hands of a few major industrial combines resulted in the emergence of a form of dual economy: on the one hand, a modern industry characterized by up-to-date methods and massive government subsidies, and on the other, a traditional manufacturing sector characterized by conservative methods and small-scale production techniques.

Concentration of wealth also led to growing economic inequalities. As we have seen, economic growth had been achieved at the expense of the peasants, many of whom fled to the cities to escape rural poverty. That labor surplus benefited the industrial sector, but the urban proletariat was still poorly paid and ill-housed. Rampant inflation in the price of rice led to food riots shortly after World War I. A rapid increase in population (the total population of the Japanese islands increased from an estimated 43 million in 1900 to 73 million in 1940) led to food shortages and the threat of rising unemployment. Intense competition and the global recession in the early 1920s led to a greater concentration of industry and a perceptible rise in urban radicalism. In the meantime, those left on the farm continued to suffer. As late as the beginning of World War II, an estimated half of all Japanese farmers were tenants.

Shidehara Diplomacy

A final problem for Japanese leaders in the post-Meiji era was the familiar capitalist dilemma of finding sources of raw materials and foreign markets for the nation's manufactured goods. Until World War I, Japan had dealt with the problem by seizing territories such as Taiwan, Korea, and southern Manchuria and transforming them into colonies or protectorates of the growing Japanese empire. That policy had succeeded brilliantly, but it had also begun to arouse the concern and, in some cases, the hostility of the Western nations. China was also becoming apprehensive; as we have seen, Japanese demands for Shandong Province at the Paris Peace Conference in 1919 aroused massive protests in major Chinese cities.

The United States was especially concerned about Japanese aggressiveness. Although the United States had been less active than some European states in pursuing colonies in the Pacific, it had a strong interest in keeping the area open for U.S. commercial activities. American anxiety about Tokyo's twenty-one demands on China in 1915 led to a new agreement with Japan in 1917, which essentially repeated the compromise provisions of the agreement reached nine years earlier.

In 1922, in Washington, D.C., the United States convened a major conference of nations with interests in the Pacific to discuss problems of regional security. The Washington Conference led to agreements on several issues, but the major accomplishment was the conclusion of a nine-power treaty recognizing the territorial integrity of China and the Open Door. The other participants induced Japan to accept these provisions by accepting its special position in Manchuria.

During the remainder of the 1920s, Japanese governments attempted to play by the rules laid down at the Washington Conference. Known as Shidehara diplomacy, after the foreign minister (and later prime minister) who attempted to carry it out, this policy sought to use diplomatic and economic means to realize Japanese interests in Asia. But this approach came under severe pressure as Japanese industrialists began to move into new areas of opportunity, such as heavy industry, chemicals, mining, and the manufacturing of appliances and automobiles. Because such industries desperately needed resources not found in abundance locally, the Japanese government came under increasing pressure to find new sources abroad.

THE RISE OF MILITANT NATIONALISM In the early 1930s, with the onset of the Great Depression and growing tensions in the international arena, nationalist forces rose to dominance in the Japanese government. These elements, a mixture of military officers and ultranationalist politicians, were convinced that the diplomacy of the 1920s had failed and advocated a more aggressive approach to protecting national interests in a brutal and competitive world. We shall discuss the factors involved and the impact of these developments on the international scene in the next chapter.

Nationalism and Dictatorship in Latin America

Because most of Latin America had won its independence from European control during the nineteenth century, nationalism and political change took different forms in this area in the years following World War I than they did in Asia and the Middle East. But the region was by no means isolated from the trends occurring throughout the rest of the world. National sentiment in opposition to foreign political and economic influence—and especially U.S. influence—was sometimes intense. And when the Great Depression struck in the late 1920s, the political equation in Latin America was affected in profound ways.

A Changing Economy

At the beginning of the twentieth century, the economy of Latin America was based largely on the export of foodstuffs and raw materials. Some countries relied on the export earnings of only one or two products. Argentina, for example, depended heavily on the sale of beef and wheat; Chile, on nitrates and copper; Brazil and the Caribbean nations, on sugar; and the Central American states, on bananas. Such exports brought large profits to a few, but for the majority of the population, the returns were meager.

During World War I, exports of some products, such as Chilean nitrates (used to produce explosives), increased dramatically. In general, however, the war led to a decline in European investment in Latin America and a rise in the U.S. role in the local economies. The United States had already begun to intervene in Latin American politics in the early years of the twentieth century during its construction of the Panama Canal, which dramatically reduced the time and distance needed for ships to pass between the Atlantic and Pacific Oceans.

THE ROLE OF THE YANKEE DOLLAR By the late 1920s, the United States had replaced Great Britain as the foremost source of foreign investment in Latin America. Unlike the British, however, U.S. investors put their funds directly into production enterprises, causing large segments of the area's export industry to fall into American hands. A number of Central American states, for example, were popularly labeled "banana republics" because of the power and influence of the U.S.-owned United Fruit

Company. American firms also dominated the copper mining industry in Chile and Peru and the oil industry in Mexico, Peru, and Bolivia.

Increasing economic power served to reinforce the traditionally high level of U.S. political influence in Latin America, especially in Central America, a region that many Americans considered vital to U.S. national security. American troops occupied parts of both Nicaragua and Honduras to put down unrest or protect U.S. interests there. The growing U.S. presence in the region aroused hostility among Latin Americans, who resented their dependent relationship on the United States, which they viewed as an aggressive imperialist power. Some charged that Washington worked, sometimes through U.S. military intervention, to keep ruthless dictators, such as Juan Vicente Gómez of Venezuela and Fulgencio Batista of Cuba, in power to preserve U.S. economic influence. In a bid to improve relations with Latin American countries, in 1933 President Franklin D. Roosevelt promulgated the **Good Neighbor policy**, which rejected the use of U.S. military force in the region. To underscore his sincerity, Roosevelt ordered the withdrawal of U.S. marines from the island nation of Haiti in 1936. For the first time in thirty years, there were no U.S. occupation troops in Latin America.

Because so many Latin American nations depended for their livelihood on the export of raw materials and food products, the Great Depression of the 1930s was a disaster for the region. In 1930, the value of Latin American exports fell to only half the amount that had been exported in each of the previous five years. Spurred by the decline in foreign revenues, Latin American governments began to encourage the development of new industries to reduce dependence on imports. In some cases—the steel industry in Chile and Brazil, the oil industry in Argentina and Mexico—government investment made up for the absence of local sources of capital.

The Effects of Dependency

During the late nineteenth century, most governments in Latin America had been dominated by landed or military elites, who governed by the blatant use of military force. This trend continued during the 1930s as domestic instability caused by the effects of the Great Depression led to the creation of military dictatorships throughout the region, especially in Argentina and Brazil and, to a lesser degree, in Mexico—three countries that together possessed more than half of the land and wealth of Latin America (see Map 5.2).

ARGENTINA By no means were all of Latin America's problems the product of foreign influence. Some were self-imposed. In Argentina, autocratic rule by an elite minority had disastrous effects. The government of Argentina, controlled by landowners who had benefited from the export of beef and wheat, was slow to recognize the need to establish a local industrial base. In 1916, Hipólito Irigoyen (1852–1933), head of the Radical Party, was elected president on a program to improve conditions for the middle and lower classes. Little was achieved, however, as the party became increasingly corrupt and identified with the interests of the large landowners. In 1930, the army overthrew Irigoyen's government, but its effort to return to the past and suppress the growing influence of labor unions failed, and in 1946, General Juan Perón—claiming the support of the *descamisados* ("shirtless ones")— seized sole power (see Chapter 8).

BRAZIL Brazil followed a similar path. In 1889, the army overthrew the Brazilian monarchy, installed by Portugal decades before, and established a republic. But it was dominated by landed elites, many of whom had grown wealthy through their ownership of coffee plantations. By 1900, three-quarters of the world's coffee was grown in Brazil. As in Argentina, the ruling oligarchy ignored the importance of establishing an urban industrial base. When the Great Depression ravaged profits from coffee exports, a wealthy rancher, Getúlio Vargas (1883–1954), seized power and served as president from 1930 to 1945. At first, Vargas sought to appease the workers by instituting an eight-hour workday and a minimum wage, but influenced by the apparent success of fascist regimes in Europe, he ruled by increasingly autocratic means and relied on a police force that used torture to silence his opponents. His industrial policy was successful, however, and by the end of World War II, Brazil had become Latin America's major industrial power. In 1945, the army, concerned that Vargas was turning increasingly to leftist elements for support, forced him to resign.

MEXICO In the early years of the twentieth century, Mexico was in a state of turbulence. Under the rule of the longtime dictator Porfirio Díaz (see Chapter 1), the real wages of the working class had declined. Moreover, 95 percent of the rural population owned no land, and about a thousand families ruled almost all of Mexico. Much of the manufacturing sector, and most of the important export industries, was in the hands of foreign owners.

The first rumblings of discontent appeared among members of the intellectual elite, who in the early years of the century began to agitate for political reforms to introduce representative government. They also favored the adoption of measures to improve the lot of the urban and rural poor. In the meantime, violent protests erupted

© Cengage Learning

MAP 5.2 Latin America in the First Half of the Twentieth Century. Shown here are the boundaries dividing the countries of Latin America after the independence movements of the nineteenth century.

Q *Which areas remained under European rule?*

structure and on occasion even crossed the border to launch raids on small towns in the United States.

The growing specter of rural revolt caused great concern among the Mexican power elite, and in 1910 Díaz was forced to resign in favor of the reformist politician Francisco Madero (1873–1913). The latter sought to carry out a program of political reform, but he was unable to keep pace with the rapid change taking place throughout the country. In 1913, Madero was deposed and assassinated by one of Díaz's military subordinates.

For the next several years, Zapata and Pancho Villa continued to be important political forces in Mexico, publicly advocating measures to redress the economic grievances of the poor. But neither had a broad grasp of the challenges facing the country, and power eventually gravitated to a more moderate group of reformists around the Constitutionalist Party. The latter were intent on breaking the power of the great landed families and powerful U.S. corporations, but without engaging in radical land reform or the nationalization of property. After a bloody conflict that cost the lives of thousands, the moderates were able to consolidate power, and in 1917 the party promulgated a new constitution that established a strong presidency, initiated land reform policies, established limits on foreign investment, and set an agenda for social welfare programs. The United States had resisted many of these measures but eventually saw the wisdom of recognizing a government that had successfully avoided the hazards of a vast social revolution, such as had occurred in Russia.

In 1920, the Constitutionalist Party leader Alvaro Obregón assumed the presidency and began to carry out a reform program. But real change did not take place until the presidency of General Lázaro Cárdenas (1895–1970) in

in the countryside. In the poverty-stricken state of Chiapas, the rebel leader Emiliano Zapata (1879–1919) aroused landless peasants, who began seizing the haciendas of wealthy landowners. Eventually, Zapata (later made famous to U.S. audiences by the 1952 film *Viva Zapata*, starring Marlon Brando) was able to set up a local revolutionary regime under his own leadership. In the state of Chihuahua, farther to the north, the bandit leader Pancho Villa (1878–1923) terrorized the local power

1934. Cárdenas won wide popularity among the peasants by ordering the redistribution of 44 million acres of land controlled by landed elites. He also seized control of the oil industry, which had hitherto been dominated by major U.S. oil companies. Alluding to the Good Neighbor policy, President Roosevelt refused to intervene, and eventually Mexico agreed to compensate the U.S. oil companies for their lost property. It then set up PEMEX, a governmental organization, to run the oil industry. By now, the revolution was democratic in name only, as the ruling political party, known as the Institutional Revolutionary Party (PRI), controlled the levers of power throughout society. Every six years, for more than half a century, PRI presidential candidates automatically succeeded each other in office.

Latin American Culture

The first half of the twentieth century witnessed a dramatic increase in literary activity in Latin America, a result in part of its ambivalent relationship with Europe and the United States. Many authors, while experimenting with imported modernist styles, felt compelled to proclaim their region's unique identity through the adoption of Latin American themes and social issues. In *The Underdogs* (1915), for example, Mariano Azuela (1873–1952) presented a sympathetic but not uncritical portrait of the Mexican Revolution as his country entered an era of unsettling change.

In their determination to express Latin America's distinctive characteristics, some writers focused on the promise of the region's vast virgin lands and the diversity of its peoples. In *Don Segundo Sombra*, published in 1926, Ricardo Guiraldes (1886–1927) celebrated the life of the ideal *gaucho* (cowboy), defining Argentina's hope and strength through the enlightened management of its fertile earth. Likewise, in *Dona Barbara*, Rómulo Gallegos (1884–1969) wrote in a similar vein about his native Venezuela. Other authors pursued the theme of solitude and detachment, a product of the region's physical separation from the rest of the world.

Latin American artists followed their literary counterparts in joining the Modernist movement in Europe, yet they too were eager to promote the emergence of a new regional and national essence. In Mexico, where the government provided financial support for painting murals on

Struggle for the Banner. Like Diego Rivera, David Alfaro Siqueiros (1896–1974) decorated public buildings with large murals that celebrated the Mexican Revolution and the workers' and peasants' struggle for freedom. Beginning in the 1930s, Siqueiros expressed sympathy for the exploited and downtrodden peoples of Mexico in dramatic frescoes such as this one. He painted similar murals in Uruguay, Argentina, and Brazil and was once expelled from the United States, where his political art and views were considered too radical.

public buildings, the artist Diego Rivera (1886–1957) began to produce a monumental style of mural art that served two purposes: to illustrate the national past by portraying Aztec legends and folk customs and to popularize a political message in favor of realizing the social goals of the Mexican Revolution. His wife, Frida Kahlo (1907–1954), incorporated Surrealist whimsy in her own paintings, many of which were portraits of herself and her family.

CONCLUSION

THE TURMOIL BROUGHT ABOUT by World War I not only resulted in the destruction of several of the major Western empires and a redrawing of the map of Europe but also opened the door to political and social upheavals elsewhere in the world. In the Middle East, the decline and fall of the Ottoman Empire led to the creation of the secular republic of Turkey and several other new states carved out of the carcass of the old empire.

Other parts of Asia also witnessed the rise of movements for national independence. In India, Gandhi and his campaign of civil disobedience played a crucial role in his country's bid to be free of British rule. China waged its own dramatic struggle to establish a modern nation as two dynamic political organizations—the Nationalists and the Communists—competed for legitimacy as the rightful heirs of the old order. Japan continued to follow its own path to modernization, which, although successful from an economic point of view, took a menacing turn during the 1930s.

The nations of Latin America faced their own economic problems because of their dependence on exports. Increasing U.S. investments in Latin America contributed to growing hostility against the powerful neighbor to the north. The Great Depression forced the region to begin developing new industries, but it also led to the rise of authoritarian governments, some of them modeled after the fascist regimes of Italy and Germany.

By demolishing the remnants of their old civilization on the battlefields of World War I, Europeans had inadvertently encouraged the subject peoples of their vast colonial empires to begin their own movements for national independence. The process was by no means completed in the two decades following the Treaty of Versailles, but the bonds of imperial rule had been severely strained. Once Europeans began to weaken themselves in the even more destructive conflict of World War II, the hopes of colonial peoples for national independence and freedom could at last be realized. It is to that devastating world conflict that we now turn.

TIMELINE

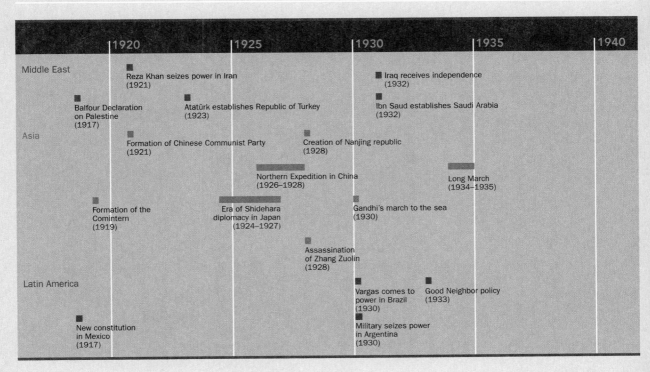

CHAPTER NOTES

1. Quoted in M. Gettleman, ed., *Vietnam: History, Documents, and Opinion on a Major World Crisis* (New York, 1965), p. 32.
2. Ts'ai Yuan-p'ei, "Ta Lin Ch'in-nan Han," in *Ts'ai Yuan-p'ei Hsiensheng Ch'uan-chi* [Collected Works of Mr. Ts'ai Yuan-p'ei] (Taipei, 1968), pp. 1057–1058.
3. Quoted in Nicholas Rowland Clifford, *Spoilt Children of Empire: Westerners in Shanghai and the Chinese Revolution of the 1920s* (Hanover, N.H., 1991), p. 16.
4. Quoted in William Theodore de Bary et al., eds., *Sources of Chinese Tradition* (New York, 1963), p. 783.
5. Lu Xun, "Diary of a Madman," in *Selected Works of Lu Hsun* (Beijing, 1957), vol. 1, p. 20.
6. On my first trip into mainland China in the 1970s, it was still not unusual to see older Chinese women with bound feet, especially in rural areas.

6

The Crisis Deepens: The Outbreak of World War II

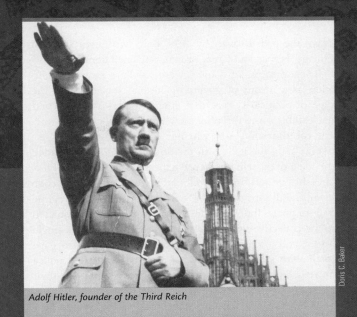

Adolf Hitler, founder of the Third Reich

Doris C. Baker

AFTER THE END of World War I, many Germans were unwilling to accept that their nation's armed forces had been vanquished on the battlefield, giving rise to the widespread belief that defeat had come about as the result of a "stab in the back" by traitorous elements within the German population. To some, there was no secret as to who those treasonous elements were: they were to be found in the country's Jewish population. Jews were prominent in many professions, including law, medicine, and education, and were active in the financial and banking sector as well. Widely envied and resented, they were ripe targets for attack by revenge-seeking revanchist groups within the country.

In the early 1930s, the nationalist firebrand Adolf Hitler took advantage of these sentiments to seize power in a country wracked by the Great Depression. In a relatively short period of time, Hitler, at the head of his National Socialist (Nazi) Party, installed himself as the dictator of what was termed the Third Reich. He soon embarked on a path to cleanse the country of its internal enemies and make Germany once again the dominant force in Europe. The ensuing conflict, which eventually spread worldwide, repeated the horrors of the previous "war to end all wars" and resulted in an even more decisive defeat for German forces on the battlefield. When World War II came to an end in 1945, there could be no further cries of a "stab in the back." Germany had been decisively defeated and its capital of Berlin lay in ruins. ◂

┌─ **CRITICAL THINKING** ─────────────

 What was the relationship between World War I and World War II, and how did the ways in which the wars were fought differ?

The Rise of Dictatorial Regimes

On February 3, 1933, only four days after he had been appointed chancellor of Germany, Adolf Hitler (1889–1945) met secretly with Germany's leading generals. He revealed to them his desire to remove the "cancer of democracy," create a new authoritarian leadership, and forge a new domestic unity. His foreign policy objectives were equally striking. Since Germany's living space was too small for its people, Hitler said, Germany must rearm and prepare for "the conquest of new living space in the east and its ruthless Germanization."

The rise of Adolf Hitler to supreme power in Germany was not an isolated incident, but part of a pattern that had spread throughout Europe and other parts of the world in the wake of the Great Depression. The apparent triumph of liberal democracy in 1919 had proven to be extremely short-lived. Italy had installed a fascist regime in the 1920s, and the Soviet Union under Joseph Stalin was a repressive dictatorial state. A host of other European states, and Latin American countries as well, adopted authoritarian systems, while a militarist regime in Japan moved that country down the path to war. By 1939, only two major states in Europe, France and Great Britain, remained democratic.

Dictatorships, of course, were hardly a new phenomenon as a means of governing human societies, but the type of political system that emerged after World War I did exhibit some ominous new characteristics. The modern **totalitarian state**, whether of the right (as in Germany) or of the left (as in the Soviet Union), transcended the ideal of passive obedience expected in a traditional dictatorship or authoritarian monarchy. It required the active loyalty and commitment of all its citizens to the regime and its goals. Individual freedom was to be subordinated to the collective will of the masses, represented by a single leader and a single party. Modern technology also gave totalitarian states the ability to use unprecedented police powers and communication techniques to impose their wishes on their subjects.

What explains the emergence of this frightening new form of government at a time when the Enlightenment and the Industrial Revolution had offered such bright hopes for the improvement of the human condition? According to the philosopher Hannah Arendt, in her renowned study, *The Origins of Totalitarianism* (1951), the totalitarian state was a direct product of the modern age. At a time when traditional sources of identity, such as religion and the local community, were in decline, alienated intellectuals found fertile ground for their radical ideas among rootless peoples deprived of their communal instincts and their traditional faiths by the corrosive effects of the Industrial Age. The Great Depression, which threw millions into poverty and sowed doubts about the viability of the capitalist system, made many observers even more vulnerable to prescriptions calling for a remaking of the human condition.

The Birth of Fascism

In the early 1920s, in the wake of economic turmoil, political disorder, and the general insecurity and fear stemming from World War I, Benito Mussolini (1883–1945) burst upon the Italian scene with the first **fascist** movement in Europe. Mussolini began his political career as a socialist but was expelled from the Socialist Party after supporting Italy's entry into World War I, a position contrary to the socialist principle of ardent neutrality in imperialist wars. In 1919, he established a new political group, the *Fascio di Combattimento*, or League of Combat. It received little attention in the parliamentary elections of 1919, but subsequently when worker strikes and a general climate of class violence broke out, alarmed conservatives turned to the Fascists, who formed armed squads to attack socialist offices and newspapers. On October 29, 1922, after Mussolini and the Fascists threatened to march on Rome if they were not given power, King Victor Emmanuel III (r. 1900–1946) capitulated and made Mussolini prime minister of Italy.

By 1926, Mussolini had established the institutional framework for his Fascist dictatorship. Press laws gave the government the right to suspend any publication that fostered disrespect for the Catholic Church, the monarchy, or the state. The prime minister was made "head of government" with the power to legislate by decree. A police law empowered the police to arrest and confine anybody for both nonpolitical and political crimes without due process of law. In 1926, all anti-Fascist parties were outlawed. By the end of 1926, Mussolini ruled Italy as *Il Duce*, the leader.

Mussolini's regime attempted to mold Italians into a single-minded community by developing Fascist organizations. By 1939, about two-thirds of the population between the ages of eight and eighteen had been enrolled in some kind of Fascist youth group. Activities for these groups included Saturday afternoon marching drills and calisthenics, seaside and mountain summer camps, and youth contests. Beginning in the 1930s, all young men were given some kind of premilitary exercises to develop discipline and provide training for war.

The Fascists also sought to reinforce traditional social attitudes, as is evident in their policies toward women. The Fascists portrayed the family as the pillar of the state and women as the foundation of the family. "Woman into the home" became the Fascist slogan. Women were to be homemakers and baby producers, "their natural and fundamental mission in life," according to Mussolini, who viewed population growth as an indicator of national strength. The Fascist attitude toward women also reflected a practical consideration: working women would compete with males for jobs in the depression economy of the 1930s. Eliminating women from the market reduced male unemployment.

Hitler and Nazi Germany

As Mussolini began to lay the foundations of his Fascist state in Italy, a young admirer was harboring similar dreams in Germany. Born on April 20, 1889, Adolf Hitler was the son of an Austrian customs official. He did poorly in secondary school and eventually made his way to Vienna to become an artist. Through careful observation of the political scene, Hitler became an avid German nationalist who learned from his experience in mass politics in Austria how political parties could use propaganda and terror effectively. But it was only after World War I, during which he served as a soldier on the Western Front, that Hitler became actively involved in politics. By then, he had become convinced that the German defeat had been caused by the Jews, for whom he now developed a fervent hatred.

THE ROOTS OF ANTI-SEMITISM Anti-semitism, of course, was not new to European civilization. Since the Middle Ages, Jews had been portrayed as the murderers of Christ and were often subjected to mob violence and official persecution. Their rights were restricted, and they were physically separated from Christians in separate urban sectors known as ghettos. By the nineteenth century, however, as a result of the ideals of the Enlightenment and the French Revolution, Jews were increasingly granted legal equality in many European countries. Many Jews left the ghettos to which they had been restricted and become assimilated into the surrounding Christian population. Some entered what had previously been the closed world of politics and the professions. Many Jews became successful as bankers, lawyers, scientists, scholars, journalists, and stage performers. Nowhere in Europe did Jews play a more active role in society than in Germany.

All too often, however, their achievements provoked envy and distrust. During the last two decades of the nineteenth century, German conservatives began to found parties that used dislike of Jews to win the votes of traditional lower-middle-class groups who felt threatened by changing times. Such parties also played on the rising sentiment of racism in German society. Spurred on by the widespread popularity of social Darwinism, rabid German nationalists promoted the concept of the *Volk* (nation, people, or race) as an underlying idea in German history since the medieval era. Portraying the German people as the successors of the pure "Aryan" race, the true and original creators of Western culture, nationalist groups called for Germany to take the lead in a desperate struggle to save European civilization from the destructive assaults of such allegedly lower races as Jews, blacks, Slavs, and Asians.

HITLER'S RISE TO POWER, 1919–1933 At the end of World War I, Hitler joined the obscure German Workers' Party and transformed it into a new organization called the National Socialist German Workers' Party (NSDAP), or Nazi for short. Hitler worked assiduously to develop the party into a mass political movement with flags, party badges, uniforms, its own newspaper, and its own police force or party militia known as the SA—the *Sturmabteilung*, or Storm Troops. The SA added an element of force and terror to the growing Nazi movement. Hitler's own oratorical skills as well as his populist message were largely responsible for attracting an increasing number of followers.

In November 1923, Hitler staged an armed uprising against the government in Munich, but the so-called Beer Hall Putsch was quickly crushed, and Hitler was sentenced to prison. During his brief stay in jail, he wrote *Mein Kampf (My Struggle)*, an autobiographical account of his movement and its underlying ideology. Virulent German nationalism, anti-Semitism, and anticommunism were linked together by a social Darwinian theory of struggle that stressed the right of superior nations to **Lebensraum** ("living space") through expansion and the right of superior individuals to secure authoritarian leadership over the masses.

After Hitler's release from prison, the Nazi Party rapidly expanded to all parts of Germany, increasing from 27,000 members in 1925 to 178,000 by the end of 1929. By 1932, the Nazi Party had 800,000 members and had become the largest party in the Reichstag, the German parliament. No doubt, Germany's economic difficulties were a crucial factor in the Nazis' rise to power. Unemployment had risen dramatically, from 4.35 million in 1931 to 6 million by the winter of 1932. The economic and psychological impact of the Great Depression made extremist parties more attractive. Hitler's appeal to national pride, national honor, and traditional militarism struck chords of emotion in his listeners, and the raw energy projected by his Nazi Party contrasted sharply with the apparent ineptitude emanating from its democratic rivals. As the conservative elites of Germany came to see Hitler as the man who could save Germany from a Communist takeover, President Paul von Hindenburg agreed to allow Hitler to become chancellor on January 30, 1933, and form a new government.

Within two months, Hitler had convinced Hindenburg to issue a decree suspending all basic rights for the full duration of the emergency—declared after a mysterious fire destroyed the Reichstag building in downtown Berlin— thus enabling the Nazis to arrest and imprison anyone without redress. When the Reichstag empowered the government to dispense with constitutional forms for four years while it issued laws that dealt with the country's problems, Hitler became a dictator appointed by the parliamentary body itself. The final step came on August 2, 1934, when Hindenburg died. The office of Reich president was abolished, and Hitler became sole ruler of Germany. Public officials and soldiers were all required to take a personal oath of loyalty to Hitler as the "Führer (leader) of the German Reich and people."

THE NAZI STATE, 1933–1939 Having smashed the Weimar Republic, Hitler now turned to his larger objective, the creation of a totalitarian state that would dominate Europe and possibly the world for generations to come. Mass demonstrations and spectacles were employed to integrate the German nation into a collective fellowship and to mobilize it as an instrument for Hitler's policies. In the economic sphere, the Nazis pursued the use of public works projects and "pump-priming" grants to private construction firms to foster employment and end the depression. But there is little doubt that rearmament contributed far more to solving the unemployment problem. Unemployment, which had stood at 6 million in 1932, dropped to 2.6 million in 1934 and fell below 500,000 in 1937. Although Hitler himself had little interest in either economics or administration, his prestige undoubtedly benefited enormously from spontaneous efforts undertaken throughout the country by his followers.

For its enemies, the Nazi totalitarian state had its instruments of terror and repression. Especially important was the SS (*Schutzstaffel*, or "protection echelon"). Originally created as Hitler's personal bodyguard, the SS, under the direction of Heinrich Himmler (1900–1945), came to control all of the regular and secret police forces. Other institutions, including the Catholic and Protestant churches,

The Führer Makes History! A common characteristic of modern totalitarian movements is their effort to mold all citizens from their earliest years into obedient servants of the state. In Nazi Germany, the vehicle responsible for training young minds was the *Hitler Jugend* (Hitler Youth). In this photograph, Adolf Hitler inspects members of the organization at a ceremony held sometime during the 1930s. On graduation, each member took an oath: "I swear to devote all my energies and my strength to the savior of our country, Adolf Hitler. I am willing and ready to give up my life for him, so help me God."

primary and secondary schools, and universities, were also brought under the control of the state. Nazi professional organizations and leagues were formed for civil servants, teachers, women, farmers, doctors, and lawyers; youth organizations—the *Hitler Jugend* (Hitler Youth) and its female counterpart, the *Bund Deutscher Mädel* (League of German Maidens)—were given special attention.

The Nazi attitude toward women was largely determined by ideological considerations. To the Nazis, the differences between men and women were quite natural. Men were warriors and political leaders, while women were destined to be wives and mothers. Certain professions, including university teaching, medicine, and law, were considered inappropriate for women. Instead, women were encouraged to pursue professional occupations that had direct practical application, such as social work and nursing.

A key goal of the Nazi regime was to resolve "the Jewish question." In September 1935, the Nazis announced new racial laws at the annual party rally in Nuremberg. These laws excluded Jews from German citizenship and forbade marriages and extramarital relations between Jews and German citizens. A more violent phase of anti-Jewish activity was initiated on November 9–10, 1938, the infamous *Kristallnacht*, or night of shattered glass. The assassination of a German diplomat in Paris became the excuse for a Nazi-led destructive rampage against the Jews; synagogues were burned, 7,000 Jewish businesses were destroyed, and at least one hundred Jews were killed. Moreover, 20,000 Jewish males were rounded up and sent to concentration camps. Jews were now barred from all public buildings and prohibited from owning, managing, or working in any retail store. Hitler would soon turn to more gruesome measures.

The Spread of Authoritarianism in Europe

Nowhere had the map of Europe been more drastically altered by World War I than in eastern Europe. The new states of Austria, Poland, Czechoslovakia, and Yugoslavia adopted parliamentary systems, and the preexisting kingdoms of Romania and Bulgaria gained new parliamentary constitutions in 1920. Greece became a republic in 1924. Hungary's government was parliamentary in form but controlled by its landed aristocrats. Thus, at the beginning of the 1920s, the future of political democracy seemed promising. Yet almost everywhere in eastern Europe, parliamentary governments soon gave way to authoritarian regimes.

Several factors helped create this situation. Eastern European states had little tradition of liberalism or parliamentary politics and no substantial middle class to support them. Then, too, these states were predominantly rural and agrarian. Many of the peasants were largely illiterate, and much of the land was still dominated by large land-owners who feared the growth of agrarian peasant parties with their schemes for land redistribution. Ethnic conflicts also threatened to tear these countries apart. Fearful of land reform, Communist agrarian upheaval, and ethnic conflict, powerful landowners, the churches, and even some members of the small middle class looked to author-itarian governments to maintain the old system. Only Czechoslovakia, with its substantial middle class, liberal tradition, and strong industrial base, maintained its politi-cal democracy.

In Spain, democracy also failed to survive. Fearful of the rising influence of left-wing elements in the government, in July 1936 Spanish military forces led by General Francisco Franco (1892–1975) launched a brutal and bloody civil war that lasted three years. Foreign intervention complicated the situation. Franco's forces were aided by arms, money, and men from Italy and Germany, and the government was assisted by 40,000 foreign volunteers and trucks, planes, tanks, and military advisers from the Soviet Union. After Franco's forces captured Madrid on March 28, 1939, the Spanish Civil War finally came to an end. General Franco soon established a dictatorship that favored large landowners, businessmen, and the Catholic clergy.

The Rise of Militarism in Japan

The rise of militant forces in Japan resulted not from a sei-zure of power by a new political party but from the grow-ing influence of nationalist elements at the top of the political hierarchy. During the 1920s, a multiparty system based on democratic practices appeared to be emerging. Two relatively moderate political parties, the Minseito and the Seiyukai, dominated the Diet and took turns pro-viding executive leadership in the cabinet. Radical ele-ments existed at each end of the political spectrum, but neither militant nationalists nor violent revolutionaries appeared to present a threat to the stability of the system.

In fact, the political system was probably weaker than it seemed at the time. Both of the major parties were deeply dependent on campaign contributions from power-ful corporations (the *zaibatsu*), and conservative forces connected to the military or the old landed aristocracy were still highly influential behind the scenes. As in the Weimar Republic in Germany during the same period, the actual power base of moderate political forces was weak, and politicians unwittingly undermined the fragility of the system by engaging in bitter attacks on each other.

Political tensions in Japan increased in 1928 when Chiang Kai-shek's forces seized Shanghai and several provinces in central China. In the next few years, Chiang engaged in negotiations with the remaining warlords north of the Yangtze River and made clear his intention to integrate the region, including the three provinces in Manchuria, into the new Nanjing republic. This plan rep-resented a direct threat to military strategists in Japan, who viewed resource-rich Manchuria as the key to their country's expansion onto the Chinese mainland. When Zhang Xueliang, son and successor of the Japanese puppet Zhang Zuolin (see Chapter 5), resisted Japanese threats and decided to integrate Manchuria into the Nanjing republic, the Japanese were shocked. "You forget," Zhang told one Japanese official, "that I am Chinese."[1] Appeals from Tokyo to Washington for a U.S. effort to restrain Chiang Kai-shek were rebuffed. Militant nationalists, out-raged at Japan's loss of influence in Manchuria, began to argue that the Shidehara policy of peaceful cooperation with other nations in maintaining the existing interna-tional economic order had been a failure.

THE MUKDEN INCIDENT In September 1931, acting on the pretext that Chinese troops had attacked a Japanese railway near the northern Chinese city of Mukden, Japanese military units stationed in the area seized con-trol throughout Manchuria. Although Japanese military authorities in Manchuria announced that China had pro-voked the action, the "Mukden incident," as it was called, had actually been carried out by Japanese saboteurs. Even-tually, worldwide protests against the Japanese action led the League of Nations to send an investigative commis-sion to Manchuria. When the commission issued a report condemning the seizure, Japan angrily withdrew from the League. Over the next several years, the Japanese con-solidated their hold on Manchuria, renaming it Manchu-kuo and placing it under the titular authority of former Chinese emperor and now Japanese puppet, Pu Yi.

Although no one knew it at the time, the Mukden inci-dent would later be singled out by some observers as the opening shot of World War II. The failure of the League of Nations to take decisive action sent a strong signal to Japan and other potentially aggressive states that they might pursue their objectives without the risk of united opposition by the major world powers. Despite its agoniz-ing efforts to build a system of peace and stability that would prevent future wars, the League had failed to resolve the challenges of the postwar era.

DEMOCRACY IN CRISIS Civilian officials in Tokyo had been horrified by the unilateral actions undertaken by ultranational Japanese military elements in Manchuria, but were cowed into silence. Despite doubts about the wisdom of the Mukden incident, the cabinet was too divided to disavow it, and military officers in Manchuria increasingly acted on their own initiative.

During the early 1930s, civilian cabinets were also struggling to cope with the economic challenges presented by the Great Depression. Already suffering from the decline of its business interests on the mainland, Japan began to feel the impact of the Great Depression after 1929 when the United States and major European nations raised their tariffs against Japanese imports in a desperate effort to protect local businesses and jobs. The value of Japanese exports dropped by 50 percent from 1929 to 1931, and wages dropped nearly as much. Hardest hit were the farmers as the prices of rice and other staple food crops plummeted. By abandoning the gold standard, Prime Minister Inukai Tsuyoshi was able to lower the price of Japanese goods on the world market, and exports climbed back to earlier levels. But the political parties were no longer able to stem the growing influence of militant nationalist elements.

In May 1932, Inukai Tsuyoshi was assassinated by right-wing extremists. He was succeeded by a moderate, Admiral Saito Makoto, but ultranationalist patriotic societies began to terrorize opponents, assassinating businessmen and public figures identified with the policy of conciliation toward the outside world. Some, like the publicist Kita Ikki, were convinced that the parliamentary system had been corrupted by materialism and Western values and should be replaced by a system that would return to traditional Japanese values and imperial authority. His message "Asia for the Asians" had not won widespread support during the relatively prosperous 1920s but increased in popularity after the Great Depression, which convinced many Japanese that capitalism was unsuitable for Japan.

During the mid-1930s, the influence of the military and extreme nationalists over the government steadily increased. Minorities and left-wing elements were persecuted, and moderates were intimidated into silence. Terrorists put on trial for their part in assassination attempts portrayed themselves as selfless patriots and received light sentences. Japan continued to hold national elections, and moderate candidates continued to receive substantial popular support, but the cabinets were dominated by the military or advocates of Japanese expansionism. In February 1936, junior officers in the army led a coup in the capital city of Tokyo, briefly occupying the Diet building and other key government installations and assassinating several members of the cabinet. The ringleaders were quickly tried and convicted of treason, but widespread sympathy for the defendants further strengthened the influence of the military in the halls of power.

The Path to War in Europe

When Hitler became chancellor on January 30, 1933, Germany's situation in Europe seemed weak. The Versailles Treaty had created a demilitarized zone on Germany's western border that would allow the French to move into the heavily industrialized parts of Germany in the event of war. To Germany's east, smaller states such as Poland and Czechoslovakia had defensive treaties with France. The Versailles Treaty had also limited Germany's army to 100,000 troops with no air force and only a small navy.

Posing as a man of peace in his public speeches, Hitler insisted that Germany wished only to revise the unfair provisions of Versailles by peaceful means and to take its rightful place among the European states. On March 9, 1935, he announced the creation of a new air force and, one week later, the introduction of a military draft that would expand Germany's army (the *Wehrmacht*) from 100,000 to 550,000 troops. France, Great Britain, and Italy condemned Germany's unilateral repudiation of the Versailles Treaty but took no concrete action.

On March 7, 1936, buoyed by his conviction that the Western democracies had no intention of using force to maintain the Treaty of Versailles, Hitler sent German troops into the demilitarized Rhineland. Under the treaty, the French had the right to use force against any violation of the demilitarized Rhineland. But France would not act without British support, and the British viewed the occupation of German territory by German troops as a reasonable action by a dissatisfied power. The London *Times*, reflecting the war-weariness that had gripped much of the European public since the end of the Great War, noted that the Germans were only "going into their own back garden."

Meanwhile, Hitler gained new allies. In October 1935, Mussolini committed Fascist Italy to imperial expansion by invading Ethiopia. Angered by French and British opposition to his invasion, Mussolini welcomed Hitler's support and began to draw closer to the German dictator he had once called a buffoon. The joint intervention of Germany and Italy on behalf of General Franco in the Spanish Civil War in 1936 also drew the two nations closer together. In October 1936, Mussolini and Hitler concluded an agreement that recognized their common political and economic interests. One month later, Germany and Japan concluded the Anti-Comintern Pact and agreed to maintain a common front against communism.

Stalin Seeks a United Front

From behind the walls of the Kremlin in Moscow, Joseph Stalin undoubtedly observed the effects of the Great Depression with a measure of satisfaction. During the early 1920s, once it became clear that the capitalist states in Europe had managed to survive without socialist revolutions, Stalin decided to improve relations with the outside world as a means of obtaining capital and technological assistance in promoting economic growth in the Soviet Union. But Lenin had predicted that after a brief period of stability in Europe, a new crisis brought on by overproduction and intense competition was likely to occur in the capitalist world. That, he added, would mark the beginning of the next wave of revolution. In the meantime, he declared, "We will give the capitalists the shovels with which to bury themselves."

To Stalin, the onset of the Great Depression was a signal that the next era of turbulence in the capitalist world was at hand, and during the early 1930s, Soviet foreign policy returned to the themes of class struggle and social revolution. When the influence of the Nazi Party reached significant levels in the early 1930s, Stalin viewed it as a pathological form of capitalism and ordered the Communist Party in Germany not to support the fragile Weimar Republic. Hitler would quickly fall, he reasoned, leading to a Communist takeover.

By 1935, Stalin had become uneasily aware that Hitler was not only securely in power in Berlin but also represented a serious threat to the Soviet Union. That summer, at a meeting of the Communist International held in Moscow, Soviet officials announced a shift in policy. The Soviet Union would now seek to form united fronts with capitalist democratic nations in Europe against the common danger of Nazism and fascism. Communist parties in capitalist countries and in colonial areas were instructed to cooperate with "peace-loving democratic forces" in forming coalition governments called **Popular Fronts**.

In most capitalist countries, Stalin's move was greeted with suspicion, but in France, a coalition of leftist parties—Communists, Socialists, and Radicals—fearful that rightists intended to seize power, formed a Popular Front government in June 1936. The new government succeeded in launching a program for workers. It included the right of collective bargaining, a forty-hour workweek, two-week paid vacations, and minimum wages. But

such policies failed to bring an end to the depression, and although it survived until 1938, the Front was for all intents and purposes dead before then. Moscow signed a defensive treaty with France and reached an agreement with three non-Communist states in eastern Europe (Czechoslovakia, Romania, and Yugoslavia), but talks with Great Britain achieved little result. The Soviet Union, rebuffed by London and disappointed by Paris, feared that it might be forced to face Hitler alone.

Decision at Munich

By the end of 1936, the Treaty of Versailles had been virtually scrapped, and Germany had erased much of the stigma of defeat. Hitler, whose foreign policy successes had earned him much public acclaim, was convinced that neither the French nor the British could effectively oppose his plans and decided in 1938 to annex Austria, where pro-German sentiment was strong. By threatening Austria with invasion, Hitler coerced the Austrian chancellor into putting Austrian Nazis in charge of the government. The new government promptly invited German troops to enter Austria and assist in maintaining law and order. One day later, on March 13, 1938, Austria formally became a part of Germany.

The annexation of Austria without objections from other European nations put Germany in position for Hitler's next objective—the destruction of Czechoslovakia. Although Czechoslovakia was quite prepared to defend itself and was supported by pacts with France and the Soviet Union, Hitler believed that its allies would not use force to defend it against a German attack.

His gamble succeeded. On September 15, 1938, Hitler demanded the cession to Germany of the Sudetenland (an area in western Czechoslovakia that was inhabited largely by ethnic Germans) and expressed his willingness to risk "world war" if he was refused. Instead of objecting, the British, French, Germans, and Italians—at a hastily arranged conference at Munich—reached an agreement that essentially met all of Hitler's demands. German troops were allowed to occupy the Sudetenland as the Czechs, abandoned by their Western allies as well as by the

Annexed Sudetenland, October 1938

Occupied Bohemia and Moravia, March 1939

Poland and Hungary

Annexed Czech territory, 1938 and 1939

© Cengage Learning

Central Europe in 1939

OPPOSING ✕ VIEWPOINTS

The Munich Conference

At the Munich Conference, the leaders of France and Great Britain capitulated to Hitler's demands on Czechoslovakia. When British Prime Minister Neville Chamberlain defended his actions at Munich as necessary for peace, another British statesman, Winston Churchill, characterized the settlement at Munich as "a disaster of the first magnitude." After World War II, political figures in western Europe and the United States would cite the example of appeasement at Munich to encourage vigorous resistance to expansionism by the Soviet Union.

Winston Churchill, Speech to the House of Commons (October 5, 1938)

I will begin by saying what everybody would like to ignore or forget but which must nevertheless be stated, namely, that we have sustained a total and unmitigated defeat, and that France has suffered even more than we have. . . . The utmost my right honorable Friend the Prime Minister . . . has been able to gain for Czechoslovakia and in the matters which were in dispute has been that the German dictator, instead of snatching his victuals from the table, has been content to have them served to him course by course. . . . And I will say this, that I believe the Czechs, left to themselves and told they were going to get no help from the Western Powers, would have been able to make better terms than they have got. . . .

We are in the presence of a disaster of the first magnitude which has befallen Great Britain and France. Do not let us blind ourselves to that. . . .

And do not suppose that this is the end. This is only the beginning of the reckoning. This is only the first sip, the first foretaste of a bitter cup which will be proffered to us year by year unless by a supreme recovery of moral health and martial vigor, we arise again and take our stand for freedom as in the olden time.

Neville Chamberlain, Speech to the House of Commons (October 6, 1938)

That is my answer to those who say that we should have told Germany weeks ago that, if her army crossed the border of Czechoslovakia, we should be at war with her. We had no treaty obligations and no legal obligations to Czechoslovakia. . . . When we were convinced, as we became convinced, that nothing any longer would keep the Sudetenland within the Czechoslovakian State, we urged the Czech Government as strongly as we could to agree to the cession of territory, and to agree promptly. . . . It was a hard decision for anyone who loved his country to take, but to accuse us of having by that advice betrayed the Czechoslovakian State is simply preposterous. What we did was save her from annihilation and give her a chance of new life as a new State, which involves the loss of territory and fortifications, but may perhaps enable her to enjoy in the future and develop a national existence under a neutrality and security comparable to that which we see in Switzerland today. Therefore, I think the Government deserves the approval of this House for their conduct of affairs in this recent crisis, which has saved Czechoslovakia from destruction and Europe from Armageddon.

 What were the opposing views of Churchill and Chamberlain on how to respond to Hitler's demands at Munich? Do these arguments have any wider relevance for other world crises?

SOURCES: *Parliamentary Debates, House of Commons* (London: His Majesty's Stationery Office, 1938), vol. 339, pp. 361–369; Neville Chamberlain, *In Search of Peace* (New York: Putnam, 1939), pp. 215, 217.

Soviet Union, stood by helplessly. The Munich Conference was the high point of Western **appeasement** of Hitler. British Prime Minister Neville Chamberlain returned to England from Munich boasting that the agreement meant "peace in our time." Hitler had promised Chamberlain that he had made his last demand (see the box above).

In fact, Munich confirmed Hitler's perception that the Western democracies were weak and would not fight. He was increasingly convinced of his own infallibility and had by no means been satisfied at Munich. In March 1939, Hitler occupied the Czech lands (Bohemia and Moravia), and with his encouragement, the Slovaks, who had always resented the condescending attitude of the more sophisticated Czechs, declared their independence of the Czechs and set up the German puppet state of Slovakia. On the evening of March 15, 1939, Hitler triumphantly declared in Prague that he would be known as the greatest German of them all.

The Western states were now alarmed by the Nazi threat. Hitler's naked aggression had made it clear that his promises were utterly worthless. When he began to demand the return to Germany of Danzig (a primarily German city that had been made a free city by the Treaty of Versailles to serve as a seaport for Poland), Britain recognized the danger and offered to protect Poland in the event of war. Both France and Britain realized that they needed Soviet help to contain Nazi aggression and began political and military negotiations with Stalin. Their distrust of Soviet communism, however, made an alliance unlikely.

Meanwhile, Hitler pressed on in the belief that Britain and France would not go to war over Poland. To preclude an alliance between the western European states and the Soviet Union, which would create the danger of a two-front war, Hitler, ever the opportunist, approached Stalin, who had given up hope of any alliance with Britain and France. The announcement on August 23, 1939, of the Nazi-Soviet Nonaggression Pact shocked the world. The treaty with the Soviet Union gave Hitler the freedom he sought, and on September 1, German forces invaded Poland. A secret protocol divided up the nation of Poland between the two signatories. Two days later, Britain and France declared war on Germany. Europe was again at war.

The Path to War in Asia

In the years immediately following the Japanese seizure of Manchuria in the fall of 1931, Japanese military forces began to expand gradually into North China. Using the tactics of military intimidation and diplomatic bullying rather than all-out attack, Japanese military authorities began to carve out a new "sphere of influence" south of the Great Wall.

Not everyone in Tokyo agreed with this aggressive policy—the young Emperor Hirohito, who had succeeded to the throne in 1926, was initially nervous about possible international repercussions—but right-wing terrorists assassinated some of its key critics and intimidated others into silence. The United States refused to recognize the Japanese takeover of Manchuria, which Secretary of State Henry L. Stimson declared an act of "international outlawry," but was unwilling to threaten the use of

force. Instead, the Americans sought to avoid confrontation in the hope of encouraging moderate forces in Japanese society. As one senior U.S. diplomat with long experience in Asia warned in a memorandum to the president:

> Utter defeat of Japan would be no blessing to the Far East or to the world. It would merely create a new set of stresses, and substitute for Japan the USSR—as the successor to Imperial Russia—as a contestant (and at least an equally unscrupulous and dangerous one) for the mastery of the East. Nobody except perhaps Russia would gain from our victory in such a war.[2]

For the moment, the prime victim of Japanese aggression was China. Nevertheless, Chiang Kai-shek attempted to avoid a confrontation with Japan so that he could deal with what he considered the greater threat from the Communists. When clashes between Chinese and Japanese troops broke out, he sought to appease the Japanese by granting them the authority to administer areas in North China. But, as the Japanese moved steadily southward, popular protests in Chinese cities against Japanese aggression intensified. In December 1936, Chiang was briefly kidnapped by military forces commanded by General Zhang Xueliang, who compelled him to end his military efforts against the Communists in Yan'an and form a new united front against the Japanese. After Chinese and Japanese forces clashed at Marco Polo Bridge, south of Beijing, in July 1937, China refused to apologize, and hostilities spread.

A Monroe Doctrine for Asia

Japan had not planned to declare war on China, but neither side would compromise, and the 1937 incident eventually turned into a major conflict. The Japanese advanced up the Yangtze valley and seized the Chinese capital of Nanjing, raping and killing thousands of innocent civilians in the process. The full enormity of the horrendous slaughter, which continued for several weeks, only emerged many years after the end of the war. The "Nanjing incident" aroused a deep-seated anger against Japan among the Chinese people that continues to affect relations between the two countries to this day.

But Chiang Kai-shek refused to capitulate and moved his government upriver to Hankou. When the Japanese seized that city, he

Japanese Advances into China, 1931–1939

MANCHURIA

Beijing

(1931–1938)

(1938–1939)

Hankou ■ Nanjing ■ ■ Shanghai

Chungking

© Cengage Learning

Keystone/Hulton Archive/Getty Images

A Japanese Victory in China. After consolidating its authority over Manchuria, Japan began to expand into northern China. Direct hostilities between Japanese and Chinese forces began in 1937. This photograph shows victorious Japanese forces in January 1938 riding under the arched Chungshan Gate in Nanjing after they had conquered the Chinese capital city. By 1939, Japan had conquered most of eastern China.

moved further upriver to Chungking, in remote Sichuan Province. Japanese strategists had hoped to force Chiang to join a Japanese-dominated **New Order in East Asia**, comprising Japan, Manchuria, and China. Now they established a puppet regime in Nanjing that would cooperate with Japan in driving Western influence out of East Asia. Tokyo hoped eventually to seize resource-rich Soviet Siberia and to create a new **Monroe Doctrine for Asia**, under which Japan would guide its Asian neighbors on the path to development and prosperity. After all, who better to instruct Asian societies on modernization than the one Asian country that had already achieved it?

Tokyo's "Southern Strategy"

During the late 1930s, Japan began to cooperate with Nazi Germany on a plan to launch a joint attack on the Soviet Union and divide up its resources between them. But when Germany surprised Tokyo by signing the nonaggression pact with the Soviets in August 1939, Japanese strategists were compelled to reevaluate their long-term objectives. Japan was not strong enough to defeat the Soviet Union alone, as a small but bitter border war along the Siberian frontier near Manchukuo had amply demonstrated. So the Japanese began to shift their gaze

southward to the vast resources of Southeast Asia—the oil of the Dutch East Indies, the rubber and tin of Malaya, and the rice of Burma and Indochina.

A move southward, of course, would risk war with the European colonial powers and the United States. Japan's attack on China in the summer of 1937 had already aroused strong criticism abroad, particularly in Washington, where President Franklin D. Roosevelt threatened to "quarantine" the aggressors after Japanese military units bombed a U.S. naval ship operating in China. The public's fear of involvement forced the president to draw back, but when Japan demanded the right to occupy airfields and exploit economic resources in French Indochina in the summer of 1940, the United States warned the Japanese that it would impose economic sanctions unless Japan withdrew from the area and returned to its borders of 1931.

Tokyo viewed the U.S. threat of retaliation as an obstacle to its long-term objectives. Japan badly needed liquid fuel and scrap iron from the United States. If they were cut off, Japan would have to find them elsewhere. The Japanese were thus caught in a vise. To obtain guaranteed access to the natural resources needed to fuel the Japanese military machine, Japan must risk being cut off from its current source of the raw materials that would be needed in the event of a conflict. After much debate, the Japanese decided to launch a surprise attack on U.S. and European colonies in Southeast Asia in the hope of a quick victory that would cement Japanese dominance in the region.

The World at War

On September 1, 1939, German forces suddenly attacked Poland. Using the tactics of **blitzkrieg**, or "lightning war," hundreds of tanks, supported by airplanes, broke quickly through Polish lines and encircled the bewildered Polish troops, whose courageous cavalry units were no match for the mechanized forces of their adversary. Conventional infantry units then moved in to hold the newly conquered territory. Within four weeks, Poland had surrendered. On September 28, 1939, Germany and the Soviet Union officially divided Poland between them. To Hitler's surprise, France and Britain declared war on Germany but took no action during a period of watchful waiting (dubbed the "phony war").

The War in Europe

Although France had joined with Great Britain in declaring war on Germany after the latter's attack on Poland, the French were ill prepared for the challenge. The political class was badly divided over both domestic and foreign policy (many conservatives openly preferred Nazi Germany over the left-leaning Socialists), and the country's military leaders had failed to appreciate the effectiveness of the new mechanized warfare. France therefore took little action when Germany launched a blitzkrieg against Denmark and Norway on April 9, 1940. One month later, the Germans attacked the Netherlands, Belgium, and France. German tank divisions broke through the weak French defensive positions in the Ardennes forest and raced across northern France, splitting the Allied armies and trapping French troops and the entire British army on the beaches of Dunkirk. Only by heroic efforts, and the German military commanders' crucial failure to exploit their advantage, did the British succeed in a gigantic evacuation of 330,000 Allied (mostly British) troops. The French capitulated on June 22. German armies occupied about three-fifths of France while the French hero of World War I, Marshal Philippe Petain (1856–1951), established a puppet regime (known as Vichy France) over the remainder. Germany was now in control of western and central Europe (see Map 6.1). Britain had still not been defeated, but it was reeling, and a new wartime cabinet under Prime Minister Winston Churchill debated whether to seek a negotiated peace settlement. Churchill, who doubted that Hitler could be trusted, was opposed.

THE BATTLE OF BRITAIN Encouraged by his stunning victories on the Continent, Hitler turned his attention to the invasion of Great Britain, an operation known as Sealion. An amphibious invasion of Britain could succeed only if Germany gained control of the air. In early August 1940, the *Luftwaffe* (German air force) launched a major offensive against British air and naval bases, harbors, communication centers, and war industries. The British fought back doggedly, supported by an effective radar system that gave them early warning of German attacks. Nevertheless, the British air force suffered critical losses and was probably saved by Hitler's change in strategy. In

September, in retaliation for a British air attack on Berlin, Hitler ordered a shift from military targets to massive bombing of cities to break British morale. The British rebuilt their air strength quickly and were soon inflicting major losses on *Luftwaffe* bombers. By the end of September, Germany had lost the Battle of Britain, and the invasion of the British Isles had to be abandoned.

The successful outcome of the Battle of Britain provided an enormous boost to British morale in a time of great peril. But behind the scenes, another development was unfolding that would eventually deal a more grievous blow to German prospects for victory. One of the most important weapons in the Allied arsenal was the ability to break the codes produced by the German code machine, known as Enigma. The product of code breakers from several countries, the Ultra project, as it eventually was called, had been initiated a decade earlier but only began to provide consistent access to German plans and actions by the summer of 1940. Eventually, it became an important, if not crucial, factor in several major Allied victories in World War II.

Thwarted in the west by the failure of Operation Sealion, Nazi leaders now pursued a new strategy, which called for Italian troops to capture Egypt and the Suez Canal, thereby closing the Mediterranean to British ships and shutting off Britain's supply of oil. This strategy failed when the British routed the Italian army. Although Hitler then sent German troops to the North African theater of war, his primary concern lay elsewhere; he had already reached the decision to fulfill his longtime obsession with the acquisition of territory in the east. In *Mein Kampf*, Hitler had declared that future German expansion must lie in the vast plains of southern Russia.

THE RUSSIAN CAMPAIGN Hitler was now convinced that Britain was remaining in the war only because it expected Soviet support. If the Soviet Union were smashed, Britain's last hope would be eliminated. Moreover, the German general staff was convinced that the Soviet Union, whose military leadership had been decimated by Stalin's purge trials, could be defeated quickly and decisively. The invasion of the Soviet Union was scheduled for spring 1941 but was delayed because of problems in the Balkans. Mussolini's disastrous invasion of Greece in October 1940 had exposed Italian forces to attack from British air bases in that country. To secure their Balkan flank, German troops seized both Yugoslavia and Greece in April 1941. Berlin had already obtained the political cooperation of Hungary, Bulgaria, and Romania. Now reassured, Hitler ordered an invasion of the Soviet Union on June 22, 1941, in the belief that the Soviets

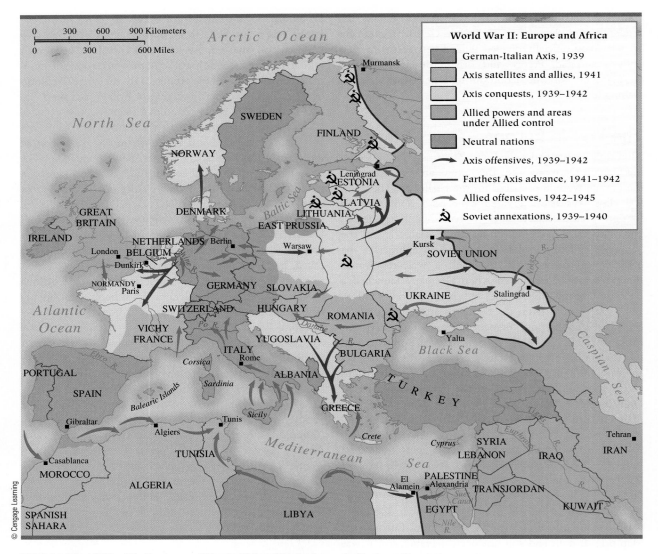

MAP 6.1 World War II in Europe and North Africa. With its fast and effective military, Germany quickly overwhelmed much of western Europe. Hitler had overestimated his country's capabilities, however, and underestimated those of his foes. By late 1942, his invasion of the Soviet Union was failing, and the United States had become a major factor in the war. The Allies successfully invaded Italy in 1943 and France in 1944.

 Which countries were neutral, and how did geography help make their neutrality an option?

could still be decisively defeated before winter set in. It was a fateful miscalculation.

The massive attack stretched out along an 1,800-mile front. German troops, supported by powerful armored units, advanced rapidly, capturing 2 million Russian soldiers. By November, one German army group had swept through Ukraine, and a second was besieging Leningrad; a third approached within 25 miles of Moscow, the Russian capital. An early winter and unexpected Soviet

resistance, however, brought a halt to the German advance. For the first time in the war, German armies had been stopped. A counterattack in December 1941 by Soviet army units newly supplied with U.S. weapons came as an ominous ending to the year for the Germans. Alarmed by the rapidity of the German advances in Europe, the Roosevelt administration had begun to provide military assistance (known as Lend-Lease) to the Soviet Union via shipments sent around northern

Scandinavia to the Soviet port of Murmansk. "We knew we were in trouble," one German war veteran remarked to me many years later, "when we became aware that many Russian soldiers were armed with American rifles."

The New Order in Europe

By the fall of 1941, the Nazi empire stretched across continental Europe from the English Channel in the west to the outskirts of Moscow in the east. The conquered territories were organized in two different ways. Some areas, such as western Poland, were annexed and transformed into German provinces. Most of occupied Europe, however, was administered indirectly by German officials with the assistance of collaborationist regimes.

Racial considerations played an important role in how conquered peoples were treated. German civil administrations were established in Norway, Denmark, and the Netherlands because the Nazis considered their peoples to be Aryan, or racially akin to the Germans, and hence worthy of more lenient treatment. Latin peoples, such as the occupied French, were given military administrations. But all the occupied territories were exploited for material goods and manpower for Germany's labor needs.

Because the conquered lands in the east contained the living space for German expansion and were populated in Nazi eyes by racially inferior Slavic peoples, Nazi administration there was considerably more ruthless. One million Poles were uprooted and dumped in southern Poland. Hundreds of thousands of ethnic Germans (descendants of Germans who had migrated years earlier from Germany to different parts of southern and eastern Europe) were encouraged to colonize designated areas in Poland. Hitler's grand vision called for a colossal project of social engineering after the war, in which Poles, Ukrainians, and Russians would become slave labor while German peasants settled on the abandoned lands and Germanized them.

Labor shortages in Germany led to a policy of ruthless mobilization of foreign labor. After the invasion of the Soviet Union, the 4 million Russian prisoners of war captured by the Germans, along with more than 2 million workers conscripted in France, became a major source of manpower. By the summer of 1944, 7 million foreign workers had been shipped to Germany, where they constituted 20 percent of Germany's labor force. Another 7 million were supplying forced labor in their own countries on farms, in industries, and even in military camps.

THE HOLOCAUST No aspect of the **Nazi New Order** was more tragic than the deliberate attempt to exterminate the Jewish people of Europe. Until 1939, Nazi policy focused on promoting the "emigration" of German Jews from Germany. Once the war began in September 1939, the so-called Jewish problem took on new dimensions. Evetually, Nazi leaders settled on what was called the **Final Solution** to the Jewish problem—the annihilation of the Jewish people. Reinhard Heydrich (1904–1942), head of the SS's Security Service, was given administrative responsibility to carry it out. After the defeat of Poland, Heydrich ordered his special strike forces—the *Einsatzgruppen*—to round up all Polish Jews and concentrate them in ghettos established in a number of Polish cities.

After the invasion of the Soviet Union in June 1941, the *Einsatzgruppen* were transformed into mobile killing units. These death squads followed the regular army's advance into the Soviet Union. Their job was to round up Jews in the villages and execute and bury them in mass graves, often giant pits dug by the victims themselves before they were shot. Even this approach to solving the Jewish problem was soon perceived as inadequate. Instead, the Nazis opted for the systematic annihilation of the European Jewish population in specially built death camps. Jews from occupied countries were rounded up, packed like cattle into freight trains, and shipped to Poland, where six extermination centers were built for this purpose. The largest and most famous was Auschwitz-Birkenau. Zyklon B (the commercial name for hydrogen cyanide) was selected as the most effective gas for quickly killing large numbers of people in gas chambers designed to look like shower rooms to facilitate the cooperation of the victims.

By the spring of 1942, the death camps were in operation. Although initial priority was given to the elimination of the ghettos in Poland, Jews were soon also being shipped from France, Belgium, and the Netherlands and eventually from Greece and Hungary. Despite desperate military needs, the Final Solution had priority in using railroad cars to transport Jews to the death camps.

By the end of the war, the Germans had killed between 5 and 6 million Jews, more than 3 million of them in the death camps. Virtually 90 percent of the Jewish populations of Poland, the Baltic countries, and Germany were exterminated. Overall, the **Holocaust** was responsible for the death of nearly two of every three European Jews.

The Nazis were also responsible for the death by shooting, starvation, or overwork of at least another 9 to 10 million people. Because the Nazis considered the Gypsies (like the Jews) an alien race, they were systematically rounded up for extermination. Civic leaders in many Slavic countries were also arrested and executed. The Nazis also singled out homosexuals for persecution, and thousands lost their lives in concentration camps.

The Holocaust: An Image from Buchenwald. When Allied troops began to occupy Nazi concentration camps in Germany, Austria, and Poland at the end of World War II, they were stunned by the horrific scenes of inhumanity that they observed there: ovens still filled with the charred remains of prisoners, piles of bodies rotting in uncovered graves, and emaciated survivors who greeted the troops with vacant eyes and frequently died within hours or days of their liberation. Some of the most poignant images were deceptively simple, though frightening in their connotations—piles of shoes, eyeglasses, and even children's toys, all left by the victims of the Nazi terror. Shown here are thousands of wedding rings found in a cave near the camp at Buchenwald.

War Spreads in Asia

On December 7, 1941, Japanese carrier-based aircraft attacked the U.S. naval base at Pearl Harbor in the Hawaiian Islands. The same day, other units launched assaults on the Philippines and began advancing toward the British colony of Malaya. Shortly thereafter, Japanese forces seized the British island of Singapore, invaded the Dutch East Indies, and occupied a number of islands in the Pacific Ocean. In some cases, as on the Bataan peninsula and the island of Corregidor in the Philippines, resistance was fierce, but by the spring of 1942, almost all of Southeast Asia and much of the western Pacific had fallen into Japanese hands. Placing the entire region under Japanese tutelage, Japan announced its intention to liberate Southeast Asia from Western rule. For the moment, however, Tokyo needed the resources of the region for its war machine and placed its conquests under its rule on a wartime footing.

Japanese leaders had hoped that their strike at American bases would destroy the U.S. Pacific Fleet and persuade the Roosevelt administration to accept Japanese domination of the Pacific. The American people, in the eyes of Japanese leaders, had been made soft by material indulgence. But the Japanese had miscalculated. Although the administration's apparent failure to anticipate the scope and direction of the Japanese attack has aroused legitimate criticism, the attack on Pearl Harbor galvanized American opinion and won broad support for Roosevelt's war policy. The United States now joined with European nations and the embattled peoples of Nationalist China in a combined effort to defeat Japan's plan to achieve hegemony in the Pacific.

U.S. STRATEGY IN THE PACIFIC On December 11, 1941, four days after the Japanese attack on Pearl Harbor, Germany committed a major error by declaring war on the United States. Confronted with the reality of a two-front war, President Roosevelt decided that because of the overwhelming superiority of the *Wehrmacht* in Europe, the war effort in that theater should receive priority over the conflict with Japan in the Pacific. Accordingly, U.S. war strategists drafted plans to make maximum use of their new ally in China. An experienced U.S. military commander, Lieutenant General Joseph Stilwell, was appointed as Roosevelt's special adviser to Chiang Kai-shek. His objective was to train Chinese Nationalist forces in preparation for an Allied advance through mainland China toward the Japanese islands. By the fall of 1942, Allied forces were beginning to gather for offensive operations into South China from Burma, while U.S. cargo planes continued to fly "over the hump" through the Himalaya Mountains to supply the Chinese government in Chungking with desperately needed war supplies.

In the meantime, the tide of battle began to turn in the Pacific. In the Battle of the Coral Sea in early May 1942, U.S. naval forces stopped the Japanese advance in the Dutch East Indies and temporarily relieved Australia of the threat of invasion. On June 4, American carrier planes destroyed all four of the attacking Japanese aircraft carriers near Midway Island and established U.S. naval superiority in the Pacific, even though almost all of the American planes were shot down in the encounter. The ability of U.S. intelligence operatives to break the Japanese military code by using an offshoot of the Ultra project, code-named "Magic," played a significant role in the victory. Farther to the south, U.S. troops under the command of General Douglas MacArthur launched their own campaign (dubbed "island hopping") by invading the Japanese-held island of New Guinea, at the eastern end of the Dutch East Indies. After a series of bitter engagements in the Solomon Islands from August to November 1942, Japanese fortunes in the area began to fade (see Map 6.2).

The New Order in Asia

Once their military takeover was completed, Japanese policy in the occupied areas of Asia became essentially defensive, as Japan hoped to use its new possessions to meet its burgeoning needs for raw materials, such as tin, oil, and rubber, as well as an outlet for Japanese manufactured goods. To provide an organizational structure for a new Great East Asia Co-Prosperity Sphere, a Ministry for Great East Asia, staffed by civilians, was established in Tokyo in October 1942 to handle relations between Japan and the conquered territories (see the box on p. 136).

ASIA FOR THE ASIANS? The Japanese conquest of Southeast Asia had been accomplished under the slogan "Asia for the Asians," and many Japanese sincerely believed that their government was liberating the peoples of southern Asia from European colonial rule. Japanese officials in the occupied territories made contact with nationalist elements and promised that independent governments would be established under Japanese tutelage. Such

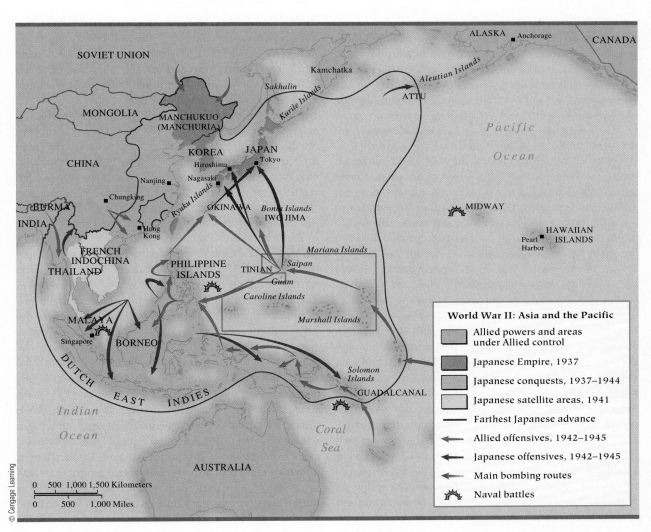

MAP 6.2 World War II in Asia and the Pacific. In 1937, Japan invaded northern China, beginning its effort to create the "Great East Asia Co-Prosperity Sphere." Further expansion led the United States to end iron and oil sales to Japan. Deciding that war with the United States was inevitable, Japan engineered a surprise attack on Pearl Harbor.

Q Why was control of the islands in the western Pacific of great importance both to the Japanese and to the Allies?

Japan's Plan for Asia

The Japanese objective in World War II was to create a vast Great East Asia Co-Prosperity Sphere to provide Japan with needed raw materials and a market for its exports. The following passage is from a secret document produced by a high-level government committee in January 1942.

Draft Plan for the Establishment of the Great East Asia Co-Prosperity Sphere

The Plan. The Japanese empire is a manifestation of morality and its special characteristic is the propagation of the Imperial Way. It is necessary to foster the increased power of the empire, to cause East Asia to return to its original form of independence and co-prosperity by shaking off the yoke of Europe and America, and to let its countries and peoples develop their respective abilities in peaceful cooperation and secure livelihood.

The Form of East Asiatic Independence and Co-Prosperity. The states, their citizens, and resources, comprised in those areas pertaining to the Pacific, Central Asia, and the Indian Oceans formed into one general union are to be established as an autonomous zone of peaceful living and common prosperity on behalf of the peoples of the nations of East Asia. The area including Japan, Manchuria, North China, lower Yangtze River, and the Russian Maritime Province, forms the nucleus of the East Asiatic Union. The Japanese empire possesses a duty as the leader of the East Asiatic Union.

The above purpose presupposes the inevitable emancipation or independence of Eastern Siberia, China, Indo-China, the South Seas, Australia, and India. . . .

Outline of East Asiatic Administration. It is intended that the unification of Japan, Manchoukuo, and China in neighborly friendship be realized by the settlement of the Sino-Japanese problems through the crushing of hostile influences in the Chinese interior, and through the construction of a new China. . . . Aggressive American and British influences in East Asia shall be driven out of the area of Indo-China and the South Seas, and this area should be brought into our defense sphere. The war with Britain and America shall be prosecuted for that purpose. . . .

Chapter 3: Political Construction

Basic Plan. The realization of the great ideal of constructing Greater East Asia Co-Prosperity requires not only the complete prosecution of the current Greater East Asia War but also presupposes another great war in the future. . . .

The following are the basic principles for the political construction of East Asia. . . .

The desires of the peoples in the sphere for their independence shall be respected, and endeavors shall be made for their fulfillment, but proper and suitable forms of government shall be decided for them in consideration of military and economic requirements and of the historical, political, and cultural elements peculiar to each area.

It must also be noted that the independence of various peoples of East Asia should be based on the idea of constructing East Asia as "independent countries existing within the New Order of East Asia" and that this conception differs from an independence based on the idea of liberalism and national self-determination. . . .

Western individualism and materialism shall be rejected, and a moral worldview, the basic principle of whose morality shall be the Imperial Way, shall be established. The ultimate object to be achieved is not exploitation but co-prosperity and mutual help, not competitive conflict but mutual assistance and mild peace, not a formal view of equality but a view of order based on righteous classification, not an idea of rights but an idea of service, and not several worldviews but one unified worldview.

 What were Japan's proposals for a Japanese-led Asia? What distinction did the government committee that drafted this document draw between "Western individualism and materialism" and the "Imperial Way"? Based on this document, were individualism and materialism a part of the Imperial Way?

Source: From *Sources of Japanese Tradition* by Wm. Theodore de Bary. Copyright © 1958 by Columbia University Press. Reprinted with permission of the publisher.

governments were eventually set up in Burma, the Dutch East Indies, Vietnam, the Philippines, and even India.

In fact, however, real power rested with the Japanese military authorities in each territory, and the local Japanese military command was directly subordinated to the Army General Staff in Tokyo. The economic resources of the colonies were exploited for the benefit of the Japanese war machine, while local peoples were recruited to serve in local military units or conscripted to work on public works projects. In some cases, the people living in the occupied areas were subjected to severe hardships. In Indochina, for example, forced requisitions of rice by the local Japanese authorities for shipment abroad created a food shortage that caused the starvation of more than a million Vietnamese in 1944 and 1945.

The Japanese planned to implant a new moral and social order as well as a new political and economic order in the occupied areas. Occupation policy stressed traditional values such as obedience, community spirit, filial piety, and discipline that reflected the prevailing political and cultural bias in Japan, while supposedly Western values such as materialism, liberalism, and individualism were strongly discouraged.

At first, many Asian nationalists took Japanese promises at face value and agreed to cooperate with their new masters. In Burma, an independent government was established in 1943 and subsequently declared war on the Allies. But as the exploitative nature of Japanese occupation policies became increasingly clear, sentiment turned against the new order. Japanese officials sometimes unwittingly provoked resentment by their arrogance and contempt for local customs. In the Dutch East Indies, for example, Indonesians were required to bow in the direction of Tokyo and recognize the divinity of the Japanese emperor, practices that were repugnant to Muslims. In Burma, Buddhist pagodas were sometimes used as military latrines. A generation later, many male Vietnamese still expressed anger at the memory of being severely punished by Japanese officials for urinating in public.

Like German soldiers in occupied Europe, Japanese military forces often had little respect for the lives of their subject peoples and viewed the Geneva Convention governing the treatment of prisoners of war as little more than a fabrication of the Western countries to tie the hands of their adversaries. In their conquest of northern and central China, the Japanese freely used poison gas and biological weapons, leading to the deaths of thousands of Chinese citizens. The Japanese occupation of the one-time Chinese capital of Nanjing, described earlier, was especially brutal.

Japanese soldiers were also savage in their treatment of Koreans. Almost 800,000 Koreans were sent overseas, most of them as forced laborers, to Japan. Tens of thousands of Korean women were forced to be "comfort women" (prostitutes) for Japanese troops. The Japanese also made extensive use of both prisoners of war and local peoples on construction projects for their war effort. In building the Burma-Thailand railway in 1943, for example, the Japanese used 61,000 Australian, British, and Dutch prisoners of war and almost 300,000 workers from Burma, Malaya, Thailand, and the Dutch East Indies. An inadequate diet and appalling work conditions in an unhealthy climate led to the deaths of 12,000 Allied prisoners of war and 90,000 local workers by the time the railway was completed. The conditions were later graphically portrayed in the award-winning movie, *The Bridge on the River Kwai*.

Such Japanese behavior created a dilemma for many nationalists, who had no desire to see the return of the colonial powers. Some turned against the Japanese, and others lapsed into inactivity. Indonesian patriots tried to have it both ways, feigning support for Japan while attempting to sabotage the Japanese administration. In Indochina, Ho Chi Minh's Indochinese Communist Party established contacts with American military units in South China and agreed to provide information on Japanese troop movements and rescue downed American fliers in the area. In Malaya, where Japanese treatment of ethnic Chinese residents was especially harsh, many joined a guerrilla movement against the occupying forces. By the end of the war, little support remained in the region for the erstwhile "liberators."

The Turning Point of the War, 1942–1943

The entry of the United States into the war created a coalition, called the Grand Alliance, that ultimately defeated the Axis Powers (Germany, Italy, and Japan). Nevertheless, the three major Allies—Britain, the United States, and the Soviet Union—had to overcome mutual distrust before they could operate as an effective alliance. President Roosevelt and Prime Minister Churchill had already agreed on a set of war aims—calling for the self-determination of all peoples—in a meeting held off the coast of Newfoundland in August 1941. But this accord, known as the **Atlantic Charter**, had not been cleared with Moscow. In a bid to allay Stalin's suspicion of U.S. intentions, President Roosevelt declared that the defeat of Germany should be the first priority of the alliance. The United States, through its Lend-Lease program, also sent large amounts of military aid, including $50 billion worth of trucks, planes, and other arms, to the Soviet Union. In 1943, the Allies agreed to fight until the **unconditional surrender** of the Axis Powers. This had the effect of making it nearly impossible for Hitler to divide his foes.

Victory, however, was only in the distant future for the Allied leaders at the beginning of 1942. As Japanese forces advanced into Southeast Asia and the Pacific after crippling the American naval fleet at Pearl Harbor, Axis forces continued the war in Europe against Britain and the Soviet Union. Reinforcements in North Africa enabled the Afrika Korps under General Erwin Rommel to break through the British defenses in Egypt and advance toward Alexandria. In the spring of 1942, a renewed German offensive in the Soviet Union led to the capture of the entire Crimean peninsula, causing Hitler to boast that in two years, German divisions would be on the border of India.

THE BATTLE OF STALINGRAD By that fall, however, the war had begun to turn against the Germans. In North Africa, British forces stopped Rommel's troops at El Alamein in the summer of 1942 and then forced them back across the desert. In November, U.S. forces landed in French North Africa and forced the German and Italian troops to surrender in May 1943. Allied war strategists drew up plans for an invasion of Italy, on the "soft underbelly" of Europe. But the true turning point of the war undoubtedly occurred on the Eastern Front, where the German armed forces suffered 80 percent of their casualties during the entire war. After capturing the Crimea, Hitler's generals wanted him to concentrate on the Caucasus and its oil fields, but Hitler decided that Stalingrad, a major industrial center on the Volga, should be taken as well. Accordingly, German forces advancing in the southern Soviet Union were divided. After three months of bitter fighting, German troops occupied the city of Stalingrad, but Soviet troops in the area, using a strategy of encirclement, now counterattacked. Besieged from all sides, the Germans were forced to surrender on February 2, 1943. The entire German Sixth Army of 300,000 men was lost, with the survivors sent off to prison camps. Soviet casualties were estimated at nearly one million, more than the United States lost in the entire war. By spring, long before Allied troops landed on the European continent, even Hitler knew that the Germans would not defeat the Soviet Union. The *Wehrmacht* was now in full retreat all across the Eastern Front.

ARSENAL OF DEMOCRACY Although the Battle of Stalingrad was probably the most important single battle in the war, an equally significant development was taking place across the Atlantic, where the growing industrial might of the United States was gradually being transformed from peaceful to wartime uses. By 1943, the United States had become the arsenal of the Allied Powers, producing the military equipment they needed. At the height of war production in 1943, the nation was constructing six ships a day and $6 billion worth of war-related goods a month. The output of American factories was dispatched not only to the U.S. forces overseas, but to Great Britain, the Soviet Union, and other Allies as well. Much of the industrial labor was done by American women, who, despite some public opposition, willingly took jobs in factories to replace husbands and brothers who had gone off to war. In addition, more than one million African Americans migrated from the rural South to the industrial cities of the North and West to find jobs in industry.

The Last Years of the War

By the beginning of 1943, the tide of battle had begun to turn against the Axis. On July 10, the Allies crossed the Mediterranean and carried the war to Italy. After taking Sicily, Allied troops began the invasion of mainland Italy in September.

© Dmitri Baltermants/The Dmitri Baltermants Collection/CORBIS

The Battle of Stalingrad. The Battle of Stalingrad was a major turning point on the Eastern Front. The Germans suffered a total defeat and the loss of the entire Sixth Army. This photograph shows thousands of captured soldiers being marched across frozen Soviet soil to prison camps. The soldiers in white fur hats are Romanian. Fewer than 6,000 captured soldiers survived to go home; the remainder—almost 85,000 prisoners—died in captivity.

Following the ouster and arrest of Mussolini, a new Italian government offered to surrender to Allied forces. But the Germans, in a daring raid, liberated Mussolini and set him up as the head of a puppet German state in northern Italy while German troops occupied much of Italy. The new defensive lines established by the Germans in the hills south of Rome were so effective that the Allied advance up the Italian peninsula was slow and marked by heavy casualties. Rome finally fell on June 4, 1944. By that time, the Italian war had assumed a secondary role as the Allies opened their long-awaited second front in western Europe. In the meantime, Allied war planners had stepped up their bombing raids on German cities, damaging the Nazi industrial capacity but killing thousands of civilians in the process.

OPERATION OVERLORD Since the autumn of 1943, under considerable pressure from Stalin, the Allies had been planning a cross-channel invasion of France (known as Operation Overlord) from Great Britain. Under the direction of U.S. General Dwight D. Eisenhower (1890–1969), five assault divisions landed on the Normandy beaches on June 6, 1944, in history's greatest naval invasion. An initially indecisive German response, due in part to effective Allied disinformation activities, enabled the Allied forces to establish a beachhead, although casualties were heavy. Within three months, they had landed 2 million men and a half-million vehicles that pushed inland and broke through the German defensive lines. Among them were French troops loyal to the French military commander Charles de Gaulle. After the puppet Vichy government was established in the summer of 1940, Colonel de Gaulle had fled the country and founded a Free French movement dedicated to cooperating with the Allies to overturn Nazi domination of the European continent.

After the breakout, Allied troops moved inland, liberating Paris by the end of August. By March 1945, they had crossed the Rhine and advanced into Germany. The Allied advance northward through Belgium encountered greater resistance, as German troops launched a desperate counterattack known as the Battle of the Bulge. The operation introduced a new generation of "King Tiger" tanks more powerful than anything the Allied forces could array against them. The Allies weathered the German attack, however, and in late April, they finally linked up with Soviet units at the Elbe River.

ADVANCE IN THE EAST The Soviets had come a long way since the Battle of Stalingrad in 1943. In the summer of 1943, Hitler had gambled on taking the offensive by making use of the first generation of "King Tiger" tanks. At the Battle of Kursk (July 5–12), the greatest engagement of World War II, involving competing forces numbering more than 3.5 million men, the Soviets soundly defeated the German forces. Soviet forces, now supplied with their own "T-34" heavy tanks, began a relentless advance westward. The Soviets reoccupied Ukraine by the end of 1943; lifted the siege of Leningrad, where more than one million people, the vast majority of them civilians, had died; and moved into the Baltic states by the beginning of 1944. Advancing along a northern front, Soviet troops occupied Warsaw in January 1945 and entered Berlin in April. Meanwhile, Soviet troops along a southern front swept through Hungary, Romania, and Bulgaria.

In January 1945, Hitler moved into a bunker 55 feet under Berlin to direct the final stages of the war. He committed suicide on April 30, two days after Mussolini was shot by partisan Italian forces. On May 7, German commanders surrendered. The war in Europe was over.

The Peace Settlement in Europe

In November 1943, Stalin, Roosevelt, and Churchill, the leaders of the Grand Alliance, met at Tehran (the capital of Iran) to decide the future course of the war. Their major strategic decision involved approval for an American-British invasion of the Continent through France, which Stalin had demanded; it was scheduled for the spring of 1944. The acceptance of this plan had important consequences. It meant that Soviet and British-American forces would meet in defeated Germany along a north-south dividing line and that eastern Europe would most likely be liberated by Soviet forces. The Allies also agreed to a partition of postwar Germany until denazification could take place. Roosevelt privately assured Stalin that Soviet borders in Europe would be moved westward to compensate for the loss of territories belonging to the old Russian Empire after World War I. Poland would receive lands in eastern Germany to make up for territory lost in the east to the Soviet Union.

The Yalta Agreement

In February 1945, the three Allied leaders met once again at Yalta, on the Crimean peninsula of the Soviet Union. Since the defeat of Germany was by now a foregone conclusion, much of the attention focused on the war in the

Pacific. At Tehran, Roosevelt had sought Soviet military help against Japan, and Stalin had assured him that Soviet forces would be in a position to enter the Pacific war three months after the close of the conflict in Europe. At Yalta, FDR reopened the subject. Development of the atomic bomb was not yet assured, and U.S. military planners feared the possibility of heavy casualties in amphibious assaults on the Japanese home islands. Roosevelt therefore agreed to Stalin's price for military assistance against Japan: possession of Sakhalin and the Kurile Islands, as well as two warm-water ports and railroad rights in Manchuria.

The creation of a new United Nations to replace the now discredited League of Nations was a major U.S. concern at Yalta. Roosevelt hoped to ensure the participation of the Big Three powers in a postwar international organization before difficult issues divided them into hostile camps. After a number of compromises, both Churchill and Stalin accepted Roosevelt's plans for the United Nations organization and set the first meeting for San Francisco in April 1945.

The issues of Germany and eastern Europe were treated less decisively and with considerable acrimony. The Big Three reaffirmed that Germany must surrender unconditionally and created four occupation zones. German reparations were set at $20 billion. A compromise was also worked out in regard to Poland. Stalin agreed to free elections in the future to determine a new government. But the issue of free elections in eastern Europe would ultimately cause a serious rift between the Soviets and the Americans and also become a source of political controversy in the United States. The Allied leaders agreed on an ambiguous statement that interim governments "broadly representative of all democratic elements in the population" would be formed in advance of the scheduling of free elections "responsive to the will of the people."[3] It would soon be clear that Moscow and Washington interpreted the provisions in different ways, a reality that would eventually lead to harsh criticism of Roosevelt's performance at Yalta from his opponents in the United States. For his part, FDR was determined to avoid the poisonous feelings left by the Treaty of Versailles after World War I and hoped to win Stalin's confidence as a means of maintaining the Grand Alliance at the close of the war.

Confrontation at Potsdam

Even before the next conference at Potsdam, Germany, took place in July 1945, Western relations with the Soviets had begun to deteriorate rapidly. The Grand Alliance had been one of necessity in which ideological incompatibility had been subordinated to the pragmatic concerns of the war. The Allied Powers' only common aim was the defeat of Nazism. Once this aim had been all but accomplished, the many differences that antagonized East-West relations came to the surface.

The Potsdam Conference of July 1945, the last Allied conference of World War II, consequently began under a cloud of mistrust. Roosevelt had died on April 12 and had been succeeded as president by Harry Truman. During the conference, Truman received word that the atomic bomb had been successfully tested. Some historians have argued that this knowledge stiffened Truman's resolve against the Soviets. Whatever the reasons, there was a new coldness in the relations between the Soviets and the Americans. At Potsdam, Truman demanded free elections throughout eastern Europe. After a bitterly fought and devastating war, however, Stalin sought absolute military security, which in his view could be ensured only by the presence of Communist states in eastern Europe. Free elections might result in governments hostile to the Soviet Union. By the middle of 1945, only an invasion by Western forces could undo developments in eastern Europe, and in the immediate aftermath of the world's most destructive conflict, few people favored such a policy. But the stage was set for a new confrontation, this time between the two major victors of World War II.

The War in the Pacific Ends

During the spring and early summer of 1945, the war in Asia continued, although with a significant change in approach. Allied war planners had initially hoped to focus their main effort on an advance through China with the aid of Chinese Nationalist forces trained and equipped by the United States. But Roosevelt became disappointed with Chiang Kai-shek's failure to take the offensive against Japanese forces in China and eventually approved a new strategy to strike toward the Japanese home islands directly across the Pacific. This "island-hopping" approach took an increasing toll on enemy resources, especially at sea and in the air (see the Film & History feature on p. 141). Meanwhile, new U.S. long-range B-29 bombers unleashed a wave of destruction on all major cities in the Japanese homeland. One massive firebombing raid on Tokyo in March 1945 killed more than 80,000 Japanese and caused such an enormous updraft that a U.S. aviator in one of the last B-29s to fly over the city was thrown into the air and broke his arm.

ENTERING THE NUCLEAR AGE As Allied forces drew inexorably closer to the main Japanese islands in the

FILM & HISTORY

Letters from Iwo Jima (2006)

In February 1945, U.S. forces launched an attack on Iwo Jima, a 5-mile-long volcanic island, located about 650 miles southeast of Tokyo. With its three airstrips, Iwo Jima was an important element in the ring of defenses protecting Japan, and the Allies intended to use it as an air base from which to bomb the main Japanese islands.

The Battle of Iwo Jima is the subject of two films directed by Clint Eastwood and released in 2006: *Flag of Our Fathers* presented the battle from the American viewpoint, and *Letters from Iwo Jima* presented the Japanese perspective. The second film won numerous awards, including a nomination for Best Picture. *Letters from Iwo Jima* is a realistic portrayal of the Japanese defense of the island. The plot focuses on two characters: the fictional Private Saigo (Kazunari Ninomiya), an ordinary soldier whose desire is to return home to his wife and daughter, and Lieutenant General Tadamichi Kuribayashi (Ken Watanabe), the actual commander of the Japanese forces on Iwo Jima. Kuribayashi is accurately portrayed as a man who shared the hardships of his men and had gained firsthand experience of the United States while spending three years there as a military attaché . Kuribayashi was largely responsible for the Japanese strategy of letting the U.S. Marines land on the beaches of Iwo Jima before attacking them with flanking fire from forces that were well protected in pillboxes and the miles of caves that permeated the island. The strategy proved very effective. The Japanese force of 22,000 men took a devastating toll on the Americans: out of the landing force of 110,000 men, 6,800 were killed and more than 17,000

General Tadamichi Kuribayashi (Ken Watanabe) prepares for the U.S. invasion of Iwo Jima.

were wounded. The assault that the U.S. military had expected to last only fourteen days dragged on instead for thirty-six.

The film also realistically portrays the code of *bushido* that motivated the Japanese forces. Based on an ideal of loyalty and service, the code emphasized the obligation to honor and defend emperor, country, and family, and to sacrifice one's life if one failed in this sacred mission. Before committing suicide, Captain Tanida (Takumi Bando) says to his men, "Men, we are honorable soldiers of the emperor. Don't ever forget that. The only way left for us is to die with honor." But the film also presents another, more human view of the Japanese soldiers that differs from the stereotype found in many American movies about World War II. For the most part, the Japanese and American soldiers are portrayed as being much the same: as men who were willing to kill and die, but who would prefer to simply go home and be with their families. ■

summer of 1945, President Harry Truman had an excruciatingly difficult decision to make. Should he use atomic weapons (at the time, only two bombs were available, and their effectiveness had not been demonstrated) to bring the war to an end without the necessity of an

Allied invasion of the Japanese homeland? The invasion of the island of Okinawa in April had resulted in thousands of casualties on both sides, with many Japanese troops committing suicide rather than surrendering to enemy forces.

After an intense debate within the administration, Truman approved the use of America's new superweapon. The first bomb was dropped on the city of Hiroshima on August 6. Truman then called on Japan to surrender or expect a "rain of ruin from the air." When the Japanese did not respond, a second bomb was dropped on Nagasaki three days later. The destruction in Hiroshima was incredible. Of 76,000 buildings near the center of the explosion, 70,000 were flattened, and 140,000 of the city's 400,000 inhabitants died by the end of 1945. By the end of 1950, another 50,000 had perished from the effects of radiation. The dropping of the first atomic bomb introduced the world to the nuclear age.

The nuclear attack on Japan, combined with the news that Soviet forces had launched an attack on Japanese-held areas in Manchuria, did have its intended effect, however.

Japan surrendered unconditionally on August 14. World War II was finally over.

In the years following the end of the war, Truman's decision to approve the use of nuclear weapons to compel Japan to surrender was harshly criticized, not only for causing thousands of civilian casualties but also for introducing a frightening new weapon that could threaten the survival of the human race. Some have even charged that Truman's real purpose in ordering the nuclear strikes was to intimidate the Soviet Union. Defenders of the decision argue that the human costs of invading the Japanese home islands would have been infinitely higher had the bombs not been dropped and that the Soviet Union would have had ample time to consolidate its control over Manchuria and command a larger role in the postwar occupation of Japan.

CONCLUSION

WORLD WAR II WAS THE MOST DEVASTATING total war in human history. Germany, Italy, and Japan had been utterly defeated. Tens of millions of people—soldiers and civilians—had been killed in only six years. Although accurate figures are impossible to come by, Soviet losses alone during the war have been estimated as high as 50 million.[4] In Asia and Europe, cities had been reduced to rubble, and millions of people faced starvation as once fertile lands stood neglected or wasted. Untold millions of people had become refugees.

What were the underlying causes of the war? One direct cause was the effort by two rising capitalist powers, Germany and Japan, to make up for their relatively late arrival on the scene by carving out their own global empires. Key elements in both countries had resented the agreements reached after the end of World War I that divided the world in a manner favorable to their rivals and hoped to overturn them at the earliest opportunity. Equally important, neither Germany nor Japan possessed a strong tradition of political pluralism; to the contrary, in both countries, the legacy of a feudal past marked by a strong military tradition still wielded great influence over the political system and the mind-set of the entire population. It is no

surprise that under the impact of the Great Depression, the effects of which were severe in both countries, fragile democratic institutions were soon overwhelmed by militant forces determined to enhance national wealth and power.

Why did the Axis Powers lose the war? The standard answer, of course, is that the Allied countries occupied the moral high ground in the conflict, and that conclusion is certainly not to be dismissed. But other more prosaic factors may have played a role as well. The ability of Allied intelligence agencies to break the German and Japanese code systems, enabling the Allies to anticipate the moves of their adversary on several occasions, was certainly a significant advantage. Equally important, Axis military leaders made a number of crucial strategic misjudgments, some of which have been noted in this chapter. Hitler's confidence in his own strategic genius, in particular, led him badly astray on several occasions. In the last analysis, however, the tendency of both German and Japanese leaders to underestimate the enormous capacity of the United States and the Soviet Union to harness their industrial and human resources in the war effort was perhaps their greatest mistake. They would pay dearly for their complacency.

TIMELINE

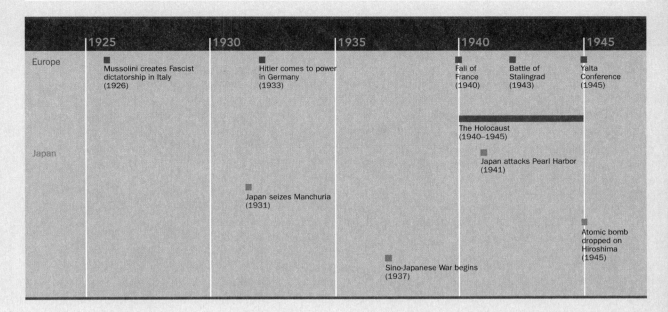

	1925	1930	1935	1940	1945

Europe

■ Mussolini creates Fascist dictatorship in Italy (1926)

■ Hitler comes to power in Germany (1933)

■ Fall of France (1940)

■ Battle of Stalingrad (1943)

■ Yalta Conference (1945)

The Holocaust (1940–1945)

Japan

■ Japan attacks Pearl Harbor (1941)

■ Japan seizes Manchuria (1931)

■ Atomic bomb dropped on Hiroshima (1945)

■ Sino-Japanese War begins (1937)

CHAPTER NOTES

1. Cited in Jonathon Fenby, *Chiang Kai-shek: China's Generalissimo and the Nation He Lost* (New York, 2003), p. 180.
2. John Van Antwerp MacMurray, quoted in Arthur Waldron, *How the Peace Was Lost: The 1935 Memorandum: "Developments Affecting American Policy in the Far East"* (Stanford, Calif., 1992), p. 5.
3. Cited in Ruhl Bartlett, *The Record of American Diplomacy* (New York, 1952), p. 665.
4. Cited in B. Schwarz, "A Job for Rewrite: Stalin's War," *New York Times*, February 2, 2004.

BY 1945, THE ERA OF GLOBAL HEGEMONY by the European imperialist nations was over. As World War I was followed by the Bolshevik Revolution, the Great Depression, the rise of Adolf Hitler, and the destructiveness of World War II, it appeared that the nations at the heart of traditional Western civilization would no longer serve as the main arbiters of world affairs. Instead, two new superpowers from outside the heartland of Europe—the United States and the Soviet Union—took their place. With the decline of the Old World, a new era of global relationships was about to begin.

THE TWO FACES OF NATIONALISM What were the underlying causes of the astounding spectacle of self-destruction that engaged the European powers in two bloody internecine conflicts within a period of less than a quarter of a century? One factor was the rise of nationalism. The spirit of nationalism had originally been praised by many Europeans as a positive development in the struggle to create peaceful and unified nation-states throughout the Continent. During the last quarter of the nineteenth century, however, it had instead become a divisive force,

loud and chauvinistic in tone, that created bitter disputes within a number of countries—especially in eastern Europe—and contributed to the growing rivalry among nations that eventually led to two world wars.

In fact, as many of its early advocates blissfully ignored, nationalism was also inherently divisive in its political ramifications. Most European countries consisted of a patchwork of various ethnic, linguistic, and religious communities, a product of centuries of migrations, wars, and dynastic alliances. How could a system of stable nation-states, each based on a single national community, ever emerge from such a bewildering amalgam of cultures and peoples? The peace treaties signed after the Great War replaced one set of territorial boundaries with another, but hardly resolved the underlying problem—the unending competition for resources and living space within the confines of a crowded continent. World War II was the tragic result.

THE TRANSFORMATION OF WARFARE Another factor that contributed to the violence of the early twentieth

century was the Industrial Revolution. Technology transformed the nature of war itself. New weapons of mass destruction created the potential for a new kind of warfare that reached beyond the battlefield into the very heartland of the enemy's territory, while the concept of nationalism transformed war from the sport of kings to a matter of national honor and commitment. This trend was amply demonstrated in the two world wars of the twentieth century. Each was a product of antagonisms that had been unleashed by economic competition and growing national consciousness. Each resulted in a level of destruction that severely damaged the material foundations and eroded the popular spirit of the participants, the victors as well as the vanquished.

In the end, then, industrial power and the driving force of nationalism, the very factors that had created the conditions for European global dominance, contained the seeds for the decline of that dominance. These seeds germinated during the 1930s, when the Great Depression sharpened international competition and mutual antagonisms, and then sprouted in the ensuing conflict, which embraced the entire globe. By the time World War II came to an end, the once-powerful countries of Europe were exhausted, leaving the door ajar not only for the emergence of the United States and the Soviet Union to global dominance but also for the collapse of the European colonial empires.

IMPERIALISM AND ITS DISCONTENTS If in Europe the dominant motif of the opening decades of the twentieth century had been the intense rivalry among the leading states over primacy in global affairs, in the rest of the world it was undoubtedly the challenge of dealing with the consequences of that struggle. By the early years of the century, a handful of European powers, increasingly challenged by Japan and the United States, had achieved political mastery over virtually the entire remainder of the world. While the overall effect of imperialism on the subject

peoples is still open to debate, it seems clear that for much of the population in colonial or semicolonial areas, imperialist domination was rarely beneficial and often destructive. Although a limited number of merchants, large landowners, and traditional hereditary elites undoubtedly prospered under the umbrella of the expanding imperialist economic order, the majority of people, urban and rural alike, suffered considerable hardship as a result of the policies adopted by their foreign rulers. The effects of the Industrial Revolution on the poor had been felt in Europe, too, but there the pain was eased somewhat by the fact that the industrial era had laid the foundations for future technological advances and material abundance. In the colonial territories, the importation of modern technology was limited, while most of the profits from manufacturing and commerce fled abroad. For too many, the "white man's burden" was shifted to the shoulders of the colonial peoples.

In response, the latter paradoxically turned to another European import, the spirit of nationalism. Some European historians have argued that nationalism was an artificial flower in much of the non-Western world, where allegiance was more often directed to the local community, the kinship group, or a religious faith. Even if that contention is justified—and the examples of Japan, Vietnam, and Thailand certainly appear exceptions to the rule—the concept of nationalism served a useful role in many countries in Asia and Africa. There it provided colonial peoples with a sense of common purpose that later proved vital in knitting together diverse elements to oppose colonial regimes and create the conditions for future independent states. At first, such movements had relatively little success, but they began to gather momentum in the second quarter of the twentieth century, when full-fledged nationalist movements began to appear throughout the colonial world to lead their people in the struggle for independence.

Beyond the question of national independence, of course, was the problem of adopting new institutions and values appropriate to the needs of a changing world. Western notions of representative government and individual freedom had their advocates in colonial areas well before the end of the nineteenth century. Countless Asians and Africans were exposed to such ideas in schools set up by the colonial regime or in the course of travel to Europe or the United States. Many of the nationalist parties founded in colonial territories espoused democratic principles and attempted to apply them when they took power after the restoration of independence.

As time went on, however, alternative ideas began to achieve popularity, especially during the late 1920s and 1930s when new ideologies such as communism and fascism began to take hold in a world ripped apart by the Great Depression. Even in Europe and the United States, confidence in the viability of democratic institutions was seriously undermined by the economic crisis that lasted until the outbreak of World War II.

For the time being, of course, the question was moot. Except in Latin America, where independent states attempted with varying degrees of success to grapple with foreign influence over their national economies, the imperialist powers showed no inclination to grant freedom to their subject peoples. Not until the end of World War II, when the era of European hegemony had clearly come to an end in the ashes of a devastated continent, would the colonial peoples begin to grasp the opportunity to take charge of their own destiny. In Part III, we will begin to address these issues. ❧

Across the Ideological Divide

Nixon lectures Soviet Communist Party chief Nikita Khrushchev on the technology of the U.S. kitchen

AP Images

East and West in the Grip of the Cold War

The victorious Allied leaders at Yalta

OUR MEETING HERE IN THE CRIMEA has reaffirmed our common determination to maintain and strengthen in the peace to come that unity of purpose and of action which has made victory possible and certain for the United Nations in this war. We believe that this is a sacred obligation which our Governments owe to our peoples and to all the peoples of the world.[1]

With these ringing words, drafted at the Yalta Conference in February 1945, President Franklin D. Roosevelt, Marshal Joseph Stalin, and Prime Minister Winston Churchill affirmed their common hope that their Grand Alliance, which had brought them victory in World War II, could be sustained in the postwar era. Only through the continuing and growing cooperation and understanding among the three victorious allies, the statement asserted, could a secure and lasting peace be realized that, in the words of the Atlantic Charter, would "afford assurance that all the men in all the lands may live out their lives in freedom from fear and want."

Roosevelt hoped that the decisions reached at Yalta would provide the basis for a stable peace in the postwar era. Allied occupation forces—American, British, and French in the west and Soviet in the east—were to bring about the end of Axis administration and organize free elections that would lead to democratic governments throughout Europe. To foster an attitude of mutual trust and end the suspicions that had marked relations between the capitalist world and the Soviet Union prior to World War II, Roosevelt tried to reassure Stalin that Moscow's legitimate territorial aspirations

and genuine security needs would be adequately met in a durable peace settlement.

It was not to be. Within months after the German surrender, the mutual trust among the victorious allies—if it had ever existed—rapidly disintegrated, and the dream of a stable peace was replaced by the specter of a nuclear holocaust. As the **Cold War** conflict between Moscow and Washington intensified, Europe was divided into two armed camps, and the two superpowers, glaring at each other across a deep ideological divide, held the survival of the entire world in their hands.

CRITICAL THINKING

Q How have historians answered the question of whether the United States or the Soviet Union bears the primary responsibility for the Cold War, and what evidence can be presented on each side of the issue?

The Collapse of the Grand Alliance

The problems started in Europe. At the end of the war, Soviet military forces occupied all of Eastern Europe and the Balkans (except for Greece, Albania, and Yugoslavia), while U.S. and other Allied forces completed their occupation of the western part of the Continent. Roosevelt had hoped that free elections administered by "democratic and peace-loving forces" would lead to the creation of democratic governments responsive to the aspirations of the local population. But it soon became clear that Moscow and Washington interpreted the Yalta agreement differently. When Soviet occupation authorities began forming a new Polish government in Warsaw, Stalin refused to accept the Polish government in exile—headquartered in London during the war and consisting primarily of representatives of the landed aristocracy who harbored a deep distrust of the Soviets—and instead installed a government composed of Communists who had spent the war in Moscow. Roosevelt complained to Stalin but, preoccupied with other problems, eventually agreed to a compromise whereby two members of the exile government in London were included in the new Communist-dominated regime. A week later, Roosevelt was dead of a cerebral hemorrhage, leaving the challenge to a new U.S. president, Harry Truman (1884–1972), who lacked experience in foreign affairs.

The Iron Curtain Descends

Similar developments took place elsewhere in Eastern Europe as all of the states occupied by Soviet troops became part of Moscow's sphere of influence. Coalitions of all political parties (except fascist or right-wing parties) were formed to run the government, but within a year or two, the Communist Party in each coalition had assumed the lion's share of power. The next step was the creation of one-party Communist governments. The timetables for these takeovers varied from country to country, but between 1945 and 1947, Communist governments became firmly entrenched in East Germany, Bulgaria, Romania, Poland, and Hungary. In Czechoslovakia, with its strong tradition of democratic institutions, the Communists did not achieve their goals until 1948. In the elections of 1946, the Communist Party became the largest party but was forced to share control of the government with non-Communist rivals. When it appeared that the latter might win new elections early in 1948, the Communists seized control of the government on February 25. All other parties were dissolved, and the Communist leader Klement Gottwald (1896–1953) became the new president of Czechoslovakia.

Yugoslavia was a notable exception to the pattern of growing Soviet dominance in Eastern Europe. The Communist Party there had led the resistance to the Nazis during the war and easily took over power when the war ended. Josip Broz, known as Tito (1892–1980), the leader of the Communist resistance movement, appeared to be a loyal Stalinist. After the war, however, he moved to establish an independent Communist state in Yugoslavia. Stalin had hoped to take control of Yugoslavia, just as he had done in other Eastern European countries. But Tito refused to capitulate to Stalin's demands and gained the support of the people (and some sympathy in the West) by portraying the struggle as one of Yugoslav national freedom. In 1948, Stalin had Yugoslavia formally expelled from the Soviet bloc, and from that point, the country embarked on a neutralist policy in the Cold War. In 1958, the Yugoslav party congress asserted that Yugoslav Communists did not see themselves as deviating from communism, only from Stalinism. They considered their more decentralized economic and political system, in which workers could manage themselves and local communes could exercise some political power, closer to the Marxist-Leninist ideal.

To Stalin (who had once boasted, "I will shake my little finger, and there will be no more Tito"), the creation of pliant pro-Soviet regimes throughout Eastern Europe to serve as a buffer zone against the capitalist West may simply have represented his interpretation of the Yalta peace agreement and a reward for sacrifices suffered during the war. Recent evidence suggests that Stalin did not decide to tighten Communist control over the new Eastern European governments until U.S. actions—notably the promulgation of the Marshall Plan (see "The Marshall Plan" below)—threatened to undermine Soviet authority in the region. If the Soviet leader had any intention of promoting future Communist revolutions in Western Europe—and there is some indication that he did—such developments would have to await the appearance of a new capitalist crisis a decade or more into the future. As Stalin undoubtedly recalled, Lenin had always maintained that revolutions come in waves.

The Truman Doctrine and the Beginnings of Containment

In the United States, the Soviet takeover of Eastern Europe represented an ominous development

Eastern Europe in 1948

Neutral nations

that threatened Roosevelt's vision of a durable peace. Public suspicion of Soviet intentions grew rapidly, especially among the millions of Americans who still had relatives living in Eastern Europe. Winston Churchill was quick to put such fears into words. In a highly publicized speech given to an American audience at Westminster College in Fulton, Missouri, in March 1946, the former British prime minister declared that an "Iron Curtain" had "descended across the Continent," dividing Germany and Europe itself into two hostile camps. Stalin responded by branding Churchill's speech a "call to war with the Soviet Union." But he need not have worried. Although public opinion in the United States placed increasing pressure on Washington to devise an effective strategy to counter Soviet advances abroad, the American people were in no mood for another war.

The first threat of a U.S.-Soviet confrontation took place in the Middle East. During World War II, British and Soviet troops had been stationed in Iran to prevent Axis occupation of the rich oil fields in that country. Both nations had promised to withdraw their forces after the war, but at the end of 1945, there were ominous signs that Moscow might attempt to use its troops as a bargaining chip to annex Iran's northern territories—known as Azerbaijan—to the Soviet Union. When the government of Iran, with strong U.S. support, threatened to take the issue to the United Nations, the Soviets backed down and removed their forces from that country in the spring of 1946.

A civil war in Greece created another potential arena for confrontation between the superpowers and an opportunity for the Truman administration to take a stand. Communist guerrilla forces supported by Tito, who hoped to create a Balkan federation under Yugoslav domination, had taken up arms against the pro-Western government in Athens. Great Britain had initially assumed primary responsibility for promoting postwar reconstruction in the eastern Mediterranean, but in 1947, postwar economic problems caused the British to withdraw from the active role they had been playing in both Greece and Turkey. President Truman, alarmed by British weakness and the possibility of Soviet expansion into the eastern Mediterranean, responded with the **Truman Doctrine**, which said in essence that the United States would provide financial aid to countries that claimed they were threatened by Communist expansion (see the box on p. 151). If the Soviets were not stopped in Greece, Truman declared, then the United States would have to face the spread of communism throughout the free world. As Dean Acheson, the American secretary of state, explained, "Like apples in a barrel infected by disease, the corruption of Greece would infect Iran and all the East . . . likewise

Africa . . . Italy . . . France. . . . Not since Rome and Carthage has there been such a polarization of power on this earth."[2]

The U.S. suspicion that Moscow was actively supporting the insurgent movement in Greece was inaccurate. Stalin was apparently unhappy that Tito was promoting the conflict, not only because he suspected that the latter was attempting to create his own sphere of influence in the Balkans but also because it risked provoking a direct confrontation between the Soviet Union and the United States in an area that was clearly within the American sphere of influence. "The rebellion in Greece," Stalin declared, "must be crushed."[3] The White House, however, was ignorant of Stalin's views.

THE MARSHALL PLAN The proclamation of the Truman Doctrine was soon followed in June 1947 by the European Recovery Program, better known as the **Marshall Plan**. Intended to rebuild prosperity and stability, this program included $13 billion for the economic recovery of war-torn Europe. Underlying the program was the belief that an economic revival would insulate the peoples of Europe from the appeal of international communism.

From the Soviet perspective, the Marshall Plan was nothing less than capitalist imperialism, a thinly veiled attempt to buy the support of the smaller European countries, which in return would be expected to submit to economic exploitation by the United States. The White House indicated that the Marshall Plan was open to the Soviet Union and its Eastern European satellite states, but they refused to participate. The Soviets, however, were in no position to compete financially with the United States and could do little to counter the Marshall Plan except to tighten their control in Eastern Europe.

Europe Divided

By 1947, the split in Europe between East and West had become a fact of life. At the end of World War II, the Truman administration had favored a quick end to its commitments in Europe, but fears of Soviet aims caused the United States to play an increasingly important role in European affairs. In an article in *Foreign Affairs* in July 1947, George Kennan, a well-known U.S. diplomat with much knowledge of Soviet affairs, advocated a policy of **containment** against further aggressive Soviet moves. Kennan favored the "adroit and vigilant application of counter-force at a series of constantly shifting geographical and political points, corresponding to the shifts and maneuvers of Soviet policy." After the Soviet blockade of Berlin in 1948, containment of the Soviet Union became formal U.S. policy.

The Truman Doctrine

By 1947, the battle lines in the Cold War had been clearly drawn. This excerpt is taken from a speech by President Harry Truman to the U.S. Congress in which he justified his request for aid to Greece and Turkey. Truman expressed the urgent need to contain the expansion of communism. Compare this statement with that of Soviet leader Leonid Brezhnev presented on p. 200.

Truman's Speech to Congress, March 12, 1947

The peoples of a number of countries of the world have recently had totalitarian regimes forced upon them against their will. The Government of the United States has made frequent protests against coercion and intimidation, in violation of the Yalta agreement, in Poland, Rumania, and Bulgaria. I must also state that in a number of other countries there have been similar developments.

At the present moment in world history nearly every nation must choose between alternative ways of life. The choice is too often not a free one.

One way of life is based upon the will of the majority, and is distinguished by free institutions, representative government, free elections, guarantees of individual liberty, freedom of speech and religion, and freedom from political oppression.

The second way of life is based upon the will of a minority forcibly imposed upon the majority. It relies upon terror and oppression, a controlled press and radio, fixed elections, and the suppression of personal freedoms.

I believe that it must be the policy of the United States to support free peoples who are resisting attempted subjugation by armed minorities or by outside pressures.

I believe that we must assist free peoples to work out their own destinies in their own way.

I believe that our help should be primarily through economic and financial aid which is essential to economic stability and orderly political processes. . . . I therefore ask the Congress for assistance to Greece and Turkey in the amount of $400,000,000.

 How did President Truman defend his request for aid to Greece and Turkey? What role did this decision play in intensifying the Cold War?

SOURCE: U.S. Congress, *Congressional Record*, 80th Congress, 1st Session (Washington, D.C.: U.S. Government Printing Office, 1947), Vol. 93, p. 1981.

The fate of Germany had become a source of heated contention between East and West. Aside from **denazification** and the partitioning of Germany (and Berlin) into four occupied zones, the Allied Powers had agreed on little with regard to the conquered nation. The Soviet Union, hardest hit by the war, took reparations from Germany in the form of booty. By the summer of 1946, nearly six hundred factories in the East German zone had been shipped to the Soviet Union. At the same time, the German Communist Party was reestablished under the control of Walter Ulbricht (1893–1973) and was soon in charge of the political reconstruction of the Soviet zone in eastern Germany.

THE BERLIN BLOCKADE Although the foreign ministers of the four occupying powers (the United States, the Soviet Union, Great Britain, and France) kept meeting in an attempt to arrive at a final peace treaty with Germany, they grew further and further apart. In response, the British, French, and Americans gradually began to merge their zones economically and by February 1948 were making plans for the formation of a national government. The Soviet Union responded with a blockade of West Berlin that prevented all traffic from entering the city's three western zones through Soviet-controlled territory in East Germany. The Soviets hoped to prevent the creation of a separate West German state, which threatened Stalin's plan to create a reunified Germany that could eventually be placed under Soviet control.

The Western powers faced a dilemma. Direct military confrontation seemed dangerous, and no one wished to risk World War III. Therefore, an attempt to break through the blockade with tanks and trucks was ruled out. The solution was the Berlin Airlift: supplies for the city's inhabitants were brought in by plane. At its peak, the airlift flew 13,000 tons of supplies daily into Berlin. The Soviets, who also wanted to avoid war, did not interfere and finally lifted the blockade in May 1949. But the blockade had severely increased tensions between the United States and the Soviet Union and confirmed the separation of Germany into two states. The Federal Republic of Germany (FRG) was formally created from the three Western zones in September 1949, and a month later, the separate German Democratic Republic (GDR) was established in East Germany. Berlin remained a divided city and the source of much contention between East and West.

A City Divided. In 1948, U.S. planes airlifted supplies into Berlin to break the blockade that Soviet troops had imposed to isolate the city. Shown here is "Checkpoint Charlie" (a crossing point between the Western and Soviet zones of Berlin) just as Soviet roadblocks are about to be removed. The banner at the entrance to the Soviet sector reads, ironically, "The sector of freedom greets the fighters for freedom and right of the Western sectors."

NATO AND THE WARSAW PACT The search for security in the new world of the Cold War also led to the formation of military alliances. The North Atlantic Treaty Organization (**NATO**) was formed in April 1949 when Belgium, Luxembourg, the Netherlands, France, Britain, Italy, Denmark, Norway, Portugal, and Iceland signed a treaty with the United States and Canada (see Map 7.1). All the powers agreed to provide mutual assistance if any one of them was attacked. A few years later, West Germany, Greece, and Turkey joined the alliance.

The Eastern European states soon followed suit. In 1949, they formed the Council for Mutual Economic Assistance (COMECON) for economic cooperation. Then, in 1955, Albania, Bulgaria, Czechoslovakia, East Germany, Hungary, Poland, Romania, and the Soviet Union organized a formal military alliance, the **Warsaw Pact**. Once again, Europe was tragically divided into hostile alliance systems.

WHO STARTED THE COLD WAR? There has been considerable historical debate over who bears responsibility

for starting the Cold War. In the 1950s, most scholars in the West assumed that the bulk of the blame must fall on the shoulders of Stalin, whose determination to impose Soviet rule on Eastern Europe snuffed out hopes for freedom and self-determination there and aroused justifiable fears of Communist expansion in the West. During the next decade, however, revisionist historians—influenced in part by their hostility to aggressive U.S. policies in Southeast Asia—began to argue that the fault lay primarily in Washington, where Truman and his anti-Communist advisers abandoned the precepts of Yalta and sought to encircle the Soviet Union with a tier of pliant U.S. client states. More recently, many historians have adopted a more nuanced view, noting that both the United States and the Soviet Union took some unwise steps that contributed to rising tensions at the end of World War II.

In fact, both nations were working within a framework conditioned by the past. The rivalry between the two superpowers ultimately stemmed from their different historical perspectives and their irreconcilable political

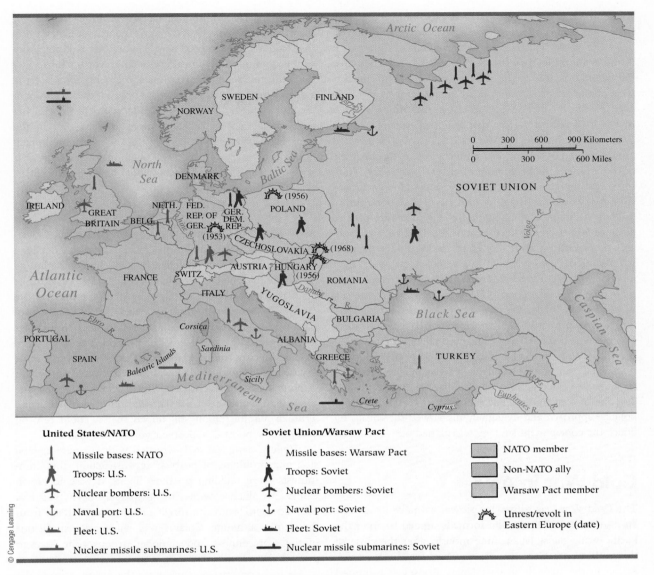

MAP 7.1 The New European Alliance Systems During the Cold War. This map shows postwar Europe as it was divided during the Cold War into two contending power blocs, the NATO alliance and the Warsaw Pact. Major military and naval bases are indicated by symbols on the map.

 Where on the map was the so-called Iron Curtain?

ambitions. As we have seen, intense competition for political and military supremacy had long been a regular feature of Western civilization. The United States and the Soviet Union were the heirs of that European tradition of power politics, and it should come as no surprise that two such different systems would seek to extend their way of life to the rest of the world. Because of its need to secure its western border, the Soviet Union was not prepared to give up the advantages it had gained in Eastern Europe

from Germany's defeat. But neither were Western leaders prepared to accept without protest the establishment of a system of Soviet satellites that not only threatened the security of Western Europe but also deeply offended Western sensibilities because of its blatant disregard of their concept of human rights.

This does not necessarily mean that both sides bear equal responsibility for starting the Cold War. Some revisionist historians have claimed that the U.S. doctrine of containment was a provocative action that aroused Stalin's suspicions and drove him into a position of hostility toward the West. This charge lacks credibility. Although it is understandable that the Soviets were concerned that the United States might use its monopoly of nuclear weapons to attempt to intimidate them, information now available from the Soviet archives and other sources makes it increasingly clear that Stalin's suspicions of the West were rooted in his Marxist-Leninist worldview and long predated Washington's enunciation of the doctrine of containment. As his foreign minister, Vyacheslav Molotov, once remarked, Soviet policy was inherently aggressive and would be triggered whenever the opportunity offered. Although Stalin apparently had no master plan to advance Soviet power into Western Europe, he was probably prepared to make every effort to do so once the next revolutionary wave arrived. Western leaders were fully justified in reacting to this possibility by strengthening their own lines of defense. On the other hand, a case can be made that in deciding to respond to the Soviet challenge in a primarily military manner, Western leaders overreacted to the situation and virtually guaranteed that the Cold War would be transformed into an arms race that could conceivably result in a new and uniquely destructive war. George Kennan, the original architect of the doctrine of containment, had initially proposed a primarily political approach and eventually disavowed the means by which the containment strategy was carried out.

Cold War in Asia

The Cold War was somewhat slower to make its appearance in Asia. At Yalta, Stalin formally agreed to enter the Pacific war against Japan three months after the close of the conflict with Germany. As a reward for Soviet participation in the struggle against Japan, Roosevelt promised that Moscow would be granted "preeminent interests" in Manchuria (interests reminiscent of those possessed by Imperial Russia prior to its defeat by Japan in 1904–1905) and the establishment of a Soviet naval base at Port Arthur. In return, Stalin promised to sign a treaty of alliance with the Republic of China, thus implicitly committing the Soviet Union not to provide the Chinese Communists with support in a possible future civil war. Although many observers would later question Stalin's sincerity in making such a commitment to the vocally anti-Communist Chiang Kai-shek, in Moscow the decision probably had a logic of its own. Stalin had no particular liking for the independent-minded Mao Zedong (he once derisively labeled the Chinese leader a "radish Communist"—red on the outside and white on the inside) and did

not anticipate a Communist victory in the eventuality of a civil war in China. Only an agreement with Chiang Kai-shek could provide the Soviet Union with a strategically vital economic and political presence in North China.

In the course of events, these agreements soon became a dead letter, and the region was sucked into the vortex of the Cold War by the end of the decade. The root of the problem lay not in the agreement at Yalta, but in the underlying weakness of Chiang Kai-shek's regime, which threatened to create a political vacuum in East Asia that both Moscow and Washington would be tempted to fill.

The Chinese Civil War

As World War II came to an end in the Pacific, relations between the government of Chiang Kai-shek in China and its powerful U.S. ally had become frayed. Although Roosevelt had hoped that China would be the keystone of his plan for peace and stability in Asia after the war, he eventually became disillusioned with the corruption of Chiang's government and his unwillingness to risk his forces against the Japanese (Chiang hoped to save them for use against the Communists after the war in the Pacific ended), and China became a backwater as the war came to a close. Nevertheless, U.S. military and economic aid to China had been substantial, and at war's end, the Truman administration still hoped that it could rely on Chiang to support U.S. postwar goals in the region.

While Chiang Kai-shek wrestled with Japanese aggression and problems of postwar reconstruction, the Communists were building up their liberated base in North China. An alliance with Chiang in December 1936 had relieved them from the threat of immediate attack from the south, although Chiang was chronically suspicious of the Communists and stationed troops near Xian to prevent them from infiltrating areas under his control.

He had good reason to fear for the future. During the war, the Communists patiently penetrated Japanese lines and built up their strength in North China. To enlarge their political base, they carried out a "mass line" policy designed to win broad popular support by reducing land rents and confiscating the lands of wealthy landlords. By the end of World War II, according to Communist estimates, 20 to 30 million Chinese were living under their administration, and their People's Liberation Army (PLA) included nearly one million troops.

As the war came to an end, world attention began to focus on the prospects for renewed civil strife in China. Members of a U.S. liaison team stationed in Yan'an during the last months of the war were impressed by the performance of the Communists, and some recommended that the United States should support them or at least remain neutral in a possible conflict between Communists and Nationalists for control of China. The Truman administration, though skeptical of Chiang's ability to forge a strong and prosperous country, was increasingly concerned about the spread of communism in Europe and tried to find a peaceful solution through the formation of a coalition government of all parties in China.

THE COMMUNIST TRIUMPH The effort failed. By 1946, full-scale war between the Nationalist government, now reinstalled in Nanjing, and the Communists resumed. Initially, most of the fighting took place in Manchuria, where newly arrived Communist units began to surround Nationalist forces occupying the major cities. Now Chiang Kai-shek's errors came home to roost. In the countryside, millions of peasants, attracted to the Communists by promises of land and social justice, flocked to serve in Mao Zedong's PLA. In the cities, middle-class Chinese, normally hostile to communism, were alienated by Chiang's brutal suppression of all dissent and his government's inability to slow the ruinous rate of inflation or solve the economic problems it caused. By the end of 1947, almost all of Manchuria was under Communist control.

The Truman administration reacted to the spread of Communist power in China with acute discomfort. Washington had no desire to see a Communist government on the mainland, but it had little confidence in Chiang Kai-shek's ability to realize Roosevelt's dream of a strong, united, and prosperous China. In December 1945, President Truman sent General George C. Marshall to China in a last-ditch effort to bring about a peaceful settlement, but anti-Communist elements in the Republic of China resisted U.S. pressure to create a coalition government with the Chinese Communist Party (CCP). During the next two years, the United States gave limited military support to Chiang's regime but refused to commit U.S. power to guarantee its survival. The administration's hands-off policy deeply angered many members of Congress, who charged that the White House was "soft on communism" and called for increased military assistance to the Nationalist government.

With morale dropping in the cities, Chiang's troops began to defect to the Communists. Sometimes whole divisions, officers as well as ordinary soldiers, changed sides. By 1948, the PLA was advancing south out of Manchuria and had encircled Beijing. Communist troops took the old imperial capital, crossed the Yangtze the following spring, and occupied the commercial hub of Shanghai (see Map 7.2). During the next few months, Chiang's government and 2 million of his followers fled to Taiwan, which the Japanese had returned to Chinese control after World War II.

With the Communist victory in China, Asia became a major theater of the Cold War and an integral element in American politics. In a white paper issued by the State Department in the fall of 1949, the Truman administration placed most of the blame for the debacle on Chiang Kai-shek's regime. Republicans in Congress, however, disagreed, arguing that Roosevelt had betrayed Chiang Kai-shek at Yalta by granting privileges in Manchuria to the Soviet Union. In their view, Soviet troops had hindered the dispatch of Nationalist forces to the area and provided the PLA with weapons to use against their rivals.

In later years, sources in Moscow and Beijing made clear that in actuality the Soviet Union gave little assistance to the CCP in its postwar struggle against the Nanjing regime. In fact, Stalin—likely concerned at the prospect of a

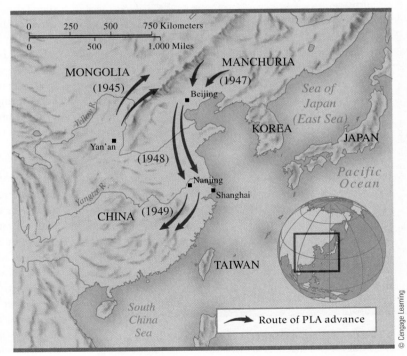

MAP 7.2 The Chinese Civil War. After the close of the Pacific war in 1945, the Nationalist government and the Chinese Communists fought a bitter civil war that ended with a Communist victory in 1949. The path of the Communist advance is shown on the map.

Q *Where did Chiang Kai-shek's government retreat to after its defeat?*

military confrontation with the United States—advised Mao against undertaking the effort. Although Communist forces undoubtedly received some assistance from Soviet occupation troops in Manchuria, their victory ultimately stemmed from conditions inside China. Nevertheless, the White House was forced to respond to its critics. During the spring of 1950, under pressure from Congress and public opinion to define U.S. interests in Asia, the Truman administration adopted a new national security policy that implied that the United States would take whatever steps were necessary to stem the further expansion of communism in the region. Containment had come to East Asia.

The New China

In their new capital at Beijing, China's Communist leaders hoped that their accession to power in 1949 would bring about an era of peace in the region and permit their new government to concentrate on domestic goals. But the desire for peace was tempered by their determination to

 Poster depicting Joseph Stalin (1879–1953) and Mao Tse-tung (1893–1976) shaking hands, c.1950 (colour litho), Russian School, (20th century)/Bibliotheque Nationale, Paris, France/Archives Charmet/The Bridgeman Art Library

A Pledge of Eternal Cooperation. After the Communist victory in the Chinese civil war, in 1950 Chairman Mao Zedong traveled to Moscow, where he negotiated a treaty of friendship and cooperation with the Soviet Union. The poster shown here trumpets the results of the meeting: "Long live and strengthen the unbreakable friendship and cooperation of the Soviet and Chinese peoples!" The two leaders, however, did not get along. Mao reportedly complained to colleagues that obtaining assistance from Stalin was "like taking meat from a tiger's mouth."

erase a century of humiliation at the hands of imperialist powers and to restore the traditional outer frontiers of the empire. In addition to recovering territories that had been part of the Manchu Empire, such as Manchuria, Taiwan, and Tibet, the Chinese leaders also hoped to restore Chinese influence in former tributary areas such as Korea and Vietnam.

It soon became clear that these two goals were not always compatible. Negotiations between Mao Zedong and Stalin held in Moscow in early 1950 were tense (see "The Sino-Soviet Dispute" below), but led to the signing of a mutual security treaty and Soviet recognition of Chinese sovereignty over Manchuria and Xinjiang (the desolate lands north of Tibet known as Chinese Turkestan because many of the peoples in the area were of Turkish origin), although the Soviets retained a measure of economic influence in both areas. Chinese troops occupied Tibet in 1950 and brought it under Chinese administration for the first time in more than a century. But in Korea and Taiwan, China's efforts to re-create the imperial buffer zone threatened to provoke new conflicts with foreign powers.

The problem of Taiwan was a consequence of the Cold War. As the civil war in China came to an end, the Truman administration appeared determined to avoid entanglement in China's internal affairs and indicated that it would not seek to prevent a Communist takeover of the island, now occupied by Chiang Kai-shek's Republic of China. But as tensions between the United States and the new Chinese government escalated during the winter of 1949–1950, influential figures in the United States began to argue that Taiwan was crucial to U.S. defense strategy in the Pacific.

The Korean War

The outbreak of war in Korea also helped bring the Cold War to East Asia. As we saw in Chapter 3, Korea, long a Chinese tributary, became part of the Japanese empire in 1908 and remained there until 1945. The removal of Korea from Japanese control had been one of the stated objectives of the Allies in World War II, and on the eve of the Japanese surrender in August 1945, the Soviet Union and the United States agreed to divide the country into two separate occupation zones at the 38th parallel. They originally planned to hold national elections after the restoration of peace to reunify Korea under an independent government. But as U.S.-Soviet relations deteriorated, two separate governments emerged in Korea, a Communist one in the north and an anti-Communist one in the south.

Tensions between the two governments ran high along the dividing line, and Kim Il-sung (1912–1994), the Communist leader in the north, asked Moscow to support his plan to unify the peninsula under his control. Stalin, however, was still unwilling to confront the United States: "If you should get kicked in the teeth," he replied, "I shall not lift a finger. You have to ask Mao for all the help."[4]

Kim, convinced that the United States lacked the stomach for a new war on the Asian mainland, was not deterred, and on June 25, 1950, North Korean troops invaded the south. The Truman administration, increasingly concerned about Communist intentions in Asia, immediately ordered U.S. naval and air forces to support South Korea, and the United Nations Security Council (with the Soviet delegate absent to protest the failure of the UN to assign China's seat to the new government in Beijing) passed a resolution calling on member nations to jointly resist the invasion in line with the security provisions in the United Nations Charter. By September, UN forces under the command of U.S. General Douglas MacArthur marched northward across the 38th parallel with the aim of unifying Korea under a single non-Communist government.

President Truman worried that by approaching the Chinese border at the Yalu River, the UN troops—the majority of whom were from the United States—could trigger Chinese intervention, but MacArthur assured him that China would not respond. In November, however, Chinese "volunteer" forces intervened on the side of North Korea and drove the UN troops southward in disarray. A static defense line was eventually established near the original dividing line at the 38th parallel, although the war continued.

To many Americans, the Chinese intervention in Korea was clear evidence that Beijing intended to promote communism throughout Asia. Immediately after the invasion, President Truman dispatched the U.S. Seventh Fleet to the Taiwan Strait to prevent a possible Chinese invasion of Taiwan. Recent evidence does suggest that Mao Zedong argued to his colleagues that they should not fear a confrontation with the United States on the Korean peninsula. But China's decision to enter the war was probably also motivated by the fear that hostile U.S. forces might be stationed on the Chinese frontier and perhaps even launch an attack across the border. MacArthur intensified such fears by calling publicly for air attacks, possibly including nuclear weapons, on Manchurian cities in preparation for an attack on Communist China.

Conflict in Indochina

A cease-fire agreement brought the hostilities in Korea to an end in July 1953, and China signaled its desire to live in peaceful coexistence with other independent countries in the region. But now a conflict on Beijing's southern flank began to intensify. The struggle had begun after Japan's surrender at the end of World War II, when the Indochinese Communist Party led by Ho Chi Minh (1890–1969), at the head of a multiparty nationalist alliance called the **Vietminh Front**, seized power in northern and central Vietnam. After abortive negotiations between Ho's government and the French over a proposed "free state" of Vietnam under French tutelage, war broke out in December 1946. French forces occupied the cities and the densely populated lowlands, while the Vietminh took refuge in the mountains.

For three years, the Vietminh waged a "people's war" of national liberation from colonial rule, gradually increasing in size and effectiveness. At the time, however, the conflict in Indochina attracted relatively little attention from world leaders. The Truman administration was uneasy about Ho's long-standing credentials as a Soviet agent but was equally reluctant to anger anticolonialist elements in the region by intervening on behalf of the French. Moscow had even less interest in the issue. Stalin—still hoping to see the Communist Party come to power in Paris—ignored Ho's request for recognition of his movement as the legitimate representative of the national interests of the Vietnamese people.

But what had begun as an anticolonial struggle by the Vietminh Front against the French became entangled in the Cold War after the CCP came to power in China. In early 1950, Beijing began to provide military assistance to the Vietminh to burnish its revolutionary credentials and protect its own borders from hostile forces. The Truman administration, increasingly concerned that a revolutionary "red tide" was sweeping through the region, decided to provide financial and technical assistance to the French, while pressuring them to prepare for an eventual transition to independent non-Communist governments in Vietnam, Laos, and Cambodia. With casualties mounting and the French public tired of fighting the

The Korean Peninsula

seemingly endless "dirty war" in Indochina, the French agreed to a peace settlement with the Vietminh at the Geneva Conference in 1954. Vietnam was temporarily divided into a northern Communist half (known as the Democratic Republic of Vietnam or DRV) and a non-Communist southern half based in Saigon (eventually to be known as the Republic of Vietnam). Elections were to be held in two years to create a unified government. Cambodia and Laos were both declared independent under neutral governments. French forces, which had suffered a major defeat at the hands of Vietminh troops at the Battle of Dien Bien Phu in the spring of 1954, were withdrawn from all three countries.

China had played an active role in bringing about the agreement and clearly hoped that a settlement would lead to a reduction of tensions in the area, but subsequent efforts to improve relations between China and the United States foundered on the issue of Taiwan. In the fall of 1954, the United States signed a mutual security treaty with the Republic of China guaranteeing U.S. military support in case of an invasion of Taiwan. When Beijing demanded U.S. withdrawal from Taiwan as the price for improved relations, diplomatic talks between the two countries collapsed.

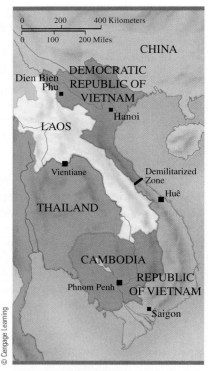

Indochina After 1954

From Confrontation to Coexistence

The 1950s opened with the world teetering on the edge of a nuclear holocaust. The Soviet Union had detonated its first nuclear device in 1949, and the two blocs—capitalist and socialist—viewed each other across an ideological divide that grew increasingly bitter with each passing year. Yet as the decade drew to a close, a measure of sanity crept into the Cold War, and the leaders of the major world powers began to seek ways to coexist in an increasingly unstable world (see Map 7.3).

Khrushchev and the Era of Peaceful Coexistence

The first clear sign of change occurred after Stalin's death in early 1953. His successor, Georgy Malenkov

(1902–1988), hoped to improve relations with the Western powers so that he could reduce defense expenditures and shift government spending to growing consumer needs. During his campaign to replace Malenkov two years later, Nikita Khrushchev (1894–1971) appealed to powerful pressure groups in the party Politburo (the governing body of the Communist Party of the Soviet Union) by calling for higher defense expenditures, but once in power, he resumed his predecessor's efforts to reduce tensions with the West and improve the living standards of the Soviet people.

In an adroit public relations touch, Khrushchev publicized Moscow's appeal for a new policy of **peaceful coexistence** with the West. In 1955, he surprisingly agreed to negotiate an end to the postwar occupation of Austria by the victorious Allies and allow the creation of a neutral country with strong cultural and economic ties with the West. He also called for a reduction in defense expenditures and reduced the size of the Soviet armed forces.

At first, Washington was suspicious of Khrushchev's motives, especially after the Soviet crackdown in Hungary in the fall of 1956 (see Chapter 9), an event that sharply increased Cold War tensions on both sides of the Iron Curtain.

THE BERLIN CRISIS A new crisis over Berlin added to the tension. The Soviets had launched their first intercontinental ballistic missile (ICBM) in August 1957, arousing U.S. fears—fueled by a partisan political debate—of a "missile gap" between the United States and the Soviet Union. Khrushchev attempted to take advantage of the U.S. frenzy over missiles to solve the problem of West Berlin, which had remained an island of prosperity inside the relatively poverty-stricken state of East Germany (the GDR). Many East Germans sought to escape to West Germany by fleeing through West Berlin—a serious blot on the credibility of the GDR and a potential source of instability in East-West relations. In November 1958, Khrushchev announced that unless the West removed its forces from West Berlin within six months, he would turn over control of the access routes to the East Germans. Unwilling to accept an ultimatum that would have abandoned West Berlin to the Communists, President

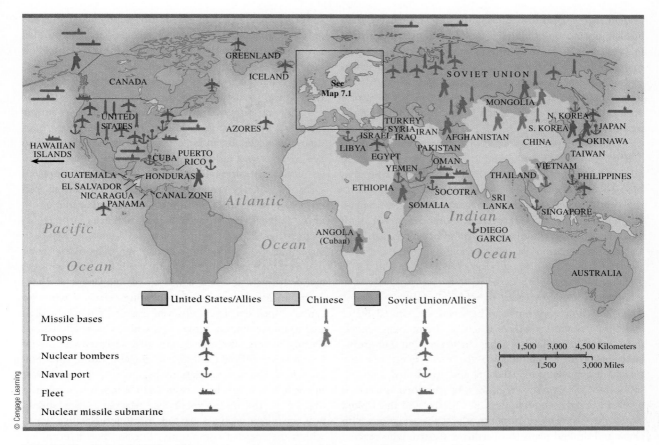

MAP 7.3 **The Global Cold War.** This map shows the location of the major military bases and missile sites maintained by the contending power blocs at the height of the Cold War.

Q *Which continents were the most heavily armed?*

Eisenhower and the West stood firm, and Khrushchev eventually backed down.

THE SPIRIT OF CAMP DAVID Despite such periodic crises in East-West relations, there were tantalizing signs that an era of true peaceful coexistence between the two power blocs could be achieved. In the late 1950s, the United States and the Soviet Union initiated a cultural exchange program to enable the peoples of the two blocs to become acquainted with each other's way of life (see the illustration on p. 147). While Leningrad's Kirov Ballet appeared at theaters in the United States, Benny Goodman and the film of Leonard Bernstein's *West Side Story* played in Moscow. In 1958, Nikita Khrushchev visited the United States and had a brief but friendly encounter with President Eisenhower at Camp David, the presidential retreat in northern Maryland. Predictions of improved future relations led reporters to laud "the spirit of Camp David."

Yet Khrushchev could rarely avoid the temptation to gain an advantage over the United States in the competition for influence throughout the world, and this resulted in an unstable relationship that prevented a lasting accommodation between the two superpowers. West Berlin was an area of persistent tension (a boil on the foot of the United States, Khrushchev derisively termed it), and in January 1961, just as newly elected president John F. Kennedy (1917–1963) took office, Moscow threatened once again to turn over responsibility for the access routes to the East German government.

Moscow also took every opportunity to promote its interests in the Third World, as the countries of Asia, Africa, and Latin America were now popularly called. Unlike Stalin, Khrushchev viewed the dismantling of colonial regimes in the area as a potential advantage for the Soviet Union and sought especially to exploit anti-American sentiment in Latin America. When neutralist leaders like Nehru in India, Tito in Yugoslavia, and Sukarno in Indonesia founded the **Nonaligned Movement** in 1955 as a means of providing an alternative to the two major power blocs, Khrushchev openly sought alliances with strategically important neutralist countries like India, Indonesia, Cuba, and Egypt at a time when Washington's ability to influence events at the United Nations had begun to wane.

In January 1961, just as Kennedy assumed the presidency, Khrushchev unnerved the new president at an informal summit meeting in Vienna by declaring that Moscow would provide active support to national liberation movements throughout the world. Increasingly, Washington was becoming concerned about Soviet meddling in such sensitive trouble spots as Southeast Asia, Central Africa, and the Caribbean.

The Cuban Missile Crisis

The Cold War confrontation between the United States and the Soviet Union reached frightening levels during the Cuban Missile Crisis. In 1959, a left-wing revolutionary named Fidel Castro (b. 1926) overthrew the Cuban dictator Fulgencio Batista and established a Soviet-supported totalitarian regime. As tensions increased between the new government in Havana and the United States, the Eisenhower administration broke relations with Cuba and drafted plans to overthrow Castro, who reacted by drawing closer to Moscow.

Soon after taking office in early 1961, Kennedy approved a plan to support an invasion of Cuba by anti-Castro exiles. But the attempt to land in the Bay of Pigs in southern Cuba was an utter failure. At Castro's request, the Soviet Union then decided to place nuclear missiles in Cuba. The Kennedy administration was not prepared to allow nuclear weapons within striking distance of the American mainland, although the United States had placed nuclear weapons in Turkey within easy range of the Soviet Union, a fact that Khrushchev was quick to point out. In October 1962, when U.S. intelligence discovered that a Soviet fleet carrying missiles was heading to Cuba, Kennedy decided to dispatch U.S. warships into the Atlantic to prevent the fleet from reaching its destination (see the Film & History feature on p. 161).

This approach to the problem was risky but had the benefit of delaying confrontation and giving the two sides time to find a peaceful solution. After a tense standoff during which the two countries came frighteningly close to a direct nuclear confrontation (the Soviet missiles already in Cuba, it turned out, were operational), Khrushchev finally sent a conciliatory letter to Kennedy agreeing to turn back the fleet if Kennedy pledged not to invade Cuba. In a

secret concession not revealed until many years later, the president also promised to dismantle U.S. missiles in Turkey. To the world, however (and to an angry Castro), it appeared that Kennedy had bested Khrushchev. "We were eyeball to eyeball," noted U.S. Secretary of State Dean Rusk, "and they blinked."

The realization that the world might have been annihilated in a matter of days had a profound effect on both sides. A communication hotline between Moscow and Washington was installed in 1963 to expedite rapid communication between the two superpowers in time of crisis. In the same year, the two powers agreed to ban nuclear tests in the atmosphere, a step that served to lessen the tensions between the two nations.

The Sino-Soviet Dispute

Nikita Khrushchev had launched his slogan of peaceful coexistence as a means of improving relations with the capitalist powers; ironically, one result of the campaign was to undermine Moscow's ties with its close ally China. During Stalin's lifetime, Beijing had accepted the Soviet Union as the official leader of the socialist camp. After Stalin's death, however, relations began to deteriorate. Part of the reason may have been Mao Zedong's contention that he, as the most experienced Marxist leader, should now be acknowledged as the most authoritative voice within the socialist community. But another determining factor was that just as Soviet policies were moving toward moderation, China's were becoming more radical.

Several other issues were involved, including territorial disputes and China's unhappiness with limited Soviet economic assistance. But the key sources of disagreement involved ideology and the Cold War. Chinese leaders were convinced that the successes of the Soviet space program confirmed that the socialists were now technologically superior to the capitalists (the East Wind, trumpeted the Chinese official press, had now triumphed over the West Wind), and they urged Khrushchev to go on the offensive to promote world revolution. Specifically, China wanted Soviet assistance in retaking Taiwan from Chiang Kai-shek. But Khrushchev was trying to improve relations with the West and rejected Chinese demands for support against Taiwan (see the box on p. 162).

By the end of the 1950s, the Soviet Union had begun to remove its advisers from China, and in 1961, the dispute broke into the open. Increasingly isolated, China voiced its hostility to what Mao described as the "urban industrialized countries" (which included the Soviet Union) and portrayed itself as the leader of the "rural underdeveloped countries" of Asia, Africa, and Latin America in a global struggle against imperialist oppression. In effect,

The Missiles of October (1973)

Never has the world been closer to nuclear holocaust than in October 1962, when U.S. and Soviet leaders found themselves in a direct confrontation over Nikita Khrushchev's decision to install Soviet missiles in Cuba, just 90 miles from the coast of the United States. When President John F. Kennedy announced that U.S. warships would intercept Soviet freighters bound for Cuban ports, the two countries teetered on the verge of war. Only after protracted and delicate negotiations was the threat defused. The confrontation sobered leaders on both sides of the Iron Curtain and led to the signing of the first test ban treaty and the opening of a hotline between Moscow and Washington.

The Missiles of October, a made-for-TV film produced in 1973, is a tense political drama that is all the more riveting because it is based on fact. Although it is less well known than the more recent *Thirteen Days*, released in 2000, it is more persuasive in many ways, and the acting is demonstrably superior. The film stars William Devane as John F. Kennedy and Martin

© Everett Collection

John Kennedy (William Devane, seated) and Robert Kennedy (Martin Sheen) confer with advisers.

Sheen as his younger brother Robert. Based in part on Robert Kennedy's book *Thirteen Days* (New York, 1969), a personal account of the crisis that was published shortly after his assassination in 1968, the film traces the tense discussions that took place in the White House as the president's key advisers debated how to respond to the Soviet challenge. President Kennedy remains cool as he reins in his more bellicose advisers to bring about a compromise solution that successfully avoids the seemingly virtual certainty of a nuclear confrontation with Moscow.

Because the film is based on the recollections of Robert Kennedy, it presents a favorable portrait of his brother's handling of the crisis, as might be expected, and the somewhat triumphalist attitude at the end of the film is perhaps a bit exaggerated. But Khrushchev's colleagues in the Kremlin and his Cuban ally, Fidel Castro, viewed the U.S.-Soviet agreement as a humiliation for Moscow that nevertheless set the two global superpowers on the road to a more durable and peaceful relationship. It was one Cold War story that had a happy ending. ■

China had applied Mao's famous concept of people's war in an international framework.

The Second Indochina War

The Eisenhower administration had opposed the peace settlement at Geneva in 1954, which divided Vietnam temporarily into two separate regroupment zones, specifically because the provision for future national elections opened up the possibility of placing the entire country under Communist rule. But President Eisenhower had been unwilling to introduce U.S. military forces to continue the conflict without the full support of the British and the French, who preferred to seek a negotiated settlement. In the end, Washington promised not to break the provisions of the agreement but refused to commit itself to the results.

During the next several months, the United States began to provide aid to a new government in South Vietnam. Under the leadership of the anti-Communist politician Ngo Dinh Diem (1901–1963), the Saigon regime began to root out dissidents while refusing to hold the national elections called for by the Geneva Accords. It was widely anticipated, even in Washington, that the Communists would win such elections. In 1959, Ho Chi Minh, despairing of the peaceful unification of the country

A Plea for Peaceful Coexistence

The Soviet leader Vladimir Lenin had contended that war between the socialist and imperialist camps was inevitable because the imperialists would never give up without a fight. That assumption had probably guided the thoughts of Joseph Stalin, who told colleagues shortly after World War II that a new war would break out in fifteen to twenty years. But Stalin's successor, Nikita Khrushchev, feared that a new world conflict could result in a nuclear holocaust and contended that the two sides must learn to coexist, although peaceful competition would continue. In this speech given in Beijing in 1959, Khrushchev attempted to persuade the Chinese to accept his views. But Chinese leaders argued that the "imperialist nature" of the United States would never change and warned that they would not accept any peace agreement in which they had no part.

Khrushchev's Speech to the Chinese, 1959

Comrades! Socialism brings to the people peace—that greatest blessing. The greater the strength of the camp of socialism grows, the greater will be its possibilities for successfully defending the cause of peace on this earth. The forces of socialism are already so great that real possibilities are being created for excluding war as a means of solving international disputes. . . .

When I spoke with President Eisenhower—and I have just returned from the United States of America—I got the impression that the President of the U.S.A.—and not a few people support him—understands the need to relax international tension. . . .

There is only one way of preserving peace—that is the road of peaceful coexistence of states with different social systems. The question stands thus: either peaceful coexistence or war with its catastrophic consequences. Now, with the present relation of forces between socialism and capitalism being in favor of socialism, he who would continue the "cold war" is moving toward his own destruction. . . .

Already in the first years of the Soviet power the great Lenin defined the general line of our foreign policy as being directed toward the peaceful coexistence of states with different social systems. For a long time, the ruling circles of the Western Powers rejected these truly humane principles. Nevertheless the principles of peaceful coexistence made their way into the hearts of the vast majority of mankind. . . .

It is not at all because capitalism is still strong that the socialist countries speak out against war, and for peaceful coexistence. No, we have no need of war at all. If the people do not want it, even such a noble and progressive system as socialism cannot be imposed by force of arms. The socialist countries therefore, while carrying through a consistently peace-loving policy, concentrate their efforts on peaceful construction; they fire the hearts of men by the force of their example in building socialism, and thus lead them to follow in their footsteps. The question of when this or that country will take the path to socialism is decided by its own people. This, for us, is the holy of holies.

 Why did Nikita Khrushchev feel that the conflict between the socialist and the capitalist camps that Lenin had predicted was no longer inevitable?

SOURCE: From G. F. Hudson et al., eds., *The Sino-Soviet Dispute* (New York: Frederick Praeger, 1961), pp. 61–63, cited in *Peking Review*, no. 40, 1959.

---

under Communist rule, returned to a policy of revolutionary war in the south. Late in the following year, a broad political organization that was designed to win the support of a wide spectrum of the population was founded in an isolated part of South Vietnam. Known as the National Liberation Front of South Vietnam, or NLF, it was under the firm leadership of Communist leaders in North Vietnam (see the box on p. 163).

By 1963, South Vietnam was on the verge of collapse. Diem's autocratic methods and inattention to severe economic inequality had alienated much of the population, and NLF armed forces, popularly known as the **Viet Cong** (Vietnamese Communists), had expanded their influence throughout much of the country. In the fall of 1963, with the approval of the Kennedy administration, South Vietnamese military officers overthrew the Diem regime. But factionalism kept the new military leadership from reinvigorating the struggle against the insurgent forces, and by early 1965, the Viet Cong, their ranks now swelled by military units infiltrating from North Vietnam, were on the verge of seizing control of the entire country. In desperation, President Lyndon B. Johnson (1908–1973) decided to launch bombing raids on the north and send U.S. combat troops to South Vietnam to prevent a total defeat for the anti-Communist government in Saigon.

Confrontation in Southeast Asia

In December 1960, the National Liberation Front of South Vietnam (NLF) was born. Composed of political and social leaders opposed to the anti-Communist government, it operated under the direction of the Communist regime in North Vietnam and served as the formal representative of revolutionary forces in the south throughout the remainder of the Vietnam War. When, in the spring of 1965, President Lyndon B. Johnson began to dispatch U.S. combat troops to Vietnam to prevent a Communist victory there, the NLF issued the declaration presented below. The second selection is from a speech that Johnson gave at Johns Hopkins University in April 1965 in response to the NLF.

Statement of the National Liberation Front of South Vietnam (1965)

American imperialist aggression against South Vietnam and interference in its internal affairs have now continued for more than ten years. More American troops and supplies, including missile units, Marines, B-57 strategic bombers, and mercenaries from South Korea, Taiwan, the Philippines, Australia, Malaysia, etc., have been brought to South Vietnam. . . .

The Saigon puppet regime, paid servant of the United States, is guilty of the most heinous crimes. These despicable traitors, these boot-lickers of American imperialism, have brought the enemy into our country. They have brought to South Vietnam armed forces of the United States and its satellites to kill our compatriots, occupy and ravage our sacred soil and enslave our people.

The Vietnamese, the peoples of all Indo-China and Southeast Asia, supporters of peace and justice in every part of the world, have raised their voice in angry protest against this criminal unprovoked aggression of the United States imperialists.

In the present extremely grave situation, the South Vietnam National Liberation Front considers it necessary to proclaim anew its firm and unswerving determination to resist the U.S. imperialists and fight for the salvation of our country. . . . [It] will continue to rely chiefly on its own forces and potentialities, but it is prepared to accept any assistance, moral and material, including arms and other military equipment, from all the socialist countries, from nationalist countries, from international organizations, and from the peace-loving peoples of the world.

Lyndon B. Johnson, "Peace Without Conquest"

The world as it is in Asia is not a serene or peaceful place.

The first reality is that North Viet-Nam has attacked the independent nation of South Viet-Nam. Its object is total conquest.

Of course, some of the people of South Viet-Nam are participating in attack on their own government. But trained men and supplies, orders and arms, flow in a constant stream from north to south.

This support is the heartbeat of the war.

And it is a war of unparalleled brutality. Simple farmers are the targets of assassination and kidnapping. Women and children are strangled in the night because their men are loyal to their government. And helpless villages are ravaged by sneak attacks. Large-scale raids are conducted on towns, and terror strikes in the heart of cities. . . .

Why are these realities our concern? Why are we in South Viet-Nam?

We are there because we have a promise to keep. Since 1954 every American President has offered support to the people of South Viet-Nam. We have helped to build, and we have helped to defend. Thus, over many years, we have made a national pledge to help South Viet-Nam defend its independence.

Our objective is the independence of South Viet-Nam, and its freedom from attack. We want nothing for ourselves—only that the people of South Viet-Nam be allowed to guide their own country in their own way.

We will do everything necessary to reach that objective. And we will do only what is absolutely necessary.

 How did the NLF justify its claim to represent the legitimate aspirations of the people of South Vietnam? What was President Johnson's counterargument?

Sources: "Statement of the National Liberation Front of South Vietnam," *New Times* (March 27, 1965), pp. 36–40. Source for Johnson's speech: *Public Papers of the Presidents of the United States: Lyndon B. Johnson, 1965*. Volume I, entry 172, pp. 394–399. Washington D.C.: Government Printing Office, 1966.

War in the Rice Paddies. The first stage of the Vietnam War consisted primarily of guerrilla conflict, as Viet Cong insurgents relied on guerrilla tactics to bring down the U.S.-supported government in Saigon. In 1965, however, in a desperate bid to prevent a Communist victory, President Lyndon Johnson ordered U.S. combat troops into South Vietnam, as shown here. Although U.S. military commanders believed that helicopters would be a key factor in defeating the insurgent forces in Vietnam, this was one instance when technological superiority did not produce a victory on the battlefied.

Hanoi responded to U.S. escalation by infiltrating more of its own regular force troops into the south, and by 1968, the war was a virtual stalemate. The Communists were not strong enough to overthrow the Saigon regime, whose weakness was shielded by the presence of half a million U.S. troops, but President Johnson was reluctant to engage in all-out war on North Vietnam for fear of provoking a global nuclear conflict. In the fall, after the Communist-led Tet offensive shook the fragile stability of the Saigon regime and aroused heightened antiwar protests in the United States, peace negotiations began in Paris.

THE ROAD TO PEACE Richard Nixon (1913–1994) came into the White House in 1969 on a pledge to bring an honorable end to the Vietnam War. With U.S. public opinion sharply divided on the issue, he began to withdraw U.S. troops while continuing to hold peace talks in Paris. But the centerpiece of his strategy was to improve relations with China and thus undercut Beijing's limited support for the North Vietnamese war effort. During the 1960s,

relations between Moscow and Beijing had reached a point of extreme tension, and thousands of troops were stationed on both sides of their long common frontier. To intimidate their Communist rivals, Soviet sources dropped the hint that they might decide to launch a preemptive strike to destroy Chinese nuclear facilities in Xinjiang. Sensing an opportunity to split the onetime allies, Nixon sent his emissary Henry Kissinger on a secret trip to China. Responding to the latter's assurances that the United States was determined to withdraw from Indochina and hoped to improve relations with the mainland regime, Chinese leaders invited President Nixon to visit China in early 1972.

Incensed at the apparent betrayal by their close allies, in January 1973 North Vietnamese leaders signed a peace treaty in Paris calling for the removal of all U.S. forces from South Vietnam. In return, the Communists agreed to seek a political settlement of their differences with the Saigon regime. But negotiations between north and south over the political settlement soon broke down, and in early 1975, convinced that Washington would not intervene, the

Communists resumed the offensive. At the end of April, under a massive assault by North Vietnamese military forces, the South Vietnamese government surrendered. A year later, the country was unified under Communist rule.

Why had the United States lost the Vietnam War? Many Americans argued that by not taking the war directly to North Vietnam, the White House had forced the U.S. armed forces to fight "with one hand tied behind their backs." Others retorted that the United States should not have gotten involved in a struggle for national liberation in the first place. Many years later, Dean Rusk, who had been secretary of state during the 1960s, declared that U.S. political leaders had underestimated the determination of the enemy and overestimated the patience of the American people. Perhaps, too, they had overestimated the ability of the Saigon government to earn the support of the people of South Vietnam.

The Communist victory in Vietnam was a humiliation for the United States, but its strategic impact was limited because of the new relationship with China. During the next decade, Sino-American relations continued to improve. In 1979, diplomatic ties were established between the two countries under an arrangement whereby the United States renounced its mutual security treaty with the Republic of China in return for a pledge from China to seek reunification with Taiwan by peaceful means. By the end of the 1970s, China and the United States had established diplomatic relations, while forging a "strategic relationship" in which each would cooperate with the other against the common threat of Soviet "hegemonism" (China's term for Soviet policy) in Asia.

An Era of Equivalence

When the Johnson administration sent U.S. combat troops to South Vietnam in 1965 in an effort to prevent the expansion of communism in Southeast Asia, Washington's primary concern was with Beijing, not Moscow. By the mid-1960s, U.S. officials viewed the Soviet Union as an essentially conservative power, more concerned with protecting its vast empire than with expanding its borders. In fact, U.S. policy makers periodically sought Soviet assistance in achieving a peaceful settlement of the Vietnam War. As long as Khrushchev was in power, they found a receptive ear in Moscow. Khrushchev did not want to risk a confrontation with the United States in Southeast Asia.

After October 1964, when Khrushchev was replaced by a new leadership headed by party chief Leonid Brezhnev (1906–1982) and Prime Minister Alexei Kosygin (1904–1980), Soviet attitudes about Vietnam became more ambivalent. On the one hand, the new Soviet leaders had no desire to see the Vietnam conflict poison relations between the great powers. On the other hand, Moscow was anxious to demonstrate its support for the North Vietnamese to deflect Chinese charges that the Soviet Union had betrayed the interests of the oppressed peoples of the world. As a result, Soviet officials voiced sympathy for the U.S. predicament in Vietnam but put no pressure on their allies to bring an end to the war. Indeed, the Soviets became Hanoi's main supplier of advanced military equipment in the final years of the war.

Still, Brezhnev and Kosygin continued to pursue the Khrushchev line of peaceful coexistence with the West and adopted a generally cautious posture in foreign affairs. By the early 1970s, a new age in Soviet-American relations had emerged, often referred to as **détente**, a French term meaning a reduction of tensions between the two sides. One symbol of the new relationship was the Anti-Ballistic Missile (ABM) Treaty, often called SALT I (for Strategic Arms Limitation Talks), signed in 1972, in which the two nations agreed to limit their missile systems.

Washington's objective in pursuing the treaty was to make it unlikely that either superpower could win a nuclear exchange by launching a preemptive strike against the other. U.S. officials believed that a policy of "equivalence," in which there was a roughly equal power balance between the two sides, was the best way to avoid a nuclear confrontation. Détente was pursued in other ways as well. When President Nixon took office in 1969, he sought to increase trade and cultural contacts with the Soviet Union. His purpose was to set up a series of "linkages" in U.S.-Soviet relations that would persuade Moscow of the economic and social benefits of maintaining good relations with the West.

The Helsinki Accords of 1975 were a symbol of that new relationship. Signed by the United States, Canada, and all European nations on both sides of the Iron Curtain, these accords recognized all borders in Central and Eastern Europe established since the end of World War II, thereby formally acknowledging for the first time the Soviet sphere of influence. The Helsinki Accords also committed the signatory powers to recognize and protect the human rights of their citizens, a clear effort by the Western states to improve the performance of the Soviet Union and its allies in that area.

An End to Détente?

Protection of human rights became one of the major foreign policy goals of the next U.S. president, Jimmy Carter (b. 1924). Ironically, just at the point when U.S. involvement in Vietnam came to an end and relations with China began to improve, the mood in U.S.-Soviet relations began to sour, for several reasons.

RENEWED TENSIONS IN THE THIRD WORLD Some Americans had become increasingly concerned about aggressive new tendencies in Soviet foreign policy. The first indication came in Africa. Soviet influence was on the rise in Somalia, across the Red Sea in South Yemen, and later in Ethiopia. Soviet involvement was also on the increase in southern Africa, where an insurgent movement supported by Cuban troops came to power in Angola, once a colony of Portugal. Then, in 1979, Soviet troops were sent to neighboring Afghanistan to protect a newly installed Marxist regime facing rising internal resistance from fundamentalist Muslims. Some observers suspected that Moscow's motive in deciding to advance into hitherto neutral Afghanistan was to extend Soviet power into the oil fields of the Persian Gulf.

To deter such a possibility, the White House promulgated the Carter Doctrine, which stated that the United States would use its military power, if necessary, to safeguard Western access to the oil reserves in the Middle East. In fact, sources in Moscow later disclosed that the Soviet advance into Afghanistan had little to do with a strategic drive toward the Persian Gulf but was an effort take advantage of the disarray in U.S. foreign policy since the defeat in Vietnam by increasing Soviet influence in a sensitive region increasingly beset with Islamic fervor. Soviet officials feared that the wave of Islamic activism could spread to the Muslim populations in the Soviet republics in central Asia and were confident that the United States was too distracted by the so-called **Vietnam syndrome** (the public fear of U.S. involvement in another Vietnam-type conflict) to respond.

Other factors also contributed to the growing suspicion of the Soviet Union in the United States. During the era of détente, Washington officials had assumed that Moscow accepted the U.S. doctrine of equivalence—the idea that both sides possessed sufficient strength to destroy the other in the event of a surprise attack. By the end of the 1970s, however, some U.S. defense analysts began to charge that the Soviets were seeking strategic superiority in nuclear weapons and argued for a substantial increase in U.S. defense spending. Such charges, combined with evidence of Soviet efforts in Africa and the Middle East and reports of the persecution of Jews and dissidents in the Soviet Union, helped undermine public support for détente in the United States. These changing attitudes were reflected in the failure of the Carter administration to obtain congressional approval of a new arms limitation agreement (SALT II) signed with the Soviet Union in 1979.

Countering the Evil Empire

The early years of the administration of President Ronald Reagan (1911–2004) witnessed a return to the harsh rhetoric, if not all of the harsh practices, of the Cold War. President Reagan's anti-Communist credentials were well known. In a speech given shortly after his election in 1980, he referred to the Soviet Union as an "evil empire" and frequently voiced his suspicion of its motives in foreign affairs. In an effort to eliminate perceived Soviet advantages in strategic weaponry, the White House began a military buildup that stimulated a renewed arms race. In 1982, the Reagan administration introduced the nuclear-tipped cruise missile, whose ability to fly at low altitudes made it difficult to detect by enemy radar. Reagan also became an ardent exponent of the Strategic Defense Initiative (SDI), nicknamed **Star Wars**. Its purposes were to create a space shield that could destroy incoming missiles and to force Moscow into an arms race that it could not hope to win.

The Reagan administration also adopted a more activist stance in the Third World. By providing military support to the anti-Soviet insurgents in Afghanistan, the White House helped maintain a Vietnam-like war in Afghanistan that would embed the Soviet Union in its own quagmire. In Central America, where the revolutionary Sandinista regime in Nicaragua was supporting a guerrilla insurgency movement in nearby El Salvador, the Reagan administration began to provide material aid to the government in El Salvador while simultaneously applying pressure on the Sandinistas by giving support to an anti-Communist guerrilla movement (the **Contras**) in Nicaragua. The administration's Central American policy caused considerable controversy in Congress, and critics charged that growing U.S. involvement there could lead to a repeat of the nation's bitter experience in Vietnam.

Toward a New World Order

In 1985, Mikhail Gorbachev (b. 1931) was elected secretary of the Communist Party of the Soviet Union in Moscow. During Brezhnev's last years and the brief tenures of his two successors (see Chapter 9), the Soviet Union had entered an era of serious economic decline, and the dynamic new party chief was well aware that drastic changes would be needed to rekindle the dreams that had inspired the Bolshevik Revolution. During the next few years, he launched a program of restructuring (*perestroika*) to revitalize the Soviet system. As part of that program, he set out to improve relations with the United States and the rest of the capitalist world. When he met with President Reagan in Reykjavik, the capital of Iceland, in 1985, the two leaders agreed to set aside their ideological differences.

Gorbachev's desperate effort to rescue the Soviet Union from collapse was too little and too late. In 1991,

Empire. Meanwhile, the string of Soviet satellites in Eastern Europe broke loose from Moscow's grip and declared their independence from Communist rule (see Chapter 9). The era of the Cold War was over.

The end of the Cold War lulled many observers into the seductive vision of a new world order that would be characterized by peaceful cooperation and increasing prosperity. Sadly, such hopes have not been realized. A bitter civil war in the Balkans in the mid-1990s graphically demonstrated that old fault lines of national and ethnic hostility still divided the post–Cold War world. Elsewhere, bloody ethnic and religious disputes broke out in Africa and the Middle East. Then, on September 11, 2001, the world entered a dangerous new era when terrorists attacked the

Mikhail Gorbachev. After graduating from the University of Moscow with a law degree in 1955, Mikhail Gorbachev rose rapidly through the ranks of the Communist Party and was elected general secretary of the party in 1985. To colleagues who questioned Gorbachev's qualifications because of his relative youth, one of his supporters remarked, "He has a nice smile, but he has iron teeth." A pragmatist at heart, Gorbachev realized that drastic reforms were needed to prevent a total collapse of the Soviet system. During the late 1980s he liberalized economic policy and sought to achieve a new openness in Soviet politics. Unintentionally, he opened the door to the disintegration of the Soviet Union.

the Soviet Union, so long an apparently permanent fixture on the global scene, suddenly disintegrated. In its place arose several new nations from the ashes of the Soviet nerve centers of U.S. power in New York City and Washington, D.C., inaugurating a new round of tension between the West and the forces of militant Islam.

CONCLUSION

AT THE END OF WORLD WAR II, the two superpowers, the United States and the Soviet Union, began to compete for political domination. The two power blocs faced each other across an ideological divide characterized by high levels of hostility and suspicion. This ideological division began in Europe but soon spread to the rest of the world as the United States fought in Korea and Vietnam to prevent the spread of communism, while the Soviet Union used its influence to prop up pro-Soviet regimes in Asia, Africa, and Latin America. To many contemporary observers, a nuclear confrontation appeared almost inevitable.

As the twentieth century entered its last two decades, however, there were tantalizing signs of a thaw in the Cold War. In 1979, China and the United States decided to establish mutual diplomatic relations, a consequence of Beijing's decision to focus on domestic reform and stop

supporting wars of national liberation in Asia. Six years later, the ascent of Mikhail Gorbachev to leadership, culminating in the collapse of the Soviet Union in 1991, brought a final end to almost half a century of bitter rivalry between the world's two superpowers.

The Cold War thus ended without the horrifying vision of a mushroom cloud. Unlike earlier rivalries that had culminated in the century's two world wars, the antagonists had gradually come to realize that the struggle for supremacy could be carried out in the political and economic arena rather than on the battlefield. And in the final analysis, it was not military superiority, but political, economic, and cultural factors that brought about the triumph of Western civilization over the Marxist vision of a classless utopia. The world's policy makers could now shift their focus to other problems of mutual concern. These issues will be addressed in the chapters that follow.

TIMELINE

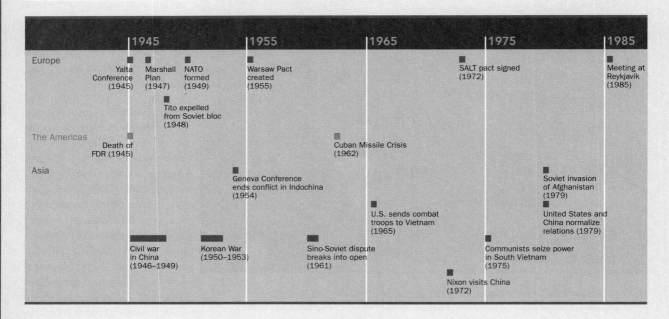

CHAPTER NOTES

1. *Department of State Bulletin*, February 11, 1945, p. 213.
2. Quoted in Joseph M. Jones, *The Fifteen Weeks, February 21–June 5, 1947*, 2nd ed. (New York, 1964), pp. 140–141.
3. Quoted in Misha Glenny, *The Balkans: Nationalism, War, and the Great Powers* (New York, 1999), pp. 543–544.
4. Cited in the *New York Review of Books*, June 9, 2011, p. 71.

The United States, Canada, and Latin America

President Lyndon Johnson at work

Everett_Glow/Glow Images

ON MAY 22, 1964, President Lyndon B. Johnson gave a policy speech before an audience of students at the University of Michigan in Ann Arbor. He used the occasion to propose a new domestic strategy—to be known as the "Great Society"—to bring about major economic and social reforms in the United States. The aim of these reforms, he said, would be to use the national wealth "to enrich and elevate our national life and to advance the quality of our American civilization."[1]

In his State of the Union address the following January, President Johnson unveiled some of the details of his plan. They included increased funding for education, urban renewal, crime fighting, disease prevention, a new Medicare program, and a war on poverty. Finally, he called for an extension of voting rights to guarantee the franchise to all citizens.

During the next few years, the U.S. Congress enacted many of the programs proposed by the Johnson administration, and the Great Society became a familiar part of the American landscape. A few years, later, however, it came under attack, as a more conservative electorate turned away from expensive welfare programs and endorsed a more modest approach to meeting the social needs of the American people. An era of active government intervention to bring about changes in the fabric of American society had come to an end. ◆

┌─ **CRITICAL THINKING** ─────────────────

Q Historians have described post–World War II politics in the United States as swinging between liberalism and conservatism like a pendulum. Why do you think U.S. politics has taken this form?

└──────────────────────────────────────

The United States Since 1945

For a generation after World War II, the legacy of Franklin Roosevelt's New Deal continued to determine the parameters of American domestic politics. The New Deal gave rise to a distinct pattern that signified a basic transformation in American society. This pattern included a dramatic increase in the role and power of the federal government; the rise of organized labor as a significant force in the economy and politics; a commitment to the welfare state, albeit a restricted one (Americans did not have access to universal health care as citizens of most other industrialized societies did); a grudging acceptance of the need to resolve problems of minority groups; and a willingness to experiment with deficit spending as a means of stimulating the economy.

An Era of Prosperity and Social Commitment

One reason for the success of New Deal policies in the postwar era was the general economic recovery that took place in the years following the resumption of peace. A shortage of consumer goods during the war had left Americans with both surplus income and the desire to purchase these goods after the war. Then, too, the growing power of organized labor enabled more and more workers to obtain the wage increases that fueled the growth of the domestic market. Increased government expenditures (justified by the theory of English economist John Maynard Keynes that government spending could stimulate a lagging economy to reach higher levels of productivity) also indirectly subsidized the American private enterprise system. Outlays on defense, especially after the Korean War began in 1950, provided money for scientific research in universities and markets for weapons industries. After 1955, tax dollars built a massive system of interstate highways, and tax deductions for mortgages subsidized homeowners. Between 1945 and 1973, real wages grew at an average rate of 3 percent a year, the most prolonged advance in American history.

Also contributing to the economic recovery was the decision by Western leaders to avoid the vicious trade wars that had taken place in the 1930s. The first stage took place in 1947, when twenty-three nations accepted the General Agreement on Tariffs and Trade (GATT); its goal was to lower tariffs and quotas in order to promote free trade on a global basis. To stimulate growth in poorer nations, the International Monetary Fund (IMF) was established to stabilize the global financial system by supervising exchange rates and providing financial and technical assistance to nations encountering economic difficulties. The World Bank was created to provide grants and loans to assist developing countries in building up their infrastructure so that they could compete more effectively in the global marketplace. As the world economy gradually recovered and demand for U.S. manufactures increased, the United States assumed the role of workshop of the world, providing jobs for millions of American servicemen returning home from the European and Pacific Theaters.

Riding the wave of popular approval for Roosevelt's progressive program, the Democratic Party controlled the White House until 1952, when the Republican candidate and war hero Dwight D. Eisenhower won election to the presidency. Ike, as he was popularly known, was by instinct a fiscal and "small government" conservative, but he tacitly accepted the fundamental premises of the New Deal and even extended them by embarking on the construction of a massive interstate highway system. Although the project was justified on the grounds of national defense, it served as a massive jobs program and stimulated the economy while improving the nation's infrastructure.

The Eisenhower years, however, were clouded by a growing sense of insecurity about the world beyond the borders of the United States. The Communist victory in China aroused fears that Communists had infiltrated the United States. A demagogic senator from Wisconsin, Joseph McCarthy, helped intensify a massive "Red scare" with unsubstantiated allegations that there were hundreds of Communists in high government positions. Congressional hearings on the matter were held by the House Un-American Activities Committee, and dozens of government officials and public figures were accused of radical sympathies or past membership in the Communist Party. A number of film actors and producers were placed on a blacklist that prevented them from finding employment in Hollywood. One U.S. senator even accused General George C. Marshall of treason for his efforts to bring about a truce in the civil war in China.

In the end, McCarthy overplayed his hand when he attacked alleged "Communist conspirators" in the U.S. Army, and he was censured by Congress in 1954. Soon afterward, his anti-Communist crusade came to an end. The pervasive fear of communism and the possibility of a nuclear war, however, remained strong. For those millions of Americans living in major metropolitan areas, the wailing of a siren in the night always conjured up latent fears of a surprise nuclear attack from the Soviet Union. The 1950s were not as tranquil as they have often been portrayed in more recent times.

TOWARD THE GREAT SOCIETY The Democrats returned to power in 1960 with the election of John F. Kennedy as president. At age forty-three, Kennedy became the youngest elected president in the history of the United States and the first born in the twentieth century. The new administration focused primarily on foreign affairs, but also inaugurated an extended period of increased economic growth, the result—in part—of lower taxes and a business-friendly atmosphere. But the bright promise of a new era of peace, progress, and prosperity was suddenly shattered on November 22, 1963, when Kennedy was assassinated under mysterious circumstances by Lee Harvey Oswald in Dallas.

Kennedy's successor, Lyndon B. Johnson, who won a new term as president in a landslide in 1964, used his stunning mandate to pursue the growth of the welfare state, first begun in the New Deal. Johnson's Great Society programs included health care for the elderly, a "war on poverty" to be fought with food stamps and a "job corps," a new Department of Housing and Urban Development to deal with the problems of the cities, and federal assistance for education.

FOCUS ON CIVIL RIGHTS Johnson's other domestic passion was the achievement of equal rights for African Americans. The **civil rights** movement began in earnest in 1954 when the U.S. Supreme Court took the dramatic step of striking down the practice of maintaining racially segregated public schools. According to Chief Justice Earl Warren, "Separate educational facilities are inherently unequal." A year later, during a boycott of segregated buses in Montgomery, Alabama, the eloquent Martin Luther King Jr. (1929–1968) surfaced as the leader of a growing movement for racial equality.

By the early 1960s, a number of groups, including King's Southern Christian Leadership Conference (SCLC), were organizing demonstrations and sit-ins across the South to end racial segregation. In August 1963, King led the March on Washington for Jobs and Freedom. This march and King's impassioned plea for racial equality had an electrifying effect on the American people (see the box on p. 172). The Kennedy administration initiated legislation to extend civil rights, but the president died before the bill was enacted into law.

On June 21, 1964, three young civil rights workers disappeared while investigating the torching of an African American church in Mississippi. A few weeks later, their bodies were discovered in a partially constructed dam nearby. President Johnson took advantage of the uproar caused by the incident to promote the cause of civil rights legislation, and in 1964, Congress enacted the Civil Rights Act, which ended segregation and discrimination in the workplace and in all public accommodations. The Voting Rights Act, passed the following year, eliminated racial obstacles to voting in southern states.

Outside the South, African Americans had had voting rights for many years, but local patterns of segregation resulted in considerably higher unemployment rates for blacks than for whites and left them segregated in huge urban ghettos. Calls for militant action by radical black nationalist leaders, such as Malcolm X of the Black Muslims, attracted more attention than the nonviolent appeals of Martin Luther King. In the summer of 1965, race riots erupted in the Watts district of Los Angeles and led to thirty-four deaths and the destruction of more than one thousand buildings. After the assassination of Martin Luther King by a white supremacist in 1968, more than one hundred cities experienced rioting, including Washington, D.C., the nation's capital. The combination of riots and provocative comments by radical black leaders led to a "white backlash" and a decline in support for civil rights issues among the white population.

A NATION DIVIDED Americans were also increasingly divided over the costly war in Vietnam (see Chapter 7).

The antiwar movement arose out of the free speech movement that began in 1964 at the University of California at Berkeley as a protest against the impersonality and authoritarianism of the large university. As the war progressed and U.S. casualties mounted, protests escalated. Teach-ins, sit-ins, and the occupation of university buildings alternated with more radical demonstrations that increasingly led to violence. Supporters contended that the antiwar movement had helped weaken the willingness of many Americans to continue the war. But the combination of antiwar demonstrations and ghetto riots in the cities also provoked many people to embrace "law and order," an appeal used by Richard M. Nixon (1913–1994), the Republican presidential candidate in 1968. With Nixon's election in 1968, a shift to the right in American politics had begun.

America Shifts to the Right

There has always been an element of tension between the concepts of liberty and equality in American society, between the desire for individual freedom and the right of every citizen to an equal opportunity to "life, liberty, and the pursuit of happiness" (in the words of the Declaration of Independence). The New Deal had followed an era of rugged individualism—epitomized by the famous remark by President Calvin Coolidge that "the business of government is business"—and had dominated the American scene for a generation. Now the pendulum was about to swing in the other direction.

NIXON AND WATERGATE Nixon owed his election, at least in part, to the disarray within the Democratic Party over the war in Vietnam, where more than 500,000 U.S. troops were now stationed, and the new president did not seek to reverse the liberal programs enacted by his predecessors. He even signed the National Environmental Policy Act, which established a national policy for the protection of the environment. Nixon also reduced U.S. involvement in Vietnam by gradually withdrawing American troops and appealing to the "silent majority" of Americans for patience in bringing the conflict to an end. He also broke with his strong anti-Communist past when he visited China in 1972 and opened the door to the eventual diplomatic recognition of that Communist state.

But on racial issues, Nixon clearly embarked on a new course. The strategy was dictated in part by the hope for political gain. A slowdown in racial desegregation appealed to southern whites, who had previously tended to vote Democratic. The Republican strategy also gained support among white Democrats in northern cities, where

"I Have a Dream"

In the spring of 1963, a bomb attack on a church that killed four African American children and the brutal fashion in which police handled black demonstrators brought the nation's attention to the policies of racial segregation in Birmingham, Alabama. A few months later, on August 28, 1963, the African American religious leader Martin Luther King Jr. led a march on Washington, D.C., and gave an inspired speech at the Lincoln Memorial that catalyzed the civil rights movement.

Martin Luther King Jr., "I Have a Dream"

Five score years ago, a great American, in whose symbolic shadow we stand today, signed the Emancipation Proclamation. This momentous decree came as a great beacon light of hope to millions of Negro slaves, who had been seared in the flames of withering injustice. It came as a joyous daybreak to end the long night of their captivity.

But one hundred years later, the Negro still is not free; one hundred years later, the life of the Negro is still sadly crippled by the manacles of segregation and the chains of discrimination; one hundred years later, the Negro lives on a lonely island of poverty in the midst of a vast ocean of material prosperity; one hundred years later, the Negro is still languished in the corners of American society and finds himself in exile in his own land. . . .

So we've come here today to dramatize a shameful condition. In a sense we've come to our nation's capital to cash a check. When the architects of our republic wrote the magnificent words of the Constitution and the Declaration of Independence, they were signing a promissory note to which every American was to fall heir. This note was the promise that all men, yes, black men as well as white men, would be guaranteed the unalienable rights of life, liberty, and the pursuit of happiness.

It is obvious today that America has defaulted on this promissory note in so far as her citizens of color are concerned. Instead of honoring this sacred obligation, America has given the Negro people a bad check, a check which has come back marked "insufficient funds." But we refuse to believe that the bank of justice is bankrupt. . . .

We have also come to this hallowed spot to remind America of the fierce urgency of now. This is no time to engage in the luxury of cooling off or to take the tranquilizing drug of gradualism. Now is the time to make real the promises of democracy; now is the time to rise from the dark and desolate valley of segregation to the sunlit path of racial justice; now is the time to lift our nation from the quicksands of racial injustice to the solid rock of brotherhood; now is the time to make justice a reality for all of God's children. It would be fatal for the nation to overlook the urgency of the moment. . . .

I say to you today, my friends, so even though we face the difficulties of today and tomorrow, I still have a dream. It is a dream deeply rooted in the American dream. I have a dream that one day this nation will rise up and live out the true meaning of its creed, "We hold these truths to be self-evident, that all men are created equal." I have a dream that one day on the red hills of Georgia, sons of former slaves and the sons of former slave owners will be able to sit down together at the table of brotherhood. . . . I have a dream that my four little children will one day live in a nation where they will not be judged by the color of their skin, but by the content of their character. . . .

This is our hope. This is the faith that I go back to the South with. With this faith we will be able to hew out of the mountain of despair a stone of hope. With this faith we will be able to transform the jangling discords of our nation into a beautiful symphony of brotherhood. With this faith we will be able to work together, to pray together, to struggle together, to go to jail together, to stand up for freedom together, knowing that we will be free one day. And this will be the day. This will be the day when all of God's children will be able to sing with new meaning, "My country 'tis of thee, sweet land of liberty, of thee I sing. Land where my father died, land of the pilgrims' pride, from every mountainside, let freedom ring." And if America is to be a great nation, this must become true. . . .

And when this happens, and when we allow freedom to ring, when we let it ring from every village and every hamlet, from every state and every city, we will be able to speed up that day when all of God's children, black men and white men, Jews and Gentiles, Protestants and Catholics, will be able to join hands and sing in the words of the old Negro spiritual: "Free at last. Free at last. Thank God Almighty, we are free at last."

 Martin Luther King Jr. was known as a highly skilled and moving orator. What are some of the rhetorically effective elements in this speech?

court-mandated busing to achieve racial integration had produced a white backlash.

But Nixon was paranoid about conspiracies and, despite a resounding victory in the presidential election in 1972, began to use illegal methods of gaining political intelligence about his political opponents. One of the president's advisers explained that their intention was to "use the available federal machinery to screw our political enemies." Nixon's zeal led to the infamous Watergate scandal—the attempted bugging of Democratic National Headquarters located at the Watergate complex in downtown Washington, D.C. Although Nixon repeatedly lied to the American public about his involvement in the affair, secret tapes of his own conversations in the White House revealed the truth. On August 9, 1974, Nixon resigned from office, an act that saved him from almost certain impeachment and conviction.

THE FIRST OIL CRISIS After Watergate, American domestic politics focused on economic issues. Gerald R. Ford (1913–2006) became president when Nixon resigned, only to lose in the 1976 election to the Democratic former governor of Georgia, Jimmy Carter, who campaigned as an outsider against the Washington establishment. Both Ford and Carter faced severe economic problems. The period from 1973 to the mid-1980s was one of economic stagnation, which came to be known as stagflation—a combination of high inflation and high unemployment. In 1984, median family income was 6 percent below that of 1973.

The economic downturn stemmed at least in part from a dramatic rise in oil prices. Oil had been a cheap and abundant source of energy in the 1950s, but by the late 1970s, half of the oil used in the United States came from the Middle East. An oil embargo imposed by the Organization of Petroleum Exporting Countries (OPEC) cartel as a reaction to the Arab-Israeli War in 1973 and OPEC's subsequent raising of prices led to a quadrupling of the cost of oil. By the end of the 1970s, oil prices had increased twentyfold, encouraging inflationary tendencies throughout the entire economy. Although the Carter administration proposed a plan for reducing oil consumption at home while spurring domestic production, neither Congress nor the American people could be persuaded to follow what they regarded as drastic measures.

By 1980, the Carter administration was facing two devastating problems. High inflation and a noticeable decline in average weekly earnings were causing a perceptible drop in American living standards. At the same time, a crisis abroad had erupted when fifty-three Americans were taken hostage by the Iranian government of Ayatollah Khomeini (see Chapter 15). Carter's inability to gain the

release of the American hostages led to the perception at home that he was a weak president. His overwhelming loss to Ronald Reagan in the election of 1980 brought forward the chief exponent of conservative Republican policies and a new political order.

DISMANTLING THE WELFARE STATE The conservative trend accelerated in the 1980s. The election of Ronald Reagan changed the direction of American policy on several fronts. Reversing decades of the expanding welfare state, Reagan cut spending on food stamps, school lunch programs, and job programs. At the same time, his administration fostered the largest peacetime military buildup in American history. Total federal spending rose from $631 billion in 1981 to more than $1 trillion by 1986. But instead of raising taxes to pay for the new expenditures, which far outweighed the budget cuts in social areas, Reagan convinced Congress to support supply-side economics. Massive tax cuts were designed to stimulate rapid economic growth and produce new revenues.

The American public, weary of high levels of government spending on social issues that never seemed to produce results, found President Reagan's approach appealing and reelected him by overwhelming margins to a second term in 1984. The country experienced an economic upturn that lasted until the end of the decade, but the administration's spending policies also resulted in record government deficits, which loomed as an obstacle to long-term growth. In 1980, the total government debt was around $930 billion; by 1988, the total debt had almost tripled, reaching $2.6 trillion. The inability of George H. W. Bush (b. 1924), Reagan's vice president and successor, to deal with an economic downturn led to the election of a Democrat, Bill Clinton (b. 1946), in November 1992.

Seizing the Political Center

The new president was a southerner who claimed to be a new Democrat—one who favored fiscal responsibility and a more conservative social agenda—a clear indication that the rightward drift in American politics had not been reversed by his victory. During his first term in office, Clinton reduced the budget deficit and signed a bill turning the welfare program back to the states while pushing measures to strengthen education and provide job opportunities for those Americans removed from the welfare rolls. By seizing the center of the American political agenda, Clinton was able to win reelection in 1996, although the Republican Party now held a majority in both houses of Congress.

President Clinton's political fortunes were helped considerably by a lengthy economic revival. Thanks to

© William J. Duiker

The Panama Canal: Lifeline to the World. Since its completion in 1914, the Panama Canal has served as one of the major maritime routes for the shipment of goods around the world. The original treaty between the United States and the Republic of Panama put the canal under U.S. control, but in 1979, operation of the canal reverted to Panamanian administration as the result of a treaty engineered by President Jimmy Carter. Today, about 1,200 ships pass through the canal each month. Annual shipping tonnage through the canal surpassed 330 million tons in 2012. Here a container ship passes through one of the locks into Gatun Lake.

President Clinton contributed to the national sense of unease by becoming the focus of a series of financial and sexual scandals that aroused concerns among many Americans that the moral fiber of the country had been severely undermined. Accused of lying under oath in a judicial hearing, he was impeached by the Republican-led majority in Congress. Although the effort to remove Clinton from office failed, his administration was tarnished, and in 2000, Republican candidate George W. Bush (b. 1946), the son of Clinton's predecessor, narrowly defeated Clinton's vice president, Albert Gore, in the race for the presidency. Bush too sought to occupy the center of the political spectrum while heeding the concerns of his conservative base.

THE POLITICS OF TERRORISM

On September 11, 2001, Muslim terrorists hijacked four commercial jet planes shortly after they took off from Boston, Newark, and Washington, D.C. Two of the planes were flown directly into the twin towers of the World Trade Center in New York City, causing both buildings to collapse; a third slammed into the Pentagon, near Washington, D.C; and the fourth crashed in a field in central Pennsylvania. About three thousand people were killed, including everyone aboard the four airliners.

The hijackings were carried out by a terrorist organization known as al-Qaeda, which had been suspected of bombing two U.S. embassies in Africa in 1998 and attacking a U.S. naval ship, the U.S.S. *Cole*, two years later. Its leader, Osama bin Laden (1957–2011), was a native of Saudi Arabia who was allegedly angry at the growing U.S. presence in the Middle East. President Bush vowed to wage an offensive war on terrorism, and in October 2001, with United Nations support, U.S. forces attacked al-Qaeda bases in Afghanistan (see Chapter 15).

The Bush administration had less success in gaining UN approval for an attack on the brutal regime of Saddam Hussein in Iraq, which the White House accused of amassing weapons of mass destruction and providing

downsizing and technological advances, major U.S. corporations began to recover the competitive edge they had lost to Japanese and European firms in previous years. At the same time, a steady reduction in the annual government budget deficit strengthened confidence in the performance of the national economy. Although wage increases were modest, inflation was securely in check, and public confidence in the future was on the rise. Reflecting that confidence in American competitiveness, the administration joined the new World Trade Organization (WTO), which replaced GATT, and signed a free trade agreement with Mexico.

Many of the country's social problems remained unresolved, however. Although crime rates were down, drug use, smoking, and alcoholism among young people remained high, and the specter of rising medical costs loomed as a generation of baby boomers (so called because they were born during the two decades after World War II when there was a dramatic spike in the number of births) neared retirement age. Americans remained bitterly divided over such issues as abortion and affirmative action programs to rectify past discrimination on the basis of gender, race, or sexual orientation.

support to terrorist groups in the region. Nevertheless, in March 2003, U.S. forces invaded Iraq and quickly overthrew the Hussein regime. Initially, the invasion had broad popular support in the United States, but as insurgent activities continued to inflict casualties on U.S. and Allied occupation forces—not to speak of the deaths of thousands of Iraqi civilians—the war became more controversial. The failure to locate the suspected weapons of mass destruction raised questions about the motives behind the administration's decision to invade Iraq. Some Americans called for an immediate pullout of U.S. troops.

The Bush administration was also dogged by an economic downturn and a number of other domestic problems, including the outsourcing of American jobs to Asian countries (especially China, which joined the WTO in 2001) and the failure to control illegal immigration from Mexico. But it benefited from the public perception that the Republican Party was more effective at protecting the American people from the threat of terrorism than its Democratic rival. Evangelical Christians—one of the nation's most vocal communities—were also drawn to the Republican Party for its emphasis on traditional moral values and the sanctity of the family and its opposition to abortion. Riding the wave of such concerns, President Bush defeated the Democratic candidate John F. Kerry in the presidential election of 2004.

After the election, the Bush administration sought to rein in the rising cost of domestic spending by presenting new proposals to reform Social Security and the Medicare program. But the public was leery of cuts to popular entitlement programs, and the plans were quickly dropped. In the meantime, the war in Iraq continued to distract the White House from other pressing issues, including a dramatic rise in the price of oil and an exploding national budget deficit. In midterm elections held in the fall of 2006, the Democratic Party seized control of both houses of Congress for the first time in twelve years.

A HISTORIC MILESTONE The presidential campaign of 2008 was historic in terms of the major candidates for high office. The nominee of the Democratic Party, Illinois senator Barack Obama (b. 1961), was an African American of mixed parentage. Senator John McCain, the Republican candidate, selected Alaska governor Sarah Palin as his running mate. The Republican Party ran strongly on issues of national security, but a sudden financial crisis, brought on by a serious downturn in the housing market and an ensuing credit crunch, put the public focus squarely on the national economy. When the votes were counted, Barack Obama had won a decisive victory over his Republican rival, while Democratic majorities increased in both houses of Congress.

Barack Obama had run on a platform of economic change and social renewal, but his immediate challenge was to reverse the sudden downturn and put the U.S. economy back on a path of steady growth. In the face of Republican opposition, his administration enacted into law a stimulus program to put millions of newly unemployed Americans back to work. But the new president was unwilling to abandon his ambitious social agenda and successfully pushed through the Patient Protection and Affordable Care Act—popularly known as Obamacare—that provided access to inexpensive health care to most U.S. citizens. Other legislative proposals, including additional stimulus projects and immigration reform, stalled in Congress after Republicans made big gains in the 2010 midterm elections.

The presidential election of 2012 was fought primarily on the state of the nation's economy, which had shown only modest improvement under Obama's stewardship. Mitt Romney, the Republican candidate, ran on a platform of low taxes and a sharp reduction in entitlement spending. But the reelection of President Obama—who called for a balanced approach combining tax increases for wealthy Americans and modest cuts in social spending—suggested that, although many Americans remained distrustful of government, liberal programs like Social Security and Medicare were still widely popular.

But if, for the time being, the pendulum rests in the "vital center" of American politics, the political arena itself is more divided than ever. Disagreements between the two major parties over a variety of fundamental issues, including the role of government, the social safety net, abortion, and gay rights, have become increasingly wide. This partisan divide threatens the ability of the political system to deal with the multiple challenges facing the nation today.

The Changing Face of American Society

Major changes have taken place in American society in the decades since World War II. New technologies such as television, jet planes, and the computer have dramatically altered the pace and nature of American life. Increased prosperity has led to the growth of the middle class, the expansion of higher education, and a rapid increase in consumer demand for the products of a mass society. The building of a nationwide system of superhighways, combined with low fuel prices during much of the period and steady improvements in the quality and operability of automobiles, has produced a highly mobile society in which the average American family moves at least once every five years, sometimes from one end of the continent to the other.

One consequence of this change has been a movement from rural areas and central cities into the suburbs. There has also been an exodus of Americans from the Northeast and Midwest to the "sunbelt" areas of the West and the South, where new industries have resulted in rapid economic growth.

A Consumer Society, a Permissive Society

These changes in the physical surroundings of the country have been matched by equally important shifts in the social fabric. Boosted by rising incomes, the baby boom generation grew up with higher expectations about their future material prospects than their parents had. The members of this new **consumer society** focused much of their attention on achieving a middle-class lifestyle, complete with a home in the suburbs, two automobiles, and ample time for leisure activities. The growing predilection for buying on the installment plan was an important factor in protecting the national economy from the cycle of "boom and bust" that had characterized the prewar period, but also increased the level of personal debt.

With the introduction of credit cards, the personal debt of the average American skyrocketed, while the savings rate plummeted to its lowest level in decades. By the end of the 1990s, adjustable rate mortgages had become increasingly popular. Inappropriate mortgages were a major factor in the financial crisis that struck the national economy in the fall of 2008, as were risky banking practices. The fact is that millions of Americans, with the encouragement of their political leaders, were spending beyond their means. When housing prices stopped rising, the number of home foreclosures increased dramatically, triggering a massive financial crisis; the ensuing leap in unemployment led to more foreclosures, and the nation faced its most serious economic recession in decades.

American social mores were also changing. Casual attitudes toward premarital sex (a product in part of the introduction of the birth control pill) and the use of drugs (a practice that increased dramatically during the Vietnam War) marked the emergence of a youth movement in the 1960s that questioned all authority and fostered rebellion against older generations.

The new standards were evident in the breakdown of the traditional nuclear family. Divorce rates increased exponentially so that by the end of the century, one of every two marriages was likely to end in divorce. Attitudes toward extramarital sex were also changing, and the stigma attached to children born out of wedlock eroded

dramatically. At the same time, Americans were also becoming more receptive to gay rights. In the 2012 elections, several states approved referendums allowing same-sex marriage, and in June 2013, the U.S. Supreme Court struck down restrictive provisions contained in the Defense of Marriage Act, while declaring that the power to define marriage resided in the individual states.

The Melting Pot in Action

One of the primary visual factors that has helped shape American society in the postwar era has been the increasing pace of new arrivals from abroad. As restrictions on immigration were loosened after World War II, millions of immigrants began to arrive from all over the world. Although the majority came from Latin America, substantial numbers came from China, Vietnam, and the countries of southern Asia. By 2003, people of Hispanic origin surpassed African Americans as the largest minority group in the country.

In recent years, illegal immigration—primarily from Mexico but also to a lesser extent from other countries in Central America—has become a controversial issue in American politics. Since many undocumented immigrants gravitate to low-paying jobs that are not attractive to most Americans, they have usually been tacitly accepted by the public as a necessary evil. Now, however, their numbers have increased dramatically, and critics point to the financial burden the new arrivals place on the nation's educational and medical systems. At the same time, recent immigrants, many of them undocumented, have became an increasingly indispensable element in the U.S. economy, comprising one-quarter of all farmworkers and 14 percent of all those employed in construction jobs. As more immigrants attain citizenship, they are having an impact on U.S. politics. The number of Hispanics living in the United States has increased to 50 million, more than 15 percent of the total population; of these, some 22 million are eligible to vote, and their political preferences have proved to be a decisive factor in some recent elections.

Women and Society

Many of the changes taking place in American life reflect the fact that the role of women has been in a state of rapid transition. In the years immediately following World War II, many women gave up their jobs in factories and returned to their traditional role as homemakers, sparking the "baby boom" of the late 1940s and 1950s. Eventually, however, many women became restive with their restrictive role as wives and mothers and began to enter the workforce at an increasing rate. Unlike the situation before the war, many of them were married. In 1900, for example, married women made up about 15 percent of the female labor force. By 1970, their number had increased to 62 percent.

American women were still not receiving equal treatment in the workplace, however, and by the late 1960s, some began to assert their rights and speak as feminists. One of the leading advocates of women's rights in the United States was Betty Friedan (1921–2006). A journalist and the mother of three children, Friedan grew increasingly unhappy with her attempt to fulfill the traditional role of housewife and mother. In 1963, she published *The Feminine Mystique*, in which she argued that women were systematically being denied equality with men. *The Feminine Mystique* became a best seller and transformed Friedan into a prominent spokeswoman for women's rights in the United States.

As women became more actively involved in public issues, their role in education increased as well. Beginning in the 1980s, women's studies programs began to proliferate on college campuses throughout the United States. In recent years, considerably more than half of all students enrolled in institutions of higher learning are women. The consequences are evident throughout society as a whole, as women are beginning to occupy senior positions in the legal profession, medicine, politics, and business. According to recent studies, in nearly 20 percent of U.S. households, the wife is the primary breadwinner.

Although women have steadily made gains in terms of achieving true equality in legal rights and economic opportunity in American society, much remains to be done. In recent years, much of the energy in the **women's liberation movement** has focused on maintaining the right to legalized abortion. In 1973, the U.S. Supreme Court's decision in *Roe v. Wade* established the legal right to abortion. That ruling, however, came under attack from those Americans who believe that an abortion is an act of murder against an unborn child, and the issue has remained an important factor in political campaigns.

The Environment

Environmental problems first began to engage public opinion in the United States during the 1950s, when high pollution levels in major cities such as Los Angeles, Chicago, and Pittsburgh, combined with the popularity of Rachel Carson's book *Silent Spring*, aroused concerns over the impact that unfettered industrialization was having on the quality of life and health of the American people. During the next several decades, federal, state, and local governments began to issue regulations directed at reducing smog in urban areas and improving the quality of rivers and streams throughout the country.

In general, most Americans reacted favorably to such regulations, but by the 1980s, the environmental movement had engendered a backlash as some people complained that excessively radical measures could threaten the pace of economic growth and cause a loss of jobs. By the end of the century, environmental issues had become deeply entangled with worries about the state of the national economy. Still, growing concerns about the potential impact of global warming kept the state of the environment alive as a serious problem in the world community (see Chapter 16). In 2006, the documentary film *An Inconvenient Truth* appeared in movie theaters across the country. Produced by Albert Gore, Clinton's vice president, it sought to arouse public awareness of

The Women's Liberation Movement. In the late 1960s, as women began once again to assert their rights, a revived women's liberation movement emerged. Feminists in the movement maintained that women themselves must alter the conditions of their lives. During this women's liberation rally, some women climbed the statue of Admiral Farragut in Washington, D.C., to exhibit their signs.

Oil: Blessing or Curse? The availability of ample supplies of liquid energy has fueled the rise of the United States as an economic powerhouse for over a century. Yet today it is widely considered a major factor in promoting global warming, thus producing rising sea levels and damaging the environment for future generations. In recent years, the challenge has acquired a new urgency, as major new sources of oil and natural gas in the Western Hemisphere reduce U.S. dependence on imports from the Middle East. Shown here is an oil derrick currently operating off the coast of South America.

came from the government. Much of this expense was funded by or for the national defense establishment. One of every four scientists and engineers trained in the decades after World War II was engaged in the creation of new weapons systems.

There was no more stunning example of how the new scientific establishment operated than the space race of the 1960s. In 1957, the Soviet Union announced that it had sent the first space satellite, *Sputnik I*, into orbit around the earth. In response, the United States launched a gigantic project to land a manned spacecraft on the moon within a decade. Massive government funding financed the scientific research and technological advances that attained this goal in 1969.

the severity of the current climatic crisis. In the presidential elections held two years later, Barack Obama made environmental issues a centerpiece of his campaign, but as the effects of the financial crisis of 2008 rippled through the economy, his administration felt compelled to put economic concerns at the front of the agenda. Climate change, however, does not fluctuate according to the vicissitudes of American politics, and the massive hurricane that struck the East Coast in the fall of 2012 was a vivid reminder that global warming is not simply a theory, as some have maintained, but a looming reality. A major challenge for the near future will be to balance the obvious benefits from the exploitation of shale oil deposits with the potential damage to the environment.

Science and Technology

After World War II, the United States emerged as the leading nation in promoting the development of science and technology. Taking advantage of wartime advances in aircraft, weaponry, and electronics, the federal government took the lead in supporting large-scale projects composed of teams of scientists working in ever-larger laboratories, many of them located on university campuses. By 1965 almost 75 percent of all scientific research funds

The postwar alliance of science and technology led to an accelerated rate of change that became a fact of life throughout Western society. The emergence of the computer, in particular, has revolutionized American business practices and transformed the way individuals go about their lives and communicate with each other. Although early computers, which required thousands of vacuum tubes to function, were quite large, the development of the transistor and the silicon chip enabled manufacturers to reduce the size of their products dramatically. By the 1990s, the personal computer had become a fixture in businesses, schools, and homes around the country. The Internet—the world's largest computer network—provides millions of people around the world with quick access to immense quantities of information as well as rapid communication and commercial transactions. The United States was initially at the forefront of this process, but in recent years, innovation has become a global phenomenon.

Science is also being harnessed to serve other social purposes, including the development of biologically engineered food products, the formulation of new medicines to fight age-old diseases, and the development of alternative fuels to replace oil and the internal combustion engine. Recent interest has focused on the invention of new automobile engines that—like the hybrid varieties now entering the market—rely on some combination of electrical power and liquid energy. To encourage this process, the Obama administration has set higher energy consumption standards for vehicles produced in the United States in future years.

The World of Culture

The changing character of American society is vividly reflected in the world of culture, where the postwar era brought forth a new popular culture increasingly oriented toward the interests of young people.

Art and Architecture

After World War II, the American art world began to experiment with a variety of styles to express reality in new ways. One group of young artists, known as **Abstract Expressionists**, painted large nonrepresentational canvases in an effort to express a spiritual essence beyond the material world. Among the first was Jackson Pollock (1912–1956), who developed the technique of dripping and flinging paint onto a canvas laid on the floor. Pollock's large paintings of swirling colors express the energy of primal forces as well as the vast landscapes of his native Wyoming.

Other artists, concerned that art was being overwhelmed by popular culture, sought to make painting more accessible to the public by portraying aspects of everyday life on canvases. The most famous practitioner of **Pop Art**, as it was called, was Andy Warhol (1930–1987), whose works featured repetitious images of daily items such as soup cans, or even faces of such well-known figures as the *Mona Lisa* and Marilyn Monroe. Another influential figure was Robert Rauschenberg (1925–2008), whose "collages" juxtaposed disparate images and everyday objects—photographs, clothing, letters, even cigarette butts—to reflect the energy and disorder of the world around us.

By the early 1970s, **Postmodernism** became the new vehicle of revolt. Convinced that art should serve society by addressing social inequities relating to race, gender, or sexual orientation, some artists began to experiment with a new technique called **conceptual art**. Using innovative techniques such as photography, video, and even "installations" (machine- or human-made objects, sometimes as large as a room), such artists produced shocking works with the intent of motivating the viewer to political action. A powerful example was the untitled installation by Robert Gober (b. 1954): in its center, a stereotypical statue of the Virgin Mary stands over an open drain while a steel pipe pierces her body. Such a violent violation of the Madonna can be viewed by Christians as depicting the resilience of faith in a world of doubt. For non-Christians, Gober's work represents the indomitable spirit of humanity, which remains intact despite a century of adversity.

In architecture as well, the postwar era has been marked by experimentation and diversity. Tiring of the repetition and impersonality of the international style, innovative American architects have created their own Postmodern skyline, with pyramidal and cupola-topped skyscrapers of blue-green glass and brick, while others have returned to the past by incorporating traditional materials, shapes, and decorative elements into their buildings. Modernist rectangular malls have tacked on Greek columns and entryways shaped like ancient Egyptian pyramids.

New Concepts in Music

Musical composers also experimented with radically new concepts. One innovator was John Cage (1912–1992), who defined music as the "organization of sound" and included all types of noise in his music. Any unconventional sound was welcomed: electronic buzzers and whines, tape recordings played at altered speeds, or percussion from any household item. His most discussed work, called *4'33"*, was four minutes and thirty-three seconds of silence—the "music" being the sounds the audience heard in the hall during the "performance," such as coughing, the rustling of programs, the hum of air conditioning, and the shuffling of feet.

In the 1960s, **minimalism** took hold in the United States. Largely influenced by Indian music, minimalist composers such as Philip Glass (b. 1937) focus on the subtle nuances in the continuous repetitions of a melodic or rhythmic pattern. Since the 1960s, there has also been much experimental electronic and computer music. Despite the excitement of such musical exploration, however, much of it is considered too cerebral and alien, even by the educated public.

One of the most accomplished and accessible contemporary American composers, John Adams (b. 1947), has labeled much of twentieth-century experimental composition as the "fussy, difficult music of transition." His music blends Modernist elements with classical traditions using much minimalist repetition interspersed with dynamic rhythms. Critics have applauded his operas *Nixon in China* (1987) and *Doctor Atomic* (2005), which dramatizes the anxious countdown to the detonation of the first atomic bomb in New Mexico in 1945.

New Trends in Literature

Fictional writing in the 1960s reflected growing concerns about the materialism and superficiality of American culture and often took the form of exuberant and comic verbal fantasies. As the pain of the Vietnam War and the ensuing social and political turmoil intensified, authors turned to satire, using black humor and cruelty in the hope of shocking the American public into a recognition of its social ills. Many of these novels—such as Thomas Pynchon's *V.* (1963), Joseph Heller's *Catch-22* (1961), and John Barth's *Sot-Weed Factor* (1960)—were wildly imaginative, highly entertaining, and very different from the writing of the first half of the century, which had detailed the "real" daily lives of small-town or big-city America.

In the 1970s and 1980s, American fiction relinquished the extravagant verbal displays of the 1960s, returning to a more sober exposition of social problems, this time related to race, gender, and sexual orientation. Much of the best fiction explored the moral dimensions of contemporary life from Jewish, African American, feminist, or gay perspectives. Bernard Malamud (1914–1986), Saul Bellow (1915–2005), and Philip Roth (b. 1933) presented the Jewish American experience, while Ralph Ellison (1914–1994), James Baldwin (1924–1987), and Toni Morrison (b. 1931) dramatized the African American struggle.

Some outstanding women's fiction was written by foreign-born writers from Asia and Latin America, who examined the problems of immigrants, such as cultural identity and assimilation into the American mainstream.

Popular Culture

Since World War II, the United States has been the most influential force in shaping popular culture in the West and, to a lesser degree, throughout the world. Motion pictures were the primary vehicle for the diffusion of American popular culture in the years immediately following World War II and continued to dominate both European and American markets in the next decades. Although developed in the 1930s, television did not become readily available until the late 1940s. By 1954, there were 32 million sets in the United States as television became the centerpiece of middle-class life. In the 1960s, as television spread around the world, American networks unloaded their products on Europe and developing countries at extraordinarily low prices. Only the establishment of quota systems prevented American television from completely inundating these countries.

The United States has also dominated popular music since the end of World War II. Jazz, blues, rhythm and blues, rock, rap, and hip-hop have been the most popular music forms in the Western world—and much of the non-Western world—during this time. Artists like the late Michael Jackson and Madonna have become superstars throughout the world. All of these music forms originated in the United States and are rooted in African American musical innovations. These forms later spread to the rest of the world, inspiring local artists, who then transformed the music in their own way.

In the postwar years, sports became a major product of both popular culture and the leisure industry in the United States. The emergence of professional football and basketball leagues, as well as the increasing popularity of their college equivalents, helped to transform sports into something akin to a national obsession. Sports became a cheap form of entertainment for consumers, as fans did not have to leave their homes to enjoy athletic competitions. In fact, some sports organizations initially resisted television, fearing that it would hurt ticket sales. The tremendous revenues possible from television contracts overcame this hesitation, however. As sports television revenue has escalated, many sports have come to receive the bulk of their yearly revenue from broadcasting contracts. Today, sports have become a major force in American society, and individual sports teams—whether amateur or professional—attract the fervent allegiance of millions of devoted supporters.

Canada: In the Shadow of Goliath

Canada experienced many of the same developments as the United States in the postwar years. For twenty-five years after World War II, Canada realized extraordinary economic prosperity as it set out on a new path of industrial development. Canada had always had a strong export economy based on its abundant natural resources. Now it also developed electronic, aircraft, nuclear, and chemical engineering industries on a large scale. Much of the Canadian growth, however, was financed by capital from the United States, which resulted in U.S. ownership of Canadian businesses. While many Canadians welcomed the economic growth, others feared U.S. economic domination of Canada and its resources.

Canada's close relationship with the United States has been a notable feature of its postwar history. In addition to fears of economic domination, Canadians have also worried about playing a subordinate role politically and militarily to their neighboring superpower. Canada agreed to join the North Atlantic Treaty Organization in 1949 and even sent military contingents to fight in Korea the following year. But to avoid subordination to the United States or any other great power, Canada has consistently and actively supported the United Nations. Nevertheless, concerns about the United States have not kept Canada from maintaining a special relationship with its southern neighbor. The North American Air Defense Command (NORAD), formed in 1957, was based on close cooperation between the air forces of the two countries for the defense of North America against aerial attack. As another example of their close cooperation, in 1972, Canada and the United States signed the Great Lakes Water Quality Agreement to regulate water quality of the lakes that border both countries.

After 1945, the Liberal Party continued to dominate Canadian politics until 1957, when John Diefenbaker (1895–1979) achieved a Conservative victory. But a major recession returned the Liberals to power, and under Lester Pearson (1897–1972), they created Canada's welfare state by enacting a national social security system (the Canada Pension Plan) and a national health insurance program.

The most prominent Liberal government, however, was that of Pierre Trudeau (1919–2000), who came to power in 1968. Although French Canadian in background, Trudeau was dedicated to Canada's federal union. In 1968, his government passed the Official Languages Act, creating a bilingual federal civil service and encouraging the growth of French culture and language in Canada. Although Trudeau's government vigorously pushed an industrialization program, high inflation and Trudeau's efforts to impose the will of the federal government on the powerful provincial governments alienated voters and weakened his government.

For Canada, the vigor of the U.S. economy in the 1980s and 1990s was a mixed blessing, for the American behemoth was all too often inclined to make use of its power to have its way with its neighbors. Economic recession had brought the Conservative Party to power in Canada in 1984, but its decision to privatize many of Canada's state-run corporations and sign a free trade agreement with the United States cost the government much of its popularity. In 1993, the ruling Conservatives were crushed in national elections, winning only two seats in the House of Commons. The Liberals took over with the charge of stimulating the nation's sluggish economy.

The new Liberal government also faced a festering crisis over the French-speaking province of Quebec. In the late 1960s, the Parti Québécois, headed by René Levesque, campaigned on a platform calling for Quebec's secession from the Canadian confederation. To pursue their dream of separation, some underground separatist groups even turned to terrorism. In 1976, the Parti Québécois won Quebec's provincial elections and called for a referendum that would enable the provincial government to negotiate Quebec's independence from the rest of Canada. But voters in Quebec rejected the plan in 1995, and debate over Quebec's status continued to divide Canada as the decade came to a close. Provincial elections held in April 2003 delivered a stunning defeat to the Parti Québécois, and in the first decade of the new century, the issue had declined as a factor in Canadian politics.

In the meantime, the ruling Liberal Party became plagued by scandals, and in 2006, national elections brought the Conservatives, under new prime minister Stephen Harper (b. 1959), to power in Ottawa. The new government sought to pursue a policy of limited government and lower tax rates, but Harper was hampered by the fact that his party did not control a majority of votes in the House of Commons. That problem was rectified in 2011, however, when national elections gave the Conservatives a resounding victory, freeing Prime Minister Harper to pursue a more aggressive agenda. Chief among the challenges is to negotiate the country's delicate economic relationship with the United States.

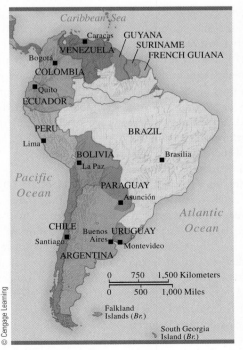

South America

Democracy, Dictatorship, and Development in Latin America Since 1945

The Great Depression of the 1930s caused political instability in many Latin American countries (see Chapter 5), but it also helped transform Latin America from a traditional to a modern economy. Since the nineteenth century, Latin Americans had exported raw materials while buying the manufactured goods of the industrialized countries. As a result of the Great Depression, however, export markets virtually vanished, and the revenues available to buy manufactured goods declined. In response, many Latin American countries encouraged the development of new industries to produce goods that were formerly imported. Due to a shortage of capital in the private sector, governments often invested in the new industries, thereby leading, for example, to government-run steel industries in Chile and Brazil and petroleum industries in Argentina and Mexico.

An Era of Dependency

In the 1960s, however, most Latin American countries were still dependent on the United States, Europe, and now Japan for the advanced technology needed for modern industries. To make matters worse, poverty in some countries limited the size of domestic markets, and many countries were unable to find markets abroad for their products.

These failures resulted in takeovers by military regimes that sought to curb the demands of the new industrial middle class and the working class that had increased in size and power as a result of industrialization. In the 1960s, repressive military regimes in Chile, Brazil, and Argentina abolished political parties and turned to export-import economies financed by foreigners while encouraging multinational corporations to come into their countries. Because these companies were primarily interested in taking advantage of Latin America's raw materials and abundant supply of cheap labor, their presence often offered little benefit to the local economy and contributed to the region's dependence on the industrially developed nations.

In the 1970s, Latin American regimes grew even more reliant on borrowing from abroad, especially from banks in Europe and the United States. Between 1970 and 1982, debt to foreigners increased from $27 billion to $315.3 billion. By 1982, a number of governments announced that they could no longer pay interest on their debts to foreign banks, and their economies began to crumble. Wages fell, and unemployment skyrocketed. Governments were forced to undertake fundamental reforms to qualify for additional loans, reducing the size of the state sector and improving agricultural production in order to stem the flow of people from the countryside to the cities and strengthen the domestic market for Latin American products. In many cases, these reforms were launched by democratic governments that began to replace the discredited military regimes during the 1980s.

In the 1990s, the opening of markets to free trade and other consequences of the globalization process began to have a growing impact on Latin American economies. As some countries faced the danger of bankruptcy, belt-tightening measures undertaken to reassure foreign investors provoked social protests and threatened to undermine the precarious political stability in the region.

Not all political parties in Latin America opted to adopt the capitalist model. In some countries, resentment at economic and social inequities led to the emergence of strong leftist movements or even to social revolution. The most prominent example was Cuba, where in the late 1950s Fidel Castro established a regime based loosely on the Soviet model. Eventually, other revolutionary movements flourished or even came to power in Chile, Uruguay, and parts of Central America as well (see "The Leftist Variant" below).

THE ROLE OF THE CATHOLIC CHURCH The Catholic Church has sometimes played a significant role in the process of social and political change. A powerful force in Latin America for centuries, the church often applied its prestige on the side of the landed elites, helping them maintain their grip on power. Eventually, however, the church adopted a middle stance in Latin American society, advocating a moderate capitalist system that would respect workers' rights, institute land reform, and provide for the poor. Some Catholics, however, took a more radical path to change by advocating a theology of liberation. Influenced by Marxist ideas, advocates of **liberation theology** believed that Christians must fight to free the oppressed, using violence if necessary. Some Catholic clergy recommended armed rebellions and even teamed up with Marxist guerrillas in rural areas. Other radical priests worked in factories alongside workers or carried on social work among the poor in the slums.

In recent years, the Catholic Church in Latin America has encountered a new challenge in the growth of evangelical Protestant sects. In Brazil, one of the reasons advanced for the rising popularity of these sects is the Vatican's stand on issues such as divorce and abortion. In a recent survey, the vast majority of Brazilian Catholics supported the right to abortion in cases of rape or danger to the mother and believed in the use of birth control to limit population growth and achieve smaller families.

THE BEHEMOTH TO THE NORTH Throughout the postwar era, the United States has cast a large shadow over Latin America. In 1948, the nations of the region formed the Organization of American States (OAS), which was intended to eliminate unilateral action by one state in the internal or external affairs of another state, while encouraging regional cooperation to maintain peace. It did not end U.S. interference in Latin American affairs, however. The United States returned to a policy of unilateral action when it believed that Soviet agents were attempting to use local Communists or radical reformers to establish governments hostile to U.S. interests. In the 1960s,

President Kennedy's Alliance for Progress encouraged social reform and economic development by providing private and public funds to elected governments whose reform programs were acceptable to the United States. But when Marxist-led insurrections began to spread throughout the region, the United States responded by providing massive military aid to anti-Communist regimes to forestall the possibility of a Soviet bastion in the Western Hemisphere.

The foremost example of U.S. interference occurred in Chile, where the Marxist Salvador Allende (1908–1973) was elected president in 1970. When Allende's government began to nationalize foreign-owned corporations, General Augusto Pinochet (1916–2006), with covert U.S. support, launched a coup d'état, which resulted in the deaths of Allende and thousands of his followers. But Pinochet's flagrant abuse of power led to unrest and eventually, in 1989, to a return of civilian rule.

Since the 1990s, the United States has played an active role in persuading Latin American governments to open their economies to the international marketplace. Though globalization has had some success in promoting prosperity in the region, it has also led to economic dislocation and hardship in some countries, provoking familiar cries of "Yanqui imperialismo" from protest groups and the election in recent years of leftist governments in several countries in the region.

Nationalism and the Military: The Examples of Argentina and Brazil

The military became the power brokers of twentieth-century Latin America. Especially in the 1960s and 1970s, military leaders portrayed themselves as the guardians of national honor and orderly progress. In the mid-1970s, only Colombia, Venezuela, and Costa Rica maintained democratic governments.

A decade later, pluralistic systems had been installed virtually everywhere except in Cuba, Paraguay, and some of the Central American states. The establishment of democratic institutions, however, has not managed to solve all the chronic problems that have plagued the states of Latin America. Official corruption continues in many countries, and the gap between rich and poor is growing, most notably in Brazil and in Venezuela, though leftist regimes in both countries have adopted policies designed to redistribute the wealth.

ARGENTINA Until World War II, a landed oligarchy, composed of wheat and cattle interests and backed by conservative elements in the military, had dominated Argentine politics. But in 1943, some leading military

officers grew restive and seized power on their own. When labor unrest broke out, the demagogic army colonel Juan Perón (1895–1974) publicly supported the workers and with their support was elected president in 1946.

Perón pursued a policy of increased industrialization to please his chief supporters—the urban middle class and the *descamisados*, or "shirtless ones," of the working class. At the same time, he sought to free Argentina from foreign investors. The government bought the railways; took over the banking, insurance, shipping, and communications industries; and assumed regulation of imports and exports. But Perón's regime was also authoritarian. His wife, Eva Perón (1919–1952), organized women's groups to support the government while Perón created fascist gangs, modeled after Hitler's Storm Troops, that used violence to intimidate his opponents. But growing corruption in the Perón government and the alienation of more and more people by the regime's excesses encouraged the military to overthrow him in September 1955. Perón went into exile in Spain.

It had been easy for the military to seize power, but they found it harder to rule, especially now that Argentina had a party of *Peronistas* clamoring for the return of the exiled leader. In the 1960s and 1970s, military and civilian governments (the latter closely watched by the military) alternated in power. When both failed to provide economic stability, military leaders decided to allow Juan Perón to return. Reelected president in September 1973, Perón died one year later. In 1976, the military installed a new regime, using the occasion to kill more than six thousand leftists in what was called the "Dirty War." With economic problems still unsolved, the regime tried to divert popular attention by invading the Falkland Islands in April 1982. Great Britain, which had controlled the islands since the nineteenth century, decisively defeated the Argentine forces. The loss discredited the military and opened the door once again to civilian rule. In 1983, Raúl Alfonsín (1927–2009) was elected president and sought to reestablish democratic processes.

In 1989, however, Alfonsín was defeated in the presidential elections by the Peronist candidate, Carlos Saúl Menem (b. 1930). Initially, the charismatic Menem won broad popularity for his ability to control the army, but when he sought to rein in rampant inflation by curbing government spending, rising unemployment and an economic recession cut into his public acclaim. Plagued with low growth, rising emigration (a growing number of descendants of European settlers were returning to live in Europe), and shrinking markets abroad, the government defaulted on its debt to the International Monetary Fund (IMF) in 2001, initiating an era of political chaos. In May 2003 with the economy in paralysis, Néstor Kirchner (1950–2010) assumed the presidency and sought to revive public confidence. The new president took decisive steps to end the crisis, adopting measures to stimulate economic growth and promote exports. By 2005, the debt to the IMF had been fully paid off. Kirchner also encouraged measures to bring the military officers who had carried out the Dirty War of the 1970s to justice. Néstor Kirchner's success in stabilizing the Argentine economy, which resulted in a 9 percent increase in the gross domestic product, was undoubtedly a factor in the presidential campaign in 2007, when his wife Cristina Fernández de Kirchner (b. 1953) was elected to succeed him in office. But growing income inequality, rising inflation—always a threat to prosperity in Argentina—and an energy crisis have tarnished the performance of the first female president in the country's history.

BRAZIL After Getúlio Vargas was forced to resign from the presidency in 1945 (see Chapter 5), a second Brazilian republic came into being. In 1949, Vargas was reelected to the presidency. But he was unable to solve Brazil's economic problems, especially its soaring inflation, and in 1954, after the armed forces called on him to resign, Vargas committed suicide. Subsequent democratically elected presidents had no better success in controlling inflation while trying to push rapid industrialization. In the spring of 1964, the military decided to intervene and took over the government.

The armed forces remained in direct control of the country for twenty years, setting a new economic course by cutting back somewhat on state control of the economy and emphasizing market forces. The new policies seemed to work, and during the late 1960s, Brazil experienced an "economic miracle" as it moved into self-sustaining economic growth, generally the hallmark of a modern economy. Promoters also pointed to the country's success in turning a racially diverse population into a relatively color-blind society.

Rapid economic growth carried with it some potential drawbacks. The economic exploitation of the Amazon River basin opened the region to farming but in the view of some critics threatened the ecological balance not only of Brazil but of the earth itself. Ordinary Brazilians hardly benefited as the gulf between rich and poor, always wide, grew even wider. At the same time, rapid development led to an inflation rate of 100 percent a year, and an enormous foreign debt added to the problems. Overwhelmed, the generals resigned from power and opened the door for a return to democracy in 1985.

In 1990, national elections brought a new president into office—Fernando Collor de Mello (b. 1949). The new administration promised to reduce inflation with a drastic reform program based on squeezing money out of the economy by stringent controls on wages and prices, drastic reductions in public spending, and cuts in the number of government employees. But Collor de Mello's efforts—reminiscent of Menem's in Argentina—were undermined by reports of official corruption, and he resigned at the end of 1992 after being impeached. In new elections two years later, Fernando Cardoso (b. 1931) was elected president by an overwhelming majority of the popular vote. Cardoso, a member of the Brazilian Social Democratic Party, introduced measures to privatize state-run industries and to reform social security and the pension system. He rode a wave of economic prosperity to reelection in 1998. But economic problems, combined with allegations of official corruption and rising factionalism within the ruling party, undermined his popularity, leading to the victory of the Workers' Party in 2002.

The new president, Luiz Inácio Lula da Silva (b. 1945), a former lathe operator, was enormously popular among the country's working masses and had come to power on a promise to introduce antipoverty programs and reverse his predecessor's policy of privatizing major industries. On taking office in 2003, however, Lula immediately cautioned his supporters that the party's ambitious plans could not be realized until urgent financial reforms had been enacted. That remark effectively summed up the challenge that the new administration faced: how to satisfy the pent-up demands of its traditional constituency—the millions of Brazilians still living in poverty—while dealing effectively with the realities of exercising power.

During the next few years, the Brazilian economy experienced dramatic growth in several areas: millions of acres of virgin lands were brought under cultivation in the interior, enabling the country to become a major exporter of agricultural products, including wheat, cotton, and soybeans. In late 2007, the government announced the discovery of significant underwater oil reserves off the southeastern coast of the country. Such successes led to growing prosperity for many Brazilian citizens, who took advantage of low interest rates to increase their purchases of automobiles, homes, and consumer goods. Ambitious social programs began to reduce the gap between wealth and poverty—always one of the most visible characteristics of Brazilian society. When Lula left office in 2010 after two terms as president, the country was poised to become a hemispheric superpower and had recently announced plans to organize a defensive alliance of Latin American countries similar to NATO.

© William J. Duiker

Renewing Rio. In accepting an invitation to host the Summer Olympic Games in 2016, the Brazilian city of Rio de Janeiro committed itself to tackling one of the city's chronic problems—the grinding poverty of many of its urban residents. Nowhere is this challenge more visible than in the vast slums, known as *favelas*, which coexist side by side with wealthy beach districts in fashionable Copacabana and Ipanema. Adding to the problem is the fact that many of these neighborhoods have long been controlled by drug gangs, who have violently resisted efforts by the city's security forces to evict them. In recent years, Rio's *favelas* have attracted the attention of Hollywood filmmakers, as this illustration subtly suggests.

rules for the registration of political parties and allowed greater freedom of debate in the press and universities. But economic problems continued to trouble Mexico.

In the late 1970s, vast new reserves of oil were discovered in Mexico. As sales of oil abroad rose dramatically, the government became increasingly dependent on oil revenues. When world oil prices dropped in the mid-1980s, Mexico was no longer able to make the payments on its foreign debt, which had reached $80 billion in 1982. The government was forced to adopt new economic policies, including the sale of publicly owned companies to private parties.

During the 1990s, Mexican leaders continued the economic liberalization policies of the previous decade, and in 1994 President Carlos Salinas (b. 1948) negotiated the North American Free Trade Agreement (NAFTA) with the United States and Canada. But although NAFTA was highly controversial in the United States because of the fear that U.S. firms would move factories to Mexico, where labor costs are cheaper and environmental standards less stringent, many Mexicans felt that NAFTA was more beneficial to the U.S. economy than to its southern neighbor. An indication of Mexico's continuing economic problems was the rising popular unrest in southern parts of the country. Unhappy farmers, many of them native Amerindians, increasingly protested the endemic poverty and widespread neglect of the needs of the indigenous peoples, who comprise about 10 percent of Mexico's total population of 100 million people.

In 2000, a national election suddenly swept the ruling PRI from power. The new president, Vicente Fox (b. 1942), came to office with high expectations and promised to address the country's many problems, including political corruption, widespread poverty, environmental concerns, and a growing population. But he was hampered both by the PRI, which still controlled many state legislatures and held a plurality in Congress, and by the protest movement in rural areas in the south. Although the movement has since faded, it aroused such a groundswell of support from around the country that Fox found himself under

Lula's protégée and chief of staff, the onetime radical activist Dilma Rousseff (b. 1947), was elected to succeed him as president in 2010 on the promise of building a new "Brazil without Misery." She has embraced the antipoverty programs of her predecessor, cleaning up the slums—known as *favelas*—that surround every major city, and recently announced an affirmative action program to increase the percentage of citizens of color in public universities. But Brazil's recent history of rapid growth has been undermined by the global recession, and her hopes to continue the successes of the Lula years face severe challenges.

The Mexican Way

During the 1950s and early 1960s, Mexico's ruling party, the Institutional Revolutionary Party (PRI), focused on industrial development. Steady economic growth combined with low inflation and real gains in wages for more and more people made those years appear to be a golden age in Mexico's economic development. But massive student protests in 1968, which turned violent and resulted in hundreds of casualties, were a clear sign of discontent beneath the surface. The protests persuaded PRI leaders to introduce political reforms. The government eased considerable pressure to deal with generations of neglect in solving the problems of Mexico.

The conservative lawyer Felipe Calderón (b. 1962) took over from Fox in December 2006 in a presidential election disputed by his rival, Andrés Manuel López Obrador. With PRI support, Calderón sought to rule from the center, while adopting measures to alleviate poverty and bring about fiscal reform. But his efforts were undermined by the economic slowdown in the United States.

In elections in 2012, the PRI returned to power. The new president, Enrique Peña Nieto (b. 1966), is a charismatic figure who reminds some observers of John F. Kennedy, but he faces enormous challenges. Forty percent of Mexicans live in poverty, and one in ten earns less than the equivalent of one U.S. dollar a day. At the same time, crime rates are soaring, despite the government's efforts to crack down on the country's influential drug cartels.

The Leftist Variant

Most of the countries in Latin America have followed the path laid out by the three examples described above. Military dictatorships have been replaced by elected governments that, at least on paper, follow standard democratic principles. In many cases, though, the influence of traditional ruling elites remains strong, leading to significant levels of popular discontent. In some countries, this has resulted in the emergence of governments dominated by leftist parties influenced by the ideas of Karl Marx. The foremost examples are Cuba and Venezuela.

THE CUBAN REVOLUTION An authoritarian regime, headed by Fulgencio Batista (1901–1973) and closely tied economically to U.S. investors, had ruled Cuba since 1934. In the early 1950s, a guerrilla movement—led by Fidel Castro (b. 1926) assisted by Ernesto "Ché" Guevara (1928–1967), an Argentinian who believed that revolutionary upheaval was necessary for change to occur—emerged in the Sierra Maestra. As the rebels gradually gained support, Batista responded with such brutality that he alienated his own supporters. The dictator fled in December 1958, and Castro's revolutionaries seized Havana on January 1, 1959.

As the new regime moved to nationalize key elements of the Cuban economy, relations between Cuba and the United States quickly deteriorated. When the Soviet Union began to provide military and economic aid to Cuba, President Eisenhower directed the Central Intelligence Agency (CIA) to "organize the training of Cuban exiles, mainly in Guatemala, against a possible future day when they might return to their homeland."[2] In October 1960, the United States declared a trade embargo of Cuba, driving Castro closer to the Soviet Union.

On January 3, 1961, the United States broke diplomatic relations with Cuba. The new U.S. president, John F. Kennedy, approved a plan originally drafted by the previous administration to launch an invasion to overthrow Castro's government, but the landing of 1,400 CIA-assisted Cubans in Cuba at the Bay of Pigs on April 17, 1961, turned into a total military disaster. This fiasco encouraged the Soviets to make an even greater commitment to Cuban independence by attempting to place nuclear missiles in the country, an act that led to a showdown with the United States (see Chapter 7).

The missile crisis persuaded Castro that the Soviet Union was unreliable. If revolutionary Cuba was to be secure and no longer encircled by hostile states tied to U.S. interests, it would have to instigate social revolution in the rest of Latin America. He believed that once guerrilla wars were launched, peasants would flock to the movement and overthrow the old regimes. Guevara attempted to launch a guerrilla war in Bolivia but was caught and killed by the Bolivian army in the fall of 1967. The Cuban strategy had failed.

In Cuba, however, Castro's socialist revolution proceeded, with mixed results. The regime provided free medical services for all citizens, and a new law code expanded the rights of women. Illiteracy was wiped out by creating new schools and establishing teacher-training institutes that tripled the number of teachers within ten years. Eschewing the path of rapid industrialization, Castro encouraged agricultural diversification. But the Cuban economy continued to rely on the production and sale of sugar. Economic problems forced the Castro regime to depend on Soviet subsidies and the purchase of Cuban sugar by Soviet bloc countries.

The disintegration of the Soviet Union was a major blow to Cuba, as the new government in Moscow no longer had a reason to continue to subsidize the onetime Soviet ally. During the 1990s, Castro began to introduce limited market reforms and to allow the circulation of U.S. dollars. But most Cubans remain locked in poverty, and although an ailing Fidel Castro was replaced in 2008 by his younger brother, Raúl Castro (b. 1931), the system of political repression remains intact. Wary of the elusive signs of liberalization in Cuba, the Obama administration has maintained its embargo on trade, although restrictions on travel between the two countries and on remittances to Cuban families from relatives in the United States have been relaxed.

VENEZUELA: THE NEW CUBA? With the discovery of oil in the small town of Cabímas in the early 1920s, Venezuela took its first step toward becoming a major exporter of oil and one of the wealthiest countries in Latin America. At first, profits from "black rain" accrued mainly to the nation's elite families, but in 1976 the oil industry was nationalized,

Hey Buddy! Wanna Buy a Used Car? After seizing power in 1959, the regime of Fidel Castro forbade the sale of automobiles in revolutionary Cuba, and even severely restricted imports from Soviet bloc nations. As a result, almost the only vehicles on the streets of Havana were vintage U.S. cars from the 1940s and 1950s, whose owners kept them running with rubber bands and bailing wire. In 2011, the regime suddenly reversed course and authorized the sale and purchase of vehicles. Cuban owners welcomed the decision, which opens up a lucrative market for antique automobiles among buyers in the United States and Europe.

"Yanqui imperialismo," he proposed resistance to U.S. proposals for a hemispheric free trade zone, charging that such an organization would operate only for the benefit of the United States. Until his death from cancer in 2013, by using his country's oil wealth as a means of promoting his political objectives, Chávez had replaced Fidel Castro as Washington's most dangerous adversary in Latin America. After Chávez's death, his vice president Nicolás Maduro (b. 1962) was elected president and vowed to continue his predecessor's policies.

Trends in Latin American Culture

Postwar literature in Latin America has been vibrant. Writers such as Jorge Luis Borges (1899–1986), Carlos Fuentes (1928–2012), and Nobel Prize winners Mario Vargas Llosa (b. 1936) and Gabriel García Márquez (b. 1927) are among the most respected literary names of the last half century. These authors often use dazzling language and daring narrative experimentation to make their point. Gabriel García Márquez from Colombia is a master of this style. In *One Hundred Years of Solitude* (1967), he explores the transformation of a small town under the impact of political violence, industrialization, and the arrival of a U.S. banana company. Especially noteworthy is his use of magical realism; the outrageous events that assail the town are related in a matter-of-fact voice, thus transforming the fantastic into the commonplace.

and Venezuela entered an era of national prosperity. But when the price of oil on world markets dropped sharply in the 1980s, the country's economic honeymoon came to an end, and in 1989 President Carlos Andrés Pérez (1922–2010) launched an austerity program that cut deeply into the living standards of much of the population.

After popular demonstrations led to an army crackdown in 1992, restive military forces launched an abortive coup to seize power. Five years later, one of the leading members of the plot—a paratroop commander named Hugo Chávez (1954–2013)—was elected president in national elections. Taking advantage of rising oil prices, Chávez launched an ambitious spending program to improve living conditions for the poor. Although such measures earned his regime broad national support, Chávez's efforts to silence critics and strengthen presidential powers—including a program to organize his supporters into "Bolivarian circles" (in honor of the nineteenth-century Venezuelan liberator Simón Bolívar) at the local level—displayed his all-too-evident dictatorial tendencies.

A longtime admirer of Fidel Castro, Chávez strengthened relations with Cuba and encouraged revolutionary movements throughout Latin America. After 2006, he acquired new allies with the election of leftist governments in Bolivia and Ecuador. As an outspoken opponent of

Unlike novelists in the United States and Western Europe, who tend to focus their attention on the interior landscape within the modern personality in an industrial society, fiction writers in Latin America, like their counterparts in Africa and much of Asia, have sought to project an underlying political message. In his epic *The War of the End of the World,* the Peruvian Mario Vargas Llosa condemns the fanaticism and the inhumanity of war. In his novel *The Feast of the Goat* (2001), he expresses his moral outrage at the cruel dictatorship of Fulgencio Trujillo in the Dominican Republic. Others, like Vargas Llosa's countryman, José Maria Arguedas (1911–1969), have championed the cause of the Amerindians and lauded the diversity that marks the ethnic mix throughout the continent. Some have run for high political office as a means of remedying social problems. Some have been women, reflecting the rising demand for sexual equality in a society traditionally marked by male domination. The memorable phrase of the Chilean poet Gabriela Mistral (1889–1957)—"I have chewed stones with woman's gums"—encapsulates the plight of Latin American women.

A powerful example of Postmodern art in Latin America is found in the haunting work of the Colombian sculptor Doris Salcedo (b. 1958). Her art evokes disturbing images of her country's endless civil war and violent drug trade. Salcedo often presents everyday wooden furniture, to which she has applied a thin layer of cement and fragments of personal mementos from the owner's past life: a remnant of lace curtain, a lock of hair, or a handkerchief. Frozen in time, these everyday souvenirs evoke the pain of those who were dragged from their homes in the middle of the night and senselessly murdered. Salcedo's work can be experienced as an impassioned plea to stop the killing of innocent civilians or as the fossilized artifact from some future archaeologist's dig, showing traces of our brief and absurd sojourn on earth.

CONCLUSION

DURING THE SECOND HALF of the twentieth century, the United States emerged as the preeminent power in the world, dominant in its economic and technological achievements as well as its military hardware. Although the Soviet Union was a serious competitor in the arms race engendered by the Cold War, its economic achievements paled in comparison with those of the U.S. behemoth.

The worldwide dominance of the United States was a product of a combination of political, economic, and cultural factors and showed no signs of abating as the new century began. But recently there are some warning signs that bear watching: an increasing gap in the distribution of wealth that could ultimately threaten the steady growth in consumer spending, an educational system that all too often fails to produce graduates with the skills needed to master the challenges of a technology-driven economy, and an increasingly dysfunctional political system that undermines the ability of the government to provide services to a nation of more than 300 million people.

For most of the twentieth century, the fortunes of the nations of Latin America were tied, for good or ill, to the United States. But in the last two decades, a number of nations in the region have emerged as economic powerhouses in their own right. Foremost among these is Brazil, which for the first time promises to live up to its reputation as the next global economic superpower. At the same time, democratic institutions are steadily taking root throughout the continent. Is Latin America finally in a position to take charge of its own destiny?

TIMELINE

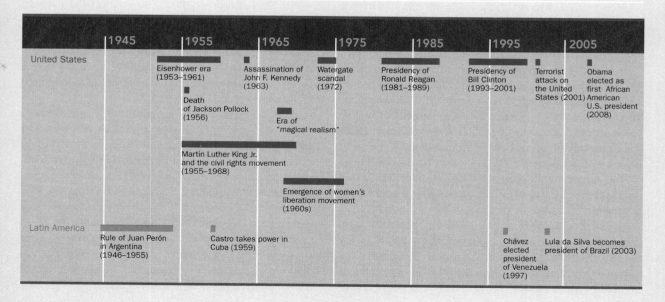

CHAPTER NOTES

1. *Public Papers of the Presidents of the United States: Lyndon B. Johnson,* Bk. 1, 1963–64 (Washington, D.C., 1965), p. 704.

2. Dwight D. Eisenhower, *The White House Years: Waging Peace, 1956–1961* (Garden City, 1965), p. 533.

Brave New World: The Rise and Fall of Communism in the Soviet Union and Eastern Europe

How to shop in Moscow

ACCORDING TO KARL MARX, capitalism is a system that involves the exploitation of man by man; under socialism, it is the other way around. That wry joke, an ironic twist on the familiar Marxist saying of the previous century, was typical of popular humor in post–World War II Moscow, where the dreams of a future Communist utopia had faded in the grim reality of life in the Soviet Union.

During the 1950s, the annual rate of economic growth in the Soviet Union exceeded 6 percent, and there were widespread predictions, even in the United States, that the Soviet Union would eventually surpass the United States as the world's preeminent economic power. But Soviet leaders had made a calculated decision to emphasize military spending at the expense of other sectors of the economy, and as growth rates dropped dramatically in the 1980s, the standard of living for Soviet citizens continued to stagnate. For much of the population in the Soviet Union and its Eastern European satellites, the "brave new world" prophesied by Karl Marx remained but a figment of his fertile imagination. ❖

CRITICAL THINKING

Q What reasons have been advanced to explain why the Soviet sytem collapsed in 1991? Which do you think are the most persuasive?

The Postwar Soviet Union

At the end of World War II, the Soviet Union was one of the world's two superpowers, and its leader, Joseph Stalin, was at the height of his power. As a result of the war, Stalin and his Soviet colleagues were now in control of a vast empire that included Eastern Europe, much of the Balkans, and territory gained from Japan in East Asia (see Map 9.1).

From Stalin to Khrushchev

World War II had devastated the Soviet Union. Twenty million citizens lost their lives, and cities such as Kiev, Kharkov, and Leningrad suffered enormous physical destruction. As the lands that had been occupied by the German forces were liberated, the Soviet government turned its attention to restoring the nation's economic structures. Nevertheless, in 1945, agricultural production was only 60 percent and steel output only 50 percent of prewar levels. The Soviet people faced incredibly difficult conditions: they worked longer hours than before the war, ate less, and were ill-housed and poorly clothed.

In the immediate postwar years, the Soviet Union removed goods and materials from occupied Germany and extorted valuable raw materials from its satellite states in Eastern Europe. More important, however, to create a new industrial base, Stalin returned to the method he had used in the 1930s—the extraction of development capital from Soviet labor. Working hard for little

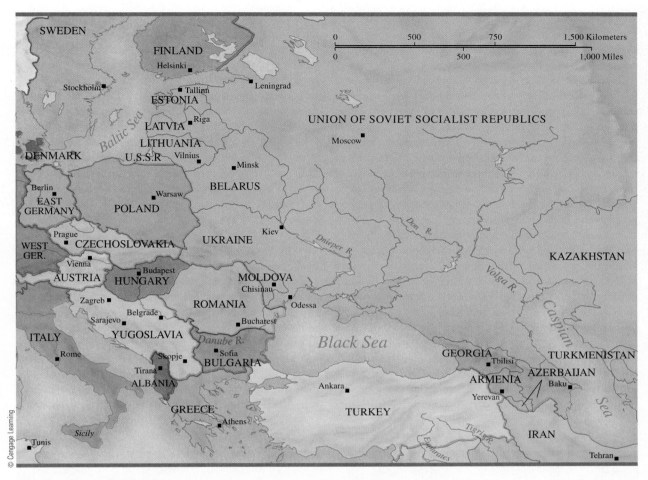

MAP 9.1 The Soviet Union. After World War II, the boundaries of Eastern Europe were redrawn as a result of Allied agreements reached at the Tehran and Yalta Conferences. This map shows the new boundaries that were established throughout the region, placing Soviet power in the center of Europe.

 How had the boundaries changed from the prewar era?

pay and for precious few consumer goods, Soviet citizens were expected to produce goods for export with little in return for themselves. The incoming capital from abroad could then be used to purchase machinery and Western technology. The loss of millions of men in the war meant that much of this tremendous workload fell upon Soviet women, who performed almost 40 percent of the heavy manual labor.

AN INDUSTRIAL POWERHOUSE The pace of economic recovery in the postwar Soviet Union was impressive. By 1947, Russian industrial production had attained 1939 levels; three years later, it had surpassed those levels by 40 percent. New power plants, canals, and giant factories were built, and new industrial enterprises and oil fields were established in Siberia and Soviet Central Asia. A new five-year plan, announced in 1946, reached its goals in less than five years. Returning to his prewar forced-draft system, Stalin had created an industrial powerhouse.

Although Stalin's economic recovery policy was successful in promoting growth in heavy industry, primarily for the benefit of the military, consumer goods remained scarce, as long-suffering Soviet citizens were still being asked to sacrifice for a better tomorrow. The development of thermonuclear weapons, MIG fighter jets, and the first space satellite (*Sputnik*) in the 1950s may have elevated the Soviet state's reputation as a world power abroad, but domestically, the Soviet people were shortchanged. Heavy industry grew at a rate three times that of personal consumption. Moreover, the housing shortage was acute, with living conditions especially difficult in the overcrowded cities.

When World War II ended, Stalin had been in power for more than fifteen years. During that time, he had removed all opposition to his rule and emerged as the undisputed master of the Soviet Union. Constantly increasing repression became the hallmark of the regime. In 1946, government decrees subordinated all forms of literary and scientific expression to the political needs of the state. Along with the anti-intellectual campaign came political terror. By the late 1940s, an estimated 9 million people were in Siberian concentration camps.

Increasingly distrustful of competitors, Stalin exercised sole authority and pitted his subordinates against one another. One of these subordinates, Lavrenti Beria, head of the secret police, controlled a force of several hundred thousand agents, leaving Stalin's colleagues completely cowed. As Stalin remarked mockingly on one occasion, "When I die, the imperialists will strangle all of you like a litter of kittens."[1]

Stalin's morbid suspicions even extended to some of his closest colleagues. In 1948, Andrei Zhdanov, his presumed successor and head of the Leningrad party organization, died under mysterious circumstances. The doctors who had attended Zhdanov were charged with causing his death (hence, the label "the doctors' plot"), but most historians believe it was done on Stalin's order. Within weeks, the Leningrad party organization was purged of several top leaders, many of whom were charged with traitorous connections with Western intelligence agencies. In succeeding years, Stalin directed his suspicion at other members of the inner circle, including Foreign Minister Vyacheslav Molotov. Known as "Old Stone Butt" in the West for his stubborn defense of Soviet security interests, Molotov had been a loyal lieutenant since the early years of Stalin's rise to power. Now Stalin distrusted Molotov and had his Jewish wife sent to a Siberian concentration camp.

THE RISE AND FALL OF NIKITA KHRUSHCHEV Stalin died—presumably of natural causes—in 1953 and, after some bitter infighting within the party leadership, was succeeded by Georgy Malenkov, a veteran administrator and ambitious member of the Politburo. Malenkov came to power with a clear agenda. In foreign affairs, he hoped to promote an easing of Cold War tensions and improve relations with the Western powers. For Moscow's Eastern European allies, he advocated a so-called **New Course** in their mutual relations and a decline in Stalinist methods of rule. Inside the Soviet Union, he hoped to reduce defense

The Portals of Doom. Perhaps the most feared location in the Soviet Union was Lyubyanka Prison, an ornate prerevolutionary building in the heart of Moscow. Taken over by the Bolsheviks after the 1917 revolution, it became the headquarters of the Soviet secret police, the Cheka, later to be known as the KGB. It was here that many Soviet citizens accused of "counterrevolutionary acts" were imprisoned and executed. The figure on the pedestal is that of Felix Dzerzhinsky, first director of the Cheka and a loyal henchman of Joseph Stalin. After the dissolution of the Soviet Union, the statue was removed.

expenditures and assign a higher priority to improving the standard of living. Such goals were laudable and probably had the support of the majority of the Russian people, but they were not necessarily appealing to key pressure groups within the Soviet Union—the army, the Communist Party, the managerial elite, and the security services (now known as the Committee for State Security, or KGB). Malenkov was soon removed from his position as prime minister, and power shifted to his rival, the new party general secretary, Nikita Khrushchev.

During his struggle for power with Malenkov, Khrushchev had outmaneuvered his rival by calling for heightened defense expenditures and a continuing emphasis on heavy industry. Once in power, however, Khrushchev showed the political dexterity displayed by many an American politician and reversed his priorities. He now resumed his predecessor's efforts to reduce tensions with the West and boost the standard of living of the Russian people. He moved vigorously to improve the performance of the Soviet economy and revitalize Soviet society. By nature, Khrushchev was a man of enormous energy as well as an innovator. In an attempt to loosen the stranglehold of the central bureaucracy over the national economy, he abolished dozens of government ministries and split up the party and government apparatus. Khrushchev also attempted to rejuvenate the stagnant agricultural sector, long the Achilles heel of the Soviet economy. He attempted to spur production by increasing profit incentives and opened "virgin lands" in Soviet Kazakhstan to bring thousands of acres of new land under cultivation.

Like any innovator, however, Khrushchev had to overcome the inherently conservative instincts of the Soviet bureaucracy, as well as of the mass of the Soviet population. His plan to remove the "dead hand" of the state, however laudable in intent, alienated much of the Soviet official class, and his effort to split the party angered those who saw it as the central force in the Soviet system. Khrushchev's agricultural schemes inspired similar opposition. Although the Kazakhstan wheat lands would eventually demonstrate their importance, progress was slow, and his effort to persuade the Russian people to eat more corn (an idea he had apparently picked up during a visit to the United States) led to the mocking nickname "Cornman." Disappointing agricultural production, combined with high military spending, hurt the Soviet economy. The industrial growth rate, which had soared in the early 1950s, declined dramatically from 13 percent in 1953 to 7.5 percent in 1964.

Khrushchev was probably best known for his policy of **de-Stalinization**. Khrushchev had risen in the party hierarchy as a Stalin protégé, but he had been deeply disturbed by his mentor's excesses and, once in a position of authority, moved to excise the Stalinist legacy from Soviet society. The campaign began at the Twentieth Congress of the Communist Party in February 1956, when Khrushchev gave a long speech criticizing some of Stalin's major shortcomings. The speech apparently had not been intended for public distribution, but it was quickly leaked to the Western press and created a sensation throughout the world (see the box on p. 194). During the next few years, Khrushchev encouraged more freedom of expression for writers, artists, and composers, arguing that "readers should be given the chance to make their own judgments" regarding the acceptability of controversial literature and that "police measures shouldn't be used."[2] At Khrushchev's order, thousands of prisoners were released from concentration camps.

Khrushchev's personality, however, did not endear him to higher Soviet officials, who frowned at his tendency to crack jokes and play the clown. Nor were the higher members of the party bureaucracy pleased when Khrushchev tried to curb their privileges. Foreign policy failures further damaged Khrushchev's reputation among his colleagues. Relations with China deteriorated badly under his leadership. His plan to install missiles in Cuba was the final straw (see Chapter 7). While he was away on vacation in 1964, a special meeting of the Soviet Politburo voted him out of office (because of "deteriorating health") and forced him into retirement. Although a group of leaders succeeded him, real power came into the hands of Leonid Brezhnev (1906–1982), the "trusted" supporter of Khrushchev who had engineered his downfall.

The Brezhnev Years, 1964–1982

The ouster of Nikita Khrushchev in October 1964 vividly demonstrated the challenges that would be encountered by any Soviet leader sufficiently bold to try to reform the Soviet system. In democratic countries, pressure on the government comes from various sources within society at large—the business community and labor unions, interest groups, and the general public. In the Soviet Union, pressure on government and party leaders originated from sources essentially operating inside the governing system—from the government bureaucracy, the party apparatus, the KGB, and the armed forces.

Leonid Brezhnev, the new party chief, was undoubtedly aware of these realities of Soviet politics, and his long tenure in power was marked, above all, by the desire to avoid changes that might provoke instability, either at home or abroad. Brezhnev was himself a product of the Soviet system. He had entered the ranks of the party leadership under Stalin, and although he was not a particularly avid believer in party ideology—indeed, his years in

Khrushchev Denounces Stalin

Three years after Stalin's death, the new Soviet premier, Nikita Khrushchev, addressed the Twentieth Congress of the Communist Party and denounced the former Soviet dictator for his crimes. This denunciation, which caused consternation in Communist parties around the world, was the beginning of a policy of de-Stalinization in the Soviet Union.

Khrushchev Addresses the Twentieth Party Congress, February 1956

Comrades, . . . quite a lot has been said about the cult of the individual and about its harmful consequences. . . . The cult of the person of Stalin . . . became at a certain specific stage the source of a whole series of exceedingly serious and grave perversions of Party principles, of Party democracy, of revolutionary legality.

Stalin absolutely did not tolerate collegiality in leadership and in work and . . . practiced brutal violence, not only toward everything which opposed him, but also toward that which seemed to his capricious and despotic character, contrary to his concepts.

Stalin abandoned the method of ideological struggle for that of administrative violence, mass repressions and terror. . . . Arbitrary behavior by one person encouraged and permitted arbitrariness in others. Mass arrests and deportations of many thousands of people, execution without trial and without normal investigation created conditions of insecurity, fear, and even desperation.

Stalin showed in a whole series of cases his intolerance, his brutality, and his abuse of power. . . . He often chose the path of repression and annihilation, not only against actual enemies, but also against individuals who had not committed any crimes against the Party and the Soviet government. . . .

Many Party, Soviet, and economic activists who were branded in 1937–38 as "enemies" were actually never enemies, spies, wreckers, and so on, but were always honest communists; they were only so stigmatized, and often, no longer able to bear barbaric tortures, they charged themselves (at the order of the investigative judges-falsifiers) with all kinds of grave and unlikely crimes.

This was the result of the abuse of power by Stalin, who began to use mass terror against the Party cadres. . . . Stalin put the Party and the NKVD [the Soviet police agency] up to the use of mass terror when the exploiting classes had been liquidated in our country and when there were no serious reasons for the use of extraordinary mass terror. The terror was directed . . . against the honest workers of the Party and the Soviet state. . . .

Stalin was a very distrustful man, sickly, suspicious. . . . Everywhere and in everything he saw "enemies," "two-facers," and "spies." Possessing unlimited power, he indulged in great willfulness and choked a person morally and physically. A situation was created where one could not express one's own will. When Stalin said that one or another would be arrested, it was necessary to accept on faith that he was an "enemy of the people." What proofs were offered? The confession of the arrested. . . . How is it possible that a person confesses to crimes that he had not committed? Only in one way— because of application of physical methods of pressuring him, tortures, bringing him to a state of unconsciousness, deprivation of his judgment, taking away of his human dignity.

 What were Stalin's major crimes, according to Khrushchev? To what degree were these problems resolved under later Soviet leaders?

SOURCE: *Congressional Record*, 84th Congress, 2nd session, vol. 102, pt. 7 (June 4, 1956), pp. 9389–9402.

power gave rise to innumerable stories about his addiction to "bourgeois pleasures," including expensive country houses in the elite Moscow suburb of Zhukovka and fast cars (many of them gifts from foreign leaders)—he was no partisan of reform.

Still, Brezhnev sought stability in the domestic arena. He and his prime minister, Alexei Kosygin (1904–1980), undertook what might be described as a program of "de-Khrushchevization," returning the responsibility for long-term planning to the central ministries and reuniting the Communist Party apparatus. Despite some cautious attempts to stimulate the stagnant farm sector by increasing capital investment in agriculture and raising food prices to increase rural income and provide additional incentives to collective farmers, there was no effort to revise the basic structure of the collective system. In the industrial sector, the regime launched a series of reforms designed to give factory managers (themselves employees of the state) more responsibility for setting prices, wages, and production quotas. These "Kosygin reforms" had little effect, however, because they were stubbornly resisted by the bureaucracy and were eventually adopted by relatively few enterprises within the vast state-owned industrial sector.

A CONTROLLED SOCIETY Brezhnev also initiated a significant retreat from Khrushchev's policy of de-Stalinization. Criticism of the "Great Leader" had angered conservatives both within the party hierarchy and among the public at large, many of whom still revered Stalin as a hero of the Soviet system and a defender of the Russian people against Nazi Germany. Many influential figures in the Kremlin feared that de-Stalinization could lead to internal instability and a decline in public trust in the legitimacy of party leadership—the hallowed "dictatorship of the proletariat." Early in Brezhnev's reign, Stalin's reputation began to revive. Although his alleged "shortcomings" were not totally ignored, he was now described in the official press as "an outstanding party leader" who had been primarily responsible for the successes achieved by the Soviet Union.

The regime also adopted a more restrictive policy toward free expression and dissidence in Soviet society. Critics of the Soviet system, such as the physicist Andrei Sakharov, were harassed and arrested or, like the famous writer Alexander Solzhenitsyn (who had written about the horrors of Soviet concentration camps), forced to leave the country. There was also a qualified return to the anti-Semitic policies and attitudes that had marked the Stalin era. Such indications of renewed repression aroused concern in the West and were instrumental in the inclusion of a statement on human rights in the 1975 Helsinki Accords, which guaranteed the sanctity of international frontiers throughout the continent of Europe (see Chapter 7). Performance in the area of human rights continued to be spotty, however, and the repressive character of Soviet society was not significantly altered.

There were, of course, no rival voices to compete with the party and the government in defining national interests. A new state constitution, promulgated in 1977, enshrined the Communist Party as "the leading and guiding force" in the Soviet Union (see the box on p. 196). The media were controlled by the state and presented only what the state wanted people to hear. The two major newspapers, *Pravda* ("Truth") and *Izvestiya* ("News"), were the agents of the party and the government, respectively. Cynics joked that there was no news in *Pravda* and no truth in *Izvestiya*. Airplane accidents in the Soviet Union were rarely publicized out of concern that they would raise questions about the quality of the Soviet airline industry. The government made strenuous efforts to prevent the Soviet people from being exposed to harmful foreign ideas, especially modern art, literature, and contemporary Western rock music. When the Summer Olympic Games were held in Moscow in 1980, Soviet newspapers advised citizens to keep their children indoors to protect them from being polluted with "bourgeois" ideas passed on by foreign visitors.

For citizens of Western democracies, such a political atmosphere would seem highly oppressive, but for the people in the Soviet republics, an emphasis on law and order was an accepted aspect of everyday life inherited from the tsarist period. Conformism was the rule in virtually every corner of Soviet society, from the educational system (characterized at all levels by rote memorization and political indoctrination) to child rearing (it was forbidden, for example, to be left-handed) and even to yearly vacations (most workers took their vacations at resorts run by their employer, where the daily schedule of activities was highly regimented). Young Americans studying in the Soviet Union reported that friends there were often shocked to hear U.S. citizens criticizing their own president and to learn that they did not routinely carry identity cards.

A STAGNANT ECONOMY Soviet leaders also failed to achieve their objective of revitalizing the national economy. Whereas growth rates during the early Khrushchev era had been impressive (prompting Khrushchev during a reception at the Kremlin in 1956 to chortle to an American guest, "We will bury you," referring to the Western countries), under Brezhnev industrial growth declined to an annual rate of less than 4 percent in the early 1970s and less than 3 percent in the period 1975–1980. Successes in the agricultural sector were equally meager. Grain production rose from less than 90 million tons in the early 1950s to nearly 200 million tons in the 1970s but then stagnated at that level (though it should be noted that Soviet statistics were notoriously unreliable).

One of the primary problems with the Soviet economy was the absence of incentives. Salary structures offered little reward for hard labor and extraordinary achievement. Pay differentials operated within a much narrower range than in most Western societies, and there was little danger of being dismissed. According to the Soviet constitution, every Soviet citizen was guaranteed an opportunity to work.

There were, of course, some exceptions to this general rule. Athletic achievement was highly prized, and a gymnast of Olympic stature would receive great rewards in the form of prestige and lifestyle. Senior officials did not receive high salaries but were provided with countless "perquisites," such as access to foreign goods, official automobiles with chauffeurs, and entry into prestigious

The Rights and Duties of Soviet Citizens

In the Soviet Union, and in other countries modeled on the Soviet system, the national constitution was viewed not as a timeless document, but as a reflection of conditions at the time it was framed. As Soviet society advanced from a state of "raw communism" to a fully socialist society, new constitutions were drafted to reflect the changes taking place in society as a whole. The first two constitutions of the Soviet Union, promulgated in 1924 and 1936, declared that the state was a "dictatorship of the proletariat" guided by the Communist Party, the vanguard organization of the working class in the Soviet Union. But the so-called Brezhnev constitution of 1977 described the Soviet Union as a "state of all the people," composed of workers, farmers, and "socialist intellectuals," although it confirmed the role of the Communist Party as the "leading force" in society. The provisions from the 1977 constitution presented here illustrate some of the freedoms and obligations of Soviet citizens. Especially noteworthy are Articles 39 and 62, which suggest that the interests and prestige of the state took precedence over individual liberties.

The Soviet Constitution of 1977

Chapter 1: The Political System

Article 6. The leading and guiding force of the Soviet society and the nucleus of its political system, of all state organizations and public organizations, is the Communist Party of the Soviet Union. The CPSU exists for the people and serves the people.

The Communist Party, armed with Marxism-Leninism, determines the general perspectives of the development of society and the course of the home and foreign policy of the USSR, directs the great constructive work of the Soviet people, and imparts a planned, systematic, and theoretically substantiated character to their struggle for the victory of communism.

Chapter 6: Equality of Citizens' Rights

Article 35. Women and men have equal rights in the USSR. Exercise of these rights is ensured by according women equal access with men to education and vocational and professional training, equal opportunities in employment, remuneration and promotion, and in social and political, and cultural activity, and by the special labor and health protection measures for women; by providing conditions enabling mothers to work; by legal protection, and material and moral support for mothers and children, including paid leaves and other benefits for expectant mothers and mothers, and gradual reduction of working time for mothers with small children.

Chapter 7: The Basic Rights, Freedoms, and Duties of Citizens of the USSR

Article 39. Citizens of the USSR enjoy in full the social, economic, political, and personal rights and freedoms proclaimed and guaranteed by the Constitution of the USSR and by Soviet laws. The socialist system ensures enlargement of the rights and freedoms of citizens and continuous improvement of their living standards as social, economic, and cultural development programs are fulfilled. Enjoyment by citizens of their rights and freedoms must not be to the detriment of the interests of society or the state, or infringe the rights of other citizens.

Article 62. Citizens of the USSR are obliged to safeguard the interests of the Soviet state, and to enhance its power and prestige. Defense of the Socialist Motherland is the sacred duty of every citizen of the USSR. Betrayal of the Motherland is the gravest of crimes against the people.

 Which of these provisions would seem out of place if they were to appear in the Constitution of the United States?

SOURCE: Excerpts from *The Soviet Constitution of 1977*. Novosti Press Agency Publishing House. Moscow, 1985.

---

institutions of higher learning for their children. For the elite, it was *blat* (influence) that most often differentiated them from the rest of the population. The average citizen, however, had little material incentive to produce beyond the minimum acceptable level. It is hardly surprising that overall per capita productivity was only about half that realized in most capitalist countries. At the same time, the rudeness of Soviet clerks and waiters toward their customers became legendary.

The problem of incentives existed at the managerial level as well, where the practice of centralized planning discouraged initiative and innovation. Factory managers, for example, were assigned monthly and annual quotas by the **Gosplan** (the "state plan," drawn up by the central planning commission). Because state-owned factories faced little or no competition, factory managers did not care whether their products were competitive in terms of price and quality, as long as the quota was attained. One of the key complaints of Soviet citizens was the low quality of most locally made consumer goods. Knowledgeable consumers quickly discovered that products manufactured at the end of the month were often of lower quality (because factory workers had to rush to meet their quotas at the end of the production cycle) and tried to avoid purchasing them.

Often consumer goods were simply unavailable. Whenever Soviet citizens saw a queue forming in front of a store, they automatically got in line, often without even knowing what the line was for, because they never knew when an item might be available again. When they reached the head of the line, most would purchase several of the same item to swap with their friends and neighbors. This "queue psychology," of course, was a time-consuming process and inevitably served to reduce the per capita rate of productivity.

Soviet citizens often tried to overcome the shortcomings of the system by operating "on the left" (the black market). Private economic activities, of course, were illegal in the socialized Soviet system, but many workers took to "moonlighting" to augment their meager salaries. An employee in a state-run appliance store, for example, would promise to repair a customer's television set on his own time in return for a payment "under the table." Otherwise, the repairs might require several weeks. Knowledgeable observers estimated that as much as one-third of the entire Soviet economy operated outside the legal system.

Another major obstacle to economic growth was inadequate technology. Except in the area of national defense, the overall level of Soviet technology was not comparable to that of the West or the advanced industrial societies of East Asia. Part of the problem, of course, stemmed from the issues already described. With no competition, factory managers had little incentive to improve the quality of their products. But another reason was the high priority assigned to defense. The military sector regularly received the most resources from the government and attracted the cream of the country's scientific talent.

There were still other reasons for the gradual slowdown in the Soviet economy. Coal mining was highly inefficient, and only about one-third of the coal extracted actually reached its final destination. Although Soviet oil reserves were estimated to be the largest in the world, for the most part they were located in inaccessible areas of Siberia where extraction facilities and transportation were inadequate. U.S. intelligence reports predicted that a leveling off of oil and gas production could cause severe problems for the future growth of the Soviet economy. Soviet planners hoped that nuclear energy would eventually take up the slack, but the highly publicized meltdown of a nuclear reactor at Chernobyl in 1986 vividly demonstrated that Soviet technology was encountering difficulties in that area as well. Finally, there were serious underlying structural problems in agriculture. Climatic difficulties (frequent flooding, drought, and a short growing season) and a lack of fertile soil (except in the renowned "black earth" regions of Ukraine) combined with a chronic shortage of mechanized farm equipment and a lack of incentives to prevent the growth of an advanced agricultural economy.

AN AGING LEADERSHIP Such problems would be intimidating for any government; they were particularly so for the elderly party leaders surrounding Leonid Brezhnev, many of whom were cautious to a fault. Although some undoubtedly recognized the need for reform and innovation, they were paralyzed by fear of instability and change. The problem worsened during the late 1970s, when Brezhnev's health began to deteriorate.

Brezhnev died in November 1982 and was succeeded by Yuri Andropov (1914–1984), a party veteran and head of the Soviet secret services. During his brief tenure as party chief, Andropov was a vocal advocate of reform, but most of his initiatives were limited to the familiar nostrums of punishment for wrongdoers and moral exhortations to Soviet citizens to work harder. At the same time, material incentives were still officially discouraged and generally ineffective. Andropov had been ailing when he was selected to succeed Brezhnev as party chief, and when he died after only a few months in office, little had been done to change the system. He was succeeded by a mediocre party stalwart, the elderly Konstantin Chernenko (1911–1985). With the Soviet system in crisis, Moscow seemed stuck in a time warp. As one concerned observer told an American journalist, "I had a sense of foreboding, like before a storm. That there was something brewing in people and there would be a time when they would say, 'That's it. We can't go on living like this. We can't. We need to redo everything.'"[3]

Ferment in Eastern Europe

The key to security along the Soviet Union's western frontier was the string of satellite states that had been created in Eastern Europe after World War II. Once Communist power had been assured in Warsaw, Prague, Sofia,

Budapest, Bucharest, and East Berlin, a series of "little Stalins" put into power by Moscow instituted Soviet-type five-year plans that emphasized heavy industry rather than consumer goods, the collectivization of agriculture, and the nationalization of industry. They also appropriated the political tactics that Stalin had perfected in the Soviet Union, eliminating all non-Communist parties and establishing the standard institutions of repression—the secret police and military forces. Dissidents were tracked down and thrown into prison, while "national Communists" who resisted total subservience to the nation were charged with treason in mass show trials and executed.

Despite such repressive efforts, however, Soviet-style policies aroused growing discontent in several Eastern European societies. Hungary, Poland, and Romania harbored bitter memories of past Russian domination and suspected that Stalin, under the guise of proletarian internationalism, was seeking to revive the empire of the Romanovs. For the vast majority of peoples in Eastern Europe, the imposition of "people's democracies" (a euphemism invented by Moscow to refer to a society in the early stage of socialist transition) resulted in economic hardship and severe threats to the most basic political liberties.

Unrest in Poland

The first signs of unrest appeared in 1953, when popular riots broke out against Communist rule in East Berlin. The riots eventually subsided, but the virus had begun to spread to neighboring countries. In Poland, public demonstrations against an increase in food prices in 1956 escalated into widespread protests against the regime's economic policies, restrictions on the freedom of Catholics to practice their religion, and the continued presence of Soviet troops (as called for by the Warsaw Pact) on Polish soil. In a desperate effort to defuse the unrest, in October the Polish party leader stepped down and was replaced by Wadyslaw Gomulka (1905–1982), a popular figure who had previously been demoted for his "nationalist" tendencies. When Gomulka took steps to ease the crisis, the new Soviet party chief, Nikita Khrushchev, flew to Warsaw to warn his Polish colleague against adopting policies that could undermine the "dictatorship of the proletariat" (the Marxist phrase for the political dominance of the party) and even weaken security links with the Soviet

Union. After a brief confrontation, during which both sides threatened to use military force to punctuate their demands, Gomulka and Khrushchev reached a compromise according to which Poland would adopt a policy labeled "internal reform, external loyalty." Poland agreed to remain in the Warsaw Pact and to maintain the sanctity of party rule. In return, Warsaw was authorized to adopt domestic reforms, such as easing restrictions on religious practice and ending the policy of forced collectivization in rural areas.

The Hungarian Uprising

The developments in Poland sent shock waves throughout the region. The impact was strongest in neighboring Hungary, where the methods of the local "little Stalin," Mátyás Rákosi, were so brutal that he had been summoned to Moscow for a lecture. In late October 1956, student-led popular riots broke out in the capital of Budapest and soon spread to towns and villages throughout the country. Rákosi was forced to resign and was replaced by Imre Nagy (1896–1958), a "national Communist" who attempted to satisfy popular demands without arousing the anger of Moscow. Unlike Gomulka, however, Nagy

How the Mighty Have Fallen. In the fall of 1956, Hungarian freedom fighters rose up against Communist domination of their country in the short-lived Hungarian Revolution. Their actions threatened Soviet hegemony in Eastern Europe, however, and in late October, Soviet leader Nikita Khrushchev dispatched troops to quell the uprising. In the meantime, the Hungarian people had demonstrated their discontent by toppling a gigantic statue of Joseph Stalin in the capital of Budapest. Statues of the Soviet dictator had been erected in all the Soviet satellites after World War II. ("W.C." identifies a public toilet in European countries.)

was unable to contain the zeal of leading members of the protest movement, who sought major political reforms and the withdrawal of Hungary from the Warsaw Pact. On November 1, Nagy promised free elections, which, given the mood of the country, would probably have brought an end to Communist rule. Moscow decided on firm action. Soviet troops, recently withdrawn at Nagy's request, returned to Budapest and installed a new government under the more pliant party leader János Kádár (1912–1989). While Kádár rescinded many of Nagy's measures, Nagy sought refuge in the Yugoslav Embassy. A few weeks later, he left the embassy under the promise of safety but was quickly arrested, convicted of treason, and executed.

The dramatic events in Poland and Hungary graphically demonstrated the vulnerability of the Soviet satellite system in Eastern Europe, and many observers throughout the world anticipated an attempt by the United States to intervene on behalf of the freedom fighters in Hungary. After all, the Eisenhower administration had promised that it would "roll back" communism, and radio broadcasts by the U.S.-sponsored Radio Liberty and Radio Free Europe had encouraged the peoples of Eastern Europe to rise up against Soviet domination. In reality, Washington was well aware that U.S. intervention could lead to nuclear war and limited itself to protests against Soviet brutality in crushing the uprising.

The year of discontent was not without its consequences, however. Soviet leaders now recognized that Moscow could maintain control over its satellites in Eastern Europe only by granting them the leeway to adopt domestic policies appropriate to local conditions. Khrushchev had already embarked on this path when, during a visit to Belgrade in 1955, he assured Tito that there were "different roads to socialism." Eastern European Communist leaders now took Khrushchev at his word and adopted reform programs to make socialism more palatable to their subject populations. Even János Kádár, derisively labeled the "butcher of Budapest," managed to preserve many of Imre Nagy's reforms to allow a measure of capitalist incentive and freedom of expression in Hungary.

The Prague Spring

Czechoslovakia did not share in the thaw of the mid-1950s and remained under the rule of Antonín Novotný (1904–1975), who had been placed in power by Stalin himself. By the late 1960s, however, Novotný's policies had led to widespread popular alienation, and in 1968, with the support of intellectuals and reformist party members, Alexander Dubček (1921–1992) was elected first secretary of the Communist Party. He immediately attempted to create what was popularly called "socialism with a human face," relaxing restrictions on freedom of speech and the press and the right to travel abroad. Reforms were announced for the economic sector, and party control over all aspects of society was reduced. A period of euphoria erupted that came to be known as the "Prague Spring."

It proved to be short-lived. Encouraged by Dubček's actions, some Czechs called for more far-reaching reforms, including neutrality and withdrawal from the Soviet bloc. To forestall the spread of this "spring fever," the Soviet Red Army, supported by troops from other Warsaw Pact states, invaded Czechoslovakia in August 1968 and crushed the reform movement. Gustáv Husák (1913–1991), a committed Stalinist, replaced Dubček and restored the old order, while Moscow justified its action by issuing what became known as the **Brezhnev Doctrine** (see the box on p. 200).

The Persistence of Stalinism in East Germany

Elsewhere in Eastern Europe, Stalinist policies continued to hold sway. The ruling Communist government in East Germany, led by Walter Ulbricht (1893–1973), consolidated its position in the early 1950s and became a faithful Soviet satellite. Industry was nationalized and agriculture collectivized. After the 1953 workers' revolt was crushed by Soviet tanks, a steady flight of East Germans to West Germany ensued, primarily through the city of Berlin. According to one estimate, some 3 million people, or almost 20 percent of the total population of the German Democratic Republic, had fled to West Germany by 1961. This exodus of mostly skilled laborers (soon only party chief Ulbricht would be left, remarked one Soviet observer sardonically) created economic problems and in 1961 led the East German government to erect the infamous Berlin Wall separating West from East Berlin, as well as even more fearsome barriers along the entire border with West Germany.

After walling off the West, East Germany succeeded in developing the strongest economy among the Soviet Union's Eastern European satellites. In 1971, Walter Ulbricht was succeeded by Erich Honecker (1912–1994), a party hard-liner who was deeply committed to the ideological battle against détente. Propaganda increased, and the use of the Stasi, the secret police, became a hallmark of Honecker's virtual dictatorship. The Stasi had more than 100,000 employees, and its files on suspected subversives reportedly took up 125 miles of shelf space.[4] Aided by this enormous police bureaucracy, Honecker ruled unchallenged for the next eighteen years.

The Brezhnev Doctrine

In the summer of 1968, when the new Communist Party leaders in Czechoslovakia were seriously considering proposals for reforming the totalitarian system there, the Warsaw Pact nations met under the leadership of Soviet party chief Leonid Brezhnev to assess the threat to the socialist camp. Soon afterward, military forces of several Soviet bloc nations entered Czechoslovakia and imposed a new government subservient to Moscow. The move was justified by the spirit of "proletarian internationalism" and was widely viewed as a warning to China and other socialist states not to stray too far from Marxist-Leninist orthodoxy, as interpreted by the Soviet Union. The principle came to be known as the Brezhnev Doctrine.

A Letter to Czechoslovakia

To the Central Committee of the Communist Party of Czechoslovakia

Warsaw, July 15, 1968

Dear comrades!

On behalf of the Central Committees of the Communist and Workers' Parties of Bulgaria, Hungary, the German Democratic Republic, Poland, and the Soviet Union, we address ourselves to you with this letter, prompted by a feeling of sincere friendship based on the principles of Marxism-Leninism and proletarian internationalism and by the concern of our common affairs for strengthening the positions of socialism and the security of the socialist community of nations.

The development of events in your country evokes in us deep anxiety. It is our firm conviction that the offensive of the reactionary forces, backed by imperialists, against your Party and the foundations of the social system in the Czechoslovak Socialist Republic, threatens to push your country off the road of socialism and that consequently it jeopardizes the interests of the entire socialist system. . . .

We neither had nor have any intention of interfering in such affairs as are strictly the internal business of your Party and your state, nor of violating the principles of respect, independence, and equality in the relations among the Communist Parties and socialist countries. . . .

At the same time we cannot agree to have hostile forces push your country from the road of socialism and create a threat of severing Czechoslovakia from the socialist community. . . . This is the common cause of our countries, which have joined in the Warsaw Treaty to ensure independence, peace, and security in Europe, and to set up an insurmountable barrier against aggression and revenge. . . . We shall never agree to have imperialism, using peaceful or nonpeaceful methods, making a gap from the inside or from the outside in the socialist system, and changing in imperialism's favor the correlation of forces in Europe. . . .

That is why we believe that a decisive rebuff of the anti-Communist forces, and decisive efforts for the preservation of the socialist system in Czechoslovakia are not only your task but ours as well. . . .

We express the conviction that the Communist Party of Czechoslovakia, conscious of its responsibility, will take the necessary steps to block the path of reaction. In this struggle you can count on the solidarity and all-round assistance of the fraternal socialist countries.

 How did Leonid Brezhnev justify the Soviet invasion of Czechoslovakia in 1968? Do you find his arguments persuasive?

SOURCE: *Moscow News,* Supplement to No. 30(917), 1968, pp. 3–6.

Culture and Society in the Soviet Bloc

In his occasional musings about the future Communist utopia, Karl Marx had predicted that a classless society would emerge to replace the exploitative and hierarchical systems of feudalism and capitalism. Workers would engage in productive activities and share equally in the fruits of their labor. In their free time, they would produce a new, advanced culture, proletarian in character and egalitarian in content.

Cultural Expression

The reality in the post–World War II Soviet Union and in Eastern Europe was somewhat different. Beginning in 1946, a series of government decrees made all forms of literary and scientific expression dependent on the state. All Soviet culture was expected to follow the party line. Historians, philosophers, and social scientists all grew accustomed to quoting Marx, Lenin, and, above all, Stalin as their chief authorities. Novels and plays, too, were supposed to portray Communist heroes and their efforts to create a better society. No criticism of existing social conditions was permitted. Even distinguished composers such as Dmitri Shostakovich (1906–1975) were compelled to heed Stalin's criticisms, including his view that contemporary Western music was nothing but a "mishmash." Some areas of intellectual activity were virtually abolished; the science of genetics disappeared, and few movies were made during Stalin's final years.

Stalin's death brought a modest respite from cultural repression. Writers and artists banned during Stalin's years were again allowed to publish. The writer Ilya Ehrenburg (1891–1967) set the tone with his novel, significantly titled *The Thaw*. Still, Soviet authorities, including Khrushchev, were reluctant to allow cultural freedom to move far beyond official Soviet ideology.

These restrictions, however, did not prevent the emergence of some significant Soviet literature, although authors paid a heavy price if they alienated the Soviet authorities. Boris Pasternak (1890–1960), who began his literary career as a poet, won the Nobel Prize in 1958 for his celebrated novel *Doctor Zhivago*, published in Italy in 1957. But the Soviet government condemned Pasternak's anti-Soviet tendencies, banned the novel from the Soviet Union, and would not allow him to accept the prize. The author had alienated the authorities by describing a society scarred by the excesses of Bolshevik revolutionary zeal.

Alexander Solzhenitsyn (1918–2008) caused an even greater furor than Pasternak. Solzhenitsyn had spent eight years in forced-labor camps for criticizing Stalin, and his *One Day in the Life of Ivan Denisovich*, which won him the Nobel Prize in 1970, was an account of life in those camps. Later, Solzhenitsyn wrote *The Gulag Archipelago*, a detailed indictment of the whole system of Soviet oppression. Soviet authorities denounced Solzhenitsyn's efforts to inform the world of Soviet crimes against humanity and arrested and expelled him from the Soviet Union after he published *The Gulag Archipelago* abroad in 1973.

Although restrictive policies continued into the late 1980s, some Soviet authors learned how to minimize battles with the censors by writing under the guise of humor or fantasy. Two of the most accomplished and popular Soviet novelists of the period, Yury Trifonov (1925–1981) and Fazil Iskander (b. 1929), focused on the daily struggle of Soviet citizens to live with dignity. Trifonov depicted the everyday life of ordinary Russians with grim realism, while Iskander used humor to poke fun at the incompetence of the Soviet regime.

The situation was similar in the Eastern European satellites, although cultural freedom varied considerably from country to country. In Poland, intellectuals had access to Western publications as well as greater freedom to travel to the West. Hungarian and Yugoslav Communists, too, tolerated a certain level of intellectual activity that was not liked but not prohibited. Elsewhere, intellectuals were forced to conform to the regime's demands.

The socialist camp did participate in modern popular culture. By the early 1970s, there were 28 million television sets in the Soviet Union, although state authorities controlled the content of the programs that the Soviet people watched. Tourism, too, made inroads into the Communist world as state-run industries provided vacation time and governments facilitated the establishment of resorts for workers on the Black Sea and Adriatic coasts.

Spectator sports became a large industry, although they were highly politicized as the

Stalinist Heroic: An Example of Socialist Realism. Under Stalin and his successors, art was assigned the task of indoctrinating the Soviet population in the public virtues, such as hard work, loyalty to the state, and patriotism. Grandiose statuary erected to commemorate the heroic efforts of the Red Army during World War II appeared in every Soviet city. Here is an example in Minsk, today the capital of Belarus. The flag reads "Forward under the banner of Lenin to the victory of Communism."

© William J. Duiker

result of Cold War divisions. Victory in international athletic events was viewed as proof of the superiority of the socialist system over its capitalist rival. Accordingly, the state provided money for the construction of gymnasiums and training camps and portrayed athletes as superheroes.

Social Changes in Eastern Europe

The imposition of Marxist systems in Eastern Europe had far-reaching social consequences. Most Eastern European countries made the change from peasant societies to modern industrialized economies. In Bulgaria, for example, 80 percent of the labor force was engaged in agriculture in 1950, but only 20 percent was still working there in 1980. Although the Soviet Union and its Eastern European satellites never achieved the high standards of living of the West, they did experience some improvement. In 1960, the average real income of Polish peasants was four times higher than before World War II. Consumer goods also became more widespread. In East Germany, only 17 percent of families had television sets in 1960, but 75 percent had acquired them by 1972.

True to their creed, Communist leaders in Eastern Europe took steps to divest traditional elites of their economic power base and replaced them with their own supporters. One route to this reversal of roles was through education.

In some countries, the desire to provide equal educational opportunities led to laws that mandated quota systems based on class. In East Germany, for example, 50 percent of the students in secondary schools had to be children of workers and peasants. The sons of manual workers constituted 53 percent of university students in Yugoslavia in 1964 and 40 percent in East Germany, compared to only 15 percent in Italy and 5.3 percent in West Germany. Social mobility also increased. In Poland in 1961, half of the white-collar workers came from blue-collar families. A significant number of judges, professors, and industrial managers stemmed from working-class backgrounds.

Education became crucial in preparing for new jobs in the Communist system and led to higher enrollments in both secondary schools and universities. In Czechoslovakia, for example, the number of students in secondary schools tripled between 1945 and 1970, and the number of university students quadrupled between the 1930s and the 1960s. The type of education that students received also changed. In Hungary before World War II, 40 percent of students studied law, 9 percent engineering and technology, and 5 percent agriculture. In 1970, the figures were 35 percent in engineering and technology, 9 percent in agriculture, and only 4 percent in law.

But as so often happens in programs aimed at creating a new society through social engineering, reality eventually intruded. As the new managers of society, regardless of class background, realized the importance of higher education, they used their power to gain special privileges for their children. By 1971, fully 60 percent of the children of white-collar workers attended a university, and even though blue-collar families constituted 60 percent of the population, only 36 percent of their children attended institutions of higher learning. Even East Germany dropped its requirement that 50 percent of secondary students had to be the offspring of workers and peasants.

This shift in educational preferences demonstrates yet another aspect of the social structure in the Communist world: the emergence of a new privileged class, made up of members of the Communist Party, state officials, high-ranking officers in the military and secret police, and a few special professional groups. The new elite not only possessed political power but also received special privileges, including the right to purchase high-quality goods in special stores, paid vacations at special resorts, access to good housing and superior medical services, and advantages in education and jobs for their children.

Women in the Soviet Bloc

The system also failed to measure up in its treatment of women. Long after the Bolshevik Revolution had called for true equality of the sexes, men continued to dominate the leadership positions of the Communist parties in the Soviet Union and Eastern Europe. Women did have greater opportunities in the workforce and even in the professions, however. In the Soviet Union, women comprised 51 percent of the labor force in 1980; by the mid-1980s, they constituted 50 percent of the engineers, 80 percent of the doctors, and 75 percent of the teachers and teachers' aides. But many of these were low-paying jobs; most female doctors, for example, worked in primary care and were paid less than skilled machinists. The chief administrators in hospitals and schools were still men.

Moreover, although women were part of the workforce, they were still expected to fulfill their traditional roles in the home. Most women worked what came to be known as the "double shift." After spending eight hours in their jobs, they came home to do the housework and take care of the children. They might spend another two hours a day in long lines at a number of stores waiting to buy food and clothes. Because of the scarcity of housing, they had to use kitchens that were shared by a number of families.

Nearly three-quarters of a century after the Bolshevik Revolution, then, the Marxist dream of an advanced, egalitarian society was as far away as ever. Although in some respects conditions in the socialist camp were an improvement over those before World War II, many problems and inequities were as intransigent as ever.

The Disintegration of the Soviet Empire

On the death of Konstantin Chernenko in 1985, party leaders selected the talented and vigorous Soviet official Mikhail Gorbachev to succeed him. The new Soviet leader had shown early signs of promise. Born into a peasant family in 1931, Gorbachev combined farmwork with school and received the Order of the Red Banner for his agricultural efforts. This award and his good school record enabled him to study law at the University of Moscow. After receiving his law degree in 1955, he returned to his native southern Russia, where he eventually became first secretary of the Communist Party in the city of Stavropol and then first secretary of the regional party committee. In 1978, Gorbachev was made a member of the party's Central Committee in Moscow. Two years later, he became a full member of the ruling Politburo and secretary of the Central Committee.

During the early 1980s, Gorbachev began to realize the immensity of Soviet problems and the crucial need to transform the system. During a visit to Canada in 1983, he discovered to his astonishment that Canadian farmers worked hard on their own initiative. "We'll never have this for fifty years," he reportedly remarked.[5] On his return to Moscow, he established a series of committees to evaluate the situation and recommend measures to improve the system.

The Gorbachev Era

With his election as party general secretary in 1985, Gorbachev seemed intent on taking earlier reforms to their logical conclusions. The cornerstone of his reform program was *perestroika*, or "restructuring." At first, it meant only a reordering of economic policy, as Gorbachev called for the beginning of a market economy with limited free enterprise and some private property. Initial economic reforms were difficult to implement, however. Radicals criticized Gorbachev for his caution and demanded decisive measures; conservatives feared that rapid changes would be too painful. In his attempt to achieve compromise, Gorbachev often pursued partial liberalization, which satisfied neither faction and also failed to work, producing only more discontent.

Gorbachev soon perceived that in the Soviet system, the economic sphere was intimately tied to the social and political spheres. Any efforts to reform the economy without political or social reform would be doomed to failure. One of the most important instruments of *perestroika* was **glasnost**, or "openness." Soviet citizens and officials were encouraged to openly discuss the strengths and weaknesses of the Soviet Union. This policy could be seen in *Pravda*, the official newspaper of the Communist Party, where disasters such as the nuclear accident at Chernobyl in 1986 and collisions of ships in the Black Sea received increasing coverage.[6] Soon this type of reporting was extended to include reports of official corruption, sloppy factory work, and protests against government policy. The arts also benefited from the new policy as previously banned works were now allowed to circulate and motion pictures began to depict negative aspects of Soviet life. Music based on Western styles, such as jazz and rock, began to be performed openly. Religious activities, previously banned by Soviet authorities, were once again tolerated.

Political reforms were equally revolutionary. In June 1987, the principle of two-candidate elections was introduced; previously, voters had been presented with only one candidate. Most dissidents, including Andrei Sakharov, who had spent years in internal exile, were released. At the Communist Party conference in 1988, Gorbachev called for the creation of a new Soviet parliament, the Congress of People's Deputies, whose members were to be chosen in competitive elections. It convened in 1989, the first such meeting since 1918. As an elected member of the Congress, Sakharov called for an end to the Communist monopoly of power, and on December 11, 1989, the day he died, he urged the creation of a new, non-Communist party. Early in 1990, Gorbachev legalized the formation of other political parties and struck out Article 6 of the Soviet constitution, which guaranteed the "leading role" of the Communist Party (see the box on p. 196). Hitherto, the position of first secretary of the party was the most important post in the Soviet Union, but as the Communist Party became less closely associated with the state, the powers of this office diminished. Gorbachev attempted to consolidate his power by creating a new state presidency, and in March 1990, he became the Soviet Union's first president. But by now his stature within the country had diminished, and reformist elements who had vociferously welcomed his policies were increasingly skeptical of success. "Russia," one erstwhile optimist lamented, "is not ready for democracy."

Eastern Europe: From Soviet Satellites to Sovereign Nations

The progressive decline of the Soviet Union had an impact on its neighbors to the west. As before, Poland was at the forefront. In the late 1970s, high food prices led to popular protests and the emergence of an independent labor union called Solidarity. Led by Lech Wałęsa (b. 1943), Solidarity rode the wave of national spirit heightened by the visit of Polish-born Pope John Paul II in June 1979 and rapidly became an influential force for change. Sensing a threat to its monopoly on power, the regime outlawed the union and declared martial law in 1981, but the movement continued to gain popular support. When Mikhail Gorbachev made it clear that Moscow would not bail it out, the Communist government bowed to the inevitable and permitted free national elections to take place, resulting in the election of Wałęsa as president of Poland in December 1990. Moscow—inspired by Gorbachev's policy of encouraging "new thinking" to improve relations with the Western powers—took no action to reverse the verdict in Warsaw.

In Hungary, as in Poland, the process of transition had begun many years earlier. After crushing the Hungarian revolution of 1956, the Communist government of János Kádár had tried to assuage popular opinion by enacting a series of far-reaching economic reforms (labeled "communism with a capitalist face-lift"), but as the 1980s progressed, the economy sagged, and in 1989, the regime permitted the formation of opposition political parties, leading eventually to the formation of a non-Communist coalition government in elections held in March 1990.

The transition in Czechoslovakia was more abrupt. After Soviet troops crushed the Prague Spring in 1968, hard-line Communists under Gustáv Husák followed a policy of massive repression to maintain their power. In 1977, dissident intellectuals, inspired in part by the Helsinki Accords, formed an organization called Charter 77 as a vehicle for protest against violations of human rights. Regardless of the repressive atmosphere, dissident activities continued to grow during the 1980s, and when massive demonstrations broke out in several major cities in 1989, Husák's government, lacking any real popular support, collapsed. At the end of December, he was replaced by Václav Havel (1936–2011), a dissident playwright who had been a leading figure in Charter 77.

But the most dramatic events took place in East Germany, where a persistent economic slump and the ongoing oppressiveness of the regime of Erich Honecker led to a flight of refugees and mass demonstrations against the regime in the summer and fall of 1989. Capitulating to popular pressure, the Communist government opened its entire border with the West. The Berlin Wall, the most tangible symbol of the Cold War, became the site of a massive celebration, and most of it was dismantled by joyful Germans from both sides of the border. In March 1990, free elections led to the formation of a non-Communist government that began to negotiate political and economic reunification with West Germany (for events in Eastern Europe since 1989, see Chapter 10).

End of Empire

The events in Eastern Europe were being watched closely in Moscow. One of Gorbachev's most serious problems stemmed from the nature of the Soviet Union. The Union of Soviet Socialist Republics was a truly multiethnic country, containing ninety-two nationalities and 112 recognized languages. Previously, the iron hand of the Communist Party, centered in Moscow, had kept a lid on the centuries-old ethnic tensions that had periodically erupted throughout the history of this region. As Gorbachev released this iron grip, tensions resurfaced as ethnic groups took advantage of the new openness to protest what they perceived to be ethnically motivated slights. As violence erupted, nationalist movements emerged in all fifteen republics of the Soviet Union. Often motivated by ethnic concerns, many of them called for sovereignty of the republics and independence from Russian-based rule centered in Moscow. The Soviet army, in disarray since the intervention in Afghanistan, appeared powerless to control the situation.

Gorbachev had made it clear that he supported self-determination but not secession, which he believed would be detrimental to the Soviet Union. Nevertheless, in December 1989, the Communist Party of Lithuania took the first step and declared itself independent of the Communist Party of the Soviet Union.

The collapse of the Soviet Union was not long in coming. On March 11, 1990, the Lithuanian Supreme Council unilaterally declared Lithuania independent. Its formal name was now the Lithuanian Republic; the adjectives *Soviet* and *Socialist* had been dropped. On March 15, the Soviet Congress of People's Deputies, though recognizing a general right to secede from the Union of Soviet Socialist Republics, declared the Lithuanian declaration null and void; proper procedures, the Congress stated, must be established and followed before secession would be acceptable.

During 1990 and 1991, Gorbachev struggled to deal with Lithuania and the other problems unleashed by his reforms. On the one hand, he tried to appease the conservative forces who complained about the growing disorder within the Soviet Union. On the other hand, he tried to accommodate the liberal forces who increasingly favored a new kind of decentralized Soviet federation. Gorbachev especially labored to cooperate more closely with Boris Yeltsin (1931–2007), elected president of the Russian Republic in June 1991. Conservative elements from the army, the party, and the KGB, however, had grown increasingly worried about the potential dissolution of the Soviet Union. On August 19, 1991, a group of these discontented rightists arrested Gorbachev and attempted to seize power. Gorbachev's unwillingness to work with the conspirators and the brave resistance in Moscow of Yeltsin and thousands of Russians who had grown accustomed to their new liberties caused the coup to disintegrate rapidly. The actions of these right-wing plotters served to accelerate the very process they had hoped to stop—the disintegration of the Soviet Union.

Despite desperate pleas from Gorbachev, all fifteen republics soon opted for complete independence (see Map 9.2). Ukraine voted for independence on December 1, 1991. A week later, the leaders of Russia, Ukraine, and Belarus announced that the Soviet Union had "ceased to exist" and would be replaced by a much looser federation, the Commonwealth of Independent States. Gorbachev resigned on December 25, 1991, and turned over his responsibilities as commander in chief to Boris Yeltsin, the president of Russia. By the end of 1991, one of the largest empires in world history had come to an end, and a new era had begun in its lands.

The New Russia: From Empire to Nation

In Russia, by far the largest of the former Soviet republics, a new power struggle soon ensued. Yeltsin, a onetime engineer who had been dismissed from the Politburo in 1987 for insubordination, was committed to introducing a free market economy as quickly as possible. In December 1991, the Congress of People's Deputies granted him temporary power to rule by decree. But former Communist Party members and their allies in the Congress were opposed to many of Yeltsin's economic reforms and tried to place new limits on his powers. Yeltsin fought back. After winning a vote of confidence on April 25, 1993, Yeltsin pushed ahead with plans for a new Russian constitution that would abolish the Congress of People's Deputies, create a two-chamber parliament, and establish a strong presidency. A hard-line parliamentary minority resisted and in early October took the offensive, urging supporters to take over government offices and the central television station. Yeltsin responded by ordering military forces to storm the parliament building and arrest hard-line opponents. Yeltsin used his victory to consolidate his power in parliamentary elections held in December.

MAP 9.2 Eastern Europe and the Former Soviet Union. After the disintegration of the Soviet Union in 1991, the fifteen constituent Soviet republics declared their independence. This map shows the states that emerged from the former Soviet Union in the 1990s and also from the former Yugoslavia, which disintegrated more slowly in the 1990s and 2000s. The breakaway region of Chechnya is indicated on the map.

Q *What new nations have appeared in the territory of the old Soviet Union since the end of the Cold War?*

During the mid-1990s, Yeltsin was able to maintain a precarious grip on power while seeking to implement reforms that would set Russia on a firm course toward a pluralistic political system and a market economy. But the new post-Communist Russia remained as fragile as ever. Burgeoning economic inequality and rampant corruption aroused widespread criticism and shook the confidence of the Russian people in the superiority of the capitalist system over the one that existed under Communist rule. A nagging war in the Caucasus—where the Muslim population of Chechnya sought national independence from Russia—drained the government's budget and exposed the decrepit state of the once vaunted Red Army. In presidential elections held in 1996, Yeltsin was reelected, but the rising popularity of a revived Communist Party and the growing strength of nationalist elements, combined with Yeltsin's precarious health, raised serious questions about the future of the country.

What had happened to derail Yeltsin's plan to transform Soviet society? According to some of his critics, he had tried to achieve too much too fast. Between 1991 and 1995, state firms that had previously provided about 80 percent of all industrial production and employment had been privatized, and the prices of goods (previously subject to government regulation) were allowed to respond to market forces. Only agriculture—where the decision to privatize collective farms had little impact in rural areas—was left substantially untouched. The immediate results were disastrous: industrial output dropped by more than one-third, and unemployment levels and prices rose dramatically. Many Russian workers and soldiers were not paid for months on end, and many social services came to an abrupt halt.

With the harsh official and ideological constraints of the Soviet system suddenly removed, corruption—labeled by one observer "criminal gang capitalism"—became rampant, and the government often appeared inept in coping with the complexities of a market economy. Few Russians appeared to grasp the realities of modern capitalism and understandably reacted to the inevitable pains that accompanied the transition from the old system by heaping all the blame on the new one. The fact is that Yeltsin had attempted to change the structure of the Soviet system without due regard for the necessity of changing the mentality of the people as well. The result was a high level of disenchantment. A new joke circulated among the Russian people: "We know now that everything they told us about communism was false. And everything they told us about capitalism was true."

THE PUTIN ERA At the end of 1999, Yeltsin suddenly resigned and was replaced by Vladimir Putin (b. 1952), a former member of the KGB. Putin vowed to bring an end to the rampant corruption and inexperience that permeated Russian political culture and to strengthen the role of the central government in managing the affairs of state. During the succeeding months, the parliament approved his proposal to centralize power in the hands of the federal government in Moscow; in early 2001, he presented a new plan to regulate political parties, which now numbered more than fifty. Parties at both extremes of the political spectrum, from those urging Western-style liberal policies to Gennadi Zyuganov's revived Communist Party, opposed the legislation—without success.

Putin also vowed to bring the breakaway state of Chechnya back under Russian authority and to adopt a more assertive role in international affairs. Growing public anger at Western plans to expand the NATO alliance into Eastern Europe and at the aggressive actions by NATO countries against Serbia in the Balkans (see Chapter 10) gave the new president an opportunity to restore Russia's position as an influential force in the world. To undercut U.S. dominance on the political scene, Moscow improved relations with neighboring China and simultaneously sought to cooperate with European nations on issues of common concern. To assuage national pride, Putin entered negotiations with such former republics of the old Soviet Union as Belarus and Ukraine to tighten mutual political and economic cooperation.

In addition, Putin steadily pursued measures to strengthen the power of the state over the political system. When critics complained that he was returning to the worst habits of the Soviet era, Putin responded forcefully, noting that while Russia was moving steadily to create conditions for building a democratic society, his government reserved the right to move forward based on its own internal circumstances. "Russia," he said, "can and will independently determine for itself the time frame and the conditions of its movement along that path."[7] Putin's determination to play an active role in that process was clearly demonstrated during the national elections in 2008. Prohibited by the constitution from serving a third term as president, he handpicked a successor—his close ally and United Russia Party member Dmitri Medvedev (b. 1965)—and agreed to serve as prime minister in the new government. Four years later, he was reelected to the presidency amid widespread claims of fraud and voter intimidation.

RUSSIA UNDER THE NEW TSAR Throughout the first decade of the new century, relations between Russia and Western nations steadily deteriorated. Western officials grew increasingly concerned that under Putin Russia was reverting to its autocratic past. They were also critical of Moscow's efforts to intimidate the new states along its perimeter, states that had once been under the firm tutelage of the Soviet Union. In turn, Moscow was irritated at U.S. and European plans to integrate Eastern European countries into the Western alliance. It was especially incensed when the United States and some European governments supported the breakaway region of Kosovo in its bid to achieve independence from Russia's traditional ally Serbia. When dissident elements in Abkhazia and South Ossetia—two restive regions in the state of Georgia—appealed to Moscow for support against alleged government efforts to engage in ethnic cleansing, Russian military forces entered Georgian territory in support of the rebel forces and extended diplomatic recognition to both regions. Although a cease-fire agreement was eventually reached, the incident strained Moscow's relations with the United States and Western Europe almost to the breaking point. When the financial crisis struck the global marketplace in the fall of 2008, Moscow initially reacted with unrestrained pleasure. Flush with foreign currency reserves from its profitable oil exports, Russian officials openly called for the emergence of a new multipolar world no longer dominated by the United States and its European allies. In a bid to fill the vacuum, Moscow sought to use its oil wealth as a political weapon and extended a hand of friendship to a number of Washington's most prominent adversaries, including Iran and Venezuela. Concerned voices in the West expressed alarm at a potential revival of the tensions of the Cold War.

Dreams in Moscow of a possible revival of the powerful Soviet empire, however, are probably misplaced. In the first place, Russia—almost totally dependent on petroleum and other natural resources for its wealth—would be among the first to suffer in the event of another serious economic downturn. In the second place, the country is suffering from a multitude of serious structural problems, including widespread corruption, bureaucratic incompetence, a technology gap, and widespread inflation.

Indeed, pride in the recent achievements of the Russian nation is muted these days. Not only have the boundaries of the old Soviet empire shrunk by one-third, but the living standards of the Russian people have declined as well. According to recent statistics, mortality rates have risen by an estimated 40 percent in the last three decades, and the national population is predicted to decline by almost 50 million in the next half-century. Since the early 1980s, marriage rates have fallen by more than 30 percent, and the rate of divorce has increased by a similar measure.

Putin has attempted to deal with the chronic problems of Russian society by centralizing his control over the system and by silencing his internal critics such as the feminist punk-rock group Pussy Riot. To those who criticize his tendency to trample on human rights, he is openly contemptuous, declaring that Russia has no intention of following the Western model. Rather, he increasingly turns to the past glories of Mother Russia. There is a widespread sense of unease in Russia today about the decline of the social order—especially the disintegration of the traditional family and the rising incidence of alcoholism, sexual promiscuity, and criminal activities—and many of Putin's compatriots express sympathy with his attempt to restore a sense of pride and discipline in Russian society. He was not alone in his feelings when in the spring of 2005 he expressed the view that the breakup of the Soviet Union was a national tragedy.

Saint Basil's Cathedral in Moscow. Under Soviet rule, religion was severely discouraged, as the Communist regime sought to neutralize potential sources of opposition to its rule. But the Russian Orthodox faith, long the official religion of Russia under the tsars, has made a comeback. The Russian Orthodox Church is now put forth as a symbol of the glories of Russian civilization, and President Vladimir Putin has wrapped himself in its mantle by appointing a monk of the church as his spiritual adviser. Saint Basil's Cathedral, located in the heart of Red Square in Moscow, is the most visible symbol of the Orthodox faith in Russia.

© William J. Duiker

CONCLUSION

THE SOVIET UNION HAD EMERGED from World War II as one of the world's two superpowers. Its armies had played an instrumental role in the final defeat of the powerful German war machine and had installed pliant Communist regimes throughout Eastern Europe. During the next four decades, the Soviet Union appeared to be secure in its power. Its military and economic performance during the first postwar decade was sufficiently impressive to create an atmosphere of incipient panic in Washington. By the mid-1980s, however, fears that the Soviet Union would surpass the United States as an economic power had long since dissipated, and the Soviet system appeared to be mired in a state of near paralysis. Economic growth had slowed to a snail's pace, corruption had reached epidemic levels, and leadership had passed to a generation of elderly party bureaucrats who appeared incapable of addressing the burgeoning problems that affected Soviet society.

What had happened to tarnish the dream that had inspired Lenin and his fellow Bolsheviks to believe they could create a Marxist paradise? Some analysts argue that the ambitious defense policies adopted by the Reagan administration forced Moscow into an arms race it could not afford and thus ultimately led to a collapse of the Soviet economy. Others suggest that Soviet problems were more deeply rooted and would have led to the disintegration of the Soviet Union even without outside stimulation. While Star Wars may have been a factor, the latter argument is surely closer to the mark. For years, if not decades, leaders in the Kremlin had disguised or ignored the massive inefficiencies of the Soviet system. It seems clear in retrospect that the Soviet command economy proved better at managing the early stages of the Industrial Revolution than at moving on to the next stage of an advanced technological society. By the 1980s, behind the powerful shield of the Red Army, the system had become an empty shell.

The perceptive Mikhail Gorbachev recognized the crucial importance of instituting radical reforms and hoped that by doing so, he could save the socialist system. By then, however, it was too late. Restive minorities that had long resented the suppression of their national or cultural identities under Moscow's heavy hand now saw their opportunity to break away from the Soviet system. Even the Russian people were no longer confident that the bright vision of a Marxist utopia could be transformed into reality.

The dissolution of the Soviet Union and its satellite system in Eastern Europe brought a dramatic end to the Cold War. At the dawn of the 1990s, a generation of global rivalry between two ideological systems had come to a close, and world leaders turned their attention to the construction of what U.S. President George H. W. Bush called the New World Order. But what sort of new order would it be?

TIMELINE

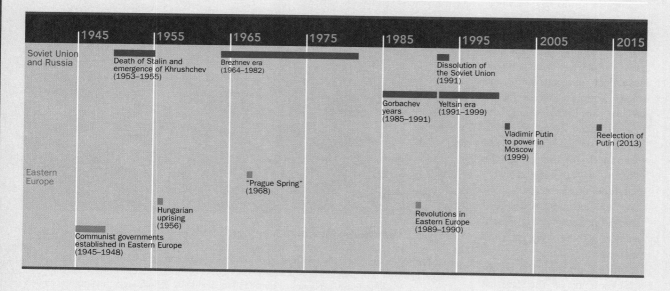

CHAPTER NOTES

1. Vladislav Zubok and Constantine Pleshakov, *Inside the Kremlin's Cold War: From Stalin to Khrushchev* (Cambridge, England, 1996), p. 166.
2. Nikita Khrushchev, *Khrushchev Remembers,* trans. Strobe Talbott (Boston, 1970), p. 77.
3. Quoted in Hedrick Smith, *The New Russians* (New York, 1990), p. 30.
4. Cited in Victor Sebestyen, *Revolution 1989: The Fall of the Soviet Empire* (New York, 2009), p. 121.
5. Smith, *The New Russians,* p. 74.
6. Not everyone got the message. Shortly after the news of the accident came out, a Soviet official claimed to me that it was nothing but "imperialist propaganda."
7. C. J. Chivers, "Russia Will Pursue Democracy, but in Its Own Way, Putin Says," *New York Times,* April 26, 2005.

Postwar Europe: On the Path to Unity?

Berlin, 1945

AT THE END OF WORLD WAR II, European civilization was in ruins. Almost 40 million people had been killed in six years. Massive air raids and artillery bombardments had reduced many of the great cities of Europe to rubble. An American general described the German capital of Berlin: "Wherever we looked, we saw desolation. It was like a city of the dead. Suffering and shock were visible in every face. Dead bodies still remained in canals and lakes and were being dug out from under bomb debris." Berlin was not alone in its devastation. Dozens of other cities around Europe had been equally damaged by Allied bombing raids during the war, as air attacks were used for the first time as a deliberate means of intimidating the enemy. Millions of Europeans now faced starvation as grain harvests were only half of what they had been in 1939. Countless others had been uprooted by the war; now they became "displaced persons," trying to find food and then their way home. The fruits of the Industrial Revolution, when mixed with the heady brew of virulent nationalism and the struggle for empire, were bitter indeed.

In the decades after 1945, Europe not only recovered from the devastating effects of World War II but also experienced an economic resurgence that seemed nothing less than miraculous. At the same time, the historical animosities that had fueled two catastrophic world wars were replaced by a determination to bring about a new united Europe, based on mutual cooperation and equal opportunity for all.

The process is by no means complete, however. As the Cold War came to an end in the early 1990s, ethnic and religious violence broke out in parts of Eastern Europe, undercutting ambitious plans to integrate the nations once isolated behind the Iron Curtain into a broader regional community. In the meantime, Europe's economic problems mounted, as generous welfare programs, combined with slower growth, resulted in growing budget deficits. In 2008, the global financial meltdown rocked the region and pushed several European nations to the edge of national bankruptcy. Today, the continent of Europe faces its most serious challenges since the end of World War II.

CRITICAL THINKING

Q What are the major challenges facing the nations of Europe today? Why?

Western Europe: Recovery and Renewal

In the immediate postwar era, the challenge was clear and intimidating. The peoples of Europe needed to rebuild their national economies and reestablish and strengthen their democratic institutions. They also needed to find the means to cooperate in the face of a potential new threat from the east in the form of the Soviet Union, whose military power had now expanded into the very center of Europe. Above all, they needed to restore their confidence in the continuing vitality and future promise of

European civilization—a civilization whose image had been badly tarnished by two bitter internal conflicts in the space of a quarter century.

In confronting the challenge, the Europeans possessed one significant trump card: the support and assistance of the United States. The United States had entered World War II as a major industrial power, but its global influence had been limited by the effects of the Great Depression and a self-imposed policy of isolation that had removed it from active involvement in world affairs. But after the United States helped bring the conflict to a close, the nation bestrode the world like a colossus. Its military power was enormous, its political influence was unparalleled, and its economic potential, fueled by the effort to build a war machine to defeat the Axis Powers, seemed unlimited. When on June 5, 1947, Secretary of State George C. Marshall told the graduating class at Harvard University that the United States was prepared to assist the nations of Europe in the task of recovery from "hunger, poverty, desperation, and chaos," he offered a beacon of hope to a region badly in need of reasons for optimism.

The Triumph of Democracy in Postwar Europe

With the economic aid of the Marshall Plan, the countries of Western Europe (see Map 10.1) recovered rapidly from the devastation of World War II. Between 1947 and 1950, European countries received $13 billion to be used for new equipment and raw materials. By the late 1970s, industrial production had surpassed all previous records, and Western Europe experienced virtually full employment. Social welfare programs included affordable health care; housing; family allowances to provide a minimum level of material care for children; increases in sickness, accident, unemployment, and old-age benefits; and educational opportunities. Despite economic recessions in the mid-1970s and early 1980s, caused in part by dramatic increases in the price of oil, the economies of Western Europe had never been so prosperous, leading some observers to label the period a "golden age" of political and economic achievement. Western Europeans were full participants in the technological advances of the age and seemed quite capable of standing up to competition from the other global economic powerhouses, Japan and the United States.

In the meantime, confidence in the democratic institutions that had been unable to confront the threat of fascism at the end of the 1930s began to revive. Although local Communist parties received wide support in national elections held in France and Italy immediately after the war, their fortunes waned as economic conditions started to improve. Even Spain and Portugal, which retained their prewar dictatorial regimes well after the end of World War II, established democratic systems in the late 1970s. Moderate political parties, especially the Christian Democrats in Italy and Germany, played a particularly important role in Europe's economic restoration. Overall, the influence of Communist parties declined, although reformist mass parties only slightly left of center, such as the Labour Party in Britain and the Social Democrats in West Germany, continued to share power. During the mid-1970s, a new variety of communism, called Eurocommunism, emerged briefly when Communist parties tried to work within the democratic system as mass movements committed to better government. But by the 1980s, internal political developments in Western Europe and events within the Communist world had combined to undermine the Eurocommunist experiment.

The Modern Welfare State: Three European Models

The European **welfare state** that began to take shape in the years following World War II represented a distinct effort to combine the social benefits provided by the reformist brand of social democracy (see Chapter 1) with the dynamic qualities of modern capitalism. The results varied from country to country, and not all political parties approved of the social democratic model. Eventually, though, virtually all the nations in Western Europe adopted some elements of the system, which differed sharply from the mostly *laissez-faire* capitalist model practiced in the United States.

France

The history of France for nearly a quarter century after the war was dominated by one man, Charles de Gaulle (1890–1970), who possessed an unshakable faith in his own historic mission to restore the greatness of the French nation. During the war, de Gaulle, then a colonel in the French army, had assumed leadership of anti-Nazi resistance groups known as the "Free French," and he played an important role in ensuring the establishment of a French provisional government after the war. But immediately following the war, the creation of the Fourth Republic, with a return to a multiparty parliamentary system that de Gaulle considered inefficient, led him to withdraw temporarily from politics. Eventually, he formed the French Popular Movement, a political organization based on conservative principles that blamed the multiparty system for France's chronic political instability and called for

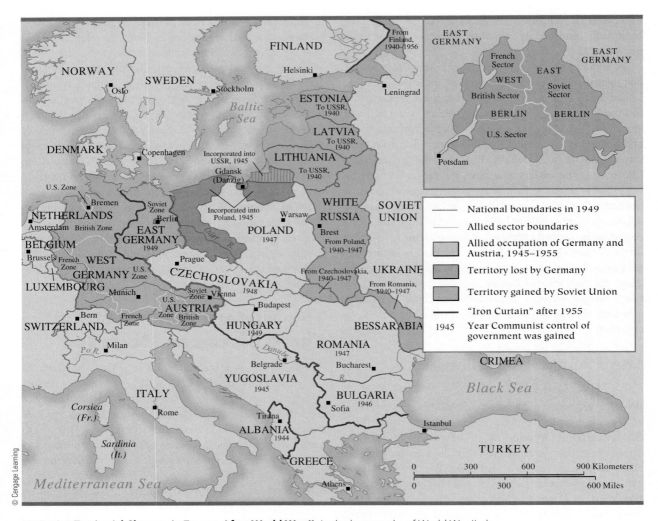

MAP 10.1 **Territorial Changes in Europe After World War II.** In the last months of World War II, the Red Army occupied much of Eastern Europe. Stalin sought pro-Soviet satellite states in the region as a buffer against future invasions from Western Europe, whereas Britain and the United States wanted democratically elected governments. Soviet military control of the territory settled the question.

 Which country gained the greatest territory at the expense of Germany?

a stronger presidency, a goal—and role—that de Gaulle finally achieved in 1958.

EXPECTATIONS OF GRANDEUR At the time of his election as president, the fragile political stability of the Fourth Republic was shaken by a crisis in Algeria, France's large North African colony. The French army, having suffered a humiliating defeat in Indochina in 1954, was determined to resist demands for independence by Algeria's Muslim majority. Independence was also opposed by the large French community living in Algeria,

whose appeals were supported by many senior French military leaders. But a strong antiwar movement among French intellectuals and church leaders led to bitter divisions in France that opened the door to the possibility of civil war. The panic-stricken leaders of the Fourth Republic offered to let de Gaulle take over the government and revise the constitution.

In 1958, de Gaulle drafted a new constitution for the Fifth Republic that greatly enhanced the power of the French president, who now had the right to choose the prime minister, dissolve parliament, and supervise

Charles de Gaulle. As president, Charles de Gaulle sought to revive the greatness of the French nation. He is shown here dressed in his military uniform during a formal state ceremony on a visit to Quebec, Canada, in July 1967.

both defense and foreign policy. As the new president, de Gaulle sought to return France to a position of power and influence. Believing that an independent role in the Cold War might enhance France's stature, he pulled France out of the NATO high command. He sought to increase French prestige in the Third World by consenting to Algerian independence despite strenuous opposition from the army and offered French colonies in Africa membership in a new French community of nations under French tutelage. France invested heavily in the nuclear arms race and exploded its first nuclear bomb in 1960.

Although the cost of the nuclear program increased the defense budget, de Gaulle did not neglect the French economy. Economic decision making was centralized, a reflection of the overall concentration of power undertaken by the Gaullist government. Between 1958 and 1968, the French gross national product (GNP) grew by 5.5 percent annually, faster than the rate of growth in the United States. By the end of the Gaullist era, France was a major industrial producer and exporter, particularly in such areas as automobiles and armaments. Nevertheless, problems remained. The expansion of traditional industries, such as coal and railroads, which had been nationalized, led to large government

deficits. The cost of living increased faster than in the rest of Europe.

SHIFT TO THE LEFT Public dissatisfaction with the government's inability to deal with these problems soon led to more violent action. In May 1968, student protests, provoked by France's anachronistic educational system as well as the ongoing war in Vietnam, were followed by a general strike by the labor unions. During the spring and summer of 1968, the whiff of tear gas and the sound of police sirens were daily occurrences on the streets of Paris. Although de Gaulle managed to restore order, the events of 1968 seriously undermined popular respect for the aloof and imperious president. Tired and discouraged, de Gaulle resigned from office in April 1969 and died within a year. Yet "le grand Charles," as he was sometimes dubbed derisively by his critics, did make a significant contribution to French governmental institutions by bringing an end to the fractious politics of the prewar era. De Gaulle's successors would enjoy the benefits of a more centralized political system that enabled the chief executive to enact major changes in French society.

During the 1970s, the French economic situation continued to decline, bringing about a political shift to the left. In 1981, the veteran Socialist leader, François Mitterrand (1916–1996), was elected president. To resolve France's economic difficulties, he froze prices and wages in the hope of reducing the huge budget deficit and high inflation. Mitterrand also introduced a number of programs to aid workers: an increased minimum wage, expanded social benefits, a mandatory fifth week of paid vacation for salaried workers, a thirty-nine-hour workweek, and higher taxes on the rich. Their success in enacting these measures convinced the Socialists that they could enact more radical reforms. Consequently, the government nationalized the steel industry, major banks, the space and electronics industries, and important insurance firms.

A SEASON OF DISCONTENT The Socialist government's efforts to reverse the country's economic decline failed, however, and in 1995 the conservative mayor of Paris, Jacques Chirac (b. 1932), was elected president. By this time, a new element had entered the equation, as public resentment against foreign-born residents had become a growing political reality in France. In 2008 there were nearly 5 million immigrants in the country, nearly 7.5 percent of the total population of 65 million. Many of the recent arrivals were Muslims from North Africa, and thus were identified in the public mind with terrorist actions committed by militant groups based in the Middle East. Spurred by such concerns, many French voters gave their support to Jean-Marie Le Pen's National Front, which openly advocated restrictions on all new immigration and limited the assimilation of immigrants already living in France. In 2002, Le Pen came in second in the race for the French presidency.

In the fall of 2005, youth riots broke out in the crowded suburbs of Paris. Many of the participants were young Muslims protesting their dismal living conditions and the lack of employment opportunities for foreign-born residents in France. After the riots subsided, government officials promised to adopt measures to respond to the complaints. Nevertheless, tensions still persist between the Muslim community and the remainder of the French population over such issues as the right of young female Muslims to wear a head scarf in public schools.

In May 2007, Nicolas Sarkozy (b. 1955) was elected president of France. As minister of the interior under the previous administration, Sarkozy had been critical of the urban protests and promised to crack down on social unrest. Once installed as president, however, he promised to adopt a Marshall Plan for troubled areas of the country. But the government's options were limited by the realities of an economy struggling with both rising inflation and anemic growth. As Europe sought to deal with the effects of the global financial meltdown, Sarkozy was defeated in his bid to win a second term in office, and in May 2012 he was replaced by the Socialist François Hollande (b. 1954). The new president took office in a country facing a sluggish economy and an unemployment rate of nearly 20 percent.

Germany: Across the Cold War Divide

The unification of the three Western zones into the Federal Republic of Germany (West Germany) became a reality in 1949. Konrad Adenauer (1876–1967), the leader of the Christian Democratic Union (CDU), served as chancellor from 1949 to 1963 and became the "founding hero" of the FRG. Adenauer, who had opposed Hitler's regime, sought to revive respect for Germany by cooperating with the United States and the other Western European nations. He was especially desirous of reconciliation with France—Germany's longtime rival. As Cold War tensions increased, concerns about German rearmament subsided, and the FRG became a member of NATO in 1955.

THE ECONOMIC MIRACLE Adenauer and his successors did not have the luxury of building upon the rich democratic traditions possessed by many of their counterparts in Western Europe. Germany's only experiment with liberal democracy had been the fragile and much maligned Weimar Republic, which had so easily succumbed to Nazi

tyranny in the 1930s. But they were able to reap the benefits of an era of economic expansion and prosperity that Weimar leaders would have envied. In fact, the Adenauer era witnessed a resurrection of the West German economy that was so remarkable it was regarded as an "economic miracle." Although West Germany had only 75 percent of the population and 52 percent of the territory of prewar Germany, by 1955 West Germany's GNP exceeded that of prewar Germany. Real wages doubled between 1950 and 1965, even though working hours were cut by 20 percent. Unemployment fell from 8 percent in 1950 to 0.4 percent in 1965. To maintain its economic expansion, West Germany imported hundreds of thousands of "guest" workers, primarily from Italy, Spain, Greece, Turkey, and Yugoslavia.

The Federal Republic had established its capital at Bonn, a sleepy market town on the Rhine River, to erase memories of the Nazi era, when the capital was at Berlin. It also began to make payments to Israel and to Holocaust survivors and their relatives to make some restitution for, in the words of German president Richard von Weizsacker, "the unspeakable sorrow that occurred in the name of Germany."

WILLY BRANDT AND *OSTPOLITIK* After the Adenauer era ended in the mid-1960s, the Social Democrats became the leading party. By forming a ruling coalition with the small Free Democratic Party, they remained in power until 1982. The first Social Democratic chancellor was Willy Brandt (1913–1992). Brandt was especially successful with his "opening toward the east" (known as *Ostpolitik*), for which he received the Nobel Peace Prize in 1972. On March 19, 1971, Brandt met with Walter Ulbricht, the leader of East Germany, and worked out the details of a treaty that was signed in 1972. This agreement did not establish full diplomatic relations with East Germany but did call for "good neighborly" relations. As a result, it led to greater cultural, personal, and economic contacts between West and East Germany. Despite this success, the discovery of an East German spy among Brandt's advisers caused his resignation in 1974.

His successor, Helmut Schmidt (b. 1918), was more of a technocrat than a reform-minded socialist and concentrated on the economic problems brought about largely by high oil prices between 1973 and 1975. Schmidt was successful in eliminating a deficit of 10 billion marks in three years. In 1982, when the coalition of Schmidt's Social Democrats with the Free Democrats fell apart over the reduction of social welfare expenditures, the Free Democrats joined with the Christian Democratic Union of Helmut Kohl (b. 1930) to form a new government.

GERMANY UNITED: THE PARTY'S OVER With the end of the Cold War, West Germany faced a new challenge. Chancellor Helmut Kohl had benefited greatly from an economic boom in the mid-1980s. Gradually, however, discontent with the Christian Democrats increased, and by 1988, their political prospects seemed diminished. But unexpectedly, the 1989 revolution in East Germany led in 1990 to the reunification of the two Germanies (see Chapter 9), making the new Germany, with its 79 million people, the leading power in Europe. Reunification, accomplished during Kohl's administration, brought rich political dividends to the Christian Democrats. In the first all-German federal election, Kohl's Christian Democrats won 44 percent of the vote, and their coalition partners, the Free Democrats, received 11 percent.

But the euphoria over reunification soon dissipated as the realization set in that the revitalization of the old German Democratic Republic (GDR) would take far more money than was originally thought, and Kohl's government was soon forced to face the politically undesirable task of raising taxes substantially. Moreover, the virtual collapse of the economy in eastern Germany led to extremely high levels of unemployment and severe discontent. Even today, unemployment in eastern Germany is double that in the old West Germany, while wages average only about 80 percent of those in the west.

Increasing unemployment in turn led to growing resentment against foreigners. For years, foreigners seeking asylum or employment found a haven in Germany because of its extremely liberal immigration laws. In 1992, more than 440,000 immigrants came to Germany seeking asylum, 123,000 of them from former Yugoslavia alone. Attacks against foreigners by right-wing extremists—many of them espousing neo-Nazi beliefs—killed seventeen people in 1992 and became an all too frequent occurrence in German life.

East Germans were also haunted by another memory from their recent past. The opening of the files of the secret police (the Stasi) showed that millions of East Germans had spied on their neighbors and colleagues, and even their spouses and parents, during the Communist era (see the Film & History feature on p. 216). A few senior Stasi officials were put on trial for their past actions, but many Germans preferred simply to close the door on an unhappy period in their lives.

As the old century came to a close, Germans struggled to cope with the challenge of building a new, united nation. To reduce the debt incurred because of economic reconstruction in the east, the government threatened to cut back on many of the social benefits Germans had long been accustomed to receiving. This in turn increased resentments that had already appeared between eastern

and western Germany (see the box on p. 217). Residents of the old East Germany still often express regrets about reunification, which is commonly referred to there by the more neutral term "Die Wende," meaning the "turn" or "change."[1]

In 1998, voters took out their frustrations at the ballot box. Helmut Kohl's conservative coalition was defeated in national elections, and a new prime minister, Social Democrat Gerhard Schröder (b. 1944), came into office. Schröder had no better luck than his predecessor at reviving the economy, however. In 2003, with nearly 5 million workers unemployed, the government announced plans to scale back welfare benefits that had long been a familiar part of life for the German people. In 2005, national elections brought the Christian Democrats back into power under the leadership of Germany's first woman chancellor, Angela Merkel (b. 1954). Having lived much of her life under communism in East Germany, Merkel supported measures to curb government spending while relying increasingly on the capitalist marketplace, but she soon encountered new challenges when Greece and other fellow members of the European Union (see "The European Union" below) were unable to pay their debts and turned to wealthy nations in northern Europe to stave off the threat of bankruptcy. Many Germans, traditionally frugal and hardworking, soon resented having to bail out their more profligate neighbors, and Merkel shared that view.

Great Britain

The end of World War II left Britain with massive economic problems. In elections held immediately after the war, the Labour Party overwhelmingly defeated Winston Churchill's Conservative Party. The Labour Party had promised far-reaching reforms, particularly in the area of social welfare—an appealing platform in a country with a tremendous shortage of consumer goods and housing. Clement Atlee (1883–1967), the new prime minister, was a pragmatic reformer rather than the leftist revolutionary that Churchill had warned against during the election campaign. His Labour government proceeded to enact reforms that created a modern welfare state.

The establishment of the British welfare state began with the **nationalization** of the Bank of England, the coal and steel industries, public transportation, and public utilities such as electricity and gas. In the area of social welfare, in 1946 the new government enacted the National Insurance Act and the National Health Service Act. The insurance act established a comprehensive social security program and nationalized medical insurance, thereby enabling the state to subsidize the unemployed, the sick, and the aged. The health act created a system of **socialized**

The Lives of Others (2006)

Directed by Florian Henckel von Donnersmarck, *The Lives of Others* is a German film (*Das Leben der Anderen*) that re-creates the depressing debilitation of East German society under its Communist regime, and especially the Stasi, the secret police. Georg Dreyman (Sebastian Koch) is a successful playwright in the German Democratic Republic (East Germany). Although he is a dedicated socialist who has not offended the authorities, they try to determine whether he is completely loyal by wiretapping his apartment, where he lives with his girlfriend, Christa-Maria Sieland (Martina Gedeck), an actress in some of Dreyman's plays. Captain Gerd Wiesler (Ulrich Mühe) of the Stasi takes charge of the spying operation. The epitome of the perfect functionary, he is a cold, calculating, dedicated professional who is convinced he is building a better society and is only too eager to fight the "enemies of socialism."

Georg Dreyman (Sebastian Koch) examines his Stasi files.

But as he listens to the everyday details of Dreyman's life, Wiesler begins to develop a conscience and becomes sympathetic to the writer. After a close friend of Dreyman's commits suicide, Dreyman turns against the Communist regime and writes an article on the alarming number of suicides in East German society that is published anonymously in *Der Spiegel*, a West German magazine. Lieutenant Colonel Grubitz (Ulrich Tukur), Wiesler's boss, suspects that Dreyman is the author. His girlfriend is brought in for questioning and provides some damning information about Dreyman's involvement. Horrified by what she has done, she commits suicide, but Wiesler, who is now determined to save Dreyman, fudges his reports and protects him from arrest. Grubitz suspects what Wiesler has done and demotes him. The film ends after the fall of the Berlin Wall when the new German government opens the Stasi files. When Dreyman reads his file, he realizes that Wiesler saved his life and writes a book dedicated to him.

The Lives of Others which won an Academy Award for Best Foreign Language Film, brilliantly depicts the stifling atmosphere of East Germany under Communist rule. The Stasi had about 90,000 employees but also recruited a network of hundreds of thousands of informers who submitted secret reports on their friends, family, bosses, and coworkers. Some volunteered the information, but as the film makes clear, others were bribed or blackmailed into collaborating with the authorities. As the movie demonstrates, the Stasi were experts at wiretapping dwellings and compiling detailed written reports about what they heard, including conversations, arguments, jokes, and even sexual activities. Ironically, Ulrich Mühe, who plays Captain Wiesler in the film, was an East German who himself had been spied on by the Stasi.

The film was praised by East Germans for accurately depicting the drab environment of their country and the role of the Stasi in fostering a society riddled by secrecy, fear, and the abuse of power. The dangers of governments that monitor their citizens are apparent and quite relevant in an age of legislation infringing on personal privacy in an attempt to fight terrorism. The police state is revealed for what it is, a soulless and hollow world with no redeeming features or values. ■

The Trabi Lives!

The unification of the two Germanies after the fall of the Berlin Wall was widely hailed as a symbol of the end of the Cold War in Europe. It even inspired fear among many Europeans living in neighboring countries that it might lead to the rise of a new and more powerful Germany. In fact, unification has given birth to a number of major political, economic, and social problems. As German citizens in the old GDR have become resentful of their wealthier counterparts in the west, a wave of "Trabi nostalgia" has set in. The Trabant, a small automobile long manufactured in East Germany, was widely scorned for its design and mechanical deficiencies, but the brand was recently revived in the east as a symbol of the "good old days" before reunification. This selection is from the transcript of a radio broadcast from Cologne in the former West Germany in 1999.

Remembrance of Things Past

There's a widespread feeling among East Germans that something new should have emerged out of unification, combining the best of both worlds.

"We suddenly saw that there is a different mentality, even a different language in some areas," says Western psychologist Uwe Wetter, "a different tradition, and cultural differences all around. But we tried to address these differences by giving our knowledge—what we thought was the best—to the Easterners. We thought that would be the way to handle the situation."

Many Easterners have not been able to reestablish the sense of identity. They pine for what they regard to be the sunny side of the former East German state: a sense of belonging, and a cozy feeling that they were being taken care of by the system. Some former East Germans continue to gather at frequently held nostalgia parties.

Stefan Winkler, from the eastern part of Berlin, is one of them: "I have mixed emotions about these nostalgia parties. I still have a GDR flag. I don't think it's for nostalgia reasons; it's more of a political statement. I think people tend to forget about the bad things after a while and only remember the good. There were a couple of really good things in East Germany. A lot of [East Germans] feel quite unsafe at the moment. Not only because they lost their jobs. It's also because many lost their identity—and that's where their nostalgia comes in."

 What might explain the difficulties that residents of the former East Germany have experienced in overcoming the challenges of reunification?

SOURCE: *World Press Review*, January 2000, p. 9.

---

medicine that forced doctors and dentists to work with state hospitals, although private practices could be maintained. This measure was especially costly for the state, but within a few years, 90 percent of the medical profession was participating.

IMPERIAL SUNSET The cost of building a welfare state at home forced the British to reduce expenses abroad. This meant dismantling the British Empire and reducing military aid to such countries as Greece and Turkey, a decision that inspired the enunciation of the Truman Doctrine in Washington (see Chapter 7). Economic necessity, and not just a belief in the concept of self-determination, brought an end to the British Empire.

Continuing economic problems brought the Conservatives back into power from 1951 to 1964. Although they favored private enterprise, the Conservatives accepted the new system and even extended it, undertaking an ambitious construction program to improve British housing. Although the British economy had recovered from the war, it had done so at a slower rate than other European countries.

This slow recovery masked a long-term economic decline caused by a variety of factors, including trade union demands for wages that rose faster than productivity and the unwillingness of factory owners to invest in modern industrial machinery and to adopt new methods. Underlying the immediate problems, however, was a deeper issue. As a result of World War II, Britain had lost much of its prewar revenue from abroad but was left with a burden of debt from its many international commitments.

Between 1964 and 1979, Conservatives and Labour alternated in power. Both parties faced seemingly intractable problems. Although separatist movements in Scotland and Wales were overcome, a dispute between Catholics and Protestants in Northern Ireland was marked by violence as the rebel Irish Republican Army (IRA) staged a series of dramatic terrorist acts in response to the suspension of Northern Ireland's parliament in 1972 and the establishment of direct rule by London. The problem of Northern Ireland remained unresolved. Nor was either party able to deal with Britain's ailing economy. Great Britain's years in the sun, it appeared, were long past.

The Modern Welfare State: Three European Models ❦ **217**

Margaret Thatcher: Entering a Man's World

In 1979, Margaret Thatcher became the first woman to serve as Britain's prime minister and went on to be its longest-serving prime minister as well. In this excerpt from her autobiography, Thatcher describes how she was interviewed by Conservative Party officials when they first considered her as a possible candidate for Parliament from Dartford. Thatcher ran for Parliament for the first time in 1950; she lost but increased the Conservative vote total in the district by 50 percent over the previous election.

Margaret Thatcher, *The Path to Power*

And they did [consider her]. I was invited to have lunch with John Miller and his wife, Phee, and the Dartford Woman's Chairman, Mrs. Fletcher, on the Saturday on Llandudno Pier. Presumably, and in spite of any reservations about the suitability of a woman candidate for their seat, they liked what they saw. I certainly got on well with them. . . . After lunch we walked back along the pier to the Conference Hall in good time for a place to hear Winston Churchill give the Party Leader's speech. . . . Foreign affairs naturally dominated his speech—it was the time of the Berlin blockade and the Western airlift—and his message was somber, telling us that only American nuclear weapons stood between Europe and communist tyranny and warning of "what seems a remorselessly approaching third world war."

I did not hear from Dartford until December, when I was asked to attend an interview. . . . With a large number of other hopefuls I turned up on the evening of Thursday 30 December for my first Selection Committee. Very few outside the political arena know just how nerve-racking such occasions are. The interviewee who is not nervous and tense is very likely to perform badly: for, as any chemist will tell you, the adrenaline needs to flow if one is to perform at one's best. I was lucky in that at Dartford there were some friendly faces around the table, and it has to be said that on such occasions there are advantages as well as disadvantages to being a young woman making her way in the political world.

I found myself short-listed, and was asked to go to Dartford itself for a further interview. Finally, I was invited . . . to address the Association's Executive Committee of about fifty people. As one of five would-be candidates, I had to give a fifteen-minute speech and answer questions for a further ten minutes.

It was the questions which were more likely to cause me trouble. There was a good deal of suspicion of woman candidates, particularly in what was regarded as a tough industrial seat like Dartford. This was quite definitely a man's world into which not just angels feared to tread. There was, of course, little hope of winning it for the Conservatives, though this is never a point that the prospective candidate even in a Labour seat as safe as Ebbw Vale would be advised to make. The Labour majority was an all but unscalable 20,000. But perhaps this unspoken fact turned to my favour. Why not take the risk of adopting the young Margaret Roberts? There was not much to lose, and some good publicity for the Party to gain.

The most reliable sign that a political occasion has gone well is that you have enjoyed it. I enjoyed that evening at Dartford, and the outcome justified my confidence. I was selected.

 In this account, is Margaret Thatcher's being a woman more important to her or to others? Why would this disparity exist?

SOURCE: Pages 62–65 from *The Path to Power* by Margaret Thatcher. Copyright © 1995 by Margaret Thatcher.

"THATCHERISM": THE CONSERVATIVES IN ASCENDANCE In 1979, after five years of Labour government and worsening economic problems, the Conservatives returned to power under Margaret Thatcher (1925–2013), the first woman prime minister in British history (see the box above). Thatcher pledged to lower taxes, reduce the government bureaucracy, limit social welfare, restrict union power, and end inflation. The "Iron Lady," as she was called, did break the power of the labor unions. Although she did not eliminate the basic components of the social welfare system, she used austerity measures to control inflation. "Thatcherism," as her economic policy was termed, improved the British economic situation, but at a price. The south of England, for example, prospered, but the old industrial areas of the Midlands and north declined and were beset by high unemployment, poverty, and sporadic violence. Cutbacks in funding for education seriously undermined the quality of British schools, long regarded as among the world's finest.

In foreign policy, Thatcher took a hard-line approach against communism. She oversaw a large military buildup aimed at replacing older technology and reestablishing Britain as a world policeman. In 1982, when Argentina attempted to take control of the Falkland Islands (one of Britain's few remaining colonial outposts, known to Argentines as the Malvinas) 300 miles off its coast, the British successfully rebuffed the Argentines, although at considerable economic cost and the loss of 255 lives. The Falklands War, however, did generate popular support for Thatcher, as many in Britain reveled in memories of the nation's glorious imperial past.

THE ERA OF TONY BLAIR While Thatcher dominated politics in the 1980s, the Labour Party, beset by divisions between its moderate and radical wings, offered little effective opposition. But in 1990, Labour's fortunes revived when the Conservative government attempted to replace local property taxes with a flat-rate tax payable by every adult to his or her local authority. Although Thatcher argued that this would make local government more responsive to popular needs, many argued that this was nothing more than a poll tax that would enable the rich to pay the same rate as the poor. After antitax riots broke out, Thatcher's once legendary popularity plummeted to an all-time low. At the end of November, a revolt within her own party caused Thatcher to resign as prime minister. Her replacement was John Major (b. 1943), whose Conservative Party won a narrow victory in the general elections held in April 1992.

The new prime minister sought to continue his predecessor's policies—privatizing the nation's railroad system in 1994—but his lackluster leadership failed to capture the imagination of many Britons, and in new elections in May 1997, the Labour Party won a landslide victory. The new prime minister, Tony Blair (b. 1953), was a moderate whose youth and energy immediately instilled a new vigor into the political scene. Adopting centrist policies reminiscent of those followed by President Bill Clinton in the United States (Blair entitled his program the "Third Way," a position somewhere between the free market practices in the United States and the paternalistic welfare systems on the Continent), his party dominated the political arena into the new century.

Riding on a wave of economic prosperity, the Labour government passed legislation to introduce a minimum wage and address child poverty. But a continued deterioration of public services—notably in the areas of education, transportation, and health care—steadily eroded Blair's popular appeal. His decision to support the U.S.-led invasion of Iraq in 2003 was also not popular with the British public. The failure of the opposition Conservative

Party to field a popular candidate kept him in power for nearly a decade, but in 2007 he stepped down from office and was replaced by his fellow Labour Party leader, Gordon Brown (b. 1951).

In 2010, in the wake of climbing unemployment and a global financial crisis, the Labour Party's thirteen-year rule ended when the Conservative Party candidate David Cameron (b. 1966) became prime minister on the basis of a coalition with the Liberal Democrats. Cameron promised to reduce the government debt by cutting government waste and social services and overhauling the health care system. Cameron's austerity measures, however, exacted a heavy price, as the British economy went into recession.

The Fall of the Iron Curtain

The collapse of the Communist governments in Eastern Europe during the revolutions of 1989 brought a wave of euphoria to Europe. In 1989 and 1990, new governments throughout the region worked diligently to scrap the remnants of the old system and introduce the democratic procedures and market systems they believed would revitalize their scarred lands (see Chapter 9). But this process proved to be neither simple nor easy.

Most Eastern European countries had little or no experience with democratic systems. Then, too, ethnic divisions, which had troubled these areas before World War II and had been forcibly submerged under Communist rule, reemerged with a vengeance. Finally, the rapid conversion to market economies also proved painful. The adoption of "shock therapy" austerity measures produced much suffering. Unemployment, for example, climbed to over 13 percent in Poland in 1992.

Nevertheless, by the beginning of the twenty-first century, many of these states were making a successful transition to both free markets and democracy. In Poland, Aleksander Kwaśniewski (b. 1954), although a former Communist, was elected president in November 1995 and pushed Poland toward an increasingly prosperous free market economy. His success brought his reelection in October 2000. In Czechoslovakia, the shift to non-Communist rule was complicated by old problems, especially ethnic issues. Czechs and Slovaks disagreed over the makeup of the new state but eventually accepted a peaceful division of the country. On January 1, 1993, Czechoslovakia split into the Czech Republic and Slovakia (see Map 10.2). Václav Havel was elected the first president of the new Czech Republic.

THE DISINTEGRATION OF YUGOSLAVIA But the most difficult transition to the post–Cold War era in Eastern Europe occurred in Yugoslavia. From its beginning in 1919, Yugoslavia had been an artificial creation composed

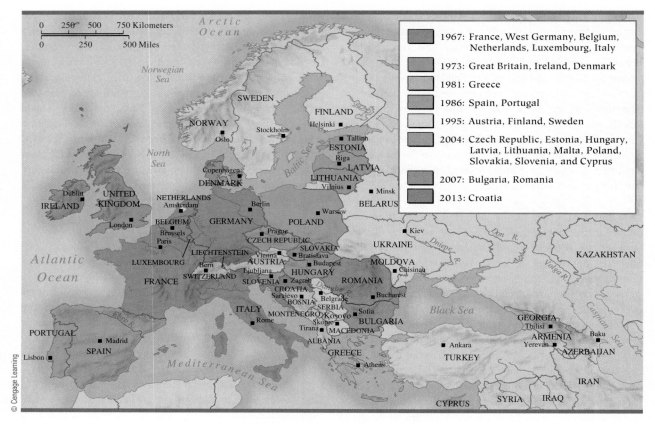

MAP 10.2 European Union, 2013. Beginning in 1957 as the European Economic Community, also known as the Common Market, the union of European states seeking to integrate their economies has gradually grown from six members to twenty-eight in 2013. The European Union has achieved two major goals—the creation of a single internal market and a common currency—although it has been less successful at working toward common political and foreign policy goals.

 What additional nations do you think will eventually join the European Union? Why?

of uneasy neighbors with a long history of mutual animosity. After World War II, the dictatorial Marshal Tito had managed to hold its six republics and two autonomous provinces together. But after his death in 1980, no strong leader emerged, and his responsibilities passed to a collective state presidency dominated by the League of Communists of Yugoslavia. At the end of the 1980s, Yugoslavia was caught up in the reform movements sweeping through Eastern Europe. The League of Communists collapsed, and new parties quickly emerged.

The Yugoslav political scene was complicated by the development of separatist movements. In 1990, the republics of Slovenia, Croatia, Bosnia-Herzegovina, and Macedonia began to lobby for a new federal structure of Yugoslavia that would fulfill their separatist desires. Slobodan Milošević (1941–2006), who had become the leader of the Serbian Communist Party in 1987 and had managed

to stay in power by emphasizing his Serbian nationalism, asserted that these republics could be independent only if new border arrangements were made to accommodate the Serb minorities in the republics who did not want to live outside the boundaries of Serbia. Serbs constituted about 12 percent of Croatia's population and 32 percent of Bosnia's.

After negotiations among the six republics failed, Slovenia and Croatia declared their independence in June 1991. Milošević's government sent the Yugoslavian army, which it controlled, into Slovenia, without much success. In September 1991, it began a full assault against Croatia. Increasingly, the Yugoslavian army was becoming the Serbian army, while Serbian irregular forces played a growing role in military operations. Before a cease-fire was arranged, the Serbian forces had captured one-third of Croatia's territory in brutal and destructive fighting.

Incident at Vukovar. In the fall of 1991, Serbian forces crossed the Danube River and put the Croatian city of Vukovar under siege. After three months of bitter fighting, Serbian troops entered the city and evacuated the Croatian members of the local population to concentration camps. Several thousand residents were killed in the fighting. After the end of the war, the city gradually began to recover, but many parts of the city have not yet been rebuilt, and houses pockmarked with bullet holes are still a common sight in much of the town center. A cemetery containing the graves of war casualties, as shown here, now sits on the outskirts of the town. Vukovar today is one of the more graphic symbols of the horrors of the recent Balkan wars.

The recognition of Slovenia, Croatia, and Bosnia-Herzegovina by many European states and the United States early in 1992 did not stop the Serbs from turning their guns on Bosnia. By mid-1993, Serbian forces had acquired 70 percent of Bosnian territory. The Serbian policy of **ethnic cleansing**—killing or forcibly removing Bosnian Muslims from their lands—revived memories of Nazi atrocities in World War II. Nevertheless, despite worldwide outrage, European governments failed to take a decisive and forceful stand against these Serbian activities, and by the spring of 1993, the Muslim population of Bosnia was in desperate straits. As the fighting spread, European nations and the United States began to intervene to stop the bloodshed, and in the fall of 1995, a fragile cease-fire agreement was reached at a conference held in Dayton, Ohio. An international peacekeeping force was stationed in the area to maintain tranquility and monitor the accords.

Peace in Bosnia, however, did not bring peace to Yugoslavia. A new war erupted in 1999 over Kosovo, which had been made an autonomous province within Yugoslavia by Tito in 1974. Kosovo's inhabitants were mainly ethnic Albanians. But many Serbs considered it sacred territory because in the fourteenth century Serbian forces had been defeated there by the Ottoman Turks in an epic battle.

In 1989, Yugoslav President Milošević stripped Kosovo of its autonomous status and outlawed any official use of the Albanian language. In 1993, some groups of ethnic Albanians founded the Kosovo Liberation Army (KLA) and began a campaign against Serbian rule in Kosovo. When Serb forces began to massacre ethnic Albanians in an effort to crush the KLA, the United States and its NATO allies sought to arrange a settlement. When Milošević refused to sign the agreement, the United States and its NATO allies began a bombing campaign that forced the Yugoslavian government into compliance. In the elections of 2000, Milošević himself was ousted from power and was later put on trial by an international tribunal for war crimes against humanity for his ethnic cleansing policies. The truncated country of Yugoslavia briefly changed its name to Serbia and Montenegro, but that union came to an end in 2006 as Montenegro and Serbia became independent states. Kosovo received its independence in 2007, against the vigorous opposition of Serbia and its traditional ally Russia. Today the region is slowly returning to peacetime conditions, although historical animosities lie just beneath the surface.

Western Europe: The Search for Unity

As we have seen, the divisions created by the Cold War led the nations of Western Europe to form the North Atlantic Treaty Organization in 1949. But military cooperation was not the only kind of unity fostered in Europe after 1945. The destructiveness of two world wars caused many thoughtful Europeans to consider the need for additional forms of integration. National feeling was still too powerful, however, for European nations to give up their political sovereignty. Consequently, the quest for unity initially focused primarily on the economic arena rather than the political one.

The Curtain Rises: The Creation of the Common Market

In 1951, France, West Germany, the Benelux countries (Belgium, the Netherlands, and Luxembourg), and Italy formed the European Coal and Steel Community (ECSC). Its purpose was to create a common market for coal and steel products among the six nations by eliminating tariffs and other trade barriers. The success of the ECSC encouraged its members to proceed further, and in 1957, they created the European Atomic Energy Community (EURATOM) to further European research on the peaceful uses of nuclear energy.

In the same year, the same six nations signed the Rome Treaty, which created the European Economic Community (EEC), also known as the Common Market. The EEC eliminated mutual customs barriers and created a large free-trade area protected from the rest of the world by a common external tariff. By promoting free trade, the EEC also encouraged cooperation and standardization in many aspects of the six nations' economies. All the member nations benefited economically.

Europeans moved toward further integration of their economies after 1970. The European Economic Community expanded in 1973 when Great Britain, Ireland, and Denmark gained membership in what its members now began to call the European Community (EC). By 1986, three more members—Spain, Portugal, and Greece—had been added. The economic integration of the members of the EC led to cooperative efforts in international and political affairs as well. The foreign ministers of the twelve members consulted frequently and provided a common front in negotiations on important issues.

The European Union

By 1992, the EC included nearly 350 million people and constituted the world's largest single trading bloc, transacting almost one-quarter of the world's commerce. In the early 1990s, EC members drafted the Treaty on European Union (known as the Maastricht Treaty, after the city in the Netherlands where the agreement was reached), seeking to create a true economic and monetary union of all members of the organization (see the box on p. 223). The treaty would not take effect, however, until all members agreed. On January 1, 1994, the European Community became the European Union (EU).

One of its first goals was to introduce a common currency, called the euro. But problems soon arose. Voters in many countries opposed the austerity measures that their governments would be compelled to take to reduce growing budget deficits. Germans in particular feared that replacing the rock-solid mark with a common European currency could lead to economic disaster. Yet the logic of the new union appeared inescapable if European nations were to improve their capacity to compete with the United States and the powerful industrializing nations of the Pacific Rim. On January 1, 2002, twelve members of the European Union (including all of the major European states except Great Britain) abandoned their national currencies in favor of the euro. The move hastened the transition of the EU into a single economic entity capable of competing in world markets with the United States and major Asian nations.

Plans for Expansion: A Bridge Too Far?

In the meantime, plans got under way to extend the EU into Eastern Europe, where several nations were just emerging from decades of domination by the Soviet Union. In December 2002, the EU voted to add ten new members—Cyprus, the Czech Republic, Estonia, Hungary, Latvia, Lithuania, Malta, Poland, Slovakia, and Slovenia. They joined the organization in 2004. Bulgaria and Romania joined in 2007, and the addition of Croatia in 2013 increased the size of the EU to twenty-eight members (see Map 10.2 on p. 220).

Yet not all are convinced that European integration is a good thing. Some Eastern Europeans fear that their countries will be dominated by investment from their prosperous neighbors, while their counterparts in Western Europe express concerns at a possible influx of low-wage workers from the newer member countries. Though Britain is an EU member, the British government, reflecting the views of many of its constituents, continues to refuse to adopt the euro and take other steps to tie its fortunes directly to the rest of the continent. All in all, a true sense of a unified Europe is still lacking among the population throughout the region, and the rising antiforeign sentiment across the continent and anger at government belt tightening are warning signs that advocates of further integration will ignore at their peril.

The application of Turkey to join the EU has only added to these concerns. Although the Turkish government has sought to assuage European criticisms of its record in the area of human rights (notably in the treatment of its Kurdish minority), many Europeans remain uneasy about the prospect of admitting an Islamic nation of more

Toward a United Europe

In December 1991, the nations of Europe took a significant step on the road to unity when they drafted the Treaty of Maastricht, which created the structure for a new European Union. The new organization, which represented a significant step beyond the forms of economic cooperation that had previously existed, envisaged integration in the fields of foreign and security policies and cooperation in the areas of justice and domestic affairs. In the years since the treaty was established, the European Union has successfully created a common currency—the euro—but resolving many of the other obstacles to unity has proved to be a severe challenge. Some of the key provisions of the treaty are presented here.

The Treaty of Maastricht

Article A

By this Treaty, the High Contracting Parties establish among themselves a European Union, hereinafter called "the Union."

This Treaty marks a new stage in the process of creating an ever closer union among the peoples of Europe, in which decisions are taken as closely as possible to the citizen.

The Union shall be founded on the European Communities, supplemented by the policies and forms of cooperation established by this Treaty. Its task shall be to organize, in a manner demonstrating consistency and solidarity, relations between the Member States and between their peoples.

Article B

The Union shall set itself the following objectives:

- to promote economic and social progress which is balanced and sustainable, in particular through the creation of an area without internal frontiers, through the strengthening of economic and social cohesion and through the establishment of economic and monetary union, ultimately including a single currency in accordance with the provisions of this Treaty;
- to assert its identity on the international scene, in particular through the implementation of a common foreign and security policy including the eventual framing of a common defence policy, which might in time lead to a common defence;
- to strengthen the protection of the rights and interests of the nationals of its Member States through the introduction of a citizenship of the Union;
- to develop close cooperation on justice and home affairs. . . .

Article F

1. The Union shall respect the national identities of its Member States, whose systems of government are founded on the principles of democracy.
2. The Union shall respect fundamental rights, as guaranteed by the European Convention for the Protection of Human Rights and Fundamental Freedoms signed in Rome on 4 November 1950 and as they result from the constitutional traditions common to the Member States, as general principles of Community law.
3. The Union shall provide itself with the means necessary to attain its objectives and carry through its policies.

 What are the key provisions of the Treaty of Maastricht? How do they appear to infringe on traditional standards of national sovereignty?

SOURCE: http://europa.eu.int/en/record/mt/titlel.html.

---

than 70 million people into an organization of predominantly Christian nations already facing serious concerns over their growing Muslim minorities. Although its application is still pending, Turkey's admission is no longer under serious consideration. In turn, many Turks now scorn the proposal to join a weakened Europe and seek to redirect their efforts to serving as a bridge to the Middle East (see Chapter 15).

Plans for a transition to a more unified Europe have also encountered resistance. In 2005, voters in several EU countries rejected the draft of a new constitution that would have strengthened the political and economic integration of the nations within the EU. Shaken by popular resistance to their proposals to strengthen the central apparatus of the EU, European leaders lowered their expectations. A new treaty, signed by all members in Lisbon in December 2007 and ratified by all members three years later, provided the organization with a permanent president who will serve for a thirty-month term and have the primary duty of representing the EU abroad. How effective the new executive will be remains to be seen.

WHAT ROLE FOR NATO? Meanwhile, the NATO alliance continues to serve as a powerful force for European unity. Yet it too faces new challenges as Moscow's former satellites in Eastern Europe have clamored for membership in the hope that it would spur economic growth and reduce the threat from a revival of Russian expansionism. In 1999, the Czech Republic, Hungary, and Poland joined the alliance, and the Baltic states—once part of the Soviet Union—followed suit several years later. Some observers have expressed concern, however, that an expanded NATO will not only reduce the cohesiveness of the organization but also provoke Russia into a new posture of hostility to the outside world. Western plans to construct U.S. missile defense sites in several Eastern European countries have encountered violent hostility in Moscow, while the Russian invasion of Georgia in 2008 inspired alarm in many Eastern European capitals over its implications for Russian expansionism in the future.

Beware of Greeks Seeking Gifts

As if the challenges discussed above were not sufficient, in the fall of 2008 the EU was sideswiped by a new crisis, as the shockwaves of the global financial meltdown began to ripple through the continent. Most affected was Greece, where the beleaguered government in Athens announced that it could no longer pay its bills.

The fragility of the Greek government's finances stemmed from a number of deep-seated factors: (1) high expenditures (an unusually high percentage of the population was on the government payroll, many in sinecures), (2) low revenues (resulting from a chronic national propensity to engage in tax evasion), and (3) a weak export market (due in part to the fact that the national currency was unrealistically based on the stronger euro). Under heavy pressure from the leaders of other EU countries, notably Germany, to adopt stringent austerity measures in order to qualify for bank loans, the Greek government sought to comply, but its efforts led to popular unrest and an economic free fall.

The EU's difficulties in dealing with the financial problems of Greece were compounded by the fact that a number of other European countries—most notably Italy, Spain, Portugal, Ireland, and Cyprus—were facing serious economic problems of their own. In fact, many EU member countries had ignored the provisions of the Treaty of Maastricht requiring them to limit their national debt and now faced the possibility of a financial meltdown that, in size and scope, could transcend that experienced by the government of Greece. The spreading crisis was a vivid reminder to European leaders of the dangers inherent in trying to apply a one-size-fits-all system to nations with highly divergent cultures and economic profiles. As the region scrambled to defuse the spreading financial epidemic, the end result could not yet be foreseen.

RETHINKING THE WELFARE STATE At the root of the current economic crisis is an incontrovertible fact: under current conditions, Europe, even more than the United States, is on a path toward bankruptcy. The slowdown in the European economy in the past two decades, combined with the changing social fabric, has already begun to erode the region's long-standing commitment to the concept of the welfare state. Aging populations, high unemployment rates, and heavy outlays for social programs have compelled European governments, even some of the wealthiest, to consider reducing some of the vaunted social benefits that their citizens view as a birthright. Measures designed to raise taxes, increase the number of working hours, and reduce pension and health benefits have run into strong popular resistance, however, and have led, in some cases, to a change in governments.

The situation is equally difficult in Eastern Europe, where nations with fragile democracies and weak economies are faced with problems of slow growth, low productivity, and high unemployment. Nations like Bulgaria, Hungary, and Romania have lost the limited economic security provided by their past membership in the Soviet bloc and must fend for themselves in a global market dominated by economic powerhouses like China, India, and Brazil. To remain competitive in global trade, several have chosen to reject the euro and maintain their own national currencies. Still, prospects for matching the economic prosperity of their western neighbors are relatively poor.

Another serious challenge facing Europe is a demographic crunch. In several nations in the EU, birthrates have fallen below replacement levels. A consequence of this uncomfortable reality has been the inflow of immigrant labor from Eastern Europe and North Africa. But equally important is the long-term impact on European retirement systems, because the number of active workers available to support each retiree is steadily declining. Today people of working age outnumber those of retirement age by only three to one. By mid-century, the ratio is predicted to decline to about two to one (by comparison, the current ratio in the United States is five to one). To counter such trends, several European governments have begun to raise the retirement age or to reduce the size of pensions for retirees. The survival of the European welfare state rests in the balance.

Aspects of Society in Postwar Europe

Socially, intellectually, and culturally, Western Europe changed significantly during the second half of the twentieth century. Although many trends represented a continuation of

Tourism: Engine of Economic Prosperity. One of the most visible consequences of the era of material prosperity that has swept across the advanced countries of the world in recent decades is the rapid growth of the travel industry. Today's tourists—circulating by all means of transport from crowded tour bus to elegant cruise ship—eagerly penetrate the far reaches of the globe in search of the ultimate travel adventure.

The financial importance of tourism is substantial—it is often the number-one source of revenue in developing countries. Yet many tourists' favorite destination is still the "Old World" of Europe, where pleasure travel began more than two hundred years ago with English aristocrats making the Grand Tour of the Continent. The eager tourists shown here, thronging the narrow streets of the city of Valletta on the island of Malta, reflect the interaction of contemporary culture and the fluidity of globalization.

prewar developments, in other cases the changes were quite dramatic, leading some observers in the 1980s to begin speaking of the gradual emergence of a postmodern age.

An Age of Affluence

Nothing changed in the postwar years as much as the material lives of Europe's inhabitants. In the decades after World War II, products such as automobiles, computers, televisions, jet planes, contraceptive devices, and advanced surgical techniques all dramatically and quickly altered the pace and nature of human life. Called variously a technocratic society, an affluent society, or the consumer society, postwar Europe was characterized by changing social values and new attitudes toward the meaning of the human experience.

The structure of European society was also altered in major respects after 1945. Especially noticeable were changes in the composition of the middle class. Traditional occupations such as merchants and the professions (law, medicine, and the universities) were greatly augmented by a new group of managers and technicians, as large companies and government agencies employed increasing numbers of white-collar supervisory and administrative personnel. In most cases, success depended on specialized knowledge acquired from some form of higher education. Since their jobs usually depended on their skills, these individuals took steps to ensure that their children would be similarly educated.

Changes occurred in other areas as well. Especially noticeable was the dramatic shift from the countryside to the cities. The number of people in agriculture declined by 50 percent. Yet the industrial working class did not expand. In West Germany, industrial workers made up 48 percent of the labor force throughout the 1950s and 1960s. Thereafter, the number of industrial workers began to dwindle as the number of white-collar service employees increased. At the same time, a substantial increase in their real wages enabled the working classes to aspire to the consumption patterns of the middle class. Buying on the installment plan, introduced in the 1930s, became widespread in the 1950s and gave workers a chance to imitate the middle class by buying such products as televisions, washing machines, refrigerators, vacuum cleaners, and stereos. But the most visible symbol of mass consumerism was the automobile. Before World War II, cars were reserved mostly for the upper classes. In 1948, there were 5 million cars in all of Europe, but by 1957, the number had tripled. By the mid-1960s, there were almost 45 million.

Rising incomes, combined with shorter working hours, created an even greater market for **mass leisure** activities. Between 1900 and 1980, the workweek was reduced from sixty hours to about forty hours (or even less in some countries), and the number of paid holidays increased. All aspects of popular culture—music, sports, media—became commercialized and offered opportunities for leisure activities, including concerts, sporting events, and television viewing.

Another very visible symbol of mass leisure was the growth of tourism. Before World War II, most people who traveled for pleasure were from the upper and middle classes. After the war, the combination of more vacation time, increased prosperity, and the flexibility provided by package tours with their lower rates and low-budget rooms enabled millions to expand their travel possibilities. By the mid-1960s, some 100 million tourists were crossing European borders each year. In recent years, the number has increased dramatically.

A Transvaluation of Values

Social change was also evident in new educational patterns. Before World War II, higher education was largely the preserve of Europe's wealthier classes. Even in 1950, only 3 or 4 percent of Western European young people were enrolled in a university. European higher education remained largely centered on the liberal arts, pure science, and preparation for the professions of law and medicine.

Much of this changed in the 1950s and 1960s. European states began to foster greater equality of opportunity in higher education by eliminating fees, and universities experienced an influx of students from the middle and lower classes. Enrollments grew dramatically. In France, 4.5 percent of young people went to a university in 1950; by 1965, the figure had increased to 14.5 percent. Overall, enrollments in European universities more than tripled between 1940 and 1960.

With growth came problems. Overcrowded classrooms, unapproachable professors, and authoritarian administrators aroused student resentment. This discontent led to an outburst of student revolts in the late 1960s. In the spring of 1968, student unrest erupted in Paris, where rampaging youths burned automobiles in the streets, took over buildings, and demanded structural changes, not only in education but in other allegedly outdated social institutions as well. When urban workers, angry at their stagnating salaries, joined the protests, the government instituted a hefty wage hike. When the workers grudgingly returned to their jobs, the government sent the gendarmes into the streets to suppress the remaining student protesters. Eventually, they too resentfully returned to their classes, leaving the streets littered with burned-out autos.

In part, the student protests were an extension of the disruptions in American universities in the mid-1960s, which were often sparked by student opposition to the Vietnam War. Protesters also criticized other aspects of Western society, such as its materialism, and expressed concern about becoming cogs in the large and impersonal bureaucratic jungles of the modern world. But other factors were important as well. One source of resentment was the lingering influence of traditional social values in European society, where a rigid code of manners and morals dating from the previous century still reigned supreme. A graffito sprayed on the wall of a building in Paris put it well: "Culture is the inversion of life." Throughout Western Europe, young people began to flout the social codes of the past, engaging publicly in casual sex and experimenting with hallucinatory drugs. Although such behavior was more prevalent in the large cities than in rural areas, the new permissiveness seeped into the culture at large. Divorce rates increased dramatically, while premarital and extramarital sexual experiences also rose substantially. Although the student revolutionaries had lost the battle in the streets of Paris, their ideas had begun to prevail in the wider world of European society.

Expanding Roles for Women

Another area that saw significant change in postwar European society was the role of women. Although some women pursued professional careers and a number of other vocations in the 1920s and 1930s, the place for most women was still in the home. Half a century later, there were almost as many women as men in the workplace, many of them employed in professions hitherto reserved for men.

But the increased number of women in the workforce has not changed some old patterns. Working-class women in particular still earn salaries lower than those paid to men for equal work. Women still tend to enter traditionally female jobs. Many European women also still face the double burden of earning income on the one hand and raising a family and maintaining the household on the other.

One consequence of the trend toward greater employment of women outside the home has been a drop in the birthrate. In many European countries, zero population growth was reached in the 1960s, and increases since then have been due solely to immigration. In Italy and Spain, the flood of women into the workplace has resulted in a dramatic reduction in the number of children born annually, leading to fears of an absolute decline in total population. In Germany, it has been estimated that nearly half a million immigrants will be required annually to maintain the current level of economic growth.

The participation of women in World Wars I and II helped them achieve one of the major aims of the nineteenth-century feminist movement—the right to vote. After World War I, governments in many countries—Sweden, Great Britain, Germany, Poland, Hungary, Austria, and Czechoslovakia—acknowledged the contributions of women to the war effort by granting them the vote. Women in France and Italy finally gained the right to vote in 1945.

After World War II, European women tended to fall back into the traditional roles expected of them, and little was heard of feminist concerns. But with the student upheavals of the late 1960s came a renewed interest in feminism, or the women's liberation movement, as it was now called. Inspired by the writings of the French author Simone de Beauvoir (1908–1986), whose feminist tract entitled *The Second Sex*, pointed out that women were second-class citizens living in a male-dominated world, women in Europe began to demand true equality with men. Realizing that women must take responsibility for transforming the fundamental conditions of their lives, feminists formed "consciousness-raising" groups to further awareness of women's issues and to campaign for the legalization of both contraception and abortion. A French law passed in 1968 legalized the sale of contraceptive devices. In 1979, abortion became legal in France. Even in countries where the Catholic Church remained strongly opposed to contraception and legalized abortion, legislation allowing them passed in the 1970s and 1980s. At the same time, European women have become more active in politics, and a number, including Angela Merkel in Germany, have reached positions of political leadership in their countries.

The Environment

By the 1970s, serious ecological problems had become all too apparent in the crowded countries of Western Europe. Air pollution, produced by nitrogen oxide and sulfur dioxide emissions from road vehicles, power plants, and industrial factories, was causing respiratory illnesses and having corrosive effects on buildings and historical monuments such as the Parthenon in Athens. Many rivers, lakes, and seas had become so polluted that they posed serious health risks. Dying forests (such as the famous Black Forest in southern Germany) and disappearing wildlife alarmed more and more people.

Although the environmental movement first began to gain broad public attention in the United States, the problem was more serious in Europe, with its higher population density and high levels of industrial production in such countries as Great Britain and West Germany. The problem was compounded by the lack of antipollution controls in the industrial sectors of the Soviet satellite states to the east.

Growing ecological awareness gave rise to Green movements and Green parties throughout Europe in the 1970s. Most started at the local level and then gradually extended their activities to the national level, where they became formally organized as political parties. As in the United States, however, the movement has been hindered by concerns that strict environmental regulations could sap economic growth and exacerbate unemployment. National rivalries and disagreements over how to deal with rising levels of pollution along international waterways such as the Rhine River have also impeded cooperation. Nevertheless, public alarm over potential effects of global warming has focused attention on the global character of environmental issues, and the members of the EU have been among the foremost supporters of efforts to

A Wind Farm in Austria. Lacking the ample reserves of liquid energy possessed by other industrial powerhouses like Russia and the United States, the nations of the European Union have sought to reduce their dependence on foreign sources of oil and natural gas by developing alternative energy supplies. Shown here is an Austrian wind farm located on the flat plains extending to the Hungarian border. A brisk wind, known locally as the *fohn*, sweeps down from the eastern slopes of the Alps and heads toward the flatlands of Eastern Europe. In past years, the *fohn* has been blamed for chronically high suicide rates in the Austrian capital of Vienna. Today it helps to reduce the region's dependence on foreign oil imports.

establish tougher standards to control environmental pollution on a worldwide basis. One of the most visible examples was the decision by the municipal government in Paris to establish a public bicycle program for use by residents and visitors to reduce carbon dioxide emissions in the city.

Aspects of Culture in Postwar Europe

Since the end of World War II, Europe has tended to follow the pattern of the United States in that a once dominant "elite" culture has gradually given way to a more **popular culture** directed toward the mass of the population. Nevertheless, even though most Europeans, like Americans, prefer popular literature, rock music, and the movies, what is sometimes called **high culture** (such as serious fiction and nonfiction, art, and classical music) continues to be produced and to exert significant influence on the broader society.

Postwar Literature

The most influential literary fashion in the immediate postwar period was **Existentialism**. The French intellectual Jean-Paul Sartre (1905–1980) was perhaps most closely identified with the Existential movement, whose fundamental premise was the absence of a god in the universe, thereby denying that humans had any preordained destiny. Humans were thus deprived of any absolute purpose or meaning, set adrift in an absurd world. Often reduced to despair and depression, the protagonists of Sartre's literary works were left with only one reason for hope—themselves and their ability to voluntarily reach out and become involved in their community. In the early 1950s, Sartre became a devout Marxist, hitching his philosophy of freedom to one of political engagement in the Communist ideal.

Sartre's contemporary, Albert Camus (1913–1960), reached similar conclusions on the meaning of life. In his seminal novel, *The Stranger* (1942), the protagonist, having stumbled through a lethargic existence, realizes just before dying that regardless of the absurdity of life, humans still have the opportunity to embrace the joyful dimensions of experience—in his case, the warmth and splendor of the Algerian skies. Neither a political activist nor an ideologue, Camus broke with Sartre and other French leftists after the disclosure of the Stalinist atrocities in the Soviet gulags.

The existentialist worldview found expression in the Paris of the 1950s in the "theater of the absurd." One of its foremost proponents was the Irish dramatist Samuel Beckett (1906–1990), who lived in France. In his trail-

blazing play *Waiting for Godot* (1952), two nondescript men eagerly await the appearance of someone who never arrives. While they wait, they pass the time exchanging hopes and fears, with humor, courage, and touching friendship. This waiting represents the existential meaning of life, which is found in the daily activities and fellowship of the here and now, despite the absence of any absolute salvation for the human condition.

POSTMODERNISM Beginning in the 1960s, many Europeans became disenchanted with political systems of any kind and began to question the validity of reason, history, progress, and universal truths. The negation of prewar ideologies, now applied to all branches of learning, fused into a new doctrine of skepticism called **deconstruction**, which described a world in which human beings have lost their status as free agents dealing with universal verities and are reduced to empty vessels programmed by language and culture.

The philosophical skepticism reflected in this new approach quickly manifested itself in European literature as authors grappled with new ways to present reality in an uncertain and nonsensical world. Whereas the Modernists at the beginning of the twentieth century had celebrated the power of art to benefit humankind, placing their faith in the written word, much of the new "Postmodern" literature reflected the lack of belief in anything, especially the written word.

Following in the footsteps of the Modernists, French authors in the 1960s experimented so radically with literary forms and language that they pushed fiction well beyond its traditional limits of rational understanding. In the "new novel," for example, authors like Alain Robbe-Grillet (1922–2008) and Nathalie Sarraute (1900–1999) delved deeply into stream-of-consciousness writing, literally abandoning the reader in the disorienting obsessions of the protagonist's unconscious mind.

Some authors, however, preferred to retrieve literary forms and values that Modernists had rejected, choosing to tell a "good" chronological story that entertained as well as delivered a moral message. Graham Greene (1904–1991) was one of Britain's more prolific, popular, and critically acclaimed authors of the century. He succeeded in combining psychological and moral depth with enthralling stories, often dealing with political conflicts set in exotic locales. A longtime critic of the United States, Greene forecast the American defeat in Vietnam in his 1955 novel *The Quiet American*.

Several other European authors also combined a gripping tale and a fresh exciting narrative with seriousness of intent. In 1959, *The Tin Drum* by Günter Grass (b. 1927) blasted German consciousness out of the complacency that had been induced by the country's postwar economic miracle. The novel reexamined Germany's infatuation with Hitler and warned German readers of the ever-present danger of repeating the evils of the past.

In *The Cave* (2001), the Portuguese novelist José Saramago (1922–2010) focused on global issues, such as the erosion of individual cultures stemming from the tyranny of globalization, which, in his view, had not only led to the exploitation of poor countries but had also robbed the world's cultures of their uniqueness. Like Grass, Saramago believed strongly in the Western humanist tradition and viewed authors as society's moral guardians and political mobilizers.

Music and the Arts

Since the end of World War II, serious music has witnessed a wide diversity of experimental movements, each searching for new tonal and rhythmic structures. Striving to go beyond Arnold Schoenberg's atonality, European composers like the French Pierre Boulez (b. 1925) and the German Karlheinz Stockhausen (1928–2007) set out to free their music from the traditional constraints of meter, form, and dynamics. They devised a new procedure called serialism, which is a mathematical ordering of musical components that, once set in motion, essentially writes itself automatically. More recently, the young British composer Thomas Adès (b. 1971) has earned critical acclaim for his musical compositions, which display radiant harmonies and pulsating energy.

In the visual arts, experimentalism, such as the recently popular installation art, is also widely practiced in Europe today, but some painters continue to use the traditional canvas to explore political and social issues relevant to their times. Some, like the Anglo-Irish painter Francis Bacon (1909–1992), sought to portray the horrors of World War II. In a 1946 canvas entitled *Painting*, Bacon portrayed the silent scream of a trapped man crouching beneath Neville Chamberlain's famous umbrella, symbol of the appeasement of Adolf Hitler. In the background, a bloody carcass on a crucifix vividly represents the butchery of war. Also of note is the German Anselm Kiefer (b. 1945), whose large canvases contrast Germany's past accomplishments with the calamity of the Holocaust. In *The Book*, he offers a desolate postapocalyptic landscape dominated by a large book made of lead. The book represents regeneration, as humankind's intellectual achievements and indomitable spirit triumph over the ravages of the twentieth century.

© William J. Duiker

Glass Pyramid at the Louvre. The Louvre, residence of French kings since the sixteenth century and an art museum since the French Revolution, has traditionally represented classical symmetry and grandeur. In 1988, under the auspices of President François Mitterrand, architect I. M. Pei added this imaginative and daring symmetrical pyramid of glass. It functions as an expedient entrance to the mammoth museum, while also allowing natural light to flood the lower floors. Its form incorporates the grandeur of Egypt with Modernist simplicity.

CONCLUSION

DURING THE IMMEDIATE POSTWAR ERA, Western Europe emerged from the ashes of World War II and achieved a level of political stability and economic prosperity unprecedented in its long history. By the 1970s, European leaders were beginning to turn their attention to bringing about further political and economic unity among the nations in the region. With the signing of the Maastricht Treaty in 1994, a schedule had been established to put the dream into effect, and many advocates of European unity were optimistic that the long era of division and mutual animosity could be put to an end.

But with the new century, the pains of transition have become more apparent, as it has become clear that long-standing structural and cultural differences stand in the way of regional unification. The decision to expand the European Union into Eastern Europe has opened up new challenges, as many of the onetime Soviet satellites do not share the economic prosperity or the democratic traditions of their neighbors to the west. In the meantime, the continent is undergoing an economic crisis, as growing budget deficits bring into question the defining feature of the EU—the concept of the welfare state. A truly united Europe still remains a long way off.

TIMELINE

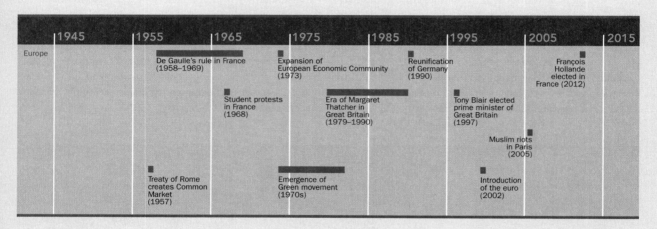

Europe

- De Gaulle's rule in France (1958–1969)
- Student protests in France (1968)
- Treaty of Rome creates Common Market (1957)
- Expansion of European Economic Community (1973)
- Era of Margaret Thatcher in Great Britain (1979–1990)
- Emergence of Green movement (1970s)
- Reunification of Germany (1990)
- Tony Blair elected prime minister of Great Britain (1997)
- Introduction of the euro (2002)
- Muslim riots in Paris (2005)
- François Hollande elected in France (2012)

1945 | 1955 | 1965 | 1975 | 1985 | 1995 | 2005 | 2015

CHAPTER NOTE

1. Cited in Michael Slackman, "For Some Germans, Unity Is Still Work in Progress," *New York Times*, October 1, 2010.

Toward the Pacific Century? Japan and the Little Tigers

General Douglas MacArthur and Emperor Hirohito, September 1945

Keystone/Hulton Royals Collection/Getty Images

THEY WERE AN UNLIKELY PAIR. The tall, lean American Douglas MacArthur looked every bit the famous warrior-general that he was as he towered over the diminutive and seemingly self-effacing Emperor Hirohito standing by his side. But the meeting between the U.S. general and the emperor of Japan on September 27, 1945, memorialized in the photograph, was a significant event in the history of post–World War II Asia. The discussions between MacArthur, recently appointed proconsul of the U.S. occupation regime in Japan, and Emperor Hirohito, the divine ruler of imperial Japan, signaled to the world that the United States' policy toward its defeated adversary would be relatively benign, rather than punitive as the Allied demand for the "unconditional surrender" of Japan had suggested. The new relationship between conqueror and conquered, which would soon blossom into a full-fledged alliance, opened the door to a series of dramatic changes in postwar East Asia.

Four decades later, Japan had emerged as the second greatest industrial power in the world, democratic in form and content and a source of stability throughout the region. Praise of the so-called Japanese miracle became a growth industry in academic circles in the United States, and Japan's achievement spawned a number of Asian imitators. Known as the "Little Tigers," the four industrializing societies of Taiwan, Hong Kong, Singapore, and South Korea achieved considerable success by following the path originally charted by Japan. Along with Japan, they became economic powerhouses and ranked among the world's top seventeen

trading nations. Other nations in Asia and elsewhere took note and began to adopt the Japanese formula. It is no wonder that observers relentlessly heralded the coming of the "Pacific Century."

CRITICAL THINKING

Q Why do you think Japan and the Little Tigers have been so successful in their efforts to build advanced industrial societies?

Japan: Asian Giant

For five years after the war in the Pacific, Japan was governed by an Allied administration under the command of U.S. General Douglas MacArthur (1880–1964). The occupation regime, which consisted of the Far Eastern Commission in Washington, D.C., and the four-power Allied Council in Tokyo, was dominated by the United States, although the country was technically administered by a new Japanese government. As commander of the occupation administration, MacArthur was responsible for demilitarizing Japanese society, destroying the Japanese war machine, trying Japanese civilian and military officials charged with war crimes, and laying the foundations of postwar Japanese society.

During the war, senior U.S. officials had discussed whether to insist on the abdication of Emperor Hirohito

(r. 1926–1989) as the symbol of Japanese imperial expansion. During the summer of 1945, the United States rejected a Japanese request to guarantee that the position of the emperor would be retained in any future peace settlement and reiterated its demand for unconditional surrender. After the war, however, the United States agreed to the retention of the emperor after he agreed publicly to renounce his divinity. Although many historians have suggested that Hirohito opposed the war policy of his senior advisers, some recent studies have contended that he fully supported it.

The Occupation Era

Under MacArthur's firm tutelage, Japanese society was remodeled along Western lines. The centerpiece of occupation policy was the promulgation of a new constitution to replace the Meiji Constitution of 1889. The new charter, which was drafted by U.S. planners and imposed on the Japanese despite their objections to some of its provisions, was designed to transform Japan into a peaceful and pluralistic society that would no longer be capable of waging offensive war. The constitution specifically renounced war as a national policy, and Japan unilaterally agreed to maintain armed forces only sufficient for self-defense. Perhaps most important, the constitution established a parliamentary form of government based on a bicameral legislature, an independent judiciary, and a universal franchise; it also reduced the power of the emperor and guaranteed human rights.

But more than a written constitution was needed to demilitarize Japan and set it on a new course. Like the Meiji leaders in the late nineteenth century, occupation administrators wished to transform Japanese social institutions and hoped their policies would be accepted by the Japanese people as readily as those of the Meiji period had been. The Meiji reforms, however, had been crafted to reflect Japanese traditions and had set Japan on a path quite different from that of the modern West. Some Japanese observers believed that a fundamental reversal of trends begun with the Meiji Restoration would be needed before Japan would be ready to adopt the Western capitalist, democratic model.

One of the sturdy pillars of Japanese militarism had been the giant business cartels, known as *zaibatsu*. Allied policy was designed to break up the *zaibatsu* into smaller units in the belief that corporate concentration, in Japan as in the United States, not only hindered competition but was inherently undemocratic and conducive to political authoritarianism. Occupation planners also intended to promote the formation of independent labor unions, lessen the power of the state over the economy, and provide a mouthpiece for downtrodden Japanese workers. Economic inequality in rural areas was to be reduced by a comprehensive land reform program that would turn the land over to the people who farmed it. Finally, the educational system was to be remodeled along American lines so that it would turn out independent individuals rather than automatons subject to manipulation by the state.

The Allied program was an ambitious and even audacious plan to remake Japanese society and has been justly praised for its clear-sighted vision and altruistic motives. Parts of the program, such as the constitution, the land reform program, and the educational system, succeeded brilliantly. But as other concerns began to intervene, changes and compromises were made that have become more controversial. In particular, with the rise of Cold War sentiment in the United States in the late 1940s, the goal of decentralizing the Japanese economy gave way to the desire to make Japan a key partner in the effort to defend East Asia against international communism. Convinced of the need to promote economic recovery in Japan, U.S. policymakers began to show more tolerance for the *zaibatsu*. Concerned at growing radicalism within the new labor movement, where left-wing elements were gaining strength, U.S. occupation authorities placed less emphasis on the independence of the labor unions.

Cold War concerns also affected U.S. foreign relations with Japan. On September 8, 1951, the United States and other former belligerent nations signed a peace treaty restoring Japanese independence. In turn, Japan renounced any claim to such former colonies or territories as Taiwan (which had been returned to the Republic of China), Korea (which, after a period of joint Soviet and U.S. occupation, had become two independent states), and southern Sakhalin and the Kurile Islands (which had been ceded to the Soviet Union). The Soviet Union refused to sign the treaty on the grounds that it had not been permitted to play an active role in the occupation. On the same day, the Japanese and Americans signed a defensive alliance and agreed that the United States could maintain military bases on the Japanese islands. Japan was now formally independent, but in a new dependency relationship with the United States.

The Transformation of Modern Japan: Politics and Government

Thus, by the early 1950s, Japan had regained at least partial control over its own destiny (see Map 11.1). Although it was linked closely to the United States through the new security treaty and the new U.S.-drafted constitution, Japan was now essentially free to move out on its own. As the world would soon discover, the Japanese adapted quickly to the new conditions. From a semifeudal society with autocratic leanings, Japan rapidly progressed into one of the most stable and advanced democracies in the world.

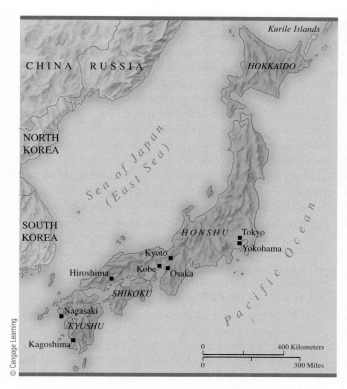

MAP 11.1 Modern Japan. Shown here are the four main islands that comprise the contemporary state of Japan.

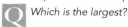 *Which is the largest?*

The Allied occupation administrators started with the conviction that Japanese expansionism was directly linked to the institutional and ideological foundations of the Meiji Constitution. Accordingly, they set out to change Japanese politics into something closer to the pluralistic approach used in most Western nations. The concepts of universal suffrage, governmental accountability, and a balance of power among the executive, legislative, and judicial branches that were embodied in the constitution of 1947 have held firm, and Japan today is a stable and mature democratic society with a literate and politically active electorate and a government that usually seeks to meet the needs of its citizens.

Yet a number of characteristics of the current Japanese political system reflect the tenacity of the traditional political culture. Although postwar Japan had a multiparty system with two major parties, the Liberal Democrats and the Socialists, in practice there was a "government party" and a permanent opposition—the Liberal Democrats, who had presided over an era of growing material prosperity, were not voted out of office for thirty years. The ruling Liberal Democratic Party included several factions, but disputes usually involved personalities rather than substantive issues.

Many of the leading Liberal Democrats controlled factions on a patron-client basis, and decisions on key issues, such as who should assume the prime ministership, were decided by a modern equivalent of the *genro* oligarchs.

That tradition changed suddenly in 1993 when the ruling Liberal Democrats, shaken by persistent reports of corruption and cronyism between politicians and business interests, failed to win a majority of seats in parliamentary elections. Morihiro Hosokawa (b. 1938), the leader of one of several newly created parties in the Japanese political spectrum, was elected prime minister. He promised to launch a number of reforms to clean up the political system. The new coalition government quickly split into feuding factions, however, and in 1995, the Liberal Democratic Party returned to power. Successive prime ministers failed to carry out promised reforms, and in 2001, Junichiro Koizumi (b. 1942), a former minister of health and welfare, was elected prime minister on a promise that he would initiate far-reaching reforms to fix the political system and make it more responsive to the needs of the Japanese people. His charisma raised expectations that he might be able to bring about significant changes, but bureaucratic resistance to reform and chronic factionalism within the Liberal Democratic Party largely thwarted his efforts. In 2009, three years after he left office, the Liberal Democrats were again voted out of power. But the massive tsunami that struck the mainland island of Honshu in 2011 highlighted the ineptitude of the ruling Democratic Party (a center-left party that had been formed in 1998), and in 2012 the Liberal Democrats returned to power under Prime Minister Shinzō Abe (b. 1954). The Abe government seeks to revive the lagging Japanese economy by stimulating competition and adopting new fiscal policies.

JAPAN, INCORPORATED One of the problems plaguing the current system has been the centralizing tendencies that it inherited from the Meiji period. The government is organized on a unitary rather than a federal basis; the local administrative units, called prefectures, have few of the powers of states in the United States. Moreover, the central government plays an active and sometimes intrusive role in various aspects of the economy, mediating management-labor disputes, establishing price and wage policies, and subsidizing vital industries and enterprises producing goods for export. This government intervention in the economy has traditionally been widely accepted and is often cited as a key reason for the efficiency of Japanese industry and the emergence of the country as an industrial giant.

In recent years, though, the tradition of active government involvement in the economy has increasingly come under fire. Japanese business, which previously sought government protection from imports, now argues that deregulation is needed to enable Japanese firms to innovate in order to keep up with the competition. Such reforms, however, have been resisted by powerful government ministries in Tokyo, which are accustomed to playing an active role in national affairs.

A third problem is that the ruling Liberal Democratic Party has long been divided into factions that seek to protect their own interests and often resist changes that might benefit society as a whole. This tradition of factionalism has tended to insulate political figures from popular scrutiny and encouraged susceptibility to secret dealing and official corruption. A number of senior politicians, including two recent prime ministers, have been forced to resign because of serious questions about improper financial dealings with business associates. Concern over political corruption continues to plague the political scene.

ATONING FOR THE PAST Lingering social problems also need to be addressed. Minorities such as the *eta* (hereditary outcasts in traditional Japan, now known as the *Burakumin*) and Korean residents in Japan continue to be subjected to legal and social discrimination. For years, official sources were reluctant to divulge that thousands of Korean women were conscripted to serve as "comfort women" (prostitutes) for Japanese soldiers during the war, and many Koreans living in Japan contend that such condescending attitudes toward minorities continue to exist. Representatives of the "comfort women" have demanded both financial compensation and a formal letter of apology from the Japanese government for the treatment they received during the Pacific War. Negotiations over the issue have been under way for several years.

The **Ainu** are another ethnic minority group that has been left behind in the country's headlong rush into modernity. Descendants of the original settlers on the islands, they were eventually overwhelmed by later arrivals from the mainland and now live for the most part in isolated communities on the northern island of Hokkaido. Long ignored by a government that sought to proclaim the ethnic homogeneity of the Japanese people, in 2008 they were finally recognized as a distinct indigenous culture. Whether their new status will enable the Ainu—currently numbering about 24,000 people—to claim compensation for past ill treatment and present neglect is still an open question.

Japan's behavior during World War II has been an especially sensitive issue. During the early 1990s, critics at home and abroad charged that textbooks printed under the guidance of the Ministry of Education did not adequately discuss the atrocities committed by the Japanese government

and armed forces during World War II. Other Asian governments were particularly incensed at Tokyo's failure to accept responsibility for such behavior and demanded a formal apology. The government expressed remorse, but only in the context of the aggressive actions of all colonial powers during the imperialist era. In the view of many Japanese, the actions of their government during the Pacific War were a form of self-defense. When new textbooks were published that openly discussed instances of Japanese wartime misconduct, including sex slavery, the use of slave labor, and the Nanjing massacre (see Chapter 6), many Japanese were outraged and initiated a campaign to delete or tone down references to atrocities committed by imperial troops during the Pacific War. At times, members of the government have exacerbated the controversy; Prime Minister Koizumi did so by attending ceremonies at shrines dedicated to the spirits of Japan's war dead, as did members of Prime Minister Abe's cabinet in 2013.

The issue is not simply an academic one, for fear of a revival of Japanese militarism is still strong in the region, where Japan's relations with other states have recently been strained by disputes with South Korea and China over ownership of small islands in the China Sea. The United States has not shared this concern, however, and applauded Japan's recent decision to enhance the ability of its self-defense forces to deal with potential disturbances within the region. The proper role of the military has provoked vigorous debate in Japan, where some observers have argued that their country should adopt a more assertive stance toward the United States and China and play a larger role in Asian affairs.

The Economy

Nowhere are the changes in postwar Japan so visible as in the economic sector, where the nation has developed into a major industrial and technological power in the space of a century, surpassing such advanced Western societies as Germany, France, and Great Britain. Here indeed is the Japanese miracle in its most concrete manifestation.

The process began a century ago in the single-minded determination of the Meiji modernizers to create a rich country and a strong state. Their initial motive was to ensure Japan's survival against Western imperialism, but this defensive urge evolved into a desire to excel and, during the years before World War II, to dominate. That desire led to the war in the Pacific and, in the eyes of some observers, still contributes to Japan's problems with its trading partners in the world today.

OCCUPATION REFORMS As we have seen, the officials of the Allied occupation identified the Meiji economic system with centralized power and the rise of Japanese militarism. Accordingly, MacArthur's planners set out to break up the *zaibatsu* and decentralize Japanese industry and commerce. But with the rise of Cold War tensions, the policy was scaled back in the late 1940s, and only the nineteen largest conglomerates were affected. In any event, the new antimonopoly law did not hinder the formation of looser ties between Japanese companies, and as a result, a new type of informal relationship, sometimes called the *keiretsu*, or "interlocking arrangement," began to take shape after World War II. Through such arrangements among suppliers, wholesalers, retailers, and financial institutions, the *zaibatsu* system was reconstituted under a new name.

The occupation administration had more success with its program to reform the agricultural system. Half of the population still lived on farms, and half of all farmers were still tenants. Under a stringent land reform program in the late 1940s, all lands owned by absentee landlords and all cultivated landholdings over an established maximum were sold on easy credit terms to the tenants. The maximum size of an individual farm was set at 7.5 acres, while an additional 2.5 acres could be leased to tenants. The reform program created a strong class of yeoman farmers, and tenants declined to about 10 percent of the rural population.

THE JAPANESE MIRACLE During the next fifty years, Japan re-created the stunning results of the Meiji era. At the end of the Allied occupation in 1950, the Japanese gross domestic product was about one-third that of Great Britain or France. Thirty years later, it was larger than both put together and well over half that of the United States. For years, Japan was the greatest exporting nation in the world, and its per capita income equals or surpasses that of most advanced Western states. In terms of education, mortality rates, and health care, the quality of life in Japan is superior to that in the United States or the advanced nations of Western Europe.

By the mid-1980s, the economic challenge presented by Japan had begun to arouse increasing concern in both official and private circles in Europe and the United States. Explanations for the phenomenon tended to fall into two major categories. Some analysts pointed to cultural factors. The Japanese are naturally group oriented and find it easy to cooperate with one another. Traditionally hardworking and frugal, they are more inclined to save than to consume, a trait that boosts the saving rate and labor productivity.[1] The Japanese are also family oriented and therefore spend less on government entitlement programs for the elderly, who normally live with their children. Like all Confucian societies, the Japanese value education,

and consequently, the labor force is highly skilled. Finally, Japan is a homogeneous society in which people share common values and respond in similar ways to the challenges of the modern world.

Others cited more practical reasons for Japanese success. Paradoxically, Japan benefited from the total destruction of its industrial base during World War II because it did not face the problem of antiquated plants that plagued many industries in the United States. Under the terms of its constitution and the security treaty with the United States, Japan spends less than 1 percent of its gross domestic product on national defense, whereas the United States spends about 5 percent. Labor productivity is high, not only because the Japanese are hard workers (according to statistics, Japanese workers spend more time on the job than workers in other advanced societies) but also because corporations reward innovation and have maintained good management-labor relations. Consequently, employee mobility and the number of days lost to labor stoppages are minimized (on an average day in the 1990s, according to one estimate, 603 Japanese workers were on strike compared with 11,956 Americans). Just as it did before World War II, the Japanese government promotes business interests rather than hindering them. Finally, some analysts have charged that Japan used unfair trade practices, subsidizing exports through the Ministry of International Trade and Industry (**MITI**), dumping goods at prices below cost to break into a foreign market, maintaining an artificially low standard of living at home to encourage exports, and unduly restricting imports from other countries.

There is some truth on both sides of the argument. Undoubtedly, Japan benefited from its privileged position beneath the U.S. nuclear umbrella as well as from its ability to operate in a free trade environment that provided both export markets and access to Western technology. The Japanese also took a number of practical steps to improve their competitive position in the world and the effectiveness of their economic system at home.

Yet many of these steps were possible precisely because of the cultural factors described here. The tradition of loyalty to the firm, for example, derives from the communal tradition in Japanese society. The concept of sacrificing one's personal interests to those of the state, though not necessarily rooted in the traditional period, was certainly fostered by the *genro* oligarchy during the Meiji era.

THE MIRACLE TARNISHED By the 1990s, however, the Japanese economy had begun to run into serious difficulties, raising the question of whether the vaunted Japanese model was as appealing as many observers had earlier declared. A rise in the value of the yen hurt exports and burst the bubble of investment by Japanese banks that had taken place under the umbrella of government protection. With a much smaller domestic market than the United States has, the Japanese economy slipped into a long-term recession that has not yet entirely abated.

These economic difficulties have placed heavy pressure on some of the highly praised features of the Japanese economy. The tradition of lifetime employment created a bloated white-collar workforce and has made downsizing difficult. Today, job security is on the decline as increasing numbers of workers are being laid off. Unfortunately, the burden has fallen disproportionately on women, who lack seniority and continue to suffer from various forms of discrimination in the workplace. On the positive side, job satisfaction is beginning to take precedence over security for many Japanese workers, and salaries are starting to reflect performance more than time on the job.

Finally, the Japanese market is slowly but inexorably beginning to open up to international competition. Foreign automakers are winning a growing share of the domestic market, and the government—concerned at the prospect of food shortages—has committed itself to facilitating the importation of rice from abroad. This last move was especially sensitive, given the almost sacred role that rice farming holds in the Japanese mind-set.

At the same time, greater exposure to foreign economic competition may improve the performance of Japanese manufacturers. In recent years, Japanese consumers have become increasingly concerned about the quality of some of their domestic products, causing one cabinet minister to complain about the "sloppiness and complacency" of Japanese firms (even the Japanese automaker Toyota has faced quality problems in its best-selling fleet of motor vehicles). One apparent reason for the quality problems is the cost-cutting measures adopted by Japanese companies to meet the challenges from abroad.

A Society in Transition

During the occupation, Allied planners set out to change social characteristics that they believed had contributed to Japanese aggressiveness before and during World War II. The new educational system removed all references to filial piety, patriotism, and loyalty to the emperor and emphasized the individualistic values of Western civilization. The new constitution and a revised civil code attempted to achieve true gender equality by removing the remaining legal restrictions on women's rights to obtain a divorce, hold a job, or change their domicile. Women were guaranteed the right to vote and were encouraged to enter politics.

THE PRESSURE TO CONFORM Such efforts to remake Japanese behavior through legislation have been only partly successful. Since the end of World War II, Japan has unquestionably become a more individualistic and egalitarian society. Freedom of choice in marriage and occupation is taken for granted, and social mobility, though less extensive than in the United States, has increased considerably. Although the Allied occupation policy established the legal framework for these developments, primary credit must be assigned to the evolution of the Japanese themselves into an urbanized and technologically advanced industrial society.

At the same time, many of the distinctive characteristics of traditional Japanese society have persisted, in somewhat altered form. The emphasis on loyalty to the group and community relationships, for example, known in Japanese as *amae*, is reflected in the strength of corporate loyalties in contemporary Japan. Even though competition among enterprises in a given industry is often quite vigorous, social cohesiveness among both management and labor personnel is exceptionally strong within each individual corporation, although, as we have seen, that attitude has eroded somewhat in recent years.

One possible product of this attitude may be the relatively egalitarian nature of Japanese society in terms of income. A chief executive officer in Japan receives, on average, about twenty times the salary of the average worker, compared with more than two hundred times in the United States. The disparity between wealth and poverty is also generally less in Japan than in most European countries and certainly less than in the United States.

Japan's welfare system also differs profoundly from its Western counterparts. Applicants are required to seek assistance first from their own families, and the physically able are ineligible for government aid. As a result, less than 1 percent of the population receives welfare benefits, compared with more than 10 percent who receive some form of assistance in the United States. Outside observers attribute the difference to several factors, including low levels of drug addiction and illegitimacy in Japan, as well as the importance of the work ethic and family responsibility.

Emphasis on the work ethic remains strong. The tradition of hard work is implanted at a young age by the educational system. The Japanese school year runs for 240 days, compared to 180 days in the United States, and work assignments outside class tend to be more extensive (according to one source, a Japanese student averages about five hours of homework per day). Competition for acceptance into universities is intense, and many young Japanese take cram courses to prepare for the "examination hell" that lies ahead. The results are impressive: the literacy rate in Japanese schools is almost 100 percent, and Japanese schoolchildren consistently earn higher scores on achievement tests than children in other advanced countries. At the same time, this devotion to success has often been accompanied by bullying by teachers and what Americans might consider an oppressive sense of conformity (see the box on p. 238).

Some young Japanese find suicide the only escape from the pressures emanating from society, school, and family. Parental pride often becomes a factor, with "education mothers" pressuring their children to work hard and succeed for the honor of the family. Ironically, once a student is accepted into college, the amount of work assigned tends to decrease because graduates of the best universities are virtually guaranteed lucrative employment offers. Nevertheless, the early training instills an attitude of deference to group interests that persists throughout life. Some outside observers, however, believe such attitudes can have a detrimental effect on individual initiative.

By all accounts, independent thinking is on the increase in Japan, and some schools are beginning to emphasize creativity over rote learning. In some cases, it leads to antisocial behavior, such as crime or membership in a teen gang. Usually, it is expressed in more indirect ways, such as the recent fashion among young people of dyeing their hair brown (known in Japanese as "tea hair"). Because the practice is banned in many schools and generally frowned on by the older generation (one police chief dumped a pitcher of beer on a student with brown hair that he noticed in a bar), many young Japanese dye their hair as a gesture of independence and a means of gaining acceptance among their peers. When seeking employment or getting married, however, they return their hair to its natural color.

WOMEN IN JAPANESE SOCIETY One of the more tenacious legacies of the past in Japanese society is sexual inequality. Although women are now legally protected against discrimination in employment, very few have reached senior levels in business, education, or politics. In the words of one Western scholar, they remain "acutely disadvantaged," though, ironically, in a recent survey of Japanese business executives, a majority declared that women were smarter than men. Women now make up more than 50 percent of the workforce, but most are in retail or service occupations, and on average they are paid only about half as much as men.[2] There is a feminist movement in Japan, but it has none of the vigor and mass support of its counterpart in the United States.

Most women in Japan consider being a homemaker the ideal position. In the home, a Japanese woman has considerable responsibility. She is expected to be a "good wife and wise mother" and has the primary responsibility for managing the family finances and raising the children. Japanese husbands (known derisively in Japan as the "wet

From Conformity to Counterculture. Traditionally, schoolchildren in Japan have worn uniforms to promote conformity with the country's communitarian social mores. In the photo on the left, young students dressed in identical uniforms are on a field trip to Kyoto's Nijo Castle, built in 1603 by Tokugawa Ieyasu. Recently, however, a youth counterculture has emerged in Japan. On the right, fashion-conscious teenagers with "tea hair"—heirs of Japan's long era of affluence—revel in their expensive hip-hop outfits, platform shoes, and layered dresses. Such dress habits symbolize the growing revolt against conformity in contemporary Japan.

Growing Up in Japan

Japanese schoolchildren are exposed to a much more regimented environment than U.S. children experience. Most Japanese schoolchildren, for example, wear black-and-white uniforms to school. These regulations are examples of rules adopted by middle school systems in various parts of Japan. The Ministry of Education in Tokyo concluded that these regulations were excessive, but they are probably typical.

School Regulations: Japanese Style

1. Boys' hair should not touch the eyebrows, the ears, or the top of the collar.
2. No one should have a permanent wave, or dye his or her hair. Girls should not wear ribbons or accessories in their hair. Hair dryers should not be used.
3. School uniform skirts should be _____ centimeters above the ground, no more and no less (differs by school and region).
4. Keep your uniform clean and pressed at all times. Girls' middy blouses should have two buttons on the back collar. Boys' pant cuffs should be of the prescribed width. No more than 12 eyelets should be on the shoes. The number of buttons on a shirt and tucks in a shirt are also prescribed.
5. Wear your school badge at all times. It should be positioned exactly.
6. Going to school in the morning, wear your book bag strap on the right shoulder; in the afternoon on the way home, wear it on the left shoulder. Your book case thickness, filled and unfilled, is also prescribed.
7. Girls should wear only regulation white underpants of 100% cotton.
8. When you raise your hand to be called on, your arm should extend forward and up at the angle prescribed in your handbook.
9. Your own route to and from school is marked in your student rule handbook; carefully observe which side of each street you are to use on the way to and from school.
10. After school you are to go directly home, unless your parent has written a note permitting you to go to another location. Permission will not be granted by the school unless the other location is a suitable one. You must not go to coffee shops. You must be home by _____ o'clock.
11. It is not permitted to drive or ride a motorcycle, or to have a license to drive one.
12. Before and after school, no matter where you are, you represent our school, so you should behave in ways we can all be proud of.

 What is the apparent purpose of these regulations? How do they differ from standards of behavior in schools in the United States?

SOURCE: *The Material Child: Coming of Age in Japan and America* by Merry White.

---

leaf tribe") perform little work around the house, spending an average of nine minutes a day on housework, compared to twenty-six minutes for American husbands. At the same time, Japanese divorce rates are well below those of the United States.

THE DEMOGRAPHIC CRISIS Many of Japan's current dilemmas stem from its growing demographic problems. Today, Japan has the highest proportion of people older than sixty-five of any industrialized country—almost 23 percent of the country's total population. By the year 2024, an estimated one-third of the Japanese population will be over the age of sixty-five, and the median age will be fifty, ten years older than the median in the United States. This demographic profile is due both to declining fertility and a low level of immigration. Immigrants make up only 1 percent of the total population of Japan. Together, the aging population and the absence of immigrants are creating the prospect of a dramatic labor shortage in coming years. Nevertheless, prejudice against foreigners persists in Japan, and the government remains reluctant to ease restrictions against immigrants from other countries in the region.

Japan's aging population has many implications for the future. Traditionally, it was the responsibility of the eldest child in a Japanese family to care for aging parents, but that system is beginning to break down because of limited housing space and the growing tendency of working-age women to seek jobs in the marketplace. The proportion of Japanese older than sixty-five years of age who live with their children has dropped from 80 percent in 1970 to about 50 percent today. At the same time, public and private pension plans are under increasing financial pressure, partly because of the low birthrate and the graying population.

Religion and Culture

As in the West, increasing urbanization has led to a decline in the practice of organized religion in Japan, although evangelical sects have proliferated in recent years. The largest and best-known sect is Soka Gakkai, a lay Buddhist organization that has attracted millions of followers and formed its own political party, the Komeito. Many Japanese also follow **Shinto**, a traditional faith based on the belief in the existence of spirits in Nature that was once identified with reverence for the emperor and the state.

Western literature, art, and music have also had a major impact on Japanese society. After World War II, many of the writers who had been active before the war resurfaced, but now their writing reflected demoralization. Many were attracted to existentialism, and some turned to hedonism and nihilism. For these disillusioned authors, defeat was compounded by fear of the Americanization of postwar Japan. One of the best examples of this attitude was the novelist Yukio Mishima (1925–1970), who led a crusade to stem the tide of what he described as America's "universal and uniform 'Coca-Colonization'" of the world in general and Japan in particular.[3] Mishima's ritual suicide in 1970 was the subject of widespread speculation and transformed him into a cult figure.

One of Japan's most serious-minded contemporary authors is Kenzaburo Oe (b. 1935). His work, rewarded with a Nobel Prize for Literature in 1994, focuses on Japan's ongoing quest for modern identity and purpose. His characters reflect the spiritual anguish precipitated by the collapse of the imperial Japanese tradition and the subsequent adoption of Western culture—a trend that Oe contends has culminated in unabashed materialism, cultural decline, and a moral void. Yet unlike Mishima, Oe does not wish to restore the imperial traditions of the past but rather seeks to regain spiritual meaning by retrieving the sense of communality and innocence found in rural Japan.

Since the 1970s, increasing affluence and a high literacy rate have contributed to a massive quantity of publications, ranging from popular potboilers to first-rate fiction. Much of this new literature deals with the common concerns of all affluent industrialized nations, including the effects of urbanization, advanced technology, and mass consumption. A wildly popular genre is the "art-manga," or graphic novel. Some members of the youth counterculture have used manga to rebel against Japan's rigid educational and conformist pressures.

Other aspects of Japanese culture have also been influenced by Western ideas, although without the intense preoccupation with synthesis that is evident in literature. Western music is very popular in Japan, and scores of Japanese classical musicians have succeeded in the West. Even rap music has gained a foothold among Japanese youth, although without the association with sex, drugs, and violence that it has in the United States. Although some of the lyrics betray an attitude of modest revolt against the uptight world of Japanese society, most lack any such connotations.

The Japanese Difference

Whether the unique character of modern Japan will endure is unclear. Confidence in the Japanese "economic miracle" has been shaken by the long recession, and there are indications of a growing tendency toward hedonism and individualism among Japanese youth. Older Japanese frequently complain that the younger generation lacks their sense of loyalty and willingness to sacrifice. There are also signs that the concept of loyalty to one's employer may be beginning to erode among Japanese youth. Some observers have predicted that with increasing affluence Japan will become more like the industrialized societies in the West. Although Japan is unlikely to evolve into a photocopy of the United States, the image of millions of dedicated "salarymen" heading off to work with their briefcases and their pinstriped suits may no longer be an accurate portrayal of reality in contemporary Japan.

Taiwan: The Other China

It did not take long for other countries in East Asia to attempt to imitate the Japanese success. To Japan's south, the Republic of China on the island of Taiwan was one of the first to do so.

After retreating to Taiwan following their defeat by the Communists, Chiang Kai-shek and his followers established a new capital at Taipei and set out to build a strong and prosperous nation based on Chinese traditions and the principles of Sun Yat-sen. The government, which continued to refer to itself as the Republic of China (ROC), contended that it remained the legitimate

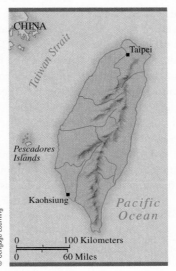

Modern Taiwan

representative of the Chinese people and that it would eventually return in triumph to the mainland.

The Nationalists had much more success on Taiwan than they had achieved on the mainland. In the relatively secure environment provided by a security treaty with the United States, signed in 1954, and the comforting presence of the U.S. Seventh Fleet in the Taiwan Strait, the ROC was able to concentrate on economic growth without worrying about a Communist invasion. The regime possessed a number of other advantages that it had not enjoyed in Nanjing. Fifty years of efficient Japanese rule had left behind a relatively modern economic infrastructure and an educated population, although the island had absorbed considerable damage during World War II and much of its agricultural produce had been exported to Japan at low prices. With only a small population to deal with (about 7 million in 1945), the ROC could make good use of foreign assistance and the efforts of its own energetic people to build a modern industrialized society.

The government moved rapidly to create a solid agricultural base. A land reform program, more effectively designed and implemented than the one introduced in the early 1930s on the mainland, led to the reduction of rents, while landholdings larger than 3 acres were purchased by the government and resold to the tenants at reasonable prices. As in Meiji Japan, the previous owners were compensated by government bonds. The results were gratifying: food production doubled over the next generation and began to make up a substantial proportion of exports.

In the meantime, the government strongly encouraged the development of local manufacturing and commerce. By the 1970s, Taiwan was one of the most dynamic industrial economies in East Asia. The agricultural proportion of the gross domestic product declined from 36 percent in 1952 to only 9 percent thirty years later. At first, the industrial and commercial sector was composed of relatively small firms engaged in exporting textiles and food products, but the 1960s saw a shift to heavy industry, including shipbuilding, steel, petrochemicals, and machinery, and a growing emphasis on exports. The government played a major role in the process, targeting strategic industries for support and investing in infrastructure. At the same time, as in Japan, the government stressed the importance of private enterprise and encouraged foreign investment and a high rate of internal saving. By the mid-1980s, more than three-quarters of the population lived in urban areas.

Taiwan Under Nationalist Rule

In contrast to the People's Republic of China (PRC) on the mainland, the ROC actively maintained Chinese tradition, promoting respect for Confucius and the ethical principles of the past, such as hard work, frugality, and filial piety. Although there was some corruption in both the government and the private sector, income differentials between the wealthy and the poor were generally less than elsewhere in the region, and the overall standard of living increased substantially. Health and sanitation improved, literacy rates were quite high, and an active family planning program reduced the rate of population growth. Nevertheless, the total population on the island increased to about 20 million in the mid-1980s.

In one respect, however, Chiang Kai-shek had not changed: increasing prosperity did not lead to the democratization of the political process. The Nationalists continued to rule by emergency decree and refused to permit the formation of opposition political parties on the grounds that the danger of invasion from the mainland had not subsided. Propaganda material from the PRC was rigorously prohibited, and dissident activities (promoting either rapprochement with the mainland or the establishment of an independent Republic of Taiwan) were ruthlessly suppressed. Although representatives to the provincial government of the province of Taiwan were chosen in local elections, the central government (technically representing the entire population of China) was dominated by mainlanders who had fled to the island with Chiang in 1949.

Some friction developed between the mainlanders (as the new arrivals were called), who numbered about 2 million, and the indigenous Taiwanese, who, except for a few aboriginal peoples in the mountains, were mostly ethnic Chinese whose ancestors had emigrated to the island during the Qing dynasty. While the mainlanders were dominant in government and the professions, the indigenous Taiwanese were prominent in commerce. Mainlanders tended to view the local population with a measure of condescension, and at least in the early years, intermarriage between members of the two groups was rare. Many Taiwanese remembered with anger the events of March 1947, when Nationalist troops had killed hundreds of Taiwanese demonstrators in Taipei. More than one thousand leading members of the local Taiwanese community were arrested and killed in the subsequent repression. By the 1980s, however, these fissures in Taiwanese society had begun to diminish; by that time, an ever-higher proportion of the population had been born on the island and identified themselves as Taiwanese.

The Chiang Kai-shek Memorial Hall in Taipei. While the Chinese government on the mainland attempted to destroy all vestiges of traditional culture, the Republic of China on Taiwan has sought to preserve the cultural heritage as a link between past and present. This policy is graphically displayed in the mausoleum for Chiang Kai-shek in downtown Taipei, shown in this photograph. The mausoleum, with its massive entrance gate, not only glorifies the nation's leader, but recalls the grandeur of old China. In 2007, the mausoleum was controversially renamed the National Taiwan Democracy Memorial Hall in a bid by the government to downplay the island's historical ties to the mainland. In 2008 the name was changed to the National Chiang Kai-shek Memorial Hall.

Crafting a Taiwanese Identity

During the 1980s, the ROC slowly began to evolve toward a more representative form of government—a process that was facilitated by the death of Chiang Kai-shek in 1975. Chiang Ching-kuo (1910–1988), his son and successor, was less concerned about the danger from the mainland and more tolerant of free expression. On his death, he was succeeded as president by Lee Teng-hui (b. 1923), a native Taiwanese. By the end of the 1980s, democratization was under way, including elections and the formation of legal opposition parties. The first fully free national elections, held in 1992, resulted in a bare majority for the Nationalists over strong opposition from the Democratic Progressive Party (DPP).

But political liberalization had its dangers; some leading Democratic Progressives began to agitate for an independent Republic of Taiwan, a possibility that aroused concern within the Nationalist government in Taipei and frenzied hostility in the PRC. In the spring of 2000, DPP candidate Chen Shui-bian (b. 1950) was elected to the presidency, ending half a century of Nationalist Party rule on Taiwan. His elevation to the position angered Beijing, which noted that in the past he had called for an independent Taiwanese

state. Chen backed away from that position and called for the resumption of talks with the PRC, but Chinese leaders remain suspicious of his intentions and reacted with hostility to U.S. plans to provide advanced military equipment to the island. In the meantime, charges of official corruption and economic problems began to erode support for the DPP on the island. The return to power of the Nationalist Party under Ma Ying-jeou (b. 1950) in 2008 and his reelection as president in 2012 have, at least for the time being, eased relations with mainland China.

Whether Taiwan will remain an independent state or be united with the mainland is impossible to predict. Certainly, the outcome depends in good measure on developments in the PRC. During his visit to China in 1972, U.S. President Richard Nixon said that this was a question for the Chinese people to decide (see Chapter 8). In 1979, President Jimmy Carter abrogated the mutual security treaty between the United States and the ROC that had been in force since 1954 and switched U.S. diplomatic recognition from the Republic of China to the PRC. But the United States continues to provide defensive military assistance to the Taiwanese armed forces and has made it clear that it supports self-determination for the people of Taiwan and that it expects the final resolution of the Chinese civil war to be by peaceful means. In the meantime, economic and cultural contacts between Taiwan and the mainland are steadily increasing, making the costs of any future military confrontation increasingly expensive for both sides. Nevertheless, the Taiwanese have shown no inclination to accept the PRC's offer of "one country, two systems," under which the ROC would accept the PRC as the legitimate government of China in return for autonomous control over the affairs of Taiwan. The unresolved future of the island remains one of the most delicate problems in the region of East Asia.

South Korea: A Peninsula Divided

While the world was focused on the economic miracle occurring on the Japanese islands, another miracle of sorts was taking place on the Asian mainland. In 1953, the Korean peninsula was exhausted from three years of bitter fraternal war, a conflict that took the lives of an estimated 4 million Koreans on both sides of the 38th parallel and turned as much as one-quarter of the population into refugees. Although a cease-fire was signed at Panmunjom in July 1953, it was a fragile peace that left two heavily armed and mutually hostile countries facing each other suspiciously.

North of the truce line was the Democratic People's Republic of Korea (PRK), a police state under the dictatorial rule of Communist leader Kim Il-sung (1912–1994). To the south was the Republic of Korea, under the equally autocratic President Syngman Rhee (1875–1965), a fierce anti-Communist who had led the resistance to the northern invasion and now placed his country under U.S. military protection. But U.S. troops could not protect Rhee from his own people, many of whom resented his reliance on the political power of the wealthy landlord class. After several years of harsh rule, marked by government corruption, fraudulent elections, and police brutality, demonstrations broke out in the capital city of Seoul in the spring of 1960 and forced him into retirement.

The Korean Model

The Rhee era was followed by a brief period of multiparty democratic government, but in 1961, General Park Chung Hee (1917–1979) came to power through a coup d'état. The

The Korean Peninsula Since 1953

new regime promulgated a new constitution, and in 1963, Park was elected president of a civilian government. He set out to foster an economic recovery after decades of foreign occupation and civil war. Adopting the nineteenth-century Japanese slogan "Rich Country and Strong State," Park built up a strong military while relying on U.S. and later Japanese assistance to help build a strong manufacturing base in what had been a predominantly agricultural society. Because the private sector had been relatively weak under Japanese rule, the government played an active role in the process by instituting a series of five-year plans that targeted specific industries for development, promoted exports, and funded infrastructure development. Under a land reform program, large landowners were required to sell all their farmland above 7.4 acres to their tenants at low prices.

The program was a solid success. Benefiting from the Confucian principles of thrift, respect for education, and hard work (during the 1960s and 1970s, South Korean workers spent an average of sixty hours a week at their jobs), as well as from Japanese capital and technology, Korea gradually emerged as a major industrial power in East Asia. The economic growth rate rose from less than 5 percent annually in the 1950s to an average of 9 percent under Park. The largest corporations—including Samsung, Daewoo, and Hyundai—were transformed into massive conglomerates called *chaebol*, the Korean equivalent of the *zaibatsu* of prewar Japan. Taking advantage of relatively low wages and a stunningly high rate of saving, Korean businesses began to compete actively with the Japanese for export markets in Asia and throughout the world. Per capita income also increased dramatically, from less than $90 (in U.S. dollars) annually in 1960 to $1,560 (twice that of Communist North Korea) twenty years later.

But like many other countries in the region, South Korea was slow to develop democratic principles. Although his government functioned with the trappings of democracy, Park continued to rule by autocratic means and suppressed all forms of dissidence. In 1979, Park was assassinated. But after a brief interregnum of democratic rule, in 1980 a new military government under General Chun Doo Hwan (b. 1931) seized power. The new regime was as authoritarian as its predecessors, but after student riots in 1987, by the end of the decade opposition to autocratic rule had spread to much of the urban population.

National elections were finally held in 1989, and South Korea reverted to civilian rule. Successive presidents sought to rein in corruption while cracking down on the *chaebols* and initiating contacts with the Communist regime in the PRK on possible steps toward eventual reunification of the peninsula. After the Asian financial crisis in 1997, economic conditions temporarily worsened, but they have since recovered, and the country is increasingly competitive in world markets today. In elections held in 2012, South Korea elected its first woman president—Park Guen-hye (b. 1952), the daughter of Park Chung Hee.

In the meantime, relations with North Korea, now on the verge of becoming a nuclear power, remain tense. Multinational efforts to persuade the regime to suspend its nuclear program continue, although North Korea claimed to have successfully conducted a nuclear test in 2009. To add to the uncertainty, the regime faced a succession crisis, when Kim Jong-il (1941–2011), the son and successor of founder Kim Il-sung, died suddenly in 2011 and was replaced by his inexperienced son, Kim Jong-un (b. 1984). In the uncertainty following the emergence of a new leader in North Korea, tensions with the South erupted once again, although they have recently subsided.

to 2012, to enforce a five-day workweek was motivated, in part, by the same considerations.

Whether the Korean people's drive to get ahead in life is seen as a benefit or a disadvantage, there is no doubt that, like many of its counterparts in East Asia, South Korea is changing rapidly. A predominantly rural nation at the end of World War II, it is now a manufacturing powerhouse. Though it has historically had a homogeneous population, it now hosts a growing foreign population, many of whom are low-wage workers and young women brought in from other parts of Asia to marry Koreans living in rural areas, where the shortage of marriageable Korean women is acute. The traumatic effect of the transformation of South Korea from a rural to an urban society is ably described by author Kyung-Sook Shin (b. 1963) in her recent novel entitled *Please Look After Mom*. The disappearance of the protagonist's mother in the book represents the loss of the country's traditional values and lifestyles.

Singapore and Hong Kong: The Littlest Tigers

The smallest but by no means the least successful of the Little Tigers are Singapore and Hong Kong. Both are

South Korea: The Little Tiger with Sharp Teeth

South Korea today is one of the most competitive economies in the world. Its manufactures rival in popularity those of other East Asian nations for predominance in global markets. Japanese observers complain about the country's "hungry spirit," which steals jobs from Japanese workers. Some critics inside the country, however, worry that Koreans put too much emphasis on achieving success and that many children spend so much time preparing for college entrance examinations that they are deprived of a normal childhood. The recent effort by Lee Myung-bak (b. 1941), who served as president from 2008

© William J. Duiker

Mending the Safety Net in South Korea. Until recently, it was common for South Korean parents to live with their eldest son's family in their senior years, a practice that was viewed as a reward for their past sacrifices in raising their children. But with the country now transformed into an industrial and urbanized society, this social contract has eroded. As their children move into the cities, older Koreans are often left to fend for themselves in rural areas. Because the government has not yet established an adequate social security network, the elderly are often left in desperate straits. Shown here are a group of elderly women visiting a Buddhist shrine in Pusan.

essentially city-states with large populations densely packed into small territories. Singapore, once a British crown colony and briefly a part of the state of Malaysia, is now an independent nation. Hong Kong was a British colony until it was returned to PRC control, but with autonomous status, in 1997. In recent years, both have emerged as industrial powerhouses with standards of living well above the level of their neighbors.

The success of Singapore must be ascribed in good measure to the will and energy of its political leaders. When it became independent in August 1965, Singapore was in a state of transition. Its longtime position as an entrepôt for trade between the Indian Ocean and the South China Sea was declining in importance. With only 618 square miles of territory, much of it marshland and tropical jungle, Singapore had little to offer but the frugality and industriousness of its predominantly overseas Chinese population. But a recent history of political radicalism, fostered by the rise of influential labor unions, had frightened away foreign investors.

Within a decade, Singapore's role and reputation had dramatically changed. Under the leadership of Prime Minister Lee Kuan-yew (b. 1923), once the firebrand leader of the radical People's Action Party, the government encouraged the growth of an attractive business climate while engaging in massive public works projects to feed, house, and educate the nation's 2 million citizens. The major components of success have been shipbuilding, oil refineries, tourism, electronics, and finance—the city-state has become the banking hub of the entire region.

Like the other Little Tigers, Singapore has relied on a combination of government planning, entrepreneurial spirit, export promotion, high productivity, and an exceptionally high rate of saving to achieve industrial growth rates of nearly 10 percent annually during the last quarter of the twentieth century. Unlike some other industrializing countries in the region, it has encouraged multinational corporations to provide much needed capital and technological input. Population growth has been controlled by a stringent family planning program, and literacy rates are among the highest in Asia.

As in the other Little Tigers, an authoritarian political system has provided a stable environment for economic growth. Until his retirement in 1990, Lee Kuan-yew and his People's Action Party dominated Singaporean politics, and opposition elements were intimidated into silence or arrested. The prime minister openly declared

that the Western model of pluralist democracy was not appropriate for Singapore and lauded the Meiji model of centralized development. Confucian values of thrift, hard work, and obedience to authority have been promoted as the ideology of the state. The government has had a passion for cleanliness and at one time even undertook a campaign to persuade its citizens to flush the public urinals. In 1989, the local *Straits Times*, a government mouthpiece, published a photograph of a man walking sheepishly from a row of urinals. The caption read "Caught without a flush: Mr. Amar Mohamed leaving the Lucky Plaza toilet without flushing the urinal."[4]

But economic success is beginning to undermine the authoritarian foundations of the system as a more sophisticated citizenry begins to demand more political freedoms and an end to government paternalism. Lee Kuan-yew's successor, Goh Chok Tong (b. 1941), promised a "kinder, gentler" Singapore, and political restrictions on individual behavior are gradually being relaxed. In the spring of 2000, the government announced the opening of a speaker's corner, where citizens would be permitted to express their views, provided they obtained a permit and did not break the law. While this was a small step, it provided a reason for optimism that a more pluralistic political system will gradually emerge under the current prime minister, Lee Hsien-loong (b. 1952), the son of Lee Kuan-yew. After he assumed office in 2004, the government announced plans to relax restrictions on freedom of speech and assembly in the small island-state.

The future of Hong Kong is not so clear-cut. As in Singapore, sensible government policies and the hard work of its people have enabled Hong Kong to thrive. At first, the prosperity of the colony depended on a plentiful supply of cheap labor. Inundated with refugees from the mainland during the 1950s and 1960s, the population of Hong Kong burgeoned to more than 6 million. Many of the newcomers were willing to work for starvation wages in sweatshops producing textiles, simple appliances, and toys for the export market. More recently, Hong Kong has benefited from increased tourism, manufacturing, and the growing economic prosperity of neighboring Guangdong Province, the most prosperous region of the PRC. In one respect, Hong Kong has differed from the other societies discussed in this chapter in that it has relied on an unbridled free market system rather than active state intervention in the economy. At the same time, by allocating substantial funds for

The Republic of Singapore

transportation, sanitation, education, and public housing, the government has created favorable conditions for economic development.

Unlike the other Little Tigers, Hong Kong remained under colonial rule until very recently. British authorities did little to foster democratic institutions or practices, and most residents of the colony cared more about economic survival than political freedoms. In talks between representatives of Great Britain and the PRC, the Chinese leaders made it clear they were determined to have Hong Kong return to mainland authority in 1997, when the British ninety-nine-year lease over the New Territories, the food basket of the colony of Hong Kong, ran out. The British agreed, on condition that satisfactory arrangements could be made for the welfare of the population. The Chinese promised that for fifty years, the people of Hong Kong would live under a capitalist system and be essentially self-governing. Recent statements and actions by Chinese leaders, however, have raised questions about the degree of autonomy Hong Kong will receive under Chinese rule, which began on July 1, 1997 (see the box on p. 246). Opposition forces have been periodically harassed, and in 2012 the Hong Kong government, which normally reflects pressures from Beijing, sought to install new educational guidelines similar to those applied in China. Faced with severe public protests, local officials rescinded the order.

Hong Kong

On the Margins of Asia: Postwar Australia and New Zealand

Technically, Australia and New Zealand are not part of Asia, and throughout their short history, both countries have identified culturally and politically with the West rather than with their Asian neighbors. Their political institutions and values are derived from Europe, and their economies resemble those of the advanced countries of the world rather than the preindustrial societies of much of Southeast Asia. Both are currently members of the British Commonwealth and of the U.S.-led ANZUS (Australia, New Zealand, and the United States) alliance.

Yet trends in recent years have been drawing both states, especially Australia, closer to Asia. In the first place, immigration from East and Southeast Asia has increased rapidly. More than one-half of current immigrants to Australia come from East Asia, and about 7 percent of the population of about 18 million people is now of Asian descent. In New Zealand, residents of Asian descent represent only about 3 percent of the population of 3.5 million, but about 12 percent of the population are Maoris, Polynesian peoples who settled on the islands about a thousand years ago. Second, trade relations with Asia are increasing rapidly. About 60 percent of Australia's export markets today are in East Asia, and the region is the source of about one-half of its imports. Asian trade with New Zealand is also on the increase. Concern about China's rising strength in the region is cause for concern, however, and was undoubtedly a factor in the agreement reached in 2011 to station 2,500 U.S. troops in Australia.

The Hong Kong Skyline. Hong Kong reverted to Chinese sovereignty in 1997 after a century of British rule. To commemorate the occasion, the imposing Conference Center, shown here in the foreground, was built on reclaimed shoreland in the Hong Kong harbor.

Return to the Motherland

After lengthy negotiations, in 1984 China and Great Britain agreed that on July 1, 1997, Hong Kong would return to Chinese sovereignty. Key sections of the agreement are included here. In succeeding years, authorities of the two countries held further negotiations. Some of the discussions raised questions in the minds of residents of Hong Kong as to whether their individual liberties would indeed be respected after the colony's return to China.

The Joint Declaration on Hong Kong

The Hong Kong Special Administrative Region will be directly under the authority of the Central People's Government of the People's Republic of China. The Hong Kong Special Administrative Region will enjoy a high degree of autonomy, except in foreign and defense affairs, which are the responsibility of the Central People's Government.

The Hong Kong Special Administrative Region will be vested with executive, legislative, and independent judicial power, including that of final adjudication. The laws currently in force in Hong Kong will remain basically unchanged.

The Government of the Hong Kong Special Administrative Region will be composed of local inhabitants. The chief executive will be appointed by the Central People's Government on the basis of the results of elections or consultations by the chief executive of the Hong Kong Special Administrative Region for appointment by the Central People's Government. . . .

The current social and economic systems in Hong Kong will remain unchanged, and so will the lifestyle. Rights and freedoms, including those of the person, of speech, of the press, of assembly, of association, of travel, of movement, of correspondence, of strike, of choice of occupation, of academic research, and of religious belief will be ensured by law. . . . Private property, ownership of enterprises, legitimate right of inheritance, and foreign investment will be protected by law.

 To what degree are the people of Hong Kong self-governing under these regulations? How do the regulations infringe on the freedom of the population?

SOURCE: Kevin Rafferty, *City on the Rocks* (New York: Penguin, 1991).

CONCLUSION

WHAT EXPLAINS THE STRIKING ABILITY of Japan and the four Little Tigers to transform themselves into export-oriented societies capable of competing with the advanced nations of Europe and the Western Hemisphere? Some analysts point to the traditional character traits of Confucian societies, such as thrift, a work ethic, respect for education, and obedience to authority. In a recent poll of Asian executives, more than 80 percent expressed the belief that Asian values differ from those of the West, and most said that these values have contributed significantly to the region's recent success. Others placed more emphasis on deliberate steps taken by government and economic leaders to meet the political, economic, and social challenges their societies face.

There seems no reason to doubt that cultural factors connected to East Asian social traditions have contributed to the economic success of these societies. Certainly, habits such as frugality, industriousness, and subordination of individual desires have all played a role in their governments' ability to concentrate on the collective interest.

Political elites in these countries have been highly conscious of these factors and willing to use them for national purposes. Prime Minister Lee Kuan-yew of Singapore deliberately fostered the inculcation of such ideals among the citizens of his small nation and lamented the decline of Confucian values among the young.

As this chapters has shown, however, without active encouragement by political elites, such traditions cannot be effectively harnessed for the good of society as a whole. As we will see in Chapter 12, the creative talents of the Chinese people, for example, were not efficiently utilized under Mao Zedong during the frenetic years of the Cultural Revolution. Only when Deng Xiaoping and other pragmatists took charge and began to place a high priority on economic development were the stunning advances of recent decades achieved.

To some observers, economic growth in the region has sometimes been achieved at the cost of political freedom and individual human rights. Until recently, government repression of opposition has been common throughout East Asia except in Japan. In addition, the rights of national minorities and women are often still limited in comparison with the advanced countries of the West. Some commentators in the region take vigorous exception to such criticism and argue that pluralistic political systems could be very dangerous and destabilizing in the heterogeneous societies that currently exist in the region.

In any event, it should be kept in mind that progress in political pluralism and human rights has not always been easy to achieve in Europe and North America and even now frequently fails to match expectations. A rising standard of living, increased social mobility, and a changing regional environment brought about by the end of the Cold War should go far to enhance political freedoms and promote social justice in the countries bordering the western Pacific.

TIMELINE

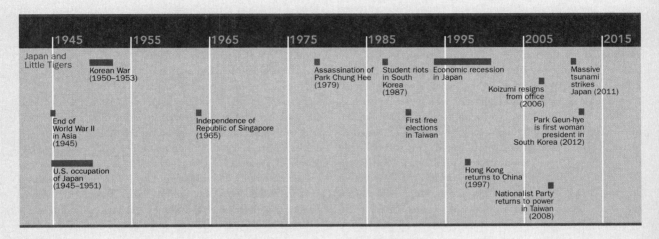

CHAPTER NOTES

1. Younger Japanese save only about 6 percent of their annual income, whereas their parents saved 25 percent. *Far Eastern Economic Review*, April 2005.

2. In 2003, only about 8 percent of managers in Japanese firms were women, compared with 46 percent in the United States. *New York Times*, July 25, 2003.

3. Yukio Mishima and Geoffrey Bownas, eds., *New Writing in Japan* (Harmondsworth, England, 1972), p. 16.

4. Stan Seser, "A Reporter at Large," *New Yorker*, January 13, 1992, p. 44.

AS WORLD WAR II CAME to an end, the survivors of that bloody struggle could afford to face the future with at least a measure of cautious optimism. With the death of Adolf Hitler in his bunker in Berlin, there were reasons to hope that the bitter rivalry that had marked relations among the Western powers would finally be put to an end and that the wartime alliance of the United States, Great Britain, and the Soviet Union could be maintained into the postwar era. In the meantime, the peoples of Asia and Africa could envision the possibility that the colonial system would soon end, ushering in a new era of political stability and economic development on a global scale.

These hopes have been only partly realized. In the decades following the war, the capitalist nations managed to recover from the extended economic depression that had

contributed to the start of World War II and advanced to a level of economic prosperity never before seen in world history. The bloody conflicts that had erupted among European nations during the first half of the twentieth century came to an end, and Germany and Japan were fully integrated into the world community. At the same time, the colonial era gradually came to a close, enabling newly independent nations in Africa and Asia to seek to regain control over their own destinies.

THE IRON CURTAIN DESCENDS The prospects for a stable, peaceful world and an end to balance-of-power politics, however, were dashed by the emergence of the grueling and sometimes tense ideological struggle between the socialist and capitalist blocs, a competition headed by the only remaining great powers, the Soviet Union and the United States. Although the two superpowers were able to avoid a nuclear confrontation, the postwar world was divided into two heavily armed camps in a balance of terror that on one occasion—the Cuban Missile Crisis—brought the world briefly to the brink of nuclear holocaust.

Europe again became divided into hostile camps as the Cold War rivalry between the United States and the Soviet Union forced the European nations to ally with one or the other of the superpowers. The creation of two mutually antagonistic military alliances—NATO in 1949 and the Warsaw Pact in 1955—confirmed the new division of Europe, while a divided Germany, and within it a divided Berlin, remained the Cold War's most visible symbols. Repeated crises over the status of Berlin only intensified the fears on both sides of the ideological divide.

In the midst of this rivalry, the Western European nations, with the assistance of the United States, made a remarkable economic recovery from the destruction of World War II and were able to strengthen and revitalize the democratic institutions and values that had been brutally swept aside during the years of Nazi occupation. In Eastern Europe, there were few reasons for optimism. Soviet domination, both political

and economic, had snuffed out the first stirrings of democracy in that region and seemed so complete that many doubted it could ever be undone. Although popular uprisings in Poland and Hungary in 1956 and in Czechoslovakia in 1968 were vivid reminders that a utopian society remained only a dream, communism appeared, at least for the time being, too powerful to be dislodged. The Helsinki Accords, signed in 1975, appeared to be a tacit admission by the West that the Iron Curtain had taken on a near-permanent status.

The confrontation between Washington and Moscow soon had repercussions throughout the world, for although the Cold War had begun in Europe, it soon spread to Asia as the Communist Party rose to power in China. By the mid-1950s, the bitter ideological rivalry between the two camps had taken on such a global character that events in such disparate areas as Southeast Asia, Central America, and the Middle East could send shock waves through world capitals everywhere. To most knowledgeable observers, the Cold War between the socialist and the capitalist blocs had become a permanent condition that was likely to affect the destiny of the human experiment for decades, if not generations, to come.

AND THE WALL CAME TUMBLING DOWN Nevertheless, in the late 1980s, the Soviet Union and its system of satellites abruptly collapsed, leading to the end of the multinational Soviet Empire and the emergence of a string of truly independent states in Eastern Europe. The

Communist Party in China managed to remain in power, but only by abandoning the key tenets of its longtime leader Mao Zedong and adopting major components of the capitalist system (see Chapter 12).

The sudden end of the Cold War spurred hopes for the emergence of a "new world order," marked by rising global prosperity and peaceful cooperation among nations. But it soon became clear that such optimistic expectations of an "end to history" (that is, an end to the rivalry and conflict among nations that had existed for centuries) were unjustified. The collapse of the Soviet system did not lead to a new era of peace, but instead unleashed long-dormant ethnic and religious forces in various parts of the world, producing a new round of civil conflicts and a rising level of terrorist activity reminiscent of the latter part of the nineteenth century. We shall explore the impact of these events in Part IV of this book. In the meantime, the Enlightenment belief in a coming age of technological achievement and human progress also came into question, as new challenges began to emerge within the ranks of the advanced capitalist nations themselves.

AFFLUENCE AND ITS DISCONTENTS In the advanced Western nations, as well as in Japan and a small number of other industrializing societies in Asia, the combination of domestic tranquillity and rapid economic growth brought an unprecedented level of prosperity to millions of people who were now able to enjoy the "good life" that had once been restricted to a small minority of the population. In the United States, the ability to "buy on the installment plan" or use a credit card made it possible for average Americans, for the first time, to spend well beyond their means. Soon other countries began to follow the American example, thereby laying the groundwork for a global network of material consumption.

By no means, however, did all residents of the advanced countries in the capitalist world share in the affluence of the last half of the twentieth century. Many lacked access to the cornucopia of goods produced by the capitalist machine. This was especially the case for members of minority groups and people who made a living by manual labor. Although political leaders sometimes tried to extend the benefits of affluence to their disadvantaged constituents, they had only limited success, and virtually all the advanced capitalist nations still had areas of poverty as the twentieth century came to an end.

The financial crisis that began in the fall of 2008 only widened the gap between rich and poor. Wages for middle-income and poorer workers have stagnated over the past few years, and unemployment has sometimes reached dangerous proportions. Even those currently living on a comfortable income worry that their prospects for retirement security may be threatened by the growing deficits run up in many of the advanced capitalist countries. The welfare state, many observers fear, may soon by a thing of the past.

Equally important, economic affluence has given rise to its own set of problems. The single-minded focus on the accumulation of material possessions, an intrinsic characteristic of the capitalist ethos, has helped to promote high levels of productivity in offices and factories, but at the same time it has produced a spiritual malaise among individual members of society, who increasingly ask whether life has any meaning and purpose beyond the sheer accumulation of things. While the spread of scientific knowledge has eroded religious belief in some sectors of society, it has caused others to question the value of science and to retreat into the certainties of faith.

At the same time, increasing social mobility has undermined the traditional basic structural units of human society—the family and the community. The individual feels increasingly cast off into the sea of life with no moorings. Modernity, as postwar society in the advanced countries is now commonly described, appears to have no answer to the search for meaning in life beyond an unconfirmed and complacent belief in the Enlightenment doctrine of progress. We shall examine some of these issues, and how they will affect the peoples of the world in the new millennium, in Part V of this book. ✸

PART IV

Third World Rising

Pudong district, Shanghai

William J. Duiker

The East Is Red: China Under Communism

Red Guards parade a victim wearing a dunce cap through the streets of Beijing during the Cultural Revolution.

"**A REVOLUTION IS NOT A DINNER PARTY**, or writing an essay, or painting a picture, or doing embroidery; it cannot be so refined, so leisurely and gentle, so temperate and kind, courteous, restrained, and magnanimous. A revolution is an insurrection, an act of violence by which one class overthrows another."[1] With these words—written in 1926, at a time when the Communists, in cooperation with Chiang Kai-shek's Nationalist Party, were embarked on their Northern Expedition to defeat the warlords and reunify China—the young revolutionary Mao Zedong warned his colleagues that the road to victory in the struggle to build a Communist society would be arduous and would inevitably involve acts of violence against the class enemy.

In the mid-1960s, more than fifteen years after the Communist seizure of power in China, Mao's words continued to resonate, as the country entered a new era of revolutionary violence, known as the Great Proletarian Cultural Revolution. For several years, legions of his supporters, many of them young activists known as Red Guards, scoured Chinese society for traitorous elements who supposedly opposed Mao's teachings by "following the capitalist road." The cataclysm, which led to the death or imprisonment of millions, did not end until Mao Zedong's death in 1976. ◆

CRITICAL THINKING

Q Why do you think communism has survived in China, when it failed to survive in the Soviet Union?

China Under Mao Zedong

The first signs were reassuring. In the fall of 1949, China was at peace for the first time in twelve years. The newly victorious Chinese Communist Party (CCP), under the leadership of its chairman, Mao Zedong, turned its attention to consolidating its power base and healing the wounds of war. Its long-term goal was to construct a socialist society, but its leaders realized that popular support for the revolution was based on the party's platform of honest government, land reform, social justice, and peace rather than on the utopian goal of a classless society. Accordingly, the new regime followed Soviet precedent in adopting a moderate program of political and economic recovery known as New Democracy.

New Democracy

Under **New Democracy**—patterned roughly after Lenin's New Economic Policy in Soviet Russia in the 1920s (see Chapter 4)—the capitalist system of ownership was retained in the industrial and commercial sectors. A program of land redistribution was adopted, but the collectivization of agriculture was postponed. Only after the CCP had consolidated its rule and brought a degree of prosperity to the national economy would the difficult transformation to a socialist society begin.

In following Soviet precedent, Chinese leaders tacitly recognized that time and extensive indoctrination would be needed to convince the Chinese people of the superiority of socialism. In the meantime, the party would rely on capitalist profit incentives to spur productivity. Manufacturing and commercial firms were permitted to remain in private hands, but they were placed under stringent government regulations and were encouraged to form "joint enterprises" with the government. To win the support of the poorer peasants, who made up the majority of the population, the land reform program that had long been in operation in "liberated areas" was now expanded throughout the country. This strategy was designed not only to win the gratitude of the rural masses but also to undermine the political and economic influence of counterrevolutionary elements still loyal to Chiang Kai-shek.

In some ways, New Democracy was a success. About two-thirds of the peasant households in the country received property under the land reform program and thus had reason to be grateful to the new regime. Spurred by official tolerance for capitalist activities and the end of the civil war, the national economy began to rebound, although agricultural production still lagged behind both official targets and the growing population, which was increasing at an annual rate of more than 2 percent. But the picture had a number of blemishes. In the course of carrying out land redistribution, thousands, if not millions, of landlords and rich farmers lost their lands, their personal property, their freedom, and sometimes their lives. Many of those who died had been tried and convicted of "crimes against the people" in tribunals set up in towns and villages around the country. As Mao himself later conceded, many were innocent of any crime, but in the eyes of the party, their deaths were necessary to destroy the power of the landed gentry in the countryside (see the box on p. 254). "You can't make an omelet," he remarked laconically, "without breaking eggs."

The Transition to Socialism

Originally, the CCP's leaders intended to follow the Leninist formula of delaying the building of a fully socialist society until China had a sufficient industrial base to permit the mechanization of agriculture. In 1953, they launched the nation's first five-year plan (patterned after earlier Soviet plans), which called for substantial increases in industrial output. Lenin had believed that the promise of mechanization would give Russian peasants an incentive to join collective farms, which, because of their greater size, could better afford to purchase expensive farm machinery. But the enormous challenge of providing tractors and reapers for millions of rural villages eventually convinced Mao Zedong and some of his colleagues that it would take years, if not decades, for China's infant industrial base to meet the burgeoning needs of a

modernizing agricultural sector. He therefore decided to begin collectivization immediately, in the hope that collective farms would increase food production and release land, labor, and capital for the industrial sector.

Accordingly, beginning in 1955, the Chinese government launched a new program to build a socialist society. Virtually all private farmland was collectivized, although peasant families were allowed to retain small plots for their private use (a Chinese version of the private plots adopted in the Soviet Union). In addition, most industry and commerce were nationalized.

Collectivization was achieved without arousing the massive peasant unrest that had occurred in the Soviet Union during the 1930s, perhaps because the Chinese government followed a policy of persuasion rather than compulsion (Mao remarked that Stalin had "drained the pond to catch the fish") and because the land reform program had already earned the support of millions of rural Chinese. But the hoped-for production increases did not materialize, and in 1958, at Mao's insistent urging, party leaders approved a more radical program known as the **Great Leap Forward**. Existing rural collectives, normally the size of a traditional village, were combined into vast "people's communes," each containing more than 30,000 people. These communes were to be responsible for all administrative and economic tasks at the local level. The party's official slogan promised "Hard work for a few years, happiness for a thousand."[2]

Mao hoped this program would mobilize the population for a massive effort to accelerate economic growth and ascend to the final stage of communism before the end of the twentieth century. It is better, he said, to "strike while the iron is hot" and advance the revolution without interruption. Some party members were concerned that this ambitious program would threaten the government's rural base of support, but Mao argued that Chinese peasants were naturally revolutionary in spirit:

> [The Chinese rural masses are] first of all, poor, and secondly, blank. That may seem like a bad thing, but it is really a good thing. Poor people want change, want to do things, want revolution. A clean sheet of paper has no blotches, and so the newest and most beautiful words can be written on it, the newest and most beautiful pictures can be painted on it.[3]

Those words, of course, were *socialism* and *communism*.

The Great Leap Forward was a disaster. Administrative bottlenecks, bad weather, and peasant resistance to the new system (which, among other things, attempted to eliminate work incentives and destroy the traditional family as the basic unit of Chinese society) combined to drive food production downward, and over the next few

Land Reform in Action

One of the great achievements of the new Communist regime was the land reform program, which succeeded in distributing farmland to almost two-thirds of the rural population in China. The program consequently won the gratitude of millions of Chinese and illustrates one of Mao Zedong's most effective propaganda techniques—the concept of "speak bitterness." Chinese peasants had historically "eaten their bitterness" (that is, suffered in silence) out of fear of retribution by powerful elements in their villages. By encouraging them to voice their anger, Mao hoped to enlist them through a "blood oath" in the service of the revolution. But the program also had a dark side as local land reform tribunals routinely convicted "wicked landlords" of crimes against the people and then put them to death. The following passage, written by a foreign observer, describes the process in one village.

Revolution in a Chinese Village

T'ien-ming [a CCP official] called all the active young cadres and the militiamen of Long Bow [village] together and announced to them the policy of the county government, which was to confront all enemy collaborators and their backers at public meetings, expose their crimes, and turn them over to the county authorities for punishment. He proposed that they start with Kuo Te-yu, the puppet village head. Having moved the group to anger with a description of Te-yu's crimes, T'ien-ming reviewed the painful life led by the poor peasants during the occupation and recalled how hard they had all worked and how as soon as they harvested all the grain the puppet officials, backed by army bayonets, took what they wanted, turned over huge quantities to the Japanese devils, forced the peasants to haul it away, and flogged those who refused.

As the silent crowd contracted toward the spot where the accused man stood, T'ien-ming stepped forward. . . . "This is our chance. Remember how we were oppressed. The traitors seized our property. They beat us and kicked us. . . ."

"Let us speak out the bitter memories. Let us see that the blood debt is repaid. . . . "

He paused for a moment. The peasants were listening to every word but gave no sign as to how they felt. . . .

"Come now, who has evidence against this man?"

Again there was silence.

Kuei-ts'ai, the new vice-chairman of the village, found it intolerable. He jumped up, struck Kuo Te-yu on the jaw with the back of his hand. "Tell the meeting how much you stole," he demanded.

The blow jarred the ragged crowd. It was as if an electric spark had tensed every muscle. Not in living memory had any peasant ever struck an official. . . .

The people in the square waited fascinated as if watching a play. They did not realize that in order for the plot to unfold they themselves had to mount the stage and speak out what was on their minds.

That evening T'ien-ming and Kuei-ts'ai called together the small groups of poor peasants from various parts of the village and sought to learn what it was that was really holding them back. They soon found the root of the trouble was fear of the old established political forces and their military backers. The old reluctance to move against the power of the gentry, the fear of ultimate defeat and terrible reprisal that had been seared into the consciousness of so many generations, lay like a cloud over the peasants' minds and hearts.

Emboldened by T'ien-ming's words, other peasants began to speak out. They recalled what Te-yu had done to them personally. Several vowed to speak up and accuse him the next morning. After the meeting broke up, the passage of time worked its own leaven. In many a hovel and tumble-down house talk continued well past midnight. Some people were so excited they did not sleep at all. . . .

On the following day the meeting was livelier by far. It began with a sharp argument as to who would make the first accusation, and T'ien-ming found it difficult to keep order. Before Te-yu had a chance to reply to any questions, a crowd of young men, among whom were several militiamen, surged forward ready to beat him.

 What was the Communist Party's main purpose in carrying out the land reform program in China? How did the tactics employed here support that strategy?

SOURCE: Richard Solomon, *Mao's Revolution and the Chinese Political Culture*, pages 198–199. Copyright © 1971 Center for Chinese Studies, University of Michigan.

years, as many as 15 million people may have died of starvation. Many peasants were reportedly reduced to eating the bark off trees and in some cases allowing infants to starve. In 1960, the commune experiment was essentially abandoned. Although the commune structure was retained, ownership and management were returned to the collective level. Mao was severely criticized by some of his more pragmatic colleagues (one remarked bitingly that "one cannot reach Heaven in a single step"), causing him to complain that he had been relegated to the sidelines "like a Buddha on a shelf."

The Great Proletarian Cultural Revolution

But Mao, still an imposing figure within the CCP, was not yet ready to abandon either his power or his dream of an egalitarian society. In 1966, he returned to the attack, mobilizing discontented youth and disgruntled party members into revolutionary units soon to be known as Red Guards who were urged to take to the streets to cleanse Chinese society—from local schools and factories to government ministries in Beijing—of impure elements who in Mao's mind were guilty of "taking the capitalist road." Supported by his wife, Jiang Qing (1914–1991), and other radical party figures, Mao launched China on a new forced march toward communism.

The so-called **Great Proletarian Cultural Revolution** lasted for ten years, from 1966 to 1976. Some Western observers interpreted it as a simple power struggle between Mao and some of his key rivals such as head of state Liu Shaoqi (1898–1969) and Deng Xiaoping (1904–1997), the party's general secretary. Both were removed from their positions, and Liu later died, allegedly of torture, in a Chinese prison. But real policy disagreements were involved. One reason Mao had advocated the Great Leap Forward was to bypass the party and government bureaucracy, which in his view had lost their revolutionary zeal and were primarily concerned with protecting their power. Now he and his supporters feared that capitalist values and the remnants of "feudalist" Confucian ideas and practices would undermine ideological fervor and betray the revolutionary cause. Mao himself was convinced that only an atmosphere of constant revolutionary fervor, or **uninterrupted revolution** as he called it, could enable the Chinese to overcome their past lethargy and achieve the final stage of utopian communism. "I care not," he once wrote, "that the winds blow and the waves beat. It is better than standing idly in a courtyard."

His opponents worried that Mao's "heaven-storming" approach could delay economic growth and antagonize the people. They argued for a more pragmatic strategy that would give priority to nation building over the ultimate Communist goal of spiritual transformation. But with Mao's supporters now in power, the CCP carried out vast economic and educational reforms that virtually eliminated any remaining profit incentives, established a new school system that emphasized "Mao Zedong thought," and stressed practical education at the elementary level at the expense of specialized training in science and the humanities in the universities. School learning was discouraged as a legacy of capitalism, and Mao's famous *Little Red Book* (a slim volume of Maoist aphorisms to encourage good behavior and revolutionary zeal) was hailed as the most important source of knowledge in all areas.

The radicals' efforts to destroy all vestiges of traditional society were reminiscent of the Reign of Terror in revolutionary France, when the Jacobins sought to destroy organized

Chairman Mao is the Red Sun in our Hearts, August 1969 (colour litho), Chinese School, (20th century)/Private Collection/© The Chambers Gallery, London/The Bridgeman Art Library

毛主席是我们心中的红太阳
（庆祝建国十七周年）
大型彩色文献纪录片　　　中央新闻纪录电影制片厂　　八一电影制片厂 联合摄制　　　中国电影发行放映公司发行

The Red Sun in Our Hearts. During the Great Proletarian Cultural Revolution, Chinese art was restricted to topics that promoted revolution and the thoughts of Chairman Mao Zedong. All the knowledge that the true revolutionary required was to be found in Mao's *Little Red Book*, a collection of his sayings on proper revolutionary behavior. In this painting, Chairman Mao's portrait hovers above a crowd of his admirers, who wave copies of the book as a symbol of their total devotion to him and his vision of a future China.

The Last Emperor (1987)

On November 14, 1908, the Chinese emperor Guangxu died in Beijing. One day later, Empress Dowager Cixi—the real power behind the throne—passed away as well. A three-year-old boy, to be known in history as Henry Puyi, ascended the throne. Four years later, the Qing dynasty collapsed, and the deposed monarch lived out the remainder of his life in a China lashed by political turmoil and violence. He finally died in 1967 at the height of the Great Proletarian Cultural Revolution.

The Last Emperor (1987), directed by the Italian filmmaker Bernardo Bertolucci and winner of nine Academy Awards, is a brilliant portrayal of the experience of one hapless individual in a nation caught up in the throes of a seemingly endless revolution. The film evokes the fading majesty of the last days of imperial China but also the chaos of the warlord era and the terrors of the Maoist period, when the last shreds of the ex-emperor's personality were shattered under the pressure of Communist brainwashing techniques. The film's portrayal of the regime's thought reform program provides a frightening example of how Mao and his colleagues obtained compliance from Chinese

Three-year-old Puyi (Richard Vuu), the last emperor of China, watches an emissary approach at the Imperial Palace.

citizens for their revolutionary objectives. Puyi (John Lone), who never appears to grasp what is happening to his country, lives and dies a nonentity.

The film, based on Puyi's autobiography, benefits from having been filmed partly on site in the Imperial City. In addition to the Chinese American actors John Lone and Joan Chen, the cast includes the veteran film star Peter O'Toole, who plays Puyi's tutor when he was an adolescent. ∎

religion and even created a new revolutionary calendar to replace the traditional Christian system. Red Guards rampaged through the country attempting to eradicate the "four olds" (old thought, old culture, old customs, and old habits). They destroyed temples and religious sculptures; they tore down street signs and replaced them with new ones carrying revolutionary names. At one point, the city of Shanghai even ordered that the significance of colors in stoplights be changed so that red (the revolutionary color) would indicate that traffic could move.

But a mood of revolutionary enthusiasm is difficult to sustain. Key groups, including party bureaucrats, urban professionals, and many military officers, did not share Mao's belief in the benefits of uninterrupted revolution

and constant turmoil. Many were alienated by the arbitrary actions of the Red Guards, who indiscriminately accused and brutalized their victims in a society where legal safeguards had almost entirely vanished (see the Film & History feature above). Whether the Cultural Revolution led to declining productivity is a matter of debate. Inevitably, however, the sense of anarchy and uncertainty caused popular support for the movement to erode, and when the end came with Mao's death in 1976, the vast majority of the population may well have welcomed its demise.

Personal accounts by young Chinese who took part in the Cultural Revolution show that their initial enthusiasm often turned to disillusionment. In *Son of the Revolution*,

Liang Heng tells how at first he helped friends organize Red Guard groups: "I thought it was a great idea. We would be following Chairman Mao just like the grown-ups, and Father would be proud of me. I suppose I too resented the teachers who had controlled and criticized me for so long, and I looked forward to a little revenge."[4] Later, he had reason to repent. His sister ran off to join the local Red Guard group. Prior to her departure, she denounced her mother and the rest of her family as "rightists" and enemies of the revolution. The family home was regularly raided by Red Guards, and their father was severely beaten and tortured for having three neckties and "Western shirts." Books, paintings, and writings were piled in the center of the floor and burned before his eyes. On leaving, a few of the Red Guards helped themselves to his monthly salary and his transistor radio.

From Mao to Deng

In September 1976, Mao Zedong died at the age of eighty-three. After a short but bitter succession struggle, the pragmatists led by Deng Xiaoping seized power from the radicals and brought the Cultural Revolution to an end. Mao's widow, Jiang Qing, and three other radicals (derisively called the "Gang of Four" by their opponents) were put on trial and sentenced to death or to long terms in prison. The egalitarian policies of the previous decade were reversed, and a new program emphasizing economic modernization was introduced.

The Four Modernizations

Under the leadership of Deng, who installed his supporters in key positions throughout the party and the government, attention focused on what were called the **Four Modernizations**: industry, agriculture, technology, and national defense. Deng had been a leader of the faction that opposed Mao's program of rapid socialist transformation, and during the Cultural Revolution, he had been forced to perform menial labor to "sincerely correct his errors." But Deng continued to espouse the pragmatic approach and reportedly once remarked, "Black cat, white cat, what does it matter so long as it catches the mice?" Under the program of Four Modernizations, many of the restrictions against private activities and profit incentives were eliminated, and people were encouraged to work hard to benefit themselves and Chinese society. The government popularized the idea that all Chinese would prosper, although not necessarily at the same speed. Familiar slogans such as "Serve the people" and "Uphold the banner of Marxist-Leninist-Maoist thought" were replaced by new ones repugnant to the

tenets of Mao Zedong thought: "Create wealth for the people" and "Time is money." The party announced that China was still at the "primary stage of socialism" and might not reach the state of utopian communism for generations.

Crucial to the program's success was the government's ability to attract foreign technology and capital. For more than two decades, China had been isolated from technological advances taking place elsewhere in the world. Although China's leaders understandably prided themselves on their nation's capacity for "self-reliance," their isolationist policy had been exceedingly costly for the national economy. China's post-Mao leaders blamed the country's backwardness on the "ten lost years" of the Cultural Revolution, but the "lost years," at least in technological terms, extended back to 1949 and in some respects even before. Now, to make up for lost time, the government encouraged foreign investment and sent thousands of students and specialists abroad to study capitalist techniques.

By adopting this pragmatic approach in the years after 1976, China made great strides in ending its chronic problems of poverty and underdevelopment. Per capita income roughly doubled during the 1980s; housing, education, and sanitation improved; and both agricultural and industrial output skyrocketed. Clearly, China had begun to enter the Industrial Age.

But critics, both Chinese and foreign, complained that Deng Xiaoping's program had failed to achieve a "fifth modernization": democracy. Official sources denied such charges and spoke proudly of restoring "socialist legality" by doing away with the arbitrary punishments applied during the Cultural Revolution. Deng himself encouraged the Chinese people to speak out against earlier excesses. In the late 1970s, ordinary citizens began to paste posters criticizing the abuses of the past on the so-called Democracy Wall near Tiananmen Square in downtown Beijing.

Yet it soon became clear that the new leaders would not tolerate any direct criticism of the CCP or of Marxist-Leninist ideology. Dissidents were suppressed, and some were sentenced to long prison terms. Among them was the well-known astrophysicist Fang Lizhi, who spoke out publicly against official corruption and the continuing influence of Marxist-Leninist concepts in post-Mao China, telling an audience in Hong Kong that "China will not be able to modernize if it does not break the shackles of Maoist and Stalinist-style socialism." Fang immediately felt the weight of official displeasure. He was refused permission to travel abroad, and articles that he submitted to official periodicals were rejected.

The problem began to intensify in the late 1980s, as more Chinese began to study abroad and more information about Western society reached educated individuals inside the country. Rising expectations aroused by the economic improvements of the early 1980s led to increasing pressure from students and other urban residents for better living conditions, relaxed restrictions on study abroad, and increased freedom to select employment after graduation.

Incident at Tiananmen Square

As long as economic conditions for the majority of Chinese were improving, other classes did not share the students' discontent, and the government was able to isolate them from other elements in society. But in the late 1980s, an overheated economy led to rising inflation and growing discontent among salaried workers, especially in the cities. At the same time, corruption, nepotism, and favored treatment for senior officials and party members were provoking increasing criticism. In May 1989, student protesters carried placards demanding Science and Democracy (reminiscent of the slogan of the May Fourth Movement, whose seventieth anniversary was celebrated in the spring of 1989), an end to official corruption, and the resignation of China's aging party leadership. These demands received widespread support from the urban population and led to massive protests in Tiananmen Square.

The demonstrations in Beijing and other major cities were greeted with less enthusiasm in rural areas, where economic conditions had been steadily improving during the 1980s and where memories of the disruptive era of the Great Proletarian Cultural Revolution were still strong. In my own travels through central China during the Tiananmen crisis, I encountered much enthusiasm for the protest movement among urban young people, but many older Chinese reacted to the events with unease or even with disdain. Several remarked to me that the student protests reminded them of the unruly behavior of the Red Guards twenty years previously, and some declared that it was the responsibility of young Chinese to remain in school. The legacy of the Cultural Revolution may be one reason why many Chinese today continue to prize social stability over individual freedom.

The demonstrations divided the Chinese leaders. Reformist elements around party general secretary Zhao Ziyang were sympathetic to the protesters, but veteran leaders such as Deng saw the students' demands for more democracy as a disguised call for an end to the CCP's rule (see the box on p. 259). After some hesitation, the government sent tanks and troops into Tiananmen Square to crush the demonstrators. Dissidents were arrested, and the regime once again began to stress ideological purity and socialist values. Although the crackdown provoked widespread criticism abroad, Chinese leaders insisted that economic reforms could only take place in conditions of party leadership and political stability.

Deng and other aging party leaders turned to the army to protect their base of power and suppress what they described as "counterrevolutionary elements." Deng was undoubtedly counting on the fact that many Chinese, particularly in rural areas, feared a recurrence of the disorder of the Cultural Revolution and craved economic prosperity more than political reform. In the months following the confrontation, the government issued new regulations requiring courses on Marxist-Leninist ideology in the schools, winnowed out dissidents in the intellectual community, and made it clear that while economic reforms would continue, the CCP's monopoly of power would not be allowed to decay. Harsh punishments were imposed on those accused of undermining the Communist system and supporting its enemies abroad.

Back to Confucius?

In the 1990s, the Chinese government began to nurture urban support by reducing the rate of inflation and guaranteeing the availability of consumer goods in great demand among the rising middle class. Under Deng Xiaoping's successor, Jiang Zemin (b. 1926), who occupied the positions of both party chief and president of China, the government promoted rapid economic growth while cracking down harshly on political dissent. That policy paid dividends in bringing about a perceptible decline in alienation among the residents of the cities. Industrial production continued to increase rapidly, leading to predictions that China would become one of the economic superpowers of the twenty-first century. But discontent in rural areas began to grow, as lagging farm income, high taxes, and official corruption sparked resentment in the countryside.

Partly out of fear that such developments could undermine the socialist system and the rule of the CCP, conservative leaders attempted to curb Western influence and restore faith in Marxism-Leninism. In what may have been a tacit recognition that Marxist exhortations were no longer an effective means of enforcing social discipline, the party sought to make use of Confucianism. Ceremonies celebrating the birth of Confucius now received official sanction, and the virtues promoted by the Master, such as righteousness, propriety, and filial piety, were widely cited as an antidote to the tide of antisocial behavior. As a further indication of its willingness to employ traditional themes to further its national interest, the Chinese government has begun to sponsor the establishment of Confucian centers in countries around the world to promote its view that Confucian humanism is destined to replace traditional religious faiths in coming decades.

In effect, Chinese leaders have tacitly conceded that Marxism is increasingly irrelevant to today's China, which

Students Appeal for Democracy

In the spring of 1989, thousands of students gathered in Tiananmen Square in downtown Beijing to provide moral support to their many compatriots who had gone on a hunger strike in an effort to compel the Chinese government to reduce the level of official corruption and enact democratic reforms, opening the political process to the Chinese people. The first selection is from an editorial published on April 26 by the official newspaper *People's Daily*. Fearing that the student demonstrations would get out of hand, as had happened during the Cultural Revolution, the editorial condemned the protests for being contrary to the Communist Party. On May 17, student leaders distributed flyers explaining the goals of the movement to participants and passersby, including the author of this text. The second selection is from one of these flyers.

Student protesters gather in Tiananmen Square in May 1989.

People's Daily Editorial, April 26, 1989

This is a well-planned plot . . . to confuse the people and throw the country into turmoil. . . . Its real aim is to reject the Chinese Communist Party and the socialist system at the most fundamental level. . . . This is a most serous political struggle that concerns the whole Party and nation.

"Why Do We Have to Undergo a Hunger Strike?"

By 2:00 P.M. today, the hunger strike carried out by the petition group in Tiananmen Square has been under way for 96 hours. By this morning, more than 600 participants have fainted. When these democracy fighters were lifted into the ambulances, no one who was present was not moved to tears.

Our petition group now undergoing the hunger strike demands that at a minimum the government agree to the following two points:

1. To engage on a sincere and equal basis in a dialogue with the "higher education dialogue group." In addition, to broadcast the actual dialogue in its entirety. We absolutely refuse to agree to a partial broadcast, to empty gestures, or to fabrications that dupe the people.

2. To evaluate in a fair and realistic way the patriotic democratic movement. Discard the label of "trouble-making" and redress the reputation of the patriotic democratic movement.

It is our view that the request for a dialogue between the people's government and the people is not an unreasonable one. Our party always follows the principle of seeking truths from actual facts. It is therefore only natural that the evaluation of this patriotic democratic movement should be done in accordance with the principle of seeking truths from actual facts.

Our classmates who are going through the hunger strike are the good sons and daughters of the people! One by one, they have fallen. In the meantime, our "public servants" are completely unmoved. Please, let us ask where your conscience is.

 What were the key demands of the protesters in Tiananmen Square? Were they approved by the Chinese government?

SOURCES: "People's Daily" Editorial from *People's Daily* Editorial, April 26, 1989; from a flyer in the archives of William J. Duiker.

responds much more forcefully to the siren call of nationalism. In a striking departure from the precepts of Marxist internationalism, official sources in Beijing cite Confucian tradition to support their assertion that China is unique and will not follow the path of "peaceful evolution" (to use their term) toward a future democratic capitalist society.

That attitude is also reflected in foreign policy, as China is playing an increasingly active role in the region. To some of its neighbors, including Japan, India, and Russia, China's new posture is disquieting and raises suspicions that China is once again preparing to flex its muscle as it did in the imperial era. The first example of this new attitude took place as early as 1979, when Chinese forces briefly invaded Vietnam as punishment for the Vietnamese occupation of neighboring Cambodia. More recently, China has aroused concern in the region by claiming sole ownership over the Spratly Islands in the South China Sea and over the Diaoyu Islands (also claimed by Japan, which calls them the Senkakus) near Taiwan (see Map 12.1). Although seldom mentioned, the substantial oil reserves in the waters around these archipelagoes are a significant factor in the dispute.

To Chinese leaders, who in other circumstances maintain that China does not represent a threat to its neighbors, such actions represent legitimate efforts to resume the country's rightful role in the affairs of the region. After a century of humiliation at the hands of the Western powers and neighboring Japan, the nation, in Mao's famous words of 1949, "has stood up," and no one will be permitted to humiliate it again. For the moment, at least, a fervent patriotism seems to be on the rise in China, actively promoted by the party as a means of holding the country together. The decision by the International Olympic Committee to award the 2008 Summer Games to Beijing led to widespread celebrations throughout the country. The event symbolized China's emergence as a major national power on the world stage.

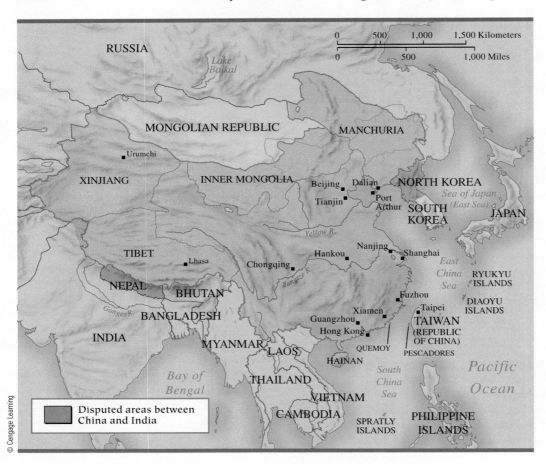

MAP 12.1 The People's Republic of China. This map shows China's current boundaries. Major regions are indicated in capital letters.

Q *In which regions are there movements against Chinese rule?*

Pumping up the spirit of patriotism, however, is not the solution to all problems. Unrest is growing among China's national minorities: in Xinjiang, where restless Muslim peoples are observing with curiosity the emergence of independent Islamic states in Central Asia, and in Tibet, where the official policy of quelling separatist sentiment has led to the violent suppression of Tibetan culture and an influx of thousands of ethnic Chinese immigrants. In the meantime, the growing popularity of organized religion, including both Christianity and indigenous faiths, is an additional indication that with the disintegration of the old Maoist utopia, the Chinese people will need more than a pallid version of Marxism-Leninism or a revived Confucianism to fill the gap.

Whether the current leadership will be able to prevent further erosion of the party's power and prestige is unclear. In the short term, efforts to slow the process of change may succeed because many Chinese are understandably fearful of punishment and concerned for their careers. And high economic growth rates can sometimes obscure a multitude of problems as many individuals will opt to chase the fruits of materialism rather than the less tangible benefits of personal freedom. But in the long run, the party leadership must resolve the contradiction between political authoritarianism and economic prosperity.

New leaders installed in 2002 and 2003 appeared aware of the magnitude of the problem. Hu Jintao (b. 1943), who replaced Jiang Zemin as CCP general secretary and head of state, called for further reforms to open up Chinese society, reduce the level of corruption, and bridge the yawning gap between rich and poor. In recent years, the government has shown a growing tolerance for the public exchange of ideas, which has surfaced with the proliferation of bookstores, avant-garde theater, experimental art exhibits, and the Internet. In 2005, an estimated 27 percent of all Chinese citizens possessed a cellphone, and the number has increased dramatically since then. Today, despite the government's efforts to restrict access to certain websites, more people are "surfing the Net" in China than in any other country on earth. The Internet is wildly popular with those under thirty, who use it for online games, downloading videos and music, and instant messaging. It also provides a forum for dissidents to voice their views and enables countless ordinary people to post information on incidents and issues that official sources wish to suppress. Party leaders, in short, no longer control access to what is taking place inside China and in the world at large. The potential impact of this new reality is enormous.

The party leadership is aware of the challenge and is seeking to rise to the occasion. At the CCP's Seventeenth National Congress in October 2007, President Hu emphasized the importance of adopting a "scientific view of development," a vague concept calling for social harmony, improved material prosperity, and a reduction in the growing income gap between rich and poor in Chinese society. But he insisted that the Communist Party must remain the sole political force in charge of carrying out the revolution. Ever fearful of chaos, party leaders are convinced that only a firm hand at the tiller can keep the ship of state from crashing onto the rocks.

But will the guiding hand remain firm? When party elders gathered in the fall of 2012 to select a new slate of leaders for the next decade, signs of division had begun to appear in the form of a neo-leftist challenge led by Sichuan party chief Bo Xilai. Although he was removed from office on a charge of corruption and disloyalty, the underlying issues have not yet been resolved, and the new president Xi Jinping (b. 1953) takes office at a time when party unity can no longer be viewed as a fait accompli.

Serve the People: Chinese Society Under Communism

Enormous changes took place in Chinese society after the Communist rise to power in 1949. Yet beneath the surface of rapid change were tantalizing hints of the survival of elements of the old China. Despite all the efforts of Mao Zedong and his colleagues, the ideas of "Confucius and sons" had still not been irrevocably discarded. China under communism remained a society that was still in many respects enthralled by its past.

The Politics of the Mass Line

Nowhere was this uneasy balance between the old and the new more clearly demonstrated than in politics and government. In its broad outlines, the new political system followed the Soviet pattern. Yet from the start, CCP leaders made it clear that the Chinese model would differ from the Soviet in important respects. Whereas the Bolsheviks had severely distrusted nonrevolutionary elements in Russia and established a minority government based on the radical left, Mao and his colleagues were more confident that they possessed the basic support of the majority of the Chinese people. Under New Democracy, the party attempted to reach out to all progressive classes in the population to maintain the alliance that had brought it to power in the first place.

The primary link between the regime and the population was the system of "mass organizations," representing peasants, workers, women, religious groups, writers, and artists. The party had established these associations during the 1920s to mobilize support for the revolution. Now they served as a conduit between party and people, enabling the leaders to assess the attitude of the masses while at the same time seeking their support for the party's programs. Behind this facade of representative institutions stood the awesome power of the CCP.

Initially, this "mass line" system worked fairly well. Although opposition to the regime was ruthlessly suppressed and there was no pretense at Western-style democracy, China finally had a government that appeared to be "for the people." Corrupt officials and bureaucratic mismanagement and arrogance had by no means been entirely eliminated, but the new ruling class came preponderantly from the workers and peasants and was more willing than its predecessors to listen to the complaints and aspirations of its constituents.

But the adoption of the Great Leap Forward betrayed a fundamental weakness in the policy of the mass line. While declaring his willingness to listen to the concerns of the population, Mao was also determined to build a utopian society based on Marxist-Leninist principles. Popular acceptance of nationalization and collectivization during the mid-1950s indicates that the Chinese people were not entirely hostile to socialism, but when those programs were carried to an extreme during the Great Leap Forward, many Chinese, even within the party, resisted and forced the government to abandon the program.

The failure of the Great Leap Forward split the CCP and led to the revolutionary disturbances of the following decade. Some of Mao's associates had opposed his radical approach and now sought to adopt a more cautious road to nation building. To Mao, such views were a betrayal of the party's revolutionary principles. The Cultural Revolution, which he launched in 1966, can be seen above all as his attempt to cleanse the system of its impurities and put Chinese society back on the straight road to egalitarian communism.

Many of his compatriots evidently shared his beliefs. Young people in particular, alienated by the lack of job opportunities, flocked to his cause and served with enthusiasm in the Red Guard organizations that became the shock troops of the revolution. But the enthusiasms aroused by the Cultural Revolution did not last, and a period of reaction inevitably set in. In China, revolutionary fervor gave way to a new era in which belief in socialist ideals was replaced by a more practical desire for material benefits.

Economics in Command

Deng Xiaoping recognized the need to restore a sense of "socialist legality" and credibility to a system that was on the verge of breakdown and hoped that rapid economic growth would satisfy the Chinese people and prevent them from demanding political reforms. The post-Mao leaders demonstrated a willingness to emphasize economic performance over ideological purity. To stimulate the stagnant industrial sector, which had been under state control since the end of the era of New Democracy, they reduced bureaucratic controls over state industries and allowed local managers to have more say over prices, salaries, and quality control. Productivity was encouraged by permitting bonuses to be paid for extra effort, a policy that had been discouraged during the Cultural Revolution. State firms were no longer guaranteed access to precious resources and were told to compete with each other for public favor and even to export goods on their own initiative. The regime also tolerated the emergence of a small private sector. Unemployed youth were encouraged to set up restaurants, bicycle or radio repair shops, and handicraft shops on their own initiative. At first, such enterprises were legally limited to seven

Creeping Capitalism in a Socialist Paradise. In the late 1970s, the Communist government in Beijing began to encourage its citizens to engage in limited private activities as a means of reviving the moribund Chinese economy. The Chinese people, who had suffered through decades of material scarcity, took up the challenge with enthusiasm, as the smile on the face of this woman—who is selling her dumplings to passersby in Shandong province—vividly attests. Her padded coat and cloth shoes were typical attire for most Chinese during the early years of economic rebound.

employees—to prevent exploitation—but eventually the restrictions were relaxed.

Finally, the regime opened up the country to foreign investment and technology. The Maoist policy of self-reliance was abandoned, and China openly sought the advice of foreign experts and the money of foreign capitalists. Special economic zones were established in urban centers near the coast (ironically, many were located in the old nineteenth-century treaty ports), where lucrative concessions were offered to encourage foreign firms to build factories. The tourist industry was encouraged, and students were sent abroad to study.

The new leaders especially stressed educational reform. The system adopted during the Cultural Revolution, emphasizing practical education and ideology at the expense of higher education and modern science, was rapidly abandoned (Mao's *Little Red Book* was even withdrawn from circulation and could no longer be found on bookshelves), and a new system based generally on the Western model was instituted. Admission to higher education was based on success in merit examinations, and courses on science and mathematics received high priority.

AGRICULTURAL REFORM No economic reform program could succeed unless it included the countryside. Three decades of socialism had done little to increase food production or to lay the basis for a modern agricultural

sector. China, with a population numbering one billion in the mid-1970s, could still barely feed itself. Peasants had little incentive to work and few opportunities to increase production through mechanization, the use of fertilizer, or better irrigation.

Under Deng Xiaoping, agricultural policy made a rapid about-face. Under the new **rural responsibility system**, adopted shortly after Deng had consolidated his authority, collectives leased land on contract to peasant families, who paid a quota as rent to the collective. Anything produced on the land above that payment could be sold on the private market or consumed. To soak up excess labor in the villages, the government encouraged the formation of so-called sideline industries, a modern equivalent of the traditional cottage industries in premodern China. Peasants raised fish or shrimp, made consumer goods, and even assembled living room furniture and appliances to sell to their newly affluent compatriots.

The reform program had a striking effect on rural production. Grain production increased rapidly, and farm income doubled during the 1980s. Yet it also created problems. In the first place, income at the village level became more unequal as some enterprising farmers (known locally as "ten thousand dollar" households) earned profits several times those realized by their less fortunate or less industrious neighbors. When some farmers discovered they could earn more by growing cash crops or other

The Three Gorges Dam. The damming of the Yangtze River over the past two decades is one of the most massive and ambitious construction projects in human history. Designed to increase the amount of farmland in the Yangtze River valley and enable precious water resources to be redistributed to drought-prone regions of the country, the project has also caused considerable environmental damage throughout the Yangtze River valley and displaced several million Chinese from their ancestral homes. Shown here is the famous Three Gorges Dam at Yichang, a modern wonder of the world.

AP Images/Xinhua Photo, Xia Lin

specialized commodities, they devoted less land to rice and other grain crops, thereby threatening to reduce the supply of China's most crucial staple. Finally, the agricultural policy threatened to undermine the government's population control program, which party leaders viewed as crucial to the success of the Four Modernizations.

THE POPULATION CONTROL PROGRAM Since a misguided period in the mid-1950s when Mao had argued that more laborers would result in higher productivity, China had been attempting to limit the growth of its population, which chronically threatened to outstrip the country's food supply. By 1970, the government had launched a stringent family planning program—including education, incentives, and penalties for noncompliance—to persuade the Chinese people to limit themselves to one child per family. The program did have some success, and the rate of population growth was drastically reduced in the early 1980s. The rural responsibility system, however, undermined the program because it encouraged farm families to pay the penalties for having additional children in the belief that their labor would increase the family income and provide the parents with greater security in their old age. Eventually, the program was relaxed, and rural families were legally permitted to have a second child if the first child was a girl. Nevertheless, the basic program continued, and in 2008 the regime announced that it would remain in force for at least another decade. By that time, China's population, estimated at about 1.3 billion in 2012, was projected to begin to decline.

Evaluating the Four Modernizations

The overall effects of the modernization program have been impressive. The standard of living improved for the majority of the population. Whereas a decade earlier, the average Chinese had struggled to earn enough to buy a bicycle, radio, watch, or washing machine, by the late 1980s, many were able to purchase videocassette recorders, refrigerators, and color television sets. Yet the rapid growth of the economy created its own problems: inflationary pressures, greed, envy, increased corruption, and—most dangerous of all for the regime—rising expectations. Young people in particular resented restrictions on employment (most young people in China were still required to accept the jobs that are offered to them by the government or school officials) and opportunities to study abroad. Disillusionment ran high, especially in the cities, where lavish living by officials and rising prices for goods aroused widespread alienation and cynicism and laid the groundwork for the massive protest demonstrations in 1989.

During the 1990s, growth rates in the industrial sector continued to be high as domestic capital became increasingly available to compete with the growing presence of foreign enterprises. The government finally recognized the need to close down inefficient state enterprises, and by the end of the decade, the private sector, with official encouragement, accounted for more than 10 percent of the nation's gross domestic product. A stock market opened, and with the country's entrance into the World Trade Organization (WTO) in 2001, China's prowess in the international marketplace improved dramatically.

Today, China has the second-largest economy in the world and is the largest exporter of goods. It possesses a large and increasingly affluent middle class and a burgeoning domestic market for consumer goods. More than 80 percent of all urban Chinese, who now number almost half the population, own a color television set, a refrigerator, and a washing machine. One-third own their homes, and nearly as many have an air conditioner. For the more affluent, a private automobile is increasingly a possibility, and in 2010, more vehicles were sold in China than in the United States. Even the global economic crisis that struck the world in the fall of 2008 did not derail the Chinese juggernaut, which quickly recovered from the sudden drop in demand for Chinese goods in countries still suffering from the economic downturn.

THE COSTS OF ECONOMIC GROWTH But as Chinese leaders have discovered, rapid economic change never comes without cost. The closing of state-run factories led to the dismissal of millions of workers each year, and the private sector, although growing at more than 20 percent annually, initially struggled to absorb them. Poor working conditions and low salaries in Chinese factories resulted in periodic outbreaks of labor unrest. Demographic conditions, however, are changing. The reduction in birthrates since the 1980s is creating a labor shortage, which is putting upward pressure on workers' salaries. As a result, China is facing inflation in the marketplace and increased competition from exports produced by factories located in lower-wage countries in South and Southeast Asia.

Discontent has also been increasing in the countryside, where farmers earn only about half as much as their urban counterparts (the government tried to increase the official purchase price for grain but rescinded the order when it became too expensive). China's entry into the World Trade Organization was greeted with great optimism but has been of little benefit to farmers facing the challenges of cheap foreign imports. Taxes and local corruption add to their complaints, and land seizures by the government or by local officials are a major source of anger in rural communities. In desperation, millions of rural

Silk Workers of the World, Unite! In recent years, many critics have charged that Chinese factories are able to market their goods at cheap prices abroad because their employees are paid low wages and often must work in abysmal conditions. The silk industry, which produces one of China's key high-end exports, is a case in point. At this factory in Wuxi, women workers spend ten-hour days with their hands immersed in boiling water as they unwind filaments from cocoons onto a spool of silk yarn. Their blistered red hands testify to the difficulty of their painful task.

Chinese have left for the big cities, where many of them are unable to find steady employment and are forced to live in squalid conditions in crowded tenements or in the sprawling suburbs. Millions of others remain on their farms and attempt to augment their income by producing for the market or, despite the risk of stringent penalties, by increasing the size of their families. A new land reform law passed in 2008 authorizes farmers to lease or transfer land use rights, although in principle all land in rural areas belongs to the local government.

AN ENVIRONMENTAL TIME BOMB Another factor hindering China's rush to economic advancement is the impact on the environment. With the rising population, fertile land is in increasingly short supply (China's population has doubled since 1950, but only two-thirds as much irrigable land is available). Soil erosion is a major problem, especially in the north, where the desert is encroaching on farmlands. Water is also a problem. An ambitious plan to transport water by canals from the Yangtze River to the more arid northern provinces has run into a number of roadblocks. Another massive project to construct dams on the Yangtze River has sparked protests from environmentalists, as well as from local peoples forced to migrate from the area (see the photo on p. 263). Air pollution is ten times the level in the United States, contributing to growing health concerns. To add to the challenge, more than 700,000 new cars and trucks appear on the country's roads each year. To reduce congestion on roadways, China is constructing an extensive rail network for high-speed bullet trains that will connect all the major regions in the country.

Chinese Society in Flux

At the root of Marxist-Leninist ideology is the idea of building a new citizen free from the prejudices, ignorance, and superstition of the "feudal" era and the capitalist desire for self-gratification. This new citizen would be characterized not only by a sense of racial and sexual equality but also by a selfless desire to contribute his or her utmost for the good of all. In the words of Mao Zedong's famous work "The Foolish Old Man Who Removed the Mountains," the people should "be resolute, fear no sacrifice, and surmount every difficulty to win victory."[5]

OUT WITH THE OLD, IN WITH THE NEW! For Mao and his colleagues, the first order of business was to remake Chinese society as a means of creating the new citizen. Like the progressive intellectuals of the New Culture movement a generation previously, the leaders of the new regime believed that old values, old attitudes, and old customs were the foremost obstacle to their ambitious political objectives. At the root of the problem, in their view, was the time-honored Confucian emphasis on the family, headed by the patriarch, as the key component in Chinese society. To the Communists, loyalty to the family, a crucial element in the Confucian social order, undercut loyalty to the state and to the dictatorship of the proletariat. Thus, their long-run objective was to destroy the influence of the traditional family system (see the box on p. 266).

During the early 1950s, they took a number of steps to bring a definitive end to the old system in China. Women were permitted to vote and encouraged to become active in the political process. At the local level, an increasing number of women became active in the CCP and in collective organizations. In 1950, a new marriage law guaranteed women equal rights with men. Most important, perhaps, it permitted women for the first time to initiate divorce proceedings against their husbands. Within a year, nearly one million divorces had been granted.

At the same time, however, the government moved carefully at first on other family issues to avoid alienating its supporters in the countryside unnecessarily. When collective farms were established in the mid-1950s, each member

Love and Marriage in China

"What men can do, women can also do." So said Chairman Mao as he "liberated" and masculinized Chinese women to work alongside men. Women's individuality and sexuality were sacrificed for the collective good of his new socialist society. Marriage, which had traditionally been arranged by families for financial gain, was now dictated by duty to the state. The Western concept of romantic love did not enter into a Chinese marriage, as this interview of a schoolteacher by the reporter Zhang Xinxin in the mid-1980s illustrates. According to recent surveys, the same is true today.

Zhang Xinxin, *Chinese Lives*

My husband and I never did any courting—honestly! We registered our marriage a week after we'd met. He was just out of the forces and a worker in a building outfit. They'd been given a foreign-aid assignment in Zambia, and he was selected. He wanted to get his private life fixed up before he went, and someone introduced us. Seeing how he looked really honest, I accepted him.

No, you can't say I didn't know anything about him. The person who introduced us told me he was a Party member who'd been an organization commissar. Any comrade who's good enough to be an organization cadre is politically reliable. Nothing special about our standing of living—it's what we've earned. He's still a worker, but we live all right, don't we?

He went off with the army as soon as we'd registered our marriage and been given the wedding certificates. He was away three years. We didn't have the wedding itself before he went because we hadn't got a room yet.

Those three years were a test for us. The main problem was that my family was against it. They thought I was still only a kid and I'd picked the wrong man. What did they have against him? His family was too poor. Of course I won in the end—we'd registered and got our wedding certificates. We were legally married whether we had the family ceremony or not.

We had our wedding after he came back in the winter of 1973. His leaders and mine all came to congratulate us and give us presents. The usual presents those days were busts of Chairman Mao. I was twenty-six and he was twenty-nine. We've never had a row.

I never really wanted to take the college entrance exams. Then in 1978 the school leadership got us all to put our names forward. They said they weren't going to hold us back: the more of us who passed, the better it would be for the school. So I put my name forward, crammed for six weeks, and passed. I already had two kids then. . . .

I reckoned the chance for study was too good to miss. And my husband was looking after the kids all by himself. I usually only came back once a fortnight. So I couldn't let him down.

My instructors urged me to take the exams for graduate school, but I didn't. I was already thirty-four, so what was the point of more study? There was another reason too. I didn't want an even wider gap between us: he hadn't even finished junior middle school when he joined the army.

It's bad if the gap's too wide. For example, there's a definite difference in our tastes in music and art, I have to admit that. But what really matters? Now we've set up this family we have to preserve it. Besides, look at all the sacrifices he had to make to see me through college. Men comrades all like a game of cards and that, but he was stuck with looking after the kids. He still doesn't get any time for himself—it's all work for him.

We've got a duty to each other. Our differences? The less said about them the better. We've always treated each other with the greatest respect.

Of course some people have made suggestions, but my advice to him is to respect himself and respect me. I'm not going to be like those men who ditch their wives when they go up in the world.

I'm the head of our school now. With this change in my status I've got to show even more responsibility for the family. Besides, I know how much he's done to get me where I am today. I've also got some duties in the municipal Women's Federation and Political Consultative Conference. No, I'm not being modest. I haven't done anything worth talking about, only my duty.

We've got to do a lot more educating people. There have been two cases of divorce in our school this year.

 Do you think the marriage described here is successful? Why or why not? What do you think this woman feels about her marriage?

SOURCE: From *Chinese Lives: An Oral History of Contemporary China*, by Zhang Xinxin and Sang Ye, copyright © 1987 by W. J. F. Jenner and Delia Davin.

of a collective accumulated "work points" based on the number of hours worked during a specified time period. Payment for work points was made not to the individual but to the family head. The payments, usually in the form of ration coupons, could then be spent at the collective community store. Because the payments went to the head of the family, the traditionally dominant position of the patriarch was maintained. When people's communes were established in the late 1950s, however, payments went to the individual.

During the radical era of the Great Leap Forward, children were encouraged to report to the authorities any comments by their parents that criticized the system. Such practices continued during the Cultural Revolution, when children were expected to report on their parents, students on their teachers, and employees on their superiors. Some have suggested that Mao deliberately encouraged such practices to bring an end to the traditional "politics of dependency." According to this theory, historically the famous **five relationships** forced individuals to swallow their anger and frustration ("to eat bitterness" in the Chinese phrase) and accept the hierarchical norms established by Confucian ethics (the five relationships were the subordination of son to father, wife to husband, younger brother to older brother, and subject to ruler, and the proper relationship of friend to friend). By encouraging the oppressed elements in society—the young, the female, and the poor—to voice their bitterness, Mao was breaking down the tradition of dependency. Such denunciations had been issued against landlords and other "local tyrants" in the land reform tribunals of the late 1940s and early 1950s. Later, during the Cultural Revolution, they were applied to other authority figures in Chinese society.

THE FAMILY REVIVES The post-Mao era has brought a decisive shift away from revolutionary utopianism and a return to the pragmatic approach to nation building. For the vast majority of Chinese, this is undoubtedly a welcome development; the era of generational warfare destroyed millions of lives, and few lamented its passing. Under the post-Mao leadership, family relationships have once more become a private affair.

As with all social changes, however, the return to a more traditional approach has had a price. Although in the large cities attitudes toward women, marriage, and the family have evolved in line with trends in Western countries, in rural areas the old norms about filial piety and the five relationships sometimes still hold sway. Arranged marriages, nepotism, and the mistreatment of females (for example, under the one-child program, many parents in rural areas reportedly killed female infants in hope that the next child would be a son) have returned,

although such behavior most likely persisted under the cloak of revolutionary purity for a generation. Expensive weddings are now increasingly common, along with the payment of a dowry to the family of the groom. Prostitution and sex crimes against women also appear to be on the rise. To discourage sexual abuse, the government now seeks to provide free legal services for women living in rural areas.

Women in China today do possess some advantages compared to their Western counterparts. Because men outnumber women in Chinese society (among infants, there are 118 males to every 100 females in today's China), women can afford to be more particular in selecting a husband. Young men often complain that without an automobile or an apartment to offer as an incentive, they find it difficult to locate a wife. Indeed, the problem of rootless young males, often with limited employment opportunities, is an issue of increasing concern for China's leaders today.

FROM MAO TO MOD With the end of the Great Proletarian Cultural Revolution, the party leadership turned away from the Maoist-inspired puritanical ethic and embraced the ideal of material consumption. Following the new slogans that urged them to "create wealth for the people" (a new version of the revolutionary slogan "serve the people") and proclaimed "to get rich is glorious," enterprising Chinese began to concentrate on improving their standard of living. For the first time, millions of Chinese saw the prospect of a house or an urban flat with a washing machine, television set, and indoor plumbing. Young people whose parents had given them patriotic names such as Build the Country, Protect Mao Zedong, and Assist Korea began to choose more elegant and cosmopolitan names for their own children. Some names, such as Surplus Grain or Bring a Younger Brother, expressed hope for the future.

The new attitudes were also reflected in physical appearance. For a generation after the civil war, clothing had been restricted to the traditional baggy "Mao suit" in olive drab or dark blue, but by the 1980s, young people craved such fashionable Western items as designer jeans, trendy sneakers, and sweat suits (or reasonable facsimiles). Cosmetic surgery to create a more buxom figure or a more Western facial look became increasingly common among affluent young women in the cities. Many had the epicanthic fold over their eyelids removed or even enlarged their noses—a curious decision in view of the tradition of referring derogatorily to foreigners as "big noses."

Much of the new prosperity is a consequence of the trend toward privatization and a more capitalistic free enterprise system. But there is also a price to pay for this change. Under the Maoist system, the elderly and the sick received retirement benefits and health care from the state or the collective organizations. Today, with the collectives no longer playing such a social role and more workers operating in the private sector, the safety net has been removed. No longer does every Chinese citizen have an "iron rice bowl" (guaranteed employment as well as health, education, and retirement benefits). The government has attempted to fill the gap by enacting a social security law, but because of a lack of funds, eligibility has been limited primarily to individuals in the cities. Those living in the countryside—who still represent over half of the population—have essentially been left to their own devices, although the government has promised to provide improved education, medical care, and other social services to the rural population.

Demographic changes will add complexity to the challenge. Because of the reduction in the birthrate since the 1980s, China will eventually face a labor shortage, resulting in upward pressure on workers' salaries and inflation in the marketplace. The median age will rise from 33 in 2005 to 45 at midcentury. In the process, the ratio of workers to retirees will drop from 6 to 1 to about 2 to 1. Under those circumstances, the lack of a nationwide retirement system represents a potential time bomb.

The shift from Marxism toward consumerism has also unleashed a sense of anomie and rootlessness in Chinese society, especially among the young, who did not live through the difficult years before Mao's death. Incidents of random terrorism are on the rise, and many young people are openly materialistic in their attitude and correspondingly cynical about politics. The growing popularity of organized religion mentioned earlier is undoubtedly another consequence.

China's Changing Culture

During the first half of the twentieth century, Chinese culture was strongly influenced by currents from the West (see Chapter 5). The rise to power of the Communists in 1949 added a new dimension to the debate over the future of culture in China. The new leaders rejected the Western attitude of "art for art's sake" and, like their Soviet counterparts, viewed culture as an important instrument of indoctrination. The standard would no longer be aesthetic quality or the personal preference of the artist but "art for life's sake," whereby culture would serve the interests of socialism.

Culture in a Revolutionary Era

At first, the new emphasis on socialist realism did not entirely extinguish the influence of traditional culture.

Mao and his colleagues tolerated—and even encouraged—efforts by artists to synthesize traditional ideas with socialist concepts and Western techniques. During the Cultural Revolution, however, all forms of traditional culture came to be viewed as reactionary. Socialist realism became the only acceptable standard in literature, art, and music. All forms of traditional expression were forbidden, and the deification of Mao and his central role in building a Communist paradise became virtually the only acceptable form of artistic expression.

Characteristic of the changing cultural climate in China was the experience of author Ding Ling. Born in 1904 and educated in a school for women set up by leftist intellectuals during the hectic years after the May Fourth Movement, she became involved in party activities in the 1930s. She then settled in Yan'an, where she wrote her most famous novel, *The Sun Shines over the Sangan River* (1948), which described the CCP's land reform program in favorable terms. It was awarded the Stalin Prize three years later.

During the early 1950s, Ding Ling was one of the most prominent literary lights of the new China, but in the more ideological climate at the end of the decade, she was attacked for her individualism and her criticism of the party. Although temporarily rehabilitated, during the Cultural Revolution she was sentenced to hard labor on a commune in the far north and was not released until the late 1970s after the death of Mao. Crippled and in poor health, she died in 1981. Ding Ling's fate mirrored the fate of thousands of progressive Chinese intellectuals who, despite their efforts, were not able to satisfy the constantly changing demands of a repressive regime.

Art and Architecture

After Mao's death, Chinese culture was finally released from the shackles of socialist realism. In painting, where for a decade the only acceptable standard for excellence was praise for the party and its policies, the new permissiveness led to a revival of interest in both traditional and Western forms. Although some painters continued to blend Eastern and Western styles, others imitated trends from abroad, experimenting with a wide range of previously prohibited art styles, including Cubism and abstract painting.

In the 1980s, some of the more avant-garde examples of contemporary art shocked the Chinese public and provoked the wrath of the party, leading the government to declare that henceforth it would regulate all art exhibits. More recently, some Chinese artists, such as the world-famous Ai Weiwei (b. 1957), have aggressively challenged the government's authority. In response, the government razed Ai's art studio in Shanghai in 2011. Eventually he was taken into police custody on charges related to tax evasion. He was subsequently released, but the government is maintaining a close watch on his activities. Nonetheless, Chinese contemporary art has expanded exponentially, attracting international attention and commanding exorbitant prices on the world market.

In recent years, China has invested heavily in transportation infrastructure and has erected endless blocks of apartment complexes to house the steady stream of migrants into the cities. This has led to an explosive building boom, highlighted by the projects connected with the 2008 Olympic Games in Beijing and spreading outward to China's many megacities. At a dizzying pace, renowned architects, both Chinese and foreign, are executing some of the new century's most original and experimental architectural designs. The gleaming forest of skyscrapers currently rising in Shanghai's Pudong district is the quintessential example.

Literature

The limits on freedom of expression have been most apparent in literature. During the early 1980s, party leaders encouraged Chinese writers to express their views on the mistakes of the past, and a new "literature of the wounded" began to describe the brutal and arbitrary character of the Cultural Revolution. One of the most prominent writers was Bai Hua, whose film script *Bitter Love* was made into the movie *The Sun and the People* (1980). It described the life of a young Chinese painter who joined the revolutionary movement during the 1940s but whose work was condemned as counterrevolutionary during the Cultural Revolution.

In criticizing the excesses of the Cultural Revolution, Bai Hua was only responding to Deng Xiaoping's appeal for intellectuals to speak out, but he was soon criticized for failing to point out the essentially beneficial role of the CCP in recent Chinese history. The film was withdrawn from circulation in 1981, and Bai Hua was compelled to recant his errors and to state that the great ideas of Mao Zedong on art and literature were "still of universal guiding significance today."[6]

Conservatives are especially incensed by the tendency of many writers to dwell on the shortcomings of the socialist system and to come uncomfortably close to direct criticism of the role of the CCP. One such writer is Mo Yan (the pen name of Guan Moye) (b. 1955), whose novels *The Garlic Ballads* (1988) and *Life and Death Are Wearing Me Out* (2008) expose the rampant corruption of contemporary Chinese society, the roots of which he attributes to one-party rule. He received the Nobel Prize in Literature in 2012. Like Mo Yan, Yan Lianke (b. 1958) addresses the suffering of the Chinese peasants. In *Dream of Ding Village* (2011), which was banned by the government, he exposes the real-life AIDS epidemic that resulted from tainted blood provided by a dishonest blood donor business. In the gripping novel *Wolf Totem* (2007), Jiang Rong (the pen name of Lü Jiamin) (b. 1946) describes an example of rural injustice in Inner Mongolia, as traditional ecological practices are sacrificed on the altar of rapid economic growth.

Since the 1990s, Chinese culture has been dramatically transformed by the nation's adoption of a market economy and the invasive spread of the Internet. A new mass literature, much of it written by and intended for China's new urban youth, explores the aspirations and frustrations of a generation obsessed with material consumption.

CONCLUSION

For four decades after the end of World War II, the two major Communist powers appeared to have become permanent features on the international landscape. Suddenly, in the late 1980s, both entered a period of internal crisis that shook the foundations of both countries. Soon thereafter, the Soviet Union collapsed, but the Communist Party survived in China and today stands at the height of its power.

Why were the outcomes so different? Although the role of human action should not be ignored, it is clear that cultural differences were also an important factor. Although the doctrine of Marxism-Leninism originated in Europe, many of its main precepts, such as the primacy of the community over the individual and the denial of the concept of private property, run counter to the trends in Western civilization. This inherent conflict is especially evident in the societies of central and western Europe, which were strongly influenced by Enlightenment philosophy and the Industrial Revolution. These forces were weaker in the countries farther to the east, but both had begun to penetrate tsarist Russia by the end of the nineteenth century.

By contrast, Marxism-Leninism found a more receptive climate in China and other countries in the region influenced by Confucian tradition. In its political culture, the Communist system exhibits many of the same characteristics as traditional Confucianism—a single truth, an elite governing class, and an emphasis on obedience to the community and its governing representatives—while feudal attitudes regarding female inferiority, loyalty to the family, and bureaucratic arrogance are hard to break. On the surface, China today bears a number of uncanny similarities to the China of the past.

Yet these similarities should not blind us to the real changes that are taking place. The China of today is fundamentally different from that of the late Qing or even the early republic. Literacy rates and the standard of living, on balance, are far higher; the pressures of outside powers are less threatening; and China has entered the opening stages of its own industrial and technological revolution. For many Chinese, independent talk radio and the Internet are a greater source of news and views than the official media. Where Sun Yat-sen, Chiang Kai-shek, and even Mao Zedong broke their lances on the rocks of centuries of tradition, poverty, and ignorance, China's present leaders rule a country much more aware of the world and its place in it.

TIMELINE

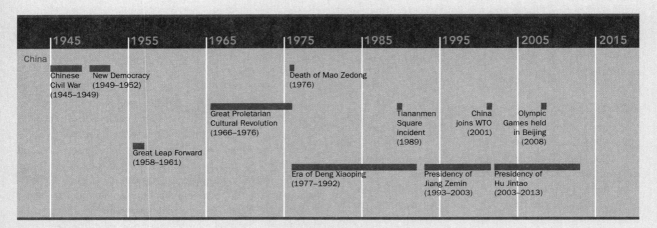

CHAPTER NOTES

1. "Report on an Investigation of the Peasant Movement in Hunan (March 1927)," *Quotations from Chairman Mao Tse-tung* (Beijing, 1976), p. 12.

2. Quoted in Stanley Karnow, *Mao and China: Inside China's Revolution* (New York, 1972), p. 95.

3. Quoted from an article by Mao Zedong in the journal *Red Flag*, June 1, 1958. See Stuart R. Schram, *The Political Thought of Mao Tse-tung* (New York, 1963), p. 253. The quotation "strike while the iron is hot" is from Karnow, *Mao and China*, p. 93.

4. Liang Heng with Judith Shapiro, *Son of the Revolution* (New York, 1983).

5. "The Foolish Old Man Who Removed the Mountains," *Quotations from Chairman Mao*, p. 182.

6. Quoted in Jonathan Spence, *Chinese Roundabout: Essays in History and Culture* (New York, 1992), p. 285.

13

Nationalism Triumphant: The Emergence of Independent States in South and Southeast Asia

The Petronas Towers in Kuala Lumpur, Malaysia

FIRST-TIME VISITORS to the Malaysian capital of Kuala Lumpur are astonished to observe a pair of twin towers thrusting up above the surrounding buildings into the clouds. The Petronas Towers rise 1,483 feet from ground level; they were the world's tallest buildings at the time of their completion in 1998. (They have since been surpassed by other structures such as Taipei 101, in Taiwan, and Burj Khalifa, in Dubai.)

Beyond their status as an architectural achievement, the Petronas Towers announced the emergence of Southeast Asia as a major player on the international scene. It is no accident that the foundations were laid on the site of the Selangor Cricket Club, symbol of British colonial hegemony in Southeast Asia. "These towers," commented one local official, "will do wonders for Asia's self-esteem and confidence, which I think is very important, and which I think at this moment are at the point of takeoff."[1]

A little more a year after that remark, Malaysia and several of its neighbors were mired in a financial crisis that threatened to derail their rapid advance to economic affluence and severely undermined the "self-esteem" that the Petronas Towers were meant to symbolize. For years after the buildings were completed, many of their offices stood empty. Today, however, the region is once again on the march. The nations of Southeast Asia have recovered from their brief economic malaise, while to their west, India, the world's largest democracy, is beginning to shake off decades of economic lethargy and emerge as a vibrant force in the global marketplace. Though not untouched by the global recession

that began in 2008, the countries of southern Asia appear to have suffered less than many other regions of the world.

The Petronas Towers, then, serve as a vivid demonstration in steel and glass of the dual face of modern Asia: a region seeking to compete with the advanced nations of the West while still struggling to overcome a legacy of economic underdevelopment and colonial rule. As Asian leaders have discovered, the path is strewn with hidden obstacles but also opportunities.

CRITICAL THINKING

Q What differences and similarities do you see in the performances of the nations of South, Southeast, and East Asia since World War II? What do you think accounts for the differences?

South Asia

In 1947, nearly two centuries of British colonial rule came to an end when two new independent nations, India and Pakistan, came into being. Under British authority, the subcontinent of South Asia had been linked ever more closely to the global capitalist economy. Yet as in other areas of Asia and Africa, the experience brought only limited benefits to the local peoples. Little industrial development took place, and the bulk of the profits went into the pockets of Western entrepreneurs.

For half a century, nationalist forces had been seeking reforms in colonial policy and the eventual overthrow of colonial power. But the peoples of South Asia did not regain their independence until after World War II.

The End of the British Raj

During the 1930s, the nationalist movement in India was severely shaken by factional disagreements between Hindus and Muslims. The outbreak of World War II subdued these sectarian clashes, but they erupted again after the war ended in 1945. Battles between Hindus and Muslims broke out in several cities, and Muhammad Ali Jinnah (1876–1948), leader of the Muslim League, demanded the creation of a separate state for each group. Meanwhile, the Labour Party, which had long been critical of the British colonial legacy on both moral and economic grounds, had come to power in Britain, and the new prime minister, Clement Attlee, announced that power would be transferred to "responsible Indian hands" by June 1948. But the imminence of independence did not dampen communal strife. As riots escalated, the British reluctantly accepted the inevitability of partition and declared that on August 15, 1947, two independent nations—predominantly Hindu India and Muslim Pakistan—would be established. Pakistan would be divided between the main area of Muslim habitation in the Indus River valley in the west and a separate territory in eastern Bengal 2,000 miles to the east. Although Mohandas "Mahatma" Gandhi warned that partition would provoke "an orgy of blood,"[2] he was increasingly regarded as a figure of the past, and his views were ignored.

The British instructed the rulers in the princely states to choose which state they would join by August 15, but problems arose in predominantly Hindu Hyderabad, where the nawab (governor) was a Muslim, and mountainous Kashmir, where a Hindu prince ruled over a Muslim population. After independence was declared, millions of Hindus and Muslims fled across the borders, resulting in violence and the deaths of more than a million people. One of the casualties was Gandhi, who was assassinated on January 30, 1948, as he was going to morning prayer. The assassin, a Hindu militant, was apparently motivated by Gandhi's opposition to a Hindu India.

Independent India

With independence, the Indian National Congress, now renamed the Congress Party, moved from opposition to the responsibility of power under Jawaharlal Nehru (1889–1964), the new prime minister. The prospect must have been intimidating. The vast majority of India's 400 million people were poor and illiterate. The new nation encompassed a significant number of ethnic groups and fourteen major languages. Although Congress leaders spoke bravely of building a new nation, Indian society still bore the scars of past wars and divisions.

The government's first problem was to resolve disputes left over from the transition period. The rulers of Hyderabad and Kashmir had both followed their own preferences rather than the wishes of their subject populations. Nehru was determined to include both states within India. In 1948, Indian troops invaded Hyderabad and annexed the area. India also occupied most of Kashmir, but at the cost of creating an intractable problem that has poisoned relations with Pakistan to the present day.

AN EXPERIMENT IN DEMOCRATIC SOCIALISM Under Nehru's leadership, India adopted a political system on the British model, with a figurehead president and a parliamentary form of government. A number of political parties operated legally, but the Congress Party, with its enormous prestige and charismatic leadership, was dominant at both the central and the local levels. It was ably assisted by the Indian civil service, which had been created during the era of British colonial rule and provided solid expertise in the arcane art of bureaucracy.

Nehru had been influenced by British socialism and patterned his economic policy roughly after the program of the British Labour Party. The state took over ownership of the major industries and resources, transportation, and utilities, while private enterprise was permitted at the local and retail levels. Farmland remained in private hands, but rural cooperatives were officially encouraged. The government also sought to avoid excessive dependence on foreign investment and technological assistance. All businesses were required by law to have majority Indian ownership.

In other respects, Nehru was a devotee of Western materialism. He was convinced that to succeed, India must industrialize. In advocating industrialization, Nehru departed sharply from Gandhi, who believed that materialism was morally corrupting and that only simplicity and nonviolence (as represented by the traditional Indian village and the symbolic spinning wheel) could save India, and the world itself, from self-destruction (see the box on p. 273). Gandhi, Nehru complained, "just wants to spin and weave."

The primary themes of Nehru's foreign policy were anticolonialism and antiracism. Under his guidance, India took a neutral stance in the Cold War and sought to provide leadership to all newly independent nations in Asia, Africa, and Latin America. At the Bandung Conference, held in Indonesia in 1955, India promoted the concept of

Two Visions for India

Although Jawaharlal Nehru and Mahatma Gandhi agreed on their desire for an independent India, their visions of the future of their homeland were dramatically different. Nehru favored industrialization to build material prosperity, whereas Gandhi praised the virtues of local self-government. The first excerpt is from a speech by Nehru; the second is from an article written by Gandhi and now published in his *Collected Works*.

Nehru's Socialist Creed

I am convinced that the only key to the solution of the world's problems and of India's problems lies in socialism, and when I use this word I do so not in a vague humanitarian way but in the scientific economic sense.... I see no way of ending the poverty, the vast unemployment, the degradation and the subjection of the Indian people except through socialism. That involves vast and revolutionary changes in our political and social structure, the ending of vested interests in land and industry, as well as the feudal and autocratic Indian states system. That means the ending of private property, except in a restricted sense, and the replacement of the present profit system by a higher ideal of cooperative service.... In short, it means a new civilization, radically different from the present capitalist order. Some glimpse we can have of this new civilization in the territories of the U.S.S.R. Much has happened there which has pained me greatly and with which I disagree, but I look upon that great and fascinating unfolding of a new order and a new civilization as the most promising feature of our dismal age.

Mahatma Gandhi, "Nonviolent Democracy: Control by the People of Themselves and Their Government"

Independence must begin at the bottom. Thus, every village will be a republic or *panchayat* [traditional village council] having full powers. It follows, therefore, that every village has to be self-sustained and capable of managing its affairs even to the extent of defending itself against the whole world.... Ultimately, it is the individual who is the unit....

In this structure composed of innumerable villages, there will be ever widening, never ascending circles. Life will not be a pyramid with the apex sustained by the bottom. But it will be an oceanic circle whose centre will be the individual always ready to perish for the village, the latter ready to perish for the circle of villagers, till at last the whole becomes one life composed of individuals, never aggressive in their arrogance but ever humble, sharing the majesty of the oceanic circle of which they are integral units.

Therefore, the outermost circumference [that is, the national government] will not wield power to crush the inner circle but will give strength to all within and derive its own strength from it.

 What are the key differences between these two views of the future of India? Why do you think Nehru's vision triumphed over that of Mahatma Gandhi?

SOURCES: From *Sources of Indian Tradition*, 2nd ed. Edited by Stephen Hay, vol. II (New York: Columbia University Press, 1988), pp. 256, 317–318.

a bloc of "Third World" countries that would provide a balance between the capitalist world and the Communist bloc. It also sought good relations with the new People's Republic of China. India's neutrality put it at odds with the United States, which during the 1950s was trying to mobilize all nations against what it viewed as the menace of international communism.

Relations with Pakistan continued to be troubled. India refused to consider Pakistan's claim to Kashmir, even though the majority of the people there were Muslim. Tension between the two countries persisted, erupting into war in 1965. In 1971, when riots against the Pakistani government broke out in East Pakistan, India intervened on the side of East Pakistan, which declared its independence as the new nation of Bangladesh (see Map 13.1).

THE POST-NEHRU ERA Nehru's death in 1964 aroused concern that Indian democracy was dependent on the Nehru mystique. When his successor, a Congress Party veteran, died in 1966, Congress leaders selected Nehru's daughter, Indira Gandhi (no relation to Mahatma Gandhi), as the new prime minister. Gandhi (1917–1984) was

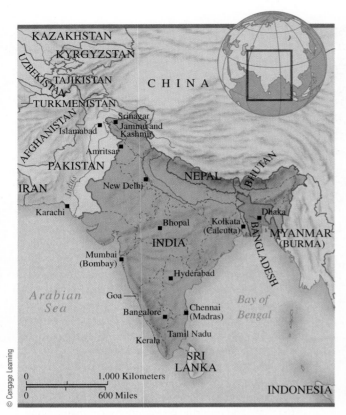

MAP 13.1 Contemporary South Asia. This map shows the boundaries of all the states in contemporary South Asia. India, the largest in area and population, is highlighted.

Q *Which of the countries on this map have a Muslim majority?*

inexperienced in politics, but she quickly showed the steely determination of her father.

Like Nehru, Gandhi embraced democratic socialism and a policy of neutrality in foreign affairs, but she was more activist than her father. To combat rural poverty, she nationalized banks, provided loans to peasants on easy terms, built low-cost housing, distributed land to the landless, and introduced electoral reforms to enfranchise the poor.

Gandhi was especially worried by India's growing population and in an effort to curb the growth rate adopted a policy of forced sterilization. This policy proved unpopular, however, and, along with growing official corruption and Gandhi's authoritarian tactics, led to her defeat in the general election of 1975, the first time the Congress Party had failed to win a majority at the national level.

A minority government of procapitalist parties was formed, but within two years, Gandhi was back in power. She now faced a new challenge, however, in the rise of religious strife. The most dangerous situation was

in the Punjab, where militant **Sikhs** were demanding autonomy or even independence from India (the Sikh religion was created in the sixteenth century to combine the best elements of Islam and Hinduism). Gandhi did not shrink from a confrontation and attacked Sikh rebels hiding in their Golden Temple in the city of Amritsar. The incident aroused widespread anger among the Sikh community, and in 1984, Sikh members of Gandhi's personal bodyguard assassinated her.

By now, Congress politicians were convinced that the party could not remain in power without a member of the Nehru family at the helm. Gandhi's son Rajiv (1944–1991), a commercial airline pilot with little interest in politics, was persuaded to replace his mother as prime minister. Rajiv lacked the strong ideological and political convictions of his mother and grandfather and allowed a greater role for private enterprise. But his government was criticized for cronyism, inefficiency, and corruption, as well as insensitivity to the poor.

Rajiv Gandhi also sought to play a role in regional affairs, mediating a dispute between the government in Sri Lanka and Tamil rebels (known as the **Elam Tigers** or Tamil Tigers), who were ethnically related to the majority population in southern India. The decision cost him his life: while campaigning for reelection in 1991, he was assassinated by a member of the Tiger organization. India faced the future without a member of the Nehru family as prime minister.

During the early 1990s, Congress remained the leading party, but the powerful hold it had once had on the Indian electorate was gone. New parties, such as the militantly Hindu Bharatiya Janata Party (BJP), actively vied with Congress for control of the central and state governments. Growing political instability at the center was accompanied by rising tensions between Hindus and Muslims.

When a coalition government formed under Congress leadership collapsed, the BJP, under Prime Minister A. B. Vajpayee (b. 1924), ascended to power in 1998 and played on Hindu sensibilities to build its political base. The new government based its success on an aggressive program of privatization in the industrial and commercial sectors and made a major effort to promote the nation's small but growing technological base. But BJP leaders had underestimated the discontent of India's less affluent citizens (an estimated 350 million Indians earn less than one U.S. dollar a day), and in the spring of 2004, a stunning defeat in national elections forced the Vajpayee government to resign. The Congress Party returned to power at the head of a coalition government based on a commitment to maintain economic growth while carrying out reforms in rural areas, including public works projects and hot lunch programs for all primary school children. But sectarian strife between Hindus and Muslims, as well as pervasive official corruption, continued to bedevil the government. In the fall of 2008, a terrorist attack in the city of Mumbai left nearly two hundred dead and raised serious questions about the effectiveness of Indian security procedures. Indian officials charged that the inspiration for the attack came from Pakistan. The Congress Party remained in power after national elections held in the spring of 2009, but serious problems, including pervasive official corruption and sectarian strife, continue to bedevil the government.

The Land of the Pure: Pakistan Since Independence

When Pakistan achieved independence in August 1947, it was, unlike its neighbor India, in all respects a new nation, based on religious conviction rather than historical or ethnic tradition. The unique state united two separate territories 2,000 miles apart. West Pakistan, including the Indus River basin and the West Punjab, was perennially short of water and was populated by dry crop farmers and peoples of the steppe. East Pakistan was made up of the marshy deltas of the Ganges and Brahmaputra Rivers. Densely populated with rice farmers, it was the home of the artistic and intellectual Bengalis.

The peoples of West Pakistan were especially diverse and included, among others, Pushtuns, Baluchis, and Punjabis. The Pushtuns are organized on a tribal basis and have kinship ties with the majority population across the border in neighboring Afghanistan. Many are nomadic and cross the border on a regular basis with their flocks. The Baluchis straddle the border with Iran, while the region of Punjab was divided between Pakistan and India at the moment of independence.

Even though the new state was an essentially Muslim society, its first years were marked by intense internal conflicts over religious, linguistic, and regional issues. Muhammad Ali Jinnah's vision of a democratic state that would assure freedom of religion and equal treatment for all was opposed by those who advocated a state based on Islamic principles.

Even more dangerous was the division between east and west. Many in East Pakistan felt that the government, based in the west, ignored their needs. In 1952, riots erupted in East Pakistan over the government's decision to adopt Urdu, a language derived from Hindi and used by Muslims in northern India, as the national language of the entire country. Most East Pakistanis spoke Bengali, an unrelated language. Tensions persisted, and in March 1971, East Pakistan declared its independence as the new nation of Bangladesh. Pakistani troops attempted to restore the central government's authority in the capital of Dhaka, but rebel forces supported by India went on the offensive, and the government bowed to the inevitable and recognized independent Bangladesh.

The breakup of the union between East and West Pakistan undermined the fragile authority of the military regime that had ruled Pakistan since 1958 and led to its replacement by a civilian government under Zulfikar Ali Bhutto (1928–1979). But now religious tensions came to the fore, despite a new constitution that made a number of key concessions to conservative Muslims. In 1977, a new military government under General Zia ul Ha'q (1924–1988) came to power with a commitment to make Pakistan a truly Islamic state. Islamic law became the basis for social behavior as well as for the legal system. Laws governing the consumption of alcohol and the role of women were tightened in accordance with strict Muslim beliefs. But after Zia was killed in a plane crash, Pakistanis elected Benazir Bhutto (1953–2007), the daughter of Zulfikar Ali Bhutto and a supporter of secularism who had been educated in the United States. She too was removed from power by a military regime, in 1990, on charges of incompetence and corruption. Reelected in 1993, she attempted to crack down on opposition forces but was removed once again amid renewed charges of official corruption. Her successor soon came under fire for the same reason and in 1999 was ousted by a military coup led by General Pervez Musharraf (b. 1943), who promised to restore political stability and honest government.

In September 2001, Pakistan became the focus of international attention when a coalition of forces arrived in neighboring Afghanistan to overthrow the Taliban regime and destroy the al-Qaeda terrorist network. Despite considerable support for the Taliban among the local population, President Musharraf pledged his help in bringing terrorists to justice. He also promised to return his country to the secular principles espoused by Muhammad Ali Jinnah. His situation was complicated by renewed tensions with India over Kashmir and a series of violent clashes between Muslims and Hindus in India. In 2003, relations began to improve as both sides promised to seek a peaceful solution to the Kashmir dispute.

By then, however, problems had begun to escalate on the domestic front. As Musharraf sought to fend off challenges from radical Muslim groups—some of them allied with Taliban forces in Afghanistan—secular opposition figures criticized the authoritarian nature of his regime. When Benazir Bhutto returned from exile to present herself as a candidate in presidential elections to be held early in 2008, she was assassinated, leading to widespread suspicions of official involvement. In September 2008, amid growing political turmoil, Benazir Bhutto's widower, Asif Ali Zardari (b. 1955), was elected president of Pakistan as the head of a civilian government composed of an uneasy coalition of several political parties.

The government faces a number of challenges in coping with the multitude of problems affecting the country today. Half of the entire population of 150 million lives in poverty, and illiteracy is widespread. Massive flooding of the Indus River in 2010 killed nearly two thousand people and left millions homeless.

In a nation where much of the rural population still professes loyalty to traditional tribal leaders, the sense of nationalism remains fragile, while military elites, who have long played a central role in Pakistani politics, continue to press their own agenda. The internal divisions within the country's ruling class became painfully apparent when the al-Qaeda leader Osama bin Laden was killed in a U.S. raid on his compound in the spring of 2011. The terrorist leader had been living secretly in a villa in the military town of Abbottabad, within two hours' drive of the national capital of Islamabad. Many observers suspected that elements within the Pakistan military were aware of his presence there, and the raid further exacerbated tensions between the United States and its reputed ally.

Poverty and Pluralism in South Asia

The leaders of the new states that emerged in South Asia after World War II faced a number of problems. The peoples of South Asia were still overwhelmingly poor and illiterate, and the sectarian, ethnic, and cultural divisions that had plagued Indian society for centuries had not dissipated.

THE POLITICS OF COMMUNALISM Perhaps the most sincere effort to create democratic institutions was in India, where the new constitution called for social justice, liberty, equality of status and opportunity, and fraternity. All citizens were guaranteed protection from discrimination on the grounds of religious belief, race, caste, gender, or place of birth.

In theory, then, India became a full-fledged democracy on the British parliamentary model. In actuality, a number of distinctive characteristics made the system less than fully democratic in the Western sense but may also have enabled it to survive. As we have seen, India became in essence a one-party state. By leading the independence movement, the Congress Party had gained massive public support, which enabled it to retain its preeminent position

in Indian politics for three decades. The party also avoided being identified as a party exclusively for the Hindu majority by including prominent non-Hindus among its leaders and favoring measures to protect minority groups such as Sikhs, untouchables, and Muslims from discrimination.

After Nehru's death in 1964, however, problems emerged that had been disguised by his adept maneuvering. One problem was the familiar one of a party too long in power. Party officials became complacent and all too easily fell prey to the temptations of corruption and pork-barrel politics.

Another problem was **communalism**. Beneath the surface unity of the new republic lay age-old ethnic, linguistic, and religious divisions. Because of India's vast size and complex history, no national language had ever emerged. Hindi was the most prevalent, but it was the native language of less than one-third of the population. During the colonial period, English had served as the official language of government, and many non-Hindi speakers suggested making it the official language. But English was spoken only by the educated elite, and it represented an affront to national pride. Eventually, India recognized fourteen official tongues, making the parliament sometimes sound like the Tower of Babel.

Divisiveness increased after Nehru's death, and under his successors, official corruption grew. Only the lack of appeal of its rivals and the Nehru family charisma carried on by his daughter Indira Gandhi kept the Congress Party in power. But she was unable to prevent the progressive disintegration of the party's power base at the state level, where regional or ideological parties won the allegiance of voters by exploiting ethnic or social revolutionary themes.

During the 1980s, religious tensions began to intensify. As we have seen, Gandhi's uncompromising approach to Sikh separatism led to her assassination in 1984. Under her son, Rajiv Gandhi, Hindu militants demanded the destruction of a mosque built on a traditional Hindu holy site at Ayodhya, in northern India, where a Hindu temple had previously existed. In 1992, Hindu demonstrators destroyed the mosque and erected a temporary temple at the site, provoking clashes between Hindus and Muslims throughout the country. In protest, rioters in neighboring Pakistan destroyed a number of Hindu shrines in that country. In 2010, an Indian court ordered that the land that had contained the mosque be divided between the Hindu and Muslim plaintiffs.

In recent years, communal divisions have intensified as militant Hindu groups agitate for a state that caters to the Hindu majority, now numbering more than 700 million people. In 2006, Muslim activists launched a terrorist attack on commuter trains that killed scores of Indians in the city of Mumbai. In the eastern state of Orissa, pitched battles have broken out between Hindus and Christians over efforts by the latter to win converts to their faith. Manmohan Singh (b. 1932), India's prime minister since 2004, has lamented what he labels an assault on India's "composite culture."[3]

THE ECONOMY Nehru's answer to the social and economic inequality that had long afflicted the subcontinent was socialism. He instituted a series of five-year plans, which led to the creation of a relatively large and reasonably efficient industrial sector, centered on steel, vehicles, and textiles. Industrial production almost tripled between 1950 and 1965, and per capita income rose by 50 percent between 1950 and 1980, although it was still less than $300 (in U.S. dollars).

By the 1970s, however, industrial growth had slowed. The lack of modern infrastructure was a problem, as was the rising price of oil, most of which had to be imported. The relative weakness of the state-owned sector, which grew at an annual rate of only about 2 percent in the 1950s and 1960s, versus 5 percent for the private sector, also became a serious obstacle.

India's major economic weakness, however, was in agriculture. At independence, mechanization was almost unknown, fertilizer was rarely used, and most farms were small and uneconomical because of the Hindu tradition of dividing the land equally among all male children. As a result, the vast majority of the Indian people lived in conditions of abject poverty. Landless laborers outnumbered landowners by almost two to one. The government attempted to relieve the problem by redistributing land to the poor, limiting the size of landholdings, and encouraging farmers to form voluntary cooperatives. But all three programs ran into widespread opposition and apathy.

Another problem was overpopulation. Even before independence, the country had had difficulty supporting its people. In the 1950s and 1960s, the population grew by more than 2 percent annually, twice the nineteenth-century rate. Beginning in the 1960s, the Indian government sought to curb population growth. Indira Gandhi instituted a program combining monetary rewards and compulsory sterilization, but popular resistance undermined the program, which was scaled back in the 1970s. One factor in the continued population growth has been a decline in the death rate, especially the rate of infant mortality. Nevertheless, as a result of media popularization and better government programs, the trend today, even in poor rural villages, is toward smaller families. The average number of children a woman bears has been reduced from six in 1950 to three today. As has occurred elsewhere, the decline in family size began among the educated and is gradually spreading throughout Indian society. Still, India is on target to surpass China and become the world's most populous nation by the year 2025.

The so-called **green revolution** that began in the 1960s helped reduce the severity of the population problem. The introduction of more productive, disease-resistant strains of rice and wheat doubled grain production between 1960 and 1980. But the green revolution also increased rural inequality. Only the wealthier farmers were able to purchase the necessary fertilizer, while poor peasants were often driven off the land. Millions fled to the cities, where they lived in vast slums, working at menial jobs or even begging for a living.

After the death of Indira Gandhi in 1984, her son Rajiv proved more receptive to foreign investment and a greater role for the private sector in the economy. India began to export more manufactured goods, including computer software. The pace of change has accelerated under Rajiv Gandhi's successors, who have continued to transfer state-run industries to private hands. These policies have stimulated the growth of a prosperous new middle class, now estimated at more than 100 million. Consumerism has soared, and sales of television sets, automobiles, DVD players, and cellphones have increased dramatically. Equally important, Western imports are being replaced by new products manufactured in India with Indian brand names.

One consequence of India's entrance into the industrial age is the emergence of a small but vibrant technological sector that provides many important services to the world's advanced nations. The city of Bangalore in southern India has become an important technological center, benefiting from low wages and the presence of skilled labor with proficiency in the English language. It has also become a symbol of the "outsourcing" of jobs from the United States and Europe that has led to an increase in middle-class unemployment throughout the Western world.

Nevertheless, Nehru's dream of a socialist society remains strong. State-owned enterprises still produce about half of all domestic goods, and high tariffs continue to stifle imports. Nationalist parties have played on the widespread fear of foreign economic influence to make it difficult for large multinational corporations, such as the retail giant Walmart, to break into the Indian market. A combination of religious and environmental groups attempted unsuccessfully to prevent Kentucky Fried Chicken from establishing outlets in major Indian cities (see the box on p. 278).

Say No to McDonald's and KFC!

One of the consequences of Rajiv Gandhi's decision to deregulate the Indian economy has been an increase in the presence of foreign corporations, including U.S. fast-food restaurant chains. Their arrival set off a storm of protest in India: from environmentalists concerned that raising grain for chickens is an inefficient use of land, from religious activists angry at the killing of animals for food, and from nationalists anxious to protect the domestic market from foreign competition. The protests went unheeded, however, and fast-food restaurants, many of them under Indian ownership, have become an increasingly visible presence on the urban scene. Most cater to local tastes by avoiding beef products and offering many vegetarian dishes. This piece, which appeared in the *Hindustan Times*, was written by Maneka Gandhi, a daughter-in-law of Indira Gandhi and a onetime minister of the environment who has emerged as a prominent rival of Sonia Gandhi, the widow of Rajiv Gandhi and the Congress Party president.

Why India Doesn't Need Fast Food

India's decision to allow Pepsi Foods Ltd. to open 60 restaurants in India—30 each of Pizza Hut and Kentucky Fried Chicken—marks the first entry of multinational, meat-based junk-food chains into India. If this is allowed to happen, at least a dozen other similar chains will very quickly arrive, including the infamous McDonald's.

The implications of allowing junk-food chains into India are quite stark. As the name denotes, the foods served at Kentucky Fried Chicken (KFC) are chicken-based and fried. This is the worst combination possible for the body and can create a host of health problems, including obesity, high cholesterol, heart ailments, and many kinds of cancer. Pizza Hut products are a combination of white flour, cheese, and meat—again, a combination likely to cause disease....

Then there is the issue of the environmental impact of junk-food chains. Modern meat production involves misuse of crops, water, energy, and grazing areas. In addition, animal agriculture produces surprisingly large amounts of air and water pollution.

KFC and Pizza Hut insist that their chickens be fed corn and soybeans. Consider the diversion of grain for this purpose. As the outlets of KFC and Pizza Hut increase in number, the poultry industry will buy up more and more corn to feed the chickens, which means that the corn will quickly disappear from the villages, and its increased price will place it out of reach for the common man. Turning corn into junk chicken is like turning gold into mud....

It is already shameful that, in a country plagued by famine and flood, we divert 37 percent of our arable land to growing animal fodder. Were all of that grain to be consumed directly by humans, it would nourish five times as many people as it does after being converted into meat, milk, and eggs....

Of course, it is not just the KFC and Pizza Hut chains of Pepsi Foods Ltd. that will cause all of this damage. Once we open India up by allowing these chains, dozens more will be eagerly waiting to come in. Each city in America has an average of 5,000 junk-food restaurants. Is that what we want for India?

 Why does the author of this article oppose the introduction of Western-style fast-food restaurants in India? Do you think her complaints apply in the United States as well?

Source: From *World Press Review* (September 1995), p. 47.

As in the industrialized countries of the West, economic growth has been accompanied by environmental damage. Water and air pollution has led to illness and death for many people, and an environmental movement has emerged. Some critics, reflecting the traditional anti-imperialist attitude of Indian intellectuals, blame Western capitalist corporations for the problem, as in the highly publicized case of leakage from a foreign-owned chemical plant at Bhopal. Much of the problem, however, comes from state-owned factories erected with Soviet aid. And not all the environmental damage can be ascribed to industrialization. The Ganges River is so polluted by human overuse that it is risky for Hindu believers to bathe in it.

Moreover, many Indians have not benefited from the new prosperity. Although the growth rate of the Indian national economy has averaged about 6 percent during the last few years, nearly one-third of the population lives below the national poverty line. Millions continue to live in urban slums, such as the famous "City of Joy" in Kolkata (Calcutta), and most farm families remain desperately poor. Despite the socialist rhetoric of India's leaders, the inequality of wealth in India is as pronounced as it is in capitalist nations in the West. Indeed, India has been described as two nations: an educated urban India of 100 million people surrounded by more than 900 million impoverished peasants in the countryside. In an effort to reduce the chronic poverty in rural areas, the current Congress government has launched a number of public works programs, increased local access to credit, and sought improvements in health and education for the poor. Nevertheless, about one-quarter of all Indians continue to subsist on less than one U.S. dollar per day.

Such problems are even more serious in neighboring Pakistan and Bangladesh. The overwhelming majority of Pakistan's citizens are poor, and at least half are illiterate. The recent flooding along the Indus River had a devastating effect on people living in the region and was described by a United Nations official as the worst humanitarian crisis in the sixty-five years of the UN's existence. Prospects for the future are not bright, for Pakistan lacks a modern technological sector to serve as a magnet for the emergence of a modern middle class.

CASTE, CLASS, AND GENDER Drawing generalizations about the life of the average Indian is difficult because of ethnic, religious, and caste differences, which are compounded by the vast gulf between town and country.

Although the constitution of 1950 guaranteed equal treatment and opportunity for all, regardless of caste, and prohibited discrimination based on untouchability, prejudice is hard to eliminate. Untouchability persists, particularly in the villages, where *harijans*, now called **dalits**, still perform menial tasks and are often denied fundamental human rights.

In general, urban Indians appear less conscious of caste distinctions. Material wealth rather than caste identity is increasingly defining status. Still, color consciousness based on the age-old distinctions between upper-class Aryans and lower-class Dravidians remains strong. Class-conscious Hindus still express a distinct preference for light-skinned marital partners.

In recent years, low-caste Indians (who represent more than 80 percent of the voting public) have begun to demand affirmative action programs to expand their opportunities and give them a more equal share of the national wealth. In particular, they want equality in education and employment opportunities. In response, the government has enacted a number of laws guaranteeing access to education and employment, regardless of caste affiliation, and many individuals of low caste, especially in the south, have attained high positions in Indian society. Old habits and prejudices are hard to break, however, and throughout the breadth of the country, the struggle for equal treatment continues.

Gender equality has also been difficult to achieve. In few societies was the life of women more restricted than in traditional India. Hindu favoritism toward men was compounded by the Muslim custom of *purdah* (the seclusion of women from public view) to create a society in which males were dominant in virtually all aspects of life. Females received no education and had no inheritance rights. They were restricted to the home and tied to their husbands for life. Widows were expected to shave their heads and engage in a life of religious meditation or even to practice **sati**, immolating themselves on their deceased husband's funeral pyre.

After independence, India's leaders sought to equalize treatment of the sexes. The constitution expressly forbade discrimination based on gender and called for equal pay for equal work. Laws prohibited child marriage and the payment of a dowry by the bride's family. Women were encouraged to attend school and enter the labor market.

Young Hindu Bride in Gold Bangles. Awaiting the marriage ceremony, a young bride sits with her female relatives at the Meenakshi Hindu temple, one of the largest in southern India. Although child marriage is illegal, Indian girls are still married at a young age. With the marital union arranged by the parents, this young bride may never have met her future husband. Bedecked in gold jewelry and rich silks—part of her dowry—she nervously awaits the priest's blessing before she moves to her husband's home. There she will begin a life of servitude to her in-laws' family.

Such laws, along with the dynamics of economic and social change, have had a major impact on the lives of many Indian women. Middle-class women in urban areas are much more likely to seek employment outside the home, and many hold managerial and professional positions. Some Indian women, however, continue to play a dual role—a modern one in their work and in the marketplace and a more submissive, traditional one at home.

Nothing more strikingly indicates the changing role of women in South Asia than the fact that in recent decades, three of the major countries in the area—India, Pakistan, and Sri Lanka—have had women prime ministers. It is worthy of mention, however, that all three—Indira Gandhi, Benazir Bhutto, and Sirimavo Bandaranaike—came from prominent political families and owed their initial success to a husband or a father who had served as prime minister before them.

Like other aspects of life, the role of women has changed much less in rural areas. In the early 1960s, many villagers still practiced the institution of *purdah*. A woman who went about freely in society would get a bad reputation. Female children are still much less likely to receive an education. The overall literacy rate in India today is about 60 percent, but it is less than 50 percent among women. Laws relating to dowry, child marriage, and inheritance are routinely ignored in the countryside. There have also been a few highly publicized instances of *sati*, although undoubtedly more women die of mistreatment at the hands of their husband or of other members of his family. Abusive treatment of women is not limited to the countryside, however; there have been several brutal and much publicized rape cases in urban areas in recent years.

Perhaps the most tragic aspect of continued sexual discrimination in India is the high mortality rate among girls. One-quarter of the female children born in India die before the age of fifteen as a result of neglect or even infanticide. Others are aborted before birth after gender-detection examinations. The results are striking. In most societies, the number of women equals or exceeds that of men; in India, according to one estimate, there are only 933 females for every 1,000 males.

South Asian Art and Literature Since Independence

Recent decades have witnessed a prodigious outpouring of literature in India. Most works have been written in one of the Indian languages and have not been translated into a foreign tongue. Many authors, however, choose to write in English for the Indian elite or for foreign audiences. For that reason, some critics charge that such literature lacks authenticity.

Because of the vast quantity of works published (India is currently the third-largest publisher of English-language books in the world), only a few of the most prominent fiction writers can be mentioned here. Anita Desai (b. 1937) was one of the first female Indian writers to achieve prominence. Her writing focuses on the struggle of Indian women to achieve a degree of independence. In her first novel, *Cry, the Peacock* (1963), the heroine finally seeks liberation by murdering her husband, preferring freedom at any cost to remaining a captive of traditional society.

The most controversial Indian-born writer today is Salman Rushdie (b. 1947). In *Midnight's Children*, published in 1981, the author linked his protagonist, born on the night of independence, to the history of modern India, its achievements and its frustrations. Like his contemporaries Günter Grass and Gabriel García Márquez, Rushdie used the technique of magical realism to jolt his audience into a recognition of the inhumanity of modern society and the need to develop a sense of moral concern for the fate of the Indian people and for the world as a whole.

Rushdie's later novels have tackled such problems as religious intolerance, political tyranny, social injustice, and greed and corruption. His attack on Islamic fundamentalism in *The Satanic Verses* (1988) won plaudits from literary critics but provoked widespread criticism among Muslims, including a death sentence by Ayatollah Khomeini in Iran. *The Moor's Last Sigh* (1995) examined the alleged excesses of Hindu nationalism. A number of younger writers are following Rushdie's lead and are providing their own critiques of India's evolving social problems. In *The White Tiger* (2008), Indian author Aravind Adiga (b. 1974) addresses the greed and corruption among India's newly rich as he traces the darkly mordant rise of a rickshaw driver to a wealthy entrepreneur.

What Is the Future of India?

Indian society looks increasingly Western in form, if not in content. As in a number of other Asian and African societies, the distinction between traditional and modern, or indigenous and Westernized, sometimes seems to be a simple dichotomy between rural and urban. The major cities appear modern and Westernized, but the villages have changed little since precolonial days.

Yet traditional practices appear to be more resilient in India than in many other societies, and the result is often a synthesis rather than a clash between conflicting institutions and values. Unlike China under Mao Zedong, India did not reject its past but merely adjusted it to meet the needs of the present. Clothing styles in the streets where the *sari* and *dhoti* continue to be popular, religious practices in the temples, and social relationships in the home all testify to the importance of tradition in India.

One disadvantage of the eclectic approach, which seeks to blend the old and the new rather than choosing one over the other, is that sometimes contrasting traditions cannot be reconciled. In his book *India: A Wounded Civilization*, V. S. Naipaul (b. 1932), a Trinidadian of Indian descent who received the Nobel Prize for Literature in 2001, charged that Mahatma Gandhi's glorification of poverty and the simple Indian village was an obstacle to efforts to overcome the poverty, ignorance, and degradation of India's past and build a prosperous modern society. Gandhi's vision of a spiritual India, Naipaul complained, was a balm for defeatism and an excuse for failure.

Yet the appeal of Gandhi's philosophy remains a major part of the country's heritage. In July 2006, at a time when growing despair at economic conditions in the countryside resulted in a rash of suicides by poor farmers, Prime Minister Manmohan Singh called on the Indian people to reject the American model of "wasteful" consumer spending and return to the frugal teachings and spiritual vision of Mahatma Gandhi, which were, in his words, a "necessity" for a country as poor in material goods as India.[4]

Certainly, India faces a difficult dilemma. As historian Martha Nussbaum points out in *The Clash Within: Democracy, Religious Violence, and India's Future*, many in India's rural population continue to hold traditional beliefs, such as the concept of *karma* and inherent caste distinctions, that are incompatible with the capitalist work ethic and the democratic belief in equality before the law. Yet these beliefs provide a measure of identity and solace often lacking in other societies where such traditional spiritual underpinnings have eroded.

India, like Pakistan, also faces a number of other serious challenges. The Congress Party's vision of a diverse society composed of many distinct ethnic and religious communities is increasingly at odds with the virulent spirit of nationalism and religious identity sweeping the

Fetching Water at the Village Well. The scarcity of water will surely become one of the planet's most crucial problems. It will affect all nations, developed and developing, rich and poor. The problem will be particularly acute in India, where the vagaries of the monsoon season and the rapidly expanding population are creating a potential environmental crisis. Although many Indians must live with an inadequate water supply, these women are fortunate to have a well in their village. A more typical image is an Indian woman dressed in a colorful *sari* and encircled by children, carrying a heavy pail of water on her head as she trudges to her distant home.

region today. It also must cope with severe environmental difficulties, including land erosion, overcrowding, and a scarcity of water and other vital resources, which will place severe limitations on the country's ability to transform itself into an economic powerhouse. As a democratic and pluralistic society, India is unable to launch major programs without popular consent and thus cannot move as quickly or often as effectively as an authoritarian system like China's. Whether India will be able to meet its challenges remains an open question.

Southeast Asia

The Japanese wartime occupation had a great impact on attitudes among the peoples of Southeast Asia. It demonstrated the vulnerability of colonial rule in the region and showed that an Asian power could defeat Europeans. The Allied governments themselves also contributed—sometimes unwittingly—to rising aspirations for independence by promising self-determination for all peoples at the end of the war. Although Winston Churchill later said that the Atlantic Charter did not apply to the colonial peoples, it would be difficult to put the genie back in the bottle again.

The End of the Colonial Era

Some did not try. In July 1946, the United States granted total independence to the Philippines. The Americans maintained a military presence on the islands, however, and U.S. citizens retained economic and commercial interests in the new country.

The British, too, under the Labour Party, were willing to bring an end to a century of imperialism in the region. In 1948, the Union of Burma received its independence. Malaya's turn came in 1957, after a Communist guerrilla movement had been suppressed.

The French and the Dutch, however, both regarded their colonies in the region as economic necessities as well as symbols of national grandeur and refused to turn them over to nationalist movements at the end of the war. The Dutch attempted to suppress a rebellion in the East Indies led by Sukarno (1901–1970), leader of the Indonesian Nationalist Party. But the United States, which feared a Communist victory there, pressured the Dutch to grant independence to Sukarno and his non-Communist forces, and in 1950, the Dutch finally agreed to recognize the new Republic of Indonesia.

THE FRANCO-VIETMINH WAR The situation was somewhat different in Vietnam, where the leading force in the anticolonial movement was the local Indochinese Communist Party (ICP) led by the veteran Moscow-trained revolutionary Ho Chi Minh (1890–1969). In August 1945, virtually at the moment of Japanese surrender, the Vietminh Front, an alliance of patriotic forces under secret ICP leadership that had been founded to fight the Japanese in 1941, launched a general uprising and seized power throughout most of Vietnam.

In early September, Ho Chi Minh was declared president of a new provisional republic in Hanoi. In the meantime, French military units began arriving in Saigon, with the permission of the British occupation command there. The new government in Hanoi, formally known as the Democratic Republic of Vietnam (DRV), appealed to the victorious Allies for recognition but received no response, and by late fall, the southern part of the country was back under French rule. Ho signed a preliminary agreement with the French recognizing Vietnam as a "free state" within the French Union, but negotiations over the details broke down in the summer of 1946, and war between the two parties broke out in December. The French occupied the cities, while the Vietminh retreated into the countryside and began to carry out a guerrilla struggle. After eight years of bitter conflict, the French were exhausted, and at the Geneva Conference in 1954, they agreed to withdraw from all Indochina. Two new states then emerged in Vietnam—a Communist one under Ho Chi Minh in the North and a non-Communist one, under the nationalist politician Ngo Dinh Diem, in the South (see Chapter 7).

In the Shadow of the Cold War

Many of the leaders of the newly independent states in Southeast Asia (see Map 13.2) admired Western political institutions and hoped to adapt them to their own countries. New constitutions were patterned on Western democratic models, and multiparty political systems quickly sprang into operation.

THE SEARCH FOR A NEW POLITICAL CULTURE By the 1960s, most of these budding experiments in pluralist democracy had been abandoned or were under serious threat. Some had been replaced by military or one-party autocratic regimes. In Burma, a moderate government based on the British parliamentary system and dedicated to Buddhism and nonviolent Marxism had given way to a military dictatorship. In Thailand, too, the military ruled. In the Philippines, President Ferdinand Marcos (1917–1989) discarded democratic restraints and established his own centralized control. In South Vietnam, under pressure from Communist-led insurgents, Ngo Dinh Diem and his successors paid lip service to the Western democratic model but ruled by authoritarian means.

One problem faced by most of these states was that independence had not brought material prosperity or ended economic inequality and the domination of the local economies by foreign interests. Most economies in the region were still characterized by tiny industrial sectors; they lacked technology, educational resources, capital investment, and leaders trained in developmental skills.

The presence of widespread ethnic, linguistic, religious, and economic differences also made the transition to Western-style democracy difficult. In Malaya, for example, the majority Malays—most of whom were farmers and virtually all of whom were (and still are) Muslims—feared economic and political domination by the local Chinese minority, who were much more experienced in industry and commerce. In 1961, the Federation of Malaya, whose ruling party was dominated by Malays, integrated former British possessions on the island of Borneo into the new Union of Malaysia in a move to increase the non-Chinese proportion of the country's population. Yet periodic conflicts persisted as the Malaysian government attempted to guarantee Malay control over politics and a larger role in the economy.

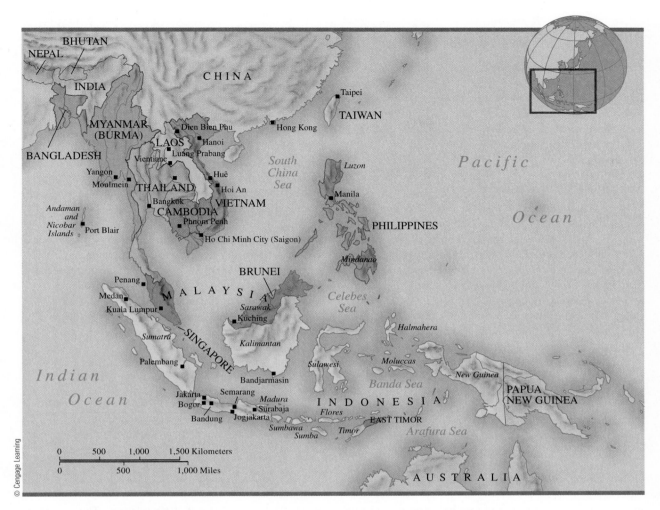

MAP 13.2 **Contemporary Southeast Asia.** Shown here are the countries of contemporary Southeast Asia. The major islands that make up the Republic of Indonesia are indicated in yellow.

Q *Which of the countries in Southeast Asia have functioning democratic governments? Which appear to be the most prosperous?*

Finally, the new nations of Southeast Asia were seeking to realize their ambitious objectives in a time of intense political turmoil throughout Asia. While their political leaders were under severe pressure to take sides in the ideological Cold War, revolutionary parties—many of them influenced by the Maoist strategy of "people's war"—operated outside the system as they sought to bring about drastic change on the model of the new China.

SUKARNO AND "GUIDED DEMOCRACY" The most prominent example of a failed experiment in democracy was in Indonesia. In 1950, the new leaders drew up a constitution creating a parliamentary system under a titular presidency. Sukarno was elected the first president.

A spellbinding orator, Sukarno played a major role in creating a sense of national identity among the disparate peoples of the Indonesian archipelago (see the box on p. 284).

But Sukarno grew exasperated at the incessant maneuvering among devout Muslims, Communists, and the army, and in the late 1950s, he dissolved the constitution and attempted to rule on his own through what he called **guided democracy**. As he described it, guided democracy was closer to Indonesian traditions and superior to the Western variety. The weakness of the latter was that it allowed the majority to dominate the minority, whereas guided democracy would reconcile different opinions and points of view in a government operated by consensus. Highly suspicious of the West, Sukarno nationalized

The Golden Throat of President Sukarno

President Sukarno of Indonesia was a spellbinding speaker and a charismatic leader of his nation's struggle for independence. These two excerpts are from speeches in which Sukarno promoted two of his favorite projects: Indonesian nationalism and "guided democracy." The force that would guide Indonesia, of course, was to be Sukarno himself.

Sukarno on Indonesian Greatness

What was Indonesia in 1945? What was our nation then? It was only two things, only two things. A flag and a song. That is all. (Pause, finger held up as afterthought.) But no, I have omitted the main ingredient. I have missed the most important thing of all. I have left out the burning fire of freedom and independence in the breast and heart of every Indonesian. That is the most important thing—this is the vital chord—the spirit of our people, the spirit and determination to be free. This was our nation in 1945—the spirit of our people!

And what are we today? We are a great nation. We are bigger than Poland. We are bigger than Turkey. We have more people than Australia, than Canada, we are bigger in area and have more people than Japan. In population now we are the fifth-largest country in the world. In area, we are even bigger than the United States of America. The American Ambassador, who is here with us, admits this. Of course, he points out that we have a lot of water in between our thousands of islands. But I say to him—America has a lot of mountains and deserts, too!

Sukarno on Guided Democracy

Indonesia's democracy is not liberal democracy. Indonesian democracy is not the democracy of the world of Montaigne or Voltaire. Indonesia's democracy is not à la America, Indonesia's democracy is not the Soviet—NO! Indonesia's democracy is the democracy which is implanted in the breasts of the Indonesian people, and it is that which I have tried to dig up again, and have put forward as an offering to you.... If you, especially the undergraduates, are still clinging to and being borne along the democracy made in England, or democracy made in France, or democracy made in America, or democracy made in Russia, you will become a nation of copyists!

 How did Sukarno justify his claim that Indonesia is as large as the United States?

SOURCE: From Howard Jones, *Indonesia: The Possible Dream* (New York: Harcourt Brace Jovanovich, Hoover Institute, 1971), pp. 223, 237.

---

foreign-owned enterprises and sought economic aid from China and the Soviet Union while relying for domestic support on the Indonesian Communist Party.

The army and many devout Muslims resented Sukarno's increasing reliance on the Communists, and the Muslims were further upset by his refusal to consider a state based on Islamic principles. In 1965, military officers launched a coup d'état that provoked a mass popular uprising, which resulted in the slaughter of several hundred thousand suspected Communists, many of whom were overseas Chinese, long distrusted by the Muslim majority (see the Film & History feature on p. 285). In 1967, a military government under General Suharto (1921–2008) was installed.

The new government made no pretensions of reverting to democratic rule, but it did restore good relations with the West and sought foreign investment to repair the country's ravaged economy. But it also found it difficult to placate Muslim demands for an Islamic state. In a few areas, including western Sumatra, militant Muslims took up arms against the state.

FROM PEACE TO WAR IN INDOCHINA The one country in Southeast Asia that consistently rejected the Western model was North Vietnam. Ho Chi Minh and his colleagues opted for the Stalinist pattern of national development, based on Communist Party rule and socialist forms of ownership. In 1958, stimulated by the success of collectivization in neighboring China, the government launched a three-year plan to lay the foundation for a socialist society. Collective farms were established, and all industry and commerce above the family level were nationalized. By the first years of the following decade, however, party leaders in Hanoi began to provide support to insurgent forces in the South (see Chapter 7). Developmental plans were abandoned, as the entire country shifted to a wartime footing.

On the Road to Political Reform

With the end of the Vietnam War and the gradual rapprochement between China and the United States in the late 1970s, the ferment and uncertainty that had

The Year of Living Dangerously (1983)

President Sukarno of Indonesia was one of the most prominent figures in Southeast Asia in the first two decades after World War II. A key figure in the nationalist movement while the country was under Dutch colonial rule, he was elected president of the new republic when it was granted formal independence in 1950. The charismatic Sukarno initially won broad popular support for his efforts to end colonial dependency and improve living conditions for the impoverished local population. But the government's economic achievements failed to match his fiery oratory, and when political unrest began to spread through Indonesian society in the early 1960s, Sukarno dismantled the parliamentary system that had been installed at independence and began to crack down on dissidents.

These conditions are the setting for the Australian film *The Year of Living Dangerously* (1983). Based on a novel of the same name by Christian Koch, the movie takes place in the summer of 1965, at a time when popular unrest against the dictatorial government had reached a crescendo and the country appeared about to erupt in civil war. The newly arrived Australian reporter Guy Hamilton (Mel Gibson) is befriended by a diminutive Chinese Indonesian journalist Billy Kwan, effectively played by Linda Hunt, who received an Academy Award for her performance. Kwan, who has become increasingly disenchanted with Sukarno's failure to live up his promises, introduces Hamilton to the seamy underside of Indonesian society as well as to radical elements connected to the Communist Party who are planning a coup to seize power in Jakarta.

The movie reaches a climax as Hamilton—a quintessentially ambitious reporter out to get a scoop on the big story—inadvertently becomes involved in the Communist plot and arouses the suspicion of government authorities. As Indonesia appears ready to

Photographer Billy Kwan (Linda Hunt) and reporter Guy Hamilton (Mel Gibson) film a political protest.

descend into chaos, Hamilton finally recognizes the extent of the danger and manages to board the last plane from Jakarta. Others are not so fortunate, as Sukarno's security police crack down forcefully on critics of his regime.

The Year of Living Dangerously (the title comes from a remark made by Sukarno during his presidential address in August 1964) is an important if underrated film that dramatically portrays a crucial incident in a volatile region caught in the throes of the global Cold War. The beautiful scenery (the film was shot in the Philippines because the story was banned in Indonesia) and a haunting film score help create a mood of tension spreading through a tropical paradise. ■

marked the first three decades of independence in Southeast Asia gradually gave way to an era of greater political stability and material prosperity. In the Philippines, the dictatorial regime of Ferdinand Marcos was overthrown by a massive public uprising in 1986 and replaced by a democratically elected government under President Corazon Aquino (1933–2009), the widow of a popular politician assassinated a few years earlier. Aquino was unable to resolve many of the country's chronic economic and social difficulties, however, and

political stability remained elusive. One of her successors, Joseph Estrada (b. 1937), a former actor, was forced to resign on the charge of corruption, and Muslims in the southern island of Mindanao have mounted a terrorist campaign in their effort to obtain autonomy or independence.

In other nations, the trends have been equally mixed. Malaysia is a practicing democracy, although tensions persist between Malays and Chinese as well as between secular and orthodox Muslims who seek to create an Islamic state. In neighboring Thailand, the military has found it expedient to hold national elections for civilian governments, but the danger of a military takeover is never far beneath the surface. In the fall of 2008, massive protests launched by opponents of the existing government closed the Bangkok airport for several days and threatened to throw Thai society into a state of paralysis.

INDONESIA AFTER SUHARTO

For years, a major exception to the trend toward political pluralism in the region was Indonesia, where Suharto ruled without restraints. But in 1996 and 1997, protests by students demanding increased freedoms and by Muslims demanding a larger role for Islam in society prompted Suharto's government to arrest many dissidents. In 1997, popular anger against the government (several members of Suharto's family had reportedly used their positions to amass considerable wealth) led to violent street riots and demands for his resignation. Forced to step down in the spring of 1998, Suharto was replaced by his deputy B. J. Habibie (b. 1936), who called for the establishment of a national assembly to select a new government based on popular aspirations. The assembly selected a moderate Muslim leader as president, but he was charged with corruption and incompetence and was replaced in 2001 by his vice president, Sukarno's daughter Megawati Sukarnoputri (b. 1947).

The new government faced internal challenges from dissident elements seeking autonomy or separation from the republic, as well as from religious forces seeking to transform the country into an Islamic state. Under pressure from the international community, Indonesia agreed to grant independence to the onetime Portuguese colony of East Timor, where the majority of the people are Roman Catholics. But violence provoked by pro-Indonesian militia units forced many refugees to flee the country. Religious tensions also erupted between Muslims and Christians elsewhere in the archipelago, and Muslim rebels in western Sumatra continue to agitate for a new state based on strict adherence to fundamentalist Islam. In 2002, a terrorist attack directed at tourists on the island of Bali aroused fears that the Muslim nation had become a haven for terrorist elements throughout the region.

In direct elections held in 2004, General Susilo Yudhyono (b. 1949) defeated Megawati Sukarnoputri and ascended to the presidency. The new chief executive promised a new era of political stability, honest government, and economic reform while ceding more authority to the country's thirty-three provinces. Pressure from traditional Muslims to abandon the nation's secular tradition and move toward the creation of an Islamic state continues, but the level of religious and ethnic tension has declined somewhat. In elections held in 2009, Yudhyono won a second term in office, while popular support for Islamic parties dropped from 38 percent to 26 percent. That the country was able to hold democratic elections in the midst of such tensions holds some promise for the future.

THE EXCEPTIONS: VIETNAM AND MYANMAR

As always, Vietnam is a special case. After achieving victory over South Vietnam with the fall of Saigon in the spring of 1975 (see Chapter 7), the Communist government in Hanoi pursued the rapid reunification of the two zones under Communist Party rule and laid plans to carry out a socialist transformation throughout the country, now renamed the Socialist Republic of Vietnam. The result was an economic disaster, and in 1986, party leaders followed the example of Mikhail Gorbachev in the Soviet Union and introduced their own version of *perestroika* in Vietnam (see Chapter 9). The trend in recent years has been toward a mixed capitalist-socialist economy along Chinese lines and a greater popular role in the governing process. Elections for the unicameral parliament are more open than in the past. The government remains suspicious of Western-style democracy, however, and represses any opposition to the Communist Party's guiding role over the state.

Only in Burma (in 1989 renamed Myanmar), where the military has been in control since the early 1960s, were the forces of greater popular participation largely silenced. Even there, however, the power of the ruling regime of General Ne Win (1911–2002) and his successors, known first as SLORC and after 1997 as the State Peace and Development Council (SPDC), was vocally challenged by Aung San Suu Kyi (b. 1945), the admired daughter of one of the heroes of the country's struggle for national liberation after World War II. In 2011, the SPDC was officially abolished and replaced by a new constitution and an elected president, Thein Sein (b. 1945), a retired military officer. Nevertheless, the military remained in control, and opposition parties such as that led by Aung San Suu Kyi did not participate in the elections. In the 2012 by-elections, however, Aung San Suu Kyi was elected to parliament, and her party, the National League for Demcracy, won forty-three of forty-five vacant seats. The military still controlled approximately 80 percent of the seats in parliament, however.

FINANCIAL CRISIS AND RECOVERY

The trend toward more representative systems of government in the region has been due in part to increasing prosperity and the growth of an affluent and educated middle class. Although Myanmar and the three Indochinese states (Cambodia, Laos, and Vietnam) are still overwhelmingly agrarian,

© William J. Duiker

Build a Better Tomorrow! One of the more familiar sights in countries ruled by Communist parties is the placard breathlessly exhorting the citizenry to fulfill the party's economic and social goals. Vietnam is one of the more enthusiastic practitioners of the art. This billboard calls on passersby to "resolutely determine to build a modern and cultured Ho Chi Minh City." The happy faces on the billboard represent all of the country's major social classes and ethnic groups: men, women, children, workers, peasants, students, office workers, soldiers, and the national minorities—all of them, by implication, enthusiastically supportive of the Communist party as the leading force in the nation.

Indonesia, Malaysia, and Thailand have been undergoing relatively rapid economic development.

In the late summer of 1997, however, these economic gains were threatened, and popular faith in the ultimate benefits of globalization was shaken as a financial crisis swept through the region. The crisis was triggered by a number of problems, including growing budget deficits caused by excessive government expenditures on ambitious development projects, irresponsible lending and investment practices by financial institutions, and an overvaluation of local currencies relative to the U.S. dollar. An underlying cause of these problems was the prevalence of backroom deals between politicians and business leaders that temporarily enriched both groups at the cost of eventual economic dislocation.

As local currencies plummeted in value, the International Monetary Fund agreed to provide assistance, but only on the condition that the governments concerned permit greater transparency in their economic systems and allow market forces to operate more freely, even at the price of bankruptcies and the loss of jobs. By the early 2000s, there were signs that the economies in the region had weathered the crisis and were beginning to recover. The massive tsunami that struck the region in December

2004 was a setback, as well as a human tragedy of enormous proportions, but as the decade wore on, progress resumed, and today the nations of Southeast Asia, with a few exceptions, are among the fastest growing in the world.

Indonesia is one of the region's foremost success stories. Blessed with abundant natural resources, including oil reserves, precious metals, and a variety of tropical products, it has surmounted the recent global economic slowdown and currently enjoys an annual growth rate of more than 6 percent. Indonesia continues to face a number of problems, including urban poverty and environmental pollution, but its prospects are brighter than could have been anticipated even a decade ago.

Regional Conflict and Cooperation: The Rise of ASEAN

Another problem for the Southeast Asian states has been the serious tensions that have arisen among them. Some of these tensions were a consequence of historical rivalries and territorial disputes that had been submerged during the long era of colonial rule. In the 1960s, Indonesian president Sukarno briefly launched a policy of confrontation with the Federation of Malaya, contending that the Malay peninsula had once been part of empires based on the Indonesian islands. The claim was dropped after Sukarno's fall from power in 1965. Another chronic border dispute has long existed between Cambodia and its two neighbors, Thailand and Vietnam, both of which once exercised suzerainty over Cambodian territories. The frontiers established at the moment of Cambodian independence were originally drawn up by French colonial authorities for their own convenience.

After the reunification of Vietnam under Communist rule in 1975, the lingering border dispute between Cambodia and Vietnam erupted again. In April 1975, a brutal revolutionary regime under the leadership of the Khmer Rouge dictator Pol Pot (1925–1988) came to power in Cambodia and proceeded to carry out the massacre of more than one million Cambodians. Then, claiming that vast territories in the Mekong delta had been seized from Cambodia by the Vietnamese in previous centuries, the Khmer Rouge regime launched attacks across the common border. In response, Vietnamese forces invaded

Holocaust in Cambodia. When the Khmer Rouge seized power in Cambodia in April 1975, they immediately emptied the capital of Phnom Penh and systematically began to eliminate opposition elements throughout the country. Thousands were tortured in the infamous Tuol Sleng prison and then marched out to the countryside, where they were massacred. Their bodies were thrown into massive pits. The succeeding government disinterred the remains, which are now displayed at an outdoor museum on the site.

for disagreements with Western countries over global economic issues and the rising power of China will present major challenges in coming years. The admission of Vietnam into ASEAN in 1995 provided both Hanoi and its neighbors with greater leverage in dealing with their powerful neighbor to the north, whose claims of ownership over islands in the South China Sea have aroused widespread concern throughout the region.

Daily Life: Town and Country in Contemporary Southeast Asia

The urban-rural dichotomy observed in India is also found in Southeast Asia, where the cities resemble those in the West while the countryside often appears little changed from precolonial days. In cities such as Bangkok, Manila, and Jakarta, broad boulevards lined with skyscrapers alternate with muddy lanes passing through neighborhoods packed with wooden shacks topped by thatch or rusty tin roofs. Nevertheless, in recent decades, millions of Southeast Asians have fled to these urban slums. Although most available jobs are menial, the pay is better than in the villages.

TRADITIONAL CUSTOMS, MODERN VALUES The urban migrants change not only their physical surroundings but their attitudes and values as well. Sometimes the move leads to a decline in traditional religious faith. Belief in natural and ancestral spirits, for example, has declined among the urban populations of Southeast Asia. In Thailand, Buddhism has come under pressure from the rising influence of materialism, although temple schools still educate thousands of rural youths whose families cannot afford the cost of public education.

Nevertheless, Buddhist, Muslim, and Confucian beliefs remain strong, even in cosmopolitan cities such as Bangkok, Jakarta, and Singapore. This preference for the traditional also shows up in lifestyle. Traditional dress—or

Cambodia in December 1978 and installed a pro-Hanoi regime in Phnom Penh. Fearful of Vietnam's increasing power in the region, China launched a brief attack on Vietnam to demonstrate its displeasure.

The outbreak of war among the erstwhile Communist allies aroused the concern of other countries in the neighborhood. In 1967, several non-Communist countries had established the Association of Southeast Asian Nations, or **ASEAN**. Composed of Indonesia, Malaysia, Thailand, Singapore, and the Philippines, ASEAN at first concentrated on cooperative social and economic endeavors, but after the end of the Vietnam War, it cooperated with other states in an effort to force the Vietnamese to withdraw from Cambodia. In 1991, the Vietnamese finally withdrew, and a new government was formed in Phnom Penh.

The growth of ASEAN from a weak collection of diverse states into a stronger organization whose ten members—Vietnam, Laos, Myanmar, Thailand, and Brunei have joined the original five countries—cooperate militarily and politically has helped provide the nations of Southeast Asia with a more cohesive voice to represent their interests on the world stage. They will need it,

You Can Take It with You. In traditional China, wealthy Chinese buried clay models of personal possessions to accompany the departed to the next world, but ordinary people burned paper effigies, which were transported to the afterlife by means of the rising smoke. This custom survives in many Chinese communities today, as this photograph taken in modern-day Malaysia demonstrates. Some merchants make their living by manufacturing paper replicas of elaborate houses as seen here, often featuring such embellishments as television sets, elegant furniture, and even BMW automobiles.

an eclectic blend of Asian and Western dress—is still common. Asian music, art, theater, and dance remain popular, although Western music has become fashionable among the young, and Indonesian filmmakers complain that Western films are beginning to dominate the local market.

The increasing inroads made by Western culture have caused anxiety in some countries. In Malaysia, for example, fundamentalist Muslims criticize the prevalence of pornography, hedonism, drugs, and alcohol in Western culture and have tried to limit their presence in their own country. The Malaysian government has attempted to limit the number of U.S. entertainment programs shown on local television stations and has replaced them with shows on traditional themes.

CHANGING ROLES FOR WOMEN   One of the most significant changes that has taken place in Southeast Asia in recent decades is in the role of women in society. In general, women in the region have historically faced fewer restrictions on their activities and enjoyed a higher status than women elsewhere in Asia. Nevertheless, they were not the equal of men in every respect. With independence, Southeast Asian women gained new rights. Virtually all of the constitutions adopted by the newly independent states granted women full legal and political rights, including the right to work. Today, women have increased opportunities for education and have entered careers previously reserved for men. Women have become more

active in politics, and as we have seen, some have served as heads of state.

Yet women are not truly equal to men in any country in Southeast Asia. Sometimes the distinction is simply a matter of custom. In Vietnam, women are legally equal to men, yet until recently no women had served in the Communist Party's ruling Politburo. In Thailand, Malaysia, and Indonesia, women rarely hold senior positions in government service or in the boardrooms of major corporations. Similar restrictions apply in Myanmar, although Aung San Suu Kyi is the leading figure in the democratic opposition movement.

Sometimes, too, women's rights have been undermined by a social or religious backlash. The revival of Islamic fundamentalism has had an especially strong impact in Malaysia, where Malay women are expected to cover their bodies and wear the traditional Muslim headdress. Even in non-Muslim countries, women are expected to behave demurely and exercise discretion in all contacts with the opposite sex.

Cultural Trends

In most countries in Southeast Asia, writers, artists, and composers are attempting to synthesize international styles and themes with local tradition and experience. The novel has become increasingly popular as writers seek to find the best medium to encapsulate the dramatic changes that have taken place in the region in recent decades.

The best-known writer in postwar Indonesia—at least to readers abroad—was Pramoedya Toer (1925–2006). Born in eastern Java, he joined the Indonesian nationalist movement in his early twenties. Arrested in 1965 on the charge of being a Communist, he spent the next several years in prison. While incarcerated, he began writing his four-volume *Buru Quartet*, which recounts in fictional form the story of the struggle of the Indonesian people for freedom from colonial rule and the autocratic regimes of the independence period.

Among the most talented of contemporary Vietnamese novelists is Duong Thu Huong (b. 1947). A onetime member of the Vietnamese Communist Party who served on the front lines during the Sino-Vietnamese war in 1979, she later became outspoken in her criticism of the party's failure to carry out democratic reforms and was briefly imprisoned in 1991. Undaunted by official pressure, she has written several novels that express the horrors experienced by guerrilla fighters during the Vietnam War and the cruel injustices perpetrated by the regime in the cause of building socialism. She has recently written a fictional biography of Ho Chi Minh entitled *The Zenith* (2012).

CONCLUSION

THE IMAGE OF SOUTHEAST ASIA mired in the Vietnam conflict and the tensions of the Cold War has become a distant memory. In ASEAN, the states in the region have created the framework for a regional organization that can serve their common political, economic, technological, and security interests. A few members of ASEAN are already on the road to advanced development. The remainder are showing signs of undergoing a similar process within the next generation. Although ethnic and religious tensions continue to exist in most ASEAN states, there are promising signs of increasing political stability and pluralism throughout the region.

To be sure, there are also challenges to overcome. The global recession that erupted in the fall of 2008 continues to test the resilience of all countries in the region, especially those like Malaysia and Singapore that are highly dependent on exports to Western markets. Myanmar (Burma) is only beginning to emerge from a period of isolation and appears mired in a state of chronic underdevelopment. The three states of Indochina remain potentially unstable and have not yet been fully integrated into the region as a whole. Finally, terrorist activity within the region, especially in Indonesia, has not been brought to an end. Although most Muslims in Southeast Asia have traditionally embraced moderate political, social, and religious views, radical agitators have made inroads through their presence in Muslim schools in the region.

All things considered, however, the situation is more promising today than would have seemed possible a generation ago. The nations of Southeast Asia appear capable of coordinating their efforts to erase the internal divisions and conflicts that have brought so much tragedy to the peoples of the region for centuries. Most have joined the steadily growing ranks of developing nations.

To some observers, though, the region's economic success has come at a high price, in the form of political authoritarianism and a lack of attention to human rights. Still, a look at the historical record suggests that political pluralism is often a by-product of economic advances and that political values and institutions evolve in response to changing societal conditions. In the end, the current growing pains in Southeast Asia may prove to be beneficial in their overall impact on societies in the region.

TIMELINE

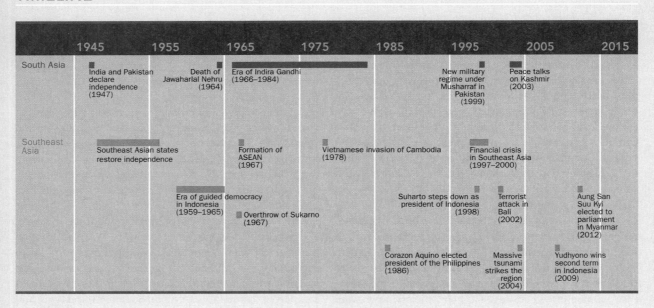

CHAPTER NOTES

1. *New York Times*, May 2, 1996.
2. Quoted in Larry Collins and Dominique Lapierre, *Freedom at Midnight* (New York, 1975), p. 252.
3. Cited in Somini Sengupta, "In World's Largest Democracy, Tolerance Is a Weak Pillar," *New York Times*, October 29, 2008.
4. From Pankaj Mishra, "Impasse in India," *New York Review of Books*, June 28, 2007, p. 51.

14

Emerging Africa

Morning in Timbuktu

© Ruth Petzold

ON TAKING OVER THE CITY, they began to terrorize the inhabitants—cutting off the hands of suspected thieves, stoning adulterous couples to death, forbidding the playing of any kind of musical instrument, and desecrating the shrines of local Sufi mystics. The invaders were fanatical tribal warriors who sought to impose their strict version of Islam on the population throughout the region. The city was Timbuktu, once a fabled caravan stop on a major trade route snaking through the Sahara and more recently a sleepy river port in the Central African country of Mali. The time was January 2013.

Timbuktu lies in the **Sahel**, a grassy region just south of the Sahara that stretches from the western tip of the African continent to the Nile River valley in the east. Historically a geographic fault line between the arid desert and the rich tropical forest lands along the Atlantic coast to the south, in recent times the Sahel has become a political and ideological battleground as well, as Muslim pastoralists compete with Christian and animist farmers for scarce fertile land and access to precious water reserves. The struggle has been going on for centuries, but it has intensified in recent years as a result of the increasing desiccation of the region. It is one of the challenges that many nations in Africa face today. ◆

CRITICAL THINKING

Q To what degree have the nations of Africa managed to achieve political stability and economic prosperity since achieving independence after World War II?

Uhuru: The Struggle for Independence in Africa

After World War II, some European governments reluctantly recognized that the end result of colonial rule in Africa would be African self-government, if not full independence. Accordingly, the African population would have to be trained to handle the responsibilities of representative government. As a result, during the 1950s most British colonies introduced reforms that increased the representation of the local population. Members of legislative and executive councils were increasingly chosen through elections, and Africans came to constitute a majority of these bodies. Elected councils at the local level were introduced in the 1950s to reduce the power of the chiefs and clan heads, who had controlled local government under indirect rule. An exception was South Africa, where European domination continued. In the Union of South Africa, the franchise was restricted to whites except in the former territory of the Cape Colony, where persons of mixed ancestry had enjoyed the right to vote since the mid-nineteenth century. Black Africans did win some limited electoral rights in Northern and Southern Rhodesia (now Zambia and Zimbabwe, respectively), although whites generally dominated the political scene.

A similar process of political liberalization was taking place in the French colonies. At first, the French tried to integrate the African peoples into French culture. By the 1920s, however, racist beliefs in Western cultural superiority and the tenacity of traditional beliefs and practices among Africans had somewhat discredited this ideal. The French therefore substituted a more limited program of assigning a limited number of French-educated elites as administrators at the local level as a link to the rest of the population. The remaining European colonial powers, notably Belgium and Portugal, made little effort to prepare their subject peoples for independence.

The Colonial Legacy

As in Asia, colonial rule had a mixed impact on the societies and peoples of Africa. The Western presence brought a number of short-term and long-term benefits to Africa, such as improved transportation and communication facilities, and in a few areas laid the foundation for a modern industrial and commercial sector. Improved sanitation and medical care increased life expectancy. The introduction of selective elements of Western political systems laid the groundwork for the gradual creation of democratic societies.

Yet the benefits of Westernization were distributed very unequally, and the vast majority of Africans found their lives little improved, if at all. Only South Africa and French-held Algeria, for example, developed modern industrial sectors, extensive railroad networks, and modern communications systems. In both countries, European settlers were numerous, most investment capital for industrial ventures was European, and whites comprised almost the entire professional and managerial class. Members of the local population were generally restricted to unskilled or semiskilled jobs at wages less than one-fifth of those enjoyed by Europeans.

Many colonies concentrated on export crops—peanuts in Senegal and Gambia, cotton in Egypt and Uganda, coffee in Kenya, palm oil and cocoa products in the Gold Coast. In some cases, the crops were grown on plantations, which were usually owned by Europeans. But plantation agriculture was not always suitable in Africa, and much farming was done by free or tenant farmers. In some areas, where land ownership was traditionally vested in the community, the land was owned and leased by the corporate village. The vast majority of the profits from the exports, however, accrued to Europeans or to merchants from other foreign countries, such as India and the Arab emirates.

While a fortunate few benefited from the increase in exports, the vast majority of Africans continued to be subsistence farmers growing food for their own consumption. The gap was particularly wide in places like Kenya, where the best lands were reserved for European settlers to make the colony self-sufficient. As in other parts of the world, the early stages of the Industrial Revolution were especially painful for the rural population, and ordinary subsistence farmers reaped few benefits from colonial rule. To make matters worse, in some areas—notably in West Africa—the cultivation of cash crops eroded the fragile soil base and turned farmland into desert.

The Rise of Nationalism

Political organizations for African rights did not arise until after World War I, and then only in a few areas, such as British-ruled Kenya and the Gold Coast. At first, organizations such as the National Congress of British West Africa (formed in 1919 in the Gold Coast) and Jomo Kenyatta's Kikuyu Central Association focused on improving living conditions in the colonies rather than on national independence. After World War II, however, following the example of independence movements elsewhere, these groups became organized political parties with independence as their objective. In the Gold Coast, Kwame Nkrumah (1909–1972) led the Convention People's Party, the first formal political party in black Africa. In the late 1940s, Jomo Kenyatta (1894–1978) founded the Kenya African National Union (KANU), which focused on economic issues but had an implied political agenda as well.

For the most part, these political activities were nonviolent and were led by Western-educated African intellectuals. Their constituents were primarily urban professionals, merchants, and members of labor unions. But the demand for independence was not restricted to the cities. In Kenya, for example, the widely publicized Mau Mau movement among the Kikuyu people used guerrilla tactics as an element of its program to achieve *uhuru* (Swahili for "freedom") from the British. One of the primary reasons for the revolt was to protest against the unlawful seizure of African lands by European plantation owners. Although only about a hundred Europeans were killed compared with an estimated two thousand Africans who died at the hands of either Mau Mau units or the British, the specter of a nationwide revolt alarmed the European population and convinced the British government in 1959 to promise eventual independence.

In South Africa and Algeria where the political system was also dominated by European settlers, the transition to independence was more complicated. In South Africa, political activity by local Africans began with the formation of the African National Congress (ANC) in 1912. Initially, the **ANC** was dominated by Western-oriented intellectuals and had limited mass support. Its goal was to achieve economic and political reforms, including full equality for educated Africans, within the framework of the existing system. But the ANC's efforts met with little success, while conservative white parties managed to stiffen the segregation laws and impose a policy of full legal segregation, called **apartheid**, in 1948. In response, the ANC became increasingly radicalized, and by the 1950s, the prospects for violence rather than conciliation were growing.

In Algeria, resistance to French rule by Berbers and Arabs in rural areas had never ceased. After World War II, urban agitation intensified, leading to a widespread rebellion against colonial rule in the mid-1950s. At first, the French government tried to maintain its authority in Algeria, which was considered an integral part of metropolitan France. But when Charles de Gaulle became president of France in 1958, he reversed French policy, and Algeria became an independent republic four years later, with Ahmad Ben Bella (1918–2004) as its president. The armed struggle in Algeria hastened the transition to statehood in its neighbors as well. Tunisia won its independence in 1956 after some urban agitation and rural unrest but retained close ties with Paris. The French attempted to suppress the nationalist movement in French Morocco by sending Sultan Muhammad V into exile, but the effort failed, and in 1956, he returned as the ruler of the independent state of Morocco.

Most black African nations achieved their independence in the late 1950s and 1960s, beginning with the Gold Coast, renamed Ghana, in 1957 (see Map 14.1). It was soon followed by Nigeria; the Belgian Congo, renamed Zaire and then the Democratic Republic of the Congo; Kenya; Tanganyika, later joined with Zanzibar and renamed Tanzania; and several other countries. Most of the French colonies agreed to accept independence within the framework of de Gaulle's French Community. By the late 1960s, only parts of southern Africa and the Portuguese possessions of Mozambique and Angola remained under European rule.

Independence thus came later to Africa than to most of Asia. Several factors help explain the delay. For one thing, colonialism was established in Africa somewhat later than in most areas of Asia, and the inevitable reaction from the local population was consequently later in coming. Furthermore, with the exception of a few areas in West Africa and along the Mediterranean, coherent states with a strong sense of cultural, ethnic, and linguistic unity did not exist in most of Africa. Most traditional states, such as Ashanti in West Africa, Songhai in the southern Sahara, and Kongo in the Congo River basin, were collections of heterogeneous peoples with little sense of national or

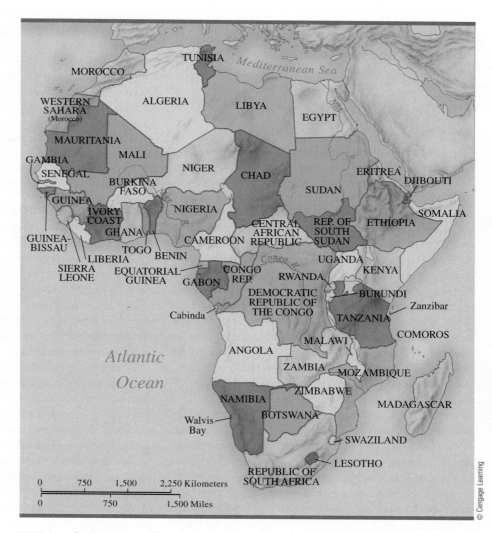

MAP 14.1 Contemporary Africa. This map shows the independent states of Africa today.

Q *Why was unity so difficult to achieve in African regions?*

cultural unity. Even after colonies were established, the European powers often practiced a policy of "divide and rule," and the British encouraged political decentralization by retaining the authority of the traditional local chieftains. It is hardly surprising that when opposition to colonial rule emerged, unity was difficult to achieve.

The Era of Independence

The newly independent African states faced intimidating challenges. They had been profoundly affected by colonial rule, but the experience had been highly unsatisfactory in most respects. Although Western political institutions, values, and technology had been introduced, at least in the cities, the exposure to European civilization had been superficial at best for most Africans and tragic for many. At the outset of independence, most African societies were still primarily agrarian and traditional, and their modern sectors depended mainly on imports from the West.

The Destiny of Africa: Unity or Diversity?

Like their counterparts in South and Southeast Asia, most of Africa's new leaders came from the urban middle class. They had studied in Europe or the United States and spoke and read European languages. Although most were profoundly critical of colonial policies, they appeared for the most part to accept the Western model of governance and Western democratic values.

Their views on economics were somewhat more diverse. Some, like Jomo Kenyatta of Kenya and General Mobutu Sese Seko (1930–1997) of Zaire, were advocates of Western-style capitalism. Others, like Julius Nyerere (1922–1999) of Tanzania, Kwame Nkrumah of Ghana, and Sékou Touré (1922–1984) of Guinea, preferred an "African form of socialism," which bore scant resemblance to the Marxist-Leninist socialism practiced in the Soviet Union. According to its advocates, it was descended from traditional communal practices in precolonial Africa.

At first, most of the new African leaders accepted the national boundaries established during the colonial era. But as we have noted, these boundaries were artificial creations of the colonial powers. Virtually all of the new states included widely diverse ethnic, linguistic, and territorial groups. Zaire, for example, was composed of more than two hundred territorial groups speaking seventy-five different languages. Such conditions posed a severe challenge to the task of forming cohesive nation-states.

A number of leaders—including Nkrumah of Ghana, Touré of Guinea, and Nyerere of Tanganyika—were enticed by **Pan-Africanism**, the concept of a continental unity that transcended national boundaries. Nkrumah in particular hoped that a pan-African union could be established that would unite all of the new countries of the continent in a broader community. His dream was not widely shared by other African political figures, however, who eventually settled on a more innocuous concept of regional cooperation on key issues. The concrete manifestation of this idea was the Organization of African Unity (OAU), founded in Addis Ababa in 1963.

Dream and Reality: Political and Economic Conditions in Independent Africa

The program of the OAU called for an Africa based on freedom, equality, justice, and dignity and on the unity, solidarity, prosperity, and territorial integrity of African states. It did not take long for reality to set in. Vast disparities in education and wealth and the lingering effects of colonial domination made it hard to establish material prosperity in much of Africa. Expectations that independence would lead to stable political structures based on "one person, one vote" were soon disappointed as the initial phase of pluralistic governments gave way to a series of military regimes and one-party states. Between 1957 and 1982, more than seventy leaders of African countries were overthrown by violence.

THE PROBLEM OF NEOCOLONIALISM Part of the problem was the residual impact of colonialism. Most new countries in Africa were dependent on the export of a single crop or natural resource. When prices fluctuated or dropped, these countries were at the mercy of the international market. In several cases, the resources were still controlled by foreigners, leading to the charge that colonialism had been succeeded by **neocolonialism**, in which Western domination was maintained primarily by economic rather than political or military means.

World trade patterns often exacerbated these problems. Most African states had to import technology and manufactured goods from the West, and the prices of those goods rose more rapidly than those of the export products. Many of the exports were raw materials, and their prices were often subject to rapid fluctuations.

The new states contributed to their own problems. Treasury funds were squandered on military equipment or expensive consumer goods rather than applied to building up the infrastructure to support and sustain an industrial economy. Corruption, a painful reality throughout the modern world, became almost a way of life in Africa as bribery became necessary to obtain even the most basic services (see the box on p. 295).

Stealing the Nation's Riches

After 1965, African novelists transferred their anger from the foreign oppressor to their own national leaders, deploring their greed, corruption, and inhumanity. One of the most pessimistic expressions of this betrayal of newly independent Africa is found in *The Beautiful Ones Are Not Yet Born*, a novel published by the Ghanaian author Ayi Kwei Armah in 1968. The author decried the government of Kwame Nkrumah and was unimpressed with the rumors of a military coup, which, he predicted, would simply replace the regime with a new despot and his entourage of "fat men." Ghana today has made significant progress in reducing the level of corruption.

Ayi Kwei Armah, *The Beautiful Ones Are Not Yet Born*

The net had been made in the special Ghanaian way that allowed the really big corrupt people to pass through it. A net to catch only the small, dispensable fellows, trying in their anguished blindness to leap and to attain the gleam and the comfort the only way these things could be done. And the big ones floated free, like all the slogans. End bribery and corruption. Build Socialism. Equality. Shit. A man would just have to make up his mind that there was never going to be anything but despair, and there would be no way of escaping it. . . .

In the life of the nation itself, maybe nothing really new would happen. New men would take into their hands the power to steal the nation's riches and to use it for their own satisfaction. That, of course, was to be expected. New people would use the country's power to get rid of men and women who talked a language that did not flatter them. There would be nothing different in that. That would only be a continuation of the Ghanaian way of life. But here was the real change. The individual man of power now shivering, his head filled with the fear of the vengeance of those he had wronged. For him everything was going to change. And for those like him who had grown greasy and fat singing the praises of their chief, for those who had been getting themselves ready for the enjoyment of hoped-for favors, there would be long days of pain ahead. The flatterers with their new white Mercedes cars would have to find ways of burying old words. For those who had come directly against the old power, there would be much happiness. But for the nation itself there would only be a change of embezzlers and a change of the hunters and the hunted. A pitiful shrinking of the world from those days Teacher still looked back to, when the single mind was filled with the hopes of a whole people. A pitiful shrinking, to days when all the powerful could think of was to use the power of a whole people to fill their own paunches. Endless days, same days, stretching into the future with no end anywhere in sight.

 According to Ayi Kwei Armah, who was to blame for conditions in his country?

Source: From *The Beautiful Ones Are Not Yet Born* by Ayi Kwei Armah (Heinemann, 1989).

AFRICA IN THE COLD WAR Many of the problems encountered by the new nations of Africa have also been ascribed to the fact that independence did not end Western interference in Africa's political affairs. Many African leaders were angered when Western powers led by the United States conspired to overthrow the left-leaning politician Patrice Lumumba (1925–1961) in the Congo in the early 1960s. Lumumba, who had been educated in the Soviet Union, aroused fears in Washington that he might promote Soviet influence in Central Africa. Eventually, he was assassinated under mysterious circumstances.

The episode was a major factor influencing African leaders to form the OAU as a means of reducing Western influence on the continent, but the strategy achieved few results. Although many African leaders agreed to adopt a neutral stance in the Cold War, competition between Moscow and Washington throughout the region was fierce, often undermining the efforts of fragile governments to build stable new nations. To make matters worse, African states had difficulty achieving a united position on many issues, and their disagreements left the region vulnerable to external influence and conflict. Border disputes festered in many areas of the continent, and in some cases—as with Morocco and a rebel movement in Western Sahara and between Kenya and Uganda—flared into outright war.

Even within many new African nations, the concept of nationhood was undermined by the lingering force of regionalism or ethnic rivalries. Nigeria, with the largest population on the continent, was rent by civil strife during the late 1960s when dissident Ibo groups in the southeast attempted unsuccessfully to form the independent state of Biafra. Another force undermining nationalism in Africa was that of **pan-Islamism**. Its prime exponent in Africa was the Egyptian president Gamal Abdul Nasser. After Nasser's death in 1970, the torch of Islamic unity in Africa was carried by the Libyan president Muammar Qaddafi

(1942–2011), whose ambitions to create a greater Muslim nation in the Sahara under his authority led to conflict with neighboring Chad. The Islamic resurgence has also surfaced in Nigeria and other nations of West Africa, where divisions between Muslims and Christians have recently erupted into violence (see "Tensions in the Desert" later in this chapter).

THE POPULATION BOMB Finally, rapid population growth crippled efforts to create modern economies. By the 1980s, annual population growth averaged nearly 3 percent throughout Africa, the highest rate of any continent. Drought conditions and the inexorable spread of the Sahara (usually known as **desertification**), caused partly by overcultivation of the land, led to widespread hunger and starvation, first in West African countries such as Niger and Mali and then in Ethiopia, Somalia, and the Sudan.

Predictions are that the population of Africa will increase by at least 200 million over the next ten years, but that estimate does not take into account the prevalence of AIDS, which has reached epidemic proportions in Africa. According to a United Nations study, at least 5 percent of the entire population of sub-Saharan Africa is infected with the virus, including a high percentage of the urban middle class. More than 65 percent of the AIDS cases reported around the world are on the continent of Africa. Some observers estimate that without measures to curtail the effects of the disease, it will have a significant impact on several African countries by reducing population growth.

Today poverty is widespread in Africa, particularly among the three-quarters of the population still living off the land. Urban areas have grown tremendously, but as in much of Asia, most are surrounded by massive squatter settlements of rural peoples who have fled to the cities in search of a better life. The expansion of the cities has overwhelmed fragile transportation and sanitation systems and led to rising pollution and perpetual traffic jams, while millions are forced to live without running water and electricity. Meanwhile, the fortunate few (all too often government officials on the take) live the high life and emulate the consumerism of the West (in a particularly expressive phrase, the rich in many East African countries are known as *wabenzi*, or "Mercedes-Benz people").

In "Pedestrian, to Passing Benz-Man," the Kenyan poet Albert Ojuka voiced the popular discontent with economic inequality in the 1970s:

> You man, lifted gently
> out of the poverty and suffering
> we so recently shared; I say—
> why splash the muddy puddle on to
> my bare legs, as if, still unsatisfied
> with your seated opulence
> you must sully the unwashed
> with your diesel-smoke and mud-water
> and force him to buy, beyond his means
> a bar of soap from your shop?
> a few years back we shared a master
> today you have none, while I have
> exchanged a parasite for something worse.
> But maybe a few years is too long a time.[1]

It is a lament still voiced today.

© William J. Duiker

Manioc, Food for the Millions. Manioc (also called cassava or yuca), a tuber like the potato, was brought to Africa from South America soon after the voyages of Columbus. Although low in nutrient value, it can be cultivated in poor soil with little moisture and is the staple food for nearly one-third of the population of sub-Saharan Africa. Manioc is also widely grown in tropical parts of Asia and South America and is familiar to Westerners as the source of tapioca. In this photograph, village women in Senegal rhythmically pound manioc to remove traces of naturally occurring cyanide that would otherwise poison those who rely on the tuber as a basic commodity. As the threat of chronic drought becomes an ever more common reality in parts of Africa, dry crops like manioc will acquire increasing importance in the diet of the African people.

The Search for Solutions

While the problems of nation building described here have to one degree or another afflicted all of the emerging states of Africa, each has sought to deal with the challenge in its own way, sometimes with strikingly different consequences. Some African countries have made dramatic improvements in the past two decades, but others have encountered increasing difficulties. Despite all its shared problems, Africa today remains one of the most diverse regions of the globe.

TANZANIA: AN AFRICAN ROUTE TO SOCIALISM

Concern over the dangers of economic inequality inspired a number of African leaders to restrict foreign investment and nationalize the major industries and utilities while promoting democratic ideals and values. Julius Nyerere of Tanzania was the most consistent, promoting the ideals of socialism and self-reliance through his Arusha Declaration of 1967, which set forth the principles for building a socialist society in Africa. Nyerere did not seek to establish a Leninist-style dictatorship of the proletariat in Tanzania, but neither was he a proponent of a multiparty democracy, which in his view would be divisive under the conditions prevailing in Africa:

> Where there is one party—provided it is identified
> with the nation as a whole—the foundations
> of democracy can be firmer, and the people can
> have more opportunity to exercise a real choice,
> than when you have two or more parties.

To import the Western parliamentary system into Africa, he argued, could lead to violence because the opposition parties would be viewed as traitors by the majority of the population.[2]

Taking advantage of his powerful political influence, Nyerere placed limits on income and established village collectives to avoid the corrosive effects of economic inequality and government corruption. Sympathetic foreign countries provided considerable economic aid to assist the experiment, and many observers noted that levels of corruption, political instability, and ethnic strife were lower in Tanzania than in many other African countries. Nyerere's vision was not shared by all of his compatriots, however. Political elements on the island of Zanzibar, citing the stagnation brought by two decades of socialism, agitated for autonomy or even total separation from the mainland. Tanzania also has poor soil, inadequate rainfall, and limited resources, all of which have contributed to its slow growth and continuing rural and urban poverty.

In 1985, Nyerere voluntarily retired from the presidency. In his farewell speech, he confessed that he had failed to achieve many of his ambitious goals to create a socialist society in Africa. In particular, he admitted that his plan to collectivize the traditional private farm (*shamba*) had run into strong resistance from conservative peasants. "You can socialize what is not traditional," he remarked. "The *shamba* can't be socialized." But Nyerere insisted that many of his policies had succeeded in improving social and economic conditions, and he argued that the only real solution was to consolidate the multitude of small countries in the region into a larger East African Federation. Today, a quarter of a century later, Nyerere's party, the Party of the Revolution, continues to rule the country. The current president, Jakaya Kikwete (b. 1950), was reelected in 2010 by a comfortable margin, although there were charges of electoral fraud.

KENYA: THE PERILS OF CAPITALISM

The countries that opted for capitalism faced their own dilemmas. Neighboring Kenya, blessed with better soil in the highlands, a local tradition of aggressive commerce, and a residue of European settlers, welcomed foreign investment and profit incentives. The results have been mixed. Kenya has a strong current of indigenous African capitalism and a substantial middle class, mostly based in the capital, Nairobi. But landlessness, unemployment, and income inequities are high, even by African standards (almost one-fifth of the country's 41 million people are squatters, and unemployment is currently estimated at 40 percent). The rate of population growth—about 2.5 percent annually—is one of the higher rates in the world. Almost 80 percent of the population remains rural, and 50 percent of the people live below the poverty line. The result has been widespread unrest in a country formerly admired for its successful development.

Kenya's problems have been exacerbated by chronic disputes between disparate ethnic groups and simmering tensions between farmers and pastoralists, leading some to question whether the country is capable of achieving political stability (see the box on p. 298). For many years, the country maintained a fragile stability under the dictatorial rule of President Daniel arap Moi (b. 1924), one of the most authoritarian of African leaders. Plagued by charges of corruption, Moi finally agreed to retire in 2002, but under his successor, Mwai Kibaki (b. 1931), the twin problems of political instability and widespread poverty continue to afflict the country. When presidential elections held in December 2007 led to a victory for Kibaki's party, opposition elements—angered by the government's perceived favoritism toward Kibaki's Kikuyu constituency—launched numerous protests, and violent riots occurred throughout the country. A fragile truce was eventually put in place, but popular anger at current conditions smolders just beneath the surface. In March 2013, another disputed presidential election resulted in a victory for Uhuru Kenyatta (b. 1961), the son of the country's first president.

ANGOLA AND ETHIOPIA: EXPERIMENTS IN MARXISM

Beginning in the mid-1970s, a few African nations decided to adopt Soviet-style Marxism-Leninism. In Angola and Ethiopia, Marxist parties followed the Soviet model and attempted to create fully socialist societies with the assistance of Soviet experts and Cuban troops and advisers. Economically, the results were disappointing, and both countries faced severe internal opposition. In Ethiopia, the

Meeting the Challenges of Independence

Tom Mboya (1930–1969) was an inspiring political figure in Kenya during the era of early independence. As minister of labor during the transition to statehood, he urged his fellow Kenyans to believe in the prospect of independence, while calming the anxieties of European residents by assuring them that their lives and property would not be threatened or confiscated. This selection is from a speech he delivered in July 1962, in which he recognized the challenges of independence while expressing confidence that the experiment would inevitably succeed. In 1969, Mboya was assassinated by a political opponent.

Tom Mboya, "Kenya as a Nation," July 23, 1962

It is suggested by some people that there is no such thing as a Kenya nation. All kinds of arguments and recriminations are thrown up to try to prove that any nationalist ambitions for Kenya must encounter more difficulties than could ever be overcome. Noisy minorities in all walks of life, both here and in their contact with overseas interests, keep plugging away at their "no confidence" theme. Some people say that Kenya is heading for economic disaster and political chaos and tribal war. . . .

When I talk now about a "Kenya nation," I am not speaking as a political romantic, but as a realist. Any sincere politician or leader must have some vision in front of him. There must be something much more than notoriety to attract him toward unceasing work, the bitterness of struggle, the temptations, and the pressures. There must be a factor of dedication, an undeniable impulse to build and to serve. In this he must satisfy himself. There are very few other rewards.

It is not only the vision of the leaders that dictates our struggle. There are the deep-rooted aspirations of our people. These people may appear simple and uneducated; they may not be articulate, but they are human beings and not stones. They have an inborn pride and a genuine desire for self-improvement and self-fulfillment. These are facts which may have dodged many people in the past but with which we all must reckon in the future. To ignore this force would be to lead to frustrations and explosions—indeed we have already had such an experience in Kenya.

It is not, however, the fear of this force that should dictate our decisions. There is the positive side of this force, namely, its ability to face the challenge of nation building. We have to release this force of our people for new and constructive purposes. We have to harness the enthusiasm for self-improvement to form the spearhead in our efforts for nation-building.

True, we have tribal differences and sensitivities. So often people point at the Congo and warn that Kenya is doomed to become another Congo. I do not share this view. We have passed the stage when this could have happened. We have passed through more trials than most African countries, and I believe we have come to appreciate freedom to a point where we would be prepared to defend it with our lives. We do not intend to exchange British colonialism for either local dictatorship or Soviet and American colonialism.

 Why was Mboya confident that the people of Kenya could surmount the challenges of nationhood?

SOURCE: R. Collins (ed.), *African History in Documents: East African History* (Princeton, 1997), pp. 166–170, from T. Mboya, *The Challenges of Nationhood: A Collection of Speeches and Writings* (London, 1970), pp. 41–47.

---

revolt by Muslim guerrilla fighters in the province of Eritrea led to the fall of the Marxist leader Mengistu Haile Mariam (b. 1937) and his regime in 1990 and the eventual independence of Eritrea. A similar revolt erupted against the government in Angola, with the rebel group UNITA controlling much of the rural population and for a time threatening the capital city of Luanda. With the death of the rebel leader Julius Savimbi in 2002, the civil war finally appeared to be at an end.

SOUTH AFRICA: AN END TO APARTHEID Perhaps Africa's greatest success story is in South Africa, where the white government, which long maintained a policy of racial segregation (apartheid) and restricted black sovereignty to a series of small "Bantustans" in relatively infertile areas of the country, finally accepted the inevitability of African involvement in the political process and the national economy. A key factor in the decision was growing international pressure in the form of a campaign to persuade foreign investors to withdraw funds from the country. In 1990, the government of President F. W. (Frederik Willem) de Klerk (b. 1936) released African National Congress leader Nelson Mandela (b. 1918) from prison, where he had been held since 1964. In 1993, the two leaders agreed to hold democratic national elections the following spring. In the meantime, ANC representatives agreed to take part in a transitional coalition government with de Klerk's National Party. Those elections resulted in a substantial majority for the ANC, and Mandela became president.

In May 1996, a new constitution was approved, calling for a multiracial state. The National Party immediately went into opposition, claiming that the new charter did not adequately provide for joint decision making by members of the coalition. But the new ANC-dominated government won broad support from many groups within the country, and in 1999, a major step toward political stability was taken when Nelson Mandela stepped down from the presidency and was replaced by his longtime disciple Thabo Mbeki (b. 1942). The new president faced a number of intimidating problems, including rising unemployment, widespread lawlessness, chronic corruption, and an ominous flight of capital and professional personnel from the country. Mbeki's conservative economic policies earned the support of some white voters and the country's new black elite but were criticized by labor unions, which contended that the benefits of the new black leadership were not seeping down to the poor. The government's promises to carry out an extensive land reform program—aimed at providing farmland to the nation's 40 million black farmers—were not fulfilled, leading some squatters to seize unused private lands near Johannesburg.

In 2008, Mbeki was forced out of office by disgruntled ANC party members. A year later, his onetime vice president and rival Jacob Zuma (b. 1942) was elected president. Although the country faces serious challenges, South Africa remains the wealthiest and most industrialized state in Africa and the best hope that a multiracial society can succeed on the continent. The country's black elite now number nearly one-quarter of its wealthiest households, compared with only 9 percent in 1991.

NIGERIA: A NATION DIVIDED If the situation in South Africa provides grounds for modest optimism, the situation in Nigeria provides reason for serious concern. Africa's largest country in terms of population and one of its wealthiest because of substantial oil reserves, Nigeria was for many years in the grip of military strongmen. During his rule, General Sani Abacha (1943–1998) ruthlessly suppressed all opposition and in late 1995 ordered the execution of author Ken Saro-Wiwa (1941–1995) despite widespread protests from human rights groups abroad. Saro-Wiwa had criticized environmental damage caused by foreign oil interests in southern Nigeria, but the regime's major concern was his support for separatist activities in the area that had launched the Biafran insurrection in the late 1960s. When Abacha died in 1998 under mysterious circumstances, national elections led to the creation of a civilian government under Olusegun Obasanjo (b. 1937).

Civilian leadership has not been a panacea for Nigeria's problems, however. Although Obasanjo promised reforms to bring an end to the corruption and favoritism that had long plagued Nigerian politics, the results were disappointing (the state power company—known as NEPA—was so inefficient that Nigerians joked that the initials stood for "never expect power again"). When presidential elections held in 2007 led to the election of Umaru Yar'Adua (1951–2010), an obscure member of Obasanjo's ruling political party, opposition forces and neutral observers complained that the vote had been seriously flawed. After Yar'Adua died from an illness in 2010, he was succeeded by his vice president, Goodluck Jonathan (b. 1951), who was elected president in his own right in 2011.

One of the most critical problems facing the Nigerian government in recent years has its roots in religious disputes. In early 2000, riots between Christians and Muslims broke out in several northern cities as a result of the decision by Muslim provincial officials to apply *Shari'a* throughout their jurisdictions. The violence temporarily abated as local officials managed to craft compromise policies that limited the application of some of the harsher aspects of Muslim law, but the dispute continues to threaten the fragile unity of Africa's most populous country. The election of Goodluck Jonathan, a Christian, in 2011 led to new protests among Muslims in the northern part of the country. The unrest has been fueled in part by the terrorist activities of Boko Haram, an al-Qaeda affiliate active in the region.

TENSIONS IN THE DESERT The religious tensions that erupted in Nigeria have spilled over into neighboring states on the border of the Sahara. Pressure to apply *Shari'a* has spread to the neighboring state of Mali, where a radical Islamic group has seized power in the northern part of the country, applying strict punishments on local residents for alleged infractions against *Shari'a* law and destroying Muslim shrines in the historic city of Timbuktu. French military units were dispatched to the region in January 2013 and drove the rebels out of the major population centers, but the threat of Islamic radicalism has not subsided.

A similar rift has been at the root of the lengthy civil war that has been raging in Sudan. Conflict between Muslim pastoralists—supported by the central government in Khartoum—and predominantly Christian black farmers in the southern part of the country raged for years until the government finally agreed to permit a plebiscite in the south under the sponsorship of the United Nations to determine whether the local population there wished to secede from the country. In elections held in early 2011, voters overwhelmingly supported independence as the new nation of the Republic of South Sudan, but clashes along the disputed border continue to provoke tensions.

The dispute between Muslims and Christians throughout the southern Sahara is a contemporary African variant of the traditional tensions that have existed between farmers and pastoralists throughout recorded history. Muslim cattle herders, migrating southward to escape the increasing desiccation of the grasslands south of the Sahara, compete for precious land with primarily Christian farmers. As a result of the religious revival now under way throughout the continent, the confrontation often leads to outbreaks of violence with strong religious and ethnic overtones.

CENTRAL AFRICA: CAULDRON OF CONFLICT The most tragic situation is in the Central African states of Rwanda and Burundi, where a chronic conflict between the minority Tutsis and the Hutu majority has led to a bitter civil war, with thousands of refugees fleeing to the neighboring Congo. The Tutsis, supported by the colonial Belgian government, had long dominated the sedentary Hutu population. The Hutus' attempt to bring an end to Tutsi domination initiated the most recent conflicts, which have been marked by massacres on both sides. In the meantime, the presence of large numbers of foreign troops and refugees intensified centrifugal forces inside Zaire, where General Mobutu Sese Seko had long ruled with an iron hand. In 1997, military forces led by Mobutu's longtime opponent Laurent-Désiré Kabila (1939–2001) managed to topple the general's corrupt government. Once in power, Kabila renamed the country the Democratic Republic of the Congo and promised a return to democratic practices. The new government systematically suppressed political dissent, however, and in January 2001, Kabila was assassinated. He was succeeded by his son Joseph Kabila (b. 1971). Peace talks to end the conflict began that fall, but the fighting has continued, leading to horrific casualties among the civilian population.

Africa: A Continent in Flux

The brief survey of events in some of the more important African countries provided here illustrates the enormous difficulty that historians of Africa face in drawing any general conclusions about the pace and scope of change that has taken place in the continent in recent decades. Progress in some areas has been countered by growing problems elsewhere, and signs of hope in one region contrast with feelings of despair in another.

The shifting fortunes experienced throughout the continent are most prominently illustrated in the political arena. Over the past two decades, the collapse of one-party regimes has led to the emergence of fragile democracies in several countries. In other instances, however, democratic governments erupted in civil war or were replaced by authoritarian leaders. One prominent example of the latter is the Ivory Coast, long considered one of West Africa's most stable and prosperous countries. After the death of President Félix Houphouet-Boigny in 1993, long-simmering resentment between Christians in the south and newly arrived Muslim immigrants in the north erupted into open conflict. National elections held in 2010 led to sporadic violence and a standoff between opposition forces and the sitting president, who was forced to resign the following year. By contrast, in Liberia, a bitter civil war recently gave way to the emergence of a stable democratic government under Ellen Johnson-Sirleaf (b. 1938), the continent's first female president.

The economic picture in Africa has also been mixed. It is clear that African societies have not yet begun to

Problems of Transport. The lack of efficient transportation is a serious problem throughout the developing world. Because of the dearth of railroads and private vehicles, especially in rural areas, Africans often choose to travel by bus. In many instances, however, that choice results in a serious lack of personal comfort and reliability. Shown here is a typically overloaded bus in Senegal. On the roof, a herd of goats is about to embark on a journey to an unknown destination.

© Claire L. Duiker

surmount the challenges they have faced since independence. Most African states are still poor and their populations illiterate. Moreover, African concerns continue to carry little weight in the international community. A recent agreement by the World Trade Organization (WTO) on the need to reduce agricultural subsidies in the advanced nations has been widely ignored. In 2000, the General Assembly of the United Nations passed the Millennium Declaration, which called for a dramatic reduction in the incidence of poverty, hunger, and illiteracy worldwide by the year 2015. So far, however, efforts to realize these ambitious goals have been limited. At a conference on the subject in September 2005, the participants squabbled over how to fund the effort. Some delegations, including that of the United States, argued that external assistance cannot succeed unless the nations of Africa adopt measures to bring about good government and sound economic policies.

Despite the African continent's chronic economic problems, however, there are signs of hope. The overall rate of economic growth for the region as a whole is twice what it was during the 1980s and 1990s. African countries were also less affected by the recent economic downturn than was much of the rest of the world. Although poverty, AIDs, and a lack of education and infrastructure are still major impediments in much of the region, rising commodity prices—most notably, an increase in oil revenues—are enabling many countries to make additional investments and reduce their national debt. One promising sign is that the African people as a whole are not about to despair. In a recent survey of public opinion throughout the continent, the majority of respondents were optimistic about the future and confident that they would be economically better off in five years.

Certainly, part of the solution to the continent's multiple problems must come from within. Although there are gratifying signs of progress toward political stability in some countries, others are still governed by brutal dictatorships or racked by civil strife. Corruption and political inexperience are serious problems as well. But many of Africa's difficulties are a consequence of interference by foreign governments and international corporations. Efforts by Western governments to protect their local farmers by providing subsidies or levying high tariffs have hurt African growers in countries where agricultural products are a major export crop. Foreign corporations interfere in local politics and impede the normal political process, often to the detriment of local populations.

THE AFRICAN UNION: A GLIMMER OF HOPE A significant part of the problem is that Africans must find better ways to cooperate with one another and to protect and promote their own interests. A first step in that direction was taken in 1991, when the OAU agreed to establish the African Economic Community (AEC). In 2001, the OAU was replaced by the **African Union**, which is intended to provide greater political and economic integration throughout the continent on the pattern of the European Union (see Chapter 10). The new organization has already sought to mediate several of the conflicts in the region.

As Africa evolves, it is useful to remember that economic and political change is often an agonizingly slow and painful process. Introduced to industrialization and concepts of Western democracy only a century ago, African societies are still groping for ways to graft Western political institutions and economic practices onto a structure still significantly influenced by traditional values and attitudes.

Continuity and Change in Modern African Societies

In general, the impact of the West has been greater on urban and educated Africans and more limited on their rural and illiterate compatriots. One reason is that the colonial presence was first and most firmly established in the cities. Many cities, including Dakar, Lagos, Johannesburg, Cape Town, Brazzaville, and Nairobi, are direct products of the colonial experience. Most African cities today look like their counterparts elsewhere in the world. They have high-rise buildings, blocks of residential apartments, wide boulevards, neon lights, movie theaters, and traffic jams.

Education

The educational system has been the primary means of introducing Western values and culture. In the precolonial era, formal schools did not really exist in Africa except for parochial schools in Christian Ethiopia and academies to train young males in Islamic doctrine and law in Muslim societies in North and West Africa. For the average African, education took place at the home or in the village courtyard and stressed socialization and vocational training. Traditional education in Africa was not necessarily inferior to that in Europe. Social values and customs were transmitted to the young by storytellers, often village elders, who could gain considerable prestige through their performance.

Europeans introduced modern Western education into Africa in the nineteenth century. At first, the schools concentrated on vocational training, with some instruction in European languages and Western civilization. Eventually, pressure from Africans led to the introduction of professional training, and the first institutes of higher learning were established in the early twentieth century.

Learning the ABCs in Niger. Educating the young is one of the most crucial problems for many African societies today. Few governments are able to allocate the funds necessary to meet the challenge, so religious organizations—Muslim or Christian—often take up the slack. In this photo, students at a madrasa—a Muslim school designed to teach the Qur'an—are learning how to read Arabic, the language of Islam's holy scripture. Madrasas are one of the most prominent forms of schooling in Muslim societies in West Africa today.

less impact. Millions of people throughout Africa (as in Asia) live much as their ancestors did, in thatched huts without modern plumbing and electricity: they farm or hunt by traditional methods, practice time-honored family rituals, and believe in the traditional deities. Even here, however, change is taking place. Slavery has been eliminated, for the most part, although there have been persistent reports of raids by slave traders on defenseless villages in the southern Sudan. Economic need, though, has brought about massive migrations as some leave to work on plantations, others move to the cities, and still others flee abroad or to refugee camps to escape starvation. Migration itself is a wrenching experience, disrupting familiar family and village ties and enforcing new social relationships.

With independence, African countries established their own state-run schools. The emphasis was on the primary level, but high schools and universities were established in major cities. The basic objectives have been to introduce vocational training and improve literacy rates. Unfortunately, both funding and trained teachers are scarce in most countries, and few rural areas have schools. As a result, illiteracy remains high, estimated at about 40 percent of the population across the continent. There has been a perceptible shift toward education in the vernacular languages. In West Africa, only about one in four adults is conversant in a Western language.

Nowhere, in fact, is the dichotomy between old and new, local and foreign, rural and urban so clear and painful as in Africa. Urban dwellers regard the village as the repository of all that is backward in the African past, while rural peoples view the growing urban areas as a source of corruption, prostitution, hedonism, and the destruction of communal customs and values. The tension between traditional ways and Western culture is particularly strong among African intellectuals, many of whom are torn between their admiration for things Western and their desire to retain an African identity.

Urban and Rural Life

The cities are where the African elites live and work. Affluent Africans, like their contemporaries in other developing countries, have been strongly attracted to the glittering material aspects of Western culture. They live in Western-style homes or apartments and eat Western foods stored in Western refrigerators, and those who can afford it drive Western cars. It has been said, not wholly in praise, that there are more Mercedes-Benz automobiles in Nigeria than in Germany, where they are manufactured.

Outside the major cities, where about three-quarters of the continent's inhabitants live, Western influence has had

African Women

As noted in Chapter 2, one of the consequences of colonialism in Africa was a change in the relationship between men and women. Some of these changes could be described as beneficial, but others were not. Women were often introduced to Western education and given legal rights denied to them in the precolonial era. But they also became a labor source and were sometime recruited or compelled to work on construction projects.

Independence also had a significant impact on gender roles in African society. Almost without exception, the new governments established the principle of sexual equality and permitted women to vote and run for political office.

Building His Dream House. In Africa, the houses of rural people are often constructed with a wood frame, known as wattle, daubed with mud, and then covered with a thatched roof. Such houses are inexpensive to build and remain cool in the hot tropical climate. In this Kenyan village not far from the Indian Ocean, a young man is applying mud to the wall of his future home. Houses are built in a similar fashion throughout the continent, as well as in much of southern Asia.

Yet as elsewhere, women continue to operate at a disability in a world dominated by males. Politics remains a male preserve, and although a few professions, such as teaching, child care, and clerical work, are dominated by women, most African women are employed in menial positions such as agricultural labor, factory work, and retail trade or as domestics. Education is open to all at the elementary level, but women comprise less than 20 percent of students at the upper levels in most African societies today.

URBAN WOMEN Not surprisingly, women have made the greatest strides in the cities. Most urban women, like men, now marry on the basis of personal choice, although a significant minority are still willing to accept their parents' choice. After marriage, African women appear to occupy a more equal position than their counterparts in most Asian countries. Each marriage partner tends to maintain a separate income, and women often have the right to possess property separate from their husbands. Though many wives still defer to their husbands in the traditional manner, others are like the woman in Abioseh Nicol's story "A Truly Married Woman," who, after years of living as a

common law wife with her husband, is finally able to provide the price and finalize the marriage. After the wedding, she declares, "For twelve years I have got up every morning at five to make tea for you and breakfast. Now I am a truly married woman, [and] you must treat me with a little more respect. You are now my husband and not a lover. Get up and make yourself a cup of tea."[3]

In the cities, a feminist movement is growing, but it is firmly based on conditions in the local environment. Many African women writers, for example, opt for a brand of African feminism much like that of Ama Ata Aidoo (b. 1942), a Ghanaian novelist, whose ultimate objective is to free African society as a whole, not just its female inhabitants. After receiving her education at a girls' school in the preindependence Gold Coast and attending Stanford University in the United States, she embarked on a writing career. Every African woman and every man, she insists, "should be a feminist, especially if they believe that Africans should take charge of our land, its wealth, our lives, and the burden of our development. Because it is not possible to advocate independence for our continent without also believing that African women must have the best that the environment can offer."[4]

WOMEN IN RURAL AREAS Feminism has had less impact on women in rural areas, where traditional attitudes continue to exert a strong influence. In some societies, female genital mutilation, the traditional rite of passage for a young girl's transit to womanhood, is still widely practiced. Polygamy is also not uncommon, and arranged marriages are still the rule rather than the exception. In some Muslim societies, efforts to apply *Shari'a* law have led to greater restrictions on the freedom of women. In northern Nigeria, a woman was recently sentenced to death for committing adultery. The sentence was later reversed on appeal.

The dichotomy between rural and urban values can lead to acute tensions. Many African villagers regard the cities as the fount of evil, decadence, and corruption. Women in particular have suffered from the tension between the pull of the city and the village. As men are drawn to the cities in search of employment and excitement, their wives and girlfriends are left behind, both literally and figuratively, in the village. Fortunately, there are some signs of change. In 2006, Ellen Johnson-Sirleaf was elected president of Liberia—the first woman to be elected chief executive of a country on the African continent.

African Culture

Inevitably, the tension between traditional and modern, local and foreign, and individual and communal that has

Salt of the Earth. During the precolonial era, many West African societies were forced to import salt from Mediterranean countries in exchange for tropical products and gold. Today, the people of Senegal satisfy their domestic needs by mining salt deposits contained in lakes like this one in the interior of the country. These lakes are the remnants of vast seas that covered the region of the Sahara in prehistoric times. Note that women are doing much of the heavy labor, while men occupy the managerial positions.

permeated contemporary African society has spilled over into culture. In general, in the visual arts and music, utility and ritual have given way to pleasure and decoration. In the process, Africans have been affected to a certain extent by foreign influences but have retained their distinctive characteristics. Wood carving, metalwork, painting, and sculpture, for example, have preserved their traditional forms but are now increasingly adapted to serve the tourist industry and the export market.

LITERATURE No area of African culture has been so strongly affected by political and social events as literature. Except for Muslim areas in North and East Africa, precolonial Africans did not have a written literature, although their tradition of oral storytelling served as a rich repository of history, custom, and folk culture. The first written literature in the vernacular or in European languages emerged during the nineteenth century in the form of novels, poetry, and drama.

Angry at the negative portrayal of Africa in Western literature (see the box on p. 305), African authors initially wrote primarily for a European audience as a means of establishing black dignity and purpose. In response to condescending Western attitudes about African history, many glorified the emotional and communal aspects of the traditional African experience. The Nigerian Chinua Achebe

(1930–2013) is considered the first major African novelist to write in the English language. In his writings, he attempted to interpret African history from an African perspective and to forge a new sense of African identity. In his trailblazing novel *Things Fall Apart* (1958), he recounted the story of a Nigerian who refused to submit to the new British order and eventually committed suicide. Criticizing his contemporaries who accepted foreign rule, the protagonist lamented that the white man "has put a knife on the things that held us together and we have fallen apart."

In recent decades, the African novel has taken a dramatic turn, shifting its focus from the brutality of the foreign oppressor to the shortcomings of the new African leaders. Having gained independence, African politicians are portrayed as mimicking and even outdoing the injustices committed by their colonial predecessors. A prominent example of this genre is the work of the Kenyan Ngugi Wa Thiong'o (b. 1938). His first novel, *A Grain of Wheat*, takes place on the eve of independence. Although Ngugi mocks local British society for its racism, snobbishness, and superficiality, his chief interest lies in the unsentimental and even unflattering portrayal of ordinary Kenyans in their daily struggle for survival.

Like most of his predecessors, Ngugi initially wrote in English, but he eventually decided to write in his native Kikuyu as a means of broadening his readership. For that reason, perhaps, in the late 1970s, he was placed under house arrest for writing subversive literature. There, he secretly wrote *Devil on the Cross*, which urged his compatriots to overthrow the ruling government. Published in 1980, the book sold widely and was eventually read aloud by storytellers throughout Kenyan society. Fearing an attempt on his life, Ngugi has since lived in exile.

Many of Ngugi's contemporaries have followed his lead and focused their frustration on the failure of the continent's new leadership to carry out the goals of independence. One of the most outstanding is the Nigerian

Africa: Dark Continent or Radiant Land?

Colonialism camouflaged its economic objectives under the cloak of a "civilizing mission," which in Africa was aimed at illuminating the so-called Dark Continent with Europe's brilliant civilization. In 1899, the Polish-born English author Joseph Conrad (1857–1924) fictionalized his harrowing journey up the Congo River in the novella *Heart of Darkness*. Conrad's protagonist, Marlow, travels upriver to locate a Belgian trader who has mysteriously disappeared. The novella describes Marlow's gradual recognition of the egregious excesses of colonial rule, as well as his realization that such evil lurks in everyone's heart. The story concludes with a cry: "The horror! The horror!" Voicing views that expressed his Victorian perspective, Conrad described an Africa that was incomprehensible, sensual, and primitive.

Over the years, Conrad's work has provoked much debate. Author Chinua Achebe, for one, lambasted *Heart of Darkness* as a racial diatribe. Since independence, many African writers have been prompted to counter Conrad's portrayal by reaffirming the dignity and purpose of the African people. One of the first to do so was the Guinean author Camara Laye (1928–1980), who in 1954 composed a brilliant novel, *The Radiance of the King*, which can be viewed as the mirror image of Conrad's *Heart of Darkness*. In Laye's work, Clarence, another European protagonist, undertakes a journey into the impenetrable heart of Africa. This time, however, he is enlightened by the process, obtaining self-knowledge and ultimately salvation.

Joseph Conrad, *Heart of Darkness*

We penetrated deeper and deeper into the heart of darkness. It was very quiet there. At night sometimes the roll of drums behind the curtain of trees would run up the river and remain sustained faintly, as if hovering in the air high over our heads, till the first break of day. Whether it meant war, peace, or prayer we could not tell. . . . But suddenly, as we struggled round a bend,

there would be a glimpse of rush walls, of peaked grass-roofs, a burst of yells, a whirl of black limbs, a mass of hands clapping, of feet stamping, of bodies swaying, of eyes rolling, under the droop of heavy and motionless foliage. The steamer toiled along slowly on the edge of a black and incomprehensible frenzy. The prehistoric man was cursing us, praying to us, welcoming us—who could tell? We were cut off from the comprehension of our surroundings; we glided past like phantoms, wondering and secretly appalled, as sane men would be before an enthusiastic outbreak in a madhouse.

Camara Laye, *The Radiance of the King*

At that very moment the king turned his head, turned it imperceptibly, and his glance fell upon Clarence. . . .

"Yes, no one is as base as I, as naked as I," he thought. "And you, lord, you are willing to rest your eyes upon me!" Or was it because of his very nakedness? . . . "Because of your very nakedness!" the look seemed to say. "That terrifying void that is within you and which opens to receive me; your hunger which calls to my hunger; your very baseness which did not exist until I gave it leave; and the great shame you feel. . . ."

When he had come before the king, when he stood in the great radiance of the king, still ravaged by the tongue of fire, but alive still, and living only through the touch of that fire,

Clarence fell upon his knees, for it seemed to him that he was finally at the end of his seeking, and at the end of all seekings.

 Compare the depiction of the continent of Africa in these two passages. Is Laye making a response to Conrad? If so, what is it?

SOURCES: "Joseph Conrad Selection": From *Heart of Darkness* by Joseph Conrad. Penguin Books, 1991. "Camara Laye Selection": From *The Radiance of the King* by Camara Laye, translated from the French by James Kirkup. New York: Vintage, 1989.

Wole Soyinka (b. 1934). His novel *The Interpreters* (1965) lambasted the corruption and hypocrisy of Nigerian politics. Succeeding novels and plays have continued that tradition, resulting in a Nobel Prize in Literature in 1986. In 1994, however, Soyinka barely managed to escape arrest, and he entered a self-imposed exile abroad until the

Abacha regime in Nigeria came to an end. In a protest against the brutality of the regime, he published from exile a harsh exposé of the crisis. His book, *The Open Sore of a Continent*, placed the primary responsibility for failure not on Nigeria's long list of dictators but on the very concept of the modern nation-state, which was introduced to Africa arbitrarily by Europeans. A nation, he contends, can only emerge spontaneously from below, as the expression of the moral and political will of the local inhabitants; it cannot be imposed artificially from above.

A number of Africa's most prominent writers today are women. Traditionally, African women were valued for their talents as storytellers, but writing was strongly discouraged by both traditional and colonial authorities on the grounds that women should occupy themselves with their domestic obligations. In recent years, however, a number of women have emerged as prominent writers of African fiction. Two examples are Buchi Emecheta (b. 1940) of Nigeria and Ama Ata Aidoo of Ghana. Beginning with *Second Class Citizen* (1975), which chronicled the breakdown of her own marriage, Emecheta has published numerous works exploring the role of women in contemporary African society and decrying the practice of polygamy. Ata Aidoo has focused on the identity of today's African women and the changing relations between men and women in society. In her novel *Changes: A Love Story* (1991), she chronicles the lives of three women, none presented as a victim but all caught up in the struggle for survival and happiness. Of late, two young authors have garnered great acclaim for their novels about Nigeria's political and social upheavals—Chimamanda Ngozi Adichie (b. 1977) in *Half a Yellow Sun* (2006) and Sefi Atta (b. 1964) in *Everything Good Will Come* (2005).

MUSIC Contemporary African music also reflects a hybridization or fusion with Western culture. Having traveled to the Americas via the slave trade centuries earlier, African drum beats evolved into North American jazz and Latin American dance rhythms, only to return to reenergize African music. In fact, today music is one of Africans' most effective weapons for social and political protest. Easily accessible to all, African music, whether Afro-beat in Nigeria, rai in Algeria, or reggae in Benin, represents the "weapon of the future," say contemporary musicians; "it helped free Nelson Mandela" and "will put Africa back on the map." Censored by all the African dictatorial regimes, these courageous musicians persist in their struggle against corruption, what one singer calls the second slavery, "the cancer that is eating away at the system." Their voices echo the chorus "Together we can build a nation / Because Africa has brains, youth, knowledge."[5]

CONCLUSION

Nowhere in the developing world is the dilemma of continuity and change more agonizing than in Africa. Mesmerized by the spectacle of Western affluence yet repulsed by the bloody trail from slavery to World War II and the atomic bombs over Hiroshima and Nagasaki, African intellectuals have been torn between the dual images of Western materialism and African uniqueness. For the average African, of course, such intellectual dilemmas pale before the daily challenge of survival. But the fundamental gap between traditional and modern is perhaps wider in Africa than anywhere else in the world and may well be harder to bridge.

What is the future of Africa? It seems almost foolhardy to seek an answer to such a question, given the degree of ethnic, linguistic, and cultural diversity that exists throughout the vast continent. Not surprisingly, visions of the future are equally diverse. Some Africans still yearn for the dreams embodied in the program of the OAU. Novelist Ngugi Wa Thiong'o calls for "an internationalization of all the democratic and social struggles for human equality, justice, peace, and progress."[6]

Others have discarded the democratic ideal and turned their attention to systems based on the subordination of the individual to the community as the guiding principle of national development. Like all peoples, Africans must ultimately find their own solutions within the context of their own traditions, not by seeking to imitate the example of others.

TIMELINE

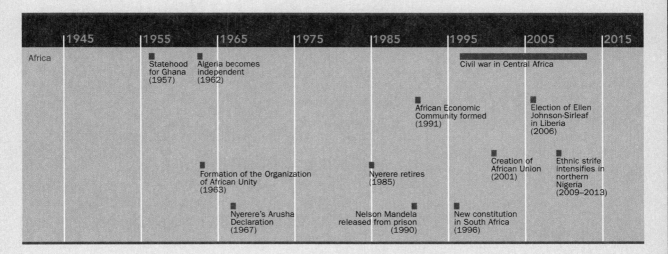

CHAPTER NOTES

1. Albert Ojuka, "Pedestrian, to Passing Benz-Man," quoted in A. Roscoe, *Uhuru's Fire: African Literature East to South* (Cambridge, England, 1977), p. 103.
2. Cited in Martin Meredith, *The Fate of Africa* (New York, 2004), p. 168.
3. Abioseh Nicol, *"A Truly Married Woman" and Other Stories* (London, 1965), p. 12.
4. Ama Ata Aidoo, *No Sweetness Here* (New York, 1995), p. 136.
5. Gilles Médioni, "Stand Up, Africa!" *World Press Review*, July 2002, p. 34.
6. Ngugi Wa Thiong'o, *Decolonising the Mind: The Politics of Language in African Literature* (Portsmouth, N.H., 1986), p. 103.

Ferment in the Middle East

Answering the call of the muezzin

© William J. Duiker

"WE MUSLIMS ARE OF ONE FAMILY even though we live under different governments and in various regions."[1] So said Ayatollah Ruholla Khomeini, the Islamic religious figure and leader of the 1979 revolution that overthrew the shah in Iran. Although some dismissed the ayatollah's remark as just a pious wish by a religious mystic, it does in fact illustrate one crucial aspect of the political dynamics in the region.

If the concept of cultural uniqueness has been presented as a potential alternative to the system of nation-states in Africa, a similar role has been played in the Middle East by the religion of Islam. In both regions, a yearning for a sense of community beyond national borders tugs at the emotions and intellect of their inhabitants and counteracts the dynamic pull of nationalism that has provoked political turmoil and conflict in much of the rest of the world. ❧

┌─ **CRITICAL THINKING** ──────────

Q What factors can be advanced to explain the chronic instability and internal conflict that have characterized conditions in the Middle East since World War II?

Crescent of Conflict

A dramatic example of the powerful force of pan-Islamic sentiment took place on September 11, 2001, when Muslim terrorists hijacked four U.S. airliners and turned them into missiles aimed at the center of world capitalism. Although the headquarters of the organization that carried out the attack—known as al-Qaeda—was located in Afghanistan, the militants themselves came from several different Muslim states. In the months that followed, popular support for al-Qaeda and its mysterious leader, Osama bin Laden (1957–2011), intensified throughout the Muslim world. To many observers, it appeared that the Islamic peoples were embarking on an era of direct confrontation with the entire Western world.

What were the sources of Muslim anger? In a speech released on videotape shortly after the attack, bin Laden declared that it was a response to the "humiliation and disgrace" that have afflicted the Islamic world for more than eighty years, a period dating back to the end of World War I. Although that was clearly not the only motive, there seems little doubt that the rage that has spread through much of the Islamic world has deep historical roots and will not be easily quenched.

For the Middle East, the period between the two world wars was an era of transition. With the fall of the Ottoman and Persian Empires, new modernizing regimes emerged in Turkey and Iran, and a more traditionalist but fiercely independent government was established in Saudi Arabia. Elsewhere, however, European influence continued to be strong; the French and British had mandates in Syria, Lebanon, Jordan, and Palestine, and British influence persisted in Iraq and southern Arabia and throughout the Nile valley. **Pan-Arabism**—the concept of the unity of all Arab peoples—was on the rise, but it lacked focus and coherence.

During World War II, the Middle East became the cockpit of European rivalries, as it had been during World War I. The region was more significant to the warring powers than previously because of the growing importance of oil and the Suez Canal's position as a vital sea route. For a brief period, the Afrika Korps, under the command of the brilliant German general Erwin Rommel, threatened to seize Egypt and the Suez Canal, but British troops defeated the German forces at El Alamein, west of Alexandria, in 1942 and gradually drove them westward until their final defeat after the arrival of U.S. troops in Morocco under the field command of General George S. Patton. From that time until the end of the war, the entire region from the Mediterranean Sea eastward was under secure Allied occupation.

The Question of Palestine

With the end of World War II, a number of independent states emerged in the Middle East. Jordan, Lebanon, and Syria, all European mandates before the war, became independent. Egypt, Iran, and Iraq, though still under a degree of Western influence, became increasingly autonomous. Sympathy for the idea of Arab unity led to the formation of the Arab League in 1945, but different points of view among its members prevented it from achieving anything of substance.

The one issue on which all Muslim states in the area could agree was the question of Palestine. As tensions between Jews and Arabs in that mandate intensified during the 1930s, the British attempted to limit Jewish immigration into the area and firmly rejected proposals for independence, despite the promise made in the 1917 Balfour Declaration (see Chapter 5).

After World War II ended, the situation drifted rapidly toward crisis, as thousands of Jewish refugees, many of them from displaced persons camps in Europe, sought to migrate to Palestine despite Arab complaints and British efforts to prevent their arrival (see the box on p. 310). As violence between Muslims and Jews intensified in the fall of 1947, the issue was taken up in the United Nations General Assembly. After an intense debate, the assembly voted to approve the partition of Palestine into two separate states, one for the Jews and one for the Arabs. The city of Jerusalem was to be placed under international control. A UN commission was established to iron out the details and determine the future boundaries.

During the next several months, growing hostility between Jewish and Arab forces—the latter increasingly supported by neighboring Muslim states—caused the British to announce that they would withdraw their own peacekeeping forces by May 15, 1948. Shortly after the stroke of midnight, as the British mandate formally came to a close, the **Zionist** leader David Ben-Gurion (1886–1973) announced the independence of the state of Israel. Later that same day, the new state was formally recognized by the United States, while military forces from several neighboring Muslim states—all of which had vigorously opposed the formation of a Jewish state in the region—entered Israeli territory but were beaten back. Thousands of Arab residents of the new state fled. Internal dissonance among the Arabs, combined with the strength of Jewish resistance groups, contributed to the failure of the invasion, but the bitterness between the two sides did not subside. The Muslim states refused to recognize the new state of Israel, which became a member of the United Nations, legitimizing it in the eyes of the rest of the world. The stage for future conflict was set.

The exodus of thousands of Palestinian refugees into neighboring Muslim states had repercussions that are still felt today. Jordan, which had become an independent kingdom under its Hashemite ruler, was flooded by the arrival of one million urban Palestinians. They overwhelmed the country's half million residents, most of whom were Bedouins. To the north, the state of Lebanon had been created to provide the local Christian community with a country of their own, but the arrival of the Palestinian refugees upset the delicate balance between Christians and Muslims. Moreover, the creation of Lebanon had angered the Syrians, who had lost that land as well as other territories to Turkey as a result of European decisions before and after the war.

Nasser and Pan-Arabism

The dispute over Palestine placed Egypt in an uncomfortable position. Technically, Egypt was not an Arab state. King Farouk (1920–1965), who had acceded to power in 1936, had frequently declared support for the Arab cause, but the Egyptian people were not Bedouins and shared little of the culture of the peoples across the Red Sea. Nevertheless, Farouk committed Egyptian armies to the disastrous war against Israel.

In 1952, King Farouk, whose corrupt habits had severely eroded his early popularity, was overthrown by a military coup engineered by young military officers ostensibly under the leadership of Colonel Muhammad Nagib. The real force behind the scenes was Colonel Gamal Abdul Nasser (1918–1970), the son of a minor government functionary who, like many of his fellow officers, had been angered by the army's inadequate preparation for the war against Israel four years earlier. In 1953, the monarchy was replaced by a republic.

The Arab Case for Palestine

As more and more Jews immigrated to Palestine after World War II, the world powers began to discuss how to handle the growing tensions in the area. In 1946, the Arab Office in Jerusalem issued a statement outlining its case against the Zionist proposal to transform Palestine into a Jewish state. The statement declared that any solution to the Palestinian problem "must recognize the right of the indigenous inhabitants of Palestine to continue in occupation of the country and to preserve its traditional character." Further, it stated, any representative government in Palestine "should be based upon the principle of absolute equality of all citizens irrespective of race and religion." The following selection is an excerpt from this document.

The Problem of Palestine

1. The whole Arab People is unalterably opposed to the attempt to impose Jewish immigration and settlement upon it, and ultimately to establish a Jewish State in Palestine. Its opposition is based primarily upon right. The Arabs of Palestine are descendants of the indigenous inhabitants of the country, who have been in occupation of it since the beginning of history; they cannot agree that it is right to subject an indigenous population against its will to alien immigrants, whose claim is based upon a historical connection which ceased effectively many centuries ago. Moreover they form the majority of the population; as such they cannot submit to a policy of immigration which if pursued for long will turn them from a majority into a minority in an alien state; and they claim the democratic right of a majority to make its own decisions in matters of urgent national concern....

2. In addition to the question of right, the Arabs oppose the claims of political Zionism because of the effects which Zionist settlement has already had upon their situation and is likely to have to an even greater extent in the future. Negatively, it has diverted the whole course of their national development. Geographically Palestine is part of Syria; its indigenous inhabitants belong to the Syrian branch of the Arab family of nations; all their culture and tradition link them to the other Arab peoples; and until 1917 Palestine formed part of the Ottoman Empire which included also several of the other Arab countries. The presence and claims of the Zionists, and the support given them by certain Western Powers have resulted in Palestine being cut off from the other Arab countries and subjected to a regime, administrative, legal, fiscal, and educational, different from that of the sister-countries. Quite apart from the inconvenience to individuals and the dislocation of trade which this separation has caused, it has prevented Palestine participating fully in the general development of the Arab world.

 How did the authors of this document justify their opposition to the establishment of an independent Jewish state in Israel? What counterarguments could be advanced against their position?

SOURCE: Akram Khater, *Sources in the History of the Modern Middle East*, 2nd ed. (Cengage, 2011), pp. 179–190.

In 1954, Nasser seized power in his own right and immediately instituted a land reform program. He also adopted a policy of neutrality in foreign affairs and expressed sympathy for the Arab cause. The British presence had rankled many Egyptians for years, for even after granting Egypt independence, Britain had retained control over the Suez Canal to protect its route to the Indian Ocean. In 1956, Nasser suddenly nationalized the Suez Canal Company, which had been under British and French administration. Seeing a threat to their route to the Indian Ocean, the British and the French launched a joint attack on Egypt to protect their investment. They were joined by Israel, whose leaders had grown exasperated at sporadic Arab commando raids on Israeli territory and now decided to strike back. But the Eisenhower administration in the United States, concerned that the attack smacked of a revival of colonialism, supported Nasser and brought about the withdrawal of foreign forces from Egypt and of Israeli troops from the Sinai peninsula.

THE UNITED ARAB REPUBLIC Nasser now turned to pan-Arabism. In 1958, Egypt united with Syria in the United Arab Republic (UAR). The union had been proposed by members of the Ba'ath Party, which advocated the unity of all Arab states in a new socialist society. In 1957, the Ba'ath Party assumed power in Syria and opened talks with Egypt on a union between the two countries, which took place in March 1958 following a plebiscite. Nasser, despite his reported ambivalence about the union, was named president of the new state.

Egypt and Syria hoped that the union would eventually include all Arab states, but other Arab leaders, including young King Hussein of Jordan and the kings of Iraq and Saudi Arabia, were suspicious. The latter two in particular understandably feared pan-Arabism on the assumption that they would be asked to share their vast oil revenues with the poorer states of the Middle East.

Nasser opposed the existing situation, in which much of the wealth of the Middle East flowed into the treasuries of a handful of wealthy feudal states or, even worse, the pockets of foreign oil interests. In his view, through Arab unity, this wealth could be put to better use to improve the standard of living in the area. To achieve a more equitable division of the wealth of the region, natural resources and major industries would be nationalized; central planning would ensure that resources were exploited efficiently, but private enterprise would continue at the local level.

In the end, however, Nasser's determination to extend state control over the economy brought an end to the UAR. When the government announced the nationalization of a large number of industries and utilities in 1961, a military coup overthrew the Ba'ath leaders in Damascus, and the new authorities declared that Syria would end its relationship with Egypt.

The breakup of the UAR did not end Nasser's dream of pan-Arabism. In 1962, Algeria finally received its independence from France and, under its new president, Ahmad Ben Bella (1918–2004), established close relations with Egypt, as did a new republic in Yemen. During the mid-1960s, Egypt took the lead in promoting Arab unity against Israel. At a meeting of Arab leaders held in Jerusalem in 1964, the Palestine Liberation Organization (PLO) was set up under Egyptian sponsorship to represent the interests of the Palestinians. According to the charter of the PLO, only the Palestinian people (and thus not Jewish immigrants from abroad) had the right to form a state in the old British mandate. A guerrilla movement called al-Fatah, led by the dissident PLO figure Yasir Arafat (1929–2004), began to launch terrorist attacks on Israeli territory, prompting Israel to raid PLO bases in Jordan in 1966.

The Arab-Israeli Dispute

The growing Arab hostility was a constant threat to the security of Israel. In the years after independence, Israeli leaders dedicated themselves to creating a Jewish homeland. Aided by reparations paid by the postwar German government and private funds provided by Jews living abroad, notably in the United States, the government attempted to build a democratic and modern state that would be a magnet for Jews throughout the world and a symbol of Jewish achievement.

Ensuring the survival of the tiny state surrounded by antagonistic Arab neighbors was a considerable challenge, made more difficult by divisions within the Israeli population. Some were immigrants from Europe, while others came from countries of the Middle East. Some were secular and even socialist in their views, while others were politically conservative and stressed religious orthodoxy. The state was also home to Christians as well as many Muslim Palestinians who had not fled to other countries. To balance these diverse interests, Israel established a parliament, called the Knesset, on the European model, with proportional representation based on the number of votes each party received in the general election. The parties were so numerous that none ever received a majority of votes, and all governments had to be formed from a coalition of several parties. As a result, moderate secular leaders such as longtime prime minister David Ben-Gurion had to cater to more marginal parties composed of conservative religious groups.

THE SIX-DAY WAR During the late 1950s and 1960s, the dispute between Israel and other states in the Middle East escalated in intensity. Essentially alone except for the sympathy of the United States and several Western European countries, Israel adopted a policy of determined resistance and immediate retaliation against PLO and Arab provocations. By the spring of 1967, relations between Israel and its Arab neighbors had deteriorated as Nasser attempted to improve his standing in the Arab world by intensifying military activities and imposing a blockade against Israeli commerce through the Gulf of Aqaba.

Concerned that it might be isolated, and lacking firm support from Western powers (which had originally guaranteed Israel the freedom to use the Gulf of Aqaba), in June 1967 Israel suddenly launched air strikes against Egypt and several of its Arab neighbors. Israeli armies then broke the blockade at the head of the Gulf of Aqaba and occupied the Sinai peninsula. Other Israeli forces attacked Jordanian territory on the West Bank of the Jordan River (Jordan's King Hussein had recently signed an alliance with Egypt and placed his army under Egyptian command), occupied the whole of Jerusalem, and seized Syrian military positions in the Golan Heights along the Israeli-Syrian border.

Despite limited Soviet support for Egypt and Syria, in a brief six-day war, Israel had mocked Nasser's pretensions of Arab unity and tripled the size of its territory, thus enhancing its precarious security (see Map 15.1). Yet

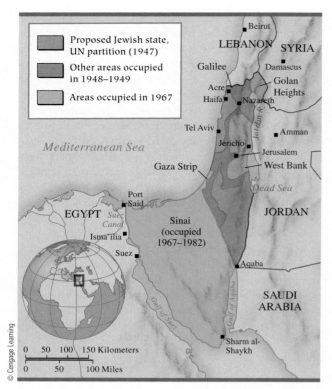

© Cengage Learning

MAP 15.1 Israel and Its Neighbors. This map shows the evolution of the state of Israel since its founding in 1948. Areas occupied by Israel after the Six-Day War in 1967 are indicated in green.

Q *What is the significance of the West Bank?*

Israel had also aroused more bitter hostility among the Arabs and brought an additional million Palestinians inside its borders, most of them living on the West Bank.

During the next few years, the focus of the Arab-Israeli dispute shifted as Arab states demanded the return of the territories lost during the 1967 war. Meanwhile, many Israelis argued that the new lands improved the security of the beleaguered state and should be retained. Concerned that the dispute might lead to a confrontation between the superpowers, the Nixon administration tried to achieve a peace settlement. The peace effort received a mild stimulus when Nasser died of a heart attack in September 1970 and was succeeded by his vice president, ex-general Anwar al-Sadat (1918–1981). Sadat soon showed himself to be more pragmatic than his predecessor, dropping the now irrelevant name United Arab Republic in favor of the Arab Republic of Egypt and replacing Nasser's socialist policies with a new strategy based on free enterprise and encouragement of Western investment. He also agreed to sign a peace treaty with Israel on the condition that Israel withdraw to its pre-1967 frontiers. Concerned that other Arab

countries would refuse to make peace and take advantage of its presumed weakness, Israel refused.

Rebuffed in his offer of peace, smarting from criticism of his moderate stand from other Arab leaders, and increasingly concerned over Israeli plans to build permanent Jewish settlements in the West Bank, Sadat attempted once again to renew Arab unity through a new confrontation with Israel. In 1973, on Yom Kippur (the Jewish Day of Atonement), an Israeli national holiday, Egyptian forces suddenly launched an air and artillery attack on Israeli positions in the Sinai just east of the Suez Canal. Syrian armies attacked Israeli positions in the Golan Heights. After early Arab successes, the Israelis managed to recoup some of their losses on both fronts. As a superpower confrontation between the United States and the Soviet Union loomed, a cease-fire was finally reached. In the next years, a fragile peace was maintained, marked by U.S. "shuttle diplomacy" (carried out by Secretary of State Henry Kissinger) and the rise to power in Israel of the militant Likud Party under Prime Minister Menachem Begin (1913–1992).

THE CAMP DAVID AGREEMENT After his election as U.S. president in 1976, Jimmy Carter began to press for a compromise peace based on Israel's return of territories occupied during the 1967 war and Arab recognition of the state of Israel. In September 1978, Sadat and Begin met with Carter at Camp David in the United States and agreed on a framework for peace in the region. A year later, in the first treaty signed with a Muslim state, Israel agreed to withdraw from the Sinai, but not from other occupied territories unless it was recognized by other Arab countries.

The promise of the Camp David agreement was not fulfilled, however. One reason was the assassination of Sadat by Islamic militants in October 1981. But there were deeper causes, including the continued unwillingness of many Muslim governments to recognize Israel and the Israeli government's encouragement of Jewish settlements in the occupied West Bank.

THE PLO AND THE *INTIFADA* During the early 1980s, the militancy of the Palestinians increased, leading to rising unrest, popularly labeled the ***intifada*** (uprising), among PLO supporters living inside Israel. To control the situation, a new Israeli government under Prime Minister Itzhak Shamir (1915–2012) invaded southern Lebanon to destroy PLO commando bases near the Israeli border. The invasion aroused controversy abroad and further destabilized the perilous balance between Muslims and Christians in Lebanon. As the 1990s began, Israel and a number of its neighbors engaged in U.S.-sponsored peace talks, but progress was slow. Terrorist attacks by Palestinian militants resulted in heavy casualties and shook the confidence of many Jewish citizens that their security needs could be protected. National elections held in 1996 led to the formation of a new government under Benjamin Netanyahu (b. 1949), which adopted a tougher stance in negotiations with the Palestinian Authority under Yasir Arafat.

In 1999, a new Labour government under Prime Minister Ehud Barak (b. 1942) sought to revitalize the peace process. Negotiations resumed with the PLO and also got under way with Syria over a peace settlement in Lebanon and the possible return of the Golan Heights. But the talks broke down over the future of the city of Jerusalem, leading to massive riots by Palestinians and a dramatic increase in bloodshed on both sides. The death of Yasir Arafat in 2004 and his replacement by Palestinian moderate Mahmoud Abbas (b. 1935), as well as the withdrawal of Israeli settlers from Gaza in 2005, raised modest hopes for progress, but the victory of **Hamas**, a radical organization dedicated to the destruction of the state of Israel, in Palestinian elections in 2006 undermined the search for peace. Also in 2006, radical Muslim forces operating in southern Lebanon launched massive attacks on Israeli cities. In response, Israeli troops crossed the border in an effort to wipe out the source of the assault. Two years later, Hamas militants in the Gaza Strip launched their own rocket attacks on sites in southern Israel. The latter responded forcefully, thereby raising the specter of a wider conflict. As attitudes hardened, Israeli elections in early 2009 led to the return to office of former prime minister Benjamin Netanyahu and a virtual stalemate in the peace process. Netanyahu was reelected in 2012 amid indications that both sides had despaired of bringing an end to the conflict.

© William J. Duiker

The Temple Mount at Jerusalem. The Temple Mount is one of the most sacred places in the city of Jerusalem. Originally, it was the site of a temple built during the reign of Solomon, king of the Israelites, about 1000 B.C.E. The Western Wall, built during the reign of King Herod, is shown in the foreground. Beyond the wall is the Dome of the Rock complex, built on the place from which Muslims believe that Muhammad ascended to heaven. Sacred to both religions, the Temple Mount is now a major bone of contention between Muslims and Jews and a prime obstacle to a final settlement of the Arab-Israeli dispute.

Revolution in Iran

The Arab-Israeli dispute also spilled over into international politics. In 1960, a number of oil-producing states formed the Organization of Petroleum Exporting Countries (OPEC) to gain control over oil prices, but the organization was not recognized by the foreign oil companies. In the 1970s, a group of Arab oil states established the Organization of Arab Petroleum Exporting Countries (OAPEC) to use as a weapon to force Western governments to abandon pro-Israeli policies. During the 1973 Yom Kippur War, some OPEC nations announced significant increases in the price of oil to foreign countries. The price hikes were accompanied by an apparent oil shortage and created serious economic problems in the United States and Europe, as well as in the Third World.

One of the key oil-exporting countries was Iran. Under the leadership of Shah Mohammad Reza Pahlavi (1919–1980), who had taken over from his father in 1941, Iran

© Cengage Learning

Iran

had become one of the richest countries in the Middle East. Although relations with the West had occasionally been fragile (especially after Prime Minister Mohammad Mosaddeq had briefly attempted to nationalize the oil industry in 1951), during the next twenty years, Iran became a prime ally of the United States in the Middle East. With encouragement from the United States, which hoped that Iran could become a force for stability in the Persian Gulf, the shah attempted to carry through a series of social and economic reforms to transform the country into the most advanced in the region.

Statistical evidence implied that his efforts were succeeding. Per capita income increased dramatically, literacy rates improved, a modern communications infrastructure took shape, and an affluent middle class emerged in the capital of Tehran. Under the surface, however, trouble was brewing. Despite an ambitious land reform program, many peasants were still landless, unemployment among intellectuals was dangerously high, and the urban middle class was squeezed by high inflation. Housing costs had skyrocketed, in part because of a massive influx of foreigners attracted by oil money.

Some of the unrest took the form of religious discontent as millions of devout Shi'ite Muslims looked with distaste at a new Iranian civilization based on greed, sexual license, and material accumulation. Conservative *ulama* (Muslim scholars) opposed rampant government corruption, the ostentation of the shah's court, and the extension of voting rights to women. Some opposition elements resorted to terrorism against wealthy Iranians or foreign residents in an attempt to initiate social and political disorder. In response, the shah's U.S.-trained security police, the SAVAK, imprisoned and sometimes tortured thousands of dissidents.

THE FALL OF THE SHAH Leading the opposition was Ayatollah Ruholla Khomeini (1900–1989), an austere Shi'ite cleric who had been exiled to Iraq and then to France because of his outspoken opposition to the shah's regime. From Paris, Khomeini continued his attacks in print, on television, and in radio broadcasts. By the late 1970s, large numbers of Iranians began to respond to Khomeini's diatribes against the "satanic regime," and demonstrations by his supporters were repressed with ferocity by the police. But workers' strikes (some of them in the oil fields, which reduced government revenue) grew in intensity. In January 1979, the shah appointed a moderate, Shapur Bakhtiar (1914–1991), as prime minister and then left the country for medical treatment.

Bakhtiar attempted to conciliate the rising opposition and permitted Khomeini to return to Iran, where he demanded the government's resignation. With rising public unrest and incipient revolt within the army, the government collapsed and was replaced by a hastily formed Islamic republic. The new government, which was dominated by Shi'ite *ulama* under the guidance of Ayatollah Khomeini, immediately began to introduce traditional Islamic law (see the Film & History feature on p. 315). A new reign of terror ensued as supporters of the shah were rounded up and executed.

Though much of the outside world focused on the U.S. embassy in Tehran, where militants held a number of foreign hostages, the Iranian Revolution involved much more. In the eyes of the ayatollah and his followers, the United States was "the great Satan," the powerful protector of Israel, and the enemy of Muslim peoples everywhere. Furthermore, it was responsible for the corruption of Iranian society under the shah. Now Khomeini demanded that the shah be returned to Iran for trial and that the United States apologize for its acts against the Iranian people. In response, the Carter administration stopped buying Iranian oil and froze Iranian assets in the United States.

The effects of the disturbances in Iran quickly spread beyond its borders. Sunni militants briefly seized the holy places in Mecca and began to appeal to their brothers to launch similar revolutions in Islamic countries around the world, including far-off Malaysia and Indonesia. At the same time, ethnic unrest emerged among the Kurdish minorities along the border. In July 1980, the shah died of cancer in Cairo. With economic conditions in Iran rapidly deteriorating, the Islamic revolutionary government finally agreed to free the hostages in return for the release of Iranian assets in the United States. During the next few years, the intensity of the Iranian Revolution moderated slightly, as the government displayed a modest tolerance for a loosening of clerical control over freedom of expression and social activities. But rising criticism of rampant official corruption and a high rate of inflation sparked a new wave of government repression; newspapers were censored, the universities were purged of disloyal or "un-Islamic" elements, and religious militants raided private homes in search of blasphemous activities. In 1997, however, Mohammad Khatami (b. 1943), a moderate Islamic cleric, was elected president. During the next few years, press censorship was relaxed, and restrictions on women's activities were loosened, though hard-liners continued to reject proprosals to expand civil rights.

The presidential elections in 2004 brought a new leader, Mahmoud Ahmadinejad (b. 1956), to power in Tehran. He immediately inflamed the situation by calling publicly for the destruction of the state of Israel, while his government aroused unease throughout the world by proclaiming its determination to develop a nuclear energy

Persepolis (2007)

The Iranian author Marjane Satrapi (b. 1969) has re-created *Persepolis*, her autobiographical graphic novel, as an enthralling animated film of the same name. Using simple black-and-white animation, the movie recounts key stages in the turbulent history of modern Iran as seen through the eyes of a spirited young girl, also named Marjane. The dialogue is in French with English subtitles (a version dubbed in English is also available), and the voices of the characters are rendered beautifully by Danielle Darrieux, Catherine Deneuve, Chiara Mastroianni, and other European film stars.

In the film, Marjane is the daughter of middle-class left-wing intellectuals who abhor the dictatorship of the shah and actively participate in his overthrow in 1979. After the revolution, however, the severity of the ayatollah's Islamic rule arouses their secularist and democratic impulses. Encouraged by her loving grandmother, who reinforces her modernist and feminist instincts, Marjane resents having to wear a head scarf and the educational restrictions imposed by the puritanical new Islamic regime, but to little avail. Emotionally exhausted and fearful of political retribution from the authorities, her family finally sends her to study in Vienna.

Study abroad, however, is not a solution to Marjane's problems. She is distressed by the nihilism and emotional shallowness of her new Austrian school friends, who seem oblivious to the contrast between their privileged lives and her own experience of living under the shadow of a tyrannical regime. Disillusioned by the loneliness of exile and several failed love affairs, she descends into a deep depression and then decides to return to Tehran. When she discovers that her family is still suffering from political persecution, however, she decides to leave the country permanently and settles in Paris.

Observing the events, first through the eyes of a child and then through the perceptions of an innocent schoolgirl, the viewer of the film is forced to fill in the blanks, as Marjane initially cannot comprehend the meaning of the adult conversations swirling around her. As Marjane passes through adolescence into adulthood, the realization of the folly of human intransigence and superstition becomes painfully clear, both to her and to the audience. Although animated films have long been a staple in the cinema, thanks in part to Walt Disney, both the novel and the film *Persepolis* demonstrate how graphic design can depict a momentous event in history with clarity and compassion. ■

program. Iran has also provided support for terrorist groups in Lebanon and elsewhere in the region. In the meantime, economic conditions at home grew steadily worse. In 2009, Ahmadinejad was reelected in a disputed vote that brought thousands into the streets of Tehran in protest. Ahmadinejad was limited to two terms in office by the Iranian constitution, and in June 2013, Hassan Rouhani (b. 1948), a Muslim cleric who received support from some moderate and reformist groups and ran on the motto "Moderation," was elected president.

Crisis in the Persian Gulf

Although much of the Iranians' anger was directed against the United States during the early phases of the revolution, Iran had equally hated enemies closer to home. To the north, the immense power of the Soviet Union, driven by atheistic communism, was viewed as a modern-day version of the Russian threat of previous centuries. To the west was a militant and hostile Iraq, now under the leadership of the ambitious Saddam Hussein (1937–2006). Problems from both directions appeared shortly after Khomeini's rise to power. Soviet military forces occupied Afghanistan to prop up a weak Marxist regime there. The following year, Iraqi forces suddenly attacked along the Iranian border.

Iraq and Iran had long had an uneasy relationship, fueled by religious differences (Iranian Islam is predominantly Shi'ite, while the ruling class in Iraq was Sunni) and a perennial dispute over borderlands adjacent to the Persian Gulf, the vital waterway for the export of oil from both countries (see Map 15.2). Like several of its neighbors, Iraq had long dreamed of unifying the Arabs but had been hindered by internal factions and suspicion among its neighbors.

During the mid-1970s, Iran gave some support to a Kurdish rebellion in the mountains of Iraq. In 1975, the government of the shah agreed to stop aiding the rebels in return for territorial concessions at the head of the gulf. Five years later, however, the Kurdish revolt had been suppressed, and President Saddam Hussein, who had assumed power in Baghdad in 1979, accused Iran of violating the

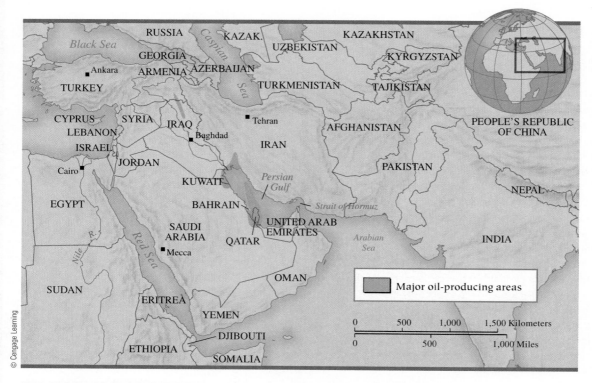

MAP 15.2 The Modern Middle East. Shown here are the boundaries of the independent states in the contemporary Middle East.

 Which are the major oil-producing countries?

territorial agreement and launched an attack on his neighbor. The war was a bloody one and lasted nearly ten years; poison gas was used against civilians, and children were sent out to clear minefields. Other countries, including the two superpowers, watched nervously in case the conflict spread throughout the region. Finally, with both sides virtually exhausted, a cease-fire was arranged in the fall of 1988.

THE VISION OF SADDAM HUSSEIN The bitter conflict with Iran had not slaked Saddam Hussein's appetite for territorial expansion in the form of a Ba'athist state that would dominate the Middle East. In early August 1990, Iraqi military forces suddenly moved across the border and occupied the small neighboring country of Kuwait at the head of the gulf. The immediate pretext was the claim that Kuwait was pumping oil from fields inside Iraqi territory. Baghdad was also angry over the Kuwaiti government's demand for repayment of loans it had made to Iraq during the war with Iran. But the underlying reason was Iraq's contention that Kuwait was legally a part of Iraq. Kuwait had been part of the Ottoman Empire until the beginning of the twentieth century, when the local prince had agreed to place his patrimony under British protection. When Iraq became independent in 1932, it

claimed the area on the grounds that the state of Kuwait had been created by British imperialism, but opposition from major Western powers and other countries in the region, which feared the consequences of a "greater Iraq," prevented an Iraqi takeover.

OPERATION DESERT STORM The Iraqi invasion of Kuwait in 1990 sparked an international outcry, and the United States amassed an international force that liberated the country and destroyed a substantial part of Iraq's armed forces. But the allied forces did not occupy Baghdad at the end of the war because allied leaders feared that doing so would cause a total breakup of the country, an eventuality that would operate to the benefit of Iran. They hoped instead that the Hussein regime would be ousted by an internal revolt. In the meantime, harsh economic sanctions were imposed on the Iraqi government as the condition for peace. The anticipated overthrow of Saddam Hussein did not materialize, however, and his tireless efforts to evade the conditions of the cease-fire continued to bedevil the administrations of Presidents Bill Clinton and George W. Bush.

CONFLICTS IN AFGHANISTAN AND IRAQ The terrorist attacks launched against U.S. cities in September

2001 added a new dimension to the Middle Eastern equation. After the failure of the Soviet Union to quell the rebellion in Afghanistan during the 1980s (see Chapter 7), a fundamentalist Muslim group known as the Taliban, supported covertly by the United States, seized power in Kabul and ruled the country with a fanaticism reminiscent of the Cultural Revolution in China. Backed by conservative religious forces in Pakistan, the Taliban provided a base of operations for Osama bin Laden's al-Qaeda terrorist network (see the box on p. 318). After the attacks of September 11, a coalition of forces led by the United States overthrew the Taliban and attempted to build a new and moderate government. But the country's history of bitter internecine warfare among tribal groups remained a severe challenge to those efforts, and Taliban forces have managed to regroup and continue to operate in the mountainous region adjacent to the Pakistani border. The terrorist threat from al-Qaeda, however, was dealt a major blow in May 2011, when Osama bin Laden was killed by U.S. special operations forces during a raid on his hideout in northern Pakistan.

After moving against the Taliban at the end of 2001, the administration of George W. Bush, charging that Iraqi dictator Saddam Hussein had not only provided support to bin Laden's terrorist organization but also stockpiled weapons of mass destruction for use against his enemies, threatened to invade Iraq and remove him from power. It was the president's hope that the overthrow of the Iraqi dictator would promote the spread of democracy throughout the region. The plan, widely debated in the media and opposed by many of the United States' traditional allies, disquieted Arab leaders and fanned anti-American sentiment throughout the Muslim world. Nevertheless, in March 2003, U.S.-led forces attacked Iraq and overthrew Saddam Hussein's regime. In the months that followed, occupation forces sought to restore stability to the country while setting out plans on which to build a democratic society.

Afghanistan

Predominantly Sunni areas
Predominantly Shi'ite areas
Predominantly Kurdish areas

Iraq

But although Saddam Hussein was captured by U.S. troops and later executed, armed resistance by militant Muslim elements continued.

When Barack Obama came into office in 2009, he promised to bring about the withdrawal of U.S. combat forces from Iraq, while training an Iraqi military force capable of defeating the remaining insurgents. In the meantime, a fragile government has been formed in Baghdad, the embryo of a possible pro-Western state that could serve as an emblem of democracy in the Middle East. Squabbling among Sunni, Shi'ite, and Kurdish elements within the country, however, continued as the last U.S. combat troops were withdrawn in the fall of 2011.

Revolution in the Middle East

In the early months of 2011, popular protests against current conditions broke out in several countries in the Middle East. Beginning in Tunisia, the riots spread rapidly to Egypt—where they brought about the abrupt resignation of longtime president Hosni Mubarak (b. 1929)—and then to other countries in the region, including Syria, Libya, and Yemen, where political leaders sought to quell the unrest, often by violent means.

In Libya, the bloody regime of dictator Muammar Qaddafi was overthrown by a popular revolt with the assistance of NATO air strikes, but the unrest in Syria has expanded into a brutal civil war. The uprisings (dubbed the "Arab Spring") created hopes around the world that the seeds of democracy had been planted in a region long dominated by autocratic governments, but also aroused widespread concern that unstable conditions could lead to further violence and a rise in international terrorism. Two years after the outbreak of unrest, the prognosis for the future of the region is still unclear as the continuing conflict in Syria threatens to inflame the entire region.

I Accuse!

In 1998, Osama bin Laden was virtually unknown outside the Middle East. But this scion of a wealthy industrialist from Saudi Arabia was on a mission—to avenge the hostile acts perpetrated on his fellow Muslims by the United States and its allies. Having taken part in the successful guerrilla war against Soviet occupation troops in Afghanistan during the 1980s, Osama now turned his ire on the tyrannical regimes in the Middle East and their great protector, the United States. In the following excerpts from a 1998 interview, he defends the use of terror against those whom he deems enemies of Islam. Three years later, his followers launched the surprise attacks that led to more than three thousand deaths on September 11, 2001.

Interview with Osama bin Laden by His Followers (1998)

What is the meaning of your call for Muslims to take up arms against America in particular, and what is the message that you wish to send to the West in general?

The call to wage war against America was made because America has spearheaded the crusade against the Islamic nation, sending tens of thousands of its troops to the land of the two Holy Mosques [Saudi Arabia], over and above its meddling in its affairs and its politics and its support of the oppressive, corrupt, and tyrannical regime that is in control. These are the reasons behind the singling out of America as a target. And not exempt from responsibility are those Western regimes whose presence in the region offers support to the American troops there. We know at least one reason behind the symbolic participation of the Western forces and that is to support the Jewish and Zionist plans for expansion of what is called the Great Israel. Surely, their presence is not out of concern over their interests in the region. . . . Their presence has no meaning save one and that is to offer support to the Jews in Palestine who are in need of their Christian brothers to achieve full control over the Arab Peninsula which they intend to make an important part of the so called Greater Israel.

Many of the Arabic as well as the Western mass media accuse you of terrorism and of supporting terrorism. What do you have to say to that?

Every state and every civilization and culture has to resort to terrorism under certain circumstances for the purpose of abolishing tyranny and corruption. Every country in the world has its own security system and its own security forces, its own police, and its own army. They are all designed to terrorize whoever even contemplates an attack on that country or its citizens. The terrorism we practice is of the commendable kind for it is directed at the tyrants and the aggressors and the enemies of Allah, the tyrants, the traitors who commit acts of treason against their own countries and their own faith and their own prophet and their own nation. Terrorizing those and punishing them are necessary measures to straighten things and to make them right. Tyrants and oppressors who subject the Arab nation to aggression ought to be punished. . . . America heads the list of aggressors against Muslims. The recurrence of aggression against Muslims everywhere is proof enough. For over half a century, Muslims in Palestine have been slaughtered and assaulted and robbed of their honor and of their property. Their houses have been blasted, their crops destroyed. And the strange thing is that any act by them to avenge themselves or to lift the injustice befalling them causes great agitation in the United Nations, which hastens to call for an emergency meeting only to convict the victim and to censure the wronged and the tyrannized whose children have been killed and whose crops have been destroyed and whose farms have been pulverized. . . .

In today's wars, there are no morals, and it is clear that mankind has descended to the lowest degrees of decadence and oppression. They rip us of our wealth and of our resources and of our oil. Our religion is under attack. They kill and murder our brothers. They compromise our honor and our dignity and if we dare to utter a single word of protest against the injustice, we are called terrorists. This is compounded injustice. And the United Nations insistence to convict the victims and support the aggressors constitutes a serious precedent that shows the extent of injustice that has been allowed to take root in this land.

 What reasons does Osama bin Laden present to justify the terrorist attacks carried out by his followers around the world? How would you respond to his charges?

SOURCE: From Khater, SOURCES IN THE HISTORY OF THE MODERN MIDDLE EAST, 2E. © 2011 Cengage Learning.

Claudia Wiens/Alamy

Tahrir Square: Ground Zero for the Arab Spring. When popular demonstrations broke out against the regime of Egyptian president Hosni Mubarak in early 2011, Tahrir Square, in the heart of the teeming metropolis of Cairo, was at the epicenter of the protests. For weeks, supporters and opponents of the regime clashed periodically in the square, resulting in severe casualties. After the overthrow of Mubarak, the square continued to provide a venue for public protests against the new government of President Mohamed Morsi, leader of the Muslim Brotherhood, and when public protests against the latter escalated, the army stepped in to depose President Morsi.

To be sure, there have been some variations in government throughout the region. In some societies, traditional authority has been replaced by charismatic one-party rule or military dictatorships. Nasser's Egypt was a single-party state where the leader won political power by the force of his presence or personality. The regimes of Ayatollah Khomeini in Iran, Muammar Qaddafi in Libya, and Saddam Hussein in Iraq could also trace much of their power to the personal appeal of the leader.

In other states, charismatic rule has given way to modernizing bureaucratic regimes. Examples include the governments of Syria, Yemen, Turkey, and Egypt since Nasser, where Anwar al-Sadat and his successor, Hosni Mubarak, focused on performance. Most of these regimes have remained highly autocratic in character, however, except in Turkey, where free elections and the sharing of power have become more prevalent in recent years. Only in the Jewish state of Israel are democratic institutions firmly established.

A few Arab nations, such as Bahrain, Kuwait, and Jordan, have engaged in limited forms of democratic experimentation. Most of the region's recent leaders, however, have maintained that Western-style democracy is not appropriate for their societies. Bashar al-Assad (b. 1965), the president of Syria, once remarked that he would tolerate only "positive criticism" of his policies. "We have to have our own democracy to match our history and culture," he said, "arising from the needs of our people and our reality."[2] President Mubarak of Egypt often insisted to foreign critics that only authoritarian rule could prevent the spread of Islamic radicalism throughout his country.

For many years, most world leaders accepted the logic of these contentions, provoking some critics to charge that Western governments coddled Middle Eastern dictatorships as a means of maintaining stability in the region and preserving their access to the vast oil reserves located on the Arabian peninsula. For their part, authoritarian leaders in the region sought to deflect,

Society and Culture in the Contemporary Middle East

In the Middle East today, all aspects of society and culture—from political and economic issues to literature, art, and the role of the family—are intertwined with questions of religious faith.

Varieties of Government: The Politics of Islam

To many seasoned observers, the strategy applied by President George W. Bush in Iraq appeared unrealistic, since democratic values are not deeply rooted in the culture of the Middle East. In many countries, feudal rulers remain securely in power. The kings of Saudi Arabia, for example, continue to govern by traditional precepts and, citing the distinctive character of Muslim society, have been reluctant to establish representative political institutions. These rulers insist that strict observance of traditional customs be maintained. Religious police are responsible for enforcing the Muslim dress code, maintaining the prohibition against alcohol, and making sure that offices close during the time of prayer.

Society and Culture in the Contemporary Middle East ❧ **319**

often with great success, popular discontent with local conditions onto the West.

The recent outbreak of popular unrest that has erupted from North Africa to the Arabian peninsula raises questions about the potential for democratic changes to emerge in the countries throughout the region. Are democratic institutions and the principles of human freedom truly antithetical to the culture of the Middle East and the principles of Islam? The success of the Muslim Brotherhood in recent elections in Egypt, elevating its candidate Mohamed Morsi (b. 1951) to the presidency in 2012, is a dramatic case in point. When the new government sought to pursue its Islamist agenda, opposition forces took to the streets once more in protest, and the military took action to seize power. As the world awaits future events, the fate of the region hangs in the balance (see the box on p. 321).

The Economics of the Middle East: Oil and Sand

Few areas exhibit a greater disparity of individual and national wealth than the Middle East. While millions live in abject poverty, a fortunate few rank among the wealthiest people in the world. The primary reason for this disparity is oil. Unfortunately for most of the peoples of the region, oil reserves are distributed unevenly and all too often are located in areas where the population density is low (see Map 15.2 on p. 316). Egypt and Turkey, with more than 75 million inhabitants apiece, have almost no oil reserves. The combined population of Kuwait, the United Arab Emirates, and Saudi Arabia is about 35 million people. This disparity in wealth inspired Nasser's quest for Arab unity but has also posed a major obstacle to that unity.

ECONOMICS AND ISLAM Not surprisingly, considering their different resources and political systems, the states of the Middle East have adopted diverse approaches to the problem of developing strong and stable economies. Some, like Nasser in Egypt and the leaders of the Ba'ath Party in Syria, attempted to create a form of Arab socialism, favoring a high level of government involvement in the economy to relieve the inequities of the free enterprise system. Others turned to the Western capitalist model to maximize growth while using taxes or massive development projects to build a modern infrastructure, redistribute wealth, and maintain political stability and economic opportunity for all.

Whatever their approach, all the states have attempted to develop their economies in accordance with Islamic beliefs. Although the Qur'an has little to say about economics and cannot be said to be either capitalist or socialist, it is clear in its opposition to charging interest and in its concern for the material welfare of the Muslim community, the **umma**. How these goals are to be achieved, though, is a matter of interpretation.

Socialist theories of economic development such as Nasser's were often suggested as a way to promote economic growth while meeting the requirements of Islamic doctrine. State intervention in the economic sector would bring about rapid development, while land redistribution and the nationalization or regulation of industry would minimize the harsh inequities of the marketplace. In general, however, the socialist approach has had little success, and most governments, including those of Egypt and Syria, eventually shifted to a more free enterprise approach while encouraging foreign investment to compensate for a lack of capital or technology.

AGRICULTURAL POLICIES Although the amount of arable land is relatively small, most countries in the Middle East rely on farming to supply food for their growing populations. Much of the fertile land was owned by wealthy absentee landlords, but land reform programs in several countries have attempted to alleviate this problem.

The most comprehensive and probably the most successful land reform program was instituted in Egypt, where Nasser and his successors managed to reassign nearly a quarter of all cultivable lands by limiting the amount a single individual could hold. Similar programs in Iran, Iraq, Libya, and Syria generally had less effect. After the 1979 revolution in Iran, many farmers forcibly seized lands from the landlords, raising questions of ownership that the revolutionary government has tried to resolve with only minimal success.

Agricultural productivity throughout the region has been plagued by a lack of water. With populations growing at more than 2 percent annually on average in the Middle East (more than 3 percent in some countries), several governments have tried to increase the amount of water available for irrigation. Many attempts have been sabotaged by government ineptitude, political disagreements, and territorial conflicts, however. For example, disputes between Israel and its neighbors over water rights and between Iraq and its neighbors over the exploitation of the Tigris and Euphrates Rivers have caused serious tensions in recent years. Today, the dearth of water in the region is reaching crisis proportions.

MIGRATORY WORKERS Another way that governments have attempted to deal with rapid population growth is to encourage emigration. Oil-producing states with small populations, such as Saudi Arabia and the United Arab Emirates, have imported labor from other countries in the

Islam and Democracy

One of George W. Bush's key objectives in launching the invasion of Iraq in 2003 was to promote the emergence of democratic states throughout the Middle East. According to U.S. officials, one of the ultimate causes of the formation of terrorist movements in Muslim societies is the prevalence in such countries of dictatorial governments that do not serve the interests of their citizens. According to the author of this editorial, an Indian Muslim, the problem lies as much with the actions of Western countries as it does with political attitudes in the Muslim world.

M. J. Akbar, "Linking Islam to Dictatorship"

Let us examine a central canard, that Islam and democracy are incompatible. This is an absurdity. There is nothing Islamic or un-Islamic about democracy. Democracy is the outcome of a political process, not a religious process.

It is glibly suggested that "every" Muslim country is a dictatorship, but the four largest Muslim populations of the world—in Indonesia, India, Bangladesh, and Turkey—vote to change governments. Pakistan could easily have been on this list.

Voting does not make these Muslims less or more religious. There are dictators among Muslims just as there are dictators among Christians, Buddhists, and Hindus (check out Nepal). . . . Christian Latin America has seen ugly forms of dictatorship, as has Christian Africa.

What is unique to the Muslim world is not the absence of democracy but the fact that in 1918, after the defeat of the Ottoman Empire, every single Muslim in the world lived under foreign subjugation.

Every single one, from Indonesia to Morocco via Turkey. The Turks threw out their invaders within a few years under the great leadership of Kemal Atatürk, but the transition to self-rule in other Muslim countries was slow, uncertain, and full of traps planted by the world's preeminent powers.

The West, in the shape of Britain, France, or America, was never interested in democracy when a helpful dictator or king would serve. When people got a chance to express their wish, it was only logical that they would ask for popular rule. It was the street that brought Mosaddeq to power in Iran and drove the shah of Iran to tearful exile in Rome. Who brought the shah of Iran and autocracy back to Iran? The CIA.

If Iranian democracy had been permitted a chance in 1953, there would have been no uprising led by Ayatollah Khomeini in 1979. In other countries, where the struggle for independence was long and brutal, as in Algeria and Indonesia, the militias who had fought the war institutionalized army authority. In other instances, civilian heroes confused their own well-being with national health. They became regressive dictators. Once again, there was nothing Islamic about it.

Muslim countries will become democracies, too, because it is the finest form of modern governance. But it will be a process interrupted by bloody experience as the street wrenches power from usurpers.

Democracy has happened in Turkey. It has happened in Bangladesh. It is happening in Indonesia. It almost happened in Pakistan, and the opportunity will return. Democracy takes time in the most encouraging environments.

Democracy has become the latest rationale for the occupation of Iraq. . . . Granted, democracy is always preferable to tyranny no matter how it comes. But Iraqis are not dupes. They will take democracy and place it at the service of nationalism. A decade ago, America was careless about the definition of victory. Today it is careless about the definition of democracy.

There is uncertainty and apprehension across the Muslim nations: uncertainty about where they stand, and apprehension about both American power and the repugnant use of terrorism that in turn invites the exercise of American power. There is also anger that a legitimate cause like that of Palestine can get buried in the debris of confusion. Muslims do not see Palestinians as terrorists.

 How does the author answer the charge that democracy and Islam are incompatible? To what degree is the West responsible for the problems of the Middle East?

Source: From M. J. Akbar, "Linking Islam to Dictatorship" in *World Press Review*, May 2004. Reprinted by permission.

region, mostly to work in the oil fields. Since the mid-1980s, the majority of the population in those states has been composed of foreign nationals, who often send the bulk of their salaries back to their families in their home countries. When oil revenues declined in the 1980s and 1990s, however, several governments took measures to reduce their migrant population. Today migrant workers are a volatile force in the politics of the region.

Scott E. Barbour/The Image Bank/Getty Images

Dubai: A Las Vegas on the Persian Gulf. While many of the countries in the Middle East are relatively poor by world standards, a favored few have amassed great wealth as a result of their fortunate geographic location. Such is the case with the United Arab Emirates, a small country situated strategically on the eastern edge of the Arabian peninsula and located directly over some of the most abundant oil reserves in the world. The modern city of Dubai, resplendent in its opulence, serves today as a playground for the super-rich and a vivid symbol of the wealth that has flowed into the region because of the world's thirst for liquid energy.

urban areas. They had less influence in the countryside, among the poor, and among devout elements within the clergy. Many of the clerics believed that Western influence in the cities had given birth to political and economic corruption, sexual promiscuity, hedonism, individualism, and the prevalence of alcohol, pornography, and drugs. Although such practices had long existed in the Middle East, they were now far more visible and socially acceptable.

RETURN TO TRADITION Reaction among conservatives against the modernist movement was quick to emerge in several countries and reached its zenith in the late 1970s

The Islamic Revival

In recent years, developments in the Middle East have often been described in terms of a resurgence of traditional values and customs in response to Western influence. Indeed, some conservative religious forces in the area have consciously attempted to replace foreign culture and values with allegedly "pure" Islamic forms of belief and behavior.

MODERNIST ISLAM Initially, many Muslim intellectuals responded to Western influence by trying to create a "modernized" set of Islamic beliefs and practices that would not clash with the demands of the twentieth century. This process took place to some degree in most Islamic societies, but it was especially prevalent in Turkey, Egypt, and Iran. Mustafa Kemal Atatürk embraced the strategy when he attempted to secularize the Islamic religion in the new Turkish republic. The Turkish model was followed by Shah Reza Khan and his son Mohammad Reza Pahlavi in Iran and then by Nasser in postwar Egypt, all of whom attempted to honor Islamic values while asserting the primacy of other issues such as political and economic development. Religion, in effect, had become the handmaiden of political power, national identity, and economic prosperity.

These secularizing trends were particularly noticeable among the political, intellectual, and economic elites in

with the return of the Ayatollah Khomeini to Iran. It is not surprising that Iran took the lead in light of its long tradition of ideological purity within the Shi'ite sect as well as the uncompromisingly secular character of the shah's reforms in the postwar era. In Iran today, traditional Islamic beliefs are all-pervasive and extend into education, clothing styles, social practices, and the legal system. In recent years, for example, Iranian women have been heavily fined or even flogged for violating the Islamic dress code.

The cultural and social effects of the Iranian Revolution soon began to spread. In Algeria, the political influence of fundamentalist Islamic groups enabled them to win a stunning victory in the national elections in 1992. When the military stepped in to cancel the second round of elections and crack down on the militants, the latter responded with a campaign of terrorism against moderates that claimed thousands of lives. A similar trend emerged in Egypt, where militant groups such as the Muslim Brotherhood engaged in terrorism, including the assassination of President Anwar al-Sadat and attacks on foreign tourists, who are considered carriers of corrupt Western influence.

Even in Turkey, generally considered the most secular of Islamic societies, there has been a perceptible rise in the visibility of religion in the broader society. In 1996 a

Muslim political group took power in a coalition government. The new government adopted a pro-Arab stance in foreign affairs and threatened to reduce the country's economic and political ties to Europe. Worried moderates voiced concern that the secular legacy of Kemal Atatürk was being eroded, and eventually the government resigned under heavy pressure from the military. But a new Islamist organization, known as the Justice and Development Party (the AK Party), won elections held in 2007 and has signaled its intention to guarantee the rights of devout Muslims to display their faith publicly. In elections held in June 2011, the AK Party won a clear victory with about 50 percent of the vote.

Under AK Prime Minister Tayyip Erdogan (b. 1954), the Turkish economy has expanded steadily, and the country exudes a new self-confidence as a Muslim powerhouse in the modern Middle East. But Erdogan's apparent intent to increase the role of Islam in Turkish society has alarmed critics who fear a gradual erosion of the secular vision of past president Kemal Atatürk. As protests erupted into the streets of major cities, the government has responded by arresting demonstrators and attempting to silence its critics in the press.

This pattern has been repeated throughout the Middle East, where even governments and individuals who do not support efforts to return to pure Islamic principles have adjusted their behavior and beliefs in subtle ways. Under Mubarak, for example, the Egyptian government encouraged television programs devoted to religion in preference to comedies and adventure shows imported from the West, and alcohol was discouraged or at least consumed discreetly. A new constitution enacted under the government of Mohamed Morsi expanded the role of Islam in Egyptian society.

Women in the Middle East

Nowhere have the fault lines between tradition and modernity in Muslim societies in the Middle East been so sharp as in the ongoing debate over the role of women. At the beginning of the twentieth century, women's place in Middle Eastern society had changed little since the death of the prophet Muhammad. Women were secluded in their homes and had few legal, political, or social rights.

During the first decades of the twentieth century, advocates of modernist views began to contend that Islamic doctrine was not inherently opposed to women's rights. To modernists, Islamic traditions such as female seclusion, wearing the veil, and polygamy were actually pre-Islamic folk traditions that had been tolerated in the early Islamic era and continued to be practiced in later centuries. Such views had a considerable impact on a number of Middle Eastern societies, including Turkey and Iran. As we have seen, greater rights for women were a crucial element in the social revolution promoted by Kemal Atatürk in Turkey. In Iran, Shah Reza Khan and his son granted female suffrage and encouraged the education of women. In Egypt, a vocal feminist movement arose in educated women's circles in Cairo as early as the 1920s. With the exception of Orthodox religious communities, women in Israel have achieved substantial equality with men and are active in politics, the professions, and even the armed forces. Golda

Istanbul on the Move. In recent years, the historical city of Istanbul has taken on a facelift, as modern skyscrapers sprout up in the suburbs of the one-time capital of the Ottoman Empire. But expansion has brought problems, as many residents resent efforts by the Islamist government of Prime Minister Tayyip Erdogan to restore the glories of the Ottoman caliphate at the expense of the secular legacy of Kemal Atatürk. Discontent came to a head in the spring of 2013, when plans were announced to erect a mosque in historic Taksim Square, in the heart of the city. Protests erupted in the streets of Istanbul and other major cities, and the government responded by arresting demonstrators and jailing critics in the media.

Meir (1898–1978), prime minister of Israel from 1969 to 1974, became an international symbol of the ability of women to be world leaders.

In recent years, a more traditional view of women's role has tended to prevail in many Middle Eastern countries. Attacks by religious conservatives on the growing role of women contributed to the emotions underlying the Iranian Revolution of 1979. Iranian women were instructed to wear the veil and to dress modestly in public. Films produced in postrevolutionary Iran rarely featured women, and when they did, physical contact between men and women was prohibited. The events in Iran had repercussions in secular Muslim societies such as Egypt, Turkey, and far-off Malaysia, where women began to dress more modestly in public and criticism of open sexuality in the media became increasingly frequent.

The most conservative nation by far remains Saudi Arabia, where following Wahhabi tradition, women are not only segregated and expected to wear the veil in public but also restricted in education and forbidden to drive automobiles. Still, women's rights have been extended in a few countries. In 1999, women obtained the right to vote in Kuwait, and they have been granted an equal right with their husbands to seek a divorce in Egypt. Even in Iran, women have many freedoms that they lacked before the twentieth century; for example, they can receive military training, vote, practice birth control, and publish fiction. Most important, today nearly 60 percent of university entrants in Iran are women.

Literature and Art

As in other areas of Asia and Africa, the encounter with the West in the nineteenth and twentieth centuries stimulated a cultural renaissance in the Middle East. Muslim authors translated Western works into Arabic and Persian and began to experiment with new literary forms.

NATIONAL LITERATURES Since World War II, Iranian literature has been hampered somewhat by political considerations, since it has been expected to serve first the Pahlavi monarchy and then the Islamic republic. Nevertheless, Iran has produced one of the most prominent national literatures in the contemporary Middle East.

Despite the male-oriented nature of Iranian society, many of the new writers are women. Since the revolution, the veil and the *chador*, an all-enveloping cloak, have become the central metaphor in Iranian women's writing. Advocates praise these garments as the last bastion of defense against Western cultural imperialism and the courageous woman's weapon against Western efforts to dominate the Iranian soul. Behind the veil, the Islamic woman can breathe freely, unpolluted by foreign exploitation and moral corruption. Other Iranian women, however, consider the veil and *chador* a "mobile prison" or an oppressive anachronism from the Dark Ages. A few use the pen as a weapon in a crusade to liberate their sisters and enable them to make their own choices. As one writer, Sousan Azadi, expressed it, "As I pulled the *chador* over me, I felt a heaviness descending over me. I was hidden and in hiding. There was nothing visible left of Sousan Azadi."[3]

Like Iran, Egypt in the twentieth century experienced a flowering of literature accelerated by the establishment of the Egyptian republic in the early 1950s. The most illustrious contemporary Egyptian writer was Naguib Mahfouz (1911–2006), who won the Nobel Prize in Literature in 1988. His *Cairo Trilogy* (1952) chronicles three generations of a merchant family in Cairo during the tumultuous years between the world wars. Mahfouz was particularly adept at blending panoramic historical events with the intimate lives of ordinary human beings. Unlike many other modern

Behind the Veil. In many Islamic countries today, women living in rural areas are much more likely than their urban counterparts to cover their faces and bodies in the traditional way. In a small Berber village in the Atlas Mountains of Morocco, this woman does her daily shopping while wearing a *chador* (a long gown covering the entire body and the head, often in blue or gray), supplemented by a veil (known as a *niqab*) to cover the lower half of her face. Women living in the cities and larger towns such as Rabat and Casablanca often wear a hair covering, but leave their faces uncovered. The Berber peoples, who have lived in the mountains of North Africa for thousands of years, initially resisted the Arab conquest in the eighth century, but continue to dress in traditional ways.

© William J. Duiker

writers, his message was essentially optimistic and reflected his hope that religion and science could work together for the overall betterment of humankind. One of the most popular contemporary authors presents a more pessimistic view. In *The Yacoubian Building*, Alaa al-Aswany (b. 1957) deplores the problems of political corruption and religious fundamentalism that plagued Egypt under Mubarak's regime.

No woman writer has played a more active role in exposing the physical and psychological grievances of Egyptian women than Nawal el-Saadawi (b. 1931). For decades, she has battled against the injustices of religious fundamentalism and a male-dominated society—even enduring imprisonment for promoting her cause. In *Two Women in One* (1985), el-Saadawi follows the struggle of a young university student as she rebels against the life her father has programmed for her, striking out instead on an unchartered independent destiny.

The emergence of a modern Turkish literature can be traced to the establishment of the republic in 1923. The most popular contemporary writer is Orhan Pamuk (b. 1952), whose novels attempt to capture Turkey's unique blend of cultures. "I am living in a culture," he writes, "where the clash of East and West, or the harmony of East and West, is the lifestyle. That is Turkey."[4] His novel *Snow* (2002) dramatizes the conflict between secularism and radical Islam in contemporary Turkey. Pamuk was awarded the Nobel Prize in Literature in 2006.

Although Israeli literature arises from a totally different tradition from that of its neighbors, it shares with them certain contemporary characteristics and a concern for ordinary human beings. Early writers identified with the aspirations of the new nation, trying to find a sense of order in the new reality, voicing terrors from the past and hopes for the future.

Some contemporary Israeli authors, however, have taken controversial positions on sensitive national issues. Their works address the difficulties of the Israeli situation as well as the bitterness of Palestinians living under Israeli occupation. In his extraordinary novel, *To the End of the Land* (2010), David Grossman (b. 1954) weaves together the daily joys and sorrows of an ordinary Israeli family with the constant undercurrent of conflict and loss. Having lost his own son in battle in 2006, Grossman has been labeled by some the moral conscience of his country. With the Arabs feeling victimized by colonialism and the Jews by Nazi Germany, each side believes that it alone is the rightful proprietor of ancient Palestine.

MUSIC Popular music in the contemporary Middle East reflects worldwide trends because it blends global and local musical elements. Hip-hop is especially popular because it allows the disadvantaged to express their grievances and yearnings in hypnotic rhymes and rhythms. In Israel, some groups rely on the shock value of their music to pillory the country's political and social shibboleths. Palestinian hip-hop projects the despair and rage of the performers as they portray the misery and futility of their everyday lives. As the Arab Spring spread from Tunisia and Egypt throughout the region, many performers were inspired to use their music for openly political purposes. One song, entitled "Come on Bashar, Leave," became popular as a joyful rallying cry for dissidents in Syria.

CONCLUSION

THE MIDDLE EAST IS ONE OF the most unstable regions in the world today. As some observers point out, this turbulence is due in part to the continued interference of outsiders attracted by the massive oil reserves under the Arabian peninsula and the Persian Gulf. Outside interference not only underlines the humiliating weakness of Muslim nations in their relations with the West, but also serves to identify Western policy toward the Middle East with unpopular dictators in the region.

But, as recent events clearly suggest, internal factors are equally if not more important in provoking the chronic turmoil in the region. One divisive issue is the tug-of-war between the sense of ethnic identity in the form of nationalism and the intense longing to be part of a broader Islamic community, a dream that dates back to the time of the Prophet Muhammad. The desire to create that community—a vision threatened by the presence of the alien state of Israel—inspired Gamal Abdul Nasser in the 1950s and Saddam Hussein in Iraq. Today it is Iran's radical ayatollahs who aspire to that position.

A further reason for the current unrest in the Middle East is the intense debate over the role of religion in civil society. Muslims, of course, are not alone in deploring the moral decline that many perceive to be occurring in societies throughout the world today. And adherents of all faiths sometimes turn to religion as a means of reversing that trend. In many parts of the Middle East, however, the effort has taken an especially extremist and violent turn. The fact is that many Muslim societies in the Middle East have yet to come to terms with a world characterized by dramatic social and technological change. The result is a deep-seated sense of anger and frustration, especially among the youth, that is surging through much of the Islamic world today. This resentment is directed as much at the region's internal leadership as at allegedly hostile outside forces in the West. Today, the world is reaping the harvest of that bitterness, and the consequences cannot yet be foreseen.

TIMELINE

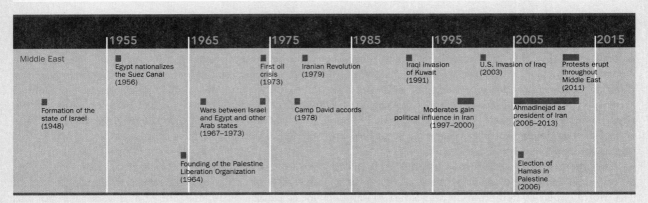

CHAPTER NOTES

1. Quoted in R. R. Andersen, R. F. Seibert, and J. G. Wagner, *Politics and Change in the Middle East: Sources of Conflict and Accommodation*, 4th ed. (Englewood Cliffs, N.J., 1982), p. 51.
2. Susan Sachs, "Assad Looks at Syria's Economy in Inaugural Talk," *New York Times*, July 18, 2000.
3. Sousan Azadi, with Angela Ferrante, *Out of Iran* (London, 1987), p. 223, quoted in *Stories by Iranian Women Since the Revolution*, ed. S. Sullivan (Austin, Tex., 1991), p. 13.
4. Brian Lavery, "In the Thick of Change Where Continents Meet," *New York Times*, August 27, 2003.

IN THE ATLANTIC CHARTER, issued after their meeting near the coast of Newfoundland in August 1941, Franklin Roosevelt and Winston Churchill set forth a joint declaration of their peace aims calling for the self-determination of all peoples and self-government and sovereign rights for all nations that had been deprived of them. Although Churchill later disavowed the assumption that he had meant these conditions to apply to colonial areas, Roosevelt on frequent occasions during the war voiced his own intention to bring about the end of colonial domination throughout the world at the close of the conflict.

It took many years to complete the process, but the promise contained in the Atlantic Charter was eventually fulfilled. Although some powers were reluctant to divest themselves of their colonies, World War II had severely undermined the stability of the colonial order, and by the end of the 1940s, most colonies in Asia had received their independence. Africa followed a decade or two later. In a few instances—notably in Algeria, Indonesia, and Vietnam—the transition to independence was a violent one, but for the most part, it was realized by peaceful means.

THREE WISHES In their own writings and public statements, the leaders of these newly liberated countries set forth three broad goals at the outset of independence: to throw off the shackles of Western economic domination and ensure material prosperity for all their citizens, to introduce new political institutions that would enhance the right of self-determination of their peoples, and to develop a sense of nationhood and establish secure territorial boundaries. Most of them opted to follow a capitalist or moderately socialist path toward economic development. Only in a few cases—North Korea and Vietnam being the most notable examples—did revolutionary leaders decide to pursue the Communist model of development.

Within a few years of the restoration of independence, however, reality had set in, as most of the new governments in Asia and Africa fell short of their ambitious goals. Virtually all remained economically dependent on the advanced industrial nations. Several faced severe problems of urban and rural poverty. At the same time, fledgling democratic governments were gradually replaced by military dictatorships or one-party regimes that dismantled representative institutions and oppressed dissident elements and ethnic minorities within their borders.

MODERNIZATION THEORY What had happened to tarnish the bright dreams of affluence, national unity, and political self-determination? During the 1950s and 1960s, one school of thought was dominant among scholars and government officials in the United States. **Modernization theory** adopted the view that the economic problems faced by the newly independent countries were a consequence of the difficult transition from a traditional agrarian to a modern industrial society. Advocates were convinced that the countries of Asia, Africa, and Latin America were destined to follow the path of the West toward the creation of modern industrial societies but would need time as well as substantial amounts of economic and technological assistance to complete the journey. In their view, it was the duty of the United States and other advanced capitalist nations to provide such assistance while encouraging the leaders of these states to follow the path already adopted by the West.

DEPENDENCY THEORY Modernization theory soon began to come under attack from a generation of younger scholars, many of whom had reached maturity during the Vietnam War and had growing doubts about the roots of the problem and the efficacy of the modernization approach. In their view, the responsibility for continued economic underdevelopment in the developing world lay not with the countries themselves but with their continued domination by the former colonial powers. In this view, known as **dependency theory**, the countries of Asia, Africa, and Latin America were the victims of the international marketplace, which charged high prices for the manufactured goods of the West while paying low prices for the raw material exports of preindustrial countries. Efforts by these countries to build up their own industrial sectors and move into the stage of self-sustaining growth were hampered because many of their resources were still  controlled by European and American corporations. To end this "neocolonial" relationship, dependency theory advocates argued, developing societies should reduce their economic ties with the West and adopt a policy of economic self-reliance, thereby taking control of their own destinies.

FROM THEORY TO PRACTICE Both of these approaches, of course, were directly linked to the ideological divisions of the Cold War and reflected the political bias of their advocates. Although modernization theorists were certainly correct in pointing out some of the key factors involved in economic development and in suggesting that some traditional attitudes and practices were incompatible with economic change, they were too quick to see the Western model of development as the only relevant one and too ready to identify economic development in the developing world with the interests of the United States and its allies.

By the same token, the advocates of dependency theory alluded correctly to the unfair and often disadvantageous relationship that continued to exist between the former colonies and the industrialized nations of the world. But they often rationalized many of the mistakes made by the leaders of developing countries while assigning all of the blame for their plight on the evil and self-serving practices of the industrialized world. At the same time, the recommendation by some dependency theorists of a policy of self-reliance was not only naive but sometimes disastrous, depriving the new nations of badly needed technology and capital resources.

Many observers today would agree that there are important truths on both sides of this debate and that no one model fits all contingencies. History has shown that there are different roads to development and that participating in the international marketplace can have both beneficial and harmful effects. Such has certainly been the case with the spread of free trade agreements in recent years. While the reduction of tariff barriers has undoubtedly spurred an increase in the exchange of goods worldwide, its disruptive effects within individual countries have often been severe, with unforeseen consequences.

THE ROCKY ROAD TO POLITICAL REFORM In the realm of politics as well, it seems evident that many observers badly underestimated the difficulties in building pluralistic political systems in societies that lacked experience with Western democratic values. Many of these new states were composed of a wide variety of ethnic, religious, and linguistic groups that found it difficult to agree on common symbols of nationalism and forms of governance. As a result, many soon began to experiment with political systems that appeared more relevant to local conditions. Although the number of countries in Asia and Africa that have adopted the democratic model has been on the increase in recent years, in many cases their democratic institutions remain fragile. At the same time, influential voices argue that such Western practices as free elections, multiple party systems, and freedom of the press are both destabilizing and destructive of other national objectives. It is still not clear that Western-style democratic values have universal relevance in our rapidly changing world.

Future trends in the developing world, then, remain difficult to predict as the impact of globalization provokes both rapid change and bitter resistance. What is not in doubt, however, is that the social and cultural assault from the West will continue unabated through its music, its movies, its television, and the growing popularity of the Internet.  Much of this influence will be felt primarily by the growing urban middle class in many societies of Asia and Africa. The members of this middle class are often strongly influenced by Western ways, and their sons and daughters ape the behavior, dress, and lifestyles of their counterparts in Europe and North America. When Reebok sneakers are worn and coveted in Lagos and Nairobi, Mumbai and Islamabad, Beijing and Hanoi, it is clear that modern Western civilization is having a universal impact. ❦

PART V

The New Millennium

The Guggenheim Museum in Bilbao, Spain

Kenneth Garrett/National Geographic Creative

The Challenge of a New Millennium

Terrorist attack on the World Trade Center in New York City, September 11, 2001

AP Images/Carmen Taylor

ON SEPTEMBER 11, 2001, two commercial airliners skyjacked by Islamic terrorists slammed into the twin towers of the World Trade Center in New York City. Another struck a side wall of the Pentagon outside Washington, D.C. A fourth crashed in a field in central Pennsylvania. These heinous attacks ushered in a new era for the United States—and the world at large. The Cold War had ended a decade earlier, encouraging pundits to predict the advent of a new world order marked by global peace and prosperity. But the fallout from the stunning attacks on the power centers of the United States, along with the unleashing of two new wars in the Middle East and President George W. Bush's declaration of a global "war on terror," aroused new questions and anxieties about the future. Would the new century bring a new era of international peace and relative stability, such as had occurred after the end of the Napoleonic wars in nineteenth-century Europe? Or would the end of the Cold War signal the rise of a new spirit of rivalry and national competitiveness, leading to destructive wars reminiscent of the last century? Would the dramatic expansion of trade among nations lead to global prosperity and material accumulation, or would the Technological Revolution already under way lead to the kinds of social and cultural ferment that had characterized the Industrial Revolution of the nineteenth century?

Certainly, at the turn of the century there were sufficient grounds to adopt any or all of these points of view. As the new millennium dawned, the United States bestrode the world like a colossus, unchallenged in its military and economic might and sufficiently confident in its destiny to play the role of global policeman. Yet there were already ominous signs—in the form of ethnic and religious clashes in Eastern Europe, the Middle East, and Africa—that the vision of a new era of peace and stability might turn out to be a mirage. By the same token, the expansion of world trade was already beginning to produce victims as well as beneficiaries. **Globalization**, like the Industrial Revolution of an earlier age, was not a tide that lifted all boats.

In the meantime, other issues—some of them virtually ignored by world leaders during the era of the Cold War—were increasingly clamoring for attention. Environmental degradation, rapid population growth, and the projected shortage of many precious natural resources, including liquid energy and fresh water, were now widely viewed as serious threats to the future success of the human experiment. And behind all of these pressing concerns lay a more existential one—how to seek out the underlying purpose and meaning of life in a world increasingly defined by the voracious accumulation of material goods. Was the rise of the consumer society the ultimate objective of all humankind, or could ultimate happiness be achieved only through the emergence of a new spiritual civilization?

Such questions were undoubtedly in the minds of many as they faced the challenges of a new millennium. Today, more than a decade later, they have taken on even greater relevance as the world faces the future with ever-increasing concern and trepidation. ◂

After the Cold War: The End of History?

With the end of superpower rivalry and the collapse of the Soviet Union in 1991, the attention of the world shifted to the new post–Cold War era. For many observers, the prognosis was excellent. U.S. President George H. W. Bush looked forward to a new era of peace and international cooperation that he labeled the "**new world order**," while pundits predicted the advent of a new "American century," marked by the victory of liberal democratic values and free enterprise capitalism.

The wave of optimism that accompanied the end of the Cold War was all too brief. After a short period of euphoria, it soon became clear that forces were now being released that had long been held in check by the ideological rigidities of the Cold War. The era of conflict that had long characterized the twentieth century was not at an end; it was simply taking a different form.

One major eruption was in the Balkans, where the Yugoslavian Federation—long held together by the transcendent personality of Marshal Tito—broke apart in a bitter conflict that has yet to be finally resolved. An even more dangerous source of discord was in the Middle East, where historical ethnic and religious animosities spread rapidly throughout the region and culminated in the outbreak of civil war in a number of countries. Farther to the east, territorial disputes between China and its neighbors threatened to embroil the Pacific region in a new round of dangerous conflicts. Under these circumstances, few today would assert that we are about to witness the emergence of a new world order.

Contemporary Capitalism and Its Discontents

The problems are by no means limited to the developing world. After a generation of rapid growth, most of the capitalist states in Europe and North America began to suffer through a general slowdown in economic performance as the new century began. This slowdown gave rise to a number of related problems, several with serious social and political implications. These problems include an increase in the level of unemployment; government belt-tightening policies to reduce social services and welfare and retirement benefits; and in many countries, growing popular resentment against minority groups or recent immigrants, who are blamed for deteriorating economic prospects.

The financial meltdown that struck with such dramatic suddenness in the fall of 2008 added a new sense of urgency to the challenges. Declining revenues resulting from the economic downturn forced business owners to cut back on their payrolls and made it more difficult for governments to meet their own financial responsibilities. At the same time, the globalization of world markets limited the ability of world leaders to insulate their peoples from the vicissitudes of the marketplace at a time of heightened instability.

Europe: Speed Bumps on the Road to Unity?

The problems were most serious in Western Europe, where growth rates have traditionally been kept artificially low because of persistent fear of inflation and where welfare payments have been more generous than in most other capitalist countries. But attempts to trim social benefits have been soundly opposed in many countries, even those such as Greece and Spain, where national governments have recently faced the possibility of bankruptcy.

Compounding the problem is the fact that the European Union (EU), as a multinational organization, lacks a centralized executive body that is authorized to make difficult decisions in a time of crisis. The nations most affected by the economic downturn have appealed for assistance from their more fortunate counterparts, notably Germany, but the Germans have been reluctant to sacrifice their own well-being in an effort to save what they regard as their more profligate neighbors. The expansion of the EU into Eastern Europe, where capitalist practices are a comparatively recent phenomenon, only adds to the complexity of the issue. Today, in both economic and structural terms, the continent of Europe is facing its most serious internal challenges since the end of World War II.

The United States: Capitalism Ascendant?

In some respects, the United States fared better than other capitalist states in the 1990s, as the economic revival at that time enabled the Clinton administration to reduce budget deficits without having to engage in substantial tax increases or a massive reduction in welfare spending. During the first decade of the new century, however, the federal deficit rose again, a consequence of growing entitlement costs and the Bush administration's policy of reducing taxes while trying to wage two wars. Although gross domestic product continued to grow, economic growth did not result in increased prosperity for all Americans. While the rich were getting richer, the poorest 20 percent of the population saw little benefit.

The financial crisis that struck in the fall of 2008 was the result of several factors, including the collapse of a housing bubble (the result of easier access to money for home mortgages), lax government regulatory procedures on lending, and a steady increase in household credit card debt. Although the Bush administration belatedly announced a major federal bailout to prevent additional losses on Wall Street, the stock market suffered its largest collapse since the Great Depression. After the presidential elections in November, the incoming Obama administration prepared a major stimulus package to jump-start the economy. Such measures were successful in reversing the downward trend in the stock market and production began slowly to recover, but growth rates were insufficient to reduce the unemployment rate, which was still close to 8 percent at the beginning of Obama's second term in office. In the meantime, the danger of political paralysis loomed, as Democrats and Republicans in Congress locked horns over the proper role of government and the relative importance of entitlement spending and deficit reduction.

Asian Miracle or Asian Myth?

One area in the capitalist world that has seemed to avoid the worst consequences of the economic slowdown in the West is East Asia, where most of the industrializing nations managed to maintain rapid economic growth with a minimum of social problems and a considerable degree of political stability. During the 1990s, pundits opined that the "East Asian miracle" was a product of the amalgamation of capitalist economic techniques and a value system inherited from Confucianism that stressed hard work, frugality, and the subordination of the individual to the community—all reminiscent of the "Puritan ethic" of the early capitalist era in the West.

The financial crisis of 1997 (see Chapter 13) demonstrated that the Pacific nations were not immune to the vicissitudes of capitalism, but (with the exception of Japan), they rapidly recovered and by the first years of the new century had resumed the steady growth that had characterized their performance during the last quarter of the twentieth century. China in particular has become a major force in the global economy, replacing Japan and Germany as the world's largest exporter of goods and serving as an engine of growth for nations throughout the region. Many observers see China, with its growing industrial base and abundant supply of cheap labor, as the most serious threat to the U.S. economic hegemony. China has a number of vulnerabilities, however (see Chapter 12), and a slowdown in its growth rates could have chilling effects on the global economy.

Eliminating World Poverty

One of the greatest failures of the global economy in the new millennium is the continued high level of poverty that persists in many parts of the world. According to recent figures, about 1.4 billion people—almost one-fifth of the entire world population—live on an income of less than $1.25 a day. An equal number are illiterate, while hundreds of thousands die annually from malnutrition, hunger, or disease. At a Millennium Summit in 2000, the United Nations adopted a plan calling for advanced nations to double their financial assistance to poorer countries, while taking measures to equalize the playing field in the realm of trade to assist the developing countries in working their way out of debt. The declared goal was to reduce the number of those suffering extreme poverty and hunger by half by the year 2015, while reducing infant mortality and ensuring basic education for all the world's children.

Five years later, the UN General Assembly returned to the issue, approving a broad list of goals to carry through on the basic commitment. But the acrimony of the debate demonstrated how difficult these goals would be to achieve, and the final results were disappointing to delegates of the poor countries. Disagreements on how to fight terrorism and protect human rights, combined with the unwillingness of industrial countries to open their markets to agricultural imports, prevented the delegates from implementing a plan. Once again, the failure to achieve concrete results demonstrated that ending widespread poverty is among the most tenacious problems facing the global community today.

One key reason for the prevalence of poverty in the Third World is the lack of educational opportunities for women. In 2006, the United Nations Development Program declared that "women's empowerment helps raise economic productivity and reduce infant mortality. It contributes to improved health and nutrition. It increases the chances for education for the next generation."[1] In their book *Half the Sky: Turning Oppression into Opportunity for Women Worldwide*, Nicholas Kristof and Sheryl WuDunn described the lack of medical facilities and the deplorable health conditions in many rural areas of Africa and Asia. In many areas, women suffer myriad illnesses as a result of cooking on traditional wood-burning stoves that produce smoke containing carbon monoxide and other pollutants. To alleviate the problem, the Global Alliance for Clean Cookstoves is developing and marketing efficient and low-cost cookstoves, with the goal of producing 100 million stoves by the year 2020.

India's Hope, India's Sorrow. In India, as in many other societies in South Asia, overpopulation is a serious obstacle to economic development. The problem is particularly serious in large cities where thousands of poor children are forced into begging or prostitution. Shown here are a few of the thousands of street children in the commercial hub of Mumbai. With the Indian economy experiencing rapid growth, the national government is aggressively addressing the issue of poverty.

From the Industrial to the Technological Revolution

As many observers have noted, the world economy as a whole is in the process of transition to what has been called a "postindustrial age," characterized by the emergence of a system that is not only increasingly global in scope but also increasingly technology intensive. This process, which futurologist Alvin Toffler has dubbed the Third Wave (the first two being the Agricultural and Industrial Revolutions), offers the promise of bringing about increased global economic growth. At the same time, however, it has caused difficulties for people in many walks of life—for blue-collar workers in the advanced societies in the West, whose high wages price them out of the market as firms move their factories abroad; for the poor and uneducated everywhere, who lack the technical skills to handle complex tasks in the contemporary economy; and even for members of the middle class, who have been fired or forced into retirement as their employers seek to slim down to compete in the global marketplace.[2]

It is now increasingly clear that the Technological Revolution, like the Industrial Revolution that preceded it, will entail enormous consequences and may ultimately give birth to a level of social and political instability that has not been seen in the developed world since the Great

Depression of the 1930s. The success of advanced capitalist states in the second half of the twentieth century was built on the foundations of a broad consensus on several propositions: (1) the importance of limiting income inequities to reduce the threat of political instability while maximizing domestic consumer demand; (2) the need for high levels of government investment in infrastructure projects such as education, communications, and transportation as a means of meeting the challenges of continued economic growth and technological innovation; and (3) the desirability of co-operative efforts in the international arena as a means of maintaining open markets for the free exchange of goods. The ultimate purpose of these principles was to create the conditions for the continued spread of the social benefits of the Industrial Revolution while at the same time minimizing the material inequities and disruptive market cycles that are endemic to the capitalist system.

Recent events graphically demonstrate that these principles remain of crucial importance as the world enters the next stage of the Technological Revolution. Yet as the new century gains momentum, all of these assumptions are increasingly coming under attack. Citizens are reacting with growing hostility to the high tax rates needed to maintain the welfare state, refusing to support education and infrastructure development, and opposing the formation of trade alliances to promote the free movement of goods and labor across national borders. Such attitudes are being expressed by individuals and groups on all sides of the political spectrum, making the traditional designations of left-wing and right-wing politics increasingly meaningless. Although most governments and political elites have continued to support most of the programs that underpin the welfare state and the global market-place, they are increasingly attacked by groups in society that feel they have been victimized by the system. The breakdown of the public consensus that brought modern capitalism to a pinnacle of achievement raises serious questions about the likelihood that the coming challenge of the Third Wave can be successfully met without increasing political and social tensions in both the domestic and international arenas.

A Transvaluation of Values

Of course, not all the problems facing the advanced human societies around the world can be ascribed directly to economic factors. It is one of the paradoxes of the modern world that at a time of almost unsurpassed political stability and relative economic prosperity for the majority of the population in the advanced capitalist states, public cynicism about the system is increasingly widespread. Alienation and drug use among young people in many Western societies are at dangerously high levels, and although crime rates have dropped slightly in some areas, the rate of criminal activities remains much higher than in the first decades after World War II.

The Family

The reasons advanced to explain this paradox vary widely. Some observers place the responsibility for many contemporary social problems on the decline of the traditional family system. The statistics are indeed disquieting. There has been a steady rise in the percentage of illegitimate births and single-parent families in countries throughout the Western world. In the United States, approximately half of all marriages end in divorce. In two-parent families, both parents often work full time, thus leaving some children to fend for themselves on their return from school.

Observers point to several factors as an explanation for these conditions: the growing emphasis in advanced capitalist states on an individualistic lifestyle devoted to instant gratification, a phenomenon promoted vigorously by the advertising media; the rise of the feminist movement, which has freed women from the servitude imposed on their predecessors, but at the expense of removing them from full-time responsibility for the care and nurturing of the next generation; and the increasing mobility of contemporary life, which disrupts traditional family ties and creates a sense of rootlessness and impersonality in the individual's relationship to the surrounding environment.

What is worth noting here is that to one degree or another, the traditional nuclear family is under attack in societies around the world, not just in the West. Even in East Asia, where the Confucian tradition of filial piety and family solidarity has been endlessly touted as a major factor in the region's economic success, the incidence of divorce and illegitimate births is on the rise, as is the percentage of women in the workforce. Older citizens frequently complain that the Asian youth of today are too materialistic, faddish, and steeped in the individualistic

values of the West. Such criticisms are now voiced in mainland China as well as in the capitalist societies around its perimeter. Although public opinion surveys suggest that some of the generational differences in Asian societies are only skin deep (when queried about their views, most young Asians express support for the same conservative values of family, hard work, and care for the elderly as their parents), the evidence suggests that the trend away from the traditional family is a worldwide phenomenon.

Religion

While some analysts cite the reduced role of the traditional family as a major factor in the widespread sense of malaise in the contemporary world, others point to the decline in religion and the increasing secularization of world society. It seems indisputable that one of the causes of the widespread feeling of alienation in many societies is the absence of any sense of underlying meaning and purpose in life, which religious faith often provides. As many specialists in world religion point out, religious faith not only provides a belief in a universal moral order, but also creates a sense of belonging among a community of believers. Historical experience suggests, however, that there is a price to pay for this enhanced sense of community, which can result in heightened intolerance of "outsiders," as the examples of Northern Ireland, Yugoslavia, and the Middle East vividly attest. Religion, by itself, cannot serve as a panacea for the problems of the contemporary world.

The issue of religion and its implications for social policy is thus quite complicated. Although the percentage of people attending church on a regular basis or professing firm religious convictions has been dropping steadily in many Western countries, the intensity of religious belief appears to be growing in many communities. This phenomenon is especially apparent in the United States, where the evangelical movement has become a significant force in politics and an influential factor in defining many social issues. But it has also occurred in Latin America, where a drop in membership in the Roman Catholic Church in some countries has been offset by significant increases in the popularity of evangelical Protestant sects. There are significant differences between the two cases, however. Whereas the evangelical movement in the United States tends to adopt conservative positions on social issues such as abortion rights, divorce, and sexual freedom, in Brazil one of the reasons advanced for the popularity of evangelical sects is the stand taken by the Vatican on issues such as divorce and abortion. In Brazil, even the vast majority of Catholics surveyed support the right to abortion in cases of rape or danger to the mother and believe in the importance of birth control to limit population growth and achieve smaller families.

In Africa and Asia as well, there are clear signs that organized religion is expanding in scope and influence. Both Christianity and Islam are gaining adherents in Africa, and the intense competition between the two faiths is one reason for the increased violence along the southern rim of the Sahara. Throughout the Muslim world, conflict between Sunnis and Shi'ites, and between traditionalists and modernizers, has reached crisis proportions in many countries. In India, Hindu revivalist groups seek to change the secular character of the Indian republic, while sporadic outbreaks of violence among Hindus, Muslims, Christians, and Sikhs are increasingly common in various parts of the country.

Even in China, where the Communist government long imposed strict limitations on the practice of any organized religion, attendance at Buddhist temples and Christian churches has been steadily increasing in recent years, especially among members of the growing and highly influential middle class, who often view their faith as a stepping-stone to higher status and achievement in Chinese society. In the meantime, dissident nationalities like the Tibetans and the Muslim minorities in Xinjiang province turn to traditional religion as a symbol for their demand for greater autonomy or independence from the People's Republic of China. Throughout the world, religion, politics, and nationality are increasingly intertwined.

A Prayer to the Buddha. Religion continues to play a major role in the lives of many peoples throughout the world today, and is even reviving in countries living under Communist rule, such as contemporary China and Vietnam. Although the practice of religion has long been officially discouraged in both countries, the government has relaxed its restrictions in recent years, and attendance at religious functions is increasing steadily. Some observers speculate that religious faith provides a sense of purpose and the meaning of life in societies where the dialectical materialism of Karl Marx has long been official doctrine. Shown here, two Vietnamese are praying at a garishly decorated Buddhist temple in the commercial center of Ho Chi Minh City—the one-time Saigon.

Technology and Society

Many people of faith around the world view religion as a hedge against the familiar—and supposedly modern—social evils of crime, drugs, and sexual excess. Others not only support a conservative social agenda but also express a strong suspicion of the role of technology and science in the contemporary world. Some Christian groups in the United States, for example, have opposed the teaching of evolutionary theory in the classroom or have demanded that public schools present the biblical interpretation of the creation of the earth. Scientists who warn of the dangers of climate change and global warming are suspected of having a partisan agenda. The sense of mutual distrust and discomfort between the world of science and the world of faith is not a new phenomenon, of course (dating back, in fact, to the early years of Christianity), but it seems to have become increasingly prevalent in recent years. Similar attitudes are held by many adherents of other world religions.

But concern about the impact of science and technology on contemporary life is by no means limited to evangelicals and other religious conservatives. Voices across the political and social spectrum have begun to suggest that scientific advances are at least partly responsible for the psychological malaise now so prevalent in much of the modern world. The criticism dates back at least to the advent of television. Television, in the eyes of its critics, has contributed to a decline in human communication and turned viewers from active participants in the experience of life into passive observers. With the advent of the computer, the process has accelerated as recent generations of young people raised on video games and surfing the Web find less and less time for personal relationships or creative activities.

Of course, the Technological Revolution has had many positive social consequences as well. The Internet provides millions of people with easy access to information

Hello, World. In the twenty-first century, the entire world is becoming wired, as peoples in the developing nations realize that economic success depends increasingly on information technology. Few countries have embraced the Internet as enthusiastically as China. Millions of Chinese citizens—sometimes to the discomfort of their government—now turn to the electronic media for their chief source of information about the wider world. In this photograph, an Apple store on a major shopping street in Shanghai displays the new iPhone (a device itself manufactured in Chinese factories) to potential buyers. The early response has been enthusiastic—about 20 percent of Apple's total revenue in 2012 came from sales of its products in China.

It has therefore robbed the whole world, human as well as natural, of its own values."[3]

At the same time, some argue that capitalism simply recognizes the acquisitive side of human nature and sets out to make a profit from it. Recent events around the world, including the Chinese Communist Party's embrace of the capitalist work ethic, suggest that efforts to suppress the acquisitive instinct are ultimately doomed to fail, no matter how stringently they are applied. It is thus left to individual human beings, families, and communities to decide how to supplement material aspirations with the higher values traditionally associated with the human experience. Perhaps it is worth observing that more than once, capitalism has demonstrated the ability to rectify its shortcomings when they threaten the survival of the system. It remains to be seen whether it can do so under current conditions. It is also not clear that the corrosive effects of contemporary materialism can ultimately be reconciled with the universal desire to find a deeper meaning in life.

and the opportunity to seek out others with common interests, as well as a means of maintaining close and frequent contact with friends and colleagues around the world. The most that can be said at the present time is that such innovations provide both an opportunity and a danger—an opportunity to explore new avenues of communication and a danger that, in the process, the nature of the human experience will be irrevocably changed.

The Impact of Capitalism

Some theorists argue that the capitalist system bears the most responsibility for the hedonism and materialism of contemporary life and has raised narcissism and conspicuous consumerism to unprecedented heights in modern consciousness. It is no doubt true that by promoting material consumption as perhaps the supreme good, modern capitalism has encouraged the acquisitive side of human nature and undermined the traditional virtues of frugality and self-denial and the life of the spirit. As Karl Marx perceptively noted more than a century ago, under capitalism money is "the universal self-constituted value of all things.

One World, One Environment

Another crucial factor that is affecting the evolution of society and the global economy is growing concern over the impact of industrialization on the earth's environment. There is nothing new about human beings causing damage to their natural surroundings. It may first have occurred when Neolithic peoples began to practice slash-and-burn agriculture or when excessive hunting thinned out the herds of bison and caribou in the Western Hemisphere. It almost certainly played a major role in the decline of the ancient civilizations in the Persian Gulf region and later of the Roman Empire.

Never before, however, has the danger of significant ecological damage been as extensive as during the past century. The effects of chemicals introduced into the atmosphere or into rivers, lakes, and oceans have increasingly threatened the health and well-being of all living species. For many years, the main focus of environmental concern was in the developed countries of the West, where industrial effluents, automobile exhausts, and the use of artificial fertilizers and insecticides led to urban smog, extensive damage to crops and wildlife, and a major reduction of the ozone layer in the upper atmosphere. In recent decades, however, as the Industrial Revolution has spread to other areas of the world, it has become clear that the problem is now global in scope and demands vigorous action in the international arena.

The opening of Eastern Europe after the revolutions of 1989 brought to the world's attention the incredible environmental destruction in that region caused by unfettered industrial pollution. Communist governments had obviously operated under the assumption that production quotas were much more important than environmental protection. The nuclear power disaster at Chernobyl in Ukraine in 1986 made Europeans acutely aware of potential environmental hazards, and 1987 was touted as the "year of the environment." In response, many European states, following the lead of the United States (see Chapter 8), implemented new regulations to protect the environment and established government ministries to oversee environmental issues. Green movements and political parties played an important role in bringing the issue to public attention.

In recent years, the problem has spread. China's headlong rush to industrialization has resulted in major ecological damage in that country. Industrial smog has created almost unlivable conditions in many cities, and hillsides denuded of their forests have experienced severe erosion that has led to the destruction of farmlands. Although the Chinese government has invested heavily in tree planting and "clean coal" technology, levels of pollution in China are already higher than in the fully developed industrial societies of the West.

Destruction of the rain forest is a growing problem in many parts of the world, notably in Brazil and in the Indonesian archipelago. With the rapid decline in the forest cover throughout the earth, there is less plant life to perform the crucial process of reducing carbon dioxide levels

Our Disappearing Forest. One of the lesser known causes of the rising levels of carbon dioxide in the earth's atmosphere is the widespread destruction of forestland that has taken place in many parts of the world in recent years. Trees are an important mechanism for absorbing harmful greenhouse gases, but the clear cutting or burning of forests—often undertaken to make room for profitable cash crops like palm oil and sugarcane—removes an important natural tool in the struggle to limit the effects of global warming in years to come. Among the most prevalent danger spots today are Southeast Asia and parts of Latin America. Shown here, a blazing forest fire destroys valuable forestland on a hillside in central Chile.

in the atmosphere. In 1997, forest fires on the Indonesian islands of Sumatra and Borneo created a blanket of smoke over the entire region, forcing schools and offices to close and causing respiratory ailments in thousands of people. Some of the damage could be attributed to the traditional slash-and-burn techniques used by subsistence farmers to clear forest cover for their farmlands, but the primary cause was the clearing of forests to create or expand palm oil plantations, one of the region's major sources of export revenue.

Facing the Issue of Global Warming

One of the few salutary consequences of such incidents that affect entire regions has been that environmental concerns have taken on a truly global character. The dangers of global warming—caused, at least in large part, by the release of certain gases into the atmosphere as a result of industrialization—and the climate change that would accompany it were the subject of an international conference in Kyoto, Japan, in December 1997. If, as many scientists predict, worldwide temperatures increase, the rise in sea levels could pose a significant threat to low-lying islands and coastal areas throughout the world, while climate change has already led to severe droughts or excessive rainfall in cultivated areas around the globe.

It is one thing to recognize a problem, however, and quite another to resolve it. So far cooperative efforts among nations to alleviate environmental problems have all too often been hindered by economic forces or by political, ethnic, and religious disputes. The 1997 conference on global warming, for example, was marked by bitter disagreement over the degree to which developing countries should share the burden of cleaning up the environment. Consequently, it achieved few concrete results. The fact is that few nations have been willing to take unilateral action that might pose an obstacle to economic development plans or lead to a rise in unemployment. Measures to reduce the release of harmful gases into the atmosphere are costly and have significant negative effects on economic growth. Thus, politicians who embrace such measures are risking political suicide.

What is most needed, of course, is international cooperation that would bring about major efforts to reduce pollution levels throughout the world. So far, there is little indication that advanced and developing nations are close to agreement on how the sacrifice should be divided. International meetings convened to discuss how to implement the agreement hammered out at the Kyoto conference have been mired in disputes and have achieved few results. Climate talks held in Durban, South Africa, in December 2011 yielded only limited agreements to preserve tropical forests and develop clean energy, but efforts by European countries to devise a plan for specific actions failed when developing nations such as China and India objected to being held to the same standards as their more industrialized counterparts. Yet, as evidence of the severity of the problem continues to accumulate, the need for a global effort to deal with the challenge is becoming increasingly clear.

The Population Debate

At the root of much of the concern about the environment is the worry that the global population could eventually outstrip the capacity of the world to feed itself. Concern over excessive population growth, of course, dates back to the early nineteenth century, when the British economist Thomas Malthus worried that the population would increase more rapidly than the food supply. Such fears peaked in the decades immediately following World War II, when a rise in world birthrates and a decline in infant mortality combined to fuel a dramatic increase in population in much of the Third World. The

concern was set aside for a period after the 1970s, when the green revolution improved crop yields and statistical evidence appeared to suggest that the rate of population growth was declining in many countries of Asia and Latin America.

Yet some experts question whether increases in food production through technological innovation (in recent years, the green revolution has been supplemented by a "blue revolution" to increase food yields from the world's oceans, seas, and rivers) can keep up indefinitely with world population growth, which continues today, though at a slightly reduced rate from earlier levels. From a total of 2.5 billion people in 1950, world population rose to 7.1 billion in 2013 and is predicted to exceed 9 billion by the middle of this century. Today, many eyes are focused on India, where the population recently surpassed 1.2 billion, and on Africa, where rapid rates of growth are expected for the foreseeable future.

Many European countries (notably France, Italy, and Russia) have the opposite problem, as low fertility rates among European-born women raise the prospect of lower population levels in the near future. A decrease in population not only would lead to labor shortages, thereby increasing the need for "guest workers" from Africa and the Middle East, but also would reduce the number of employed workers paying taxes, making it difficult to maintain expensive welfare programs. Some European countries are now providing financial incentives to encourage young citizens to have larger families.

Global Village or Clash of Civilizations?

For four decades, such global challenges were all too frequently submerged in the public consciousness as the two major power blocs competed for advantage. The collapse of the Soviet Union brought an end to the Cold War but left world leaders almost totally unprepared to face the consequences. Policymakers, scholars, and political pundits began to forecast the emergence of a "new world order." Few, however, had any real idea of what it would entail. With the sudden end to the division of the world into two squabbling ideological power blocs, there was little certainty, and much speculation, about what was going to take its place.

One hypothesis that won support in some quarters was that the decline of communism signaled that the industrial capitalist democracies of the West had triumphed in the war of ideas and would now proceed to remake the rest of the world in their own image. According to those who support this thesis, the global spread of ideas and technology—notably from the advanced Western countries to the less developed countries in Africa and Asia—will gradually lead to the erosion of traditional ideas and customs and create an international civilization based on universally held customs and values, thus creating a "global village" in the image of Western-style liberal, capitalist democracies. In a widely discussed book, *The End of History and the Last Man* (1992), the American scholar Francis Fukuyama argued that capitalism and the Western concept of liberal democracy, while hardly ideal in their capacity to satisfy all human aspirations, are at least more effective than rival doctrines in achieving them and therefore deserve consideration as the best available ideology to be applied universally throughout the globe.[4]

Fukuyama's thesis provoked a firestorm of debate. Many critics pointed out the absence of any religious component in the liberal democratic model and argued the need for a return to religious faith, with its emphasis on the life of the spirit and traditional moral values. Others, noting that greater human freedom and increasing material prosperity have led not to a heightened human achievement and emotional satisfaction but rather to increasing alienation and a crass pursuit of hedonistic pleasures, argued that a new and perhaps "postmodernist" paradigm for the human experience must be found.

The Future of Liberal Democracy

More to the point, the course of events in recent years raises serious questions about whether it is realistic to expect the Western democratic model to be transplanted to parts of the world where conditions are not especially conducive to its success. Although some of the more advanced industrialized societies in East Asia like South Korea and Taiwan have gradually introduced their own pluralistic political systems, democratic institutions in many other areas of Africa and Asia are fragile and could be seriously undermined in the event of a national crisis. Indeed, history suggests that democracy is a fragile flower in the best of circumstances and requires patience and constant care to flourish.

The most visible alternative to the democratic model in the world today is China, which has created a centralized political system based on a single dominant party that has guided the country to impressive achievements. Chinese leaders have not been shy at promoting their model to the rest of the world. In a visit to the United States in 1997, Chinese president Jiang Zemin declared that human rights were something that should be determined by individual societies on the basis of their own traditions and course of development rather than being dictated by the powerful nations of the world. To some Chinese

observers, by defining human rights almost exclusively in terms of individual freedom, Western commentators ignore the importance of providing adequate food and shelter for all members of society.

It is also possible that the liberal democratic model will become more acceptable in parts of Africa and Asia to the degree that societies in those regions proceed successfully through the advanced stages of the Industrial and Technological Revolutions and adopt the middle-class values that underlie modern civilization in the West. There is no guarantee, however, that current conditions, which have been relatively favorable to that process, will continue indefinitely or that all peoples and all societies will share equally in the benefits. Just as the Industrial Revolution exacerbated existing tensions in and among the nations of Europe, globalization and the Technological Revolution are imposing their own strains on human societies today. Should such strains become increasingly intense, they could trigger political and social conflict. Under such conditions, it is extremely difficult for liberal democracy to thrive.

Civilizations at War

In *The Clash of Civilizations and the Remaking of the World Order* (1996), political scientist Samuel P. Huntington offered his own contribution to the issue by suggesting that the post–Cold War era, far from marking the triumph of Western ideas, would be characterized by increased global fragmentation and a "**clash of civilizations**" based on ethnic, cultural, or religious differences. According to Huntington, cultural identity has replaced shared ideology as the dominant force in world affairs. As a result, he argued, the coming decades may see the world dominated by disputing cultural blocs in East Asia, Western Europe and the United States, Eurasia, and the Middle East, with the societies in each region coalescing around common cultural features against perceived threats from rival forces elsewhere around the globe. The dream of a universal order dominated by Western values, he concluded, was a fantasy.[5]

Events in recent years have provided some support for Huntington's hypothesis. The collapse of the Soviet Union led to the emergence of several squabbling new nations and a general atmosphere of conflict and tension in the Balkans and at other points along the perimeter of the old Soviet empire. Even more dramatically, the terrorist attack in September 2001 appeared to have set the advanced nations of the West and the Muslim world on a collision course.

It is certainly true that as the world becomes more global in culture and interdependent in its mutual relations, forces have been at work attempting to redefine the political, cultural, and ethnic ways in which it is divided. This process is taking place not only in developing countries but also in the West, where fear of the Technological Revolution and public anger at the impact of globalization and foreign competition have reached measurable levels. Such views are often dismissed by sophisticated commentators as atavistic attempts by uninformed people seeking to return to a mythical past. But perhaps they should more accurately be interpreted as an inevitable consequence of the rising thirst for self-protection and group identity in an impersonal and rapidly changing world. Shared culture is one defense against the impersonal world around us.

Huntington's thesis thus served as a useful corrective to the complacent tendency of many observers in Europe and the United States to see Western civilization as the zenith and the final destination of human achievement. In Western leaders' efforts to promote the concepts of universal human rights and a global marketplace, there is a recognizable element of the cultural arrogance that was reflected in the doctrine of social Darwinism at the end of the nineteenth century. Both views take as their starting point the assumption that the Western conceptualization of the human experience is universal in scope and will ultimately, inexorably spread to the rest of the world. Neither gives much credence to the view that other civilizations might have seized on a corner of the truth and thus have something to offer.

That is not to say, however, that Huntington's vision of clashing civilizations is necessarily the most persuasive characterization of the probable state of the world in the twenty-first century. In the first place, by dividing the world into competing cultural blocs, Huntington probably underestimated the centrifugal forces at work within the various regions of the world. As many critics have noted, deep-rooted cultural and historical rivalries exist among the various nations in southern and eastern Asia and in the Middle East, as well as in Africa, preventing any meaningful degree of mutual cooperation against allegedly hostile forces in the outside world.

Huntington also tended to ignore the transformative effect of the Industrial Revolution and the emerging global information network. As the Industrial and Technological Revolutions spread across the face of the earth, their impact is measurably stronger in some societies than in others, intensifying political, economic, and cultural distinctions in a given region while establishing links between individual societies in that region and their counterparts undergoing similar experiences in other parts of the world. Whereas the parallel drive to global industrial hegemony encouraged Japan and the United States to

cooperate on a variety of issues, for example, it has intensified tensions between Japan and its competitor South Korea and weakened the political and cultural ties that have historically existed between Japan and China.

Globalization: The Pros and the Cons

One major factor that will affect the course of events in the coming decades is the impact that globalization will have on the international environment. For many knowledgeable observers in the West, there is solid economic logic in pursuing the goal of increased globalization of trade. Both the Republican president George W. Bush and his Democratic predecessor, Bill Clinton, for example, supported the concept, including the creation of a free trade zone incorporating all of the nations of the Western Hemisphere. The Obama administration has followed the lead of its predecessors, and a few weeks after the beginning of Obama's second term in office, the White House stated that it planned to pursue a free trade pact with its closest partner, the European Union. The reasons are clear: the U.S. industrial machine is increasingly dependent on the importation of raw materials from abroad, and corporate profits depend heavily on sales of U.S. goods in overseas markets. Although foreign competition can sometimes lead to a loss of jobs—or entire industries—in the United States, some economists argue that the overall effect is likely to be a growing market for U.S. goods in the international marketplace.

Yet the social costs of globalization are sometimes severe and can require significant efforts by governments to alleviate the pain. In advanced industrialized countries, for example, the outsourcing of jobs in both the blue-collar and white-collar sectors of the economy to countries with lower wage rates has led to rising unemployment and a popular outcry for the protection of local industries and stricter controls of imports. As the financial crisis of 2008 rippled through world markets, several countries began to institute protectionist policies to protect local industries and their workers. In hard times, free trade is a luxury many feel they cannot afford.

The most likely scenario for the coming decades, then, is more complex than either the global village or its conceptual rival, the clash of civilizations. Although the thrust of globalization is likely to continue, resistance will be fierce in some parts of the world, where the dictates of religion and social tradition pose significant obstacles to drastic political and cultural change. And the impact of the Technological Revolution will have transformative effects on all societies, rich and poor alike. The world of the twenty-first century will be characterized by

One World, One Fashion. One of the negative aspects of tourism is the eroding of distinctive ethnic cultures, even in previously less traveled areas. Nevertheless, fashions from other lands often seem exotic and enticing. This village chief from Flores, a remote island in the Indonesian archipelago, seems very proud of his designer sunglasses.

The most appropriate label for the contemporary cultural scene, in fact, is probably pluralism. The arts today are an eclectic hybrid, combining different movements, genres, and media, as well as incorporating different ethnic or national characteristics. There is no doubt that Western culture has strongly influenced the development of the arts throughout the world in recent decades. In fact, the process has gone in both directions as art forms from Africa and Asia have profoundly enriched the cultural scene in the West. One ironic illustration is that some of the best literature in the English and French languages today is being written in the nations that were once under British or French colonial rule. Today, global interchange in the arts is playing the same creative role that the exchange of technology between different regions played in stimulating the Industrial Revolution. As one Japanese composer declared not long ago, "I would like to develop in two directions at once: as a Japanese with respect to tradition, and as a Westerner with respect to innovation.... In that way I can avoid isolation from the tradition and yet also push toward the future in each new work."[6]

simultaneous trends toward globalization and fragmentation, as the inexorable thrust of technology and information transforms societies and gives rise to counteractions by individuals and communities seeking to protect local interests and preserve a group identity and a sense of meaning and purpose in a confusing world.

The Arts: Mirror of the Age

If, as the Spanish tenor Placido Domingo once observed, the arts are the signature of their age, what has been happening in literature, art, music, and architecture in recent decades is a reflection of the evolving global response to the rapid changes taking place in human society today. This reaction has sometimes been described as Postmodernism, although today's developments are much too diverse to be placed under a single label. Some of the arts are still experimenting with the Modernist quest for the new and the radical. Others have begun to return to more traditional styles as a reaction against globalization and a response to the search for national and cultural identity in a bewildering world.

Such a globalization of culture, however, has its price. Because of the popularity of Western culture throughout the developing world, especially among young people, local cultural forms are being eroded and destroyed as a result of contamination by Western music, mass television, and commercial hype. Although what has been called the "McWorld culture" of Coca-Cola, jeans, and rock is considered merely cosmetic by some, others see it as cultural neo-imperialism and a real cause for alarm. How does a society preserve its traditional culture when the young prefer to spend their evenings at a Hard Rock Café rather than attend a traditional folk opera or *wayang* puppet theater? Although there is sometimes local resistance to outside cultural influence, especially in the Middle East where religious traditionalists see the hand of Satan in all forms of Western culture, it is an uphill battle—as we saw in Chapter 15, young Palestinians are using hip-hop to convey their anti-Israeli message. World conferences have been convened to safeguard traditional cultures from extinction, but is there sufficient time, money, or inclination to reverse the tide?

What do contemporary trends in the art world have to say about the changes that have occurred since the beginning of the twentieth century? One reply is that the euphoric optimism of artists during the age of Picasso and Stravinsky has been seriously tempered a century later. Naiveté has been replaced by cynicism or irony as protection against the underlying pessimism of the current age.

One dominant characteristic of the new art is its reticence—its reserve in expressing the dissonance and disillusioning events of the past century. It would appear that we entered the twentieth century with too many expectations, hopes that had been fueled by the promise of revolution and scientific discoveries. Yet however extraordinary the recent advances in medicine, genetics, telecommunications, computer technology, and space exploration have been, humankind seems as befuddled as ever. It is no wonder that despite the impressive recent advances in science, human beings entered the new millennium a little worn and subdued.

What, then, are the prospects for the coming years? One critic has complained that Postmodernism, "with its sad air of the parades gone by,"[7] is spent and exhausted.

Others suggest that there is nothing left to say that has not been expressed previously and more effectively. The public itself appears satiated and desensitized after a century of "shocking" art and, as in the case of world events, almost incapable of being shocked any further. Human sensibilities have been irrevocably altered by the media, by technology, and especially by the cataclysmic events that have taken place in our times. Perhaps the twentieth century was the age of revolt, representing "freedom from," while the next hundred years will be an era seeking "freedom for."

What is comforting is that no matter how pessimistic and disillusioned people claim to be, hope springs eternal as young writers, artists, and composers continue to grapple with their craft, searching for new ways to express the human condition. How can one not be astonished by architect Frank Gehry's Guggenheim Museum in Bilbao, Spain (see the photo on p. 329), with its thrusting turrets and billowing sails of titanium? Such exuberance can only testify to humanity's indomitable spirit and ceaseless imagination—characteristics that are badly needed in the world today.

CHAPTER NOTES

1. Nicholas D. Kristof and Sheryl WuDunn, *Half the Sky: Turning Oppression into Opportunity for Women Worldwide* (New York, 2009), p. xx.
2. Alvin Toffler and Heidi Toffler, *Creating a New Civilization: The Politics of the Third Wave* (Atlanta, 1995).
3. Quoted in John Cassidy, "The Return of Karl Marx," *New Yorker*, October 20, 1997, p. 250.
4. Fukuyama's original thesis was expressed in "The End of History," *National Interest*, Summer 1989. He has defended his views in Timothy Burns, ed., *After History? Francis Fukuyama and His Critics* (Lanham, Md., 1994). Fukuyama contends—rightly in my view—that his concept of the "end of history" has been widely misinterpreted. I hope I have not done so in these comments.
5. Samuel P. Huntington, *The Clash of Civilizations and the Remaking of the World Order* (New York, 1996). An earlier version was published under the title "The Clash of Civilizations?" in *Foreign Affairs*, Summer 1993.
6. The composer was Toru Takemitsu. See Robert P. Morgan, *Twentieth-Century Music* (New York, 1991), p. 422.
7. Herbert Muschamp, "The Miracle in Bilbao," *New York Times Magazine*, September 7, 1997, p. 72.

Abstract Expressionism a post–World War II artistic movement that broke with all conventions of form and structure in favor of total abstraction.

Abstract painting an artistic movement that developed early in the twentieth century in which artists focused on color to avoid any references to visual reality.

African National Congress see ANC.

African Union the organization that replaced the Organization of African Unity in 2001; designed to bring about increased political and economic integration of African states.

Ainu an ethnic minority group in Japan. Descendants of the islands' original settlers, they now live mainly on the island of Hokkaido.

amae a Japanese term referring to loyalty to and dependency on the group and community.

anarchists people who hold that all government and existing social institutions are unnecessary and advocate a society based on voluntary cooperation.

ANC the African National Congress. Founded in 1912, it was the beginning of political activity by South African blacks. Banned by the politically dominant whites in 1960, it was not officially "unbanned" until 1990. It is now the majority party in South Africa.

anti-Semitism hostility toward or discrimination against Jews.

apartheid the system of racial segregation practiced in the Republic of South Africa until the 1990s; involved political, legal, and economic discrimination against nonwhites.

appeasement the policy, followed by the European nations in the 1930s, of accepting Hitler's annexation of Austria and Czechoslovakia in the belief that meeting his demands would ensure peace and stability.

ASEAN the Association for the Southeast Asian Nations, formed in 1967 to promote the prosperity and political stability of its member nations. Currently, Brunei, Cambodia, Indonesia, Laos, Malaysia, Myanmar, the Philippines, Singapore, Thailand, and Vietnam are members. Other countries in the region participate as "observer" members.

assimilation the concept, originating in France, that the colonial peoples should be assimilated into the parent French culture.

association the concept, developed by the French colonial officials, that the colonial peoples should be permitted to retain their precolonial cultural traditions.

Atlantic Charter a policy statement, drafted by Great Britain and the United States in 1941, that set out the Allies' goals for the post–World War II world, including the self-determination of all peoples.

blitzkrieg "lightning war." A war conducted with great speed and force, as in Germany's advance at the beginning of World War II.

Bolsheviks a small faction of the Russian Social Democratic Party that was led by Lenin and dedicated to violent revolution. The Bolsheviks seized power in Russia in 1917 and were subsequently renamed the Communists.

Brezhnev Doctrine the doctrine, enunciated by Leonid Brezhnev, that the Soviet Union had a right to intervene if socialism was threatened in another socialist state; used to justify the use of Soviet troops in Czechoslovakia in 1968.

Burakumin a Japanese minority similar to *dalits* (untouchables) in Indian culture. Past and current discrimination has resulted in lower educational attainment and socioeconomic status for members of this group. Movements with objectives ranging from "liberation" to integration have tried over the years to change this situation.

cartel a combination of independent commercial enterprises that work together to control prices and limit competition.

caste system a system of rigid social hierarchy in which all members of that society are assigned by birth to specific "ranks" and inherit specific roles and privileges.

chaebol a South Korean business conglomerate similar to the Japanese *keiretsu*.

civil disobedience the tactic of using illegal but nonviolent means of protest; designed by the Indian nationalist leader Mohandas Gandhi to resist British colonial rule. The tactic was later adopted by nationalist and liberation forces in many other countries.

civil rights the basic rights of citizens, including equality before the law, freedom of speech and press, and freedom from arbitrary arrest.

civil service examination an elaborate Chinese system of selecting bureaucrats on merit, first introduced in 165 C.E., developed by the Tang dynasty in the seventh century C.E., and refined under the Song dynasty. It contributed to efficient government, upward mobility, and cultural uniformity.

clash of civilizations a hypothesis proposed by Samuel P. Huntington in 1996. He argued that the post–Cold War era would be characterized by increased global fragmentation based on ethnic, cultural, and religious differences.

Cold War the ideological conflict between the Soviet Union and the United States between the end of World War II and the early 1990s.

collective farms large farms created by combining many small holdings into large farms worked by the peasants under government supervision; created in the Soviet Union by Stalin and in China by Mao Zedong.

communalism in South Asia, the tendency of people to band together in mutually antagonistic social subgroups; elsewhere used to describe unifying trends in the larger community.

Communist International (Comintern) a worldwide organization of Communist Parties, founded by Lenin in 1919 and dedicated to the advancement of world revolution; also known as the Third International.

conceptual art an artistic movement beginning in the 1970s in which the emphasis is on conveying a concept and on the means used to create the art rather than on the object that is created.

Confucianism a system of thought based on the teachings of Confucius (551–479 B.C.E.) that developed into the ruling ideology of the Chinese state.

conquistadors "conquerors." Leaders in the Spanish conquests in the Americas, especially Mexico and Peru, in the sixteenth century.

consumer society a term applied to Western society after World War II as the working classes adopted the consumption patterns of the middle class and installment plans, credit cards, and easy credit made consumer goods such as appliances and automobiles widely available.

containment   a policy adopted by the United States during the Cold War. It called for the use of any means, short of all-out war, to limit Soviet expansion.

Contras   in Nicaragua in the 1980s, an anti-Sandinista guerrilla movement supported by the U.S. Reagan administration.

Dadaism   an artistic movement in the 1920s and 1930s by artists who were revolted by the senseless slaughter of World War I and used their "anti-art" to express contempt for the Western tradition.

daimyo   prominent Japanese landowning families who provided allegiance to the local shogun in exchange for protection; similar to feudal vassals in Europe.

dalits   the lowest level of Indian society, technically outside the caste system and considered less than human. Commonly referred to as untouchables, they were renamed *harijans* ("children of God") by Gandhi. They remain the object of discrimination despite affirmative action programs.

deconstruction (poststructuralism)   a theory formulated by Jacques Derrida in the 1960s, holding that there is no fixed, universal truth because culture is created and can therefore be analyzed in various ways.

deficit spending   the concept, developed by John Maynard Keynes in the 1930s, that in times of economic depression, governments should stimulate demand by hiring people to do public works, such as building highways, even if this increases the public debt.

denazification   after World War II, the Allied policy of rooting out all traces of Nazism in German society by bringing prominent Nazis to trial for war crimes and purging any known Nazis from political office.

dependency theory   the theory, emerging in the 1960s, that the economic underdevelopment of the developing nations of Asia, Africa, and Latin America is caused by their continued economic domination by the former colonial powers.

descamisados   the "shirtless ones." The working-class supporters of Juan Perón during his rise to power in Argentina.

desertification   the process of becoming desert, often as a result of mismanagement of the land or climate change; especially, the expansion of the Sahara.

de-Stalinization   the policy of denouncing and undoing the most repressive aspects of Stalin's regime; begun by Nikita Khrushchev in 1956.

détente   the relaxation of tension between the Soviet Union and the United States that occurred in the 1970s.

direct rule   a concept devised by European colonial governments to rule their colonial subjects without the participation of local authorities. It was most often applied in colonial societies in Africa.

Einsatzgruppen   in Nazi Germany, special strike forces in the SS that played an important role in rounding up and killing Jews.

Elam Tigers   a militant separatist organization based in northern Sri Lanka that sought to obtain a separate state for the Tamil people, an ethnic group whose members live in India and Malaysia as well as Sri Lanka; also known as the Tamil Tigers (the formal name is Liberation Tigers of Tamil Eelam).

eta   in feudal Japan, a class of hereditary slaves who were responsible for what were considered degrading occupations, such as curing leather and burying the dead; known today as the *Burakumin*.

ethnic cleansing   the policy of killing or forcibly removing people of another ethnic group; used by the Serbs against Bosnian Muslims in the 1990s.

existentialism   a philosophical movement that arose after World War II and emphasized the meaninglessness of life, born of the desperation caused by two world wars.

fascism   an ideology that exalts the nation above the individual and calls for a centralized government with a dictatorial leader, economic and social regimentation, and forcible suppression of opposition; in particular, the ideology of Mussolini's Fascist regime in Italy.

favelas   slums and shantytowns in and around urban areas in Brazil.

feminism   the belief in the social, political, and economic equality of the sexes; also, organized activity to advance women's rights.

Final Solution   the Nazis' name for their attempted physical extermination of the Jewish people during World War II.

Five Pillars of Islam   the core requirements of the Muslim faith: belief in Allah and his prophet, Muhammad; prescribed prayers; observation of Ramadan; pilgrimage to Mecca; and giving alms to the poor.

five relationships   in traditional China, the hierarchical interpersonal associations considered crucial to the social order; consisted of the subordination of son to father, wife to husband, younger brother to older brother, and subject to ruler, and the proper relationship of friend to friend.

Four Modernizations   the radical reforms of Chinese industry, agriculture, technology, and national defense instituted by Deng Xiaoping after his accession to power in the late 1970s.

genro   the ruling clique of aristocrats in Meiji Japan.

glasnost   "openness." Mikhail Gorbachev's policy of encouraging Soviet citizens to openly discuss the strengths and weaknesses of the Soviet Union.

globalization   a term referring to the trend by which peoples and nations have become more interdependent; often used to refer to the development of a global economy and culture.

Good Neighbor policy   a policy adopted by the administration of President Franklin D. Roosevelt to practice restraint in U.S. relations with Latin American nations.

Gosplan   in the Soviet Union, the "state plan" for the economy drawn up by the central planning commission.

Great Leap Forward   a short-lived radical experiment in China, started in 1958, that created vast rural communes in an attempt to replace the family as the fundamental social unit.

Great Proletarian Cultural Revolution   an attempt to destroy all vestiges of tradition in China in order to create a totally egalitarian society. Launched by Mao Zedong in 1966, it devolved into virtual anarchy and lasted only until Mao's death in 1976.

green revolution   the introduction of technological agriculture, especially in India in the late 1960s; increased food production substantially but also exacerbated rural inequality because only the wealthier farmers could afford fertilizer.

guided democracy   the name given by President Sukarno of Indonesia in the late 1950s to his style of government, which theoretically operated by consensus.

Hamas   a militant Islamic group, whose goal is to liberate the Palestinian territories from Israel. Hamas has controlled the Gaza Strip since winning elections in 2006.

harijans   "children of god." A name used by Mohandas Gandhi to refer to the *dalits* (untouchables) in India.

high culture   the literary and artistic culture of the educated and wealthy ruling classes.

Hinduism   the main religion in India. It emphasizes reincarnation, based on the results of the previous life, and the desirability of escaping this cycle. Its various forms feature both asceticism and the pleasures of ordinary life and encompass a multitude of gods as different manifestations of one ultimate reality.

Holocaust the mass slaughter of European Jews by the Nazis during World War II.

imperialism the policy of extending one nation's power either by conquest or by establishing direct or indirect economic or cultural authority over another. Generally driven by economic self-interest, it can also be motivated by a sincere (if often misguided) sense of moral obligation.

indirect rule a colonial policy of foreign rule in cooperation with local political elites. Though implemented in much of India and Malaya and in parts of Africa, it was not feasible where resistance was greater.

informal empire the growing presence of Europeans in Africa during the first decades of the nineteenth century. During this period, most African states were nonetheless still able to maintain their independence.

intifada the "uprising" of Palestinians living under Israeli control, especially in the 1980s and 1990s.

Islam the religion derived from the revelations of Muhammad, the Prophet of Allah; literally, "submission" (to the will of Allah); also, the culture and civilization based on the faith.

keiretsu a type of powerful industrial or financial conglomerate that emerged in post–World War II Japan following the abolition of the *zaibatsu*.

kowtow the ritual of prostration and touching the forehead to the ground, demanded of all foreign ambassadors to the Chinese court as a symbol of submission.

laissez-faire French for "leave it alone." An economic doctrine that holds that an economy is best served when the government does not interfere but allows the economy to self-regulate according to the forces of supply and demand.

Lebensraum "living space." A doctrine, adopted by Hitler, that holds that a nation's power depends on the amount of land it occupies. Thus, a nation must expand to be strong.

liberalism an ideology based on the belief that people should be as free from restraint as possible. Economic liberalism is the idea that the government should not interfere in the workings of the economy. Political liberalism is the idea that there should be restraints on the exercise of power so that people can enjoy basic civil rights in a constitutional state with a representative assembly.

liberation theology an activist movement, especially among Roman Catholic clergy in Latin America, that combines Marxist ideas with a call to liberate the oppressed from injustice.

maharaja originally, a king in the Aryan society of early India (a great raja); later used more generally to denote an important ruler.

Marshall Plan the European Recovery Program, under which the United States provided financial aid to European countries to help them rebuild after World War II.

Marxism the political, economic, and social theories of Karl Marx, which included the idea that history is the story of class struggle and that ultimately the proletariat will overthrow the bourgeoisie and establish a dictatorship en route to a classless society.

mass leisure forms of leisure that appeal to large numbers of people in a society, including the working classes; emerged at the end of the nineteenth century to provide workers with amusements after work and on weekends; used during the twentieth century by totalitarian states to control their populations.

mass society a society in which the concerns of the majority—the lower classes—play a prominent role; characterized by extension of voting rights, an improved standard of living for the lower classes, and mass education.

matrilinear passing through the female line—for example, from a father to his sister's son rather than to his own—as practiced in some African societies; not necessarily or even usually combined with matriarchy, in which women rule.

Meiji Restoration the period during the late nineteenth and early twentieth centuries when fundamental economic and cultural changes occurred in Japan, transforming it from a feudal and agrarian society to an industial and technological one.

Mensheviks the faction of the Russian Social Democratic Labor Party that called for the gradual achievement of socialism by democratic means and opposed Lenin's emphasis on violent revolution.

minimalism a style of music originating in the 1960s that is characterized by subtle and gradual transformations of musical phrases or rhythmic patterns that are continuously repeated.

ministerial responsibility a tenet of nineteenth-century liberalism that held that ministers of the monarch should be responsible to the legislative assembly rather than to the monarch.

mir a traditional peasant village commune in Russia.

MITI the Ministry of International Trade and Industry in Japan; responsible for formulating and directing much of Japanese industrial policy after World War II.

Modernism the artistic and literary styles that emerged in the decades before 1914 as artists rebelled against traditional efforts to portray reality as accurately as possible and writers explored new forms.

modernization theory the theory, prevalent in the 1950s and 1960s, that the world's newly independent countries would ultimately follow the Western model and create modern industrial societies and that their current economic problems were a consequence of the difficult transition from a traditional agrarian to a modern industrial economy.

Monroe Doctrine for Asia Japan's plan to end Western influence in East Asia while guiding the nations of the region to modernization and prosperity on the Japanese model.

Narodnaya Volya the "People's Will." A left-wing Russian terrorist organization that assassinated Tsar Alexander II in 1881.

nationalism a sense of national consciousness based on awareness of being part of a commmunity—a "nation"—that has common institutions, traditions, language, and customs and that becomes the focus of the individual's primary political loyalty.

nationalization the process of converting a busines or industry from private ownership to government control and ownership.

NATO the North Atlantic Treaty Organization, a military alliance formed in 1949 in which the signatories (Belgium, Canada, Denmark, France, Great Britain, Iceland, Italy, Luxembourg, the Netherlands, Norway, Portugal, and the United States) agreed to provide mutual assistance if any one of them was attacked; later expanded to include other nations, including former members of the Warsaw Pact.

natural selection Darwin's idea that organisms that are most adaptable to their environment survive and pass on the variations that enabled them to survive while less adaptable organisms become extinct; known by the shorthand expression "survival of the fittest."

Nazi New Order the Nazis' plan for their conquered territories; included the extermination of Jews and others considered inferior, ruthless exploitation of resources, German colonization in the east, and the use of Poles, Russians, and Ukrainians as slave labor.

neocolonialism the use of economic rather than political or military means to maintain Western domination of developing nations.

new course a short-lived liberalizing change in Soviet policy toward Eastern European allies instituted after Stalin's death in 1953.

New Culture Movement a protest launched by students at Beijing University after the failure of the 1911 revolution; aimed at abolishing the remnants of the old system and introducing Western values and institutions into China.

New Deal the reform program implemented by President Franklin D. Roosevelt in the 1930s; included large public works programs and the introduction of Social Security.

New Democracy the initial program of the Chinese Communist government, from 1949 to 1955; focused on honest government, land reform, social justice, and peace rather than the goal of a classless society.

New Economic Policy a modified version of the old capitalist system introduced in the Soviet Union by Lenin in 1921 to revive the economy after the ravages of the civil war and war communism.

New Order in East Asia Japan's plan in the 1930s to create a Japanese-dominated sphere of influence comprising Japan, Manchuria, and China.

new world order a term used by President George H. W. Bush to refer to the new era of peace and international cooperation that he envisioned would result after the collapse of the Soviet Union.

Nonaligned Movement an organization of neutralist nations established in the 1950s to provide a third alternative to the socialist bloc, headed by the Soviet Union, and the capitalist nations led by the United States. Jawaharlal Nehru of India, Gamal Abdul Nasser of Egypt, and Sukarno of Indonesia were the movement's chief sponsors.

Open Door Notes a series of letters sent in 1899 by U.S. Secretary of State John Hay to Great Britain, France, Germany, Italy, Japan, and Russia, calling for equal economic access to the Chinese market for all states and for the maintenance of the territorial and administrative integrity of the Chinese Empire.

organic evolution Darwin's principle that all plants and animals have evolved over a long period of time from earlier and simpler forms of life.

pan-Africanism the concept of African continental unity and solidarity in which the common interests of African countries transcend regional boundaries.

pan-Arabism a movement promoted by Egyptian president Gamal Abdul Nasser and other Middle Eastern leaders to unify all Arab peoples in a single supra-national organization. After Nasser's death in 1971, the movement languished.

pan-Islamism a movement aimed at unifying all Muslim peoples throughout Africa; promoted first by Gamal Abdul Nasser of Egypt and later by Muammar Qaddafi of Libya.

peaceful coexistence the policy adopted by the Soviet Union under Nikita Khrushchev in 1955 and continued by his successors that called for economic and ideological rivalry with the West rather than nuclear war.

perestroika "restructuring." The term applied to Mikhail Gorbachev's economic, political, and social reform in the Soviet Union.

polygny the practice of having more than one wife at a time.

Pop Art an artistic movement of the 1950s and 1960s in which artists took images of popular culture and transformed them into works of fine art; for example, Andy Warhol's paintings of Campbell's soup cans.

popular culture as opposed to high culture, the unofficial written and unwritten culture of the masses, much of which was passed down orally and was centered on public and group activities such as festivals; in the twentieth century, the entertainment, recreation, and pleasures that people purchase as part of mass consumer society.

Popular Fronts governments to be formed by coalitions of leftist parties including Communists in the 1930s as part of Stalin's strategy to form a united front with the capitalist nations against Nazism. Although the strategy did not succeed in most countries, a Popular Front government was formed in France in 1936 and survived until 1938.

Postmodernism a term used to cover a variety of artistic and intellectual styles and ways of thinking prominent since the 1970s.

poststructuralism *see* deconstruction.

priyayi the local landed aristocracy in the Dutch East Indies; used as local administrators by the Dutch East India Company.

proletariat the industrial working class; in Marxism, the class that will ultimately overthrow the bourgeoisie.

purdah the Indian term for the practice among Muslims and some Hindus of isolating women and preventing them from associating with men outside the home.

raja originally, a chieftain in the Aryan society of early India, a representative of the gods; later used more generally to denote a ruler.

reparations payments made by a defeated nation after a war to compensate another nation for damage sustained as a result of the war; required from Germany after World War I.

rural responsibility system post-Maoist land reform in China, under which collectives leased land to peasant families, who could consume or sell their surplus production and keep the profits.

Sahel the grassy semidesert region extending across Africa south of the Sahara.

samurai "retainers." Japanese warriors who usually served a particular shogun and lived by a strict code of ethics and duty; similar to European knights.

sati the Hindu ritual requiring a wife to throw herself on her deceased husband's funeral pyre.

satyagraha "hold fast to the truth." The Hindu term for the practice of nonviolent resistance advocated by Mohandas Gandhi.

self-strengthening a late-nineteenth-century Chinese policy under which Western technology would be adopted while Confucian principles and institutions were maintained intact.

sepoys local troops who formed the basis of the British Indian Army; hired by the East India Company to protect British interests in South Asia.

Shari'a a law code, originally drawn up by Muslim scholars shortly after the death of Muhammad, that provides believers with a set of prescriptions to regulate their daily lives.

Shi'ite the second largest tradition of Islam, which split from the majority Sunni soon after the death of Muhammad in a disagreement over the succession; especially significant in Iran and Iraq.

Shinto a kind of state religion in Japan, derived from beliefs in nature spirits and until recently linked with belief in the divinity of the emperor and the sacredness of the Japanese nation.

shogun   a powerful Japanese leader, originally military, who ruled under the titular authority of the emperor.

shogunate system   the system of government in Japan in which the emperor exercised only titular authority while the shoguns (regional military dictators) exercised actual political power.

Sikhism   a religion, founded in the early sixteenth century in the Punjab, that began as an attempt to reconcile the Hindu and Muslim traditions and developed into a significant alternative to both.

social Darwinism   the application of Darwin's principle of organic evolution to the social order; led to the belief that progress comes from the struggle for survival as the fittest advance and the weak decline.

socialism   an ideology that calls for collective or government ownership of the means of production and the distribution of goods.

socialized medicine   health services for all citizens provided by government assistance.

soviets   councils of workers' and soldiers' deputies formed throughout Russia in 1917; played an important role in the Bolshevik Revolution.

sphere of influence   a territory or region over which an outside nation exercises political or economic influence.

Star Wars   nickname for the Strategic Defense Initiative, proposed by President Ronald Reagan, which was intended to provide a shield that would destroy any incoming missiles; named after a popular science fiction movie series.

sultan   "holder of power." A title commonly used by Muslim rulers in the Ottoman Empire, Egypt, and elsewhere; still in use in parts of Asia, sometimes for regional authorities.

Sunni   the largest tradition of Islam, from which the Shi'ites split soon after the death of Muhammad in a disagreement over the succession.

Surrealism   an artistic movement that arose between World War I and World War II. Surrealists portrayed recognizable objects in unrecognizable relationships in order to reveal the world of the unconscious.

Swahili   a mixed African-Arab culture that developed by the twelfth century along the east coast of Africa; also, the national language of Kenya and Tanzania.

tariffs   duties (taxes) imposed on imported goods; usually imposed both to raise revenue and to discourage imports and protect domestic industries.

three obediences   the traditional duties of Japanese women, in permanent subservience: child to father, wife to husband, and widow to son.

Three People's Principles   the three principles on which the program of Sun Yat-sen's Revolutionary Alliance (Tongmenghui) was based: nationalism (meaning primarily the elimination of Manchu rule over China), democracy, and people's livelihood.

totalitarian state   a state characterized by government control over all aspects of economic, social, political, cultural, and intellectual life; subordination of the individual to the state; and insistence that the masses be actively involved in the regime's goals.

trade union   an association of workers in the same trade, formed to help members secure better wages, benefits, and working conditions.

trench warfare   warfare in which the opposing forces attack and counterattack from a relatively permanent system of trenches protected by barbed wire; characteristic of World War I.

Truman Doctrine   the doctrine, enunciated by President Harry Truman in 1947, that the United States would provide economic aid to countries that were threatened by Communist expansion.

uhuru   "freedom" in Swahili. A key slogan in African independence movements, especially in Kenya.

ulama   a convocation of leading Muslim scholars. The earliest, which took place shortly after the death of Muhammad, drew up the *Shari'a*, a law code based largely on the Qur'an and the sayings of Muhammad, to provide believers with a set of prescriptions to regulate their daily lives.

umma   the Muslim community as a whole.

unconditional surrender   complete, unqualified surrender of a nation; required of Germany and Japan by the Allies in World War II.

uninterrupted revolution   the goal of the Great Proletarian Cultural Revolution launched by Mao Zedong in 1966.

varna   Indian classes or castes. *See also* caste system.

Viet Cong   the forces of the National Liberation Front of South Vietnam (NLF) during the Vietnam War. The term is short for "Vietnamese Communists."

Vietminh Front   the multiparty national alliance led by Ho Chi Minh that took control of northern and central Vietnam after World War II and waged a "people's war" of national liberation against the French.

Vietnam syndrome   the presumption, from the 1970s on, that the U.S. public would object to a protracted military entanglement abroad, such as another Vietnam-type conflict.

war communism   Lenin's policy of nationalizing industrial and other facilities and requisitioning the peasants' produce during the civil war in Russia.

war guilt clause   the clause in the Treaty of Versailles that declared Germany (and Austria) responsible for starting World War I and ordered Germany to pay reparations for the damage the Allies had suffered as a result of the war.

Warsaw Pact   a military alliance, formed in 1955, in which Albania, Bulgaria, Czechoslovakia, East Germany, Hungary, Poland, Romania, and the Soviet Union agreed to provide mutual assistance. After it was dissolved in 1991, most former members eventually joined NATO.

welfare state   a social and political system in which the government assumes primary responsibility for the social welfare of its citizens by providing such things as social security, unemployment benefits, and health care.

women's liberation movement   the struggle for equal rights for women, which has deep roots in history but achieved new prominence under this name in the 1960s, building on the work of, among others, Simone de Beauvoir and Betty Friedan.

Young Turks   a successful Turkish reformist group in the late nineteenth and early twentieth centuries.

zaibatsu   powerful business cartels formed in Japan during the Meiji era and outlawed following World War II.

zamindars   Indian tax collectors who were assigned land from which they kept part of the revenue. The British revived the system in a misguided attempt to create a landed gentry.

Zen   a school of Buddhism particularly important in Japan, some of whose adherents stress that enlightenment (*satori*) can be achieved suddenly, whereas others emphasize lengthy meditation.

Zionism   an international movement that called for the establishment of a Jewish state or a refuge for Jews in Palestine.

INDEX

Italicized page numbers show the locations of illustrations.

Brezhnev Doctrine, 199, 200
Briand, Aristide, 86
Bridge on the River Kwai, The (movie), 137
Britain. *See* England (Britain)
British Columbia, 15
British Empire: Africa and, 43; China and,
    50–51; in India, 272; India and, 30–32;
    Sepoy Rebellion and, 96; welfare state
    and, 217. *See also* Colonies and
    colonization; England (Britain)
British raj, 272
Brown, Gordon, 219
Broz, Josip. *See* Tito, Josip Broz (Yugoslavia)
Brynner, Yul, 34
Buddhism, 282, 288
Bueno Aires, 16
Bulgaria, 13, 124, 131, 149, 152
Bulge, 139
Bund Deutscher Mädel (League of German
    Maidens), 124
Burakumin (Japan), 234
Burma (Myanmar): Christianity in, 33;
    elections in, 286; independence of, 282;
    Japanese occupation of, 137; military
    dictatorship in, 282; nationalism in, 97;
    political reform in, 286. *See also* Southeast
    Asia
Burma-Thailand railway, 137
Buru Quartet (Toer), 289
Burundi, 300
Bush, George H.W., 173
Bush, George W., 174, 317, 330, 331, 340
Bushido, 141

Caffard Cove, 38
Cage, John, 179
Cai Yuanpei, 108
Cairo Trilogy (Naguib), 324
Calcutta, 98
Calderón, Felipe, 186
Caliphate, 103, 104
Cambodia: France and, 34, 35; independence
    in, 158; Vietnam and, 287–288
Cameras, 22
Camp David, 159
Camp David Agreement, 312
Camus, Albert, 228
Can Vuong (Vietnam), 96
Canada, 180–181; elections in, 178, 181;
    liberalism in, 15; United States and,
    180–181
Canada Pension Plan, 181
Cannadine, David, 30
Canton, 50
Cape Colony, 42, 43, 43 (map), 291
Cape of Good Hope, 37, 39
Cape Verde, 39
Capitalism: in Africa, 297; after Cold War, 331;
    China and, 336; in Europe, 19; global
    impact of, 336; in Kenya, 297; Marxism
    and, 19; political parties and, 19; in
    United States, 14

Caravan routes, 26, 37, 291
Cárdenas, Lázaro, 117–118
Cardoso, Fernando, 184
Caribbean, 38
Carnegie Steel Company, 14
Carson, Rachel, 177
Cartels, 6
Carter, Jimmy, 165; Camp David Agreement
    and, 312; Taiwan and, 241
Carter Doctrine, 166
Casement, Roger, 44
Cassava, 296
Castes, 30, 279
Castro, Fidel, 160, 182, 186
Castro, Raúl, 186
Caterpillar tractor, 74
Catholics and Catholic Church, 334; abortion
    and, 198, 227, 334; contraception and,
    227; in East Timor, 286; Italy and, 17; in
    Latin America, 182; Latin America and,
    15, 182; Mexico and, 17; Nazi Germany
    and, 124; in Northern Ireland, 217; in
    Poland, 198; Spain and, 125
Caucasus, 206
Cave, The (Saramago), 229
Cayenne, 38
Central Africa, 40, 300. *See also* specific
    locations
Central America, 15, 28; economy in, 115–116;
    illegal immigrants from, 176; nationalism
    and military in, 183; Reagan and, 166. *See
    also* specific countries
Central Asia, 26, 52, 136, 261
Central Europe, 131; in 1939, 127 (map); Great
    Depression and, 87; industrialization in,
    3, 4 (map), 6; nation-states in, 11
Central Intelligence Agency, 186
Central Kingdom, 48 (map). *See also* China
Central Powers (World War I), 71, 77,
    80, 106
Ceylon. *See* Sri Lanka
Cézanne, Paul, 22–23
Chad, 296
Chador, 324
Chaebol, 242–243
Chamberlain, Neville, 128
Changes: A Love Story (Aidoo), 306
Charter 77, 204
Charter Oath of 1868 (Japan), 60
Chávez, Hugo, 187
Chechenya, 206
"Checkpoint Charlie," 152
Cheka (Russia), 85, *192*
Chen Sui-bian, 241
Chennai, 98
Chernenko, Konstantin, 197, 203
Chernobyl nuclear accident, 197, 203, 337
Chiang Ching-kuo, 241
Chiang Kai-shek, *109*, 109, 110–112, 125, 129,
    134, 154–155, 239
Chiang Kai-shek Memorial Hall, *241*
Chiapas (Mexico), 117

Chicago School, 23
Chihuahua (Mexico), 117
Child labor, 7, 61
Child marriage, in India, *279*
Chile, 183; landholding elites in, 17;
    urbanization in, 16–17
China, 51, 260 (map); agriculture in, 49,
    263–264; architecture in, 269; arts in,
    268–269; Boxer Rebellion, 54; capitalism
    and, *336*; Christianity in, 261; civil
    service, 54–55; civil war in, 154–155, 155
    (map); collectives in, 253–255;
    communism in, 112, 155–156, 253–255;
    Confucianism in, 48, 57, 113, 258;
    consumerism in, 267–268; Cultural
    Revolution in, 255–257, 262, 267; culture
    in, 268–269; current boundaries, 260
    (map); democracy and, 252–253, 339;
    demographic changes in, 268; economy
    in, 112, 262–263, 264–265, 332; elections
    in, 263; environment in, 265, 337;
    European hegemony and, 26; family in,
    267; foreign policy, 260; Four
    Modernizations in, 257–258, 264; Great
    Depression and, 112; Great Leap
    Forward in, 253, 262, 266; health care in,
    268; higher education in, 263;
    imperialism in, 52–53, 57;
    industrialization in, 49–50; Internet and,
    261; Japan and, 57–58, 62, 109, 125,
    129–130; Korea and, 62, 63; Korean War
    and, 157; labor in, 264; land reform in,
    254; literature in, 269; Long March in,
    110 (map); Macartney's mission in, 47;
    under Mao Zedong, 252–256; marriage
    in, 113, 266; mass line in, 261–262; May
    Fourth Movement in, 109; missionaries in,
    49; Nanjing Republic, 110–112; New
    Culture Movement in, 108–109; New
    Democracy in, 252–253; Nixon and, 164;
    Northern Expedition in, 110 (map);
    Olympics in (2008), 260; Open Door
    policy in, 53–54; Opium War, 50–51;
    outsourcing to, 175; population control
    in, 264; Qing Empire, 48 (map); religion
    in, 335; revolution in, 55–56, 108–113;
    rural areas in, 49; social change in, 113;
    socialism in, 253–255; society in, 56–58,
    265–268; Soviet Union and, 160–161;
    Taiping Rebellion, 51; Taiwan and,
    241–242; Tiananmen Square protests in,
    258, 259; United States and, 164–165;
    Vietnam and, 260; women in, 57–58, 113,
    267. *See also* Taiwan
Chinese Communist Party, 108, 109, 110, 155,
    252
Chinese Empire. *See* China
Chinese Turkestan, 156
Chirac, Jacques, 213
Choshu (Japan), 59
Christian Democratic Union (Germany), 214
Christian missionaries, 28, 40